GOD
MAN
AND
RELIGION

GOD MAN AND RELIGION

readings in the philosophy of religion

Keith E. Yandell

University of Wisconsin
Madison, Wisconsin

McGraw-Hill Book Company

New York   St. Louis   San Francisco   Düsseldorf   Johannesburg
Kuala Lumpur   London   Mexico   Montreal   New Delhi
Panama   Rio de Janeiro   Singapore   Sydney   Toronto

GOD
MAN
AND
RELIGION
readings in the
philosophy
of religion

1 2 3 4 5 6 7 8 9 0 D O D O 7 9 8 7 6 5 4 3 2

This book was set in Optima by Black Dot, Inc. The editors were Samuel B. Bossard and James R. Belser; the designer was Jo Jones; and the production supervisor was Sally Ellyson. The printer and binder was R. R. Donnelley & Sons Company.

Library of Congress Cataloging in Publication Data

Yandell, Keith E   1938-
   God, man, and religion.

   1. Religion—Philosophy—Collections.
2. Experience (Religion)—Collections.   3.   Ethics—Collections.   I.   Title.
BL51.Y272   200'.1   72-1978
ISBN 0-072249-8
ISBN 0-072247-1 (pbk.)

Dedicated to Karen, David, and Eric
who interrupted, but also inspired

CONTENTS

PREFACE

Interest in religion and religion-related topics is strong in both student and general populations. My purpose in this book has been to respond to that interest by selecting essays which fall into four general areas: religious experience, the sources of and responses to secularity, religion and morality, and attempted proofs and disproofs of specific religious beliefs. The current interest in religious experience seems to me to be matched by its importance. Thus we begin with this topic.

Both mystical and numinous experience, and monistic and dualistic traditions, cry out for—and get—consideration. Hence both Eastern and Western sources are represented in our first section. But it is the mystical-numinous and monistic-dualistic distinctions that are important. These conceptual and experiential contrasts are more significant than the geographical classifications which they transcend, in the sense that representatives of both sides of the conceptual and experiential bifurcations appear in each hemisphere. Information concerning the phenomenology—the felt and perceived quality—of the varieties of religious experience provides a background for what is philosophically the core question: What is the evidential value of religious experience? Representative selections from religious texts without some expert explanation will be incomprehensible to most students; expert explanation without representative selections will be too abstract; selections and explanations without analysis and appraisal will be disappointing philosophically. Hence selections, explanations, and analyses and appraisals are included. My own difficulty with other readers has been that one or more of these elements is absent.

Concerning the origin of and responses to secularity, I have chosen essays which reveal their intellectual and cultural bases and essays which illustrate what seem to be the more important of the radical responses. Less radical, or more traditional, responses appear in the other sections. Existentialism, empiricism, and ontology are represented by Bultmann, Braithwaite, and Tillich. These are chosen rather than, say, "death-of-God" theologians. The roots seem to me more worth perusal than the fruits. They also last longer.

No reader in the philosophy of religion can afford, I think, to ignore what has seemed to many to be the strongest evidence against traditional theism, the problem of evil. Rather than including essays which exemplify revisions or rejections of theism in the light of the existence of evil, I have chosen to stress the question as to whether the existence of evil *justifies* a rejection or revision of traditional theism. Essays on this topic are supplemented by some of the more interesting and sophisticated essays dealing with the connection between religion and morality written since G. E. Moore's *Principia Ethica* (1903) with its claim that a necessary rift exists between descriptive and evaluative claims, and so between religious and moral claims. This supposed rift has been among the major factors supporting the view that religion and morality must remain forever separate.

The traditional focus of philosophy of religion has been on the success or failure of proofs of God's existence and the relation, if any, between faith and reason. While this focus is too narrow, it would be folly to ignore these matters. Hence the final section deals with them.

Any anthology in the philosophy of religion probably will be reflective both of the topics currently most discussed in the area and of the issues which the editor finds most important. Thus the readings become both a description and a recommendation. At any rate, it may as well be said that this is so regarding the present selection. Obviously a teacher will edit a reader which he can comfortably use. He can only hope that he is not pedagogically unique.

Keith E. Yandell

GOD
MAN
AND
RELIGION

INTRODUCTION

The philosopher of religion necessarily casts his conceptual nets widely. He is concerned with the similarities and differences between various religions—with the varieties of religious experience and the meanings of religious beliefs. Thus in Part One, Comparative Religion and Cognitive Appraisal, I have included sample expressions of such experiences and beliefs taken from important religious texts. I have followed Ninian Smart in dividing religions according to the dominance of mystical or numinous emphasis. Also included are significant interpretations of mystical and numinous religion. Without a comprehension of what religious experiences are and how they are interpreted by their subjects, and without a knowledge of the meaning of religious beliefs in their own conceptual and behavioral settings, a philosopher of religion works in a vacuum.

But no philosopher can be satisfied simply with a description of religious experiences and beliefs. He will want to know what validity, if any, they possess. He will want to discover what value, if any, religious experiences have as evidence for religious beliefs. He will also be concerned with the bearing, if any, of psychological interpretations of religious experiences on these questions. If there are any criteria which can be rightly used to appraise competing religious systems, he will need to know what they are, on what grounds they are established as appropriate criteria, and what the result is of their correct application. Thus selections discussing all these issues have been included. Arguments for religious beliefs other than those based on religious experience are considered later (see Part Four).

Part Two considers secularity and religious responses to secularity. For our purposes, secularity is the sum of the intellectual objections and cultural impediments to religious belief. The three responses to secularity considered in Part Two are often viewed as three forms of capitulation to secularity. Whether this is a fair appraisal or not, it is rather plainly true that Rudolph Bultmann's existentialist interpretation of Christianity and his famous recommendations toward demythologizing are strongly motivated by secularity. Ronald Hepburn questions whether the results of this reinterpretation will bear rational scrutiny.

R. B. Braithwaite prefers an empirical analysis of Christian belief to an existentialist analysis. Thus he replaces a doctrinal analysandum with an observable and behavioral analysans. Since I know of no other full-dress critique of Braithwaite, I have taken the liberty of including my own essay along with a defense of Braithwaite by Kai Nielsen and my brief reply to Nielsen.

Paul Tillich offers an analysis of Christian belief in terms of what he believes is a correct ontology, or doctrine of what there is. "Ground of being" replaces "God and Father" as the crucial concept for understanding the Deity. Along with this substitution, and in support of it, Tillich offers a view of doctrinal language as symbolic rather than descriptive. William P. Alston severely questions the adequacy of Tillich's view of symbols, and Marvin Fox raises equally important questions concerning whether Tillich has really *analyzed* Christian doctrine and not simply *replaced* it by something else. One question, then, appropriate to ask about the views of Bultmann, Braithwaite, and Tillich is whether they have not, contrary to their own intentions, ceased to analyze their own religious tradition in unwitting presentations of novel doctrine. Another is whether the replacement is not itself quite as objectionable as (at least in their view) the original was. Although these issues are here presented in terms of three encounters between secularity and Christianity, other religious perspectives (most notably, perhaps, Judaism) face similar issues with similar results.

In Part Three, Religion and Morality, two perennial problems are presented. One is the problem of evil: Does the existence of evil provide conclusive, or good, evidence against the existence of God? David Hume and J. L. Mackie argue that it does; Gottfried Leibniz, Immanuel Kant, and Alvin Plantinga argue that it does not. Leibniz and especially Plantinga make appeal to the "free will defense," and Dewey Hoitenga argues that there is a better response to the challenge represented by Hume and Mackie. Hoitenga's important article has had no answer. Thus I have attempted to respond to it, contending that Plantinga's reply is superior to the alternative Hoitenga favors.

Patterson Brown argues that there is a defensible and important connection between God and the good, between religion and morality. Running contrary to most recent discussions of these issues, he takes "the good is what God wills" to be a viable and nontrivial moral principle. Anthony Flew and Keith Campbell criticize these views. Brown's essays are also relevant to the problem of evil, and he suggests a resolution, or perhaps dissolution, of the problem.

Part Four, Religion and Reason, concludes our selections. Anselm's argument that "God exists" is a necessary truth, his discussion with the dissenting monk Gaunilon, opens this section. Presentations and critiques of the argument from contingency, the argument from design, and the moral argument follow. Stephen Cahn concludes the theistic arguments of Part Four with the contention that philosophical arguments for the existence of God possess little if any relevance to actual religious belief.

Finally, W. K. Clifford argues that religious belief, since it "goes beyond the evidence" we have, is irrational. William James counters with a defense of religious belief against the charge of irrationality, and George Mavrodes in turn argues that James unwittingly presents a view not really different in its results from that of Clifford. John Hick challenges an assumption common to Clifford and James, namely, that religious belief is belief that "goes beyond the evidence." Without wishing to return to natural theology or offering proofs of the existence of God, Hick believes that such writers as Clifford and James have taken an oversimplified view of religious faith, and Hick offers his own, different analysis of faith as the adoption of a "total interpretation." If one accepts Hick's analysis —and I think there is a good deal to be said in favor of his viewpoint—the question arises of which among many available total interpretations is rationally superior. Hence the considerations discussed in Part One (among others) again become paramount.

I think it is fair to say that wherever one enters the network of issues and insights that go under the name of the philosophy of religion, one is led sooner or later to consider most of the other parts of the network. The more one can see the subject globally the better. But global understanding presupposes careful examination of various particular topics. I hope and believe that the following selections are representative of what goes on in the philosophy of religion and that anyone who masters their content and learns to think for himself about the issues they raise will have taken a long step at least toward understanding where and how philosophy and religion interact. He may even have taken a step or two toward being a more reflective and mature person—but that is up to him.

PART ONE

COMPARATIVE RELIGION AND COGNITIVE APPRAISAL

Recent years have witnessed an increase in interest and knowledge concerning comparative religion. Knowledge of Eastern religions has naturally raised questions about the similarities and differences between "Eastern" and "Western" religions. Judaism, Christianity, and Islam are "Western" religions in the sense of being the dominant religions in the West, but not of course in the sense of having originated in the Western Hemisphere. Jerusalem and Mecca are not Western cities. In fact, the selections that follow indicate that some of the most important differences between religious systems and viewpoints are not matters of "East" as opposed to "West" but theistic as opposed to nontheistic perspective and numinous as opposed to mystical experience.

Ninian Smart, in *Reasons and Faiths,* distinguishes between numinous religious experience—experience which presents itself as an encounter with an awe-inspiring Being who is different in kind from anything or anyone else the subject has experienced and who has initiated the encounter—and mystical religious experience. The response appropriate to such a Being is to worship; the character of a numinous Being makes detached scrutiny (at least during experience of Him) impossible. In one commonly used sense of "mystical," at least, many numinous experiences are mystical. Further, a belief that God exists often arises or is substantiated, at least for the subject of the experience, by the occurrence of numinous experience, so that numinous religious experience is *theistic* religious experience, experience of God.

Smart, however, uses "mystical" in another sense which, though somewhat stipulative and technical, is quite useful. He uses "mystical" to mark off experience of "satori," enlightment, or "nirvana," a sense of ultimate peace and fulfillment. Such experiential states do not present themselves as experiences of a higher being. Rather, such states are self-attained, usually through some form of discipline (physical, or moral, or intellectual), and are not *of* any external or independent being. Characterized by peace, a sense of fulfillment, and bliss, these states are often viewed as simultaneously psychologically satisfying, morally the fulfillment of one's nature, and intellectually providing insight into the real nature of the world. Nirvana is attained by one's own effort and is a state of consciousness; numinous experience is not attained but is granted by its Object, and is an encounter with a Being who exists quite independent of being experienced. Mystical experience (in Smart's sense) leads to a religion in which theism plays little or no role; numinous experience, as we have said, leads to theistic religion. We could with a point replace "leads to" by "generally takes place in the context of," for there is as it were mutual reinforcement between religious tradition and religious experience.

The opening part of this book contains selections illustrating both mystical and numinous religious experience. Mystical religious experience is illustrated by selections from Buddhist and Hindu religious writings, and William James's "marks of mysticism" and Ninian Smart's characterization of nirvana follow. (James in his characterization of mysticism uses "mysticism" in a wider sense than Smart does.) Numinous religious experience is illustrated by selections from the Hindu Bhagavad-Gita, and from the Old and New Testaments in the Bible, followed by Edmund Jacobs' description of Jehovah (or Jahweh, as the scholarly fashion now is) and C. H. Dodd's summary of apostolic Christianity.

The seven essays which conclude Part One discuss some of the issues the opening chapters raise. A brief résumé of these issues may be of some help to the reader.

Joseph Campbell notes two radically different religious frameworks. For one, God is Creator and man is creature. Man may come to know God, but cannot become God. Man's good is to attain to his full potential as made in God's image, and part of this fulfillment involves the worship of God. Human sin breaks man's fellowship with God, and God's redemptive activity in history makes possible their reconciliation. For the other, ultimate reality is apersonal, and man's religious goal is loss of his individuality and personality. By loss of individuality, one submerges himself (or what was himself) in a comprehensive apersonal whole. Individual differences are only apparent and illusory, and really "all is one." This conception is not an easy one to make at all clear, but it has been influential in various religious and philosophical traditions.

William James contrasts the impersonal viewpoint of the sciences, which (at least in popular thought) present us with an orderly universe that is unconcerned with human values, and the personal viewpoint of religion, which is deeply concerned with these values. Seeking for a common element in various religions, James emphasizes feelings and conduct and deemphasizes beliefs. Yet he expresses that (as he believes) common element in terms of "a sense that there is *something wrong about us* as we naturally stand" and "a sense that *we are saved from the wrongness* by making proper connection with the higher powers." These are surely claims or beliefs about our condition and its correction. James offers as a psychological analysis of the religious experience of persons with "more developed minds" a sense of their moral wrongness in which "the individual, so far as he suffers from his wrongness and criticises it, is to that extent consciously beyond it, and in at least possible touch with something higher, if anything higher exist." Such a person then identifies his real self with that "part" of him that criticizes his own evil, and

> he becomes conscious that this higher part is . . . continuous with a MORE of the same quality . . . operative in the universe outside of him, and which he can keep in working touch with . . . and save himself.

James believes that this experience is of great psychological utility. But, he asks, is it veridical—does such experience actually include an encounter with something in fact "more" than our own experience? The first stage of his answer is that in religious experience we, as it were, meet (i.e., are affected by) our own subconscious. But if this is all that is involved, then religious experience (at least of a numinous sort) is *not* veridical. Whether or not this *is* all is, James suggests, a matter of "overbelief"—a belief, whether in favor of or against the veracity of religious experience, that goes beyond our evidence. And religion (but also irreligion) contains overbeliefs as essential elements.

John Baillie presents his interpretation of religious experience as a sense of a demand made, and an offer extended, from One who has a right to demand our obedience and is gracious enough to offer His fellowship. For Baillie, religious experience is numinous experience, and is mediated "in, with, and under" moral experience, experience of other persons, and the reading of the Bible and related materials. Experience of God is, he suggests, not detached from our experience of moral obligations or other persons. It is in being knowingly obligated to act, or in respecting and loving another person, that we become also conscious of a Lawgiver and a Creator of persons. Tbe numinous experience is thus in Baillie's view more a matter of the *depth* of moral and personal experience than a matter of another *kind* of experience in addition to others.

Rudolf Otto, whose *Das Heilige* is probably the classic analysis of numinous experience, describes its elements in these terms: a feeling of dependence consequent upon a sense of being a creature (a created one, as it were) in contrast to the Being one is encountering—a Being who is objective, outside and independent of the self, mysterious, unique, awe-inspiring, worship-worthy, overpowering, unapproachable except on His own terms, majestic, presenting urgent demands, beyond human comprehension, and uniquely attractive and fascinating. In contrast to Baillie, Otto seems to take numinous experience as a different *kind* of experience, not simply an element of "depth" in our experience. But perhaps the difference between Otto and Baillie is only one of emphasis.

Whichever view one takes of numinous experience, Baillie's or Otto's (if they are ultimately different views), does such experience count as evidence for religious beliefs—in particular, that God exists? C. D. Broad examines the argument from religious experience to the existence of God. Roughly, the argument goes as follows: our knowledge that something exists almost always depends on our experiencing that thing ourselves or receiving reliable reports from others that they have experienced whatever is in question. Now various people have had, and reported, experience of God. These experiences are substantially alike and have occurred in a wide variety of places and times. Hence God exists.

How are we to appraise this argument? Broad suggests three possible analogies: (1) What the biologists tell us about the minute structure and changes in cells is discernible only by those who have knowledgeable access to sensitive equipment and are able to interpret the data such equipment provides. Here most men must rely on the experts. (2) What habitual drunkards tell us, based on their experience while in delirium tremens, is universally constant but hallucinatory nonetheless. (3) A group of sighted men who are a minority in a society mainly composed of blind men might not be readily believed, but their claims of what the blind men will feel when they move as instructed by their sighted brethren will tend to confirm that the sighted possess a source of information not shared by their cohorts. Which of these, if any, provides an illuminating analogy with respect to religious experience as evidence for the existence of God?

One important consideration in an attempt to answer this question is the degree to which religious experience conflicts with, is unrelated to, or is confirmed by the remainder of human experience. Broad sees only one point of conflict—that "nearly all mystics seem to be agreed that time and change and unchanging duration are unreal or extremely superficial." Broad himself does not seem to take this conflict as a serious one, saying that "temporal characteristics present very great philosophical difficulties and puzzles when we reflect upon them." Not every philosopher would agree, and of course not all religions are agreed that time and change are superficial. Nor is mystical religious experience the only sort of religious experience even if by "mystical" we mean something broader than Smart does. So long, however, as the remainder of our experience does not contradict what religious experience tells us, the second (drunkard) analogy will not do, for delirium tremens experience is nonveridical because the overwhelming evidence is that things "seen" by men in this condition do not, in fact, exist. (The relevance of evil as possible counterevidence will be considered in Part Three.)

On the other hand, Broad argues, the fact that similar training (e.g., Yoga) produces similar experiences is of no evidential value because "uniform methods of training and meditation would be likely to produce more or less similar experiences, whether these experiences were largely veridical or wholly delusive." (Nor, particularly within numinous religious traditions, can religious experience be elicited on demand or by technique. If God reveals Himself, He, not we, will decide.) So, Broad argues, analogy (1) (concerning biology) won't do either.

What then of the third analogy, the one concerning sighted men in a predominantly blind society? Broad considers the argument that the founders of religions "have made actual ethical discoveries which others can afterwards recognize to be true . . . and that this makes it reasonable for us to attach some weight to what founders of religions tell us about things which we cannot understand or verify for ourselves." And Broad concludes that unless there is reason to reject the testimony of these founders, we should accept it. As he expresses his view:

> When there is a nucleus of agreement between the experiences of men in different places, times, and traditions, and when they all tend to put much the same kind of interpretation on the cognitive content of these experiences, it is reasonable to ascribe this agreement to their all being in contact with a certain objective aspect of reality *unless* there be some positive reason to think otherwise.

In this regard, religious experience and sensory experience (Broad suggests) are alike. Now Broad does not consider whether the "ethical discoveries" of the founders of various religions are compatible or not, nor (if they are) whether this verifies or lends credence only to some of their doctrines (for these doctrines disagree significantly) and if so to which ones. Nor does he much inquire whether the deliverances of religious experience are consistent with one another. This is so, even though he recognizes that these are important issues. Instead of raising them, however, he instead asks whether there is a "positive reason" to reject whatever uniform testimony religious experience may offer. While he says some things of importance on this topic, the next essay is dedicated solely to an important aspect of this question.

William P. Alston discusses "what bearing; if any, the existence of an adequate explanation of theistic religious belief exclusively in terms of factors within the natural world would have on the acceptibility of such beliefs." As a case in point, he offers an extensive description and analysis of the Freudian theory of the origin of theistic belief and asks what effect, if any, it would have on the reasonability of theistic belief were this theory to turn out to be correct.

The question gains its point from the (at least supposed) fact that if we discover that we have accepted a belief—not because we have any reason for doing so but simply because we were taught it early in life, or due to the operations of psychological factors of which we may have hitherto had no knowledge—we regard this belief as in an importantly different position from beliefs for which we take it that we have adequate reasons. Where *P* is some statement, "reason for believing *P*" will here mean, roughly, "evidence in *P*'s favor." It is possible to have a reason for believing a statement which is a prudential reason—one will be better off in some manner if one believes. But prudential reasons are not (normally, if ever) reasons in the sense of evidence.

Now if I believe that God exists because of the operation of psychological factors which are described to me, and if I accept this explanation of my believing that God exists, is this either evidence that God does not exist or that I am unreasonable if I retain my belief that He does exist? (Assuming, for the sake of the question, that I can stop believing that He does, or that whether I can stop believing or not is not relevant to whether my belief is reasonable, or perhaps that if I *cannot* stop believing, my belief is here for *that* reason unreasonable.)

Alston argues that the answer to this question is negative. After considering in great detail a Freudian explanation of belief in God, and assuming for the sake of argument that this explanation is correct (as Alston notes, a quite debatable assumption) Alston argues that neither the Freudian nor any other explanation claims to provide an explanation (sufficient by itself) of the belief in question. Freud's explanation claims "that an individual's *tendency* to accept belief in a supernatural deity is *partly* due to a tendency to project a childhood father-image." Hence the truth of this sort of explanation is compatible with a theist having evidential reasons for his belief; so even were the Freudian explanation true, at least for some persons, it would do nothing to show that the belief of those persons was unreasonable. Alston writes:

> if we try to inflate any of the current theoretical approaches into a theory which claims to provide a specification of sufficient conditions it becomes hopelessly implausible. And thus far no one has made any plausible suggestions as to how we might develop a theory which integrates all the relevant factors.

He continues:

> Therefore, in the absence of any genuine actual example, I am going to take the psychoanalytic explanation as one which might, with suitable supplementation, be developed into the sort of theory in which I am interested, and in referring to it as an example I shall be pretending such supplementation has actually been carried out.

Suppose, then, a Freudian-like explanation were so supplemented as to be a sufficient explanation of a man's belief in God—no condition necessary to this man's believing in God is left out; whenever the relevant conditions present in this man are present in another, the other believes in God; whenever any relevant condition present in this man is absent in another, the other does not believe; and reasons and evidence play no role whatever in the explanation. What now of our question?

The question whether the existence of such an explanation has, as it were, negative impact on theistic religious belief becomes three questions, assuming for the sake of the argument that there is such an explanation of a man's religious belief:

(1a) Does this provide evidence that God does not exist, so that belief that He does is false?

(1b) Does this provide evidence that *belief in God* is unreasonable, though it would not have this consequence for any other (or only for some other) beliefs which were explicable in the same way?

(1c) Does this provide evidence that belief in God is unreasonable and the same consequence follows for any other belief explicable in the same way?

Alston answers as follows. The reply to (1a) is negative; an affirmative response would be appropriate only if "God exists" entailed "No one (or, perhaps, not everyone) who believes in God so believes due to only natural causes." But this entailment does not hold. "There seems, then, to be little reason to suppose that the fact, if it is a fact, that theistic belief is causally determined directly furnishes any evidence against theistic belief." The truth of an explanation of the Freudian sort which gave sufficient conditions for belief in God would, however, rule out direct experience of God, and is therefore incompatible with, say, Otto's reading of numinous experience.

Concerning (1b), Alston considers such claims as "Religious belief is a form of neurosis" and "Religious belief is a manifestation of infantile behavior," concluding:

In order to argue that theistic belief, since neurotic, is unworthy of serious consideration, one must be holding the term "neurosis" subject to . . . evaluative criteria. . . . But so long as all we have shown is that this belief is due to certain unconscious processes, we have no right to call it neurotic in this sense. To gain this right we would have to show that a person who has a theistic belief is less able to function effectively than he would have been without it. And no one has ever begun to show this.

Alston touches on (1c) only obliquely at the end of his essay. It raises the question of the self-applicability of the sort of Freudian explanation being considered. If being causally explicable via this sort of explanation discredits any belief, as an affirmative answer to (1c) would require, it discredits the acceptance of the view that Freudian explanations are adequate. Or if not, why not? (A problem, or paradox, of self-reference perhaps arises, but it is not very clear with what, if any, relevant consequences.)

These brief remarks do not, of course, exhaust or adequately reflect the subtlety and complexity of Alston's careful essay. For that, the reader must turn to the essay itself.

Ninian Smart holds that a choice between different and incompatible religious frameworks is not, or need not be, rationally arbitrary. There are, he holds, rationally relevant considerations in such contexts of choice. Consider, then, the view that there is one God (monotheism) and the view that there is more than one god (polytheism). Are there any rational criteria for deciding that a monotheistic view is superior to a polytheistic one, or conversely? Smart offers these considerations: monotheism gives "a more exalted view of the divine" than polytheism, is less "attached to local legend, . . . integrates better with moral insights [which are] universal in nature," and is simpler in the sense of claiming that only one deity exists. (The claim that so long as two systems are otherwise equally viable, the system whose truth requires the lesser amount of underived entities is rationally superior—the principle of parsimony–has wide acceptance, and it is to this principle that Smart appeals when he mentions simplicity.) Further, numinous experience appears more in accord with monotheism, and historically polytheism has tended to develop into monotheism. So if the choice is between monotheism and polytheism, there is good reason to be a monotheist.

But even if Smart is right about this, there are other religious choices. Some religious systems will be purely numinous, or nearly so; Islam is an example. Some religious systems will be purely mystical, or nearly so; Theravada Buddhism is an example. A numinous religious system is, in part, one in which all religious experience is taken to be numinous, mystical experience (in Smart's sense of "mystical") being interpreted, as it were, as disguised experience of God. A mystical religion is, in part, one in which all religious experience is taken to be mystical, numinous experience being interpreted, as it were, as disguised experience of an inner state. For example, a Theravada Buddhist will not be any sort of theist. He will base his religious belief on experience that is "mystical" in Smart's sense of the term—both in the sense that he will take this experience to confirm his belief and that the occurrence of this experience played a significant role historically in the development of his beliefs and in his personally adopting them—though as C. D. Broad notes there will probably have been a mutual influence of experience on belief and belief on experience. By a "mystical" experience the Theravada Buddhist will mean something like this. In ordinary experience of, say, a pencil, experience is, as it were, a relationship involving three relata—the pencil, my seeing (etc.) the pencil, and myself. There is an object of experience (the pencil), a process of experiencing (seeing the pencil), and a subject of experience (myself). Ordinary perceptual experience is subject-process-object. Moral experience fits the same model, as indeed does aesthetic experience, personal interaction, solitary reflection, or any other experiences that most people have. Even if, in such cases as feeling pain, the process-object distinction breaks down, the experience is still subject-object. But in mystical experience, in the relevant sense of "mystical," the very distinction between subject of experience and object of experience supposedly vanishes. Loss of subjecthood, of selfhood, putatively occurs. (Compare the Campbell essay in Chapter 3.)

Now one may doubt that any experience of this sort ever in fact occurs. One can claim that the "subjects" of such experiences misdescribe their experience or misunderstand its nature. There is no doubt that something of this sort can happen; the "possessor" of an experience is certainly not its infallible interpreter. (Compare Broad's second analogy of the drunkard.) A charming illustration of this fact is given in Johan Huizinga's The Waning of the Middle Ages.[1] Jean Gerson, "a

---

[1] Johan Huizinga, The Waning of the Middle Ages (New York: St. Martin's Press, 1949), p. 197.

supporter of moderate . . . mysticism," was told by a "visionary . . . that in the contemplation of God her mind had been annihilated, really annihilated, and then created anew. 'How do you know?' he asked her. 'I experienced it,' she had answered."

Mystical experience (in the present sense of "mystical") and mystical experience in which the subject-object distinction is retained, and numinous experience (under which experience which is "mystical" in the wider sense may be classed) have been held (e.g., concerning numinous experience, by Feurbach and Freud) to be cases in which the subject has misread his experience, or at least "overinterpreted" it.

Suppose, however, at least for the sake of the argument, that mystical experience of the Theravada sort does occur. What then? Mystical experience involves a sense of timelessness, of peace and bliss, of transcendence of ordinary experience. Now one can argue (as hinted above) in either of two ways. One can say that Theravada mystical experience is, as it were, a veiled (and perhaps also psychologized) sense of the presence of an eternal God who transcends nature and who gives peace and bliss. Or one can argue that numinous experience is, as it were, a veiled (perhaps also mythologized) sense of one's own inner state of peace, bliss, and timelessness. Smart is, of course, aware of this ambivalence and asks whether there are any reasons for arguing one way as opposed to the other.

He offers three such reasons—that numinous experience cannot be reduced to mystical; that for mystical experience the world of persons and things, obligations and duties, must be illusory and this conflicts with our moral experience, "the promptings of conscience, and the sentiments of justice and love"; that transcendence of the illusory (which putatively occurs in Theravada mysticism) "has less merit" than transcendence of the nonillusory (which putatively occurs in numinous experience).

So far, if Smart has argued successfully, theism is the most reasonable religious perspective. But, he argues, within a theistic system, "man . . . feels that it is he that must make expiation for his sins; while on the other hand he supposes that only God can bridge the gulf" between God and man. Smart continues: "Christ by being both man and God can achieve, through his solidarity with mankind, the expiation for mankind, and, through his Godhood, bridge the gulf."

As Smart is aware, many questions remain. Is the doctrine of atonement by the death of Christ morally defensible? Is the notion of God becoming man blasphemous? And, conversely, is not the notion that God cannot, if He wills, become a Man who redeems men itself rather the blasphemous view? Is the doctrinal complexity that results from accepting a Divine Incarnation justified by the problems solved by it? And what relevance has historical evidence at this point?

Returning to the question of theism or nontheism, is the at least implicit Theravada claim that only in mystical experience do we see the world aright at all plausible? What are we to make of the description of mystical experience as blissful and peaceful when no self remains to be in bliss or at peace? If mystical experience involves literal loss of all selfhood or personal identity, then is it not nonsense to talk about bliss or peace, and is seeking such experience not suicide and encouraging others to do so not similar to murder? Or if only an "empirical self" is lost but a "real self" discovered, then does not a subject-object distinction remain after all? And so on.

The value of Smart's essay lies in part in his illustrations of how reasoning and rational appraisal are not inappropriate in the context of comparative religion. This is, in itself, an important claim, even if (as Smart would surely grant and even insist) more remains to be done in terms of laying out the criteria for such appraisal.

Chapter
ONE

RELIGION EAST AND WEST
mystical experience

THE FOUR
HOLY TRUTHS
Buddhist Scriptures

From Edward Conze (ed. and trans.), *Buddhist Scriptures*, 1959, by permission of Penguin Books Ltd., Harmondsworth, Middlesex, England.

What then is the Holy Truth of Ill? Birth is ill, decay is ill, sickness is ill, death is ill. To be conjoined with what one dislikes means suffering. To be disjoined from what one likes means suffering. Not to get what one wants, also that means suffering. In short, all grasping at any of the five Skandas[1] involves suffering.

What then is the Holy Truth of the Origination of Ill? It is that craving which leads to rebirth, accompanied by delight and greed, seeking its delight now here, now there, i.e. craving for sensuous experience, craving to perpetuate oneself, craving for extinction.

What then is the Holy Truth of the Stopping of Ill? It is the complete stopping of that craving, the withdrawal from it, the renouncing of it, throwing it back, liberation from it, non-attachment to it.

What then is the Holy Truth of the steps which lead to the stopping of Ill? It is this holy eightfold Path, which consists of right views, right intentions, right speech, right conduct, right livelihood, right effort, right mindfulness, right concentration.

MIND-ONLY
AND SALVATION
Buddhist Texts

E. Conze, "The Mahayana," from E. Conze, I. B. Horner, D. Snellgrove, and A. Waley (eds.), *Buddhist Texts through the Ages*, 1964, by permission of Bruno Cassirer (publishers) Ltd., Oxford, England, and Harper & Row, Publishers, Incorporated, New York.

As long as consciousness does not abide in representation-only,
So long does one not turn away from the tendency towards the twofold grasping.

Commentary. As long as consciousness does not abide in the true nature of thought, which is also called 'representation-only', so long it proceeds with the object and the subject as a basis. 'The twofold grasping' means the grasping of the

---

[1][Form = body, feelings, perceptions, volitional impulses, consciousness—the supposed five elements of personality. E. Conze].

object and the grasping of the subject. 'The tendency towards it' is the germ of the future genesis of the twofold grasping, which they have placed in the store-consciousness. Until the time when the thought of the Yogin is supported on representation-only, which is marked by non-duality, so long he 'does not turn away from', does not forsake the tendency towards the twofold grasping. And here the non-forsaking of the external basis implies also the non-forsaking of the internal basis. And he thinks to himself, "I grasp at sight-objects, etc., with my eyes, etc."

Next one explains, why to take as a basis thought-only which is devoid of an object, is not sufficient for the abiding in the true nature of thought:

As long as he places something before him, taking it as a basis, saying: 'This is just representation-only', so long he does not abide in that alone.

This refers to someone who, conceited and acting on hearsay alone, thinks, "I am established in the pure representation-only." "This is mere representation-only, it is devoid of an object, there is here no external object," thus he grasps at a basis and esteems himself. 'Before him' means 'face to face with him'. 'He places', as he has heard it said, with his mind. . . . 'He does not abide in That alone', because he has not forsaken the apprehension of (his own) consciousness.

Then he (Vasubandhu) says with regard to the forsaking of the grasping at consciousness, and how thereby one becomes one who is supported by thought-only:

But when cognition no longer apprehends an object, then
It stands firmly in consciousness-only, because, where there is nothing to grasp there is no more grasping.

At the time when outside thought 'he does not apprehend', not see, not grasp, not take as real, any object whatsoever, be it the demonstration (of Dharma) and instruction (in it), or an ordinary object, like form, sound, etc.—and that because he sees that which really is, and not because he is as one born blind—at that time there is a forsaking of the grasping at consciousness, and he is established in the true nature of his own thought. The reason for this is that 'where there is nothing to grasp, there is no more grasping'. Where there is an object there is a subject, but not where there is no object. The absence of an object results in the absence also of a subject, and not merely in that of grasping. It is thus that there arises the cognition which is homogeneous, without object, indiscriminate and supramundane. The tendencies to treat object and subject as distinct and real entities are forsaken, and thought is established in just the true nature of one's own thought.

When thought thus abides in representation-only, then how can one describe it? He says:

It is without thought, without basis, and is the supramundane cognition.
The revulsion from the substratum results from the loss of the twofold corruption.

This is the element without outflows, inconceivable, wholesome and stable,
The blissful body of emancipation, the Dharma-body of the great Sage.

Vasubandhu, Trimśikā, 26–30

THE SUPREME TEACHING
The Upanishads

From Juan Mascaro (trans.), *The Upanishads,* 1965, by permission of Penguin Books Ltd., Harmondsworth, Middlesex, England.

Prologue

To Janaka king of Videha came once Yajñavalkya meaning to keep in silence the supreme secret wisdom. But once, when Janaka and Yajñavalkya had been holding a discussion at the offering of the sacred fire, Yajñavalkya promised to grant the king any wish and the king chose to ask questions according to his desire. Therefore Janaka, king of Videha, began and asked this question:

Yajñavalkya, what is the light of man?

The sun is his light, O king, he answered. It is by the light of the sun that a man rests, goes forth, does his work, and returns.

This is so in truth, Yajñavalkya. And when the sun is set, what is then the light of man?

The moon then becomes his light, he replied. It is by the light of the moon that a man rests, goes forth, does his work, and returns.

This is so in truth, Yajñavalkya. And when the sun and the moon are set, what is then the light of man?

Fire then becomes his light. It is by the light of fire that a man rests, goes forth, does his work, and returns.

And when the sun and the moon are set, Yajñavalkya, and the fire has sunk down, what is then the light of man?

Voice then becomes his light; and by the voice as his light he rests, goes forth, does his work and returns. Therefore in truth, O king, when a man cannot see even his own hand, if he hears a voice after that he wends his way.

This is so in truth, Yajñavalkya. And when the sun is set, Yajñavalkya, and the moon is also set, and the fire has sunk down, and the voice is silent, what is then the light of man?

The Soul then becomes his light; and by the light of the Soul he rests, goes forth, does his work, and returns.

What is the Soul? asked then the king of Videha.

Waking and Dreaming

Yajñavalkya spoke:

It is the consciousness of life. It is the light of the heart. For ever remaining the same, the Spirit of man wanders in the world of waking life and also in the world of dreams. He seems to wander in thought. He seems to wander in joy.

But in the rest of deep sleep he goes beyond this world and beyond its fleeting forms.

For in truth when the Spirit of man comes to life and takes a body, then he is joined with mortal evils; but when at death he goes beyond, then he leaves evil behind.

The Spirit of man has two dwellings: this world and the world beyond. There is also a third dwelling-place: the land of sleep and dreams. Resting in this borderland the Spirit of man can behold his dwelling in this world and in the other world afar, and wandering in this borderland he beholds behind him the sorrows of this world and in front of him he sees the joys of the beyond.

Dreams

When the Spirit of man retires to rest, he takes with him materials from this all-containing world, and he creates and destroys in his own glory and radiance. Then the Spirit of man shines in his own light.

In that land there are no chariots, no teams of horses, nor roads; but he creates his own chariots, his teams of horses, and roads. There are no joys in that region, and no pleasures nor delights; but he creates his own joys, his own pleasures and delights. In that land there are no lakes, no lotus-ponds, nor streams; but he creates his own lakes, his lotus-ponds, and streams. For the Spirit of man is Creator.

It was said in these verses:

Abandoning his body by the gate of dreams, the Spirit beholds in awaking his senses sleeping. Then he takes his own light and returns to his home, this Spirit of golden radiance, the wandering swan everlasting.

Leaving his nest below in charge of the breath of life, the immortal Spirit soars afar from his nest. He moves in all regions wherever he loves, this Spirit of golden radiance, the wandering swan everlasting.

And in the region of dreams, wandering above and below, the Spirit makes for himself innumerable subtle creations. Sometimes he seems to rejoice in the love of fairy beauties, sometimes he laughs or beholds awe-inspiring terrible visions.

People see his field of pleasure; but he can never be seen.

So they say that one should not wake up a person suddenly, for hard to heal would he be if the Spirit did not return. They say also that dreams are like the waking state, for what is seen when awake is seen again in a dream. What is true is that the Spirit shines in his own light.

'I give you a thousand gifts,' said then the king of Videha, 'but tell me of the higher wisdom that leads to liberation.'

When the Spirit of man has had his joy in the land of dreams, and in his wanderings there has beholden good and evil, he then returns to this world of waking. But whatever he has seen does not return with him, for the Spirit of man is free.

And when he has had his joy in this world of waking and in his wanderings here has beholden good and evil, he returns by the same path again to the land of dreams.

Even as a great fish swims along the two banks of a river, first along the eastern bank and then the western bank, in the same way the Spirit of man moves along beside his two dwellings: this waking world and the land of sleep and dreams.

Deep Sleep

Even as a falcon or an eagle, after soaring in the sky, folds his wings for he is weary, and flies down to his nest, even so the Spirit of man hastens to that place of rest where the soul has no desires and the Spirit sees no dreams.

What was seen in a dream, all the fears of waking, such as being slain or oppressed, pursued by an elephant or falling into an abyss, is seen to be a delusion. But when like a king or a god the Spirit feels 'I am all,' then he is in the highest world. It is the world of the Spirit, where there are no desires, all evil has vanished, and there is no fear.

As a man in the arms of the woman beloved feels only peace all around, even so the Soul in the embrace of Atman, the Spirit of vision, feels only peace all around. All desires are attained, since the Spirit that is all has been attained, no desires are there, and there is no sorrow.

There a father is a father no more, nor is a mother there a mother; the worlds are no longer worlds, nor the gods are gods any longer. There the *Vedas* disappear; and a thief is not a thief, nor is a slayer a slayer; the outcast is not an outcast, nor the base-born a base-born; the pilgrim is not a pilgrim and the hermit is not a hermit; because the Spirit of man has crossed the lands of good and evil, and has passed beyond the sorrows of the heart.

There the Spirit sees not, but though seeing not he sees. How could the Spirit not see if he is the All? But there is no duality there, nothing apart for him to see.

There the Spirit feels no perfumes, yet feeling no perfumes he feels them. How could the Spirit feel no perfumes if he is the All? But there is no duality there, no perfumes, apart for him to feel.

There the Spirit tastes not, yet tasting not he tastes. How could the Spirit not taste if he is the All? But there is no duality there, nothing apart for him to taste.

There the Spirit speaks not, yet speaking not he speaks. How could the Spirit not speak if he is the All? But there is no duality there, nothing apart for him to speak to.

There the Spirit hears not, yet hearing not he hears. How could the Spirit not hear if he is the All? But there is no duality there, nothing apart for him to hear.

There the Spirit thinks not, yet thinking not he thinks. How could the Spirit not think if he is the All? But there is no duality there, nothing apart for him to think.

There the Spirit touches not, yet touching not he touches. How could the Spirit not touch if he is the All? But there is no duality there, nothing apart for him to touch.

There the Spirit knows not, yet knowing not he knows. How could the Spirit not know if he is the All? But there is no duality there, nothing apart for him to know.

For only where there seems to be a duality, there one sees another, one feels another's perfume, one tastes another, one speaks to another, one listens to another, one touches another and one knows another.

But in the ocean of Spirit the seer is alone beholding his own immensity.

This is the world of Brahman, O king. This is the path supreme. This is the supreme treasure. This is the world supreme. This is the supreme joy. On a portion of that joy all other beings live.

He who in this world attains success and wealth, who is Lord of men and enjoys all human pleasures, has reached the supreme human joy.

But a hundred times greater than the human joy is the joy of those who have attained the heaven of the ancestors.

A hundred times greater than the joy of the heaven of the ancestors is the joy of the heaven of the celestial beings.

A hundred times greater than the joy of the heaven of the celestial beings is the joy of the gods who have attained divinity through holy works.

A hundred times greater than the joy of the gods who have attained divinity through holy works is the joy of the gods who were born divine, and of him who has sacred wisdom, who is pure and free from desire.

A hundred times greater than the joy of the gods who were born divine is the joy of the world of the Lord of Creation, and of him who has sacred wisdom, who is pure and free from desire.

And a hundred times greater than the joy of the Lord of Creation is the joy of the world of Brahman, and of him who has sacred wisdom, who is pure and free from desire.

This is the joy supreme, this is the world of the Spirit, O king.

'I give you a thousand gifts,' said then the king of Videha: 'but tell me of the higher wisdom that leads to liberation.'

And Yajñavalkya was afraid and thought: Intelligent is the king. He has cut me off from all retreat.

When the Spirit of man has had his joy in the land of dreams, and in his wanderings there has beholden good and evil, he returns once again to this the world of waking.

Death

Even as a heavy-laden cart moves on groaning, even so the cart of the human body, wherein lives the Spirit, moves on groaning when a man is giving up the breath of life.

When the body falls into weakness on account of old age or disease, even as a mango-fruit, or the fruit of the holy fig-tree, is loosened from its stem, so the Spirit of man is loosened from the human body and returns by the same way to Life, wherefrom he came.

As when a king is coming, the nobles and officers, the charioteers and heads of the village prepare for him food and drink and royal lodgings, saying 'The king is coming, the king is approaching,' in the same way all the powers of life wait for him who knows this and say: 'The Spirit is coming, the Spirit is approaching.'

And as when a king is going to depart, the nobles and officers, the charioteers and the heads of the village assemble around him, even so all the powers of life gather about the soul when a man is giving up the breath of life.

When the human soul falls into weakness and into seeming unconsciousness all the powers of life assemble around. The soul gathers these elements of life-fire and enters into the heart. And when the Spirit that lives in the eye has returned to his own source, then the soul knows no more forms.

Then a person's powers of life become one and people say: 'he sees no more.' His powers of life become one and people say: 'he feels perfumes no more.' His powers of life become one and people say: 'he tastes no more.' His powers of life become one and people say: 'he speaks no more.' His powers of life become one and people say: 'he hears no more.' His powers of life become one and people say: 'he thinks no more.' His powers of life become one and people say: 'he touches no more.' His powers of life become one and people say: 'he knows no more.'

Then at the point of the heart a light shines, and this light illumines the soul on its way afar. When departing, by the head, or by the eye or other parts of the body, life arises and follows the soul, and the powers of life follow life. The soul becomes conscious and enters into Consciousness. His wisdom and works take him by the hand, and the knowledge known of old.

Even as a caterpillar, when coming to the end of a blade of grass, reaches out to another blade of grass and draws itself over to it, in the same way the Soul, leaving the body and unwisdom behind, reaches out to another body and draws itself over to it.

And even as a worker in gold, taking an old ornament, moulds it into a form newer and fairer, even so the Soul, leaving the body and unwisdom behind, goes into a form newer and fairer: a form like that of the ancestors in heaven, or of the celestial beings, or of the gods of light, or of the Lord of Creation, or of Brahma the Creator supreme, or a form of other beings.

The Soul is Brahman, the Eternal.

It is made of consciousness and mind: it is made of life and vision. It is made of the earth and the waters: it is made of air and space. It is made of light and darkness: it is made of desire and peace. It is made of anger and love: it is made of virtue and vice. It is made of all that is near: it is made of all that is afar. It is made of all.

Karma

According as a man acts and walks in the path of life, so he becomes. He that does good becomes good; he that does evil becomes evil. By pure actions he becomes pure; by evil actions he becomes evil.

And they say in truth that a man is made of desire. As his desire is, so is his faith. As his faith is, so are his works. As his works are, so he becomes. It was said in this verse:

A man comes with his actions to the end of his determination.

Reaching the end of the journey begun by his works on earth, from that world a man returns to this world of human action.

Thus far for the man who lives under desire.

Liberation

Now as to the man who is free from desire.

He who is free from desire, whose desire finds fulfilment, since the Spirit is his desire, the powers of life leave him not. He becomes one with Brahman, the Spirit, and enters into the Spirit. There is a verse that says:

When all desires that cling to the heart disappear, then a mortal becomes immortal, and even in this life attains Liberation.

As the slough of a snake lies dead upon an ant-hill, even so the mortal body; but the incorporeal immortal Spirit is life and light and Eternity.

Concerning this are these verses:

I have found the small path known of old that stretches far away. By it the sages who know the Spirit arise to the regions of heaven and thence beyond to liberation.

It is adorned with white and blue, yellow and green and red. This is the path of the seers of Brahman, of those whose actions are pure and who have inner fire and light.

Into deep darkness fall those who follow action. Into deeper darkness fall those who follow knowledge.

There are worlds of no joy, regions of utter darkness. To those worlds go after death those who in their unwisdom have not wakened up to light.

When awake to the vision of the Atman, our own Self, when a man in truth can say: 'I am He', what desires could lead him to grieve in fever for the body?

He who in the mystery of life has found the Atman, the Spirit, and has awakened to his light, to him as creator belongs the world of the Spirit, for he is this world.

While we are here in this life we may reach the light of wisdom; and if we reach it not, how deep is the darkness. Those who see the light enter life eternal; those who live in darkness enter into sorrow.

When a man sees the Atman, the Self in him, God himself, the Lord of what was and of what shall be, he fears no more.

Before whom the years roll and all the days of the years, him the gods adore as the Light of all lights, as Life immortal.

In whom the five hosts of beings rest and the vastness of space, him I know as Atman immortal, him I know as eternal Brahman.

Those who know him who is the eye of the eye, the ear of the ear, the mind of the mind and the life of life, they know Brahman from the beginning of time.

Even by the mind this truth must be seen: there are not many but only One. Who sees variety and not the Unity wanders on from death to death.

Behold then as One the infinite and eternal One who is in radiance beyond space, the everlasting Soul never born.

Knowing this, let the lover of Brahman follow wisdom. Let him not ponder on many words, for many words are weariness.

Yajñavalkya went on:

This is the great Atman, the Spirit never born, the consciousness of life. He dwells in our own hearts as ruler of all, master of all, lord of all. His greatness becomes not greater by good actions nor less great by evil actions. He is the Lord supreme, sovereign and protector of all beings, the bridge that keeps the worlds apart that they fall not into confusion.

The lovers of Brahman seek him through the sacred *Vedas*, through holy sacrifices, charity, penance and abstinence. He who knows him becomes a Muni, a sage. Pilgrims follow their life of wandering in their longing for his kingdom.

Knowing this, the sages of old desired not offspring. 'What shall we do with offspring,' said they, 'we who possess the Spirit, the whole world?' Rising above the desire of sons, wealth, and the world they followed the life of the pilgrim. For the desire of sons and wealth is the desire of the world. And this desire is vanity.

But the Spirit is not this, is not this. He is incomprehensible, for he cannot be comprehended. He is imperishable, for he cannot pass away. He has no bonds of attachment, for he is free; and free from all bonds he is beyond suffering and fear.

A man who knows this is not moved by grief or exultation on account of the evil or good he has done. He goes beyond both. What is done or left undone grieves him not.

This was said in this sacred verse:

The everlasting greatness of the seer of Brahman is not greater or less great by actions. Let man find the path of the Spirit: who has found this path becomes free from the bonds of evil.

Who knows this and has found peace, he is the lord of himself, his is a calm endurance, and calm concentration. In himself he sees the Spirit, and he sees the Spirit as all.

He is not moved by evil: he removes evil. He is not burned by sin: he burns all sin. And he goes beyond evil, beyond passion, and beyond doubts, for he sees the Eternal.

This is the world of the Spirit, O king. Thus spoke Yajñavalkya.

O Master. Yours is my kingdom and I am yours, said then the king of Videha.

Epilogue

This is the great never-born Spirit of man, enjoyer of the food of life, and giver of treasure. He finds this treasure who knows this.

This is the great never-born Spirit of man, never old and immortal. This is the Spirit of the universe, a refuge from all fear.

Brihad. Up. 4. 3–4

THE MARKS OF
MYSTICAL EXPERIENCE
William James

From William James, *The Varieties of Religious Experience,* pp. 292–295, New American Library edition. The *Varieties* constituted the Gifford Lectures for 1901–1902.

Over and over again in these lectures I have raised points and left them open and unfinished until we should have come to the subject of Mysticism. Some of you, I fear, may have smiled as you noted my reiterated postponements. But now the hour has come when mysticism must be faced in good earnest, and those broken threads wound up together. One may say truly, I think, that personal religious experience has its root and centre in mystical states of consciousness; so for us, who in these lectures are treating personal experience as the exclusive subject of our study, such states of consciousness ought to form the vital chapter from which the other chapters get their light. Whether my treatment of mystical states will shed more light or darkness, I do not know, for my own constitution shuts me out from their enjoyment almost entirely, and I can speak of them only at second hand. But though forced to look upon the subject so externally, I will be as objective and receptive as I can; and I think I shall at least succeed in convincing you of the reality of the states in question, and of the paramount importance of their function.

First of all, then, I ask, What does the expression 'mystical states of consciousness' mean? How do we part off mystical states from other states?

The words 'mysticism' and 'mystical' are often used as terms of mere reproach, to throw at any opinion which we regard as vague and vast and sentimental, and without a base in either facts or logic. For some writers a 'mystic' is any person who believes in thought-transference, or spirit-return. Employed in this way the word has little value: there are too many less ambiguous synonyms. So, to keep it useful by restricting it, I will do what I did in the case of the word 'religion,' and simply propose to you four marks which, when an experience has them, may justify us in calling it mystical for the purpose of the present lectures. In this way we shall save verbal disputation, and the recriminations that generally go therewith.

1. *Ineffability.* The handiest of the marks by which I classify a state of mind as mystical is negative. The subject of it immediately says that it defies expression, that no adequate report of its contents can be given in words. It follows from this that its quality must be directly experienced; it cannot be imparted or transferred to others. In this peculiarity mystical states are more like states of feeling than like states of intellect. No one can make clear to another who has never had a certain feeling, in what the quality or worth of it consists. One must have musical ears to know the value of a symphony; one must have been in love one's self to understand a lover's state of mind. Lacking the heart or ear, we cannot interpret the musician or the lover justly, and are even likely to consider him weak-minded or absurd. The mystic finds that most of us accord to his experiences an equally incompetent treatment.

2. *Noetic quality.* Although so similar to states of feeling, mystical states seem to those who experience them to be also states of knowledge. They are states of insight into depths of truth unplumbed by the discursive intellect. They are illuminations, revelations, full of significance and importance, all inarticulate though they remain; and as a rule they carry with them a curious sense of authority for after-time.

These two characters will entitle any state to be called mystical, in the sense in which I use the word. Two other qualities are less sharply marked, but are usually found. These are:—

3. *Transiency.* Mystical states cannot be sustained for long. Except in rare instances, half an hour, or at most an hour or two, seems to be the limit beyond which they fade into the light of common day. Often, when faded, their quality can but imperfectly be reproduced in memory; but when they recur it is recognized; and from one recurrence to another it is susceptible of continuous development in what is felt as inner richness and importance.

4. *Passivity.* Although the oncoming of mystical states may be facilitated by preliminary voluntary operations, as by fixing the attention, or going through certain bodily performances, or in other ways which manuals of mysticism prescribe; yet when the characteristic sort of consciousness once has set in, the mystic feels as if his own will were in abeyance, and indeed sometimes as if he were grasped and held by a superior power. This latter peculiarity connects mystical states with certain definite phenomena of secondary or alternative personality, such as prophetic speech, automatic writing, or the mediumistic trance. When these latter conditions are well pronounced, however, there may be no recollection whatever of the phenomenon, and it may have no significance for the subject's usual inner life, to which, as it were, it makes a mere interruption. Mystical states strictly so called are never merely interruptive. Some memory of their content always remains, and a profound sense of their importance. They modify the inner life of the subject between the times of their recurrence. Sharp divisions in this region are, however, difficult to make, and we find all sorts of gradations and mixtures.

These four characteristics are sufficient to mark out a group of states of consciousness peculiar enough to deserve a special name and to call for careful study. Let it then be called the mystical group.

Our next step should be to gain acquaintance with some typical examples. Professional mystics at the height of their development have often elaborately organized experiences and a philosophy based thereupon. But you remember what I said in my first lecture: phenomena are best understood when placed within their series, studied in their germ and in their over-ripe decay, and compared with their exaggerated and degenerated kindred. The range of mystical experience is very wide, much too wide for us to cover in the time at our disposal. Yet the method of serial study is so essential for interpretation that if we really wish to reach conclusions we must use it. I will begin, therefore, with phenomena which claim no special religious significance, and end with those of which the religious pretensions are extreme.

The simplest rudiment of mystical experience would seem to be that deepened sense of the significance of a maxim or formula which occasionally sweeps over one. "I've heard that said all my life," we exclaim, "but I never realized its full meaning until now." "When a fellow-monk," said Luther, "one day repeated the words of the Creed: 'I believe in the forgiveness of sins,' I saw the Scripture in an entirely new light; and straightway I felt as if I were born anew. It was as if I had found the door of paradise thrown wide open."[1]

This sense of deeper significance is not confined to rational propositions. Single words,[2] and conjunctions of words, effects of light on land and sea, odors and musical sounds, all bring it when the mind is tuned aright. Most of us can remember the strangely moving power of passages in certain poems read when we were young, irrational doorways as they were through which the mystery of fact, the wildness and the pang of life, stole into our hearts and thrilled them. The words have now perhaps become mere polished surfaces for us; but lyric poetry and music are alive and significant only in proportion as they fetch these vague vistas of a life continuous with our own, beckoning and inviting, yet ever eluding our pursuit. We are alive or dead to the eternal inner message of the arts according as we have kept or lost this mystical susceptibility.

A more pronounced step forward on the mystical ladder is found in an extremely frequent phenomenon, that sudden feeling, namely, which sometimes sweeps over us, of having 'been here before,' as if at some indefinite past time, in just this place, with just these people, we were already saying just these things. As Tennyson writes:

> Moreover, something is or seems,
> That touches me with mystic gleams,
> Like glimpses of forgotten dreams—
>
> Of something felt, like something here;
> Of something done, I know not where;
> Such as no language may declare.[3]

Sir James Crichton-Browne has given the technical name of 'dreamy states' to

---

[1]Newman's *Securus judicat orbis terrarum* is another instance.

[2]'Mesopotamia' is the stock comic instance.—An excellent old German lady, who had done some traveling in her day, used to describe to me her *Sehnsucht* that she might yet visit 'Philadelphiä,' whose wondrous name had always haunted her imagination. Of John Foster it is said that "single words (as *chalcedony*), or the names of ancient heroes, had a mighty fascination over him. 'At any time the word *hermit* was enough to transport him.' The words *woods* and *forests* would produce the most powerful emotion." Foster's Life, by RYLAND, New York, 1846, p. 3.

[3]The Two Voices. In a letter to Mr. B. P. Blood, Tennyson reports of himself as follows:—

"I have never had any revelations through anaesthetics, but a kind of waking trance—this for lack of a better word—I have frequently had, quite up from boyhood, when I have been all alone. This has come upon me through repeating my own name to myself silently, till all at once, as it were out of the intensity of the consciousness of individuality, individuality itself seemed to dissolve and fade away into boundless being, and this not a confused state but the clearest, the surest of the surest, utterly beyond words—where death was an almost laughable impossibility—the loss of personality (if so it were) seeming no extinction, but the only true life. I am ashamed of my feeble description. Have I not said the state is utterly beyond words?"

Professor Tyndall, in a letter, recalls Tennyson saying of this condition: "By God Almighty! there is no delusion in the matter! It is no nebulous ecstasy, but a state of transcendent wonder, associated with absolute clearness of mind." Memoirs of Alfred Tennyson, ii. 473.

these sudden invasions of vaguely reminiscent consciousness.[4] They bring a sense of mystery and of the metaphysical duality of things, and the feeling of an enlargement of perception which seems imminent but which never completes itself. In Dr. Crichton-Browne's opinion they connect themselves with the perplexed and scared disturbances of self-consciousness which occasionally precede epileptic attacks. I think that this learned alienist takes a rather absurdly alarmist view of an intrinsically insignificant phenomenon. He follows it along the downward ladder, to insanity; our path pursues the upward ladder chiefly. The divergence shows how important it is to neglect no part of a phenomenon's connections, for we make it appear admirable or dreadful according to the context by which we set it off.

---

[4]The Lancet, July 6 and 13, 1895, reprinted as the Cavendish Lecture, on Dreamy Mental States, London, Baillière, 1895. They have been a good deal discussed of late by psychologists. See, for example, BERNARD-LEROY: L'Illusion de Fausse Reconnaissance, Paris, 1898.

THE NATURE OF NIRVANA
Ninian Smart

From Ninian Smart, *Reasons and Faiths*, 1958, by permission of Hillary House Publishers Ltd., New York, and Routledge & Kegan Paul, Ltd., London.

Literally, 'nirvāṇa' means 'waning away' (as of a flame) or 'cooling off',[1] and therefore suggests a connection with *taṇhā*, 'burning' or 'craving', which according to the Buddha's teaching is the cause of *dukkha*, 'suffering' or 'misery',[2] and is conducive to rebirth. Thus the Four Noble Truths declare (i) that all existence is sorrowful; (ii) that the cause of sorrow is craving; (iii) that there is a means of destroying this craving; (iv) and that the way to the destruction of craving is the Noble Eightfold Path. And with the destruction of craving, there will be no more rebirth, and one is thus freed from the ceaseless round of existence (*saṁsāra*). Thus there are four aspects of nirvāṇa which have to be noticed:

(a) Achieving the state of nirvāṇa involves destroying the fetters, depravities or intoxicating influences (*āsavas*) which implicate one in worldly existence; and thus involves the cultivation of good conduct, summed up in

---

[1]The Pāli term is *nibbāna*, but I use 'nirvana' as being more familiar to English readers. The latter, the Sanskrit expression, being one of a group meaning 'release', need not have a specifically Buddhist sense—for the Brāhmanist, nirvāṇa would be union with Brahman.
[2]*taṇhā*=Skrt. *tṛṣṇā*; *dukkha*=Skrt. *duḥkha*.

sections (iii) to (v) of the Eightfold Path as right speech, right activity and right livelihood.

(b) The destruction of the *āsavas* also involves spiritual training, summed up in sections (vi) and (vii) of the Path as right endeavour and right mindfulness (i.e. the struggle for self-mastery and continual watchfulness and self-awareness).

(c) These lead to mystical meditation (*samādhi*), summed up in section (viii) of the Path as right meditation.

(d) On death one attains to complete nirvāṇa, and there is no more rebirth.

We may thus refer to four achievements within the Eightfold Path: (a) the achievement of moral mastery; (b) the achievement of spiritual mastery; (c) the attainment of mystical bliss; (d) the arrival at death of one who has achieved the above and not fallen away (like the unfortunate Godhika who attained temporary release six times but fell away.)[3] It should be noted that spiritual mastery is held to bring knowledge or insight—insight into the truth of the Four Truths. Thus (b) and (c) are often referred to respectively as the emancipation of knowledge, and the emancipation of heart and mind.[4] The words 'nirvāṇa' and *'parinirvāṇa'* are sometimes used by Western scholars to distinguish (c) from (d), nirvāṇa being the attainment of bliss together with moral and spiritual mastery and *parinirvāṇa* being the attainment of death without falling-away. This distinction is convenient and shall be used here, even though it is strictly inaccurate, since *'parinirvāṇa'* (together with the perfect passive participle *parinibbuta* in Pāh) is used as much for (c) as (d) in the texts,[5] the only difference in Pāli being that *nibbāna* refers to the state and *parinibbāna* the attaining of the state.[6] Thus *nirvāṇa* is, in our terminology, the state of one who has attained a short-term state or states of mystical bliss and insight, but it will also be used of the latter by itself, it being understood always that this is achieved in the setting of moral and spiritual mastery.[7] It should be noted with regard to (d), that some Western scholars have thought of *parinirvāṇa* as involving some special state after death, as signifying, that is, a sort of after-life; but this is a mistake generated by the desire to see greater similarities between Hīnayāna and Western religion than in fact obtain. But the question as to what happens to a saint upon death was declared by the Buddha to be one of the undetermined questions, (*avyākatāni*): and 'What I have determined hold as determined, and what I have not determined hold as undetermined'.[8] He points out that to ask what happens to the *arahat* upon death is like asking where a flame goes when it goes out; no

---

[3] *Saṁyutta Nik.,* i.109.
[4] *ceto,* see E. J. Thomas, *The History of Buddhist Thought,* p. 121.
[5] *pari-* is an achievement-prefix; a noun referring to a state is converted thereby into a noun meaning the achievement of that state. Thus *nibbāna: parinibbāna* :: 'tranquillity' :: 'tranquillization' :: 'luminousness' :: 'illumination'. See E. J. Thomas, *op. cit.,* p. 121, n. 4.
[6] And even here the distinction can become blurred, as also in such English words as 'success' which can be used both for the achievement and the state of one who is successful. See n. 7.
[7] It becomes quite natural for the point at which the state is achieved to be called nirvāṇa.
[8] *Majjhima Nik.,* i.427.

answer fits the case and so the question should not be asked.[9] But the doctrine of *parinirvāṇa* involves that the saint cannot be held to achieve it until he is dead (compare Solon's saying as used by Aristotle: 'Call no man happy while he yet lives,[10] with the rider that this achievement involves emancipation from rebirth. To say of a man that he has achieved *parinirvāṇa* is to make a spiritual judgment to which all his behaviour up until his death is relevant. Thus the issue discussed in the *Milindapañha* as to whether a saint (i.e. one who has achieved nirvāṇa) can do wrong is in part a logical question as to whether a wrong-doing person who claims to have achieved nirvāṇa can be counted as so having attained.

Like other mystical states as reported, e.g. by Western mystics and Ṣūfīs, nirvāṇa is a goal, as is shown by the universal references to the conduct leading to them as 'the Path', 'the Way', etc. And this path involves a method (in Buddhism, right meditation). John Cassian, for example, one of the earliest Christian writers on mysticism, is insistent that mysticism involves method.[11] Again the whole concept of *yoga* (i.e. yoking) is one of controlled attainment.

Nevertheless, the goals achieved in different mystical endeavours are not in a sense the same goal. Someone who had correctly performed the injunctions laid down by the Buddha would be likely to exclaim: 'Now I have gained nirvāṇa', not 'Now I have seen God' or 'Now I am one with Brahman'. This is not accountable in the following simple ways: The Buddhist has never heard of Allah or Brahman—or: The Buddhist and the others are trying to say the same thing in different ways—or even: The Buddhist thinks he has achieved one thing when he has *really* attained another.

It is not simply a matter of not having heard of Allah, for even if he had and he were a Buddhist he would still express himself by reference to nirvāṇa. Nor is it a case of different ways of saying the same thing, for, on the contrary, the difference of language is one of the vitally important differences. It is indeed this which perhaps more than anything else distinguishes the achievement of the Buddhist monk from that of the Ṣūfī. For in many other ways there are similarities of behaviour: and the subtle divergencies are crystallized by the use of differing concepts. For, first, each is embedded in different doctrinal schemes. And second, they are partly precipitated out of the rules for attaining the goals represented by the concepts. In fact, in the case of nirvāṇa, the concept is in a very great degree bound up with the Eightfold Path (*Allah* and *union with Allah* are less tightly bound to a path, since another strand enters here too). Thus, it can hardly be said of one who has obeyed *these* rules that he has attained to the goal precipitated out of *those* rules, that the *nibbuta* has gained the peace of God. Nor that he thinks he has achieved one thing but has in fact achieved another. (Though there may be a missionary point in saying these things; but even so the real issue must be seen in the relative merits of doctrinal schemes.)

From the foregoing it will be seen that it is absurd to entertain the possibility of stumbling, all unawares, on the mystic's bliss. For the latter is defined in large part by the procedure for getting there. Thus Plotinus' remark:

---

[9] *Ibid.*, i.483–8.
[10] Reported and interpreted in *Nicomachean Ethics*, 1100 a 11.
[11] *Confessions*, xiv.

It is pointless to say 'Look to God' without giving instruction on how to look,[12]

is a stronger one than that of St. Thomas à Kempis when he said:

What will it avail thee to argue profoundly about the Trinity if thou be void of humility and therefore displeasing to the Trinity?[13]

In the first case, talk about the divine will be empty without 'unpacking' in terms of the Path; in the second, it will have content but no fruit. In the one case it will be pointless, in the other worse than pointless.

Thus propositions about the attainment of nirvāṇa need, for their verification, attention to their setting. Just as, in understanding 'He scored a goal' we must look to the setting of a game conducted according to certain rules; and in understanding 'He found the solution' we must look to a situation of search, so too with 'He attained nirvāṇa' we must attend to the setting. Even if a boy were kicking a football about by himself and then deftly shot it between the posts, we could only understand this as a goal on the supposition that he was pretending to play a game; even if someone while watching an opera were to cry 'I know the answer', we could only understand this oddly-situated solution by reference to another situation, some search that this Archimedes had been conducting. So too it would hardly make sense to speak of someone's realizing nirvāṇa unless certain conditions had previously been fulfilled, unless, so to speak, the stage had been set. Thus these conditions are not merely (or perhaps even) to be thought of as causal conditions, for unless they obtain it is *inappropriate* to say that nirvāṇa has been achieved. One must advance along the Eightfold Path. To verify the proposition 'He has attained nirvāṇa' one must consult the rules.

But it may be objected that there is a hint of an unjust comparison. For though it is true that concepts such as *goal, touch,* etc. (and others found in games-contexts), are precipitated by the rules, these rules are conventional, whereas the rules for realizing nirvāṇa constitute *advice* on how to succeed (like, not the rules of a game, but the rules for becoming proficient at it). Now in this case the goal is prior to the rules whereas in the other case this is not so. We set up the target and then seek how to hit it—the target arises neither out of our search on how to hit it nor out of conventions as to what will constitute a target. Did not the Buddha so often employ a medical analogy, suggesting that nirvāṇa was a cure and that the cure can be effected in a certain way?

There are two points here to be kept distinct. (a) What are the conditions under which we would count a change of character as ascribable to the attainment of nirvāṇa? (b) What are the causal conditions of such an attainment?

As for (b), it can be supposed that a certain pattern of life and direction of effort, as adumbrated in the Noble Eightfold Path, is likely to lead to liberation. Without delving too deeply into the foggy problem of what kind of causal connection is involved here we can at least make this modest claim. But we must nevertheless take account of one complication, namely that at least there must be

---

[12]*Enneads*, II.9.15.
[13]*Imitatio Christi*, I.I.3.

some hope or intention of uprooting the misery-producing craving within us. But this 'must' is not simply causal in import, for otherwise, if there were no such hope or intention, it would not be unlikely but absurd to speak of an achievement. Thus one logically cannot attain to nirvāṇa by accident.

As for (a), since the goal is not capable of direct definition, and since it has to be indicated by the direction in which it lies, a necessary part of its description consists of the rules to be used in order to reach it; and therefore the behaviour expected of one who travels the Path must be referred to in considering the claim to have attained it. The correct pre-arrival behaviour is therefore one of the conditions which would have to be fulfilled before one could be said to have realized nirvāṇa. Over and above this, the nature of the goal is described within the framework of the doctrinal scheme under whose aegis the spiritual activity takes place, and this will to some extent affect the rules—for example, John Cassian pays some considerable attention to mystical *prayer;* but in a faith where prayer is not used because inapplicable—since there is no God—this part of the mystic's training will not appear.[14]

We may state the matter succinctly thus: The nature of the goal is revealed in the rules enjoined for its attainment, which are affected not merely by differing conceptions of the mystical journey, but also by differing features in the doctrinal schemes. Further, the attainer of the goal must intend to, in the sense that he deliberately submits to the enjoined rules, with the hope or intention of attaining the goal. The pre-arrival conditions which have to be fulfilled before the claim to have achieved nirvāṇa can be entertained are: the attainment of moral and spiritual mastery, as under stages (i) to (vii) of the Eightfold Path. Hence the claim is not a simple one to have had some particular experience or experiences: for the setting involved in the claim stretches well before the time of blissful rapture and the achievement is the achievement of a particular sort of goal.

---

[14]*Confessions* x, xi. But Cassian's description of such prayer is, it should be noted, rather different from that of ordinary prayer, being ineffable, expressed by groanings and sighs that cannot be uttered, etc. In some respects it is not far off rapture or bliss.

Chapter
TWO

RELIGION EAST AND WEST
numinous experience

SURRENDER AND RENUNCIATION

Bhagavad-Gita

From Juan Mascaro (trans.), *The Bhagavad Gita,* 1962, by permission of Penguin Books Ltd., Harmondsworth, Middlesex, England.

Arjuna

1 Speak to me, Krishna, of the essence of renunciation, and of the essence of surrender.

Krishna

2 The renunciation of selfish works is called renunciation; but the surrender of the reward of all work is called surrender.

3 Some say that there should be renunciation of action—since action disturbs contemplation; but others say that works of sacrifice, gift and self-harmony should not be renounced.

4 Hear my truth about the surrender of works, Arjuna. Surrender, O best of men, is of three kinds.

5 Works of sacrifice, gift, and self-harmony should not be abandoned, but should indeed be performed; for these are works of purification.

6 But even these works, Arjuna, should be done in the freedom of a pure offering, and without expectation of a reward. This is my final word.

7 It is not right to leave undone the holy work which ought to be done. Such a surrender of action would be a delusion of darkness.

8 And he who abandons his duty because he has fear of pain, his surrender is of Rajas, impure, and in truth he has no reward.

9 But he who does holy work, Arjuna, because it ought to be done, and surrenders selfishness and thought of reward, his work is pure, and is peace.

10 This man sees and has no doubts: he surrenders, he is pure and has peace. Work, pleasant or painful, is for him joy.

11 For there is no man on earth who can fully renounce living work, but he who renounces the reward of his work is in truth a man of renunciation.

12 When work is done for a reward, the work brings pleasure, or pain, or both, in its time; but when a man does work in Eternity, then Eternity is his reward.

13 Know now from me, Arjuna, the five causes of all actions as given in the Sankhya wisdom, wherein is found the end of all works.

14 The body, the lower 'I am', the means of perception, the means of action, and Fate. These are the five.

15 Whatever a man does, good or bad, in thought, word or deed, has these five sources of action.

16 If one thinks that his infinite Spirit does the finite work which nature does, he is a man of clouded vision and he does not see the truth.

17 He who is free from the chains of selfishness, and whose mind is free from any ill-will, even if he kills all these warriors he kills them not and he is free.

18 In the idea of a work there is the knower, the knowing and the known. When the idea is work there is the doer, the doing and the thing done.

19 The knowing, the doer and the thing done are said in the science of the 'Gunas' to be of three kinds, according to their qualities. Hear of these three.

20 When one sees Eternity in things that pass away and Infinity in finite things, then one has pure knowledge.

21 But if one merely sees the diversity of things, with their divisions and limitations, then one has impure knowledge.

22 And if one selfishly sees a thing as if it were everything, independent of the one and the many, then one is in the darkness of ignorance.

23 When work is done as sacred work, unselfishly, with a peaceful mind, without lust or hate, with no desire for reward, then the work is pure.

24 But when work is done with selfish desire, or feeling it is an effort, or thinking it is a sacrifice, then the work is impure.

25 And that work which is done with a confused mind, without considering what may follow, or one's own powers, or the harm done to others, or one's own loss, is work of darkness.

26 A man free from the chains of selfish attachments, free from his lower 'I am', who has determination and perserverance, and whose inner peace is beyond victory or defeat—such a man has pure Sattva.

27 But a man who is a slave of his passions, who works for selfish ends, who is greedy, violent and impure, and who is moved by pleasure and pain, is a man of impure Rajas.

28 And a man without self-harmony, vulgar, arrogant and deceitful; malicious, indolent and despondent, and also procrastinating, is a man of the darkness of Tamas.

29 Hear now fully and in detail the threefold division of wisdom and steadiness, according to the three Gunas.

30 There is a wisdom which knows when to go and when to return, what is to be done and what is not to be done, what is fear and what is courage, what is bondage and what is liberation—that is pure wisdom.

31 Impure wisdom has no clear vision of what is right and what is wrong, what should be done and what should not be done.

32 And there is a wisdom obscured in darkness when wrong is thought to be right, and when things are thought to be that which they are not.

33 When in the Yoga of holy contemplation the movements of the mind and of the breath of life are in a harmony of peace, there is steadiness, and that steadiness is pure.

34 But that steadiness which, with a desire for rewards, attaches itself to wealth, pleasure, and even religious ritual, is a steadiness of passion, impure.

35 And that steadiness whereby a fool does not surrender laziness, fear, self-pity, depression and lust, is indeed a steadiness of darkness.

36 Hear now, great Arjuna, of the three kinds of pleasure. There is the pleasure of following that right path which leads to the end of all pain.

37 What seems at first a cup of sorrow is found in the end immortal wine. That pleasure is pure: it is the joy which arises from a clear vision of the Spirit.

38 But the pleasure which comes from the craving of the senses with the objects

of their desire, which seems at first a drink of sweetness but is found in the end a cup of poison, is the pleasure of passion, impure.

39 And that pleasure which both in the beginning and in the end is only a delusion of the soul, which comes from the dullness of sleep, laziness or carelessness, is the pleasure of darkness.

40 There is nothing on earth or in heaven which is free from these three powers of Nature.

41 The works of Brahmins, Kshatriyas, Vaisyas and Sudras are different, in harmony with the three powers of their born nature.

42 The works of a Brahmin are peace; self-harmony, austerity and purity; loving-forgiveness and righteousness; vision and wisdom and faith.

43 These are the works of a Kshatriya: a heroic mind, inner fire, constancy, resourcefulness, courage in battle, generosity and noble leadership.

44 Trade, agriculture and the rearing of cattle is the work of a Vaisya. And the work of the Sudra is service.

45 They all attain perfection when they find joy in their work. Hear how a man attains perfection and finds joy in his work.

46 A man attains perfection when his work is worship of God, from whom all things come and who is in all.

47 Greater is thine own work, even if this be humble, than the work of another, even if this be great. When a man does the work God gives him, no sin can touch this man.

48 And a man should not abandon his work, even if he cannot achieve it in full perfection; because in all work there may be imperfection, even as in all fire there is smoke.

49 When a man has his reason in freedom from bondage, and his soul is in harmony, beyond desires, then renunciation leads him to a region supreme which is beyond earthly action.

50 Hear now how he then reaches Brahman, the highest vision of Light.

51 When the vision of reason is clear, and in steadiness the soul is in harmony; when the world of sound and other senses is gone, and the spirit has risen above passion and hate;

52 When a man dwells in the solitude of silence, and meditation and contemplation are ever with him; when too much food does not disturb his health, and his thoughts and words and body are in peace; when freedom from passion is his constant will;

53 And his selfishness and violence and pride are gone; when lust and anger and greediness are no more, and he is free from the thought 'this is mine'; then this man has risen on the mountain of the Highest: he is worthy to be one with Brahman, with God.

54 He is one with Brahman, with God, and beyond grief and desire his soul is in peace. His love is one for all creation, and he has supreme love for me.

55 By love he knows me in truth, who I am and what I am. And when he knows me in truth he enters into my Being.

56 In whatever work he does he can take refuge in me, and he attains then by my grace the imperishable home of Eternity.

57 Offer in thy heart all thy works to me, and see me as the End of thy love, take refuge in the Yoga of reason, and ever rest thy soul in me.

58 If thy soul finds rest in me, thou shalt overcome all dangers by my grace; but if thy thoughts are on thyself, and thou wilt not listen, thou shalt perish.

59 If thou wilt not fight thy battle of life because in selfishness thou art afraid of the battle, thy resolution is in vain: nature will compel thee.

60 Because thou art in the bondage of Karma, of the forces of thine own past life; and that which thou, in thy delusion, with a good will dost not want to do, unwillingly thou shalt have to do.

61 God dwells in the heart of all beings, Arjuna: thy God dwells in thy heart. And his power of wonder moves all things—puppets in a play of shadows—whirling them onwards on the stream of time.

62 Go to him for thy salvation with all thy soul, victorious man. By his grace thou shalt obtain the peace supreme, thy home of Eternity.

63 I have given thee words of vision and wisdom more secret than hidden mysteries. Ponder them in the silence of thy soul, and then in freedom do thy will.

64 Hear again my Word supreme, the deepest secret of silence. Because I love thee well, I will speak to thee words of salvation.

65 Give thy mind to me, and give me thy heart, and thy sacrifice, and thy adoration. This is my Word of promise: thou shalt in truth come to me, for thou art dear to me.

66 Leave all things behind, and come to me for thy salvation. I will make thee free from the bondage of sins. Fear no more.

67 These things must never be spoken to one who lacks self-discipline, or who has no love, or who does not want to hear or who argues against me.

68 But he who will teach this secret doctrine to those who have love for me, and who himself has supreme love, he in truth shall come unto me.

69 For there can be no man among men who does greater work for me, nor can there be a man on earth who is dearer to me than he is.

70 He who learns in contemplation the holy words of our discourse, the light of his vision is his adoration. This is my truth.

71 And he who only hears but has faith, and in his heart he has no doubts, he also attains liberation and the worlds of joy of righteous men.

72 Hast thou heard these words, Arjuna, in the silent communion of thy soul? Has the darkness of thy delusion been dispelled by thine inner Light?

Arjuna

73 By thy grace I remember my Light, and now gone is my delusion. My doubts are no more, my faith is firm; and now I can say 'Thy will be done'.

Sanjaya

74 Thus I heard these words of glory between Arjuna and the God of all, and they fill my soul with awe and wonder.

75 By the grace of the poet Vyasa I heard these words of secret silence. I heard the mystery of Yoga, taught by Krishna the Master himself.

76 I remember, O king, I remember the words of holy wonder between Krishna and Arjuna, and again and again my soul feels joy.

77 And I remember, I ever remember, that vision of glory of the God of all, and again and again joy fills my soul.

78 Wherever is Krishna, the End of Yoga, wherever is Arjuna who masters the bow, there is beauty and victory, and joy and all righteousness. This is my faith.

CREATION AND FALL
Genesis

The Bible, King James version.

Chapter 1

In the beginning God created the heaven and the earth.

2 And the earth was without form, and void; and darkness *was* upon the face of the deep. And the Spirit of God moved upon the face of the waters.

3 And God said, Let there be light: and there was light.

4 And God saw the light, that *it was* good: and God divided the light from the darkness.

5 And God called the light Day, and the darkness he called Night. And the evening and the morning were the first day.

6 ¶ And God said, Let there be a firmament in the midst of the waters, and let it divide the waters from the waters.

7 And God made the firmament, and divided the waters which *were* under the firmament from the waters which *were* above the firmament: and it was so.

8 And God called the firmament Heaven. And the evening and the morning were the second day.

9 ¶ And God said, Let the waters under the heaven be gathered together unto one place, and let the dry *land* appear: and it was so.

10 And God called the dry *land* Earth; and the gathering together of the waters called he Seas: and God saw that *it was* good.

11 And God said, Let the earth bring forth grass, the herb yielding seed, *and* the fruit tree yielding fruit after his kind, whose seed *is* in itself, upon the earth: and it was so.

12 And the earth brought forth grass, *and* herb yielding seed after his kind, and the tree yielding fruit, whose seed *was* in itself, after his kind: and God saw that *it was* good.

13 And the evening and the morning were the third day.

14 ¶ And God said, Let there be lights in the firmament of the heaven to divide the day from the night; and let them be for signs, and for seasons, and for days, and years:

15 And let them be for lights in the firmament of the heaven to give light upon the earth: and it was so.

16 And God made two great lights; the greater light to rule the day, and the lesser light to rule the night: *he made* the stars also.

17 And God set them in the firmament of the heaven to give light upon the earth,

18 And to rule over the day and over the night, and to divide the light

from the darkness: and God saw that *it was* good.

19 And the evening and the morning were the fourth day.

20 And God said, Let the waters bring forth abundantly the moving creature that hath life, and fowl *that* may fly above the earth in the open firmament of heaven.

21 And God created great whales, and every living creature that moveth, which the waters brought forth abundantly, after their kind, and every winged fowl after his kind: and God saw that *it was* good.

22 And God blessed them, saying, Be fruitful, and multiply, and fill the waters in the seas, and let fowl multiply in the earth.

23 And the evening and the morning were the fifth day.

24 ¶ And God said, Let the earth bring forth the living creature after his kind, cattle, and creeping thing, and beast of the earth after his kind: and it was so.

25 And God made the beast of the earth after his kind, and cattle after their kind, and every thing that creepeth upon the earth after his kind: and God saw that *it was* good.

26 ¶ And God said, Let us make man in our image, after our likeness: and let them have dominion over the fish of the sea, and over the fowl of the air, and over the cattle, and over all the earth, and over every creeping thing that creepeth upon the earth.

27 So God created man in his *own* image, in the image of God created he him; male and female created he them.

28 And God blessed them, and God said unto them, Be fruitful, and multiply, and replenish the earth, and subdue it: and have dominion over the fish of the sea, and over the fowl

of the air, and over every living thing that moveth upon the earth.

29 ¶ And God said, Behold, I have given you every herb bearing seed, which *is* upon the face of all the earth, and every tree, in the which *is* the fruit of a tree yielding seed; to you it shall be for meat.

30 And to every beast of the earth, and to every fowl of the air, and to every thing that creepeth upon the earth, wherein *there is* life, *I have given* every green herb for meat: and it was so.

31 And God saw every thing that he had made, and, behold, *it was* very good. And the evening and the morning were the sixth day.

Chapter 2

Thus the heavens and the earth were finished, and all the host of them.

2 And on the seventh day God ended his work which he had made; and he rested on the seventh day from all his work which he had made.

3 And God blessed the seventh day, and sanctified it: because that in it he had rested from all his work which God created and made.

4 ¶ These *are* the generations of the heavens and of the earth when they were created, in the day that the LORD God made the earth and the heavens,

5 And every plant of the field before it was in the earth, and every herb of the field before it grew: for the LORD God had not caused it to rain upon the earth, and *there was* not a man to till the ground.

6 But there went up a mist from the earth, and watered the whole face of the ground.

7 And the LORD God formed man

of the dust of the ground, and breathed into his nostrils the breath of life; and man became a living soul.

8 ¶ And the LORD God planted a garden eastward in Eden; and there he put the man whom he had formed.

9 And out of the ground made the LORD God to grow every tree that is pleasant to the sight, and good for food; the tree of life also in the midst of the garden, and the tree of knowledge of good and evil.

10 And a river went out of Eden to water the garden; and from thence it was parted, and became into four heads.

11 The name of the first *is* Pison: that *is* it which compasseth the whole land of Havilah, where *there is* gold;

12 And the gold of that land *is* good: there *is* bdellium and the onyx stone.

13 And the name of the second river *is* Gihon: the same *is* it that compasseth the whole land of Ethiopia.

14 And the name of the third river *is* Hiddekel: that *is* it which goeth toward the east of Assyria. And the fourth river *is* Euphrates.

15 And the LORD God took the man, and put him into the garden of Eden to dress it and to keep it.

16 And the LORD God commanded the man, saying, Of every tree of the garden thou mayest freely eat:

17 But of the tree of the knowledge of good and evil, thou shalt not eat of it: for in the day that thou eatest thereof thou shalt surely die.

18 ¶ And the LORD God said, *It is* not good that the man should be alone; I will make him an help meet for him.

19 And out of the ground the LORD God formed every beast of the field, and every fowl of the air; and

brought *them* unto Adam to see what he would call them: and whatsoever Adam called every living creature, that *was* the name thereof.

20 And Adam gave names to all cattle, and to the fowl of the air, and to every beast of the field; but for Adam there was not found an help meet for him.

21 And the LORD God caused a deep sleep to fall upon Adam, and he slept: and he took one of his ribs, and closed up the flesh instead thereof;

22 And the rib, which the LORD God had taken from man, made he a woman, and brought her unto the man.

23 And Adam said, This *is* now bone of my bones, and flesh of my flesh: she shall be called Woman, because she was taken out of Man.

24 Therefore shall a man leave his father and his mother, and shall cleave unto his wife: and they shall be one flesh.

25 And they were both naked, the man and his wife, and were not ashamed.

Chapter 3

Now the serpent was more subtil than any beast of the field which the LORD God had made. And he said unto the woman, Yea, hath God said, Ye shall not eat of every tree of the garden?

2 And the woman said unto the serpent, We may eat of the fruit of the trees of the garden:

3 But of the fruit of the tree which *is* in the midst of the garden, God hath said, Ye shall not eat of it, neither shall ye touch it, lest ye die.

4 And the serpent said unto the woman, Ye shall not surely die:

5 For God doth know that in the

day ye eat thereof, then your eyes shall be opened, and ye shall be as the gods, knowing good and evil.

6 And when the woman saw that the tree *was* good for food, and that it *was* pleasant to the eyes, and a tree to be desired to make *one* wise, she took of the fruit thereof, and did eat, and gave also unto her husband with her; and he did eat.

7 And the eyes of them both were opened, and they knew that they *were* naked; and they sewed fig leaves together, and made themselves aprons.

8 And they heard the voice of the LORD God walking in the garden in the cool of the day: and Adam and his wife hid themselves from the presence of the LORD God amongst the trees of the garden.

9 And the LORD God called unto Adam, and said unto him, Where *art* thou?

10 And he said, I heard thy voice in the garden, and I was afraid, because I *was* naked; and I hid myself.

11 And he said, Who told thee that thou *wast* naked? Hast thou eaten of the tree, whereof I commanded thee that thou shouldest not eat?

12 And the man said, The woman whom thou gavest *to be* with me, she gave me of the tree, and I did eat.

13 And the LORD God said unto the woman, What *is* this *that* thou hast done? And the woman said, The serpent beguiled me, and I did eat.

14 And the LORD God said unto the serpent, Because thou hast done this, thou *art* cursed above all cattle, and above every beast of the field; upon thy belly shalt thou go, and dust shalt thou eat all the days of thy life:

15 And I will put enmity between thee and the woman, and between thy seed and her seed; it shall bruise thy head, and thou shalt bruise his heel.

16 Unto the woman he said, I will greatly multiply thy sorrow and thy conception; in sorrow thou shalt bring forth children; and thy desire *shall be* to thy husband, and he shall rule over thee.

17 And unto Adam he said, Because thou hast hearkened unto the voice of thy wife, and hast eaten of the tree, of which I commanded thee, saying, Thou shalt not eat of it: cursed *is* the ground for thy sake; in sorrow shalt thou eat *of* it all the days of thy life;

18 Thorns also and thistles shall it bring forth to thee; and thou shalt eat the herb of the field;

19 In the sweat of thy face shalt thou eat bread, till thou return unto the ground; for out of it wast thou taken: for dust thou *art,* and unto dust shalt thou return.

20 And Adam called his wife's name Eve; because she was the mother of all living.

21 Unto Adam also and to his wife did the LORD God make coats of skins, and clothed them.

22 ¶ And the LORD God said, Behold, the man is become as one of us, to know good and evil: and now, lest he put forth his hand, and take also of the tree of life, and eat, and live for ever:

23 Therefore the LORD God sent him forth from the garden of Eden, to till the ground from whence he was taken.

24 So he drove out the man; and he placed at the east of the garden of Eden Cherubims, and a flaming sword which turned every way, to keep the way of the tree of life.

DIVINE HOLINESS
Isaiah

The Bible, King James version.

Chapter 6

In the year that king Uzziah died I saw also the Lord sitting upon a throne, high and lifted up, and his train filled the temple.

2 Above it stood the seraphims: each one had six wings; with twain he covered his face, and with twain he covered his feet, and with twain he did fly.

3 And one cried unto another, and said, Holy, holy, holy, *is* the LORD of hosts: the whole earth is full of his glory.

4 And the posts of the door moved at the voice of him that cried, and the house was filled with smoke.

5 Then said I, Woe *is* me! for I am undone; because I *am* a man of unclean lips, and I dwell in the midst of a people of unclean lips: for mine eyes have seen the King, the LORD of hosts.

6 Then flew one of the seraphims unto me, having a live coal in his hand, *which* he had taken with the tongs from off the altar:

7 And he laid *it* upon my mouth, and said, Lo, this hath touched thy lips; and thine iniquity is taken away, and thy sin purged.

8 Also I heard the voice of the LORD, saying, Whom shall I send, and who will go for us? Then said I, Here *am* I; send me.

THE CRUCIFIXION AND THE RESURRECTION
The Gospel of St. Matthew

The Bible, King James version.

Chapter 27

When the morning was come, all the chief priests and elders of the people took counsel against Jesus to put him to death:

2 And when they had bound him, they led *him* away, and delivered him to Pontius Pilate the governor.

3 ¶ Then Judas, which had betrayed him, when he saw that he was condemned, repented himself, and brought again the thirty pieces of silver to the chief priests and elders,

4 Saying, I have sinned in that I have betrayed the innocent blood. And they said, What *is that* to us? see thou *to that.*

5 And he cast down the pieces of silver in the temple, and departed, and went and hanged himself.

6 And the chief priests took the silver pieces, and said, It is not lawful for, to put them into the treasury, because it is the price of blood.

7 And they took counsel, and

bought with them the potter's field, to bury strangers in.

8 Wherefore that field was called, The field of blood, unto this day.

9 Then was fulfilled that which was spoken by Jeremy the prophet, saying, And they took the thirty pieces of silver, the price of him that was valued, whom they of the children of Israel did value;

10 And gave them for the potter's field, as the Lord appointed me.

11 And Jesus stood before the governor: and the governor asked him, saying, Art thou the King of the Jews? And Jesus said unto him, Thou sayest.

12 And when he was accused of the chief priests and elders, he answered nothing.

13 Then said Pilate unto him, Hearest thou not how many things they witness against thee?

14 And he answered him to never a word; insomuch that the governor marvelled greatly.

15 Now at *that* feast the governor was wont to release unto the people a prisoner, whom they would.

16 And they had then a notable prisoner, called Barabbas.

17 Therefore when they were gathered together, Pilate said unto them, Whom will ye that I release unto you? Barabbas, or Jesus which is called Christ?

18 For he knew that for envy they had delivered him.

19 ¶ When he was set down on the judgment seat, his wife sent unto him, saying, Have thou nothing to do with that just man: for I have suffered many things this day in a dream because of him.

20 But the chief priests and elders persuaded the multitude that they should ask Barabbas, and destroy Jesus.

21 The governor answered and said unto them, Whether of the twain will ye that I release unto you? They said, Barabbas.

22 Pilate saith unto them, What shall I do then with Jesus which is called Christ? *They* all say unto him, Let him be crucified.

23 And the governor said, Why, what evil hath he done? But they cried out the more, saying, Let him be crucified.

24 ¶ When Pilate saw that he could prevail nothing, but *that* rather a tumult was made, he took water, and washed *his* hands before the multitude, saying, I am innocent of the blood of this just person: see ye *to it.*

25 Then answered all the people, and said, His blood *be* on us, and on our children.

26 ¶ Then released he Barabbas unto them: and when he had scourged Jesus, he delivered *him* to be crucified.

27 Then the soldiers of the governor took Jesus into the common hall, and gathered unto him the whole band *of soldiers.*

28 And they stripped him, and put on him a scarlet robe.

29 ¶ And when they had platted a crown of thorns, they put *it* upon his head, and a reed in his right hand: and they bowed the knee before him, and mocked him, saying, Hail, King of the Jews!

30 And they spit upon him, and took the reed, and smote him on the head.

31 And after that they had mocked him, they took the robe off from him, and put his own raiment on him, and led him away to crucify *him.*

32 And as they came out, they found a man of Cyrene, Simon by name: him they compelled to bear his cross.

33 And when they were come unto a place called Golgotha, that is to say, a place of a skull,

34 ¶ They gave him vinegar to drink mingled with gall: and when he had tasted *thereof,* he would not drink.

35 And they crucified him, and parted his garments, casting lots: that it might be fulfilled which was spoken by the prophet, They parted my garments among them, and upon my vesture did they cast lots.

36 And sitting down they watched him there;

37 And set up over his head his accusation written, THIS IS JESUS THE KING OF THE JEWS.

38 Then were there two thieves crucified with him, one on the right hand, and another on the left.

39 ¶ And they that passed by reviled him, wagging their heads,

40 And saying, Thou that destroyest the temple, and buildest *it* in three days, save thyself. If thou be the Son of God, come down from the cross.

41 Likewise also the chief priests mocking *him,* with the scribes and elders, said,

42 He saved others; himself he cannot save. If he be the King of Israel, let him now come down from the cross, and we will believe him.

43 He trusted in God; let him deliver him now, if he will have him: for he said, I am the Son of God.

44 The thieves also, which were crucified with him, cast the same in his teeth.

45 Now from the sixth hour there was darkness over all the land unto the ninth hour.

46 And about the ninth hour Jesus cried with a loud voice, saying, Eli, Eli, lama sabachthani? that is to say, My God, my God, why hast thou forsaken me?

47 Some of them that stood there, when they heard *that,* said, This *man* calleth for Elias.

48 And straightway one of them ran, and took a spunge, and filled *it* with vinegar, and put *it* on a reed, and gave him to drink.

49 The rest said, Let be, let us see whether Elias will come to save him.

50 ¶ Jesus, when he had cried again with a loud voice, yielded up the ghost.

51 And, behold, the veil of the temple was rent in twain from the top to the bottom; and the earth did quake, and the rocks rent;

52 And the graves were opened; and many bodies of the saints which slept arose,

53 And came out of the graves after his resurrection, and went into the holy city, and appeared unto many.

54 Now when the centurion, and they that were with him, watching Jesus, saw the earthquake, and those things that were done, they feared greatly, saying, Truly this was the Son of God.

55 And many women were there beholding afar off, which followed Jesus from Galilee, ministering unto him:

56 Among which was Mary Magdalene, and Mary the mother of James and Joses, and the mother of Zebedee's children.

57 When the even was come, there came a rich man of Arimathaea, named Joseph, who also himself was Jesus' disciple:

58 He went to Pilate, and begged the body of Jesus. Then Pilate commanded the body to be delivered.

59 And when Joseph had taken the body, he wrapped it in a clean linen cloth,

60 And laid it in his own new tomb, which he had hewn out in the rock: and he rolled a great stone to the door of the sepulchre, and departed.

61 And there was Mary Magdalene, and the other Mary, sitting over against the sepulchre.

62 ¶ Now the next day, that followed the day of the preparation, the chief priests and Pharisees came together unto Pilate,

63 Saying, Sir, we remember that that deceiver said, while he was yet alive, After three days I will rise again.

64 Command therefore that the sepulchre be made sure until the third day, lest his disciples come by night, and steal him away, and say unto the people, He is risen from the dead: so the last error shall be worse than the first.

65 Pilate said unto them, Ye have a watch: go your way, make *it* as sure as ye can.

66 So they went, and made the sepulchre sure, sealing the stone, and setting a watch.

Chapter 28

In the end of the sabbath, as it began to dawn toward the first *day* of the week, came Mary Magdalene and the other Mary to see the sepulchre.

2 And, behold, there was a great earthquake: for the angel of the Lord descended from heaven, and came and rolled back the stone from the door, and sat upon it.

3 His countenance was like lightning, and his raiment white as snow:

4 And for fear of him the keepers did shake, and became as dead *men.*

5 And the angel answered and said unto the women, Fear not ye: for I know that ye seek Jesus, which was crucified.

6 He is not here: for he is risen, as he said. Come, see the place where the LORD lay.

7 And go quickly, and tell his disciples that he is risen from the dead; and, behold, he goeth before you into Galilee; there shall ye see him: lo, I have told you.

8 And they departed quickly from the sepulchre with fear and great joy; and did run to bring his disciples word.

9 ¶ And as they went to tell his disciples, behold, Jesus met them, saying, All hail. And they came and held him by the feet, and worshipped him.

10 Then said Jesus unto them, Be not afraid: go tell my brethren that they go into Galilee, and there shall they see me.

11 ¶ Now when they were going behold, some of the watch came into the city, and shewed unto the chief priests all the things that were done.

12 And when they were assembled with the elders, and had taken counsel, they gave large money unto the soldiers,

13 Saying, Say ye, His disciples came by night, and stole him *away* while we slept.

14 And if this come to the governor's ears, we will persuade him, and secure you.

15 So they took the money, and did as they were taught: and this saying is commonly reported among the Jews until this day.

16 ¶ Then the eleven disciples went away into Galilee, into a mountain where Jesus had appointed them.

17 And when they saw him, they worshipped him: but some doubted.

18 And Jesus came and spake unto them, saying, All power is given unto me in heaven and in earth.

19 ¶ Go ye therefore, and teach all nations, baptizing them in the name of the Father, and of the Son, and of the Holy Ghost:

20 Teaching them to observe all things whatsoever I have commanded you: and, lo, I am with you alway, *even* unto the end of the world. Amen.

THE LIVING GOD
Edmund Jacob

What gives the Old Testament its force and unity is the affirmation of the sovereignty of God. God is the basis of all things and all that exists only exists by his will. Moreover, the existence of God is never questioned; only fools can say, "There is no God" (Ps. 14.1; 53.2; Job 2.10); and even when the prophet Jeremiah speaks of the unfaithful Israelites who denied Yahweh by saying, "It is not he" (*lo hu*) (5.12) he does not intend to speak of those who disbelieve in God but of rebels who question his sovereignty. The passages which can be invoked as proofs of the existence of God are meant to lay stress on certain aspects which can be discussed, but the reality of God imposed itself with an evidence which passed beyond all demonstration. The knowledge of God in the sense of the awareness of divine reality—and not in the profounder sense the prophets will give to it—is to be found everywhere. The entire world knows God; not only Israel but all the peoples praise him; even nature has only been created to proclaim his power (Ps. 148.9–13). Even sin itself proclaims the existence of God by contrast, for it is either desertion from God or revolt against him; the sinner is a man who turns his back on God, but who does not dream of contesting his existence.

The fact of God is so normal that we have no trace of speculation in the Old Testament about the origin or the evolution of God: whilst neighbouring religions present a theogony as the first step in the organization of chaos, the God of the Old Testament is there from the beginning. He does not evolve, and the various names which are given him are those of originally independent gods and do not mark phases of his development. The Old Testament gives us no "history" of the person of Yahweh, who nevertheless existed in another form before becoming the national God of the Israelites, and the gods of the patriarchs only have a chronological and not a genealogical connection with Yahweh. From the time that Yahweh appears he is a major God whose eternity could be affirmed (Ps. 90.2; 139.16), but the idea of eternity is secondary to that of life. God is not living because he is eternal, but he is eternal because he is living. The Israelite felt God as an active power before positing him as an eternal principle. God is never a problem, he is not the ultimate conclusion of a series of reflections; on the contrary, it is he who questions and from whom the initiative always comes. Strongly typical in this respect is the sudden and unexpected appearance on the scene of history of the prophet Elijah, who justifies his intervention simply by the words, "Yahweh is living" (1 Kings 17.1). Just as life is a mysterious reality which can only be recognized, so God is a power which imposes itself on man and comes to meet him without his being always prepared for it.

The expression "living God" (*'el chay, 'elohim chayyim*) has a less deeply imprinted theological character than other formulae such as holy God or God the

King, and so we do not agree with Baudissin[1] that it is of recent date and that it sprang into being from the polemic of Yahwism against the cult of dying and rising gods who claimed to have the monopoly of life, nor with L. Koehler[2] that it sprang up as an answer to the criticism that God had neither life nor power. To say of God that he was a living God was the elementary and primordial reaction of man in face of the experience of the power which, imposing itself on the entirety of his being, could only be envisaged as a person, that is, as a living being. It is to the power and succour of that person that the Israelites appeal when they are menaced in their own personal life, *chay Yahweh,* and when Yahweh himself wishes to confirm by an oath the dependability of his threats or promises he introduces it by the affirmation of his life: "I am living, says the Lord Yahweh. . . . I will make the effects of my oath fall upon his head" (Ezek. 17.19), but also: "I am living, oracle of the Lord Yahweh, I have no pleasure in the death of the wicked" (Ezek. 33.11).

Life is what differentiates Yahweh from other gods; before it is expressed in a well formulated monotheism, the faith of Israel is confident of the feebleness of the gods of the nations and contrasts that weakness to the living God; the gods of the nations are stupid and foolish while Yahweh is the true God and the living God (Jer. 10.9–10). Yahweh does not die: "Thou shalt not die" cries the prophet Habakkuk[3] (1.12). The idea of God as living also implies that Yahweh is the one who gives life: "As true as Yahweh lives, who has given us this *nephesh*" (Jer. 38.16). It is because they see in the Living One essentially the source of life that believers regard as the supreme aspiration of piety the ability to approach the living God (Ps. 42.3; 84.3); and finally it is belief in the living God which will lead to the affirmation of victory over death.

From a literary point of view, faith in a living God attained its best expression in anthropomorphic language; "the idea of a living God," writes F. Michaeli, "gives to the anthropomorphism of the Bible a significance quite other than that which applies to similar expressions about pagan idols . . . it is because God is living that one can speak of him as of a living man, but also in speaking of him as of a human being one recalls continually that he is living."[4] Anthropomorphism is found throughout the Old Testament; it is by no means a "primitive" way of speaking of God and it easily harmonizes with a highly spiritual theology, as, for example, in Second Isaiah: God speaks (Gen. 1.3), hears (Ex. 16.12), sees (Gen. 6.12), smells (1 Sam. 26.19), laughs (Ps. 2.4; 59.9), whistles (Is. 7.18); he makes use of the organs suited to these functions: he has eyes (Amos 9.4), hands (Ps. 139.5), arms (Is. 51.9; 52.10; Jer. 27.5), ears (Is. 22.14), and feet (Nahum 1.3; Is. 63.3) which he places on a footstool (Is. 66.1). His bearing is described with the help of the most realistic anthropomorphisms: he treads the wine-press like a grape-gatherer (Is. 63.1–6), he rides on the clouds (Dt. 33.26; Hab. 3.8), he comes down

---

[1]In *Adonis und Eshmun,* Leipzig 1911, pp. 450ff. The expression "living God" does not necessarily imply a relation to nature. Yahweh—to whom the title is given more often than to El or Elohim—is living because he is bound to a social group, which is a living reality *par excellence.*

[2]L. Koehler, *Theologie des A.T.,* p. 35.

[3]The actual form of the verse: "We shall not die" is due to a *tiqqun sopherim* designed to correct the disrespect which the mere thought of the death of God would involve.

[4]F. Michaeli, *Dieu à l'image de l'homme,* p. 147.

from heaven to see the tower of Babel and to scatter its builders with his own hands (Gen. 11.7), and he himself shuts the door of the ark behind Noah (Gen. 7.16). Figures of speech borrowed from military language are particularly frequent. Yahweh is a *gibbor* and an *'ish milchamah* (Ex. 15.3; Ps. 24.8; Zech. 9.13), because at the period which may coincide with the first age of settlement in Canaan war was the normal and even the only way for Yahweh to reveal himself.[5] Sometimes it is even the activity of animals which provides the term of comparison; when it is a matter of showing a terrifying aspect, the lion, the bear and the panther illustrate it in turn (Lam. 3.10; Hos. 5.14; 11.10; 13.7), and also the moth, which destroys more subtly but quite as surely (Hos. 5.12); yet the sacred character of animals in the majority of pagan religions was bound to hinder Israel from making too large a use of theriomorphism. Anthropomorphisms are accompanied by anthropopathisms: God feels all the emotions of human beings—joy (Zeph. 3.17), disgust (Lev. 20.23), repentance (Gen. 6.6) and above all jealousy (Ex. 20.5; Dt. 5.9).

There were mitigations of the anthropomorphism. Respect for divine transcendence led to the substituting for God of intermediaries for his communication with men, for example in the E editing of the J traditions, but it must be noted that these attenuations are attributable to ethical tendencies rather than to a spiritualizing for which the idea of a personal and present God was fundamentally unacceptable. Other limits to anthropomorphism are simply due to the fact that from the beginning Israel was aware that God was only partially the image of man. In the conception of God as a person Israel felt and expressed both the similarity and the separation, for such a person was felt not only as a different being but often indeed as a veritable obstacle; the "thou" who was God could say No! to the "I" of man, so that even while speaking of God in human terms account must be taken of the fact that one realized that between the two there was no common measure. God is not subject, like men, or at least not to the same extent as men, to changes of humour or feeling: "God is not man, that he should lie, or a son of man, that he should repent. Has he said, and will he not do it? Or has he spoken, and will he not fulfil it?" (Num. 23.19). "I am God and not man" (Hos. 11.9); and then Isaiah summarizes the irreducible difference between God and man by the terms spirit and flesh (31.3), putting the opposition not between what is spiritual or corporeal, but between what is strong and what is feeble and ephemeral. Another limit to anthropomorphism is supplied by the very conception of man in Israel. According to the anthropology dominant in the Old Testament a man only exists as a member of a community, there is no isolated man, there are only *bene 'adam*, that is, participators in that great collective personality which is constituted by humanity and, more especially, Israel. But that idea of collective personality could not be applied to God: to exist and manifest his sovereignty, God has no need of the assistance of other beings; biblical anthropomorphism thus differentiates itself clearly from ancient anthropomorphism in general where the god is not only always associated with an attendant goddess, but where he is also surrounded by an entire court of equal or inferior personages like a human family. The Old Testament is unaware of any feminine partner to Yahweh, and Hebrew does not even possess any term for goddess and uses the ambiguous

---

[5] G. von Rad, *Der Heilige Krieg im alten Israel,* 1951.

word *'elohim* (1 Kings 11.5, 33, Astarté *'elohe Sidonim*). Certainly it happened that, under the influence of the contemporary world and because of a very natural tendency of the human mind, the attempt was made to give a consort to Yahweh: Maacah, the mother of king Asa, made an idol which might serve as a feminine counterpart to Yahweh (1 Kings 15.13), and the Jews of the military colony of Elephantiné did not hesitate to associate with Yahweh the great Canaanite goddess under the name of Anat Yahu; but these are deviations which were never admitted within the framework of the orthodox faith which only knew a single consort of Yahweh, namely the people of Israel, but the union with the people is the result of an act of pure grace and in no way corresponds to a necessity of the natural order. Transcendence of sex is also shown in the absence of a son of God: the *bene ha'elohim* of Gen. 6.2 and of the prologue to Job are divine beings, but not sons in the proper sense. Finally, a last limit to anthropomorphism and one which clearly shows that anthropomorphism was unsuitable for expressing the divine personality in its fulness, is the prohibition of making a visual representation of Yahweh;[6] consistent anthropomorphism necessarily ends in plastic representations. Even if in the course of history the people of Israel sometimes had difficulty in keeping to the Mosaic order (Ex. 20.4, 22; Dt. 4.12, 15–18), it must be recognized that the prohibition on the making of images of the deity and adoring them (for an image of the divine is made to be adored) represents the main trend of Israelite religion. To make a representation of God means to desire to imprison him within certain limits and God was too great for anyone to be able for an instant to dream of setting a limit to what clearly never ceased, namely his life.

---

[6]As a God of nomadic origin and bound to a human society, Yahweh had no need like other gods of fashioned representations in animal or human form, though one must beware of equating nomadism with spirituality. But contact with the religion of Canaan, where the power of the image was very great, might have led the Israelites to use the same procedures sometimes to represent Yahweh, without there being necessarily in origin an act of infidelity. The fasioned image of a bull was not always an adoration of Baal; and the ephod itself, a human or closely human representation of Yahweh (cf. I Sam. 19.1 ff.), could appear perfectly legitimate and even necessary for affirming the power of Yahweh. But as these attempts ultimately struck at the uniqueness of Yahweh and especially at his jealousy, a radical condemnation of all images and an insistent reminder of the Mosaic requirements was brought into operation.

THE APOSTOLIC PREACHING

C. H. Dodd

From C. H. Dodd, *Apostolic Preaching and Its Development*, 1936. Used by permission of Hodder & Stoughton, Ltd., London.

We may begin with the speeches in Acts ii-iv. There are four in all. The first two (ii, 14–36, 38–39) are supposed to have been delivered by Peter to the multitude assembled on the Day of Pentecost, the third (iii. 12–26) to the people after the healing of a lame man, and the fourth (iv. 8–12) to the Sanhedrin after the arrest of the apostles. The second account of the arrest in v. 17–40 is probably a doublet from another source, and it does not betray the same traces of Aramaism. The speech said to have been delivered on this occasion (v. 29–32) does no more than recapitulate briefly the substance of the previous speeches. The speech of Peter to Cornelius in ch. x. 34–43 is akin to the earlier speeches, but has some special features, and in it the evidence for an Aramaic original is at its strongest.

We may with some confidence take these speeches to represent, not indeed what Peter said upon this or that occasion, but the *kerygma* of the Church at Jerusalem at an early period.

The first four speeches of Peter cover substantially the same ground. The phraseology and the order of presentation vary slightly, but there is no essential advance from one to another. They supplement one another, and taken together they afford a comprehensive view of the content of the early *kerygma*. This may be summarized as follows:

First, the age of fulfilment has dawned. "This is that which was spoken by the prophet" (Acts ii. 16). "The things which God foreshewed by the mouth of all the prophets, He thus fulfilled" (iii. 18). "All the prophets from Samuel and his successors told of these days" (iii. 24). It was a standing principle of Rabbinic exegesis of the Old Testament that what the prophets predicted had reference to the "days of the Messiah," that is to say, to the expected time when God, after long centuries of waiting, should visit His people with judgment and blessing, bringing to a climax His dealings with them in history. The apostles, then, declare that the Messianic age has dawned.

Secondly, this has taken place through the ministry, death, and resurrection of Jesus, of which a brief account is given, with proof from the Scriptures that all took place through "the determinate counsel and foreknowledge of God": (*a*) His Davidic descent. "David, being a prophet, and knowing that God had sworn to set one of the fruit of his loins upon his throne, foresaw (Christ)," who is therefore proclaimed, by implication, to have been born "of the seed of David" (ii. 30–31, citing Ps. cxxxii. 11). (*b*) His ministry. "Jesus of Nazareth, a man divinely accredited to you by works of power, prodigies, and signs which God did through Him among you" (Acts ii. 22). "Moses said, The Lord your God will raise up a prophet like me; him you must hear in everything that he may say to you" (Acts iii. 22, apparently regarded as fulfilled in the preaching and teaching of Jesus). (*c*) His death. "He was delivered up by the determinate counsel and foreknowledge of God, and you, by the agency of men without the law, killed Him by crucifixion" (ii. 23). "You caused Him to be arrested, and denied Him before Pilate, when he had decided to acquit Him. You denied the Holy and Righteous One, and asked for a murderer to be granted to you, while you killed the Prince of Life" (iii. 13–14). (d) His resurrection. "God raised Him up, having loosed the pangs of death, because it was not possible for Him to be held by it. For David says with reference to Him, 'Thou wilt not leave my soul in Hades, nor give Thy Holy One to see corruption'" (ii. 24–31). "God raised Him from the dead, whereof we are witnesses" (iii. 15). "Jesus of Nazareth, whom you crucified, whom God raised from the dead" (iv. 10).

Thirdly, by virtue of the resurrection, Jesus has been exalted at the right hand of God, as Messianic head of the new Israel. "Being exalted at the right hand of God" (according to Ps. cx. 1). . . . "God has made Him Lord and Christ" (ii. 33–36). "The God of our fathers has glorified His Servant Jesus" (iii. 13). "He is the Stone which was rejected by you builders, and has become the top of the corner" (iv. 11, citing Ps. cxviii. 22). Cf. "God exalted Him at His right hand, as Prince and Saviour" (v. 31).

Fourthly, the Holy Spirit in the Church is the sign of Christ's present power and glory. "Being exalted at the right hand of God, and having received the promise of the Holy Spirit from the Father, He poured out this which you see and hear" (Acts ii. 33). This is documented from Joel ii. 28–32 (Acts ii. 17–21). Cf. "We are witnesses of these things, and so is the Holy Spirit which God has given to those who obey Him" (v. 32).

Fifthly, the Messianic Age will shortly reach its consummation in the return of Christ. "That He may send the Messiah appointed beforehand for you, Jesus, whom heaven must receive until the times of the restoration of all things, of which God spoke through the mouth of His prophets from of old" (iii. 21). This is the only passage in Acts i–iv which speaks of the second advent of Christ. In Acts x this part of the *kerygma* is presented in these terms: "This is He who is appointed by God as Judge of living and dead" (x. 42). There is no other explicit reference to Christ as Judge in these speeches.

Finally, the *kerygma* always closes with an appeal for repentance, the offer of forgiveness and of the Holy Spirit, and the promise of "salvation," that is, of "the life of the Age to Come," to those who enter the elect community. "Repent and be baptized, each of you, upon the name of Jesus Christ for the remission of your sins, and you will receive the gift of the Holy Spirit. For the promise is for you and your children, and for all those far off, whom the Lord your God may call" (Acts ii. 38–39, referring to Joel ii. 32, Is. lvii. 19). "Repent therefore and be converted for the blotting out of your sins. . . . You are the sons of the prophets and of the covenant which God made with your fathers, saying to Abraham, 'And in thy seed shall all families of the earth be blessed.' For you in the first place God raised up His Servant Jesus and sent Him to bless you by turning each of you away from your sins" (Acts iii. 19, 25–26, citing Gen. xii. 3). "In no other is there salvation, for there is no other name under heaven given among men by which you must be saved" (Acts iv. 12). Cf. "God exalted Him at His right hand as Prince and Saviour, to give repentance to Israel, and remission of sins" (Acts v. 31); "To Him all the prophets bear witness, that everyone who believes in Him shall receive remission of sins through His name" (Acts x. 43).

We may take it that this is what the author of Acts meant by "preaching the Kingdom of God." It is very significant that it follows the lines of the summary of the preaching of Jesus as given in Mark i. 14–15: "Jesus came into Galilee preaching the Gospel of God, and saying, 'The time is fulfilled, and the Kingdom of God has drawn near: repent and believe the Gospel.'" This summary provides the framework within which the Jerusalem *kerygma* is set.

The first clause, "The time is fulfilled," is expanded in the reference to prophecy and its fulfilment. The second clause, "The Kingdom of God has drawn near," is expanded in the account of the ministry and death of Jesus, His resurrection and exaltation, all conceived as an eschatological process. The third clause, "Repent and believe the Gospel," reappears in the appeal for repentance and the offer of forgiveness with which the apostolic *kerygma* closes. Whether we say that the apostolic preaching was modelled on that of Jesus, or that the evangelist formulated his summary of the preaching of Jesus on the model of that of the primitive Church, at any rate the two are identical in purport. The Kingdom of God is conceived as coming in the events of the life, death, and resurrection of Jesus, and to proclaim these facts, in their proper setting, is to preach the Gospel of the Kingdom of God.

It is clear, then, that we have here, as in the preaching which we found to lie behind the Pauline epistles, a proclamation of the death and resurrection of Jesus Christ, in an eschatological setting from which those facts derive their saving significance. We may proceed to compare the two versions of the *kerygma,* in Paul and in the Acts respectively.

There are three points in the Pauline *kerygma* which do not directly appear in the Jerusalem *kerygma* of Acts:

(i) Jesus is not there called "Son of God." His titles are taken rather from the prophecies of Deutero-Isaiah. He is the holy and righteous "Servant" of God. It is noteworthy that the first person who is said in Acts to have "preached Jesus, that He is the Son of God," is Paul himself (ix. 20). It may be that this represents an actual difference of terminology. Yet the idea that Jesus, as Messiah, is Son of God is deeply embedded in the Synoptic Gospels, whose sources were in all probability not subject to Pauline influence; and the Christological formula in Rom i. 1–4 is, as we have seen, probably not Pauline in origin. The phrase "Son of God with power" there carries much the same ideas as the phrase "Lord and Christ" in the Jerusalem *kerygma,* for its significance is Missianic rather than properly theological.

(ii) The Jerusalem *kerygma* does not assert that Christ died *for our sins.* The result of the life, death, and resurrection of Christ is the forgiveness of sins, but this forgiveness is not specifically connected with His death. Since, however, Paul includes this statement in that which he "received," we may hesitate to ascribe to him the origin of the idea. Since the Jerusalem *kerygma* applies to Christ the Isaianic title of "Servant," the way was at least open to interpret His death on the lines of Isaiah liii. Acts viii. 32–35 may suggest the possibility that this step was taken explicitly by the school of Stephen and Philip, with which Paul appears to have been in touch.

(iii) The Jerusalem *kerygma* does not assert that the exalted Christ intercedes for us. It may be that in Rom. viii. 34 Paul has inserted this on his own account into the apostolic formula. But, on the other hand, the idea occurs also in Hebrews vii.

25 and seems to be implied in Matt. x. 32, so that it may not be of Pauline origin. It is perhaps, in effect, another way of saying that forgiveness is offered "in His name."

For the rest, all the points of the Pauline preaching reappear: the Davidic descent of Jesus, guaranteeing His qualification for Messiahship; His death according to the Scriptures; His resurrection according to the Scriptures; His consequent exaltation to the right hand of God as Lord and Christ; His deliverance of men from sin into new life; and His return to consummate the new Age. This coincidence between the apostolic Preaching as attested by the speeches in Acts, and as attested by Paul, enables us to carry back its essential elements to a date far earlier than a critical analysis of Acts by itself could justify; for, as we have seen, Paul must have received the tradition very soon after the death of Jesus.

With this in view, we may usefully draw attention to other points in the Jerusalem *kerygma* which reappear in the epistles of Paul, though he does not explicitly include them in his "Gospel."

The *kerygma* in Acts lays emphasis upon the Holy Spirit in the Church as the sign that the new age of fulfilment has begun. The idea of the Spirit in the Church is very prominent in the Pauline epistles. We are now justified in concluding that this was no innovation of his, but represents a part of the tradition he had received. It is to be observed that in Gal. iii. 2 Paul appeals to the evidence of the Spirit in the Church as a *datum* from which he may argue regarding the nature and conditions of salvation in Christ, and on this basis he develops his doctrine of the Spirit as the "earnest," or first instalment, of the consummated life of the Age to Come (2 Cor. i. 22, v. 5; Eph. i. 13–14). This is true to the implications of the *kerygma* as we have it in Acts.

Again, the "calling" and "election" of the Church as the "Israel of God" can now be seen to be no peculiarity of Pauline teaching. It is implied in such passages of the *kerygma* as Acts iii. 25–26, ii. 39.

There is, indeed, very little in the Jerusalem *kerygma* which does not appear, substantially, in Paul. But there is one important element which at first sight at least is absent from his preaching, so far as we can recover it from the epistles, namely, the explicit reference to the ministry of Jesus, His miracles (Acts ii. 22) and teaching (Acts iii. 22). Such references are only slight in the first four speeches of Peter, to which we have so far given most attention. But the case is different in the speech attributed to Peter in Acts x. 34–43. The principal elements of the *kerygma* can be traced in this speech—the fulfilment of prophecy, the death and resurrection of Christ, His second advent, and the offer of forgiveness. But all is given with extreme brevity, except the section dealing with the historical facts concerning Jesus. These are here treated in fairly full outline.

The Greek of x. 35–38 is notoriously rough and ungrammatical, and indeed scarcely translatable, though the general meaning is clear. This is strange in so excellent a Greek writer as the author of Acts. In some MSS. it has been improved. But Dr. Torrey has shown that if the text in its more difficult form (which on general principles of textual criticism is likely to be more original) be translated word for word into Aramaic, it becomes both grammatical and perspicuous. The case, therefore, for regarding the passage as a translation is strong. I shall here follow Dr. Torrey, and give the passage after his restored

Aramaic, being convinced that by doing so we shall come nearer to the original form.

"As for the word which He, the Lord of all, sent to the children of Israel, preaching the Gospel of peace through Jesus the Messiah, you know the thing (literally, 'the word') that happened through all Judaea, beginning from Galilee after the baptism which John preached; that God anointed Jesus of Nazareth with Holy Spirit and power; and He went about doing good and healing all who were oppressed by the devil, because God was with Him. And we are witnesses of all that He did in the country of the Jews and Jerusalem. Him they killed by hanging Him upon a tree. God raised Him up on the third day, and permitted Him to be manifest, not to all the people, but to witnesses chosen beforehand by God, namely to us, who ate and drank with Him after He rose from the dead."

It is to be observed that the first clause, "the word which He sent to the children of Israel, preaching the Gospel of peace through Jesus Christ," which forms a sort of heading to the whole, is a virtual equivalent of the term "*kerygma*" or "Gospel." The passage is therefore offered explicitly as a form of apostolic Preaching. It is represented as being delivered by Peter to a Gentile audience. It is quite intelligible in the situation presupposed that some account of the ministry of Jesus should have been called for when the Gospel was taken to people who could not be acquainted, as the Jews of Judaea were, with the main facts. We may perhaps take it that the speech before Cornelius represents the form of *kerygma* used by the primitive Church in its earliest approaches to a wider public.

In the preaching attested by Paul, although it was similarly addressed to the wider public, there does not seem to be any such comprehensive summary of the facts of the ministry of Jesus, as distinct from the facts of His death and resurrection. It would, however, be rash to argue from silence that Paul completely ignored the life of Jesus in his preaching; for, as we have seen, that preaching is represented only fragmentarily, and as it were accidentally, in the epistles. That he was aware of the historical life of Jesus, and cited His sayings as authoritative, need not be shown over again. It may be, for all we know, that the brief recital of historical facts in 1 Cor. xv. 1 *sqq.* is only the conclusion of a general summary which may have included some reference to the ministry. But this remains uncertain.

According to Acts, Paul did preach in terms closely similar to those of the Petrine *kerygma* of Acts x. The speech said to have been delivered by Paul at Pisidian Antioch (Acts xiii. 16–41) is too long to be quoted here in full, but the gist of it is as follows:

God brought Israel out of Egypt, and gave them David for their king. Of the seed of David Jesus has come as Saviour. He was heralded by John the Baptist. His disciples followed Him from Galilee to Jerusalem. There He was brought to trial by the rulers of the Jews before Pilate, who reluctantly condemned Him. He died according to the Scriptures, and was buried. God raised Him from the dead, according to the Scriptures, and He was seen by witnesses. Through Him forgiveness and justification are offered. Therefore take heed.

This is obviously of the same stuff as the *kerygma* in the early chapters of Acts. It may be compared on the one hand with the speeches in Acts ii–iv, and on the other hand with the speech in Acts x. It is a mixture of the two types. In particular, its historical *data* are fuller than those of Acts ii–iv, but less full than those of Acts x, containing no allusions to the baptism of Jesus or His miracles in Galilee. There is nothing specifically Pauline in it, except the term "justification." On the other hand, the general scheme, and the emphasis, correspond with what we have found in the epistles, and there is little or nothing in it which could not be documented out of the epistles, except the historical details in the introductory passage (xiii. 16–22) and the specific allusions to episodes in the Gospel story, and in particular to the ministry of John the Baptist (the fullest account in the New Testament outside the Gospels) and the trial before Pilate.

That these two episodes did not fall wholly outside the range of Paul's interest might perhaps be argued on the following grounds.

(i) Paul refers in his epistles to Apollos as one whom he would regard as a fellow-worker, though others set him up as a rival. Now, according to Acts, Apollos had been a follower of John the Baptist. Paul therefore must have had occasion to relate the work of the Baptist to the Christian faith.

(ii) In 1 Tim. vi. 13 we have an allusion to Christ's "confession before Pontius Pilate." Although we should probably not accept 1 Timothy as an authentic Pauline letter, yet it no doubt represents the standpoint of the Pauline circle, and the allusion to Pilate may have been derived from Paul's preaching.

These observations are far from proving that Paul would have included such references to John the Baptist and to the trial before Pilate in his preaching, but they show that it is not impossible that he may have done so, in spite of the silence of his epistles. In any case, if we recall the close general similarity of the *kerygma* as derived from the Pauline epistles to the *kerygma* as derived from Acts, as well as Paul's emphatic assertion of the identity of his Gospel with the general Christian tradition, we shall not find it altogether incredible that the speech at Pisidian Antioch may represent in a general way one form of Paul's preaching, that form, perhaps, which he adopted in synagogues when he had the opportunity of speaking there. If that is so, then we must say that he, like other early Christian preachers, gave a place in his preaching to some kind of recital of the facts of the life and ministry of Jesus.

If he did not do so, then we must say that in this respect he departed from the common model of apostolic preaching. For it seems clear that within the general scheme of the *kerygma* was included some reference, however brief, to the historical facts of the life of Jesus. These facts fall within the eschatological setting of the whole, no less than the facts of His death and resurrection. They are themselves eschatological events, in the sense that they form part of the process by which God's purpose reaches fulfilment and His Kingdom comes.

Chapter
THREE

RELIGIOUS EXPERIENCES AND DOCTRINES
analyses and appraisals

THE DIALOGUE IN MYTH
BETWEEN EAST
AND WEST

Joseph Campbell

The myth of eternal return, which is still basic to Oriental life, displays an order of fixed forms that appear and reappear through all time. The daily round of the sun, the waning and waxing moon, the cycle of the year, and the rhythm of organic birth, death, and new birth, represent a miracle of continuous arising that is fundamental to the nature of the universe. We all know the archaic myth of the four ages of gold, silver, bronze, and iron, where the world is shown declining, growing ever worse. It will disintegrate presently in chaos, only to burst forth again, fresh as a flower, to recommence spontaneously the inevitable course. There never was a time when time was not. Nor will there be a time when this kaleidoscopic play of eternity in time will have ceased.

There is therefore nothing to be gained, either for the universe or for man, through individual originality and effort. Those who have identified themselves with the mortal body and its affections will necessarily find that all is painful, since everything—for them—must end. But for those who have found the still point of eternity, around which all—including themselves—revolves, everything is acceptable as it is; indeed, can even be experienced as glorious and wonderful. The first duty of the individual, consequently, is simply to play his given role—as do the sun and moon, the various animal and plant species, the waters, the rocks, and the stars—without resistance, without fault; and then, if possible, so to order his mind as to identify its consciousness with the inhabiting principle of the whole.

The dreamlike spell of this contemplative, metaphysically oriented tradition, where light and darkness dance together in a world-creating cosmic shadow play, carries into modern times an image that is of incalculable age. In its primitive form it is widely known among the jungle villages of the broad equatorial zone that extends from Africa eastward, through India, Southeast Asia, and Oceania, to Brazil, where the basic myth is of a dreamlike age of the beginning, when there was neither death nor birth, which, however, terminated when a murder was committed. The body of the victim was cut up and buried. And not only did the food plants on which the community lives arise from those buried parts, but on all who ate of their fruit the organs of reproduction appeared; so that death, which had come into the world through a killing, was countered by its opposite, generation, and the self-consuming thing that is life, which lives on life, began its interminable course.

Throughout the dark green jungles of the world there abound not only dreadful animal scenes of tooth and claw, but also terrible human rites of cannibal communion, dramatically representing—with the force of an initiatory shock —the murder scene, sexual act, and festival meal of the beginning, when life and death became two, which had been one, and the sexes became two, which also had been one. Creatures come into being, live on the death of others, die, and become the food of others, continuing, thus, into and through the transformations of time, the timeless archetype of the mythological beginning; and the individual matters no more than a fallen leaf. Psychologically, the effect of the enactment of such a rite is to shift the focus of the mind from the individual (who perishes) to the everlasting group. Magically, it is to reinforce the ever-living life in all lives, which appears to be many but is really one; so that the growth is stimulated of the yams, coconuts, pigs, moon, and breadfruits, and of the human community as well.[. . .]

For the West, however, the possibility of such an egoless return to a state of soul antecedent to the birth of individuality has long since passed away; and the first important stage in the branching off can be seen to have occurred in that very part of the nuclear Near East where the earliest god-kings and their courts had been for centuries ritually entombed: namely Sumer, where a new sense of the separation of the spheres of god and man began to be represented in myth and ritual about 2350 B.C. The king, then, was no longer a god, but a servant of the god, his Tenant Farmer, supervisor of the race of human slaves created to serve the gods with unremitting toil. And no longer identity, but relationship, was the paramount concern. Man had been made not to *be* God but to know, honor, and serve him; so that even the king, who, according to the earlier mythological view, had been the chief embodiment of divinity on earth, was now but a priest offering sacrifice in tendance to One above—not a god returning himself in sacrifice to Himself.

In the course of the following centuries, the new sense of separation led to a counter-yearning for return—not to identity, for such was no longer possible of conception (creator and creature were not the same), but to the presence and vision of the forfeited god. Hence the new mythology brought forth, in due time, a development away from the earlier static view of returning cycles. A progressive, temporally oriented mythology arose, of a creation, once and for all, at the beginning of time, a subsequent fall, and a work of restoration, still in progress. The world no longer was to be known as a mere showing in time of the paradigms of eternity, but as a field of unprecedented cosmic conflict between two powers, one light and one dark.

The earliest prophet of this mythology of cosmic restoration was, apparently, the Persian Zoroaster, whose dates, however, have not been securely established. They have been variously placed between c. 1200 and c. 550 B.C., so that, like Homer (of about the same span of years), he should perhaps be regarded rather as symbolic of a tradition than as specifically, or solely, one man. The system associated with his name is based on the idea of a conflict between the wise lord, Ahura Mazda, "first father of the Righteous Order, who gave to the sun and stars their path," and an independent evil principle, Angra Mainyu, the Deceiver, principle of the lie, who, when all had been excellently made, entered into it in every particle. The world, consequently, is a compound wherein good and evil, light and dark, wisdom and violence, are contending for a victory. And the privilege and duty of each man—who, himself, as a part of creation, is a compound of good and evil—is to elect, voluntarily, to engage in the battle in the interest of the light. It is supposed that with the birth of Zoroaster, twelve thousand years following the creation of the world, a decisive turn was given the conflict in favor of the good, and that when he returns, after another twelve millennia, in the person of the messiah Saoshyant, there will take place a final battle and cosmic conflagration, through which the principle of darkness and the lie will be undone. Whereafter, all will be light, there will be no further history, and the Kingdom of God (Ahura Mazda) will have been established in its pristine form forever.

It is obvious that a potent mythical formula for the reorientation of the human spirit is here supplied—pitching it forward along the way of time, summoning man to an assumption of autonomous responsibility for the renovation of the universe in God's name, and thus fostering a new, potentially political (not finally contemplative) philosophy of holy war. "May we be such," runs a Persian prayer, "as those who bring on this renovation and make this world progressive, till its perfection shall have been achieved."

The first historic manifestation of the force of this new mythic view was in the Achaemenian empire of Cyrus the Great (died 529 B.C.) and Darius I (reigned c. 521–486 B.C.), which in a few decades extended its domain from India to Greece, and under the protection of which the post-exilic Hebrews both rebuilt their temple (Ezra 1:1–11) and reconstructed their traditional inheritance. The second historic manifestation was in the Hebrew application of its universal message to themselves; the next was in the world mission of Christianity; and the fourth, in that of Islam.

"Enlarge the place of your tent, and let the curtains of your habitations be stretched out; hold not back, lengthen your cords and strengthen your stakes. For you will spread abroad to the right and to the left, and your descendants will possess the nations and will people the desolate cities" (Isaiah 54:2–3; c. 546–536 B.C.).

"And this gospel of the kingdom will be preached throughout the whole world as a testimony to all nations; and then the end will come" (Matthew 24:14; c. 90 A.D.).

"And slay them wherever you catch them, and turn them out from where they have turned you out; for tumult and oppression are worse than slaughter. . . . And fight them on until there is no more tumult or oppression and there prevail justice and faith in Allah; but if they cease, let there be no hostility except to those who practice oppression" (Koran 2:191, 193; c. 632 A.D.).

Two completely opposed mythologies of the destiny and virtue of man, therefore, have come together in the modern world.[. . .]

The extent to which the mythologies—and therewith psychologies—of the Orient and Occident diverged in the course of the period between the dawn of civilization in the Near East and the present age of mutual rediscovery appears in their opposed versions of the shared mythological image of the first being, who was originally one but became two.

"In the beginning," states an Indian example of c. 700 B.C., preserved in the Brihadaranyaka Upanishad,

> this universe was nothing but the Self in the form of a man. It looked around and saw that there was nothing but itself, whereupon its first shout was, "It is I!"; whence the concept "I" arose. (And that is why, even now, when

addressed, one answers first, "It is I!" only then giving the other name that one bears.)

Then he was afraid. (That is why anyone alone is afraid.) But he considered: "Since there is no one here but myself, what is there to fear?" Whereupon the fear departed. (For what should have been feared? It is only to a second that fear refers.)

However, he still lacked delight (therefore, we lack delight when alone) and desired a second. He was exactly as large as a man and woman embracing. This Self then divided itself in two parts; and with that, there were a master and a mistress. (Therefore this body, by itself, as the sage Yajnavalkya declares, is like half of a split pea. And that is why, indeed, this space is filled by a woman.)

The male embraced the female, and from that the human race arose. She, however, reflected: "How can he unite with me, who am produced from himself? Well then, let me hide!" She became a cow, he a bull and united with her; and from that cattle arose. She became a mare, he a stallion; she an ass, he a donkey and united with her; and from that solid-hoofed animals arose. She became a goat, he a buck; she a sheep, he a ram and united with her; and from that goats and sheep arose. Thus he poured forth all pairing things, down to the ants. Then he realized: "I, actually, am creation; for I have poured forth all this." Whence arose the concept "Creation" [Sanskrit *sṛṣṭiḥ:* "what is poured forth"].

Anyone understanding this becomes, truly, himself a creator in this creation.

The best-known Occidental example of this image of the first being, split in two, which seem to be two but are actually one, is, of course, that of the Book of Genesis, second chapter, where it is turned, however, to a different sense. For the couple is separated here by a superior being, who, as we are told, caused a deep sleep to fall upon the man and, while he slept, took one of his ribs. In the Indian version it is the god himself that divides and becomes not man alone but all creation; so that everything is a manifestation of that single inhabiting divine substance: there is no other; whereas in the Bible, God and man, from the beginning, are distinct. Man is made in the image of God, indeed, and the breath of God has been breathed into his nostrils; yet his being, his self, is not that of God, nor is it one with the universe. The fashioning of the world, of the animals, and of Adam (who then became Adam and Eve) was accomplished not within the sphere of divinity but outside of it. There is, consequently, an *intrinsic,* not merely *formal,* separation. And the goal of knowledge cannot be to *see* God here and now in all things; for God is not in things. God is transcendent. God is beheld only by the dead. The goal of knowledge has to be, rather, to know the *relationship* of God to his creation, or, more specifically, to man, and through such knowledge, by God's grace, to link one's own will back to that of the Creator.

Moreover, according to the biblical version of this myth, it was only after creation that man fell, whereas in the Indian example creation itself was a fall—the fragmentation of a god. And the god is not condemned. Rather, his creation, his "pouring forth" (sṛṣṭiḥ), is described as an act of voluntary, dynamic will-to-be-more, which anteceded creation and has, therefore, a metaphysical, symbolical, not literal, historical meaning. The fall of Adam and Eve was an event within the already created frame of time and space, an accident that should not have taken place. The myth of the Self in the form of a man, on the other hand, who looked around and saw nothing but himself, said "I," felt fear, and then desired to be two, tells of an intrinsic, not errant, factor in the manifold of being, the correction or undoing of which would not improve, but dissolve, creation. The Indian point of view is metaphysical, poetical; the biblical, ethical and historical.

Adam's fall and exile from the garden was thus in no sense a metaphysical departure of divine substance from itself, but an event only in the history, or pre-history, of man. And this event in the created world has been followed throughout the remainder of the book by the record of man's linkage and failures of linkage back to God—again, historically conceived. For, as we next hear, God himself, at a certain point in the course of time, out of his own volition, moved toward man, instituting a new law in the form of a covenant with a certain people. And these became, therewith, a priestly race, unique in the world. God's reconciliation with man, of whose creation he had repented (Genesis 6:6), was to be achieved only by virtue of this particular community—in time: for in time there should take place the realization of the Lord God's kingdom on earth, when the heathen monarchies would crumble and Israel be saved, when men would "cast forth their idols of silver and their idols of gold, which they made to themselves to worship, to the moles and to the bats."

> Be broken, you peoples, and be dismayed;
>   give ear, all you far countries;
> gird yourselves and be dismayed;
>   gird yourselves and be dismayed.
> Take counsel together, but it will come to nought;
>   speak a word, but it will not stand,
>   for God is with us.

In the Indian view, on the contrary, what is divine here is divine there also; nor has anyone to wait—or even to hope—for a "day of the Lord." For what has been lost is in each his very self (ātman), here and now, requiring only to be sought. Or, as they say: "Only when men shall roll up space like a piece of leather will there be an end of sorrow apart from knowing God."

The question arises (again historical) in the world dominated by the Bible, as to the identity of the favored community, and three are well known to have developed claims: the Jewish, the Christian, and the Moslem, each supposing itself to have been authorized by a particular revelation. God, that is to say, though conceived as outside of history and not himself its substance (transcendent: not immanent), is supposed to have engaged himself miraculously in the enterprise of restoring fallen man through a covenant, sacrament, or revealed book, with a view to a general, communal experience of fulfillment yet to come. The world is corrupt and man a sinner; the individual, however, through engagement along with God in the destiny of the only authorized community, participates in the coming glory of the kingdom of righteousness, when "the glory of the Lord shall be revealed, and all flesh shall see it together."

In the experience and vision of India, on the other hand, although the holy mystery and power have been understood to be indeed transcendent ("other than the known; moreover, above the unknown"), they are also, at the same time, immanent ("like a razor in a razorcase, like fire in tinder"). It is not that the divine is every*where:* it is that the divine is every*thing.* So that one does not require any outside reference, revelation, sacrament, or authorized community to return to it. One has but to alter one's psychological orientation and recognize (re-cognize) what is within. Deprived of this recognition, we are removed from our own reality by a cerebral shortsightedness which is called in Sanskrit *māyā,* "delusion" (from the verbal root *mā,* "measure, measure out, to form, to build," denoting, in the first place, the power of a god or demon to produce illusory effects, to change form, and to appear under deceiving masks; in the second place, "magic," the production of illusions and, in warfare, camouflage, deceptive tactics; and finally, in philosophical discourse, the illusion superimposed upon reality as an effect of ignorance). Instead of the biblical exile from a geographically, historically conceived garden wherein God walked in the cool of the day, we have in India, therefore, already c. 700 B.C. (some three hundred years before the putting together of the Pentateuch), a *psychological* reading of the great theme.

The shared myth of the primal androgyne is applied in the two traditions to the same task—the exposition of man's distance, in his normal secular life, from the divine Alpha and Omega. Yet the arguments radically differ, and therefore support two radically different civilizations. For, if man has been removed from the divine through a historical event, it will be a historical event that leads him back, whereas if it has been by some sort of psychological displacement that he has been blocked, psychology will be his vehicle of return. And so it is that in India the final focus of concern is not the community (though, as we shall see, the idea of the holy community plays a formidable role as a disciplinary force), but yoga.

The Two Views of Ego

The Indian term *yoga* is derived from the Sanskrit verbal root *yuj,* "to link, join, or unite," which is related etymologically to "yoke," a yoke of oxen, and is in sense analogous to the word "religion" "to link back, or bind." Man, the creature, is by religion bound back to God. However, religion, *religio,* refers to a linking historically conditioned by way of a covenant, sacrament, or Koran, whereas yoga is the psychological linking of the mind to that superordinated principle "by which the mind knows." Furthermore, in yoga what is linked is finally the self to itself, consciousness to consciousness, for what had seemed, through *māyā,* to be two are in reality not so; whereas in religion what are linked are God and man, which are not the same.

It is of course true that in the popular religions of the Orient the gods are worshiped as though external to their devotees, and all the rules and rites of a covenanted relationship are observed. Nevertheless, the ultimate realization, which the sages have celebrated, is that the god worshiped as though without is in reality a reflex of the same mystery as oneself. As long as an illusion of ego remains, the commensurate illusion of a separate deity also will be there; and vice versa, as long as the idea of a separate deity is cherished, an illusion of ego, related to it in love, fear, worship, exile, or atonement, will also be there. But precisely that illusion of duality is the trick of *māyā*. "Thou art that" (*tat tvam asi*) is the proper thought for the first step to wisdom.

In the beginning, as we have read, there was only the Self; but it said "I" (Sanskrit, *aham*) and immediately felt fear, after which, desire.

It is to be remarked that in this view of the instant of creation (presented from within the sphere of the psyche of the creative being itself) the same two basic motivations are identified as the leading modern schools of depth analysis have indicated for the *human* psyche: aggression and desire. Carl G. Jung, in his early paper on *The Unconscious in Normal and Pathological Psychology* (1916), wrote of two psychological types: the introvert, harried by fear, and the extrovert, driven by desire. Sigmund Freud also, in his *Beyond the Pleasure Principle* (1920), wrote of "the death wish" and "the life wish": on the one hand, the will to violence and the fear of it (*thanatos, destrudo*), and, on the other hand, the need and desire to love and be loved (*eros, libido*). Both spring spontaneously from the deep dark source of the energies of the psyche, the *id,* and are governed, therefore, by the self-centered "pleasure principle": *I* want: *I* am afraid. Comparably, in the Indian myth, as soon as the self said "I" (*aham*), it knew first fear, and then desire.

But now—and here, I believe, is a point of fundamental importance for our reading of the basic difference between the Oriental and Occidental approaches to the cultivation of the soul—in the Indian myth the principle of ego, "I" (*aham*), is identified completely with the pleasure principle, whereas in the psychologies of both Freud and Jung its proper function is to know and relate to external reality (Freud's "reality principle"): not the reality of the metaphysical but that of the physical, empirical sphere of time and space. In other words, spiritual maturity, as understood in the modern Occident, requires a differentiation of *ego* from *id,* whereas in the Orient, throughout the history at least of every teaching that has stemmed from India, ego (*aham-kāra:* "the making of the sound 'I'") is impugned as the principle of libidinous delusion, to be dissolved.[. . .]

Now it is to be observed that in the version [. . .] of the temptation of the Buddha, the Antagonist represents all three of the first triad of ends (the so-called *trivarga:* "aggregate of three"); for in his character as the Lord Desire he personifies the first; as the Lord Death, the aggressive force of the second; while in his summons to the meditating sage to arise and return to the duties of his station in society, he promotes the third. And, indeed, as a manifestation of that Self which not only poured forth but permanently supports the universe, he is the proper incarnation of these ends. For they do, in fact, support the world. And in most of the rites of all religions, this triune god, we may say, in one aspect or another, is the one and only god adored.

However, in the name and achievement of the Buddha, the "Illuminated One," the fourth end is announced: release from delusion. And to the attainment of this, the others are impediments, difficult to remove, yet, for one of purpose, not invincible. Sitting at the world navel, pressing back through the welling creative force that was surging into and through his own being, the Buddha actually broke back into the void beyond, and—ironically—the universe immediately burst into bloom. Such an act of self-noughting is one of individual effort. There can be no question about that. However, an Occidental eye cannot but observe that there is no requirement or expectation anywhere in this Indian system of four ends—neither in the primary two of the natural organism and the impressed third of society, nor in the exalted fourth of release—for a maturation of the personality through intelligent, fresh, individual adjustment to the time-space world round about, creative experimentation with unexplored possibilities, and the assumption of personal responsibility for unprecedented acts performed within the context of the social order. In the Indian tradition all has been perfectly arranged from all eternity. There can be nothing new, nothing to be learned but what the sages have taught from of yore. And finally, when the boredom of this nursery horizon of "I want" against "thou shalt" has become insufferable, the fourth and final aim is all that is offered—of an extinction of the infantile ego altogether: disengagement or release (*moksa*) from both "I" and "thou."

In the European West, on the other hand, where the fundamental doctrine of the freedom of the will essentially dissociates each individual from every other, as well as from both the will in nature and the will of God, there is placed upon each the responsibility of coming intelligently, out of his own experience and volition, to some sort of relationship with—not identity with or extinction in—the all, the void, the suchness, the absolute, or whatever the proper term may be for that which is beyond terms. And, in the secular sphere likewise, it is normally expected that an educated ego should have developed away from the simple infantile polarity of the pleasure and obedience principles toward a personal, uncompulsive, sensitive relationship to empirical reality, a certain adventurous attitude toward the unpredictable, and a sense of personal responsibility for decisions. Not life as a good soldier, but life as a developed, unique individual, is the ideal. And we shall search the Orient in vain for anything quite comparable. There the ideal, on the contrary, is the quenching, not development, of ego. That is the formula turned this way and that, up and down the line, throughout the literature: a systematic, steady, continually drumming devaluation of the "I" principle, the reality function—which has remained, consequently, undeveloped, and so, wide open to the seizures of completely uncritical mythic identifications.

THE VALIDITY OF MYSTICAL EXPERIENCE

William James

From William James, *The Varieties of Religious Experience*, Lecture XX (entire), published by the New American Library, Mentor edition.

The material of our study of human nature is now spread before us; and in this parting hour, set free from the duty of description, we can draw our theoretical and practical conclusions. In my first lecture, defending the empirical method, I foretold that whatever conclusions we might come to could be reached by spiritual judgments only, appreciations of the significance for life of religion, taken 'on the whole.' Our conclusions cannot be as sharp as dogmatic conclusions would be, but I will formulate them, when the time comes, as sharply as I can.

Summing up in the broadest possible way the characteristics of the religious life, as we have found them, it includes the following beliefs:—

1. That the visible world is part of a more spiritual universe from which it draws its chief significance;

2. That union or harmonious relation with that higher universe is our true end;

3. That prayer or inner communion with the spirit thereof—be that spirit 'God' or 'law'—is a process wherein work is really done, and spiritual energy flows in and produces effects, psychological or material, within the phenomenal world.

Religion includes also the following psychological characteristics:—

4. A new zest which adds itself like a gift to life, and takes the form either of lyrical enchantment or of appeal to earnestness and heroism.

5. An assurance of safety and a temper of peace, and, in relation to others, a preponderance of loving affections.

In illustrating these characteristics by documents, we have been literally bathed in sentiment. In re-reading my manuscript, I am almost apalled at the amount of emotionality which I find in it. After so much of this, we can afford to be dryer and less sympathetic in the rest of the work that lies before us.

The sentimentality of many of my documents is a consequence of the fact that I sought them among the extravagances of the subject. If any of you are enemies of what our ancestors used to brand as enthusiasm, and are, nevertheless, still listening to me now, you have probably felt my selection to have been sometimes almost perverse, and have wished I might have stuck to soberer examples. I reply that I took these extremer examples as yielding the profounder information. To learn the secrets of any science, we go to expert specialists, even though they may be eccentric persons, and not to commonplace pupils. We combine what they tell us with the rest of our wisdom, and form our final judgment independently. Even so with religion. We who have pursued such radical expressions of it may now be sure that we know its secrets as authentically as any one can know them who learns them from another; and we have next to answer, each of us for himself, the practical question: what are the dangers in this element of life? and in what proportion may it need to be restrained by other elements, to give the proper balance?

But this question suggests another one which I will answer immediately and get it out of the way, for it has more than once already vexed us.[1] Ought it to be assumed that in all men the mixture of religion with other elements should be identical? Ought it, indeed, to be assumed that the lives of all men should show identical religious elements? In other words, is the existence of so many religious types and sects and creeds regrettable?

To these questions I answer 'No' emphatically. And my reason is that I do not see how it is possible that creatures in such different positions and with such different powers as human individuals are, should have exactly the same functions and the same duties. No two of us have identical difficulties, nor should we be expected to work out identical solutions. Each, from his peculiar angle of observation, takes in a certain sphere of fact and trouble, which each must deal with in a unique manner. One of us must soften himself, another must harden himself; one must yield a point, another must stand firm,—in order the better to defend the position assigned him. If an Emerson were forced to be a Wesley, or a Moody forced to be a Whitman, the total human consciousness of the divine would suffer. The divine can mean no single quality, it must mean a group of qualities, by being champions of which in alternation, different men may all find worthy missions. Each attitude being a syllable in human nature's total message, it takes the whole of us to spell the meaning out completely. So a 'god of battles' must be allowed to be the god for one kind of person, a god of peace and heaven and home, the god for another. We must frankly recognize the fact that we live in partial systems, and that parts are not interchangeable in the spiritual life. If we are peevish and jealous, destruction of the self must be an element of our religion; why need it be one if we are good and sympathetic from the outset? If we are sick souls, we require a religion of deliverance; but why think so much of deliverance, if we are healthy-minded?[2] Unquestionably, some men have the completer experience and the higher vocation, here just as in the social world;

---

[1]For example, on pages 116, 137, 263 above. [References are to the New American Library edition. Ed.]
[2]From this point of view, the contrasts between the healthy and the morbid mind, and between the once-born and the twice-born types, of which I spoke in earlier lectures (see pp. 137–141), cease to be the radical antagonisms which many think them. The twice-born look down upon the rectilinear consciousness of life of the once-born as being 'mere morality,' and not properly religion. "Dr. Channing," an orthodox minister is reported to have said, "is excluded from the highest form of religious life by the extraordinary rectitude of his character." It is indeed true that the outlook upon life of the twice-born—holding as it does more of the element of evil in solution—is the wider and completer. The 'heroic' or 'solemn' way in which life comes to them is a 'higher synthesis' into which healthy-mindedness and morbidness both enter and combine. Evil is not evaded, but sublated in the higher religious cheer of these persons (see pp. 53–57, 280–283). But the final consciousness which each type reaches of union with the divine has the same practical significance for the individual; and individuals may well be allowed to get to it by the channels which lie most open to their several temperaments. In the cases which were quoted in Lecture IV, of the mind-cure form of healthy-mindedness, we found

but for each man to stay in his own experience, whate'er it be, and for others to tolerate him there, is surely best.

But, you may now ask, would not this one-sidedness be cured if we should all espouse the science of religions as our own religion? In answering this question I must open again the general relations of the theoretic to the active life.

Knowledge about a thing is not the thing itself. You remember what Al-Ghazzali told us in the Lecture on Mysticism,—that to understand the causes of drunkenness, as a physician understands them, is not to be drunk. A science might come to understand everything about the causes and elements of religion, and might even decide which elements were qualified, by their general harmony with other branches of knowledge, to be considered true; and yet the best man at this science might be the man who found it hardest to be personally devout. *Tout savoir c'est tout pardonner.* The name of Renan would doubtless occur to many persons as an example of the way in which breadth of knowledge may make one only a dilettante in possibilities, and blunt the acuteness of one's living faith.[3] If religion be a function by which either God's cause or man's cause is to be really advanced, then he who lives the life of it, however narrowly, is a better servant than he who merely knows about it, however much. Knowledge about life is one thing; effective occupation of a place in life, with its dynamic currents passing through your being, is another.

For this reason, the science of religions may not be an equivalent for living religion; and if we turn to the inner difficulties of such a science, we see that a point comes when she must drop the purely theoretic attitude, and either let her knots remain uncut, or have them cut by active faith. To see this, suppose that we have our science of religions constituted as a matter of fact. Suppose that she has assimilated all the necessary historical material and distilled out of it as its essence the same conclusions which I myself a few moments ago pronounced. Suppose that she agrees that religion, wherever it is an active thing, involves a belief in ideal presences, and a belief that in our prayerful communion with them,[4] work is done, and something real comes to pass. She has now to exert her critical activity, and to decide how far, in the light of other sciences and in that of general philosophy, such beliefs can be considered *true.*

Dogmatically to decide this is an impossible task. Not only are the other sciences and the philosophy still far from being completed, but in their present state we find them full of conflicts. The sciences of nature know nothing of spiritual presences, and on the whole hold no practical commerce whatever with the idealistic conceptions towards which general philosophy inclines. The scientist, so-called, is, during his scientific hours at least, so materialistic that one may well say that on the whole the influence of science goes against the notion that religion should be recognized at all. And this antipathy to religion finds an echo within the very science of religions itself. The cultivator of this science has to

---

abundant examples of regenerative process. The severity of the crisis in this process is a matter of degree. How long one shall continue to drink the consciousness of evil, and when one shall begin to short-circuit and get rid of it, are also matters of amount and degree, so that in many instances it is quite arbitrary whether we class the individual as a once-born or a twice-born subject.

[3]Compare, e.g., the quotation from Renan on p. 46, above.

[4]'Prayerful' taken in the broader sense explained above on pp. 351 ff. ["Every kind of inward communion or conversation with the power recognized as divine."]

become acquainted with so many groveling and horrible superstitions that a presumption easily arises in his mind that any belief that is religious probably is false. In the 'prayerful communion' of savages with such mumbo-jumbos of deities as they acknowledge, it is hard for us to see what genuine spiritual work—even though it were work relative only to their dark savage obligations—can possibly be done.

The consequence is that the conclusions of the science of religions are as likely to be adverse as they are to be favorable to the claim that the essence of religion is true. There is a notion in the air about us that religion is probably only an anachronism, a case of 'survival,' an atavistic relapse into a mode of thought which humanity in its more enlightened examples has outgrown; and this notion our religious anthropologists at present do little to counteract.

This view is so widespread at the present day that I must consider it with some explicitness before I pass to my own conclusions. Let me call it the 'Survival theory,' for brevity's sake.

The pivot round which the religious life, as we have traced it, revolves, is the interest of the individual in his private personal destiny. Religion, in short, is a monumental chapter in the history of human egotism. The gods believed in—whether by crude savages or by men disciplined intellectually—agree with each other in recognizing personal calls. Religious thought is carried on in terms of personality, this being, in the world of religion, the one fundamental fact. To-day, quite as much as at any previous age, the religious individual tells you that the divine meets him on the basis of his personal concerns.

Science, on the other hand, has ended by utterly repudiating the personal point of view. She catalogues her elements and records her laws indifferent as to what purpose may be shown forth by them, and constructs her theories quite careless of their bearing on human anxieties and fates. Though the scientist may individually nourish a religion, and be a theist in his irresponsible hours, the days are over when it could be said that for Science herself the heavens declare the glory of God and the firmament showeth his handiwork. Our solar system, with its harmonies, is seen now as but one passing case of a certain sort of moving equilibrium in the heavens, realized by a local accident in an appalling wilderness of worlds where no life can exist. In a span of time which as a cosmic interval will count but as an hour, it will have ceased to be. The Darwinian notion of chance production, and subsequent destruction, speedy or deferred, applies to the largest as well as to the smallest facts. It is impossible, in the present temper of the scientific imagination, to find in the driftings of the cosmic atoms, whether they work on the universal or on the particular scale, anything but a kind of aimless weather, doing and undoing, achieving no proper history, and leaving no result. Nature has no one distinguishable ultimate tendency with which it is possible to feel a sympathy. In the vast rhythm of her processes, as the scientific mind now follows them, she appears to cancel herself. The books of natural theology which satisfied the intellects of our grandfathers seem to us quite grotesque,[5] representing, as they did, a God who conformed the largest things of

[5]How was it ever conceivable, we ask, that a man like Christian Wolff, in whose dry-as-dust head all the learning of the early eighteenth century was concentrated, should have preserved such a baby-like faith in the personal and human character of Nature as to expound her operations as he did in his work on the uses of natural things? This, for example, is the account he gives of the sun and its utility:—

nature to the paltriest of our private wants. The God whom science recognizes must be a God of universal laws exclusively, a God who does a wholesale, not a retail business. He cannot accommodate his processes to the convenience of individuals. The bubbles on the foam which coats a stormy sea are floating episodes, made and unmade by the forces of the wind and water. Our private selves are like those bubbles,—epiphenomena, as Clifford, I believe, ingeniously called them; their destinies weigh nothing and determine nothing in the world's irremediable currents of events.

"We see that God has created the sun to keep the changeable conditions on the earth in such an order that living creatures, men and beasts, may inhabit its surface. Since men are the most reasonable of creatures, and able to infer God's invisible being from the contemplation of the world, the sun in so far forth contributes to the primary purpose of creation: without it the race of man could not be preserved or continued. . . . The sun makes daylight, not only on our earth, but also on the other planets; and daylight is of the utmost utility to us; for by its means we can commodiously carry on those occupations which in the night-time would either be quite impossible, or at any rate impossible without our going to the expense of artificial light. The beasts of the field can find food by day which they would not be able to find at night. Moreover we owe it to the sunlight that we are able to see everything that is on the earth's surface, not only near by, but also at a distance, and to recognize both near and far things according to their species, which again is of manifold use to us not only in the business necessary to human life, and when we are traveling, but also for the scientific knowledge of Nature, which knowledge for the most part depends on observations made with the help of sight, and, without the sunshine, would have been impossible. If any one would rightly impress on his mind the great advantages which he derives from the sun, let him imagine himself living through only one month, and see how it would be with all his undertakings, if it were not day but night. He would then be sufficiently convinced out of his own experience, especially if he had much work to carry on in the street or in the fields. . . . From the sun we learn to recognize when it is midday, and by knowing this point of time exactly, we can set our clocks right, on which account astronomy owes much to the sun. . . . By help of the sun one can find the meridian. . . . But the meridian is the basis of our sun-dials, and generally speaking, we should have no sun-dials if we had no sun." Vernünftige Gedanken von den Absichten der natürlichen Dinge, 1782, pp. 74–84.

Or read the account of God's beneficence in the institution of "the great variety throughout the world of men's faces, voices, and handwriting," given in Derham's Physico-theology, a book that had much vogue in the eighteenth century. "Had Man's body," says Dr. Derham, "been made according to any of the Atheistical Schemes, or any other Method than that of the infinite Lord of the World, this wise Variety would never have been: but Men's Faces would have been cast in the same, or not a very different Mould, their Organs of Speech would have sounded the same or not so great a Variety of Notes; and the same Structure of Muscles and Nerves would have given the Hand the same Direction in Writing. And in this Case, what Confusion, what Disturbance, what Mischiefs would the world eternally have lain under! No Security could have been to our persons; no Certainty, no Enjoyment of our Possessions; no Justice between Man and Man; no Distinction between Good and Bad, between Friends and Foes, between Father and Child, Husband and Wife, Male or Female; but all would have been turned topsy-turvy, by being exposed to the Malice of the Envious and ill-Natured, to the Fraud and Violence of Knaves and Robbers, to the Forgeries of the crafty Cheat, to the Lusts of the Effeminate and Debauched, and what not! Our Courts of Justice can abundantly testify the dire Effects of Mistaking Men's Faces, of counterfeiting their Hands, and forging Writings. But now as the infinitely wise Creator and Ruler hath ordered the Matter, every man's Face can distinguish him in the Light, and his Voice in the Dark; his Handwriting can speak for him though absent, and be his Witness, and secure his Contracts in future Generations. A manifest as well as admirable Indication of the divine Superintendence and Management."

A God so careful as to make provision even for the unmistakable signing of bank checks and deeds was a deity truly after the heart of eighteenth century Anglicanism.

I subjoin, omitting the capitals, Derham's 'Vindication of God by the Institution of Hills and Valleys,' and Wolff's altogether culinary account of the institution of Water:—

"The uses," says Wolff, "which water serves in human life are plain to see and need not be described at length. Water is a universal drink of man and beasts. Even though men have made themselves drinks that are artificial, they could not do this without water. Beer is brewed of water and malt, and it is the

You see how natural it is, from this point of view, to treat religion as a mere survival, for religion does in fact perpetuate the traditions of the most primeval thought. To coerce the spiritual powers, or to square them and get them on our side, was, during enormous tracts of time, the one great object in our dealings with the natural world. For our ancestors, dreams, hallucinations, revelations, and cock-and-bull stories were inextricably mixed with facts. Up to a comparatively recent date such distinctions as those between what has been verified and what is only conjectured, between the impersonal and the personal aspects of existence, were hardly suspected or conceived. Whatever you imagined in a lively manner, whatever you thought fit to be true, you affirmed confidently; and whatever you affirmed, your comrades believed. Truth was what had not yet been contradicted, most things were taken into the mind from the point of view of their human suggestiveness, and the attention confined itself exclusively to the aesthetic and dramatic aspects of events.[6]

---

water in it which quenches thirst. Wine is prepared from grapes, which could never have grown without the help of water; and the same is true of those drinks which in England and other places they produce from fruit. . . . Therefore since God so planned the world that men and beasts should live upon it and find there everything required for their necessity and convenience, he also made water as one means whereby to make the earth into so excellent a dwelling. And this is all the more manifest when we consider the advantages which we obtain from this same water for the cleaning of our household utensils, of our clothing, and of other matters. . . . When one goes into a grinding-mill one sees that the grindstone must always be kept wet and then one will get a still greater idea of the use of water."

Of the hills and valleys, Derham, after praising their beauty, discourses as follows: "Some constitutions are indeed of so happy a strength, and so confirmed an health, as to be indifferent to almost any place or temperature of the air. But then others are so weakly and feeble, as not to be able to bear one, but can live comfortably in another place. With some the more subtle and finer air of the hills doth best agree, who are languishing and dying in the feculent and grosser air of great towns, or even the warmer and vaporous air of the valleys and waters. But contrariwise, others languish on the hills, and grow lusty and strong in the warmer air of the valleys.

"So that this opportunity of shifting our abode from the hills to the vales, is an admirable easement, refreshment, and great benefit to the valetudinarian, feeble part of mankind; affording those an easy and comfortable life, who would otherwise live miserably, languish, and pine away.

"To this salutary conformation of the earth we may add another great convenience of the hills, and that is affording commodious places for habitation, serving (as an eminent author wordeth it) as screens to keep off the cold and nipping blasts of the northern and easterly winds, and reflecting the benign and cherishing sunbeams, and so rendering our habitations both more comfortable and more cheerly in winter.

"Lastly, it is to the hills that the fountains owe their rise and the rivers their conveyance, and consequently those vast masses and lofty piles are not, as they are charged, such rude and useless excrescences of our ill-formed globe; but the admirable tools of nature, contrived and ordered by the infinite Creator, to do one of its most useful works. For, was the surface of the earth even and level, and the middle parts of its islands and continents not mountainous and high as now it is, it is most certain there could be no descent for the rivers, no conveyance for the waters; but, instead of gliding along those gentle declivities which the higher lands now afford them quite down to the sea, they would stagnate and perhaps stink, and also drown large tracts of land.

"[Thus] the hills and vales, though to a peevish and weary traveler they may seem incommodious and troublesome, yet are a noble work of the great Creator, and wisely appointed by him for the good of our sublunary world."

[6]Until the seventeenth century this mode of thought prevailed. One need only recall the dramatic treatment even of mechanical questions by Aristotle, as, for example, his explanation of the power of the lever to make a small weight raise a larger one. This is due, according to Aristotle, to the generally miraculous character of the circle and of all circular movement. The circle is both convex and concave; it is made by a fixed point and a moving line, which contradict each other; and whatever moves in a circle moves in opposite directions. Nevertheless, movement in a circle is the most 'natural' movement; and the long arm of the lever, moving, as it does, in the larger circle, has the greater amount of this natural

How indeed could it be otherwise? The extraordinary value, for explanation and prevision, of those mathematical and mechanical modes of conception which science uses, was a result that could not possibly have been expected in advance. Weight, movement, velocity, direction, position, what thin, pallid, uninteresting ideas! How could the richer animistic aspects of Nature, the peculiarities and

---

motion, and consequently requires the lesser force. Or recall the explanation by Herodotus of the position of the sun in winter: It moves to the south because of the cold which drives it into the warm parts of the heavens over Libya. Or listen to Saint Augustine's speculations: "Who gave to chaff such power to freeze that it preserves snow buried under it, and such power to warm that it ripens green fruit? Who can explain the strange properties of fire itself, which blackens all that it burns, though itself bright, and which, though of the most beautiful colors, discolors almost all that it touches and feeds upon, and turns blazing fuel into grimy cinders? . . . Then what wonderful properties do we find in charcoal, which is so brittle that a light tap breaks it, and a slight pressure pulverizes it, and yet is so strong that no moisture rots it, nor any time causes it to decay." City of God, book xxi. ch. iv.

Such aspects of things as these, their naturalness and unnaturalness, the sympathies and antipathies of their superficial qualities, their eccentricities, their brightness and strength and destructiveness, were inevitably the ways in which they originally fastened our attention.

If you open early medical books, you will find sympathetic magic invoked on every page. Take, for example, the famous vulnerary ointment attributed to Paracelsus. For this there were a variety of receipts, including usually human fat, the fat of either a bull, a wild boar, or a bear; powdered earthworms, the *usnia*, or mossy growth on the weathered skull of a hanged criminal, and other materials equally unpleasant—the whole prepared under the planet Venus if possible, but never under Mars or Saturn. Then, if a splinter of wood, dipped in the patient's blood, or the bloodstained weapon that wounded him, be immersed in this ointment, the wound itself being tightly bound up, the latter infallibly gets well,—I quote now Van Helmont's account,—for the blood on the weapon or splinter, containing in it the spirit of the wounded man, is roused to active excitement by the contact of the ointment, whence there results to it a full commission or power to cure its cousin-german, the blood in the patient's body. This it does by sucking out the dolorous and exotic impression from the wounded part. But to do this it has to implore the aid of the bull's fat, and other portions of the unguent. The reason why bull's fat is so powerful is that the bull at the time of slaughter is full of secret reluctancy and vindictive murmur, and therefore dies with a higher flame of revenge about him than any other animal. And thus we have made it out, says this author, that the admirable efficacy of the ointment ought to be imputed, not to any auxiliary concurrence of Satan, but simply to the energy of the *posthumous character of Revenge* remaining firmly impressed upon the blood and concreted fat in the unguent. J. B. VAN HELMONT: A Ternary of Paradoxes, translated by WALTER CHARLETON, London, 1650.—I much abridge the original in my citations.

The author goes on to prove by the analogy of many other natural facts that this sympathetic action between things at a distance is the true rationale of the case. "If," he says, "the heart of a horse, slain by a witch, taken out of the yet reeking carcase, be impaled upon an arrow and roasted, immediately the whole witch becomes tormented with the insufferable pains and cruelty of the fire, which could by no means happen unless there preceded a conjunction of the spirit of the witch with the spirit of the horse. In the reeking and yet panting heart, the spirit of the witch is kept captive, and the retreat of it prevented by the arrow transfixed. Similarly hath not many a murdered carcase at the coroner's inquest suffered a fresh haemorrhage or cruentation at the presence of the assassin?—the blood being, as in a furious fit of anger, enraged and agitated by the impress of revenge conceived against the murderer, at the instant of the soul's compulsive exile from the body. So, if you have dropsy, gout, or jaundice, by including some of your warm blood in the shell and white of an egg, which, exposed to a gentle heat, and mixed with a bait of flesh, you shall give to a hungry dog or hog, the disease shall instantly pass from you into the animal, and leave you entirely. And similarly again, if you burn some of the milk either of a cow or of a woman, the gland from which it issued will dry up. A gentleman at Brussels had his nose mowed off in a combat, but the celebrated surgeon Tagliacozzus digged a new nose for him out of the skin of the arm of a porter at Bologna. About thirteen months after his return to his own country, the engrafted nose grew cold, putrefied, and in a few days dropped off, and it was then discovered that the porter had expired, near about the same punctilio of time. There are still at Brussels eye-witnesses of this occurrence," says Van Helmont; and adds, "I pray what is there in this of superstition or of exalted imagination?"

Modern mind-cure literature—the works of Prentice Mulford, for example—is full of sympathetic magic.

oddities that make phenomena picturesquely striking or expressive, fail to have been first singled out and followed by philosophy as the more promising avenue to the knowledge of Nature's life? Well, it is still in these richer animistic and dramatic aspects that religion delights to dwell. It is the terror and beauty of phenomena, the 'promise' of the dawn and of the rainbow, the 'voice' of the thunder, the 'gentleness' of the summer rain, the 'sublimity' of the stars, and not the physical laws which these things follow, by which the religious mind still continues to be most impressed; and just as of yore, the devout man tells you that in the solitude of his room or of the fields he still feels the divine presence, that inflowings of help come in reply to his prayers, and that sacrifices to this unseen reality fill him with security and peace.

Pure anachronism! says the survival-theory;—anachronism for which dean-thropomorphization of the imagination is the remedy required. The less we mix the private with the cosmic, the more we dwell in universal and impersonal terms, the truer heirs of Science we become.

In spite of the appeal which this impersonality of the scientific attitude makes to a certain magnanimity of temper, I believe it to be shallow, and I can now state my reason in comparatively few words. That reason is that, so long as we deal with the cosmic and the general, we deal only with the symbols of reality, but *as soon as we deal with private and personal phenomena as such, we deal with realities in the completest sense of the term.* I think I can easily make clear what I mean by these words.

The world of our experience consists at all times of two parts, an objective and a subjective part, of which the former may be incalculably more extensive than the latter, and yet the latter can never be omitted or suppressed. The objective part is the sum total of whatsoever at any given time we may be thinking of, the subjective part is the inner 'state' in which the thinking comes to pass. What we think of may be enormous,—the cosmic times and spaces, for example, —whereas the inner state may be the most fugitive and paltry activity of mind. Yet the cosmic objects, so far as the experience yields them, are but ideal pictures of something whose existence we do not inwardly possess but only point at outwardly, while the inner state is our very experience itself; its reality and that of our experience are one. A conscious field *plus* its object as felt or thought of *plus* an attitude towards the object *plus* the sense of a self to whom the attitude belongs—such a concrete bit of personal experience may be a small bit, but it is a solid bit as long as it lasts; not hollow, not a mere abstract element of experience, such as the 'object' is when taken all alone. It is a *full* fact, even though it be an insignificant fact; it is of the *kind* to which all realities whatsoever must belong; the motor currents of the world run through the like of it; it is on the line connecting real events with real events. That unsharable feeling which each one of us has of the pinch of his individual destiny as he privately feels it rolling out on fortune's wheel may be disparaged for its egotism, may be sneered at as unscientific, but it is the one thing that fills up the measure of our concrete actuality, and any would-be existent that should lack such a feeling, or its analogue, would be a piece of reality only half made up.[7]

---

[7]Compare Lotze's doctrine that the only meaning we can attach to the notion of a thing as it is 'in itself' is by conceiving it as it is *for* itself; i.e., as a piece of full experience with a private sense of 'pinch' or inner activity of some sort going with it.

If this be true, it is absurd for science to say that the egotistic elements of experience should be suppressed. The axis of reality runs solely through the egotistic places,—they are strung upon it like so many beads. To describe the world with all the various feelings of the individual pinch of destiny, all the various spiritual attitudes, left out from the description—they being as describable as anything else—would be something like offering a printed bill of fare as the equivalent for a solid meal. Religion makes no such blunder. The individual's religion may be egotistic, and those private realities which it keeps in touch with may be narrow enough; but at any rate it always remains infinitely less hollow and abstract, as far as it goes, than a science which prides itself on taking no account of anything private at all.

A bill of fare with one real raisin on it instead of the word 'raisin,' with one real egg instead of the word 'egg,' might be an inadequate meal, but it would at least be a commencement of reality. The contention of the survival-theory that we ought to stick to non-personal elements exclusively seems like saying that we ought to be satisfied forever with reading the naked bill of fare. I think, therefore, that however particular questions connected with our individual destinies may be answered, it is only by acknowledging them as genuine questions, and living in the sphere of thought which they open up, that we become profound. But to live thus is to be religious; so I unhesitatingly repudiate the survival-theory of religion, as being founded on an egregous mistake. It does not follow, because our ancestors made so many errors of fact and mixed them with their religion, that we should therefore leave off being religious at all.[8] By being religious we establish ourselves in possession of ultimate reality at the only points at which reality is given us to guard. Our responsible concern is with our private destiny, after all.

You see now why I have been so individualistic throughout these lectures, and why I have seemed so bent on rehabilitating the element of feeling in religion

---

[8]Even the errors of fact may possibly turn out not to be as wholesale as the scientist assumes. We saw in Lecture IV how the religious conception of the universe seems to many mind-curers 'verified' from day to day by their experience of fact. 'Experience of fact' is a field with so many things in it that the sectarian scientist, methodically declining, as he does, to recognize such 'facts' as mind-curers and others like them experience, otherwise than by such rude heads of classification as 'bosh,' 'rot,' 'folly,' certainly leaves out a mass of raw fact which, save for the industrious interest of the religious in the more personal aspects of reality, would never have succeeded in getting itself recorded at all. We know this to be true already in certain cases; it may, therefore, be true in others as well. Miraculous healings have always been part of the supernatralist stock in trade, and have always been dismissed by the scientist as figments of the imagination. But the scientist's tardy education in the facts of hypnotism has recently given him an apperceiving mass for phenomena of this order, and he consequently now allows that the healings may exist, provided you expressly call them effects of 'suggestion.' Even the stigmata of the cross on Saint Francis's hands and feet may on these terms not be a fable. Similarly, the time-honored phenomenon of diabolical possession is on the point of being admitted by the scientist as a fact, now that he has the name of 'hystero-demonopathy' by which to apperceive it. No one can foresee just how far this legitimation of occultist phenomena under newly found scientist titles may proceed—even 'prophecy,' even 'levitation,' might creep into the pale.

Thus the divorce between scientist facts and religious facts may not necessarily be as eternal as it at first sight seems, nor the personalism and romanticism of the world, as they appeared to primitive thinking, be matters so irrevocably outgrown. The final human opinion may, in short, in some manner now impossible to foresee, revert to the more personal style, just as any path of progress may follow a spiral rather than a straight line. If this were so, the rigorously impersonal view of science might one day appear as having been a temporarily useful eccentricity rather than the definitively triumphant position which the sectarian scientist at present so confidently announces it to be.

and subordinating its intellectual part. Individuality is founded in feeling; and the recesses of feeling, the darker, blinder strata of character, are the only places in the world in which we catch real fact in the making, and directly perceive how events happen, and how work is actually done.[9] Compared with this world of living individualized feelings, the world of generalized objects which the intellect contemplates is without solidity or life. As in stereoscopic or kinetoscopic pictures seen outside the instrument, the third dimension, the movement, the vital element, are not there. We get a beautiful picture of an express train supposed to be moving, but where in the picture, as I have heard a friend say, is the energy or the fifty miles an hour?[10]

Let us agree, then, that Religion, occupying herself with personal destinies and keeping thus in contact with the only absolute realities which we know, must necessarily play an eternal part in human history. The next thing to decide is what she reveals about those destinies, or whether indeed she reveals anything distinct enough to be considered a general message to mankind. We have done as you see, with our preliminaries, and our final summing up can now begin.

I am well aware that after all the palpitating documents which I have quoted, and all the perspectives of emotion-inspiring institution and belief that my previous lectures have opened, the dry analysis to which I now advance may appear to many of you like an anticlimax, a tapering-off and flattening out of the subject, instead of a crescendo of interest and result. I said awhile ago that the religious attitude of Protestants appears poverty-stricken to the Catholic imagina-

---

[9]Hume's criticism has banished causation from the world of physical objects, and 'Science' is absolutely satisfied to define cause in terms of concomitant change—read Mach, Pearson, Ostwald. The 'original' of the notion of causation is in our inner personal experience, and only there can causes in the old-fashioned sense be directly observed and described.

[10]When I read in a religious paper words like these: "Perhaps the best thing we can say of God is that he is *the Inevitable Inference*," I recognize the tendency to let religion evaporate in intellectual terms. Would martyrs have sung in the flames for a mere inference, however inevitable it might be? Original religious men, like Saint Francis, Luther, Behmen, have usually been enemies of the intellect's pretension to meddle with religious things. Yet the intellect, everywhere invasive, shows everywhere its shallowing effect. See how the ancient spirit of Methodism evaporates under those wonderfully able rationalistic booklets (which every one should read) of a philosopher like Professor Bowne (The Christian Revelation, The Christian Life, The Atonement: Cincinnati and New York, 1898, 1899, 1900). See the positively expulsive purpose of philosophy properly so called:—

"Religion," writes M. Vacherot (La Religion, Paris, 1869, pp. 313, 436, et passim), "answers to a transient state or condition, not to a permanent determination of human nature, being merely an expression of that stage of the human mind which is dominated by the imagination. . . . Christianity has but a single possible final heir to its estate, and that is scientific philosophy."

In a still more radical vein, Professor Ribot (Psychologie des Sentiments, p. 310) describes the evaporation of religion. He sums it up in a single formula—the ever-growing predominance of the rational intellectual element, with the gradual fading out of the emotional element, this latter tending to enter into the group of purely intellectual sentiments. "Of religious sentiment properly so called, nothing survives at last save a vague respect for the unknowable x which is a last relic of the fear, and a certain attraction towards the ideal, which is a relic of the love, that characterized the earlier periods of religious growth. To state this more simply, *religion tends to turn into religious philosophy.*—These are psychologically entirely different things, the one being a theoretic construction of ratiocination, whereas the other is the living work of a group of persons, or of a great inspired leader, calling into play the entire thinking and feeling organism of man."

I find the same failure to recognize that the stronghold of religion lies in individuality in attempts like those of Professor Baldwin (Mental Development, Social and Ethical Interpretations, ch. x.) and Mr. H. R. Marshall (Instinct and Reason, chaps. viii. to xii.) to make it a purely 'conservative social force.'

tion. Still more poverty-stricken, I fear, may my final summing up of the subject appear at first to some of you. On which account I pray you now to bear this point in mind, that in the present part of it I am expressly trying to reduce religion to its lowest admissible terms, to that minimum, free from individualistic excrescences, which all religions contain as their nucleus, and on which it may be hoped that all religious persons may agree. That established, we should have a result which might be small, but would at least be solid; and on it and round it the ruddier additional beliefs on which the different individuals make their venture might be grafted, and flourish as richly as you please. I shall add my own over-belief (which will be, I confess, of a somewhat pallid kind, as befits a critical philosopher), and you will, I hope, also add your over-beliefs, and we shall soon be in the varied world of concrete religious constructions once more. For the moment, let me dryly pursue the analytic part of the task.

Both thought and feeling are determinants of conduct, and the same conduct may be determined either by feeling or by thought. When we survey the whole field of religion, we find a great variety in the thoughts that have prevailed there; but the feelings on the one hand and the conduct on the other are almost always the same, for Stoic, Christian, and Buddhist saints are practically indistinguishable in their lives. The theories which Religion generates, being thus variable, are secondary; and if you wish to grasp her essence, you must look to the feelings and the conduct as being the more constant elements. It is between these two elements that the short circuit exists on which she carries on her principal business, while the ideas and symbols and other institutions form looplines which may be perfections and improvements, and may even some day all be united into one harmonious system, but which are not to be regarded as organs with an indispensable function, necessary at all times for religious life to go on. This seems to me the first conclusion which we are entitled to draw from the phenomena we have passed in review.

The next step is to characterize the feelings. To what psychological order do they belong?

The resultant outcome of them is in any case what Kant calls a 'sthenic' affection, an excitement of the cheerful, expansive, 'dynamogenic' order which, like any tonic, freshens our vital powers. In almost every lecture, but especially in the lectures on Conversion and on Saintliness, we have seen how this emotion overcomes temperamental melancholy and imparts endurance to the Subject, or a zest, or a meaning, or an enchantment and glory to the common objects of life.[11] The name of 'faith-state,' by which Professor Leuba designates it, is a good one.[12] It is a biological as well as a psychological condition, and Tolstoy is absolutely accurate in classing faith among the forces *by which men live*.[13] The total absence of it, anhedonia,[14] means collapse.

The faith-state may hold a very minimum of intellectual content. We saw examples of this in those sudden raptures of the divine presence, or in such mystical seizures as Dr. Bucke described.[15] It may be a mere vague enthusiasm,

[11]Compare, for instance, pages 166, 178, 181, 183, 199 to 204, 218 to 220.
[12]American Journal of Psychology, vii. 345.
[13]Above, p. 153.
[14]Above, p. 124.
[15]Above, p. 307.

half spiritual, half vital, a courage, and a feeling that great and wondrous things are in the air.[16]

When, however, a positive intellectual content is associated with a faith-state, it gets invincibly stamped in upon belief,[17] and this explains the passionate loyalty of religious persons everywhere to the minutest details of their so widely differing creeds. Taking creeds and faith-state together, as forming 'religions,' and treating these as purely subjective phenomena, without regard to the question of their 'truth,' we are obliged, on account of their extraordinary influence upon action and endurance, to class them amongst the most important biological functions of mankind. Their stimulant and anaesthetic effect is so great that Professor Leuba, in a recent article,[18] goes so far as to say that so long as men can *use* their God, they care very little who he is, or even whether he is at all. "The truth of the matter can be put," says Leuba, "in this way: *God is not known, he is not understood; he is used*—sometimes as meat-purveyor, sometimes as moral support, sometimes as friend, sometimes as an object of love. If he proves himself useful, the religious consciousness asks for no more than that. Does God really exist? How does he exist? What is he? are so many irrelevant questions. Not God, but life, more life, a larger, richer, more satisfying life is, in the last analysis, the end of religion. The love of life, at any and every level of development, is the religious impulse."[19]

At this purely subjective rating, therefore, Religion must be considered vindicated in a certain way from the attacks of her critics. It would seem that she cannot be a mere anachronism and survival, but must exert a permanent function,

---

[16]Example: Henri Perreyve writes to Gratry: "I do not know how to deal with the happiness which you aroused in me this morning. It overwhelms me; I want to *do* something, yet I can do nothing and am fit for nothing. . . . I would fain do *great things.*" Again, after an inspiring interview, he writes: "I went homewards, intoxicated with joy, hope, and strength. I wanted to feed upon my happiness in solitude, far from all men. It was late; but, unheeding that, I took a mountain path and went on like a madman, looking at the heavens, regardless of earth. Suddenly an instinct made me draw hastily back—I was on the very edge of a precipice, one step more and I must have fallen. I took fright and gave up my nocturnal promenade." A. GRATRY: Henri Perreyve, London, 1872, pp. 92, 89.

This primacy, in the faith-state, of vague expansive impulse over direction is well expressed in Walt Whitman's lines (Leaves of Grass, 1872, p. 190):—

"O to confront night, storms, hunger, ridicule, accidents, rebuffs, as the trees and animals do. . . .
Dear Camerado! I confess I have urged you onward with me, and still urge you, without the least idea
what is our destination,
Or whether we shall be victorious, or utterly quell'd and defeated."

This readiness for great things, and this sense that the world by its importance, wonderfulness, etc., is apt for their production, would seem to be the undifferentiated germ of all the higher faiths. Trust in our own dreams of ambition, or in our country's expansive destinies, and faith in the providence of God, all have their source in that onrush of our sanguine impulses, and in that sense of the exceedingness of the possible over the real.

[17]Compare LEUBA: Loc. cit., pp. 346–349.

[18]The Contents of Religious Consciousness, in The Monist, xi. 536, July, 1901.

[19]Loc. cit., pp. 571, 572, abridged. See, also, this writer's extraordinarily true criticism of the notion that religion primarily seeks to solve the intellectual mystery of the world. Compare what W. BENDER says (in his Wesen der Religion, Bonn, 1888, pp. 85, 38): "Not the question about God, and not the inquiry into the origin and purpose of the world is religion, but the question about Man. All religious views of life are anthropocentric." "Religion is that activity of the human impulse towards self-preservation by means of which Man seeks to carry his essential vital purposes through against the adverse pressure of the world by raising himself freely towards the world's ordering and governing powers when the limits of his own strength are reached." The whole book is little more than a development of these words.

whether she be with or without intellectual content, and whether, if she have any, it be true or false.

We must next pass beyond the point of view of merely subjective utility, and make inquiry into the intellectual content itself.

First, is there, under all the discrepancies of the creeds, a common nucleus to which they bear their testimony unanimously?

And second, ought we to consider the testimony true?

I will take up the first question first, and answer it immediately in the affirmative. The warring gods and formulas of the various religions do indeed cancel each other, but there is a certain uniform deliverance in which religions all appear to meet. It consists of two parts:—

1. An uneasiness; and
2. Its solution.

1. The uneasiness, reduced to its simplest terms, is a sense that there is *something wrong about us* as we naturally stand.

2. The solution is a sense that *we are saved from the wrongness* by making proper connection with the higher powers.

In those more developed minds which alone we are studying, the wrongness takes a moral character, and the salvation takes a mystical tinge. I think we shall keep well within the limits of what is common to all such minds if we formulate the essence of their religious experience in terms like these:—

The individual, so far as he suffers from his wrongness and criticises it, is to that extent consciously beyond it, and in at least possible touch with something higher, if anything higher exist. Along with the wrong part there is thus a better part of him, even though it may be but a most helpless germ. With which part he should identify his real being is by no means obvious at this stage; but when stage 2 (the stage of solution or salvation) arrives,[20] the man identifies his real being with the germinal higher part of himself; and does so in the following way. *He becomes conscious that this higher part is conterminous and continuous with a* MORE *of the same quality, which is operative in the universe outside of him, and which he can keep in working touch with, and in a fashion get on board of and save himself when all his lower being has gone to pieces in the wreck.*

It seems to me that all the phenomena are accurately describable in these very simple general terms.[21] They allow for the divided self and the struggle; they involve the change of personal centre and the surrender of the lower self; they express the appearance of exteriority of the helping power and yet account for our sense of union with it;[22] and they fully justify our feelings of security and joy.

---

[20]Remember that for some men it arrives suddenly, for others gradually, whilst others again practically enjoy it all their life.

[21]The practical difficulties are: 1, to 'realize the reality' of one's higher part; 2, to identify one's self with it exclusively; and 3, to identify it with all the rest of ideal being.

[22]"When mystical activity is at its height, we find consciousness possessed by the sense of a being at once *excessive* and *identical* with the self: great enough to be God; interior enough to be *me*. The 'objectivity' of it ought in that case to be called *excessivity,* rather, or exceedingness." RÉCÉJAC: Essai sur les fondements de la conscience mystique, 1897, p. 46.

There is probably no autobiographic document, among all those which I have quoted, to which the description will not well apply. One need only add such specific details as will adapt it to various theologies and various personal temperaments, and one will then have the various experiences reconstructed in their individual forms.

So far, however, as this analysis goes, the experiences are only psychological phenomena. They possess, it is true, enormous biological worth. Spiritual strength really increases in the subject when he has them, a new life opens for him, and they seem to him a place of conflux where the forces of two universes meet; and yet this may be nothing but his subjective way of feeling things, a mood of his own fancy, in spite of the effects produced. I now turn to my second question: What is the objective 'truth' of their content?[23]

The part of the content concerning which the question of truth most pertinently arises is that 'MORE of the same quality' with which our own higher self appears in the experience to come into harmonious working relation. Is such a 'more' merely our own notion, or does it really exist? If so, in what shape does it exist? Does it act, as well as exist? And in what form should we conceive of that 'union' with it of which religious geniuses are so convinced?

It is in answering these questions that the various theologies perform their theoretic work, and that their divergencies most come to light. They all agree that the 'more' really exists; though some of them hold it to exist in the shape of a personal god or gods, while others are satisfied to conceive it as a stream of ideal tendency embedded in the eternal structure of the world. They all agree, moreover, that it acts as well as exists, and that something really is effected for the better when you throw your life into its hands. It is when they treat of the experience of 'union' with it that their speculative differences appear most clearly. Over this point pantheism and theism, nature and second birth, works and grace and karma, immortality and reincarnation, rationalism and mysticism, carry on inveterate disputes.

At the end of my lecture on Philosophy[24] I held out the notion that an impartial science of religions might sift out from the midst of their discrepancies a common body of doctrine which she might also formulate in terms to which physical science need not object. This, I said, she might adopt as her own reconciling hypothesis, and recommend it for general belief. I also said that in my last lecture I should have to try my own hand at framing such an hypothesis.

The time has now come for this attempt. Who says 'hypothesis' renounces the ambition to be coercive in his arguments. The most I can do is, accordingly, to offer something that may fit the facts so easily that your scientific logic will find no plausible pretext for vetoing your impulse to welcome it as true.

The 'more,' as we called it, and the meaning of our 'union' with it, form the nucleus of our inquiry. Into what definite description can these words be translated, and for what definite facts do they stand? It would never do for us to place ourselves offhand at the position of a particular theology, the Christian

---

[23]The word 'truth' is here taken to mean something additional to bare value for life, although the natural propensity of man is to believe that whatever has great value for life is thereby certified as true.
[24]Above, p. 346.

theology, for example, and proceed immediately to define the 'more' as Jehovah, and the 'union' as his imputation to us of the righteousness of Christ. That would be unfair to other religions, and, from our present standpoint at least, would be an over-belief.

We must begin by using less particularized terms; and, since one of the duties of the science of religions is to keep religion in connection with the rest of science, we shall do well to seek first of all a way of describing the 'more,' which psychologists may also recognize as real. The *subconscious self* is nowadays a well-accredited psychological entity; and I believe that in it we have exactly the mediating term required. Apart from all religious considerations, there is actually and literally more life in our total soul than we are at any time aware of. The exploration of the transmarginal field has hardly yet been seriously undertaken, but what Mr. Myers said in 1892 in his essay on the Subliminal Consciousness[25] is as true as when it was first written: "Each of us is in reality an abiding psychical entity far more extensive than he knows—an individuality which can never express itself completely through any corporeal manifestation. The Self manifests through the organism; but there is always some part of the Self unmanifested; and always, as it seems, some power of organic expression in abeyance or reserve."[26] Much of the content of this larger background against which our conscious being stands out in relief is insignificant. Imperfect memories, silly jingles, inhibitive timidities, 'dissolutive' phenomena of various sorts, as Myers calls them, enter into it for a large part. But in it many of the performances of genius seem also to have their origin; and in our study of conversion, of mystical experiences, and of prayer, we have seen how striking a part invasions from this region play in the religious life.

Let me then propose, as an hypothesis, that whatever it may be on its *farther* side, the 'more' with which in religious experience we feel ourselves connected is on its *hither* side the subconscious continuation of our conscious life. Starting thus with a recognized psychological fact as our basis, we seem to preserve a contact with 'science' which the ordinary theologian lacks. At the same time the theologian's contention that the religious man is moved by an external power is vindicated, for it is one of the peculiarities of invasions from the subconscious region to take on objective appearances, and to suggest to the Subject an external control. In the religious life the control is felt as 'higher'; but since on our hypothesis it is primarily the higher faculties of our own hidden mind which are controlling, the sense of union with the power beyond us is a sense of something, not merely apparently, but literally true.

---

[25]Proceedings of the Society for Psychical Research, vol. vii. p. 305. For a full statement of Mr. Myers's views, I may refer to his posthumous work, 'Human Personality in the Light of Recent Research,' which is already announced by Messrs. Longmans, Green & Co. as being in press. Mr. Myers for the first time proposed as a general psychological problem the exploration of the subliminal region of consciousness throughout its whole extent, and made the first methodical steps in its topography by treating as a natural series a mass of subliminal facts hitherto considered only as curious isolated facts, and subjecting them to a systematized nomenclature. How important this exploration will prove, future work upon the path which Myers has opened can alone show. Compare my paper: 'Frederic Myers's Services to Psychology,' in the said Proceedings, part xlii., May, 1901.

[26]Compare the inventory given above on pp. 365–6, and also what is said of the subconscious self on pp. 188–190, 193–195.

This doorway into the subject seems to me the best one for a science of religions, for it mediates between a number of different points of view. Yet it is only a doorway, and difficulties present themselves as soon as we step through it, and ask how far our transmarginal consciousness carries us if we follow it on its remoter side. Here the over-beliefs begin: here mysticism and the conversion-rapture and Vedantism and transcendental idealism bring in their monistic interpretations[27] and tell us that the finite self rejoins the absolute self, for it was always one with God and identical with the soul of the world.[28] Here the prophets of all the different religions come with their visions, voices, raptures, and other openings, supposed by each to authenticate his own peculiar faith.

Those of us who are not personally favored with such specific revelations must stand outside of them altogether and, for the present at least, decide that, since they corroborate incompatible theological doctrines, they neutralize one another and leave no fixed result. If we follow any one of them, or if we follow philosophical theory and embrace monistic pantheism on non-mystical grounds, we do so in the exercise of our individual freedom, and build out our religion in the way most congruous with our personal susceptibilities. Among these susceptibilities intellectual ones play a decisive part. Although the religious question is primarily a question of life, of living or not living in the higher union which opens itself to us as a gift, yet the spiritual excitement in which the gift appears a real one will often fail to be aroused in an individual until certain particular intellectual beliefs or ideas which, as we say, come home to him, are touched.[29] These ideas

---

[27]Compare above, pp. 321 ff.

[28]One more expression of this belief, to increase the reader's familiarity with the notion of it:—

"If this room is full of darkness for thousands of years, and you come in and begin to weep and wail, 'Oh, the darkness,' will the darkness vanish? Bring the light in, strike a match, and light comes in a moment. So what good will it do you to think all your lives, 'Oh, I have done evil, I have made many mistakes'? It requires no ghost to tell us that. Bring in the light, and the evil goes in a moment. Strengthen the real nature, build up yourselves, the effulgent, the resplendent, the ever pure, call that up in every one whom you see. I wish that every one of us had come to such a state that even when we see the vilest of human beings we can see the God within, and instead of condemning, say, 'Rise, thou effulgent One, rise thou who art always pure, rise thou birthless and deathless, rise almighty, and manifest your nature.' . . . This is the highest prayer that the Advaita teaches. This is the one prayer: remembering our nature." . . . "Why does man go out to look for a God? . . . It is your own heart beating, and you did not know, you were mistaking it for something external. He, nearest of the near, my own self, the reality of my own life, my body and my soul.—I am Thee and Thou art Me. That is your own nature. Assert it, manifest it. Not to become pure, you are pure already. You are not to be perfect, you are that already. Every good thought which you think or act upon is simply tearing the veil, as it were, and the purity, the Infinity, the God behind, manifests itself—the eternal Subject of everything, the eternal Witness in this universe, your own Self. Knowledge is, as it were, a lower step, a degradation. We are It already; how to know It?" SWAMI VIVEKANANDA: Addresses, No. XII., Practical Vedanta, part iv. pp. 172, 174, London, 1897; and Lectures, The Real and the Apparent Man, p. 24, abridged.

[29]For instance, here is a case where a person exposed from her birth to Christian ideas had to wait till they came to her clad in spiritistic formulas before the saving experience set in:—

"For myself I can say that spiritualism has saved me. It was revealed to me at a critical moment of my life, and without it I don't know what I should have done. It has taught me to detach myself from worldly things and to place my hope in things to come. Through it I have learned to see in all men, even in those most criminal, even in those from whom I have most suffered, undeveloped brothers to whom I owed assistance, love, and forgiveness. I have learned that I must lose my temper over nothing, despise no one, and pray for all. Most of all I have learned to pray! And although I have still much to learn in this domain, prayer ever brings me more strength, consolation, and comfort. I feel more than ever that I have only made a few steps on the long road of progress; but I look at its length without dismay, for I have confidence that the day will come when all my efforts shall be rewarded. So Spirtualism has a great place in my life, indeed it holds the first place there." Flournoy Collection.

will thus be essential to that individual's religion;—which is as much as to say that over-beliefs in various directions are absolutely indispensable, and that we should treat them with tenderness and tolerance so long as they are not intolerant themselves. As I have elsewhere written, the most interesting and valuable things about a man are usually his over-beliefs.

Disregarding the over-beliefs, and confining ourselves to what is common and generic, we have in *the fact that the conscious person is continuous with a wider self through which saving experiences come,*[30] a positive content of religious experience which, it seems to me *is literally and objectively true as far as it goes.* If I now proceed to state my own hypothesis about the farther limits of this extension of our personality, I shall be offering my own over-belief—though I know it will appear a sorry under-belief to some of you—for which I can only bespeak the same indulgence which in a converse case I should accord to yours.

The further limits of our being plunge, it seems to me, into an altogether other dimension of existence from the sensible and merely 'understandable' world. Name it the mystical region, or the supernatural region, whichever you choose. So far as our ideal impulses originate in this region (and most of them do originate in it, for we find them possessing us in a way for which we cannot articulately account), we belong to it in a more intimate sense than that in which we belong to the visible world, for we belong in the most intimate sense wherever our ideals belong. Yet the unseen region in question is not merely ideal, for it produces effects in this world. When we commune with it, work is actually done upon our finite personality, for we are turned into new men, and consequences in the way of conduct follow in the natural world upon our regenerative change.[31] But that which produces effects within another reality must be termed a reality itself, so I feel as if we had no philosophic excuse for calling the unseen or mystical world unreal.

God is the natural appellation, for us Christians at least, for the supreme reality, so I will call this higher part of the universe by the name of God.[32] We and God have business with each other; and in opening ourselves to his influence our deepest destiny is fulfilled. The universe, at those parts of it which our personal being constitutes, takes a turn genuinely for the worse or for the better in

---

[30]"The influence of the Holy Spirit, exquisitely called the Comforter, is a matter of actual experience, as solid a reality as that of electromagnetism." W. C. BROWNELL, Scribner's Magazine, vol. xxx. p. 112.

[31]That the transaction of opening ourselves, otherwise called prayer, is a perfectly definite one for certain persons, appears abundantly in the preceding lectures. I append another concrete example to reinforce the impression on the reader's mind:—

"Man can learn to transcend these limitations [of finite thought] and draw power and wisdom at will. . . . The divine presence is known through experience. The turning to a higher plane is a distinct act of consciousness. It is not a vague, twilight or semi-conscious experience. It is not an ecstasy; it is not a trance. It is not super-consciousness in the Vedantic sense. It is not due to self-hypnotization. It is a perfectly calm, sane, sound, rational, common-sense shifting of consciousness from the phenomena of sense-perception to the phenomena of seership, from the thought of self to a distinctively higher realm. . . . For example, if the lower self be nervous, anxious, tense, one can in a few moments compel it to be calm. This is not done by a word simply. Again I say, it is not hypnotism. It is by the exercise of power. One feels the spirit of peace as definitely as heat is perceived on a hot summer day. The power can be as surely used as the sun's rays can be focused and made to do work, to set fire to wood." The Higher Law, vol. iv. pp. 4, 6, Boston, August, 1901.

[32]Transcendentalists are fond of the term 'Over-soul,' but as a rule they use it in an intellectualist sense, as meaning only a medium of communion. 'God' is a causal agent as well as a medium of communion, and that is the aspect which I wish to emphasize.

proportion as each one of us fulfills or evades God's demands. As far as this goes I probably have you with me, for I only translate into schematic language what I may call the instinctive belief of mankind: God is real since he produces real effects.

The real effects in question, so far as I have as yet admitted them, are exerted on the personal centres of energy of the various subjects, but the spontaneous faith of most of the subjects is that they embrace a wider sphere than this. Most religious men believe (or 'know,' if they be mystical) that not only they themselves, but the whole universe of beings to whom the God is present, are secure in his parental hands. There is a sense, a dimension, they are sure, in which we are *all* saved, in spite of the gates of hell and all adverse terrestrial appearances. God's existence is the guarantee of an ideal order that shall be permanently preserved. This world may indeed, as science assures us, some day burn up or freeze; but if it is part of his order, the old ideals are sure to be brought elsewhere to fruition, so that where God is, tragedy is only provisional and partial, and shipwreck and dissolution are not the absolutely final things. Only when this farther step of faith concerning God is taken, and remote objective consequences are predicted, does religion, as it seems to me, get wholly free from the first immediate subjective experience, and bring a *real hypothesis* into play. A good hypothesis in science must have other properties than those of the phenomenon it is immediately invoked to explain, otherwise it is not prolific enough. God, meaning only what enters into the religious man's experience of union, falls short of being an hypothesis of this more useful order. He needs to enter into wider cosmic relations in order to justify the subject's absolute confidence and peace.

That the God with whom, starting from the hither side of our own extra-marginal self, we come at its remoter margin into commerce should be the absolute world-ruler, is of course a very considerable over-belief. Over-belief as it is, though, it is an article of almost every one's religion. Most of us pretend in some way to prop it upon our philosophy, but the philosophy itself is really propped upon this faith. What is this but to say that Religion, in her fullest exercise of function, is not a mere illumination of facts already elsewhere given, not a mere passion, like love, which views things in a rosier light. It is indeed that, as we have seen abundantly. But it is something more, namely, a postulator of new *facts* as well. The world interpreted religiously is not the materialistic world over again, with an altered expression; it must have, over and above the altered expression, *a natural constitution* different at some point from that which a materialistic world would have. It must be such that different events can be expected in it, different conduct must be required.

This thoroughly 'pragmatic' view of religion has usually been taken as a matter of course by common men. They have interpolated divine miracles into the field of nature, they have built a heaven out beyond the grave. It is only transcendentalist metaphysicians who think that, without adding any concrete details to Nature, or subtracting any, but by simply calling it the expression of absolute spirit, you make it more divine just as it stands. I believe the pragmatic way of taking religion to be the deeper way. It gives it body as well as soul, it makes it claim, as everything real must claim, some characteristic realm of fact as its very own. What the more characteristically divine facts are, apart from the actual inflow of energy in the faith-state and the prayer-state, I know not. But the over-belief on which I am ready to make my personal venture is that they exist. The whole drift of my education goes to persuade me that the world of our present consciousness is only one out of many worlds of consciousness that exist, and that those other worlds must contain experiences which have a meaning for our life also; and that although in the main their experiences and those of this world keep discrete, yet the two become continuous at certain points, and higher energies filter in. By being faithful in my poor measure to this over-belief, I seem to myself to keep more sane and true. I *can*, of course, put myself into the sectarian scientist's attitude, and imagine vividly that the world of sensations and of scientific laws and objects may be all. But whenever I do this, I hear that inward monitor of which W. K. Clifford once wrote, whispering the word 'bosh!' Humbug is humbug, even though it bear the scientific name, and the total expression of human experience, as I view it objectively, invincibly urges me beyond the narrow 'scientific' bounds. Assuredly, the real world is of a different temperament,—more intricately built than physical science allows. So my objective and my subjective conscience both hold me to the over-belief which I express. Who knows whether the faithfulness of individuals here below to their own poor over-beliefs may not actually help God in turn to be more effectively faithful to his own greater tasks?

THE EXPERIENCE OF GOD

John Baillie

From John Baillie, *Our Knowledge of God,* pp. 155–159 and 178–179. Copyright © 1959 by John Baillie. Reprinted by permission of Charles Scribner's Sons, New York, and Oxford University Press, London.

The witness of all true religion is that there is no reality which more directly confronts us than the reality of God. No other reality is nearer to us than He. The realities of sense are more obvious, but His is the more intimate, touching us as it does so much nearer to the core of our being. God's approach to us in Christ is the closest approach that is ever made to the inmost citadel of our souls—

> The hold that falls not when the town is got,
> The heart's heart, whose immurèd plot
> Hath keys yourself keep not![1]

"Behold, I stand at the door and knock," says Christ; and though many knockings are more obtrusive, none is so patient or in the last resort so ineluctable. God alone is omnipresent. His is the only claim that is always with us and never lets us

---

[1]Francis Thompson, *A Fallen Yew.*

go. "Whither shall I go from thy spirit? or whither shall I flee from thy presence? If I ascend up into heaven, thou art there: if I make my bed in Sheol, behold, thou art there. If I take the wings of the morning, and dwell in the uttermost parts of the sea; Even there shall thy hand lead me, and thy right hand shall hold me. If I say, Surely the darkness shall cover me; even the night shall be light about me. Yea, the darkness hideth not from thee, but the night shineth as the day: the darkness and the light are both alike to thee."[2] I am sure that, in proportion as we are honest with ourselves, we shall all have to confess to this haunting Presence. It has been with us from our youth up, and we know that it will be with us to the end. No other challenge that has ever reached us has been so insistent or so imperious. You and I have often tried to evade it; we have done many things in its despite; sometimes, when its demands were most inconvenient, we have tried to pretend that it had no right to be there at all. But in the bottom of our hearts we have never been able to doubt its right. We have always known that there is no other sovereign right but this, and no other "totalitarian" authority. We are surrounded by many glaring realities that occupy the foreground of our con-sciousness and make all sorts of claims on our attention and allegiance; but we have always known that only one obligation is absolute and one imperative categorical. Moreover, you and I have always known that this claim that was being made upon us was being made upon us for our *good,* and that in yielding to it lay our only true salvation. Even when we most tried to escape from it, we still knew that our deepest weal lay in obedience. We knew that it was sovereign Love that was here constraining us and claiming us for its own; and we knew that in the last resort it was something that was being *offered* us rather than asked of us—and that what was being asked of us was only that we should accept the offer. So when men gazed upon the figure of the Crucified Christ, they were conscious of all the rebuke it held for them, all the condemnation of their sin, all the rigour and austerity of its demands; but behind all they knew most certainly that "herein was love." "For God sent not his Son into the world to condemn the world; but that the world through him might be saved."[3]

I have already spoken of the Kantian revolution as that next following upon the Cartesian in the order of modern thought. In Kant's Critical Philosophy there is a most valuable recovery of the fundamental truth upon which I have been dwelling, yet Kant was still too much in bondage to the humanistic tradition, and particularly to the eighteenth-century stratum of that tradition, to let it appear in anything but a sadly curtailed and impoverished form. Kant's great rediscovery was that of the Primacy of the Practical Reason, as he called it. It is not in the realm of sense, he believed, that we are all really in touch with absolute objective reality, and certainly not in the realm of the supersensible objects of scientific and metaphysical speculation, but only in the realm of the practical claim that is made upon our wills by the Good. Ultimate reality meets us, not in the form of an object that invites our speculation, but in the form of a demand that is made upon our obedience. We are confronted not with an absolute object of theoretical knowledge but with an absolute obligation. We reach the Unconditional only in an unconditional imperative that reaches us. There is here, as it seems to me,

---

[2] *Psalms* cxxxix.
[3] *John* iii, 17.

most precious and deeply Christian insight. But where Kant erred, and where his eighteenth-century education was too much for him, was in his analysis of this experience into mere *respect for a law*. The eighteenth century had its own very remarkable greatness, but it also had its obvious limitations—limitations which could not, in fact, be better exemplified than in this proposal to make *law* at once the primary fact in the universe and the prime object of our *respect*. Something of this respect for law we can still conjure up as we stroll through the well-ordered palace and gardens of Versailles, or again as we wander at will through the equally well-ordered couplets of Alexander Pope's poetry; yet between us and both of these experiences stands that Romantic Revival which, in spite of all its regrettable extravagances, has taught us a delight in *fera natura* of which we shall never again be able entirely to rid ourselves. The reduction of the spiritual life of mankind to the mere respectful acceptance of a formula was, in fact, the last absurdity of the eighteenth century. It is no mere formula with which the sons of men have ever found themselves faced as they approached life's most solemn issues, but a Reality of an altogether more intimate and personal kind;[4] and respect or *Achtung* is hardly an adequate name for all the fear and the holy dread, the love and the passionate self-surrender, with which they have responded to its presence. We must indeed do Kant the justice of remembering that he discovered a process of reasoning which, as he thought, justified him in envisaging this moral law in a more concrete way as the commandment of a holy God. In this way something of the true spiritual life of mankind seems to find its way back into his scheme. Yet the loophole by which it is allowed to enter is so narrow that little or nothing of the rich reality of it succeeds in getting through. Kant's religion remained to the end a mere legalistic moralism *plus* a syllogism that allowed him to conceive of an eighteenth-century Legislator behind His eighteenth-century law. "Thus," as—to take only one example—he himself most cogently concluded, "the purpose of prayer can only be to induce in us a moral disposition. . . . To wish to converse with God is absurd: we cannot talk to one we cannot intuit; and as we cannot intuit God, but can only believe in him, we cannot converse with him."[5]

Now it seems to me that it is precisely such a sense of *converse* with the Living God as Kant thus clearly saw to be excluded by his own system that lies at the root of all our spiritual life. That life finds its only beginning in the revelation to our finite minds of One whose transcendent perfection constitutes upon our lives a claim so sovereign that the least attempt to deny it awakens in us a sense of sin and shame; and thus is initiated the sequence, ever extending itself as the revelation of the divine nature becomes deeper and fuller, of confession, repentance, forgiveness, reconciliation, and the new life of fellowship. *There is no other spiritual sequence than this.*

.   .   .   .

Yet, though we are more directly and intimately confronted with the presence of God than with any other presence, it does not follow that He is ever

---

[4] "For no law, apart from a Lawgiver, is a proper object of reverence. It is mere brute fact; and every living thing, still more every person exercising intelligent choice, is its superior. The reverence of persons can be appropriately given only to that which itself is at least personal."—Archbishop William Temple, *Nature, Man and God,* p. 255. Dr. Temple italicizes the whole passage.
[5] *Lectures on Ethics,* trans. by L. Infield, p. 99.

present to us *apart* from all other presences. And, in fact, it is the witness of experience that only "in, with and under" other presences is the divine presence ever vouchsafed to us. This aspect of the matter was referred to at the beginning of this chapter, but must now be more fully investigated.

I believe the view to be capable of defence that no one of the four subjects of our knowledge—ourselves, our fellows, the corporeal world, and God—is ever presented to us except in conjunction with all three of the others. Here, however, we need only concern ourselves with the fact that God does not present Himself to us except in conjunction with the presence of our fellows and of the corporeal world.

Taking the second point first, it seems plain that the consciousness of God is never given save in conjunction with the consciousness of things. We do not know God through the world, but we know Him with the world; and in knowing Him with the world, we know Him as its ground. Nature is not an argument for God, but it is a sacrament of Him. Just as in the sacrament of Holy Communion the Real Presence of Christ is given (if the Lutheran phrase may here be used without prejudice) "in, with and under" the bread and wine, so in a wider sense the whole corporeal world may become sacramental to us of the presence of the Triune God. The conception of a sacramental universe thus expresses the truth that lay behind St. Thomas's natural theology, while being free from the errors in which the latter became involved. No writer has done more to clarify our thought on this matter than Baron von Hügel. "Necessity of the Thing-element in Religion" is not only the title of a section in his greatest work,[6] but a constant theme in all his works. "Spirit," he tells us, "is awakened on occasion of Sense."[7] The knowledge of God, he insists, is not during this life given to us in its isolated purity, but only through "the humiliations of the material order."[8] The knowledge of God which we have on earth is of a kind that we cannot conceive to exist apart from some knowledge of things.

But it is equally certain that all our knowledge of God is given us "in, with and under" our knowledge of one another. This means, first, that the knowledge of God is withholden from those who keep themselves aloof from the *service* of their fellows. It means that "He that loveth not knoweth not God,"[9] whereas "if we love one another, God dwelleth in us."[10] And this is indeed a blessed provision by which God makes my knowledge of Himself pass through my brother's need. It means, second, that only when I am in *fellowship* with my fellow men does the knowledge of God come to me individually. It means the necessity of the Church and the rejection of religious individualism. It gives the true sense of the Cyprianic formula, *extra ecclesiam nulla salus.* "For where two or three are gathered together in my name, there am I in the midst of them."[11] Such was the promise; and its fulfilment came when the disciples "were *all* with one accord in one place" and the Spirit "sat upon *each* of them."[12] It means,

---

[6] *The Mystical Element in Religion,* 2nd edition, Vol. II, pp. 372 ff.
[7] *Essays and Addresses,* 2nd series, p. 246.
[8] See the chapter on "The Natural Order" in M. Nédoncelle's *Baron Friedrich von Hügel.*
[9] *1 John* iv. 8.
[10] *1 John* iv. 12.
[11] *Matthew* xviii. 20.
[12] *Acts* ii. 1–3.

third, the necessity of history. There is a necessary historical element in all religion, for we know of no religion that is not dependent on tradition; but Christianity is plainly an historical religion in the fullest possible sense. The Christian knowledge of God is not given to any man save in conjunction with the telling of an "old, old story." Therefore it means, lastly, the necessity of Christ, God incarnate in the flesh. "For there is one God, and one mediator between God and men, the man Christ Jesus; who gave himself a ransom for all, to be testified in due time."[13] The service of others, the fellowship with others, and the historical tradition in which I stand are all media that lead me to the Mediator, and the Mediator leads me to God. And all this mediation is part of God's gracious purpose in refusing to unite me to Himself without at the same time uniting me to my fellow men—in making it impossible for me to obey either of the two great commandments without at the same time obeying the other. This understanding of the relation of faith to history is one which has been greatly clarified for us by Dr. Gogarten and other writers of his school.[14] It is finely summarized by Dr. Brunner: "However inconceivable for us the miracle of the Incarnation may be, yet God lets us in some measure learn why his revelation happens precisely thus and in no other way. It is the wisdom and the goodness of the ruler of the world that he has revealed himself once for all at a particular place, at a particular time. Inasmuch as God, so to speak, deposits his gift of salvation at this one historical place, he compels at the same time all men who wish to share in this gift to betake themselves to this one place, and there to meet each other. . . . It is as if God had used a stratagem by so revealing himself that he can only be found when we find our brother along with him, that in order to find him we must let ourselves be bound to our brother. Only in the bond which unites me to the historical fellowship of my fellow believers—to be more exact, in the fellowship of those who believed before me—is my faith possible. . . . I must, so to speak, submit to becoming myself a member of the fellowship, if I wish to enter into relation with God. God will not bind me to himself on any other terms than these, that he binds me at the same time to my brother."[15]

Clearly, then, the immediacy of God's presence to our souls is a mediated immediacy. But I must now do what I can to resolve the apparent self-contradictoriness of this phrase.

What I must do is to ask myself how the knowledge of God first came to me. And here I can only repeat what was said in the opening pages of this book: unless my analysis of my memory is altogether at fault, the knowledge of God first came to me in the form of an awareness that I was "not my own" but one under authority, one who "owed" something, one who "ought" to be something which he was not. But whence did this awareness come to me? Certainly it did not come "out of the blue." I heard no voice from the skies. No, it came, without a doubt, from what I may call the spiritual climate of the home into which I was born. It came from my parents' walk and conversation. At the beginning it may have been merely the consciousness of a conflict between my mother's will and my own,

---

[13] *1 Timothy* ii. 5–6.
[14] See especially F. Gogarten, *Ich Glaube an den Dreieinigen Gott: eine Untersuchung über Glauben und Geschichte* (1926); *Glaube und Wirklichkeit* (1928).
[15] *God and Man*, English translation, p. 126 f.

between what I desired and what she desired of me. Yet I cannot profess to remember a time when it was merely that. I cannot remember a time when I did not already dimly know that what opposed my own wilfulness was something much more than mere wilfulness on my mother's part. I knew she had a right to ask of me what she did; which is the same as to say that I knew that what she asked of me was right and that my contrary desire was wrong. I knew, therefore, that my mother's will was not the ultimate source of the authority which she exercised over me. For it was plain that she herself was under that same authority. Indeed, it was not only from my parents' specific demands on me that this sense of authority came to me but from the way they themselves lived. Clearly they, too, were under orders, and under essentially the same orders. I cannot remember a time when I did not already know that what my parents demanded of me and what they knew to be demanded of themselves were in the last resort one and the same demand, however different might be its detailed application to our different situations. I cannot remember a time when I did not know that my parents and their household were part of a wider community which was under the same single authority. Nor, again, can I recall a time when I did not know that this authority was closely bound up with, and indeed seemed to emanate from, *a certain story.* As far back as I can remember anything, my parents and my nurses were already speaking to me of Abraham and Isaac and Jacob, of Moses and David, of God's covenant with the Israelites and of their journey through the wilderness, of the culmination of the story in the coming of Jesus Christ, God's only Son, whom He sent to earth to suffer and die for our salvation; and then of the apostles and martyrs and saints and "Scots worthies" whose golden deeds brought the story down to very recent days. And I knew that that story was somehow the source of the authority with which I was confronted. I could not hear a Bible story read without being aware that in it I was somehow being confronted with a solemn presence that had in it both sweetness and rebuke. Nor do I remember a day when I did not already dimly know that this presence was God.

It was, then, through the media of my boyhood's home, the Christian community of which it formed a part, and the "old, old story" from which that community drew its life, that God first revealed Himself to me. This is simple matter of fact. But what I take to be matter of fact in it is not only that God used these media but that in using them He actually did reveal Himself to *my* soul.

For what I seemed to know was not merely that God had declared His will to my parents and that they in their turn had declared their will to me, but also that through my parents God had declared His will to me. The story told me how God had spoken to Abraham and Moses and the prophets and apostles, but what gave the story its power over my mind and imagination and conscience was the knowledge that "in, with and under" this speaking to these others of long ago He was also now speaking to myself. That God should have revealed Himself to certain men of long ago could not in itself be of concern to me now; first, because, not being myself privy to this revelation, I could never know for sure whether it were a real or only an imagined one; second, because mere hearsay could never be a sufficient foundation for such a thing as religion, though it might be well enough as a foundation for certain other kinds of knowledge; and third, because the revelation would necessarily lack the particular authorization and relevance to my case which alone could give it power over my recalcitrant will.

What is it to me that God should have commanded David to do this or that, or called Paul to such and such a task? It is nothing at all, unless it should happen that, as I read of His calling and commanding them, I at the same time found Him calling and commanding me. If the word of God is to concern me, it must be a word addressed to me individually and to the particular concrete situation in which I am standing now. This insight into what we may perhaps venture to call the necessary "here-and-nowness"—the *hic et nunc*—of revelation is one which has emerged very strikingly from recent theological discussions. Kierkegaard's doctrine of the "existential moment"[16] has been a potent influence on many writers; but I need perhaps mention only Dr. Eberhard Grisebach's elaborate demonstration in his book called *Gegenwart*[17] that our sole touch with reality is in the present, the past and the future being alike unreal except so far as they are contained in the present moment.

In a letter to M. de Beaumont, Rousseau once asked, "Is it simple, is it natural, that God should have gone and found Moses in order to speak to Jean Jacques Rousseau?" No, it is far from simple; but what right have we to assume that truth is simple? And as to whether it is natural, have we any knowledge of what would be natural in such a region of experience apart from the witness of the experience itself? We have to take experience as we find it—though that apparently was what Rousseau was refusing to do. And especially we have to face the fact that we have here to do with an experience of an entirely unique kind, its uniqueness lying precisely in this conjunction of immediacy with mediacy—that is, in the fact that God reveals Himself to me only through others who went before, yet in so doing reveals Himself to me now.

This is, indeed, a mysterious ordering of things. Yet I would not be understood as trying to surround it with any spurious air of mystery. Mysterious though it be, it is a mystery with which all men have some degree of acquaintance. It was not *only* in the Bible stories that I was met in my youth with this peculiar conjugation of past and present. Other tales of later days were told me, and in them the same Presence seemed to be speaking to me something of the same word. Were this Presence and this word in *every* tale I was told? I think not. There were, for instance, fairy stories; and they, though they absorbed my interest and caught my imagination, seemed to have nothing to say to me, nothing to do with me. And of some other stories the same thing was true. The stories that had Presence in them for me, though they were by no means always Bible stories, were somehow of a piece with the Bible stories. Usually, indeed, they were Christian stories, and as such were definitely derivative from the Bible history. But even when that was not the case, if they had Presence in them at all, it was the same Presence as met me in the Bible. And to this day all the history that has Presence in it for me, all the history that has anything to say to me, all of the past through which I am addressed in the present, is centered in the story of the Incarnation and the Cross. All that history has to say to me is somehow related to that; and no story that was entirely out of relation to that could have any present reality in it for me at all. Every story is either B.C. or else A.D.; and that not in mere date but in its very essence; logically as well as chronologically. Indeed, the

---

[16]See especially his book *Der Augenblick* (1855).

[17]*Gegenwart, eine Kritische Ethik* (1928).

same story may be chronologically A.D. yet logically B.C., such as stories of noble deeds done within the Christian era by men of other lands whom the knowledge of Christ has not yet reached. Such deeds seem to me to look forward to the Incarnation and the Cross rather than back to them, so that the doers of them are still living as it were under the Old Dispensation. Perhaps these truths of experience on which I have been dwelling have never received better intellectual formulation than in Professor Tillich's doctrine of *die Mitte der Geschichte,* where it is taught that history can have meaning only if it have a centre, and that for the Christian that centre is necessarily Christ. "In dealing with the philosophy of history," he writes, "it is impossible to avoid the Christological problem. History and christology belong to one another as do question and answer." "Instead of the beginning and end of history determining its centre, it is its centre that determines its beginning and end. But the centre of history can only be the place where is revealed the principle that gives it meaning. History is constituted when its centre is constituted, or rather—since this is no mere subjective act—when such a centre reveals its centrality."[18]

The question may now be raised whether a story that has no Presence in it and no word to speak to us really partakes of the true nature of history at all; that is, whether anything can be history for the Christian which does not stand in relation to Christ as its centre. When Dr. Barth insists, as he does so often, that in history in general there is no revelation, since revelation interrupts history at a single point rather than informs it throughout, he is obviously thinking of history as something past and done with. Christ, he says, comes vertically into history and He *alone* reveals God; the history into which He comes does not reveal God *at all.* Thinking of history in this way, the Barthian theologians always oppose "the Christ of Faith" to "the Christ of History." History, they say, cannot give you the truth about Christ; only faith can do that. I believe this dichotomy to be radically mistaken. I believe that a historiographer who writes without faith produces *bad history.* I believe that faith is quite essential to sound historiography. And I believe Professor Tillich's doctrine of Christ as the centre round which all history arranges itself to be altogether profounder than the Barthian attempt to set the rest of history in contrast with Christ. To Professor Tillich history is nothing dead and desiccated, "the presence of the past in the present" being essential to its very nature, so that he can say that in ancient Greek thought "there is no conception of the world as history, even though history as a report on the complex of human movements and as a pattern for politicians be not lacking to it."[19] A similar view is eloquently defended by Dr. Gogarten, to whose treatment of this whole matter I have already acknowledged my debt. "However one may try to solve it," he writes, "and however one may alter its form in so doing, the problem of history is fundamentally the problem of the presentness of the past. Were the past merely past, as it is in the case of all natural events, there would be no such thing as history but only an unhistorical present—and indeed not even that. For there can be a real present only where there is something past that

---

[18]*Religiöse* Verwirklichung (1930), pp. 111, 116. The essay from which I quote is translated in *The Interpretation of History* (1936), pp. 242 ff., but I have not followed this somewhat unsatisfactory translation.
[19]*Op. cit.,* p. 112.

becomes present." "History is something that happens in the present."[20] Such, surely, is the right way of it. *It is only in the conception of history as something that happens in the present that the apparent contradiction in our doctrine of a mediated immediacy can be reasonably resolved.*

---

[20] *Ich Glaube an den Dreieinigen Gott*, pp. 71 f., 83.

THE VALIDITY OF NUMINOUS EXPERIENCE
Rudolf Otto

From Rudolf Otto, *The Idea of the Holy*, J. W. Harvey (trans.), copyright 1959. By permission of Oxford University Press, London.

The Elements in the "Numinous"

Creature-feeling. The reader is invited to direct his mind to a moment of deeply-felt religious experience, as little as possible qualified by other forms of consciousness. Whoever cannot do this, whoever knows no such moments in his experience, is requested to read no farther; for it is not easy to discuss questions of religious psychology with one who can recollect the emotions of his adolescence, the discomforts of indigestion, or, say, social feelings, but cannot recall any intrinsically religious feelings. We do not blame such an one, when he tries for himself to advance as far as he can with the help of such principles of explanation as he knows, interpreting "aesthetics" in terms of sensuous pleasure, and "religion" as a function of the gregarious instinct and social standards, or as something more primitive still. But the artist, who for his part has an intimate personal knowledge of the distinctive element in the aesthetic experience, will decline his theories with thanks, and the religious man will reject them even more uncompromisingly.

Next, in the probing and analysis of such states of the soul as that of solemn worship, it will be well if regard be paid to what is unique in them rather than to what they have in common with other similar states. To be *rapt* in worship is one thing; to be morally *uplifted* by the contemplation of a good deed is another; and it is not to their common features, but to those elements of emotional content peculiar to the first that we would have attention directed as precisely as possible. As Christians we undoubtedly here first meet with feelings familiar enough in a weaker form in other departments of experience, such as feelings of gratitude, trust, love, reliance, humble submission, and dedication. But this does not by any means exhaust the content of religious worship. Not in any of these have we got the special features of the quite unique and incomparable experience of solemn worship. In what does this consist?

Schleiermacher has the credit of isolating a very important element in such an experience. This is the "feeling of dependence." But this important discovery of Schleiermacher is open to criticism in more than one respect.

In the first place, the feeling or emotion which he really has in mind in this phrase is in its specific quality not a "feeling of dependence" in the "natural" sense of the word. As such, other domains of life and other regions of experience than the religious occasion the feeling, as a sense of personal insufficiency and impotence, a consciousness of being determined by circumstances and environment. The feeling of which Schleiermacher wrote has an undeniable analogy with these states of mind: they serve as an indication to it, and its nature may be elucidated by them, so that, by following the direction in which they point, the feeling itself may be spontaneously felt. But the feeling is at the same time also qualitatively different from such analogous states of mind. Schleiermacher himself, in a way, recognizes this by distinguishing the feeling of pious or religious dependence from all other feelings of dependence. His mistake is in making the distinction merely that between "absolute" and "relative" dependence, and therefore a difference of degree and not of intrinsic quality. What he overlooks is that, in giving the feeling the name "feeling of dependence" at all, we are really employing what is no more than a very close analogy. Anyone who compares and contrasts the two states of mind introspectively will find out, I think, what I mean. It cannot be expressed by means of anything else, just because it is so primary and elementary a datum in our psychical life, and therefore only definable through itself. It may perhaps help him if I cite a well-known example, in which the precise "moment" or element of religious feeling of which we are speaking is most actively present. When Abraham ventures to plead with God for the men of Sodom, he says (Gen. xviii. 27): "Behold now, I have taken upon me to speak unto the Lord, which am but dust and ashes." There you have a self-confessed "feeling of dependence," which is yet at the same time far more than, and something other than, *merely* a feeling of dependence. Desiring to give it a name of its own, I propose to call it "creature-consciousness" or creature-feeling. It is the emotion of a creature, submerged and overwhelmed by its own nothingness in contrast to that which is supreme above all creatures.

It is easily seen that, once again, this phrase, whatever it is, is not a *conceptual* explanation of the matter. All that this new term, "creature-feeling," can express, is the note of submergence into nothingness before an overpowering, absolute might of some kind; whereas everything turns upon the *character* of this overpowering might, a character which cannot be expressed verbally, and can only be suggested indirectly through the tone and content of a man's feeling-response to it. And this response must be directly experienced in oneself to be understood.

We have now to note a second defect in the formulation of Schleiermacher's principle. The religious category discovered by him, by whose means he professes to determine the real content of the religious emotion, is merely a category of *self*-valuation, in the sense of self-depreciation. According to him the religious emotion would be directly and primarily a sort of *self*-consciousness, a feeling concerning oneself in a special, determined relation, viz. one's dependence. Thus, according to Schleiermacher, I can only come upon the very fact of God as the result of an inference, that is, by reasoning to a cause beyond myself to account for my "feeling of dependence." But this is entirely opposed to the psychological facts of the case. Rather, the "creature-feeling" is itself a first subjective concomitant and effect of another feeling-element, which casts it like a shadow, but which in itself indubitably has immediate and primary reference to an object outside the self.[1]

Now this object is just what we have already spoken of as "the numinous." For the "creature-feeling" and the sense of dependence to arise in the mind the "numen" must be experienced as present, a *numen praesens,* as in the case of Abraham. There must be felt a something "numinous," something bearing the character of a "numen," to which the mind turns spontaneously; or (which is the same thing in other words) these feelings can only arise in the mind as accompanying emotions when the category of "the numinous" is called into play.

The numinous is thus felt as objective and outside the self. We have now to inquire more closely into its nature and the modes of its manifestation.

"Mysterium Tremendum"

The analysis of "tremendum." We said above that the nature of the numinous can only be suggested by means of the special way in which it is reflected in the mind in terms of feeling. "Its nature is such that it grips or stirs the human mind with this and that determinate affective state." We have now to attempt to give a further indication of these determinate states. We must once again endeavour, by adducing feelings akin to them for the purpose of analogy or contrast, and by the use of metaphor and symbolic expressions, to make the states of mind we are investigating ring out, as it were, of themselves.

Let us consider the deepest and most fundamental element in all strong and sincerely felt religious emotion. Faith unto salvation, trust, love—all these are there. But over and above these is an element which may also on occasion, quite apart from them, profoundly affect us and occupy the mind with a wellnigh bewildering strength. Let us follow it up with every effort of sympathy and imaginative intuition wherever it is to be found, in the lives of those around us, in sudden, strong ebullitions of personal piety and the frames of mind such ebullitions evince, in the fixed and ordered solemnities of rites and liturgies, and again in the atmosphere that clings to old religious monuments and buildings, to temples and to churches. If we do so we shall find we are dealing with something

---

[1]This is so manifestly borne out by experience that it must be about the first thing to force itself upon the notice of psychologists analysing the facts of religion. There is a certain naïveté in the following passage from William James's *Varieties of Religious Experience* (p. 58), where, alluding to the origin of the Grecian representations of the gods, he says: "As regards the origin of the Greek gods, we need not at present seek an opinion. But the whole array of our instances leads to a conclusion something like this: It is as if there were in the human consciousness *a sense of reality, a feeling of objective presence,* a *perception* of what we may call *'something there,'* more deep and more general than any of the special and particular 'senses' by which the current psychology supposes existent realities to be originally revealed." (The italics are James's own.) James is debarred by his empiricist and pragmatist standpoint from coming to a recognition of faculties of knowledge and potentialities of thought in the spirit itself, and he is therefore obliged to have recourse to somewhat singular and mysterious hypotheses to explain this fact. But he grasps the fact itself clearly enough and is sufficient of a realist not to explain it away. But this "feeling of reality," the feeling of a "numinous" *object* objectively given, must be posited as a primary immediate datum of consciousness, and the "feeling of dependence" is then a consequence, following very closely upon it, viz. a depreciation of the *subject* in his own eyes. The latter presupposes the former.

for which there is only one appropriate expression, "*mysterium tremendum.*"
(The feeling of it may at times come sweeping like a gentle tide, pervading the
mind with a tranquil mood of deepest worship. It may pass over into a more set
and lasting attitude of the soul, continuing, as it were, thrillingly vibrant and
resonant, until at last it dies away and the soul resumes its "profane," non-
religious mood of everyday experience. It may burst in sudden eruption up from
the depths of the soul with spasms and convulsions, or lead to the strangest
excitements, to intoxicated frenzy, to transport, and to ecstasy. It has its wild and
demonic forms and can sink to an almost grisly horror and shuddering. It has its
crude, barbaric antecedents and early manifestations, and again it may be
developed into something beautiful and pure and glorious. It may become the
hushed, trembling, and speechless humility of the creature in the presence
of—whom or what? In the presence of that which is a *mystery* inexpressible and
above all creatures.)

It is again evident at once that here too our attempted formulation by means
of a concept is once more a merely negative one. Conceptually *mysterium*
denotes merely that which is hidden and esoteric, that which is beyond conception or understanding, extraordinary and unfamiliar. The term does not define the
object more positively in its qualitative character. But though what is enunciated
in the word is negative, what is meant is something absolutely and intensely
positive. This pure positive we can experience in feelings, feelings which our
discussion can help to make clear to us, in so far as it arouses them actually in our
hearts.

1. *The element of awefulness.* To get light upon the positive *"quale"* of the object
of these feelings, we must analyse more closely our phrase *mysterium tremendum,* and we will begin first with the adjective.

Tremor is in itself merely the perfectly familiar and "natural" emotion of *fear.*
But here the term is taken, aptly enough but still only by analogy, to denote a
quite specific kind of emotional response, wholly distinct from that of being
afraid, though it so far resembles it that the analogy of fear may be used to throw
light upon its nature. There are in some languages special expressions which
denote, either exclusively or in the first instance, this "fear" that is more than fear
proper. The Hebrew *hiqdīsh* (hallow) is an example. To "keep a thing holy in the
heart" means to mark it off by a feeling of peculiar dread, not to be mistaken for
any ordinary dread, that is, to appraise it by the category of the numinous. But the
Old Testament throughout is rich in parallel expressions for this feeling. Specially
noticeable is the *'ēmāh* of Yahweh ("fear of God"), which Yahweh can pour forth,
dispatching almost like a daemon, and which seizes upon a man with paralysing
effect. It is closely related to the δεῖμα πανικόν of the Greeks. Compare Exod.
xxiii. 27: "I will send my fear before thee, and will destroy all the people to whom
thou shalt come . . . "; also Job ix. 34; xiii. 21 ("let not his fear terrify me"; "let
not thy dread make me afraid"). Here we have a terror fraught with an inward
shuddering such as not even the most menacing and overpowering created thing
can instil. It has something spectral in it.

In the Greek language we have a corresponding term in σεβαστός. The early
Christians could clearly feel that the title σεβαστός (*augustus*) was one that could
not fittingly be given to any creature, not even to the emperor. They felt that to
call a man σεβαστός was to give a human being a name proper only to the *numen,*

to rank him by the category proper only to the *numen,* and that it therefore amounted to a kind of idolatry. Of modern languages English has the words "awe," "aweful," which in their deeper and most special sense approximate closely to our meaning. The phrase, "he stood aghast," is also suggestive in this connexion. On the other hand, German has no native-grown expression of its own for the higher and riper form of the emotion we are considering, unless it be in a word like *erschauern,* which does suggest it fairly well. It is far otherwise with its cruder and more debased phases, where such terms as *grausen* and *Schauer,* and the more popular and telling *gruseln* ("grue"), *gräsen,* and *grässlich* ("grisly"), very clearly designate the numinous element. In my examination of Wundt's Animism I suggested the term *Scheu* (dread); but the special "numinous" quality (making it "awe" rather than "dread" in the ordinary sense) would then, of course, have to be denoted by inverted commas. "Religious dread" (or "awe") would perhaps be a better designation. Its antecedent stage is "daemonic dread" (cf. the horror of Pan) with its queer perversion, a sort of abortive offshoot, the "dread of ghosts." It first begins to stir in the feeling of "something uncanny," "eerie," or "weird." It is this feeling which, emerging in the mind of primeval man, forms the starting-point for the entire religious development in history. "Daemons" and "gods" alike spring from this root, and all the products of "mythological apperception" or "fantasy" are nothing but different modes in which it has been objectified. And all ostensible explanations of the origin of religion in terms of animism or magic or folk-psychology are doomed from the outset to wander astray and miss the real goal of their inquiry, unless they recognize this fact of our nature—primary, unique, underivable from anything else—to be the basic factor and the basic impulse underlying the entire process of religious evolution.[2]

Not only is the saying of Luther, that the natural man cannot fear God perfectly, correct from the standpoint of psychology, but we ought to go farther and add that the natural man is quite unable even to "shudder" (*grauen*) or feel horror in the real sense of the word. For "shuddering" is something more than "natural," ordinary fear. It implies that the mysterious is already beginning to loom before the mind, to touch the feelings. It implies the first application of a category of valuation which has no place in the everyday natural world of ordinary experience, and is only possible to a being in whom has been awakened a mental predisposition, unique in kind and different in a definite way from any "natural" faculty. And this newly-revealed capacity, even in the crude and violent manifestations which are all it at first evinces, bears witness to a completely new function of experience and standard of valuation, only belonging to the spirit of man.

Before going on to consider the elements which unfold as the *"tremendum"* develops, let us give a little further consideration to the first crude, primitive

---

[2]Cf. my papers in *Theologische Rundschau,* 1910, vol. i., on "Myth and Religion in Wundt's *Völkerpsychologie,"* and in *Deutsche Literaturzeitung,* 1910, No. 38. I find in more recent investigations, especially those of R. R. Marett and N. Söderblom, a very welcome confirmation of the positions I there maintained. It is true that neither of them calls attention quite as precisely as, in this matter, psychologists need to do, to the unique character of the religious "awe" and its qualitative distinction from all "natural" feelings. But Marett more particularly comes within a hair's breadth of what I take to be the truth about the matter. Cf. his *Threshold of Religion* (London, 1909), and N. Söderblom's *Das Werden des Gottesglaubens* (Leipzig, 1915), also my review of the latter in *Theol. Literaturzeitung,* Jan. 1915.

forms in which this "numinous dread" or *awe* shows itself. It is the mark which really characterizes the so-called "religion of primitive man," and there it appears as "daemonic dread." This crudely naïve and primordial emotional disturbance, and the fantastic images to which it gives rise, are later overborne and ousted by more highly developed forms of the numinous emotion, with all its mysteriously impelling power. But even when this has long attained its higher and purer mode of expression it is possible for the primitive types of excitation that were formerly a part of it to break out in the soul in all their original naïveté and so to be experienced afresh. That this is so is shown by the potent attraction again and again exercised by the element of horror and "shudder" in ghost stories, even among persons of high all-round education. It is a remarkable fact that the physical reaction to which this unique "dread" of the uncanny gives rise is also unique, and is not found in the case of any "natural" fear or terror. We say: "my blood ran icy cold," and "my flesh crept." The "cold blood" feeling may be a symptom of ordinary, natural fear, but there is something non-natural or supernatural about the symptom of "creeping flesh." And any one who is capable of more precise introspection must recognize that the distinction between such a "dread" and natural fear is not simply one of degree and intensity. The awe or "dread" *may* indeed be so overwhelmingly great that it seems to penetrate to the very marrow, making the man's hair bristle and his limbs quake. But it may also steal upon him almost unobserved as the gentlest of agitations, a mere fleeting shadow passing across his mood. It has therefore nothing to do with intensity, and no natural fear passes over into it merely by being intensified. I may be beyond all measure afraid and terrified without there being even a trace of the feeling of uncanniness in my emotion.

We should see the facts more clearly if psychology in general would make a more decisive endeavour to examine and classify the feelings and emotions according to their qualitative differences. But the far too rough division of elementary feelings in general into pleasures and pains is still an obstacle to this. In point of fact "pleasures" no more than other feelings are differentiated merely by degrees of intensity: they show very definite and specific differences. It makes a specific difference to the condition of mind whether the soul is merely in a state of pleasure, or joy, or aesthetic rapture, or moral exaltation, or finally in the religious bliss that may come in worship. Such states certainly show resemblances one to another, and on that account can legitimately be brought under a common class-concept ("pleasure"), which serves to cut them off from other psychical functions, generically different. But this class-concept, so far from turning the various subordinate species into merely different degrees of the same thing, can do nothing at all to throw light upon the essence of each several state of mind which it includes.

Though the numinous emotion in its completest development shows a world of difference from the mere "daemonic dread," yet not even at the highest level does it belie its pedigree or kindred. Even when the worship of "daemons" has long since reached the higher level of worship of "gods," these gods still retain as *numina* something of the "ghost" in the impress they make on the feelings of the worshipper, viz. the peculiar quality of the "uncanny" and "aweful," which survives with the quality of exaltedness and sublimity or is symbolized by means of it. And this element, softened though it is, does not disappear even on the highest level of all, where the worship of God is at its purest. Its disappearance would be indeed an essential loss. The "shudder" reappears in a form ennobled beyond measure where the soul, held speechless, trembles inwardly to the farthest fibre of its being. It invades the mind mightily in Christian worship with the words: "Holy, holy, holy"; it breaks forth from the hymn of Tersteegen:

> God Himself is present:
> Heart, be stilled before Him:
> Prostrate inwardly adore Him.

The "shudder" has here lost its crazy and bewildering note, but not the ineffable something that holds the mind. It has become a mystical awe, and sets free as its accompaniment, reflected in self-consciousness, that "creature-feeling" that has already been described as the feeling of personal nothingness and submergence before the awe-inspiring object directly experienced.

The referring of this feeling numinous *tremor* to its object in the numen brings into relief a property of the latter which plays an important part in our Holy Scriptures, and which has been the occasion of many difficulties, both to commentators and to theologians, from its puzzling and baffling nature. This is the ὀργή (*orgé*), the Wrath of Yahweh, which recurs in the New Testament as ὀργή θεοῦ, and which is clearly analogous to the idea occurring in many religions of a mysterious *ira deorum*. To pass through the Indian Pantheon of gods is to find deities who seem to be made up altogether out of such an ὀργή; and even the higher Indian gods of grace and pardon have frequently, beside their merciful, their "wrath" form. But as regards the "wrath of Yahweh," the strange features about it have for long been a matter for constant remark. In the first place, it is patent from many passages of the Old Testament that this "wrath" has no concern whatever with moral qualities. There is something very baffling in the way in which it "is kindled" and manifested. It is, as has been well said, "like a hidden force of nature," like stored-up electricity, discharging itself upon anyone who comes too near. It is "incalculable" and "arbitrary." Anyone who is accustomed to think of deity only by its rational attributes must see in this "wrath" mere caprice and wilful passion. But such a view would have been emphatically rejected by the religious men of the Old Covenant, for to them the Wrath of God, so far from being a diminution of His Godhead, appears as a natural expression of it, an element of "holiness" itself, and a quite indispensable one. And in this they are entirely right. This ὀργή is nothing but the *tremendum* itself, apprehended and expressed by the aid of a naïve analogy from the domain of natural experience, in this case from the ordinary passional life of men. But naïve as it may be, the analogy is most disconcertingly apt and striking; so much so that it will always retain its value and for us no less than for the men of old be an inevitable way of expressing one element in the religious emotion. It cannot be doubted that, despite the protest of Schleiermacher and Ritschl, Christianity also has something to teach of the "wrath of God."

It will be again at once apparent that in the use of this word we are not concerned with a genuine intellectual "concept," but only with a sort of illustrative substitute for a concept. "Wrath" here is the "ideogram" of a unique emotional moment in religious experience, a moment whose singularly *daunting* and awe-inspiring character must be gravely disturbing to those persons who will recognize nothing in the divine nature but goodness, gentleness, love, and a sort of confidential intimacy, in a word, only those aspects of God which turn towards the world of men.

This ὀργή is thus quite wrongly spoken of as "natural" wrath: rather it is an entirely non- or super-natural, i.e., numinous, quality. The rationalization process takes place when it begins to be filled in with elements derived from the moral reason: righteousness in requital, and punishment for moral transgression. But it should be noted that the idea of the wrath of God in the Bible is always a synthesis, in which the original is combined with the later meaning that has come to fill it in. Something supra-rational throbs and gleams, palpable and visible, in the "wrath of God," prompting to a sense of "terror" that no "natural" anger can arouse.

Beside the "wrath" or "anger" of Yahweh stands the related expression "jealousy of Yahweh." The state of mind denoted by the phrase "being jealous *for* Yahweh" is also a numinous state of mind, in which features of the *tremendum* pass over into the man who has experience of it.

2. *The element of "overpoweringness" ("majestas").* We have been attempting to unfold the implications of that aspect of the *mysterium tremendum* indicated by the adjective, and the result so far may be summarized in two words, constituting, as before, what may be called an "ideogram," rather than a concept proper, viz. "absolute unapproachability."

It will be felt at once that there is yet a further element which must be added, that, namely, of "might," "power," "absolute overpoweringness." We will take to represent this the term *majestas,* majesty—the more readily because anyone with a feeling for language must detect a last faint trace of the numinous still clinging to the word. The *tremendum* may then be rendered more adequately *tremenda majestas,* or "aweful majesty." This second element of majesty may continue to be vividly preserved, where the first, that of unapproachability, recedes and dies away, as may be seen, for example, in mysticism. It is especially in relation to this element of majesty or absolute overpoweringness that the creature-consciousness, of which we have already spoken, comes upon the scene, as a sort of shadow or subjective reflection of it. Thus, in contrast to "the overpowering" of which we are conscious as an object over against the self, there is the feeling of one's own submergence, of being but "dust and ashes" and nothingness. And this forms the numinous raw material for the feeling of religious humility.[3]

Here we must revert once again to Schleiermacher's expression for what we call "creature-feeling," viz. the "feeling of dependence." We found fault with this phrase before on the ground that Schleiermacher thereby takes as basis and point of departure what is merely a secondary effect; that he sets out to teach a consciousness of the religious *object* only by way of an inference from the shadow it casts upon *self*-consciousness. We have now a further criticism to bring against it, and it is this. By "feeling of dependence" Schleiermacher means consciousness of *being conditioned* (as effect by cause), and so he develops the implications of this logically enough in his sections upon Creation and Preserva-

---

[3]Cf. R. R. Marett, "The Birth of Humility," in *The Threshold of Religion,* 2nd ed., 1914. [Tr.]

tion. On the side of the deity the correlate to "dependence" would thus be "causality," i.e., God's character as all-causing and all-conditioning. But a sense of this does not enter at all into that immediate and first-hand religious emotion which we have in the moment of worship, and which we can recover in a measure for analysis; it belongs on the contrary decidedly to the *rational* side of the idea of God; its implications admit of precise conceptual determination; and it springs from quite a distinct source. The difference between the "feeling of dependence" of Schleiermacher and that which finds typical utterance in the words of Abraham already cited might be expressed as that between the consciousness of *created-ness*[4] and the consciousness of *creaturehood*.[5] In the one case you have the creature as the work of the divine creative act; in the other, impotence and general nothingness as against overpowering might, dust and ashes as against "majesty." In the one case you have the fact of having been created; in the other, the status of the creature. And as soon as speculative thought has come to concern itself with this latter type of consciousness—as soon as it has come to analyse this "majesty"—we are introduced to a set of ideas quite different from those of creation or preservation. We come upon the ideas, first, of the annihilation of self, and then, as its complement, of the transcendent as the sole and entire reality. These are the characteristic notes of mysticism in all its forms, however otherwise various in content. For one of the chiefest and most general features of mysticism is just this *self-depreciation* (so plainly parallel to the case of Abraham), the estimation of the self, of the personal "I," as something not perfectly or essentially real, or even as mere nullity, a self-depreciation which comes to demand its own fulfilment in practice in rejecting the delusion of selfhood, and so makes for the annihilation of the self. And on the other hand mysticism leads to a valuation of the transcendent object of its reference as that which through plenitude of being stands supreme and absolute, so that the finite self contrasted with it becomes conscious even in its nullity that "I am naught, Thou art all." There is no thought in this of any causal relation between God, the creator, and the self, the creature. The point from which speculation starts is not a "consciousness of absolute dependence"—of myself as result and effect of a divine cause—for that would in point of fact lead to insistence upon the reality of the self; it starts from a consciousness of the absolute superiority or supremacy of a power other than myself, and it is only as it falls back upon ontological terms to achieve its end—terms generally borrowed from natural science—that that element of the *tremendum,* originally apprehended as "plenitude of power," becomes transmuted into "plenitude of being."

This leads again to the mention of mysticism. No mere inquiry into the genesis of a thing can throw any light upon its essential nature, and it is hence immaterial to us how mysticism historically arose. But essentially mysticism is the stressing to a very high degree, indeed the overstressing, of the non-rational or supra-rational elements in religion; and it is only intelligible when so understood. The various phases and factors of the non-rational may receive varying emphasis, and the type of mysticism will differ according as some or others fall into the background. What we have been analysing, however, is a feature that recurs in

---

[4]*Geschaffenheit.*
[5]*Geschöpflichkeit.*

all forms of mysticism everywhere, and it is nothing but the "creature-consciousness" stressed to the utmost and to excess, the expression meaning, if we may repeat the contrast already made, not "feeling of our createdness" but "feeling of our creaturehood," that is, the consciousness of the littleness of every creature in face of that which is above all creatures.

A characteristic common to all types of mysticism is the *Identification,* in different degrees of completeness, of the personal self with the transcendent Reality. This identification has a source of its own, with which we are not here concerned, and springs from "moments" of religious experience which would require separate treatment. "Identification" alone, however, is not enough for mysticism; it must be Identification with the Something that is at once absolutely supreme in power and reality and wholly non-rational. And it is among the mystics that we most encounter this element of religious consciousness. Récéjac has noticed this in his *Essai sur les fondements de la connaissance mystique* (Paris, 1897). He writes (p. 90):

> Le mysticisme commence par la crainte, par le sentiment d'une *domination* universelle, *invincible,* et devient plus tard un désir d'union avec ce qui domine ainsi.

And some very clear examples of this taken from the religious experience of the present day are to be found in W. James (*op. cit.,* p. 66):

> The perfect stillness of the night was thrilled by a more solemn silence. The darkness held a presence that was all the more felt because it was not seen. I could not any more have doubted that *He* was there than that I was. Indeed, I felt myself to be, if possible, the less real of the two.

This example is particularly instructive as to the relation of mysticism to the "feelings of identification," for the experience here recounted was on the point of passing into it.[6]

3. *The element of "energy" or urgency.* There is, finally, a third element comprised in those of *tremendum* and *majestas,* awefulness and majesty, and this I venture to call the "urgency" or "energy" of the numinous object. It is particularly vividly perceptible in the ὀργή or "wrath"; and it everywhere clothes itself in symbolical expressions—vitality, passion, emotional temper, will, force, movement,[7] excitement, activity, impetus. These features are typical and recur again and again from the daemonic level up to the idea of the "living" God. We have here the factor that has everywhere more than any other prompted the fiercest opposition to the "philosophic" God of mere rational speculation, who can be put into a definition. And for their part the philosophers have condemned these expressions of the energy of the numen, whenever they are brought on to the scene, as sheer anthropomorphism. In so far as their opponents have for the most part themselves failed to recognize that the terms they have borrowed from

---

[6]Compare too the experience on p. 70: " . . . What I felt on these occasions was a temporary los⸢ of m own identity."

[7]The "mobilitas Dei" of Lactantius.

the sphere of human conative and affective life have merely value as analogies, the philosophers are right to condemn them. But they are wrong, in so far as, this error notwithstanding, these terms stood for a genuine aspect of the divine nature—its non-rational aspect—a due consciousness of which served to protect religion itself from being "rationalized" away.

For wherever men have been contending for the "living" God or for voluntarism, there, we may be sure, have been non-rationalists fighting rationalists and rationalism. It was so with Luther in his controversy with Erasmus; and Luther's *omnipotentia Dei* in his *De Servo Arbitrio* is nothing but the union of "majesty"—in the sense of absolute supremacy—with this "energy," in the sense of a force that knows not stint nor stay, which is urgent, active, compelling, and alive. In mysticism, too, this element of "energy" is a very living and vigorous factor, at any rate in the "voluntaristic" mysticism, the mysticism of love, where it is very forcibly seen in that "consuming fire" of love whose burning strength the mystic can hardly bear, but begs that the heat that has scorched him may be mitigated, lest he be himself destroyed by it. And in this urgency and pressure the mystic's "love" claims a perceptible kinship with the ὀργή itself, the scorching and consuming wrath of God; it is the same "energy," only differently directed. "Love," says one of the mystics, "is nothing else than quenched wrath."

The element of "energy" reappears in Fichte's speculations on the Absolute as the gigantic, never-resting, active world-stress, and in Schopenhauer's daemonic "Will." At the same time both these writers are guilty of the same error that is already found in myth; they transfer "natural" attributes, which ought only to be used as "ideograms" for what is itself properly beyond utterance, to the non-rational as real qualifications of it, and they mistake symbolic expressions of feelings for adequate concepts upon which a "scientific" structure of knowledge may be based.

In Goethe, as we shall see later, the same element of energy is emphasized in a quite unique way in his strange descriptions of the experience he calls "daemonic."

The Analysis of "Mysterium"

> *Ein begriffener Gott ist kein Gott.*
> "A God comprehended is no God."
> (TERSTEEGEN.)

We gave to the object to which the numinous consciousness is directed the name *mysterium tremendum*, and we then set ourselves first to determine the meaning of the adjective *tremendum*—which we found to be itself only justified by analogy—because it is more easily analysed than the substantive idea *mysterium*. We have now to turn to this, and try, as best we may, by hint and suggestion, to get to a clearer apprehension of what it implies.

4. *The "wholly other."* It might be thought that the adjective itself gives an explanation of the substantive; but this is not so. It is not merely analytical; it is a synthetic attribute to it; i.e., *tremendum* adds something not necessarily inherent in *mysterium*. It is true that the reactions in consciousness that correspond to the one readily and spontaneously overflow into those that correspond to the other;

in fact, anyone sensitive to the use of words would commonly feel that the idea of "mystery" (*mysterium*) is so closely bound up with its synthetic qualifying attribute "aweful" (*tremendum*) that one can hardly say the former without catching an echo of the latter, "mystery" almost of itself becoming "aweful mystery" to us. But the passage from the one idea to the other need not by any means be always so easy. The elements of meaning implied in "awefulness" and "mysteriousness" are in themselves definitely different. The latter may so far preponderate in the religious consciousness, may stand out so vividly, that in comparison with it the former almost sinks out of sight; a case which again could be clearly exemplified from some forms of mysticism. Occasionally, on the other hand, the reverse happens, and the *tremendum* may in turn occupy the mind without the *mysterium.*

This latter, then, needs special consideration on its own account. We need an expression for the mental reaction peculiar to it; and here, too, only one word seems appropriate, though, as it is strictly applicable only to a "natural" state of mind, it has here meaning only by analogy: it is the word "stupor." *Stupor* is plainly a different thing from *tremor*; it signifies blank wonder, an astonishment that strikes us dumb, amazement absolute.[8] Taken, indeed, in its purely natural sense, *mysterium* would first mean merely a secret or a mystery in the sense of that which is alien to us, uncomprehended and unexplained; and so far *mysterium* is itself merely an ideogram, an analogical notion taken from the natural sphere, illustrating, but incapable of exhaustively rendering, our real meaning. Taken in the religious sense, that which is "mysterious" is—to give it perhaps the most striking expression—the "wholly other" (θάτερον, *anyad*, *alienum*), that which is quite beyond the sphere of the usual, the intelligible, and the familiar, which therefore falls quite outside the limits of the "canny," and is contrasted with it, filling the mind with blank wonder and astonishment.

This is already to be observed on the lowest and earliest level of the religion of primitive man, where the numinous consciousness is but an inchoate stirring of the feelings. What is really characteristic of this stage is *not*—as the theory of Animism would have us believe—that men are here concerned with curious entities, called "souls" or "spirits," which happen to be invisible. Representations of spirits and similar conceptions are rather one and all early modes of "rationalizing" a precedent experience, to which they are subsidiary. They are attempts in some way or other, it little matters how, to guess the riddle it propounds, and their effect is at the same time always to weaken and deaden the experience itself. They are the source from which springs, not religion, but the rationalization of religion, which often ends by constructing such a massive structure of theory and such a plausible fabric of interpretation, that the "mystery" is frankly excluded.[9] Both imaginative "myth," when developed into a

---

[8]Compare also *obstupefacere.* Still more exact equivalents are the Greek θαμβος and θαμβειν. The sound θ α μ β (*thamb*) excellently depicts this state of mind of blank, staring wonder. And the difference between the moments of *stupor* and *tremor* is very finely suggested by the passage, Mark x. 32. . . . On the other hand, what was said above of the facility and rapidity with which the two moments merge and blend is also markedly true of θαμβος, which then becomes a classical term for the (ennobled) awe of the numinous in general. So Mark xvi. 5 is rightly translated by Luther "und sie entsetzten sich," and by the English Authorized Version "and they were affrighted."

[9]A spirit or soul that has been conceived and comprehended no longer prompts to "shuddering," as is proved by Spiritualism. But it thereby ceases to be of interest for the psychology of religion.

system, and intellectualist Scholasticism, when worked out to its completion, are methods by which the fundamental fact of religious experience is, as it were, simply rolled out so thin and flat as to be finally eliminated altogether.

Even on the lowest level of religious development the essential characteristic is therefore to be sought elsewhere than in the appearance of "spirit" representations. It lies rather, we repeat, in a peculiar "moment" of consciousness, to wit, the *stupor* before something "wholly other," whether such an other be named "spirit" or "daemon" or "deva," or be left without any name. Nor does it make any difference in this respect whether, to interpret and preserve their apprehension of this "other," men coin original imagery of their own or adapt imaginations drawn from the world of legend, the fabrications of fancy apart from and prior to any stirrings of daemonic dread.

In accordance with laws of which we shall have to speak again later, this feeling or consciousness of the "wholly other" will attach itself to, or sometimes be indirectly aroused by means of, objects which are already puzzling upon the "natural" plane, or are of a surprising or astounding character; such as extraordinary phenomena or astonishing occurrences or things in inanimate nature, in the animal world, or among men. But here once more we are dealing with a case of association between things specifically different—the "numinous" and the "natural" moments of consciousness—and not merely with the gradual enhancement of one of them—the "natural"—till it becomes the other. As in the case of "natural fear" and "daemonic dread" already considered, so here the transition from natural to daemonic amazement is not a mere matter of degree. But it is only with the latter that the complementary expression *mysterium* perfectly harmonizes, as will be felt perhaps more clearly in the case of the adjectival form "mysterious." No one says, strictly and in earnest, of a piece of clock-work that is beyond his grasp, or of a science that he cannot understand: "That is 'mysterious' to me."

It might be objected that the mysterious is something which is and remains absolutely and invariably beyond our understanding, whereas that which merely eludes our understanding for a time but is perfectly intelligible in principle should be called, not a "mystery," but merely a "problem." But this is by no means an adequate account of the matter. The truly "mysterious" object is beyond our apprehension and comprehension, not only because our knowledge has certain irremovable limits, but because in it we come upon something inherently "wholly other," whose kind and character are incommensurable with our own, and before which we therefore recoil in a wonder that strikes us chill and numb.[10]

This may be made still clearer by a consideration of that degraded off-shoot and travesty of the genuine "numinous" dread or awe, the fear of ghosts. Let us try to analyse this experience. We have already specified the peculiar feeling-element of "dread" aroused by the ghost as that of "grue," grisly horror.[11] Now this "grue" obviously contributes something to the attraction which ghost-stories

---

[10]In *Confessions*, ii. 9. I, Augustine very strikingly suggests this stiffening, benumbing element of the "wholly other" and its contrast to the rational aspect of the numen; the *dissimile* and the *simile:*

"Quid est illud, quod interlucet mihi et percutit cor meum sine laesione? Et inhorresco et inardesco. *Inhorresco*, in quantum *dissimilis* ei sum. Inardesco, in quantum similis ei sum."

("What is that which gleams through me and smites my heart without wounding it? I am both a-shudder and a-glow. A-shudder, in so far as I am unlike it, a-glow in so far as I am like it.")

[11]*gruseln, gräsen.*

exercise, in so far, namely, as the relaxation of tension ensuing upon our release from it relieves the mind in a pleasant and agreeable way. So far, however, it is not really the ghost itself that gives us pleasure, but the fact that we are rid of it. But obviously this is quite insufficient to explain the ensnaring attraction of the ghost-story. The ghost's real attraction rather consists in this, that of itself and in an uncommon degree it entices the imagination, awakening strong interest and curiosity; it is the weird thing itself that allures the fancy. But it does this, not because it is "something long and white" (as someone once defined a ghost), nor yet through any of the positive and conceptual attributes which fancies about ghosts have invented, but because it is a thing that "doesn't really exist at all," the "wholly other," something which has no place in our scheme of reality but belongs to an absolutely different one, and which at the same time arouses an irrepressible interest in the mind.

But that which is perceptibly true in the fear of ghosts, which is, after all, only a caricature of the genuine thing, is in a far stronger sense true of the "daemonic" experience itself, of which the fear of ghosts is a mere off-shoot. And while, following this main line of development, this element in the numinous conscious-ness, the feeling of the "wholly other," is heightened and clarified, its higher modes of manifestation come into being, which set the numinous object in contrast not only to everything wonted and familiar (i.e., in the end, to nature in general), thereby turning it into the "supernatural," but finally to the world itself, and thereby exalt it to the "supramundane," that which is above the whole-order.

In mysticism we have in the "beyond" (ἐπέκεινα) again the strongest stressing and over-stressing of those non-rational elements which are already inherent in all religion. Mysticism continues to its extreme point this contrasting of the numinous object (the numen), as the "wholly other," with ordinary experience. Not content with contrasting it with all that is of nature or this world, mysticism concludes by contrasting it with Being itself and all that "is," and finally actually calls it "that which is nothing." By this "nothing" is meant not only that of which nothing can be predicated, but that which is absolutely and intrinsically other than and opposite of everything that is and can be thought. But while exaggerating to the point of paradox this *negation* and contrast—the only means open to conceptual thought to apprehend the *mysterium*—mysticism at the same time retains the *positive quality* of the "wholly other" as a very living factor in its overbrimming religious emotion.

But what is true of the strange "nothingness" of our mystics holds good equally of the *sūnyam* and the *sūnyatā*, the "void" and "emptiness" of the Buddhist mystics. This aspiration for the "void" and for becoming void, no less than the aspiration of our western mystics for "nothing" and for becoming nothing, must seem a kind of lunacy to anyone who has no inner sympathy for the esoteric language and ideograms of mysticism, and lacks the matrix from which these come necessarily to birth. To such an one Buddhism itself will be simply a morbid sort of pessimism. But in fact the "void" of the eastern, like the "nothing" of the western, mystic is a numinous ideogram of the "wholly other."

These terms "supernatural" and "transcendent"[12] give the appearance of positive attributes, and, as applied to the mysterious, they appear to divest the

---

[12]Literally, supramundane: *überweltlich.*

mysterium of its originally negative meaning and to turn it into an affirmation. On the side of conceptual thought this is nothing more than appearance, for it is obvious that the two terms in question are merely negative and exclusive attributes with reference to "nature" and the world or cosmos respectively. But on the side of the feeling-content it is otherwise; that *is* in very truth positive in the highest degree, though here too, as before, it cannot be rendered explicit in conceptual terms. It is through this positive feeling-content that the concepts of the "transcendent" and "supernatural" become forthwith designations for a unique "wholly other" reality and quality, something of whose special character we can *feel,* without being able to give it clear conceptual expression.

The Element of Fascination

The qualitative *content* of the numinous experience, to which "the mysterious" stands as *form,* is in one of its aspects the element of daunting "awefulness" and "majesty," which has already been dealt with in detail; but it is clear that it has at the same time another aspect, in which it shows itself as something uniquely attractive and *fascinating.*

These two qualities, the daunting and the fascinating, now combine in a strange harmony of contrasts, and the resultant dual character of the numinous consciousness, to which the entire religious development bears witness, at any rate from the level of the "daemonic dread" onwards, is at once the strangest and most noteworthy phenomenon in the whole history of religion. The daemonic-divine object may appear to the mind an object of horror and dread, but at the same time it is no less something that allures with a potent charm, and the creature, who trembles before it, utterly cowed and cast down, has always at the same time the impulse to turn to it, nay even to make it somehow his own. The "mystery" is for him not merely something to be wondered at but something that entrances him; and beside that in it which bewilders and confounds, he feels a something that captivates and transports him with a strange ravishment, rising often enough to the pitch of dizzy intoxication; it is the Dionysiac-element in the numen.

The ideas and concepts which are the parallels or "schemata" on the rational side of this non-rational element of "fascination" are love, mercy, pity, comfort; these are all "natural" elements of the common psychical life, only they are here thought as absolute and in completeness. But important as these are for the experience of religious bliss or felicity, they do not by any means exhaust it. It is just the same as with the opposite experience of religious infelicity—the experience of the ὀργή or "wrath" of God—both alike contain fundamentally non-rational elements. Bliss or beatitude is more, far more, than the mere natural feeling of being comforted, of reliance, of the joy of love, however these may be heightened and enhanced. Just as "wrath," taken in a purely rational or a purely ethical sense, does not exhaust that profound element of *awefulness* which is locked in the mystery of deity, so neither does "graciousness" exhaust the profound element of *wonderfulness* and rapture which lies in the mysterious beatific experience of deity. The term "grace" may indeed be taken as its aptest designation, but then only in the sense in which it is really applied in the language of the mystics, and in which not only the "gracious intent" but "something more" is meant by the word. This "something more" has its antecedent phases very far back in the history of religions.

It may well be possible, it is even probable, that in the first stage of its development the religious consciousness started with only one of its poles—the "daunting" aspect of the numen—and so at first took shape only as "daemonic dread." But if this did not point to something beyond itself, if it were not but one "moment" of a completer experience, pressing up gradually into consciousness, then no transition would be possible to the feelings of positive self-surrender to the numen. The only type of worship that could result from this "dread" alone would be that of ἀπαιτεῖσθαι and ἀποτρέπειν, taking the form of expiation and propitiation, the averting or the appeasement of the "wrath" of the numen. It can never explain how it is that "the numinous" is the object of search and desire and yearning, and that too for its own sake and not only for the sake of the aid and backing that men expect from it in the natural sphere. It can never explain how this takes place, not only in the forms of "rational" religious worship, but in those queer "sacramental" observances and rituals and procedures of communion in which the human being seeks to get the numen into his possession.

Religious practice may manifest itself in those normal and easily intelligible forms which occupy so prominent a place in the history of religion, such forms as propitiation, petition, sacrifice, thanksgiving, &c. But besides these there is a series of strange proceedings which are constantly attracting greater and greater attention, and in which it is claimed that we may recognize, besides mere religion in general, the particular roots of mysticism. I refer to those numerous curious modes of behaviour and fantastic forms of mediation, by means of which the primitive religious man attempts to master "the mysterious," and to fill himself and even to identify himself with it. These modes of behaviour fall apart into two classes. On the one hand the "magical" identification of the self with the numen proceeds by means of various transactions, at once magical and devotional in character—by formula, ordination, adjuration, consecration, exorcism, &c.: on the other hand are the "shamanistic" ways of procedure, possession, indwelling, self-fulfilment in exaltation and ecstasy. All these have, indeed, their starting-points simply in magic, and their intention at first was certainly simply to appropriate the prodigious force of the numen for the natural ends of man. But the process does not rest there. Possession of and by the numen becomes an end in itself; it begins to be sought for its own sake; and the wildest and most artificial methods of asceticism are put into practice to attain it. In a word, the *vita religiosa* begins; and to remain in these strange and bizarre states of numinous possession becomes a good in itself, even a way of salvation, wholly different from the profane goods pursued by means of magic. Here, too, commences the process of development by which the experience is matured and purified, till finally it reaches its consummation in the sublimest and purest states of the "life within the Spirit" and in the noblest mysticism. Widely various as these states are in themselves, yet they have this element in common, that in them the *mysterium* is experienced in its essential, positive, and specific character, as something that bestows upon man a beatitude beyond compare, but one whose real nature he can neither proclaim in speech nor conceive in thought, but may know only by a direct and living experience. It is a bliss which embraces all those blessings that are indicated or suggested in positive fashion by any "doctrine of salvation," and it quickens all of them through and through; but these do not exhaust it. Rather by its all-pervading, penetrating glow it makes of these very blessings more than the intellect can conceive in them or affirm of them. It gives the peace that passes understanding, and of which the tongue can only stammer brokenly. Only from afar, by metaphors and analogies, do we come to apprehend what it is in itself, and even so our notion is but inadequate and confused.

THE ARGUMENT FROM RELIGIOUS EXPERIENCE
C. D. Broad

From C. D. Broad, *Religion, Philosophy and Psychical Research,* 1953, 1969. By permission of Hillary House Publishers Ltd., New York.

The Argument from Design has been criticized very fairly and thoroughly by two of the greatest European philosophers, Hume and Kant. I have nothing to add to their criticisms, and I have seen nothing in the writings of those who have tried to rehabilitate the argument which effectively rebuts their adverse verdict. I shall therefore set this argument aside. As regards arguments from ethical premises, I have said what I have to say on the logical and epistemological issues in Chapter XI of my book *The Mind and its Place in Nature.* That chapter is, indeed, concerned primarily with ethical arguments for human survival, and not for the existence of God. But the principles are the same in either case, and so I do not propose to treat the subject again here. I shall therefore confine myself in this article to specifically religious experience and the argument for the existence of God which has been based on it.

This argument differs in the following important respect from the other two empirical types of argument. The Argument from Design and the arguments from ethical premises start from facts which are common to every one. But some people seem to be almost wholly devoid of any specifically religious experience; and among those who have it the differences of kind and degree are enormous. Founders of religions and saints, e.g., often claim to have been in direct contact with God, to have seen and spoken with Him, and so on. An ordinary religious man would certainly not make any such claim, though he might say that he had had experiences which assured him of the existence and presence of God. So the first thing that we have to notice is that capacity for religious experience is in certain respects like an ear for music. There are a few people who are unable to recognize and distinguish the simplest tune. But they are in a minority, like the people who have absolutely no kind of religious experience. Most people have some slight appreciation of music. But the differences of degree in this respect are enormous, and those who have not much gift for music have to take the statements of accomplished musicians very largely on trust. Let us, then, compare tone-deaf persons to those who have no recognizable religious experience at all; the ordinary followers of a religion to men who have some taste for music but can neither appreciate the more difficult kinds nor compose; highly religious men and saints to persons with an exceptionally fine ear for music who may yet be unable to compose it; and the founders of religions to great musical composers, such as Bach and Beethoven.

This analogy is, of course, incomplete in certain important respects. Religious experience raises three problems, which are different though closely interconnected. (i) What is the *psychological analysis* of religious experience? Does it contain factors which are present also in certain experiences which are not religious? Does it contain any factor which never occurs in any other kind of experience? If it contains no such factor, but is a blend of elements each of which can occur separately or in non-religious experiences, its psychological peculiarity must consist in the characteristic way in which these elements are blended in it. Can this peculiar structural feature of religious experience be indicated and described? (ii) What are the *genetic and causal conditions* of the existence of religious experience? Can we trace the origin and development of the disposition to have religious experiences (*a*) in the human race, and (*b*) in each individual? Granted that the disposition is present in nearly all individuals at the present time, can we discover and state the variable conditions which call it into activity on certain occasions and leave it in abeyance on others? (iii) Part of the content of religious experience is alleged knowledge or well-founded belief about the nature of reality, e.g., that we are dependent on a being who loves us and whom we ought to worship, that values are somehow conserved in spite of the chances and changes of the material world at the mercy of which they seem *prima facie* to be, and so on. Therefore there is a third problem. Granted that religious experience exists, that it has such-and-such a history and conditions, that it seems vitally important to those who have it, and that it produces all kinds of effects which would not otherwise happen, is it *veridical*? Are the claims to knowledge or well-founded belief about the nature of reality, which are an integral part of the experience, *true or probable*? Now, in the case of musical experience, there are analogies to the psychological problem and to the genetic or causal problem, but there is no analogy to the epistemological problem of validity. For, so far as I am aware, no part of the content of musical experience is alleged knowledge about the nature of reality; and therefore no question of its being veridical or delusive can arise.

Since both musical experience and religious experience certainly exist, any theory of the universe which was incompatible with their existence would be false, and any theory which failed to show the connexion between their existence and the other facts about reality would be inadequate. So far the two kinds of experience are in exactly the same position. But a theory which answers to the condition that it allows of the *existence* of religious experience and indicates the *connexion* between its existence and other facts about reality may leave the question as to its *validity* quite unanswered. Or, alternatively, it may throw grave doubt on its cognitive claims, or else it may tend to support them. Suppose, e.g., that it could be shown that religious experience contains no elements which are not factors in other kinds of experience. Suppose further it could be shown that this particular combination of factors tends to originate and to be activated only under certain conditions which are known to be very commonly productive of false beliefs held with strong conviction. Then a satisfactory answer to the questions of psychological analysis and causal antecedents would have tended to answer the epistemological question of validity in the negative. On the other hand, it might be that the only theory which would satisfactorily account for the origin of the religious disposition and for the occurrence of actual religious experiences under certain conditions was a theory which allowed some of the cognitive claims made by religious experience to be true or probable. Thus the three problems, though entirely distinct from each other, may be very closely connected; and it is the existence of the third problem in connexion with religious experience which puts it, for the present purpose, in a different category from musical experience.

In spite of this essential difference the analogy is not to be despised, for it brings out at least one important point. If a man who had no ear for music were to give himself airs on that account, and were to talk *de haut en bas* about those who can appreciate music and think it highly important, we should regard him, not as an advanced thinker, but as a self-satisfied Philistine. And, even if he did not do this but only propounded theories about the nature and causation of musical experience, we might think it reasonable to feel very doubtful whether his theories would be adequate or correct. In the same way, when persons without religious experience regard themselves as being *on that ground* superior to those who have it, their attitude must be treated as merely silly and offensive. Similarly, any theories about religious experience constructed by persons who have little or none of their own should be regarded with grave suspicion. (For that reason it would be unwise to attach very much weight to anything that the present writer may say on this subject.)

On the other hand, we must remember that the possession of a great capacity for religious experience, like the possession of a great capacity for musical appreciation and composition, is no guarantee of high general intelligence. A man may be a saint or a magnificent musician and yet have very little common sense, very little power of accurate introspection or of seeing causal connexions, and scarcely any capacity for logical criticism. He may also be almost as ignorant about other aspects of reality as the non-musical or non-religious man is about musical or religious experience. If such a man starts to theorize about music or religion, his theories may be quite as absurd, though in a different way, as those made by persons who are devoid of musical or religious experience. Fortunately it happens that some religious mystics of a high order have been extremely good at introspecting and describing their own experiences. And some highly religious persons have had very great critical and philosophical abilities. St. Teresa is an example of the first, and St. Thomas Aquinas of the second.

Now I think it must be admitted that, if we compare and contrast the statements made by religious mystics of various times, races, and religions, we find a common nucleus combined with very great differences of detail. Of course the interpretations which they have put on their experiences are much more varied than the experiences themselves. It is obvious that the interpretations will depend in a large measure on the traditional religious beliefs in which various mystics have been brought up. I think that such traditions probably act in two different ways.

(i) The tradition no doubt affects the theoretical interpretation of experiences which would have taken place even if the mystic had been brought up in a different tradition. A feeling of unity with the rest of the universe will be interpreted very differently by a Christian who has been brought up to believe in a personal God and by a Hindu mystic who has been trained in a quite different metaphysical tradition.

(ii) The traditional beliefs, on the other hand, probably determine many of the details of the experience itself. A Roman Catholic mystic may have visions of the Virgin and the saints, whilst a Protestant mystic pretty certainly will not.

Thus the relations between the experiences and the traditional beliefs are highly complex. Presumably the outlines of the belief are determined by the experience. Then the details of the belief are fixed for a certain place and period by the special peculiarities of the experiences had by the founder of a certain religion. These beliefs then become traditional in that religion. Thenceforth they in part determine the details of the experiences had by subsequent mystics of that religion, and still more do they determine the interpretations which these mystics will put upon their experiences. Therefore, when a set of religious beliefs has once been established, it no doubt tends to produce experiences which can plausibly be taken as evidence for it. If it is a tradition in a certain religion that one can communicate with saints, mystics of that religion will seem to see and to talk with saints in their mystical visions; and this fact will be taken as further evidence for the belief that one can communicate with saints.

Much the same double process of causation takes place in sense-perception. On the one hand, the beliefs and expectations which we have at any moment largely determine what *interpretation* we shall put on a certain sensation which we should in any case have had then. On the other hand, our beliefs and expectations do to some extent determine and modify some of the sensible characteristics of the *sensa themselves.* When I am thinking only of diagrams a certain visual stimulus may produce a sensation of a sensibly flat sensum; but a precisely similar stimulus may produce a sensation of a sensibly solid sensum when I am thinking of solid objects.

Such explanations, however, plainly do not account for the first origin of religious beliefs, or for the features which are common to the religious experiences of persons of widely different times, races, and traditions.

Now, when we find that there are certain experiences which, though never very frequent in a high degree of intensity, have happened in a high degree among a few men at all times and places; and when we find that, in spite of differences in detail which we can explain, they involve certain fundamental conditions which are common and peculiar to them; two alternatives are open to us. (i) We may suppose that these men are in contact with an aspect of reality which is not revealed to ordinary persons in their everyday experience. And we may suppose that the characteristics which they agree in ascribing to reality on the basis of these experiences probably do belong to it. Or (ii) we may suppose that they are all subject to a delusion from which other men are free. In order to illustrate these alternatives it will be useful to consider three partly analogous cases, two of which are real and the third imaginary.

(*a*) Most of the detailed facts which biologists tell us about the minute structure and changes in cells can be perceived only by persons who have had a long training in the use of the microscope. In this case we believe that the agreement among trained microscopists really does correspond to facts which untrained persons cannot perceive. (*b*) Persons of all races who habitually drink alcohol to excess eventually have perceptual experiences in which they seem to themselves to see snakes or rats crawling about their rooms or beds. In this case we believe that this agreement among drunkards is merely a uniform hallucination. (*c*) Let us now imagine a race of beings who can walk about and touch things but cannot see. Suppose that eventually a few of them developed the power of sight. All that they might tell their still blind friends about colour would be wholly unintelligible to and unverifiable by the latter. But they would also be able to tell their blind friends a great deal about what the latter would feel if they were to walk in certain directions. These statements would be verified. This would not, of course, *prove* to the blind ones that the unintelligible statements about colour correspond to certain aspects of the world which they cannot perceive. But it would show that the seeing persons had a source of additional information about matters which the blind ones could understand and test for themselves. It would not be unreasonable then for the blind ones to believe that probably the seeing ones are also able to perceive other aspects of reality which they are describing correctly when they make their unintelligible statements containing colour-names. The question then is whether it is reasonable to regard the agreement between the experiences of religious mystics as more like the agreement among trained microscopists about the minute structure of cells, or as more like the agreement among habitual drunkards about the infestation of their rooms by pink rats or snakes, or as more like the agreement about colours which the seeing men would express in their statements to the blind men.

Why do we commonly believe that habitual excess of alcohol is a cause of a uniform delusion and not a source of additional information? The main reason is as follows. The things which drunkards claim to perceive are not fundamentally different in kind from the things that other people perceive. We have all seen rats and snakes, though the rats have generally been grey or brown and not pink. Moreover the drunkard claims that the rats and snakes which he sees are literally present in his room and on his bed, in the same sense in which his bed is in his room and his quilt is on his bed. Now we may fairly argue as follows. Since these are the sort of things which we could see if they were there, the fact that we cannot see them makes it highly probable that they are not there. Again, we know what kinds of perceptible effect would generally follow from the presence in a room of such things as rats or snakes. We should expect fox-terriers or mongooses to show traces of excitement, cheese to be nibbled, corn to disappear from bins, and so on. We find that no such effects are observed in the bedrooms of persons suffering from *delirium tremens*. It therefore seems reasonable to conclude that the agreement among drunkards is a sign, not of a revelation, but of a delusion.

Now the assertions in which religious mystics agree are not such that they conflict with what we can perceive with our senses. They are about the structure and organization of the world as a whole and about the relations of men to the rest of it. And they have so little in common with the facts of daily life that there is not much chance of direct collision. I think that there is only one important point on which there is conflict. Nearly all mystics seem to be agreed that time and change and unchanging duration are unreal or extremely superficial, whilst these seem to plain men to be the most fundamental features of the world. But we must admit, on the one hand, that these temporal characteristics present very great philosophical difficulties and puzzles when we reflect upon them. On the other hand, we may well suppose that the mystic finds it impossible to state clearly in ordinary language what it is that he experiences about the facts which underlie the appearance of time and change and duration. Therefore it is not difficult to allow that what we experience as the temporal aspect of reality corresponds in some sense to certain facts, and yet that these facts appear to us in so distorted a form in our ordinary experience that a person who sees them more accurately and directly might refuse to apply temporal names to them.

Let us next consider why we feel fairly certain that the agreement among trained microscopists about the minute structure of cells expresses an objective fact, although we cannot get similar experiences. One reason is that we have learned enough, from simpler cases of visual perception, about the laws of optics to know that the arrangement of lenses in a microscope is such that it will reveal minute structure, which is otherwise invisible, and will not simply create optical delusions. Another reason is that we know of other cases in which trained persons can detect things which untrained people will overlook, and that in many cases the existence of these things can be verified by indirect methods. Probably most of us have experienced such results of training in our own lives.

Now religious experience is not in nearly such a strong position as this. We do not know much about the laws which govern its occurrence and determine its variations. No doubt there are certain standard methods of training and meditation which tend to produce mystical experiences. These have been elaborated to some extent by certain Western mystics and to a very much greater extent by Eastern Yogis. But I do not think that we can see here, as we can in the case of microscopes and the training which is required to make the best use of them, any conclusive reason why these methods should produce veridical rather than delusive experiences. Uniform methods of training and meditation would be likely to produce more or less similar experiences, whether these experiences were largely veridical or wholly delusive.

Is there any analogy between the facts about religious experience and the fable about the blind men some of whom gained the power of sight? It might be said that many ideals of conduct and ways of life, which we can all recognize now to be good and useful, have been introduced into human history by the founders of religions. These persons have made actual ethical discoveries which others can afterwards recognize to be true. It might be said that this is at least roughly analogous to the case of the seeing men telling the still blind men of facts which the latter could and did verify for themselves. And it might be said that this makes it reasonable for us to attach some weight to what founders of religions tell us about things which we cannot understand or verify for ourselves; just as it would have been reasonable for the blind men to attach some weight to the unintelligible statements which the seeing men made to them about colours.

I think that this argument deserves a certain amount of respect, though I should find it hard to estimate how much weight to attach to it. I should be inclined to sum up as follows. When there is a nucleus of agreement between the experiences of men in different places, times, and traditions, and when they all tend to put much the same kind of interpretation on the cognitive content of these experiences, it is reasonable to ascribe this agreement to their all being in contact with a certain objective aspect of reality *unless* there be some positive reason to think otherwise. The practical postulate which we go upon everywhere else is to treat cognitive claims as veridical unless there be some positive reason to think them delusive. This, after all, is our only guarantee for believing that ordinary sense-perception is veridical. We cannot *prove* that what people agree in perceiving really exists independently of them; but we do always assume that ordinary waking sense-perception is veridical unless we can produce some positive ground for thinking that it is delusive in any given case. I think it would be inconsistent to treat the experiences of religious mystics on different principles. So far as they agree they should be provisionally accepted as veridical unless there be some positive ground for thinkng that they are not. So the next question is whether there is any positive ground for holding that they are delusive.

There are two circumstances which have been commonly held to cast doubt on the cognitive claims of religious and mystical experience. (i) It is alleged that founders of religions and saints have nearly always had certain neuropathic symptoms or certain bodily weaknesses, and that these would be likely to produce delusions. Even if we accept the premisses, I do not think that this is a very strong argument. (a) It is equally true that many founders of religions and saints have exhibited great endurance and great power of organization and business capacity which would have made them extremely successful and competent in secular affairs. There are very few offices in the cabinet or in the highest branches of the civil service which St. Thomas Aquinas could have not held with conspicuous success. I do not, of course, regard this as a positive reason *for* accepting the metaphysical doctrines which saints and founders of religions have based on their experiences; but it is relevant as a *rebuttal* of the argument which we are considering. (b) Probably very few people of extreme genius in science or art are perfectly normal mentally or physically, and some of them are very crazy and eccentric indeed. Therefore it would be rather surprising if persons of religious genius were completely normal, whether their experiences be veridical or delusive. (c) Suppose, for the sake of argument, that there is an aspect of the world which remains altogether outside the ken of ordinary persons in their daily life. Then it seems very likely that some degree of mental and physical abnormality would be a necessary condition for getting sufficiently loosened from the objects of ordinary sense-perception to come into cognitive contact with this aspect of reality. Therefore the fact that those persons who claim to have this peculiar kind of cognition generally exhibit certain mental and physical abnormalities is rather what might be anticipated if their claims were true. One might need to be slightly 'cracked' in order to have some peep-holes into the super-sensible world. (d) If mystical experience were veridical, it seems quite likely that it would *produce* abnormalities of behaviour in those who had it strongly. Let us suppose, for the sake of argument, that those who have religious experience are in frequent contact with an aspect of reality of which most men get only rare and faint glimpses. Then such persons are, as it were, living in two worlds, while the ordinary man is living in only one of them. Or, again, they might be compared to a man who has to conduct his life with one ordinary eye and another of a telescopic kind. Their behaviour may be appropriate to the aspect of reality which they alone perceive and think all-important; but, for that very reason, it may be inappropriate to those other aspects of reality which are all that most men perceive or judge to be important and on which all our social institutions and conventions are built.

(ii) A second reason which is commonly alleged for doubt about the claims of religious experience is the following. It is said that such experience always originates from and remains mixed with certain other factors, e.g., sexual emotion, which are such that experiences and beliefs that arise from them are very likely to be delusive. I think that there are a good many confusions on this point, and it will be worth while to begin by indicating some of them.

When people say that B 'originated from' A, they are liable to confuse at least three different kinds of connexion between A and B. (i) It might be that A is a necessary but insufficient condition of the existence of B. (ii) It might be that A is a necessary and sufficient condition of the existence of B. Or (iii) it might be that B simply *is* A in a more complex and disguised form. Now, when there is in fact evidence only for the first kind of connexion, people are very liable to jump to the conclusion that there is the third kind of connexion. It may well be the case, e.g., that no one who was incapable of strong sexual desires and emotions could have anything worth calling religious experience. But it is plain that the possession of a strong capacity for sexual experience is not a *sufficient* condition of having religious experience; for we know that the former quite often exists in persons who show hardly any trace of the latter. But, even if it could be shown that a strong capacity for sexual desire and emotion is *both* necessary and sufficient to produce religious experience, it would not follow that the latter is just the former in disguise. In the first place, it is not at all easy to discover the exact meaning of this metaphorical phrase when it is applied to psychological topics. And, if we make use of physical analogies, we are not much helped. A mixture of oxygen and hydrogen in presence of a spark is necessary and sufficient to produce water accompanied by an explosion. But water accompanied by an explosion is not a mixture of oxygen and hydrogen and a spark 'in a disguised form', whatever that may mean.

Now I think that the present rather vaguely formulated objection to the validity of the claims of religious experience might be stated somewhat as follows. 'In the individual religious experience originates from, and always remains mixed with, sexual desires and emotions. The other generative factor of it is the religious tradition of the society in which he lives, the teachings of his parents, nurses, schoolmasters, etc. In the race religious experience originated from a mixture of false beliefs about nature and man, irrational fears, sexual and other impulses, and so on. Thus the religious tradition arose from beliefs which we now recognize to have been false and from emotions which we now recognize to have been irrelevant and misleading. It is now drilled into children by those who are in authority over them at a time of life when they are intellectually and emotionally at much the same stage as the primitive savages among whom it originated. It is, therefore, readily accepted, and it determines beliefs and emotional dispositions which persist long after the child has grown up and acquired more adequate knowledge of nature and of himself.'

Persons who use this argument might admit that it does not definitely *prove* that religious beliefs are false and groundless. False beliefs and irrational fears in our remote ancestors *might* conceivably be the origin of true beliefs and of an appropriate feeling of awe and reverence in ourselves. And, if sexual desires and emotions be an essential condition and constituent of religious experience, the experience *may* nevertheless be veridical in important respects. We might merely have to rewrite one of the beatitudes and say 'Blessed are the *im*pure in heart, for they shall see God'. But, although it is logically possible that such causes should produce such effects, it would be said that they are most unlikely to do so. They seem much more likely to produce false beliefs and misplaced emotions.

It is plain that this argument has considerable plausibility. But it is worth while to remember that modern science has almost as humble an ancestry as contemporary religion. If the primitive witch-smeller is the spiritual progenitor of the Archbishop of Canterbury, the primitive rain-maker is equally the spiritual progenitor of the Cavendish Professor of Physics. There has obviously been a gradual refinement and purification of religious beliefs and concepts in the course of history, just as there has been in the beliefs and concepts of science. Certain persons of religious genius, such as some of the Hebrew prophets and the founders of Christianity and of Buddhism, do seem to have introduced new ethico-religious concepts and beliefs which have won wide acceptance, just as certain men of scientific genius, such as Galileo, Newton, and Einstein, have done in the sphere of science. It seems somewhat arbitrary to count this process as a continual approximation to true knowledge of the material aspect of the world in the case of science, and to refuse to regard is as at all similar in the case of religion. Lastly, we must remember that all of us have accepted the current common-sense and scientific view of the material world on the authority of our parents, nurses, masters, and companions at a time when we had neither the power nor the inclination to criticize it. And most of us accept, without even understanding, the more recondite doctrines of contemporary physics simply on the authority of those whom we have been taught to regard as experts.

On the whole, then, I do not think that what we know of the conditions under which religious beliefs and emotions have arisen in the life of the individual and the race makes it reasonable to think that they are *specially* likely to be delusive or misdirected. At any rate any argument which starts from that basis and claims to reach such a conclusion will need to be very carefully handled if its destructive effects are to be confined within the range contemplated by its users. It is reasonable to think that the concepts and beliefs of even the most perfect religions known to us are extremely inadequate to the facts which they express; that they are highly confused and are mixed up with a great deal of positive error and sheer nonsense; and that, if the human race goes on and continues to have religious experiences and to reflect on them, they will be altered and improved almost out of recognition. But all this could be said, *mutatis mutandis,* of scientific concepts and theories. The claim of any particular religion or sect to have complete or final truth on these subjects seems to me to be too ridiculous to be worth a moment's consideration. But the opposite extreme of holding that the whole religious experience of mankind is a gigantic system of pure delusion seems to me to be almost (though not quite) as far-fetched.

PSYCHOLOGICAL EXPLANATION OF RELIGIOUS BELIEF

William P. Alston

William P. Alston, "Psychoanalytic Theory and Theistic Belief," from John Hick (ed.), *Faith and the Philosophers*, 1964. By permission of Macmillan and Co., Ltd., London, The Macmillan Co. of Canada, Limited, Toronto, and St. Martin's Press, New York.

In this paper I am going to attempt to determine just what bearing, if any, the existence of an adequate explanation of theistic religious belief exclusively in terms of factors within the natural world would have on the acceptability of such beliefs; more particularly I shall examine the claims to the effect that such explanations render theistic belief unacceptable. It would be possible to proceed immediately to a consideration of this problem with no more specification of the sort of explanation in question than what I have just given. I believe, however, that the discussion will be more likely to be firmly anchored and that there will be a greater chance of focusing the discussion on real issues if the treatment of the philosophical issues is prefaced by a fairly detailed presentation of an actual example of the sort of explanation I have in mind. Indeed there may be those who, in the absence of such documentation, would suppose that the chance of success for such explanatory ventures is so remote as to render consideration of my problem useless. But I should not like to justify my prolegomenon in this way, for I fear that there is nothing in developments to date which could be relied upon to remove such a doubt.

If a man accepts a given belief that is widely accepted he is not likely to feel a need to explain the fact that it is widely accepted. But if he does not accept it, especially if it seems to him to be plainly false, he may well come to wonder why so many people do accept it. From ancient times there have been many attempts on the part of religious sceptics to answer this sort of question. To the question, 'Why do people believe in the existence of supernatural personal beings?' some of the simpler answers which have been given are:

1 Man has a natural tendency to personify things in his environment.

2 Believing that the course of events is controlled by one or more personal beings which can, by suitable devices, be persuaded to direct it in a way favourable to man, serves to alleviate man's fear of the dangers in his environment.

3 These beliefs are a survival from the earliest human attempts to explain natural phenomena.

More elaborate attempts which have been made in the last 150 years include:

4 The Marxian theory that religion is one of the ideological reflections of the current state of economic interrelations in a society.

5 Durkheim's similar but more extensively developed theory that religious belief represents a projection into another realm of the actual structure of the society. This approach has recently been considerably elaborated by G. E. Swanson.[1]

6 The Freudian theory that belief in gods arises from projections which are designed to alleviate certain kinds of unconscious conflicts.

I have chosen the Freudian theory for detailed presentation for several reasons. First, it is the only theory which attempts to spell out in any detail the psychological mechanisms involved. Although Swanson in supporting the Durkheimian theory shows by statistical studies that there is a considerable correlation between certain features of the structure of a society and certain features of its theology, neither he nor any other protagonist of this point of view has, to my knowledge, done anything to indicate what psychological processes effect the transition between one's awareness of the structure of one's society and one's readiness to accept a certain theology. Second (though this point does not distinguish this theory from *all* the others), this theory is a live issue at present; there are men who are working to develop and extend it (though not, unfortunately, to test it) and so long as psychoanalytic theory continues to develop, this explanation of religious belief will have considerable growth-potential. Third, although it should be clear that no theory which proceeds in terms of one sort of factor can possibly be a complete explanation of religious belief, I am inclined to think, without really being able to support this, that Freudian theory is in possession of a larger segment of the complete explanation than any other.

I

A

To get the fundamentals of Freud's theory, we should look first at his great work, *Totem and Taboo*,[2] and I think it will be worth our while to retrace briefly the main stages of his investigation as he sets them out there. He began by considering the notion of taboo, which is very widely diffused in primitive societies. Certain things, persons, places, etc., are credited with a mysterious sort of sanctity or uncleanness (the two are not clearly distinguished) and from this character springs a strict prohibition against contact with them, except perhaps in very special circumstances. Freud noted some strong analogies between these taboos and certain compulsion neuroses, particularly those in which prohibitions are prominent. They are alike in the following striking features. (1) The prohibition has no rational explanation, or at least its violation will give rise to anxiety out of all proportion to the reasons against violating it. (2) The prohibition has to do chiefly with the act of touching and secondarily with other sorts of contact. (3) The prohibitions are readily displaced from their primary objects to others associated with them in some way. For example a person who has violated a taboo himself becomes a taboo, and a neurotic who finds it impossible to pronounce a certain

---

[1]In *The Birth of the Gods*, University of Michigan Press, Ann Arbor, 1961.
[2]In *The Basic Writings of Sigmund Freud*, tr. A. A. Brill, The Modern Library, New York.

name will also find it impossible to have any dealings with anything on a street which bears that name. (4) Violation can be expiated by carrying out certain stereotyped procedures such as repeated washings. Now the existence of these analogies gives us some hope of explaining taboos, for psychoanalysis, Freud thinks, has discovered the explanation for compulsion neuroses of these sorts. In early childhood the individual has a strong impulse to touch, look at, or otherwise come into contact with something, e.g., his mother or certain parts of her body. Some external authority (his father) prohibited him from doing so and backed the prohibition with strong sanctions. These threats plus the authority which the father's position gave him stopped the overt actions, but the desires were not destroyed—they were merely repressed, driven into the unconscious, from which they seek satisfaction in all sorts of disguised ways. The compulsion is a result of this psychic constellation of forces. The desire, blocked from its initial object, seeks substitute objects which are connected along various paths of association with the original object; but the prohibition, which has itself become unconscious as well, opposes each substitute in turn, the opposition now being manifested as a strange and inexplicable anxiety over the carrying out of the act. Thus both the tendency to touch the object and the fear of doing so are derived from sources which have been forgotten.

To give an analogous explanation of taboos we should have to show that at some earlier period of the race man had certain strong desires which were forcibly suppressed by external authority in such a way that both the desires and their suppression were forced into the unconscious, to emerge in the form of simultaneous desires for and fears of handling certain objects which are some-how associated with the original objects of desire. But where are we to find such phenomena? At this point totemism is brought into the picture. A totemic group is one which is bound together by a special regard for a certain species of animal or plant, the totem, which is regarded somehow as the original ancestor of the group and hence of one blood with it. If we make the assumption that totemism is the oldest form of religion and social organization, then we can take the fundamental totemic taboos as the basic ones, out of which all the others are derived by various associations. These are: not to kill the totem animal, and to avoid sexual intercourse with other members of one's totemic group. But even if we can somehow derive the other taboos from these, how does that help? These taboos themselves seem as inexplicable as can be. To what primordial trauma could they be related?

At this point two important clues present themselves. First the phenomenon of the totemic feast. In many totemic societies, the first taboo is cancelled on a solemn yearly occasion on which a member of the totemic species is killed and eaten in a rigorously prescribed way. The interesting thing is that this is both an occasion of mourning (for the slain totemic ancestory) and a joyful celebration. This clearly indicates that the ambivalence typical of the compulsion neurosis is present here; there are strong tendencies to both commit and abstain from committing (and hence regret committing) the tabooed act. The second clue comes once again from psychopathology, this time from the animal phobias of children. Freud's analysis of these, particularly his famous 'Analysis of a Phobia in a Five-Year-Old Boy',[3] where the boy was afraid to even look at horses, convinced

---

[3]Sigmund Freud, *Collected Papers,* ed. Ernest Jones, Vol. III (London: Hogarth Press, 1956), pp. 149–242.

him that in each case the animal feared was a symbolic substitute for the father. If we can take the totem animal as a father substitute, then the desires against which the fundamental totemic taboos are in fact directed are those which Oedipus realized—to slay one's father and sexually possess one's mother,—and we come within sight of the possibility of explaining totemism on the basis of the Oedipus complex, which, according to Freud, is at the root of all or most neuroses.

But we still need a racial analogue of the individual's infantile conflict with the father over his mother. At this crucial point in the argument I shall quote Freud's own summary of his position, in *Moses and Monotheism* and *Totem and Taboo:*

The argument started from some remarks by Charles Darwin and embraced a suggestion of Atkinson's. It says that in primaeval times men lived in small hordes, each under the domination of a strong male. . . . The story is told in a very condensed way, as if what in reality took centuries to achieve, and during that long time was repeated innumerably, had happened only once. The strong male was the master and father of the whole horde: unlimited in his power, which he used brutally. All females were his property, the wives and daughters in his own horde as well as perhaps also those robbed from other hordes. The fate of the sons was a hard one; if they excited the father's jealousy they were killed or castrated or driven out. They were forced to live in small communities and to provide themselves with wives by robbing them from others. Then one or the other son might succeed in attaining a situation similar to that of the father in the original horde. . . . The next decisive step towards changing this first kind of 'social' organization lies in the following suggestion. The brothers who had been driven out and lived together in a community clubbed together, overcame the father and—according to the custom of those times—all partook of his body . . . we attribute to those primaeval people the same feelings and emotions that we have elucidated in the primitives in our own times, our children, by psychoanalytic research. That is to say: they not merely hated and feared their father, but also honoured him as an example to follow; in fact, each son wanted to place himself in his father's position. The cannibalistic act thus becomes comprehensible as an attempt to assure one's identification with the father by incorporating a part of him.[4]

After they [the brothers] had got rid of him, had satisfied their hatred and had put into effect their wish to identify themselves with him, the affection which had all this time been pushed under was bound to make itself felt. It did so in the form of remorse. . . . The dead father became stronger than the living one had been—for events took the course we so often see them follow in human affairs to this day. What had up to then been prevented by his actual existence was thenceforward prohibited by the sons themselves, in accordance with the psychological procedure so familiar to us in psychoanalyses under the name of 'deferred obedience'. They revoked their deed by forbidding the killing of the totem, the substitute for their father; and they renounced its fruits by resigning their claim to the women who had now been set free. They thus created out of their filial sense of guilt the two funda-

---

[4]*Moses and Monotheism*, Hogarth Press, London, 1951, pp. 130–133.

mental taboos of totemism, which for that very reason inevitably corresponds to the two repressed wishes of the Oedipus complex.[5]

Thus the dictates of the father return in a disguised form in the totemic taboos, and their strength is based not only on the original power of the father, but on the enhancement of the power of his memory, as a result of the guilt felt for his murder.

However ingenious all this may be as an explanation of totemism, what does it have to do with religion as we know it today? Well, Freud tries to use these same principles to explain the development of religion up through Christianity. The basic point is that the memory of the primaeval murder(s), together with the ambivalent tender and hostile impulses toward the father associated therewith, have been repressed, and that like all repressed material, it is constantly seeking expression; but in order that the repression be maintained, this expression must be more or less disguised. The first step in the development is the replacement of the totem animal with a person deity; in transitional stages, he still bears the countenance of the animal, or the animal may be his inseparable companion; he may sometimes transform himself into the animal, or he may have attained his status, according to the myth, by vanquishing the animal. To represent the father as a personal deity is obviously closer to the truth of the matter, closer to an actual reinstatement of the father, and Freud suggests that this development was abetted by the fact that in the course of time the bitterness against the father abated and his image became a more ideal one, especially since, as none of the brothers could attain to his power and status, that status came to be an unattainable ideal for them. But the hostility had not disappeared. Just as the totem animal was ritually killed and eaten once a year, so the practice of sacrificing divine kings, gods in human form, grew up in many forms. This side of the picture was also reflected mythically in widespread stories of the divine son who committed incest with the mother in defiance of the divine father, only first to be killed by an animal and then resurrected amid joy and celebration.

The primaeval father is most fully restored in all his grandeur in monotheism, the worship of the one and only father-deity whose power is unlimited. In *Moses and Monotheism* Freud explains the fact that it was the Jews who most decisively attained this stage as a people by supposing, with some off-beat heterodox Old Testament scholars, that Moses was an Egyptian who tried to impose monotheism on the Jews and was murdered by them for his pains. The murder of this godlike figure formed such a close parallel with the primaeval murder that the Jews were, so to say, sensitized for a more complete return of the repressed material, and so gradually came to accept the doctrines of their great leader. But this pure ethical monotheism is unstable; it tries to achieve a reconciliation with the father without taking into account the guilt of the sons, and as a result it cannot deal with the hostile tendencies and the guilt accruing therefrom; it offers them no expression. This deficiency is remedied in Christianity which takes as its starting-point man's original sin, and proclaims that the Son of God has suffered death to atone for that sin. (From Freud's standpoint, the attribution of innocence to the Son is part of the disguise.) But though the Son dies he rises again and henceforth occupies the

---

[5] *Totem and Taboo*, translated by James Strachey (London: Routledge and Kegan Paul, 1950), p. 143.

centre of attention and worship so that the hostility to the father is triumphant after all.

Such is Freud's theory as we have it in his two major works on religion. There is no doubt that as historical explanation it is fantastic. There seems to be little basis for the assumption of the primaeval horde and its violent dissolution, other than its usefulness for a psychoanalytic explanation. And other features of the account have found as little acceptance among anthropologists and historians. For example, it is not generally thought nowadays that totemism is the earliest form of religion, or that every group passed through a stage of totemism. And practically no Old Testament scholars accept the thesis that Moses was murdered by the Israelites. An even more serious difficulty concerns the way Freud treats the race, or a society, like an individual man. By analogy with individual case-histories he supposes that cultural behaviour at a certain period of history can be viewed as a disguised manifestation of impulses and memories which had been repressed because of traumatic experiences in an early stage of the race or society. This presupposes that mental contents can persist in a repressed form over many generations, indeed over many millenia, and can from time to time profoundly influence people's behaviour. Being repressed, they cannot have been transmitted from one generation to another by oral teaching or anything of that sort. Despite Freud's disclaimer of Jung's concept of the collective uncon-scious, it seems that he is committed to something like that.

But really these objections do not strike at the root of the matter. We can look on this prehistoric 'I was a Teen-Age Oedipus' story, and its unconscious sequels, as so much window-dressing to Freud's basic ideas. If we remember that, according to Freud, what the primaeval sons did is what every son wants to do but usually fails to carry out, and if we remember that, according to Freud, in the unconscious the wish is equivalent to the deed and gives rise to an equivalent guilt, we can see that the Oedipean conflict which each individual goes through in his childhood is for him an emotional equivalent of such a prehistoric deed persisting in the racial memory. Or to turn it around, we may look at Freud's narrative as a mythical exposition of the unconscious complex which every individual gets from his own early relations with his parents. By this revision we can consider Freud's theory in a form in which it can be taken more seriously as an account of the role played by individual development, rather than cultural evolution, in the formation of religious belief.

B

Unfortunately there is no canonical presentation of this more sober version of the Freudian theory. We shall have to rely on scattered and relatively undeveloped remarks in Freud, particularly in *The Future of an Illusion*,[6] supplemented with works by other psychoanalytic theorists, particularly T. Reik's *Dogma and Compulsion*[7] and *Ritual*,[8] J. C. Flugel's *Man, Morals, and Society*,[9] and M. Ostow's and B. Scharfstein's *The Need to Believe*.[10]

---

[6]Tr. W. D. Robson Scott, Liverright, New York, 1949, *also* Hogarth Press, London, 1928.
[7]Tr. B. Miall, International Universities Press, New York, 1951, *also* Bailey Bros., London.
[8]Tr. D. Bryan, W. W. Norton, New York, 1931.
[9]International Universities Press, New York, 1947, *also* Duckworth, London, 1955.
[10]International Universities Press, New York, 1954.

Translating Freud's pseudo-historical narrative into an account of those factors in the development of the individual which render him susceptible to belief in a theistic God, we get something like this. In his early life a boy's relations to his parents typically develop in such a way as to present grave problems to him. (To keep things within manageable length we are restricting ourselves to the male believer. Perhaps the religious beliefs of females cannot be causally explained!) His parents, particularly his father, appear to him as almighty all-knowing beings, and as such they are regarded as mysterious and responded to with awe. The child is dependent on them in all sorts of ways and, of course, he normally develops a close attachment to them, feeling gratitude to them for their providential care and protection and vastly enjoying their company (a great deal of the time). But, of course, they also function as disciplinarians, restricting him in various ways and punishing him for transgressions, and so they are also regarded as stern judges and harsh taskmasters whose wrath is likely to be provoked at any moment, and this harshness naturally arouses resentment and hostility. (Of course there are wide variations between different sets of parents in these regards, but these differences may loom larger to the adult observer than to the child.) Thus we have a striking surface similarity between the standard attributes of the theistic God—omnipotence, omniscience, inscrutability, providential concern and the small child's view of his parents and feelings toward them—and between the standard ways of relating oneself to the theistic God—utter dependence, awe, fear of divine punishment, gratitude for divine mercy and protection. Of course this similarity in itself is no evidence for a causal connection; at best it furnishes a clue.

So far, there is nothing to provide a decisive distinction between the parents in these regards, although it is generally assumed that the father is usually regarded as the chief source both of frustration and protection. Freud's main reason for regarding the father as the chief model for God (still restricting ourselves to the male child) comes from the Oedipean situation, and this is the chief point at which the theory of individual development parallels the 'historical' account. As all the world knows, Freud supposes that the male child at around the age of four comes to desire the mother sexually and to regard the father as a rival. Depending more or less on actual indications, the child becomes so afraid of the father's hostility that he not only abandons his sexual aims but also represses the entire complex of desires, fears, etc. (Love for the father plays a role here too.) This complex remains, in greater or less intensity, in the unconscious, and it is because the theistic God provides an external figure on which to project this material that men have as much inclination as they do to believe in such a Being and to accept the attitudes and practices that go along with this belief.

This rough sketch of the theory leaves many questions unanswered. The most important of these is: Just what does 'projecting' this unconscious material do for the individual? To answer this question we must first get a fuller idea of the nature of the material and the conditions of its existence in the unconscious.

Normally the termination of the Oedipean situation leaves the individual with a number of conflicts, the exact nature of which are hidden from him because of the repression. There is the conflict between tendencies to rebel against the father and tendencies to submit to the father. And of course there is the conflict between the desires which his father opposed and the prohibitions against satisfying these desires; many of these prohibitions have now become internalized in the form of the 'super-ego'. Since these desires, fears, prohibitions, conceptions, etc., are excluded from consciousness, they are largely unavailable for further development and so retain their childlike form. But they also retain their strength; the desires press for some sort of satisfaction and the fears and prohibitions oppose this. And the lack of satisfaction and the continual vacillation manifest themselves in various kinds of conscious distress.

The projection of the childhood father-image onto a supernatural being serves to alleviate, or at least reduce this distress in several ways. First, the mere fact of externalizing the problem is some relief in itself. Instead of mysterious discomfort with only vague intimations of its source, the individual has a clear-cut opposition between various desires of his own on the one hand and a forbidding external person on the other. At least he can understand the problem. Second, there is much less conflict because the balance has been tipped decisively in the direction of the prohibiting tendencies. (Perhaps the theory should hold that this decisive shift has to have already occurred in the unconscious before there is a very strong tendency to believe in the theistic God. See the detailed analysis from Freud below.) The external figure is so overpowering as to seriously weaken the rebellious tendencies, and on the other hand he is so idealized morally and credited with such perfect love as to render resentment and hostility much less appropriate. Third, as is suggested in our summary of Freud's historical account, the theology tends to be shaped in such a way as to give some vicarious satisfaction to the rebellious tendencies as well. Reik in *Dogma and Compulsion* carries out an elaborate analysis of the development of the Christian doctrine of the Trinity as a series of shifts in the balance of rebellious and submissive forces in the son-father conflict. And even if there are no female deities available there are feminine aspects of God, or perhaps the Virgin Mary, and in relation to these the individual may achieve some substitute satisfaction of the Oedipean desires.[11]

The Oedipean situation leaves a heavy deposit of guilt, as well as conflict, in the unconscious—guilt both for the continuing sexual desires for the mother and for the hostility against the father. Projection onto a supernatural deity can also serve to alleviate this guilt, for religion not only gets out into the open a figure, transgression against whom gave rise to the guilt and to whom reparations will have to be made, but also provides means for making the reparation and otherwise dissipating guilt—confession, penance, restrictions and renunciations of various kinds. Some Freudian writers, especially Ostow and Scharfstein, have placed the chief emphasis on this function of the religious projections in relieving guilt.

In *The Future of an Illusion,* a very chaotic work, the only clear suggestion made as to the psychological basis of theistic belief seems to be rather different from all the foregoing. There Freud speaks of the various dangers and frustrations of life, and says that the adult, in the face of these conditions, tends to regress to the infantile state in which he could rely on the love and protection of his almighty father. And since the adult can only carry this off by positing an invisible

---

[11]It is worth noting, however, that satisfaction of sexual desires in fantasy plays a very small role in Freud's account of religion, although, of course, it is primarily conflicts over sexual impulses that underlie the relationships to the father which he does take as crucial.

cosmic counterpart of the infantile image of the father he proceeds to do so.[12] Now in itself this suggestion differs from the old-age idea that belief in God is a wish-fulfilment only by invoking the well-attested mechanism of regression and calling attention to the fact that the infantile attitude toward the father provides an appropriate goal of regression. But it can also be viewed as a supplement to the Freudian theory as sketched above. In the concept of regression in the face of emotional difficulties it provides a possible way of answering questions as to the timing of conversion to or revivification of religious beliefs. The regression has three important features. First, it tends to reinstate various earlier modes of feeling toward, thinking about, and relating to, persons and things. This is the point made in the passage from *The Future of an Illusion* alluded to earlier in this paragraph. Second, it tends to strengthen the childhood desires, etc., already existing in the unconscious, thereby increasing the need for some sort of relief. Third, it lowers resistance to projection, since the further back we go in individual development the less sharp the distinction between oneself and the external world. All these factors are conducive to the sort of projection posited by the theory. We should also note that the difficulties which set off regression can themselves be intimately connected with the relevant unconscious material; for example, anxiety over intimate involvement with a woman unconsciously identified with the mother can play this role.

To sum up, Freudian theory can be construed as regarding an individual's tendency to accept belief in a supernatural personal deity (of the sort envisaged in the Judaeo-Christian tradition) as partly due to a tendency to project a childhood father-image existing in the unconscious, this projection normally following on a regression set off by emotional difficulties of one sort or another and serving to alleviate, at least in part, unconscious conflicts and unconscious guilt. It would seem that *contra* many psychoanalytic writers the conflicts and guilt so alleviated need not be restricted to the Oedipean situation. It does seem that only conflicts between the super-ego and forbidden tendencies could be alleviated by this method, rather than conflicts between different morally neutral tendencies; but this still leaves a very wide field. And it would seem that unconscious guilt arising from any source could be interpreted by the individual as due to transgressions against divine commands. Hence I do not believe that this theory of religious belief is necessarily tied to the thesis that the Oepidean situation has the absolutely central importance attributed to it by Freud; although if we are to hold that projection of an unconscious father-image underlies theistic religious belief we have to suppose that relations to the father are extremely important in the life of the young child and that in the course of these relations difficulties arise which result in considerable repression.

What reason is there to suppose that this theory is correct? There is no scientifically respectable evidence for it. Such evidence might conceivably be gathered. If we could develop reliable measures of such factors as degree of unconscious conflict, degree of unconscious guilt, strength of tendency to regress under difficulties and strength of tendency to project, we could then determine the extent to which these correlate with degree of belief in a theistic God, provided we had some reliable way of measuring the latter. But we are a

---

[12]*Op. cit.* pp. 41–42.

long way from this. Meanwhile the only backing for the theory consists of speculative extensions to religious belief of mechanisms like regression and projection, the existence and (to some extent) the conditions of which have been established elsewhere. These extensions are supported by analogies between cases of religious belief and cases of neurosis in which the operation of these mechanisms is fairly well established. The analogies are sometimes developed in great detail, as in Reik's analysis of the development of the doctrine of the Trinity, but no matter how elaborate, they remain suggestive rather than evidential. Nevertheless, the analogies and extrapolations seem to me impressive enough to make them worth taking seriously.

It may be in order to append to this rather abstract summary an actual example of an analysis by Freud of a particular case of coming to believe in God. Freud once received a letter from an American physician who had noted in a published interview with Freud a reference to the latter's lack of religious faith, and who communicated to Freud an account of his conversion experience. The account ran, in part, as follows:[13]

> . . . One afternoon while I was passing through the dissecting-room my attention was attracted to a sweet-faced dear old woman who was being carried to a dissecting-table. This sweet-faced woman made such an impression on me that a thought flashed up in my mind, 'There is no God: if there were a God he would not have allowed this dear old woman to be brought into the dissecting-room.'
>
> When I got home that afternoon the feeling I had had at the sight in the dissecting-room had determined me to discontinue going to church. The doctrines of Christianity had before this been the subject of doubts in my mind.
>
> While I was meditating on this matter a voice spoke to my soul and said that 'I should consider the step I was about to take'. My spirit replied to this inner voice saying, 'If I knew of a certainty that Christianity was truth and the Bible was the Word of God, then I would accept it'.
>
> In the course of the next few days God made it clear to my soul that the Bible was his Word, that the teachings about Jesus Christ were true, and that Jesus was our only hope. After such a clear revelation I accepted the Bible as God's word and Jesus Christ as my personal Saviour. Since then God has revealed himself to me by many infallible proofs.
>
> I beg you as a brother physician to give thought to this most important matter, and I can assure you, if you look into this subject with an open mind, God will reveal the truth to your soul, the same as he did to me and to multitudes of others. . . .

Freud proceeded to subject this account to psychoanalytic interpretation, with the following results.

We may suppose, therefore, that this was the way in which things happened. The sight of a woman's dead body, naked or on the point of being stripped,

---

[13]Sigmund Freud, *Collected Papers*, 'A Religious Experience', translated by J. Strachey (London: Hogarth Press, Vol. 5, 1950), pp. 243–246.

reminded the young man of his mother. It roused in him a longing for his mother which sprang from his Oedipus complex, and this was immediately completed by a feeling of indignation against his father. His ideas of 'father' and 'God' had not yet become widely separated; so that his desire to destroy his father could become conscious as doubt in the existence of God and could seek to justify itself in the eyes of reason as indignation about the ill-treatment of a mother-object. It is of course typical for a child to regard what his father does to his mother in sexual intercourse as ill-treatment. The new impulse, which was displaced into the sphere of religion, was only a repetition of the Oedipus situation and consequently soon met with a similar fate. It succumbed to a powerful opposing current. During the actual conflict the level of displacement was not maintained: there is no mention of arguments in justification of God, nor are we told what the infallible signs were by which God proved his existence to the doubter. The conflict seems to have been unfolded in the form of an hallucinatory psychosis: inner voices were heard which uttered warnings against resistance to God. But the outcome of the struggle was displayed once again in the sphere of religion and it was of a kind pre-determined by the fate of the Oedipus complex: complete submission to the will of God the Father. The young man became a believer and accepted everything he had been taught since his childhood about God and Jesus Christ. He had had a religious experience and had undergone a conversion.

C

I have been presenting the psychoanalytic explanation as an example of an explanation of theistic belief in terms of factors within the natural world. My central concern in this paper is to determine what bearing the adequacy of an explanation of this sort would have on the acceptability of theistic belief. But before settling down to this task, we must try to be clearer as to the defining features of the sort of theory in which we are interested and as to the extent to which the psychoanalytic explanation does or does not exemplify these features.

First, let me make more explicit what I mean by the adequacy of such an explanation. In saying of such an explanation ('causal' explanation, if you like, though I do not wish to import anything into 'causal' other than what is specified here) that it is adequate, I simply mean that it specifies conditions which are such that whenever those conditions are satisfied theistic belief exists in some specified relation to the conditions. It might be argued that in order to explain the occurrence of a belief we need something further, e.g. some intelligible relationship between the antecedent conditions and the belief. Thus it might be said that even if we found an absolutely unexceptionable correlation between theistic belief and level of blood sugar, so that on the basis of this we were convinced that wherever blood sugar is at a certain level theistic belief exists, that would not serve to *explain* such belief or to show that blood sugar *produces* such belief, for it is impossible to understand how there could be any connection between them. But if we did have a perfect correlation over a wide range of cases, then I would suppose that we should first look for intermediate factors which would bridge this conceptual gap, or, if persistent search should fail to uncover any, we should have to revise the basic principles in terms of which blood sugar level and theistic belief cannot be directly connected. This raises problems in the philosophy of science into which I cannot go.

One must recognize that Freudian theory, as it actually exists, is just not a theory of this sort. By this I do not mean that it has not been established as a theory of this sort, but that it is not put forward, and cannot plausibly be put forward, as a theory which specifies conditions sufficient to give rise to theistic belief. Remember that when I summed up the theory I presented it as claiming that an individual's *tendency* to accept belief in a supernatural deity is *partly* due to a tendency to project a childhood father-image. . . . It can aspire to explain only a *tendency* to accept the belief, rather than simply the belief, because the theory in the form in which we are considering it is dealing with a situation in which the individual finds the belief ready-made in his culture, rather than dealing with the problem of the cultural origin of the belief. Therefore the cultural configuration with which the individual is faced and the learning processes by which he assimilates this will have to form part of the explanation of the fact that a given individual acquires theistic belief. Psychoanalysis can aspire only to explain the differential readiness of different people to accept what is thus proffered. And I have said '*partly* due' because even with this restriction there are obviously many other factors which play a part in determining the degree of this readiness. Both from everyday observation and from various systematic investigations there is every reason to suppose that such things as intellectual capacity, temperamental factors such as a generalized enthusiasm or the reverse, the associations that he has formed with things religious, and the kinds of religious believers with whom he has been in personal contact, will affect an individual's readiness to accept certain beliefs with a given degree of assurance and a given sort of integration with other aspects of his personality. (Moreover, we should not lose sight of the possibility that theistic belief has very different psychological roots in different sorts of people and that psychoanalysis might give part of the explanation for some but not for all.) Given this obvious diversity in the determinants of theistic belief, if we try to inflate any of the current theoretical approaches into a theory which claims to provide a specification of sufficient conditions it becomes hopelessly implausible. And thus far no one has made any plausible suggestions as to how we might develop a theory which integrates all the relevant factors. Therefore, in the absence of any genuine actual example, I am going to take the psychoanalytic explanation as one which might, with suitable supplementation, be developed into the sort of theory in which I am interested, and in referring to it as an example I shall be pretending such supplementation has actually been carried out.

There are various other questions which might be raised concerning the boundaries of the kind of theory in which we are interested. Just what are we to count as theistic belief? For example, does the sort of religious belief which Paul Tillich says he has count? More generally, to just what extent does a Supreme Being have to be conceived as a person in order for the belief to be classified as theistic? And are we considering simply the bare belief that there exists an omnipotent perfectly good personal Being, or are we also including other typical components of a theistic theology, such as the doctrines of creation and predestination, and certain sorts of beliefs concerning human nature and destiny?

Again, will the theory try to account for variations in the strength and/or persistence of such beliefs in terms of variations in the factors, or will it be simply an explanation of presence-or-absence, defined by some cutoff point? There are many such issues which would have to be settled by someone setting out to refine and develop such theories, but for our purpose we can leave these alternatives open. We shall simply suppose that a theory has been established which defines theistic belief in a way which makes it possible to reliably determine when we have it and when we don't, and in a way which does not significantly jar with the established use of the term; and that the theory relates the existence and/or degrees of such belief to certain factors in the natural world.

There is one further restriction on the theories in which we are interested which must be made explicit. Let us suppose that there are one or more cogent arguments for the existence of God, and let us suppose that it can be shown that a grasp of one of these arguments, plus acceptance of the premises, is always sufficient to bring about theistic belief, unless certain specifiable and enumerable forms of irrationality are present. The fact that someone understands a certain argument and the fact that someone accepts certain propositions are surely facts within the natural world. Yet I suppose that no one would have the slightest inclination to say that the adequacy of this sort of explanation would have any tendency to show the belief to be unacceptable. I want to restrict my attention to possible explanations with respect to which there would be an inclination to say this. This restriction can be carried out by including a proviso that the theories specify conditions which do not include acquiring, considering or possessing good reasons for theistic belief. I shall put this by saying that these theories specify 'reason-irrelevant' conditions. This will still leave us with a wide range of examples, including the psychoanalytic theory.

II

We can now turn to the central question of this paper: Would the success of an explanation of religious belief in terms of natural factors have any tendency to show such belief to be unacceptable? We may as well begin by considering the most extreme claim which could be made on this matter, viz., that such explanations of religious beliefs as the Freudian show that these beliefs can no longer be considered serious candidates for acceptance. We can distinguish different versions of this view, depending on just what aspect of the explanation is supposed to give it this force. Presumably it will be either the general point that theistic belief is due to some reason-irrelevant natural causes[14] or other, or it will be the more specific point that it is due to the particular sort of natural causes specified in the psychoanalytic explanation. I shall consider each of these possibilities in turn.

A

Why should anyone suppose that the fact that there are casual factors within the world of nature which are responsible for theistic belief constitute any reason

---

[14]Henceforth when I use the phrase 'natural cause' or even simply 'cause' the appropriate qualifications are to be understood.

for rejecting the belief? One cannot appeal here to a general principle that any belief can be refuted by showing that it is due to natural causes. For if we accept causal determinism within the psychological sphere, and those whose positions are being considered presumably would, then such causal determinations could, in principle, be exhibited for any belief whatsoever. There would have to be something special about the belief in a theistic God which would render it specially liable to such refutation. Now there are undoubtedly some beliefs which could be refuted by showing them to be causally determined, e.g., the belief that no beliefs are causally determined (assuming that we can get around self-referential difficulties here). Similarly it might be supposed that theism has implications which are incompatible with a causal determination of theistic belief. For example, it might be claimed that it would not be in keeping with the character and/or purposes of a theistic God to allow belief or non-belief in his existence to be determined by any natural factors; that he would reserve such a sacred matter as this for his own direct jurisdiction.

I do not suppose that anyone would claim that such causal determination is *logically* incompatible with the existence of God. Surely there is nothing in the theistic notion of God which would make it impossible that God should set up the natural world in such a way that belief in his existence would be produced by certain natural mechanisms. The fact that such belief is especially important to him does nothing to establish any such conclusion. For there is no reason to doubt that he could so arrange things that the operation of such mechanisms would be such as to be in line with his purposes. Indeed there are many other things in the universe which are presumably very important to God's plans (indeed, what isn't?) which everyone admits to be causally determined, e.g. the revolution of the earth around the sun and the biological processes responsible for the functioning of plants. The most that could be claimed with any plausibility is that one would not *expect* a theistic God to arrange things so that theistic belief is so controlled. I will resist the temptation to oppose this on the grounds that no human being can have any grounds for expecting an omnipotent Creator to act in one way rather than another. For if that is the way the game is played we are also prevented from having any *a posteriori* grounds for deciding whether such a Being exists, and I would take that to be a severe blow to theistic belief. Moreover, in so far as our concept of God has any content we have some reason, on some level of generality, for expecting one thing rather than another; and if the concept has no content then religion evaporates. However, in this particular case I would like to say that I do not see that the great importance or sanctity of this matter carries any strong presumption that God would not tie the belief to natural causes. I suppose I would admit to some mild surprise at finding a theistic God operating in this manner. But if anything is clear, it is that there are many features of the world which are not quite what one would initially expect from such a deity, and that if the belief can survive those that are repeatedly brought out in discussions of the problem of evil, it has nothing to fear from the present point.

There is one stronger reason for regarding such causal determination as discordant or even strictly incompatible with theism. This is the idea that it is part of God's plan to leave decision on belief or non-belief (in this matter) to the free choice of the individual. God has created man as a free moral agent and has left him to work out his own destiny. And among the most crucial choices which each individual has to make for himself is this one—whether to recognize the divine existence, with everything that this entails, or to blind oneself to it. (This line of thought requires the assumption that the divine existence is obvious to anyone who does not *avoid* it.) But if such belief is causally determined, then the individual does not have a free choice in this matter. *Ergo.* . . . This line of argument, even if sound, does not show that causal determination of theistic belief is incompatible with certain views as to the divine purpose that are firmly entrenched in theistic thought.

This issue cannot be considered here because it raises all the fundamental problems about free will. The line of argument just sketched presupposes that if a certain belief is causally determined then one can't make a free choice as to whether to accept it or not. (I am leaving aside the further difficulty that it may be a mistake to use notions like choice and decision with respect to belief.) But whether this is so is perhaps the chief issue in discussions about free will, and there are powerful reasons for doubting that it is the case. In any event, if psychoanalytic theory comes into conflict with theism on this ground, it does so together with any view which regards human actions as causally determined. And so we are not faced here with a difficulty for theism which is in any way special to the causal determination of *theistic belief.*

But let us remember that we are dealing, not with explanations in terms of *any* natural factor, but specifically with those in terms of reason-irrelevant factors. And it might be thought that this restriction would put us in a better position to demonstrate an incompatibility. Can we suppose that a deity which is the source of rationality would structure things in such a way that theistic belief is produced by irrational factors; i.e., in such a way that those who have the belief are (or may be) without any real basis for the belief? Well one can easily construe a concept of God which would rule out such causal determination, but it is not at all clear that the concept of God in, e.g., Christianity, always or even usually is of this sort. References in Christian literature to God as the source of reason are far outnumbered by apostrophes to the inscrutability, mysteriousness or downright irrationality (by human standards) of the divine activity. God as a cosmic mathematician is a modern invention. And of course to a religious thinker like Kierkegaard rationality is the last thing in the world God is interested in promoting.

There seems, then, to be little reason to suppose that the fact, if it is a fact, that theistic belief is causally determined directly furnishes any *evidence* against theistic belief. And this is not surprising. For psychological investigations into the causation of beliefs, even this belief, is the wrong quarter in which to look for such evidence. One looks for evidence for and against the Darwinian theory of evolution not in the factors which make people accept it or the reverse, but in the results of palaeontology, comparative anatomy and the experimental production of mutations in fruit flies. And the fact that Kepler developed his heliocentric theory of the solar system under the influence of his quasi-religious sun-worship is not thought to be a relevant consideration if we are trying to determine whether his theory is correct. Of course in attempting to transfer these points to the theistic case we run into the fact that it is much more difficult here to say what would be relevant evidence. But in spite of all the problems that can be raised about the traditional arguments for the existence of God, I feel confident in saying that the order, or lack thereof, in the world, the existence of evil and the facts of human morality, are the right sort of thing to consider in a way that factors productive of theistic belief are not—if we are looking for positive or negative evidence.

I have still done nothing to rule out the possibility that a theory of the sort we are considering could do something in a more indirect way to weaken theistic belief, e.g., by showing that certain supposed reasons for acceptance are not sound ones, or by providing reasons for doubting that any adequate supporting reasons can be found. Something of the former sort is suggested by Freud in *The Future of an Illusion*.

Now, it is quite true that if anyone should argue that the existence of religious belief could only be explained by supposing that God himself had communicated it to men (that men could never have thought of all this by themselves, that the conceptions are too lofty to be initially formed by men, etc.), then showing another way in which such belief can be, and is, brought about disposes of this argument. It would nullify, e.g., the argument put forth by Descartes in his *Meditations* to the effect that the presence of the idea of God in the human mind can only be explained by supposing that God himself is ultimately responsible for putting it there. (Of course this does nothing to show that God has not in fact revealed truths to men; it only shows that we cannot hold that he has done so on *these* grounds. Note too that the sort of theory we are considering takes as one of the factors to be used in explaining the occurrence of theistic belief in the individual the existence of certain conceptions and certain beliefs in the culture to which that individual is exposed. This means that the ultimate origin of that cultural tradition is still unexplained, and as long as this is the case, a wedge is left for the revelationist.) But this is hardly a serious consequence; theism is not usually defended in this way.

There is one important way of supporting theistic belief which would certainly be adversely affected, perhaps fatally, by causal explanations. I am referring to the claim that one can be sure of the existence of God because one has directly experienced the presence of God.[15] Of course there are different sorts of experiences which have been so construed, and a complete discussion would have to take account of these differences, but for purposes of illustration we can once more revert to Freudian theory and consider a Freudian explanation of certain very pervasive features of mystical experience—(1) a breakdown of the usual boundaries of the self, a sense of a merging of oneself into the object, loss of separateness; (2) joy, which sometimes reaches rapturous intensity, combined with a profound sense of peace. If we look, as a Freudian would, for analogues of this in the development of the individual, we can find it in the experience of the infant. As reconstructed by psychoanalysis the infant's experience lacks the self-world distinction. He has to learn by hard experience what is part of him and what is outside him. Thus his consciousness is, in Freud's apt terminology, 'oceanic'. He feels an inseparable connection between himself and his environment; or rather he just feels, without referring contents to different sources.

---

[15]General explanations of theistic belief would not have any bearing on the force of this reason, except for the way in which a specification of necessary and sufficient reason-irrelevant conditions cuts off the possibility of any adequate reasons, as explained below.

Moreover, if we consider the fed, satisfied baby on the edge of sleep, we may find the prototype of the profoundly peaceful rapture with which the mystic is suffused.

Then, by invoking the familiar concepts of fixation and of regression we can suppose that such experiences arise as follows. People differ in the extent to which they outgrow the desires, modes of thought, etc., of a given stage of development, and this certainly seems to be the case with respect to the early infantile stage; consider the well-established concept of the 'oral personality'. When an adult who still has strong but repressed desires to be in the infantile situation runs into severe difficulties and frustrations, a regression will ensue. One of the things this means is that the desires appropriate to that stage will be strengthened and press even more insistently for some sort of satisfaction. One form such satisfaction could take is an hallucinatory experience in which the individual feels himself to be in something like the infantile situation, suitably reinterpreted (as immediate union with God) so as to be acceptable to one's consciously held standards. Thus we find Ostow and Scharfstein quoting the following from Porphyry's *Life of Plotinus:* 'Plotinus would tell his disciples how, at the age of eight, when he was already going to school, he still clung about his nurse and loved to bare her breasts and take suck: one day he was told he was a "perverted imp" and so was shamed out of the trick'. The authors then go on to say, 'The tendency to retreat and demand the love and security granted an infant had already been established, and his later longing to join God in a union of love was a reappearance on a new level of the old desire'.[16]

I do not want to suggest that there is any strong reason to believe that this is a correct explanation of such experiences. (There is, again, no direct evidence at all.) I simply present it as an example of the sort of explanation I wish to consider. Supposing that some such theory were established, what bearing, if any, would this have on claims that in such experiences one is directly apprehending God? There are those who maintain that the success of such explanations would constitute a refutation of the claim. So far as I can see the strongest way to support this position is to say that if we can show that there are natural factors which are sufficient to produce experiences of this sort, then one is unwarranted in claiming that divine activity or influence must be at least partly responsible for their occurrence, and hence that one has no basis for supposing that one is in contact with God when one has such an experience. To this it will, no doubt, be replied that causal origin is one thing and epistemological status another, and that answering questions about one does not suffice to answer questions about the other. More specifically, to say what one perceived on a given occasion is not to say what produced one's perception (or the sensations that were involved in the perception), and *vice versa.* Hence the fact that one's experience is produced by certain psychological factors, independently of any supernatural influence, leaves completely open the question whether one is perceiving God in that experience.

Clearly this raises fundamental questions concerning the concept of perception. There are those who affirm and those who deny that a necessary condition of perceiving x is that x be among the factors which produce the experience

---

[16]Mortimer Ostow and Ben-Ami Scharfstein, *The Need to Believe* (New York: International Universities Press, 1954), p. 118.

(sensation, awareness of sensa, etc.) involved in the supposed perception. (It is a further question whether the notion of perception can be completely analysed in such terms.) The parties to the above dispute will, of course, take opposite positions on this issue. I am unable to go into these matters here. I will only say that it seems to me plausible to say that the presence of *x* somewhere (not too far back) in the chain of causes giving rise to a certain experience is one necessary condition of that experience being involved in a perception of *x*. This principle seems to be supported by some of the procedures we use in determining whether or not someone has directly perceived something. If a thick brick wall was so placed as to prevent light waves from a house from reaching my eyes, then I could not have seen that house at that time.

It seems reasonable to take principles which are well established with respect to sense-perception, an area where we pretty much know what to say under a given set of conditions, and extend them to the discussion of purported direct experiences of God, an area where it is not at all clear what one should say. Thus I am inclined to agree that a successful explanation of certain mystical experiences in terms of purely natural factors would enable us to disallow claims that in these experiences one is directly apprehending God.

But even if there are certain ways of justifying theistic beliefs which could be discredited by psychological explanations—either of theistic belief in general or of the way in question—there would always remain the possibility that there were other modes of justification which would turn out to be valid. To do any real damage the Freudian theory would have to provide reason for supposing that no adequate justification could be given.

Construed in a certain way Freudian theory will have this consequence. Up to now I have been interpreting a causal theory in such a way that it purports to specify *sufficient* conditions of religious belief. But suppose we understand our imaginary enriched Freudianism to put forward its factors as both sufficient and necessary for religious belief. Then it follows that no adequate reasons could be given. For if there were such reasons, the grasp of them by a rational man would itself be a sufficient condition of his accepting the belief.

I am sure that many will oppose this thesis on the grounds that reasons are one thing and causes quite another. Hence to say that someone has adequate reasons for a certain belief is to say nothing about the causes of his coming to have the belief, and to say that someone's belief is due to certain causes is to say nothing about the reasons that he might or might not have for it. But this seems to me to be mistaken. Of course a reason cannot be a cause, nor can a cause be a reason. They exist in logically different realms. But that does not mean that a statement about reasons cannot have implications concerning causes and *vice versa.* It seems quite clear to me that to say that A's reason for thinking that his lawn-mower is in his garage is that he saw it there in the morning, or that B's reason for thinking that the Republicans will show gains in the 1962 elections is that the party which does not have control of the presidency generally gains in off-year elections, is to imply something about the causes which have (or might have) given rise to his having this belief, or at least something about the causes which maintain his belief. It would be absurd to say 'A has every reason to believe that *x*, but I can't imagine what led him to believe that'. Conversely, to say that A's belief that there exists an omnipotent personal Being is *wholly* due to cultural conditioning in early childhood plus a projection of an unconscious father-image onto the Being envisaged in that cultural training is to deny that he has any reason for the belief. For if he had a reason, the psychological processes involved in becoming aware of the considerations involved in the reason, and in connecting them to the belief in question, would be at least part of what led him to have or retain the belief.

But this is a hollow triumph for the psychoanalytic critic of theistic religion. For the psychoanalytic factors could be established as necessary as well as sufficient conditions only if we could be sure that no one could acquire sufficient reasons for the belief; for if he could the belief could be produced in some other way.[17] Since the establishment of reason-irrelevant necessary and sufficient conditions presupposes that no sound reasons can be given, it can hardly be used to warrant that claim.

Now if we are dealing only with an established claim that there are reason-irrelevant causal factors which are sufficient to produce that belief (and furthermore are in general what is responsible for producing it), then what? Of course it follows that anyone whose belief is produced in this way lacks any sound basis for the belief. But what implication should I draw from it for *my* state of religious belief? Well, if I have adequate reasons for the belief myself it will do nothing to shake my confidence in those grounds. And justifiably. Why should I abandon what I can see to be sound reason for the belief just because it has been shown that many other people hold the belief without having any such grounds? It may be said that the demonstration that the belief is generally held as a result of unconscious projections might well make me suspicious of the cogency of my reasons. My belief might be caused by similar projections and I might be deceiving myself into thinking that I have good reasons in order to put a good face on the matter. And so I might. I would agree that the psychoanalytic results would properly make me suspicious and that in the light of this the reasonable thing for me to do would be to scrutinize my reasons very carefully. But if I have looked on them and have seen that they are good, what more is there for me to do.[18] And if I do not have adequate reasons for the belief, we have already seen that the existence of reason-irrelevant sufficient conditions does nothing to show that there could not be adequate reasons for the belief.

There still remains one way in which the success of a theory of the sort we are considering might have some relevance. If a man has no grounds of any magnitude for deciding the question of the existence of God one way or the other, he might be faced with the question of whether this is an issue which is worth considering further. After all, there are many important theses which at present we are unable to either prove or disprove, and we only have a limited amount of time and energy to devote to such matters. In this instance, he might take note of the fact that there are many people, including many intelligent and

---

[17]It is significant that in *The Future of an Illusion* Freud prefaces his presentation of his explanation of theistic belief with a chapter in which he argues that there is no sound ground for the belief. Though if I am correct he should have gone further and argued that there *could be* no sound ground.

[18]There is also the case in which I came to the belief *via* the Freudian route and then subsequently found really adequate reasons. In this case we should not say that in the later stages the belief is *really* due to the psychoanalytic factors alone. For now the situation has changed in such a way that even if the unconscious pressures should cease to operate I would still have a strong tendency to retain the belief.

thoughtful people, who accept this belief, and this might lead him to conclude that it is a matter which should be looked into further. But now if it could be shown that, so far as we can tell, what leads these peoole to adopt this belief is something which is quite irrelevant to its truth or falsity, this would nullify the above reason for taking the issue seriously. Thus a causal explanation could, under these conditions, properly have the effect of counteracting a possible reason for regarding the question as one which is worth exploring further. Not much of a consequence, but something.

Thus I am forced to conclude that the fact, if it is a fact, that reason-irrelevant causal factors are sufficient to produce theistic belief has little or no tendency to show that the belief is false, unlikely to be true, or not worthy of serious consideration. And remember that we have arrived at this conclusion with respect to an imagined theory which would present at least sufficient conditions for the belief. As for theories of the sort we actually have, which can reasonably claim nothing more than a certain degree of correlation between theistic belief and certain factors, the case would be even worse. For such theories leave ample room for the operation of awareness of reasons in the production of the belief. And here there is even less reason to think that a theistic God would not set things up so that such partial correlations would not obtain.

B

Thus far we have simply been considering Freudian theory as an example of the general claim that theistic belief is in general due solely to reason-irrelevant causal factors. But the Freudian theory has some special features which distinguish it from some of the other theories of this class and some of these might be relevant to our problem. More specifically, the theory tends to assimilate religious belief to infantile modes of thought and to neurotic manifestations. Remember that, according to the theory, theistic belief, like many neuroses, is based on a regression to infantile modes of psychic organization and that it bears traces of this regression in the way it conceives God and in the ways it leads men to feel toward God. Moreover, as Reik points out in elaborate detail in his two books on the subject, religion exhibits many of the features of neurotic compulsions both in its ritual and in its doctrinal aspects. Michael Argyle summarizes the points of similarity as follows:

(a) . . . obsessions and compulsions simultaneously allow some substitute gratification both of the desire and of its prohibition. . . . Reik . . . similarly traces the development of ideas about the Trinity as a compromise between ideas of filial rebellion and veneration for the father.

(b) The neurotic's rituals have a compulsive character, in that he must carry them out conscientiously and experiences guilt if he fails to do so: this is to some extent true of religious rituals too.

(c) In religion there are taboos—of Sunday work, food before communion, and so forth: neurotics also have things which they must avoid touching or thinking about. . . . Reik . . . points out that the taboos surrounding religious dogma develop as a defence against scepticism: at the same time the dogma is developed in absurd detail, reflecting an underlying contempt for it.

(d) The real conflict in neurotics becomes displaced on to trivial details and verbal matters; this is also the case with religion, where the dogmas and rituals become elaborated in enormous detail, minute parts of which may become the basis for schisms and persecutions.[19]

On the basis of all this it is argued, or more often suggested, that beliefs which have this status, which are essentially infantile and/or neurotic in character could not be taken seriously by rational, adult individuals. This sort of claim is clearly different from the one based on the mere existence of *some* sort of causal determination, and it must be examined separately.

But first note that it is not at all clear that *this* argument requires that we suppose the psychoanalytic theory inflated into a complete statement of causal conditions. It would seem plausible to suggest that the existence of substantial correlations between theistic belief and such factors as degree of unconscious conflict, tendency to regression, etc., would do as much, or almost as much, to show that theistic belief has an infantile and/or neurotic *character* as would the development of a complete theory integrating these factors with others. For presumably the other factors that would have to be included—degree of intelligence, cultural training, etc., would not add anything to the force of the diagnosis. Hence in this section we can work with the theory as we actually have it.

In evaluating this claim we must first make some important distinctions which are generally overlooked. First we must, as noted earlier, distinguish between the existence of similarities between the *forms* taken by theistic belief and the *forms* of infantile and neurotic behaviour, and the existence of causal factors for theistic belief of an infantile or neurotic kind. A great deal of the psychoanalytic discussion of religion consists simply of pointing out similarities, as with the similarities between obsessional neurosis and theistic belief listed above, and supposing that this shows that the two are fundamentally the same sort of thing. But such surface similarities are radically insufficient to bear the weight of such a conclusion. A man 'obsessed' with a radically new idea, who is constantly preoccupied with thinking it through, seeing its implications, devising ways to test it, etc., exhibits striking similarities to obsessional neurotics, but it would be a great mistake to dismiss his theorizing on this basis. And in fact, despite the obvious similarities in patterns of overt behaviour, his 'obsession' with the idea may be psychologically quite a different thing and may have very different psychological roots from the obsession of the neurotic. When I look at a snake in a zoo my experience may be phenomenally quite similar to that of a man suffering from hallucinations in delirium tremens, but it would be a great mistake to conclude from this that my experience is really an hallucination, or that this shows that there are really no such things as snakes. Surface similarities can be misleading.

But with respect to the charge that religion is a neurosis, the Freudian theory goes beyond these similarities and posits similar underlying mechanisms. But here, too, we must distinguish between two views which are not always distinguished. (1) Among the important causal factors producing theistic belief is

---

[19]Michael Argyle, *Religious Behaviour* (London: Routledge and Kegan Paul, 1958), p. 165.

always some neurosis of a commonly recognized sort. (2) Some of the important causal factors here are the same as some which play a crucial role in producing certain neuroses. There seems to be no evidence at all for (1), not even if we restrict our sample to neurotic believers! I shall confine my attention to (2).

If the Freudian theory as presented earlier is to be adequate, there are common causal conditions for neurosis and theistic belief—a substantial amount of unconscious conflict, a tendency to regression, etc. But the question remains as to whether this justifies Freud in terming religion 'the universal obsessional neurosis of humanity'.[20] Why should we not rather say that given these common causal conditions there are two ways in which the individual may respond—either by a neurosis or by religious faith? Of course we could say with Freud that this is just the difference between an idiosyncratic neurosis and a socially approved neurosis. But we might also say, with Jung, that a religious orientation is an alternative to neurosis, or even constitutes a prophylaxis against, or cure for, a neurosis. How can we choose between these positions?

In considering this question we are forced to get clearer about the term 'neurosis', and more particularly about the sense of this term, if any, in which there would be any plausibility in saying that the fact that a belief arises out of a neurosis shows that we do not have to take it seriously. There are various ways of defining 'neurosis' and more general terms like 'psychological abnormality'. If we define a neurosis in terms of underlying causal factors, as is often done, e.g., in terms of the amount of conflict which is unconscious and therefore not resoluble by rational deliberation, then in order to show that a belief can be dismissed from serious consideration on the grounds that it arises out of a neurosis we would need a supplementary argument to the effect that any belief so produced is unlikely to be correct. But we know too little about the effects of unconscious processes to have any confidence in any such principle. Moreover, if we widen the sphere to cover kinds of disguised resolutions of unconscious conflicts other than beliefs, we can think of many such cases which would not be classified as harmful or undesirable—e.g. (to take a couple of favourite textbook examples) the resolution of unconscious conflict over aggression by developing skill as a surgeon or resolution of unconscious conflict over love of one's mother by specializing in painting madonnas.

Therefore it seems that if we are to draw negatively evaluative implications from connection with a neurosis we shall have to build some negative evaluations into the concept of neurosis. And I believe that this is usually what is done. Included in the commonly-used working criteria for calling a state a neurosis is the requirement that this state have the effect of hampering the individual in his 'adjustments to the environment' or in his attempts to achieve his aims in life. If that is part of the definition of a neurosis, then there is some plausibility in holding that a belief which arises from a neurosis is, *ipso facto,* unlikely to be correct. For if a neurosis has the effect of hampering the individual's attempts to get along in his environment, then the hampering would presumably involve among other things, producing false beliefs about the environment, or suppressing or warping true beliefs. And in fact this is one of the prominent features of

---

[20]Sigmund Freud, *The Future of an Illusion,* translated by W. D. Robson-Scott (New York: Liveright, 1953), p. 76.

neurosis. But now what happens is this. As people develop confidence in a theory of the causal basis of states which satisfy the initial criteria for neurosis, we get the familiar phenomenon of transition from synthetic to analytic connections; the underlying causal mechanisms come to be themselves used as criteria. It is then easy to assume unquestioningly, with respect to anything which satisfies these latter criteria, that it will have the unfortunate effects which were among the initial criteria. But, of course, the proposition that anything which results from certain sorts of unconscious processes will hamper the individual's pursuit of his goals is a generalization which must be tested separately for each new range of cases.

Hence the matter stands as follows. In order to argue that theistic belief, since neurotic, is unworthy of serious consideration, one must be holding the term 'neurosis' subject to the evaluative criteria mentioned earlier. But so long as all we have shown is that this belief is due to certain unconscious processes, we have no right to call it neurotic in this sense. To gain this right we would have to show that a person who has a theistic belief is less able to function effectively than he would have been without it. And no one has ever begun to show this.

Moreover, there are some profound difficulties which intrude themselves when we consider the possibility of establishing such a conclusion. A psychoana·lytically-minded writer who set out to do so would, presumably, proceed by determining whether religious believers were less able to establish satisfying personal relations, get ahead in their professions, etc., than non-religious believers who were identical in other respects. But even if this could be established the theist might complain we have been too restrictive in our survey of the 'environment' and of what constitutes 'success' or 'effective functioning' therein. If we include the 'supernatural environment' in our survey, it would seem plausible to suppose that theistic belief would be a powerful, or rather indispensable, aid to effective functioning with respect to *it*. And if we did not include it, our opponent might accuse us of stacking the cards against him. 'You are', he would say, 'using a criterion of effective functioning which already presupposes that my beliefs are false. For if they are not false, it would be quite reasonable to suppose that the conditions which were conducive to effective functioning and accurate apprehension with respect to two such different realms would be radically different.' As James put it, 'If there were such a thing as inspiration from a higher realm, it might well be that the neurotic temperament would furnish the chief condition of the requisite receptivity'.[21]

It is hard to know what to say about this issue. This may be one point at which there is, in the nature of the case, a complete *impasse* between the theist and his psychoanalytic critic.

To sum up, even if the psychoanalytic theory of the causal basis of theistic belief is correct, there seems to be no reason to say that therefore religion is a happy alternative to a neurosis; and therefore there is no reason for suggesting, on these grounds, that theistic belief is false, probably false, or unworthy of serious consideration.

The charge that theistic belief can be dismissed as infantile in character can be handled more briefly. This is based solely on the surface similarities between

[21] *The Varieties of Religious Experience* (Longmans, London, 1952, *and* New American Library, New York, 1958).

the theistic conception of God, and the believer's feelings and attitudes toward him, and the child's conception of, and feeling and attitude toward, his father. (The matter of regression to an infantile orientation has already been handled as part of the grounds for regarding religion as a neurosis.) Such similarities may be admitted. But the theist might well reply that whether such conceptions, attitudes, etc., are warranted is wholly a matter of whether his beliefs are true. It would be unworthy of an adult human being to take up such attitudes toward another human being. But if theism is correct, we do as a matter of fact, stand in a relation to God very similar to that in which we stood to our fathers in early childhood, and therefore, if theism is correct, such attitudes and feelings are quite appropriate. In view of this fact one could hardly use such similarities as a basis for rejecting theistic claims. In general, a set of facts which are perfectly compatible with a theory can do nothing to weaken the plausibility of that theory.

We should note that here too it makes a difference whether the theory is asserting only sufficient, or necessary and sufficient, conditions. If it is the former (and we have seen that this is the only form of the theory which is not clearly unjustified), then in addition to the moves already considered it is open to the theist to hold that although many people may hold religious beliefs as the result of the unconscious mechanisms in question, the belief can and sometimes is, held as a result of other factors. That is, it is open to him to distinguish between quasi-neurotic and non-quasi-neurotic ways of being religious. Of course he may not be able to show any sufficient conditions of the latter sort, but at least the theory in the weaker form does nothing to indicate that this would be impossible.

III

In this paper I have been considering the possible bearing of causal explanations of theistic belief on the question of whether there are, or might be, adequate reasons for or against such beliefs. What emerges from the foregoing discussion is the, by no means novel, conclusion that in religion as elsewhere there is no substitute for the detailed examination of evidence which has a direct bearing on the truth or falsity of a given belief, and that, in particular, investigations of the factors which generally produce the belief is no such substitute. As I say, this conclusion is nothing new; if the present discussion has added anything to previous discussions it is by way of considering more thoroughly and patiently some of the relevant distinctions.

But there is another way in which causal theories might be relevant to a decision on the acceptability of theistic belief. Consider the position of James in *The Will to Believe,* or the more extreme position of Kierkegaard, according to both of whom believing in God is somehow justifiable, even though no adequate reasons can be presented either for or against the proposition that God exists. (That is, even though we cannot discover adequate reasons in support of the proposition that God exists, we can discover adequate reasons for the proposition that it is justifiable to believe that God exists.) Such support may be of different sorts. In *The Will to Believe* James says that we are going to take some position on this problem without having adequate reasons for it in any event, so 'hat we may as well recognize the inevitable and accept it with good grace.

Kierkegaard supposes that if he presents the stance of faith and contrasting stances in sufficient concreteness, the reader will see that the former is the only possible stance for one who resolutely faces the facts of the human situation. One might wonder whether a psychoanalytic explanation of theistic belief, if established, would properly have any bearing on one's response to the position of these authors. That is, would an acceptance of the psychoanalytic explanation properly influence my decision as to whether or not it is justifiable to believe in God without adequate evidence for his existence?

This question presents very different problems from those already considered, problems that I cannot really discuss at the tail-end of a paper that is already too long. To settle the question we would have to decide what sorts of considerations properly influence a decision as to the justifiability of accepting a proposition under these conditions. I do not know how to lay down a criterion which will separate proper from improper considerations here, and perhaps no such separation can be made. Perhaps if we have abandoned the attempt to show that the proposition is true or false and are still trying to decide whether it is all right to believe it, then anything goes. But even if there still is a distinction between relevant and irrelevant considerations, it is hard to see how facts about the usual causal basis of the belief could be excluded. If one is to admit as relevant facts about the psychological consequences of accepting the belief, about the relative or absolute inevitability of taking some stand or other on a question, and about the way acceptance of the belief will have logical implications for the way various enquiries can and cannot be carried out (and facts of all these sorts have been adduced by philosophers who have discussed this sort of question), it is hard to see how facts about the causal basis of the belief can be excluded. Thus it might be quite pertinent, if not conclusive, in this sort of context to deny that theistic belief is justifiable, on the grounds that it involves acquiescing in a regression to an infantile mode of thought.

IV

There is one other sort of way in which causal explanations might be relevant to the status of theism, but, although I feel that this dimension of the problem is quite important, I am unable to formulate it clearly enough to even begin to determine just how much it does come to. It is often remarked that the general climate of thought in which supernaturalistic theology flourishes is very different from that in which intellectual endeavour is largely devoted to searching out empirically testable causal generalizations. Not that there is any logical incompatibility between a sophisticated theism and the search for such generalizations, or even between theism and a dogmatic determinism. It is just that the general cast of thought which naturally lead to taking the one or the other very seriously are quite different. So long as the search for natural causes shies away from human thought, experience and behaviour, it is relatively easy to distinguish the physical world, investigated by science, from the supernatural realm, which makes contact with man through religion. But when the search for natural causes extends to man, including religious thought, experience and behaviour, such compartmentalization is not so easy. It is still possible, as we have seen in the various moves made in the body of this paper, to distinguish causal explanation of a belief from a disproof of that belief. But to carry it through introduces more and more strain. Therefore it seems that the thorough-going success of a theory like the Freudian would help to render the climate of thought even more antithetical to full-blooded theistic belief. But what implications, if any, this has on the justifiability of theistic belief, I do not know.

CRITERIA FOR APPRAISAL IN COMPARATIVE RELIGION
Ninian Smart

Ninian Smart, "Revelation, Reason and Religion," from Ian Ramsay (ed.), *The Prospect for Metaphysics*, reprinted by permission of the publishers, George Allen & Unwin, Ltd., London, © 1956; and Philosophical Library, New York, © 1961.

Natural theology is the Sick Man of Europe. In view of the subtle and exhaustive objections adduced by Hume, Kant and modern empiricists against the traditional arguments for God's existence, it is no longer reasonable to rely upon these particular supports for theistic belief. But the alternative is not irrationalism, for this can give us no guidance as to what we should choose: why be Christian rather than Hindu, or religious rather than atheistical? But if we can rely neither on metaphysical reasoning nor on unreasoning, we might feel tempted to write off religion altogether. Yet its truth-suggesting fascination in daily life and the testimony of many profound and holy men is not lightly to be disregarded. It is not my present task, however, to produce the theologian's stone, the long-searched-for argument that will convince the outsider. Rather I wish to consider whether there is a middle way between traditional natural theology and some simple appeal to revelation (or to any other authority). I wish, in effect, to adumbrate the religious reasons for holding doctrines. For I believe on the one hand, with the revelationists, that one cannot excogitate religious truth: one has to judge what is given, in the form of revelations and teachings—since ordinary philosophers and theologians are neither prophets nor Buddhas. But I believe on the other hand, with the rationalistically inclined, that one can still detect considerations favouring one position rather than another.

But first a word about philosophical analysis. I take it that the job of the philosopher here is to elucidate, as far as possible, the manner in which religious propositions[1] have meaning. This involves connecting up doctrines and experience. Now of course there is no special reason for philosophers to confine themselves to Christian doctrines and life; indeed, to be fair it is necessary to

---

[1] I use the word 'proposition' here as a generic term to cover statements, commands, etc.

consider other luminous teachings, such as those of Buddhism. Nor can it be pretended that all the great religions are saying the same thing—even if some; times their doctrines overlap. But in a way this is fortunate, since contrasts help us to see the reasons for them, and in the comparative study of religions one is not merely enabled to view religious teachings (especially one's own) afresh, but one is also offered the chance to gain some further insight into the relation between beliefs and experiences. In brief, if one regards philosophical analysis here as a rather specialized branch of the comparative study of religion, one can acquire a little more clarity about the religious reasons implicit in revelation. But so far, the philosopher is being a neutral in the conflict of faiths. There is no absolute taboo, however, upon his descending into the dusty arena of general apologetic. I propose here to illustrate what can be done in this way in general defence of Christian doctrine. Admittedly, this need not be the job for a philosopher. But on the other hand, the purism of thinking that philosophical analysis is the only proper employment for philosophers is excessive. Intellectual compartmentaliza-tion, though often good at the start, may be sterile at the finish.

Thus, one job a philosopher may do is general apologetic. And so the above remarks can be placed in a different context. One way of refurbishing traditional metaphysics is to claim that it expresses, or even evokes, intuitions or disclosures of the divine Being. Now an appeal to such notions must lead in the direction along which I have already pointed. For if the intuition is utterly bare, it can guarantee nothing which can be formulated in words, and is therefore of no use in supporting doctrines. It must at least lead more naturally to one's saying certain things rather than others, and must therefore (albeit in a weak sense) be expressible. On the other hand, it is scarcely realistic to suppose that such an intuition bears a label containing a detailed and legible inscription. If it did, intuitionism would be with difficulty distinguished from, and hardly more plausible than, fundamentalism. It seems, then, to follow that if there are such intuitions, they are dimly suggestive of certain doctrines rather than others; but only *dimly* suggestive. But further, if we appeal to metaphysical intuitions and disclosures we are already indulging in phenomenology; and there seems to be no good reason for confining ourselves to certain intuitions which may or may not arise in certain intellectual (or allegedly intellectual)[2] contexts, but rather ought to contemplate the whole field of religious phenomenology. If, for instance, we are speaking about God, it is reasonable to consider those experiences or disclosures which occur in specifically religious contexts, and which, though considerably ineffable, are dim pointers to certain forms of divine discourse rather than to others.

It might be objected that phenomenology involves merely the description of the psychological content of states of mind, whereas the whole point about an intuition is that it is cognitive, and thus cannot be considered merely as a psychological item. Consequently, it may be argued, an appeal to intuitions does not involve indulging in phenomenology (just as, when we are judging the report of an eyewitness, we are not dragged into a discussion of the psychology of

---

[2]It may be wondered whether an intuition arising through an argument (such as one of the Five Ways) which can no longer be treated as valid in any straightforward way can properly be described as intellectual; but in any case, it is rather artificial to distinguish between different faculties of the mind.

perception). Nevertheless, the contrast seems unrealistic, in the present instance, for a number of reasons. First, to say that an intuition is cognitive is to say that one knows (or claims to know) something in virtue of it; but the same would be true of many numinous experiences (although it must be confessed that more needs to be done to make the notion of 'knowing' in religious contexts perspicuous). Second, intuitions of God only become plausible if they chime in with what is yielded in revelations and disclosures of God (for otherwise why talk of them as 'of God'?); but this already suggests at least some resemblance between revelations and intuitions. Third, even though one can draw a contrast between epistemology and the psychology of perception, the facts pertaining to the latter are by no means irrelevant to the former. Fourth, where rules of reasoning are not clear (and they are not clear in religion) the distinction between what is to count as cognitive and what counts as merely an item in psychology (or social history, etc.) becomes quite blurred. Fifth, it seems more in accord with common sense to discuss religious truth not merely in the context of supposed intuitions but also in the milieu of those experiences and activities which give religion its living power. I therefore turn to consider specifically religious experiences and disclosures.

For example, the numinous experience analysed by Otto, though hardly definitive in its pronouncements, nevertheless provides the impulse to speak about gods or God. And again, rather differently, mystical experience (by which I mean the interior and imageless visions of the great Western mystics, the *samādhi* attained by the *yogin,* and so on, and which must be distinguished from those experiences mainly discussed by Otto),[3] though various in its flavours and interpretations, does have certain formal characteristics which suggest certain ways of speaking about that which is realized. In the ensuing, I am necessarily crude in my phenomenology, for this kind of task as I have set myself here cannot too well be attempted in so brief a compass.[4]

There is one further preliminary point before I proceed, namely that a defence of religion by appeal to intuitions or disclosures (the merits of different terms here have to be canvassed) need not entail that *all* people have such experiences. I am inclined to feel that there may be some intimation of divinity which every man may have; but such intimations *may* not occur to all, and in any case may well be of less evidential value than certain profounder revelations to the comparatively few.

Christianity presents an ideologically significant picture of the world which is not derivable from scientific investigations. The elaboration, systematization and general defence of this view of the world can not unreasonably be called an exercise in metaphysics. There does not appear to me to be any clear line between theology and speculation: for both are concerned with the kind of cosmos we live in. And at least it makes for explicitness to count Christian metaphysics as not an essay in the exercise of pure reason (which happens to be on the side of the angels), but a defence of a position which cannot be worked

---

[3]For a discussion of Otto's term 'numinous' and the distinct characters of the numinous and the mystical, see my 'Numen, Nirvana and the Definition of Religion' in *Church Quarterly Review,* April-June 1959, pp. 216–25.
[4]At least, however, I have the excuse of having treated these matters more fully in my *Reasons and Faiths* (London, 1958).

out by reason alone. Moreover, this is (in a broad, very broad, sense) an empirical approach, since we consider what is given rather than legislate for reality.

Christianity claims to be monotheistic. Of course, the doctrine of the Trinity seems at first sight to belie this fact, and it is a common accusation by Muslims that the belief in the Incarnation, by identifying God with a visible person, is setting up another God beside God. However, we shall return to this *prima facie* blasphemous and polytheistic character of Christianity in a moment. Meanwhile let us consider the reasons for preferring monotheism to polytheism. People may simply say, of course, that the truth just is that there is one God and that polytheists are heathens. But bad names get us nowhere. Perhaps certain intimations or intuitions tell men that there is something divine which glimmers in the world. But why one divine Being rather than many?

Can we not gain some insight into this matter? Perhaps the following considerations may help. First, monotheism gives us a more exalted view of the divine. But what if the divine is not that much exalted? All we can say here, maybe, is that the more profound and tremendous experiences of the numinous point in this direction. For the notion of discrete divinities, often clashing, hardly matches up to the overwhelming character of certain theophanies. Second, monotheism is simpler, and other things being equal we prefer the simpler hypothesis. Third, polytheism is more attached to local legend and therefore is less adaptable to those living outside the magic circle; and it is hard to believe that the experiences on which beliefs in the gods are based are so various in such distinct detail. Fourth, whether or not primeval religion was monotheistic, early religion is polytheistic, but shows a tendency to evolve towards monotheism or monism. Fifth, monotheism integrates better with moral insights (universal in nature) than does fragmentary polytheism, especially as the chaotic legends clustering around the gods may be far from edifying. Sixth, the mysterious and overwhelming presence can be linked aesthetically to the cosmological unease, the sense of the aweful contingency of the world. Seventh, monotheism, as we shall observe, chimes in, to some degree, with mystical experience.

It will be apparent that these comments on the religions of worship are somewhat aesthetic in character—rather formal explications of considerations which can be employed to back judgement. But if anything is to count as the adducing of reasons in religion, this is, I think, where we have to start.

But what of pantheism or monism? Do not all the above arguments favour such views as much as they do monotheism? And certainly the dividing line between pantheism and monotheism is shadowy. For example, how do we distinguish sharply between a picture of the divine Being concealed *within* all things and that of the divine Being as *beyond* them? It is not a matter simply of whether you have a three- or two-dimensional model (both admittedly not literal)? All, I think, that can be said is that again the monotheistic picture is more intensely numinous. It expresses more strongly and vividly the gulf fixed between worshipper and the object of worship, and thus gives more intense expression to that which is met with in theophany. Again, the astonishment incorporated in the cosmological argument, namely that it is not the case that nothing exists, fits in better with a monotheistic picture than with the pantheistic; for divine fiat links with contingency, whereas emanation hints at necessity.

Yet all these points might well pass the Buddhist by. For in Theravād·

Buddhism (not to mention the original teachings of Gautama) there is no doctrine of a divine Creator, no worship of a Supreme Being. Instead there is the interior mystical quest culminating in the attainment of *nirvāna*. Mystical quest, you may say? But is not mysticism a union with God? But that is looking at the matter theistically. And assuredly this is not the Buddhist notion, that there is a union between persons. Nevertheless, there are certain loose resemblances between the mystical goal (even in Buddhism) and the object of worship. These resemblances, while not necessitating a theistic interpretation, make it in some degree plausible. For in the mystical state, even on an agnostic interpretation, there is a timelessness reminiscent of divine immortality, a transcendence over mundane experience reminiscent of the otherness of the Supreme Being, a bliss which links up with the fascination of the numinous and with the notion of a divine *summum bonum,* a lack of ordinary perceptions which hints at the invisibility of the Creator, a power suggestive of grace—and so on. It is true that the lack of distinction between subject and object in the mystical state leads to doctrines of deification and union with God which may be thought to be blasphemous by the ordinary worshipper. And not unconnectedly, pantheism chimes in with the mystical quest: for if God be within all things, it is not absurd to look within ourselves. Still, though there are such difficulties, certainly mysticism can be suggestively interpreted by the theist as a kind of vision of God (and incidentally is less amenable to a polytheistic interpretation, since the comparatively 'this-wordly' aspect of the gods is less in accord with the imperceptibility and transcendence of the mystical goal, etc.).

Nevertheless, the Theravāda is splendid in its doctrinal simplicity. It eschews metaphysical speculations about Creation and immortality, but concentrates almost exclusively upon inner insight and peace and is not complicated by divine ritual. If we praise monotheism for its simplicity, why not praise this form of Buddhism likewise? Why not indeed? Let us do so. But the later history of Buddhism is instructive. The austere simplicity is replaced in the Mahāyāna by the proliferation of a doctrinally complex faith—one where many of the concepts of theism show themselves: the worship of Avalokiteśvara, doctrines of grace (or the transfer of merit), the Three-Body doctrine (so reminiscent of Christianity), and so on. The intimations of the numinous were perhaps not to be denied. If the Lesser Vehicle, like early Islām in a different way, is glorious in its single-mindedness, it is thereby less rich. The Advaita Vedānta, Ṣūfism and mystical Christianity, as well as the Mahāyāna, are, though complex in welding together different religious insights, more accommodating. Maybe this will be thought to be no great gain. But we can only judge from the experience of spiritual men; and at least in these teachings there is a fairly convincing weaving together of diverse strands of religious language and experience. The outer God who is concealed from our gaze by the visible cosmos reappears at the depths of the soul. The unspeakably majestic object of worship is found in the ineffability of interior insight. Where directions are not literal, we may perchance attain the same place by transcending the world outwards and inwards.

Admittedly it is hard to argue against such a doctrine as that of the Advaita, where the picture of God is relegated firmly to second place, and where the Godhead is described somewhat impersonally in accordance, *prima facie,* with the insights of the mystical vision. (Not for nothing was Śaṅkara called a crypto-Buddhist.) Here the picture of the personal Lord is itself implicated in the grand illusion of *māyā*. And one must note that this kind of illusionist idealism is naturally generated by mystical withdrawal. The Christian apologist can appeal merely to three points here. First, the strength and vividness of numinous experience may not warrant the relegation of the personal picture of the Lord to second place. Second, realism about the cosmos fits in better with moral insight; for the promptings of conscience and the sentiments of justice and love fade somewhat where all things are illusory. And third, transcendence of the unreal has less merit than transcendence of the real.[5]

So far, then, I have adduced what may be called religious reasons for a monotheism which can, so to speak, accommodate the mystical vision. Thereby two main insights of religion are blended appropriately.

But theism generates a problem. For the exalted view of the divine holiness is reflected in reverse among the devotees. Who can confront this almighty splendour without feeling the converse of holiness? The worshipper so confronted repents in self-debasement. He recognizes not merely holiness in God, but unholiness in himself. The purity of the Godhead reveals the sinfulness of men. And this the more so because in theism morals and religion come together in a most intimate manner, so that religious impurity and moral defect coalesce. Thus the very glory of theism is liable to bring in its train a particular view of man, as sinful and removed from God's face by a great gulf fixed. How to bridge it?

Men have tried sacrifice, and even a broken spirit. But is it in accord with the supreme blinding majesty of God that puny men should pretend to proffer an adequate expiation, whether by good works or otherwise? The worshipper here must feel that salvation or holiness can only come from the supreme source of holiness. Only God is holy, and so only God can bring holiness. So Allah is said, for all his terror, to be merciful; and here is a deep insight. But is it enough that men should merely live in hope of the divine compassion? Man still feels that it is he that must make expiation for his sins; while on the other hand he supposes that only God can bridge the gulf.

Theism thus brings a religious problem. Yet this is, so to speak, solved by Christianity. For Christ by being both man and God can achieve, through his solidarity with mankind, the expiation for mankind, and, through his Godhood, bridge the gulf. The two requirements are met. Hence too the reaction of the Church against docetism. For though doctrines such as the latter seem to preserve monotheism better they destroy the whole point of Christianity.

But Gāndhi said that the uniqueness of the Incarnation was a great stumbling-block to his acceptance of Christ. Why only one Incarnation? Why the scandal of particularity? First, the Christian doctrine, though it involves a seeming blasphemy, is the simplest of its kind. It is hard, perhaps, for the monotheist to accept what at first sight seems an abrogation of his belief; and it would be blasphemous to do it lightly. Second, multiple incarnations, as in Vaiṣṇavism, seem ill in accord with the majesty of God, especially where animal manifestations are produced through legend. Third, they tend in the direction of docetism, for a person who appears in many forms cannot be thought to *be* one of those forms in the full sense: they are likely to be regarded more as appearances than as

---

[5]I owe this point to Mr T. S. Gregory, in discussion.

realities. Thus the need for atonement will not easily be met by multiple incarnations. Fourth, historical data may be relevant, though I do not propose to examine these directly here.

But history reminds us of a problem. Even supposing that the doctrine of Incarnation strikes a deep chord, how do we recognize the divine human? What are the grounds, for instance, for calling Jesus God? True, we would only here be being wise after the event; but there are certain suggestive things to which we can point. Miracle-working is an intimation of omnipotence; signs of sinlessness correspond to the purity of the Holy One; the actions of an apparent Saviour chime in with the thought that only God can save; and the claim to divinity supervenes rather startlingly on all these. Not only so but, looking further afield, the pattern of history fits in with the Messianic life.

Moreover, just as monotheism itself harmonizes more easily with the moral insights of men than does polytheism, so the Incarnation has a moral significance but dimly adumbrated in pure monotheism of the Jewish or Muslim variety: for Christ in making himself a sacrifice not merely fulfils, as it were, a profound religious function, but illuminates the field of morality by his example. The Suffering Servant helps us to understand the significance of love blended with humility. This is not to deny that elsewhere there are similar conceptions, as in Buddhist compassion; but it may well be claimed that in Christianity there is a striking tragic realism which weaves together the insights of numinous religion, mysticism and morality.

Perhaps all this balancing of insights is precarious and indeed flavoured with subjective preferences. I concede that the basic points, namely the superior richness of Christianity, the emphasis on theism and the religion of worship, the need for atonement and the attractiveness of *agapē,* constitute no knockdown arguments. And there are certainly counter-arguments, such as the imperilling of pure monotheism in Christianity and, perhaps, its Judaic dogmatism whereby little credit is given to the intuitions of the polytheist. Nevertheless, a sympathetic Buddhist or Hindu would, I suggest, regard the arguments as at least relevant. Maybe one can gain no more certainty in such matters than in, say, literary or artistic criticism. But one would not for this reason deny that there are relevant insights (or reasons) in regard to revelations. In any event, it is incumbent upon us to try to give such reasons, for they make explicit our religious value-judgements. The trouble about a great deal of comparative apologetic is that it is not thus explicit.

So much, albeit briefly, for what I mean by religious reasons. There are, however, other tasks for the apologist. Revelations, for various reasons, give different pictures of this world. And some of these apply more easily than others. Or at any rate there are problems about their application which must concern us. I use the term 'application' here for the following reason. On the view here presented, certain revelations or revelatory experiences are basically what are appealed to in defence of a religious position. I do not myself believe that one can gain a knowledge of God simply by observing the physical world. Nevertheless the doctrines themselves present a picture of the cosmos which has to square with reality. That is, we do not see that a daffodil is divine (save perhaps in peculiar contemplations) and thus come to believe in God. But our belief gives us the notion that the daffodil has a divine flavour. (A like remark applies to morality too.) Regarding problems of application, the purposive view of history, for example, implicit in Christianity can be contrasted with the cyclical and repetitive picture provided in Indian religion. More importantly, cosmology poses difficulties of application.

We find that there are billions of stars in countless galaxies. Some of these stars are suns; and some of these will perhaps have planets like ours. The theory of evolution and the possibility of the synthesis of organic from inorganic matter may suggest that it is not incredible (and perhaps even probable) that there is life elsewhere in the universe and that there are in other places reasoning organisms. Such speculations would create acute difficulties about the scandal of particularity: the scandal might indeed seem an outrage. Hinduism and Buddhism, with their florid imaginings of beings of all sorts in all kinds of worlds, find the task of applying themselves to this vast universe less difficult. For the Trinity Doctrine, as a final expression of truth about the Godhead, may suffer if there are men elsewhere to be saved through Incarnation. Agreed, all this is highly speculative, but it is a matter for the philosopher, *qua* metaphysical apologist, to discuss.

Again, there are certain more traditional metaphysical problems concerned with the application of doctrines to the world which ought to be discussed. Notably, there is the problem of free will, which links up with the truth or otherwise of scientific materialism. More precisely, it connects not only with the conceptual problem of whether one could adapt language in such a way as to remove the dualistic ontology which seems implicit in current usage, but also with informed speculation as to the possibility of a unified scientific theory of human behaviour. To this latter recent advances in cybernetics, brain physiology and so forth are obviously relevant.

What then is the situation? First, there is philosophical analysis, which helps to illuminate the structure and epistemology of doctrines, East and West. As such it is best regarded as a peculiar way of doing the comparative study of religions. Then there is general apologetics, the giving (in the present instance) of religious reasons for a certain view of the cosmos; and this might as well be done by the sympathetic philosopher as by anyone else. Here historical facts may enter in, but these already have to be interpreted by reference to certain religious insights. Then there arise questions of a general nature, which though not pure exercises in the *a priori* nevertheless ought to engage philosophers' attention, regarding the application of doctrines to the cosmos as we know it. And all this, save neutral philosophical analysis, can be termed 'metaphysics'. Or it is a sort of natural theology—it is natural, since it does not merely expound revelation but attempts to give reasons on behalf of a revelation; and it is theology because it involves religious beliefs and ways of speaking. But perhaps I am here being a Pickwick, for this is not natural theology in the old sense. It is a soft, rather than the old hard, variety.

Yet what of the glimmering abstractions of yesteryear? What of the Five Ways and the superb claims of reason? Here, I can only feel that the hard metaphysics of the old days, where Aristotle and others conspire with faith, has to be left on one side. It is true that there are uneasinesses about the cosmos which the traditional arguments for God's existence enshrine—in particular the cosmological worry of why anything exists at all. But the rules of argument in this connexion are so debatable that it is absurd to pretend that we have either strong inductions or deductions here. In short, traditional natural theology can supply hunches which perhaps reinforce the insights of religious phenomenology, but it cannot stand on its own.

The main point of this paper may be put in another way by saying that any appeal to religious experience (whether intuitive or otherwise) must inevitably lead to a consideration of the experience not merely of Christians but of Buddhists and others, and thereby to an examination of the way experience is linked to different sorts of doctrines. Through this investigation one is bound to ask what the criteria are for choosing between different formulations of religious belief. And from the apologetic point of view it is necessary to give reasons for accepting one's own faith rather than some other. Since natural theology in the old form appears to me to be gravely suspect, and since an irrationalist appeal to revelation alone (whether fundamentalist or not) is utterly self-defeating, our only choice is to work with the notion of religious reasons of the kind which I have sketched.

All this may seem somewhat programmatic. But even programmes are sometimes useful, and I have tried to illustrate part of the programme of Christian metaphysics. I said at the outset that natural theology is the Sick Man of Europe. I do not profess to have cured him. But at least I have tried to give advice on how to live with one's coronary.

PART
TWO

RELIGION AND SECULARITY

This part begins with the reasons and causes of secularity, at least as interpreted by H. J. Paton and F. L. Baumer. Thus Paton lists as "impediments to religion" the divergence of doctrinal claims among themselves, the apparent conflict between various doctrinal claims and the "results" of scientific research, the conception of the world as "governed throughout by unvarying law," the conviction that only by following scientific methods can we gain knowledge or reasonable belief, the challenge of biology and the social sciences to the religious view that man is a unique creation of God, the Freudian and other psychological interpretations of religious experience and religious views of man, the view of history for which "history" means "what historical research can substantiate" and for which historical research can interpret or include only events which are analogous to other events within ordinary human experience and challenges from Logical Positivism and other versions of extreme empiricism to the meaningfulness (intelligibility) of religious discourse. It seems fair to say that no one of these matters is by itself fatal to religious belief. Indeed, it may be that together, and rightly understood, none of these matters provides any substantial *evidence* against religious belief. But each of the perspectives from which the plausibility of religious belief is challenged is also an expression of a general point of view, a way of looking at man and nature which is mainly unreceptive to traditional religious belief. Perhaps, then, "modern man"—insofar as he is not a creation of scholars or a projection by troubled thinkers of their own doubts upon the world at large—drinks in an antireligious view with his mother's milk. Often, students take religious belief to be, not *false,* but *irrelevant.*

Baumer sees this as in good part the result of the "radical tenor of nineteenth-century scepticism." Among the influences leading to this scepticism about religious belief Baumer identifies the concern only with the social utility of religion, the willingness of agnostics to do without religious knowledge, the influence of purely naturalistic views of man in the "new" sciences biology and anthropology, the naturalistic approach to religion in such writers as David Hume and James Frazer, Feuerbach's psychological and Marx's economic interpretations of religion, the sort of "historicism" for which "opinions are counted rather as phenomena to be explained, than as matters of truth and falsehood," and the effects of "Higher Criticism" of the Biblical writings. These, then, are some at least of the most important sources of secularity—the tendency to reject religious belief or to view it as irrelevant.

Rudolph Bultmann, R. B. Braithwaite, and Paul Tillich are much influenced by secularity but also wish to retain religious belief—in this case, to remain Christian. Hence they reinterpret Christian doctrine in a way in which, as each believes, what is essential or most important to Christian belief is retained. While any attempt to put their viewpoints briefly is chancey, the following seems to capture their quite different tactics.

Bultmann argues that the New Testament puts Christian belief in "mythological" terms—a view of the world as the scene of the activity of God, angels, and demons; in which miracles occur; in which men are in slavery to Satan, sin, and death; in which history progresses toward a final resurrection and judgment which will send all men to either eternal salvation or damnation; in which Christ, Himself a preexistent Divine Being, comes sent from God to die on the cross to atone for men's sins and to rise again as the victorious Lord who will return to execute Final Judgment. Bultmann cannot accept this view, but rather than simply saying that he is not a Christian he endeavors to "demythologize" Christianity. Acknowledging that the "modern view" of the world is not unchallengeable or unalterable, he nonetheless tries to reinterpret the doctrines just noted as not expressing claims about God, sin, Christ, and so on, but rather as expressing man's understanding of himself in the world in which he lives. Myth should be interpreted not cosmically, but anthropologically, or better still, existentially.

In sum, the New Testament is to be radically reinterpreted along the lines of existentialist philosophy—with the hope that as a result man will thereby gain "an understanding of himself which will challenge him to a genuine existential decision."

One of Bultmann's purposes is to escape problems which arise, in his opinion, when one considers traditional Christian belief. He says (though it is hard to see that he is right on these points) that the doctrine of the Virgin Birth of Christ is inconsistent with that of His preexistence (how so, if the birth is the means by which the preexistent Son becomes man?) and that the doctrine that God created the world is incompatible with the doctrine that there are evil rulers of this world, spiritual beings who are evil and exercise their power in human affairs. (Why is the existence of an omnipotent Creator logically incompatible with the existence of other beings who are permitted to exercise their power?) But suppose for the sake of the argument that Bultmann is right. One move would be to *reject* at least one of the doctrines in each case of logical conflict. Bultmann chooses instead to "demythologize" *both* beliefs, and so to retain both beliefs (or some semblance of them). Why adopt the latter alternative rather than the former? Ronald Hepburn raises this important question, and a number of others, in his critique of Bultmann. Some of his argument is summarized in the following paragraphs.

If the answer to Hepburn's question is that by demythologizing we get existentialist insights, how are we sure that it is insights and not delusions that we receive? Will appeal to such "insights" escape the "peril of failing to emerge from the subjectivist circle?" To what degree will this appeal open us to the wide-scale and unnecessary acceptance of paradoxes, if not sheer contradictions? And won't we still have to face the question of whether the demythologized claims of traditional belief are true?

Other problems arise with respect to Bultmann's apparently inconsistent, or at least ambiguous, use of the word "mythology," his tendency not to distinguish between a purely linguistic reform and a change of view about matters of fact (for—as Hepburn notes—to say that an event is "amenable to demythologizing . . . is to say something not only about the language in which the 'event' is described, but to decide also about the actual status of the event itself"); and Bultmann manifests a persistent tendency to avoid the question of evidence for or against the theses he forwards. In sum, Hepburn seems to be saying, Bultmann has not so much faced up to (let alone solved) the problems of religious belief as bypassed them.

As I have included an appraisal of R. B. Braithwaite in which I attempt to make clear his particular analysis of traditional religious claims, I shall only refer the reader to Braithwaite's own clear statement of it and my exchange with Kai Nielsen concerning the value and success of Braithwaite's enterprise.

Paul Tillich contends that "religious symbols need no justification if their meaning is understood." He holds that five characteristics distinguish genuine symbols from symbols so called: a symbol "points beyond itself" to (represents) something else, it "participates in the reality of" what it represents (points to, symbolizes), it cannot be created at will (is not simply conventional), it opens up "dimensions of reality . . . which otherwise are covered," and it has integrating (or disintegrating) power for societies and for individuals. Further, every religious symbol is intended "to point to that which transcends finitude."

As Tillich realizes, this raises some questions. How can I know that there is something that corresponds to, or is represented by, a symbol? If *only* symbolic knowledge of *x* is possible, is *any* knowledge of *x* possible? And what might "symbolic knowledge" or "knowledge through symbols" mean? There are, Tillich suggests, two ways of attempting to answer these questions, the phenomenological way and the ontological way. The former "tries to find the referent of religious symbolism . . . in a particular experience, that of the holy and of the ultimate concern implied in the holy." The ontological way "tries to find the referent of religious symbolism . . . in the character of being as such . . . it gives an analysis of the encountered world with respect to its finitude and finds through this analysis its [the world's] self-transcending quality, its pointing beyond its finitude."

Tillich distinguishes between primary and secondary religious symbols. Only primary symbols "point directly to the referent of all religious symbolism." Thus "In the Psalmist's phrase 'The Lord is my shepherd,' the word 'Lord' is a genuine and primary religious symbol, the word 'shepherd' is a poetic metaphor." A particular symbol may change its status, a primary symbol becoming secondary, or conversely.

There are three kinds or levels of primary symbols. One sort refers the highest degree of such qualities as personality, power, love, justice, etc., to a "highest being"—not as descriptions of this being but as a way of stressing its transcendence of all being. Another sort refers actions such as creation, providence, miracles, incarnation, etc., to this being—not as things which are *done* by this being, but symbolically. A final sort refers finite objects to this being, taking them as manifestations of the holy. Thus objects, persons, and events (not, or not only, words) are symbols.

But if "God is personal and loving" does not *describe* God, and if He does not literally create the world and govern it providentially, what is one to make of "personal," "loving," "Creator," and "Providence" as *symbols?* What does, for example, "God loves us" *say?* And what will count as a reason for believing what it says (if it says or means anything)? Tillich is aware of these issues, of course. He himself attempts to deal with the meaning and truth of religious symbols. This was the point of the essay at hand.

As to the truth of religious symbols, the degree to which (as Tillich puts it) a symbol "reaches the referent of all religious symbols," Tillich has three comments. A symbol is *authentic* if it is "adequate to" the religious experience it expresses. (I suppose the idea is that one who had the experience could in some manner tell whether a symbol was "adequate to" the experience, perhaps somewhat in the way that one who has a sensory experience, or a moral or aesthetic experience, can often at least tell whether a description of that experience is fully, somewhat, or not at all adequate or accurate to that experience.) (2) A symbol is, in part, true to the degree that it itself makes clear the distinction between itself and what it symbolizes. But (1) does not help much, since if only (subjective) phenomenological adequacy is in question, this could be attained *without knowing* whether there was a holy being which was experienced or whether there only *seemed* to be one. And if "phenomenology adequacy" is to include "having a referent," (1) will be decidable only if we already know there is a referent. The defect of (2) comes out when we note that so far Tillich has not given us any reason for not adding to it the two words "if any." "Self-negating" symbols may fail to represent or refer to anything actual. So the third comment must bear considerable weight—the weight of giving a reason for supposing that an authentic and self-negating symbol does correspond to something to which it is the appropriate pointer.

The third comment by Tillich goes as follows: (3) "The positive criterion for the truth of a symbol (e.g., creation) is the degree to which it includes the valuation in an ultimate perspective of the individual persons." In short, the truth of a symbol is the degree to which it expresses the "ultimate concern" of its user. And again it would appear that a symbol could be eminently successful in this regard without there being anything that was, in fact, symbolized.

The difficulty here arises, it seems clear, because of the restrictions Tillich feels forced to make concerning the meaning of religious symbols. Were "God loves us" and "God created the world" to partially but literally describe what God is and does, then, he believes, religious doctrine would conflict with "the scientific interpretation of reality." Further, God would thereby be treated as another being, not as "beyond all being." And thus, he supposes, on the one hand religious belief would be shown false (because it conflicts with a scientific interpretation of things) and on the other hand religious belief would be idolatrous because it confused the symbol with the thing symbolized. He is thus confident that the truth of religious symbols, and their meaning, can be discerned only in religious experience, an awareness of the pointing-beyond-itself of any being or of the "holiness" of any being. But one may suspect that something has gone wrong in Tillich's analysis—that the questions of meaning and truth have perhaps been put off but not answered. This, at least, is the view of William P. Alston.

Alston notes that "God is being-itself" is for Tillich a nonsymbolic statement, although anything else that can be said about God will be symbolic. No property can be ascribed to God. So no statement ascribing a property to God, e.g., no proposition saying that God is good, can be shown to be true (or false) by appeal to design (or evil). And further "there is no ground for considering one sort of attitude or feeling more appropriate [to God] . . . than another." If God is all-knowing, all-powerful, all-good, Creator and Providence, presumably it is right to worship Him. But God is *not* any of these things for Tillich. "God" in the traditional Judeo-Christian theology is but another symbol. The God who is being-itself apparently is immune to being the *appropriate* object of *any* behavioral or attitudinal response (including "ultimate concern"). As Alston pointedly asks, "What would it mean to love being-itself?"

Alston notes that Tillich's answer to this question is that the object of ultimate concern is being-itself as it is manifested "in and through" some symbol or other.

But this raises all over again the question as to what "being manifested in and through a symbol" tells us (if anything) about being-itself.

Alston's conclusion is that

> If we are not satisfied with a purely naturalistic account of religious symbols, there is no short cut around the traditional scheme, which makes their justification rest, at least in part, on the truth of those nonsymbolic assertions which specify their symbolizanda.

This conclusion is reinforced by Marvin Fox's different, but also penetrating, discussion of Tillich's views.

It is hard, I think, not to feel that the advantage in these discussions lies very much on the side of the critics—though of course the reader will have to decide for himself whether this is correct. If so, three typical and important responses to secularity have failed. As Fox puts it, they fall between the extremes they attempt to unite. And if this is so, then presumably either secularity itself must be challenged or traditional religion simply abandoned. Or, perhaps, one must distinguish between the "assured results" to which secularity appeals (asking how "assured" they are and whether they are in fact evidence against traditional religious belief) and the psychological milieu that secularity creates (which is presumably *philosophically* irrelevant).

Chapter

FOUR

THE MEANING
AND SCOPE
OF SECULARITY

INTELLECTUAL IMPEDIMENTS TO RELIGIOUS BELIEF

H. J. Paton

From H. J. Paton, *The Modern Predicament,* reprinted by permission of The Macmillan Company, First Collier Paperback, 1962, and George Allen & Unwin, Ltd., London.

§ 1. Different Types of Impediment

There are many impediments to religion. Among these human wickedness—or human sinfulness, if we use the language of theology—is the most formidable, but it is by no means the only one; and under this head we ought not to include the sin of thinking about religion, as is sometimes done by those who are guilty of the sin of thinking too little. Another obstacle is to be found in the aberrations of religion itself and in the unworthiness of its professed followers. These impediments are patent enough from the religious point of view. We must now take a more detached standpoint and consider some of the alleged incompatibilities between religious belief and the rest of our knowledge. This ungrateful task may be described as a study of the *intellectual* impediments to religion. The views with which we have to deal are commonplace among thinkers, and are dimly apprehended even by the unthinking masses, so that it would be foolish, and indeed wrong, to pass them over in silence or to pretend that they are not serious.

§ 2. Religion and Science

Intellectual impediments to religion are made possible by the intellectual element in religion itself. Every religion, and certainly every developed religion, offers us a doctrine of man, a doctrine of history, a doctrine of the universe, and a doctrine of God. The exact status of such doctrines may be difficult to determine, and obsession with theory may be one of the major religious aberrations. Nevertheless religion cannot get on without some sort of doctrine, even if this can be reduced to the barest minimum.

Doctrine necessarily claims to be true, and this means that it enters into competition with other doctrines also claiming to be true. We may hold that one doctrine is true from one point of view and another from another; but ultimately there can be only one truth, or one comprehensive system of truths, in which divergent points of view are reconciled. We may not be able to effect this reconciliation, but to abandon the belief that such a reconciliation is possible is to abandon reason altogether and to have no defence against lunacy.

What are the doctrines with which religion, so far as it is doctrinal, may, and does, come into conflict? They can all be summed up in one word—science. But this bald statement is in need of some further elucidation.

In the first place, science has to be interpreted widely. It includes, not only the natural sciences, but also the mental and social sciences, such as psychology and anthropology. It covers also the modern methods of historical and literary criticism. The development of all these disciplines in the last four hundred years has brought religion face to face with a situation very different from any that existed before.

In the second place, it may be objected that there is no such thing as science—there are only sciences in the plural—and that all this talk about a conflict between religion and science is too vague to be profitable.

In such an objection there is some truth, and we ought always to be chary of those who are in the habit of telling us that Science (with a capital S) teaches us this or that and admits of no further argument. Assertions of this kind often spring, not directly from science, but from semi-popular philosophy, and some of the impediments to religion may fall under this description. Nevertheless we are blind if we fail to see that in method, in outlook, and in what can be described as atmosphere, science—all science—may be opposed to religion. Even if scientific knowledge is ultimately compatible with religion, it does not appear to be so at first sight; and indeed it seems to contradict a great deal formerly considered by theologians to be necessary for a saving faith. Furthermore, whatever may be true as regards logical compatibility, there is at least a psychological opposition between the scientific and the religious attitude. The gradual spread of the scientific outlook—and we are all affected by it even if the scientists say we are not nearly as much affected as we ought to be—has tended, not so much to refute religious belief, but rather to make it fade and wither. To quote Professor Price: 'it has led to that inner emptiness and lack of faith . . . which is our fundamental and, as it seems, incurable disease'.

It may be replied that all this is very much out of date—a mere survival of Victorian rationalism long ago abandoned. Those who comfort themselves thus are, I am afraid, deceived. It is true that science to-day—apart from the followers of Karl Marx, who was more of a prophet than a scientist—is not so cocksure as it once was about the finality of its teaching and is more prepared for revolutionary discoveries. It is also true that the note of hostility to religion is often, though by no means always, less strident than it was in the past. All this is to the good, but the main reason for the lesser stridency is that the modern rationalist no longer considers himself to be battling for victory: he supposes that the victory is already won. The greater amiability of present-day discussions is no doubt a straw that can help to show which way the wind is blowing; but those who clutch at that straw may only give the impression that they are drowning men.

§ 3. Religion and Physics

The tide of science which threatens to submerge religion began to flow when Copernicus discovered that the earth was not the centre of the physical universe, but only one of the planets revolving round the sun. This tidal movement became more perceptible when Galileo confirmed his discovery and began to develop the modern methods of observation and measurement which have led to such astonishing triumphs. As if aware of the impending danger, the Church reacted violently, and condemned these doctrines as incompatible with Holy Scripture.

Yet in spite of its utmost endeavours the tide has flowed relentlessly for more than four hundred years. Its rise has continuously accelerated and is certain—unless there is a world catastrophe—to accelerate more and more. During the whole of this period—if we may change the metaphor—religion has been fighting a rearguard action, abandoning one position after another till it is uncertain how much is left.

Why is it that the amazing achievements of modern physics and astronomy have seemed so inimical to religion? It is not merely that they overthrow primitive Biblical speculations about the physical universe—although, when a book has been regarded as divinely inspired throughout, to contradict the least part of it may seem to destroy the authority of the whole. Nor is it merely that man is seen as the creature of a day, clinging precariously to a whirling planet in a solar system which is itself utterly insignificant amid the vast reaches of interstellar space and astronomical time. These and many other considerations all play their part; but perhaps the main impediments to religion arise from two things—from the character of scientific method and from the conception of the world as governed throughout by unvarying law.

On scientific method little need here be said, although psychologically it may be the strongest influence of all. A scientific training makes it difficult or impossible to accept statements on authority, to be satisfied with second- or third-hand evidence, to believe in marvels which cannot be experimentally repeated, or to adopt theories which cannot be verified by empirical observation. There may be exceptions to this rule; for some scientists seem to lose their critical power once they stray beyond the narrow limits of their own subject. But there can be no doubt that in this respect the influence of science is both powerful and pervasive, and that it is unfavourable to much that passes for religion. How far that influence may in its turn lead to error or extravagance it is not here necessary to enquire. For our present purpose it is enough to recognize that the whole attitude, not merely of scientists, but of thoughtful men brought up in a scientific age, towards all the problems of life, whether secular or sacred, has been affected to an extent which it is almost impossible to exaggerate. Here may be found perhaps the greatest impediment to the unquestioning acceptance of any simple and traditional religious faith.

It is more difficult to gauge the effects which follow from conceiving the physical universe as subject to laws which admit of no exceptions. As late as the eighteenth century many thinkers regarded the discovery of physical laws as a revelation of the divine plan by which the universe is governed; and the very simplicity and comprehensiveness of the plan was taken to be a proof of divine benevolence and wisdom. Yet at least as early as Descartes it was already realized that physical laws were independent of, if not opposed to, the idea of purpose in the universe. It is this second interpretation which has prevailed. When Laplace, speaking of the existence of God, said 'I have no need of that hypothesis', he meant that the conception of God's activity or purpose played no part in his formulation of scientific law, as it had done in the work of other thinkers, including the great Isaac Newton himself. In that specific sense the dictum of Laplace is the universal assumption of science to-day.

If modern physics is unfavourable to belief in a divine purpose or plan, it is still more unfavourable to belief in miracles. So far as these are considered to be breaches of physical laws, they cannot be accepted without rejecting the most fundamental presuppositions of science. Hence it is not surprising that they have become somewhat of an embarrassment to religion. At one time they were invoked to guarantee the truth of revelation. Now, if they are defended at all, it is revelation that is invoked to guarantee the truth of miracles, and their occurrence is explained as the manifestation of some higher law.

So far as physics is incompatible with miracles and has no use for a divine purpose in the universe, it is hard to see how we can retain the idea of providence in general and of special providences in particular. But this is not the worst. The character of scientific law appears to require a universal determinism which applies to the movements of human bodies as much as to the movement of the smallest electron or the remotest star. This cuts at the roots of all morality and so of religion as well.

There are some who seek to escape from this gloomy situation by reminding us that the old-fashioned mechanical views of physics are now abandoned. The concepts of mechanical cause and effect have been given up, and in place of causal laws we are left only with statistical averages. Physics itself even recognizes a principle of indeterminacy and so leaves at least a chink for human freedom. Hence perhaps the future before religion is not quite so black as it has been painted.

Without any wish to be dogmatic on these difficult subjects we must still ask ourselves whether those who find comfort in such considerations may not also be clutching at straws. To abandon the old-fashioned view of causation is by no means to give up the universality of law: all it amounts to is that the laws have a different character. The microscopic space left open by the principle of indeterminacy is far too small for the exercise of human freedom—if indeed we can conceive human freedom at all as manifested only in the apparent chinks and interstices of the physical universe. The late Professor Susan Stebbing was right when she said 'It cannot be maintained that all that is required for human freedom is some amount of uncertainty in the domain of microphysics'. And if we wish to argue that the new physics is less unfavourable to religion than the old, we must take into our reckoning what is called the second law of thermodynamics, according to which the universe is steadily running down. It is hard to see how this can offer any ground either for moral optimism or for religious faith.

The general effect of the modern scientific outlook is summed up in the eloquent, and by now familiar, words of Mr. Bertrand Russell. 'That man is the product of causes which had no prevision of the end they were achieving; that his origin, his growth, his hopes and fears, his loves and beliefs, are but the outcome of accidental collocations of atoms; that no fire, no heroism, no intensity of thought and feeling, can preserve an individual life beyond the grave; that all the labours of the ages, all the inspiration, all the noon-day brightness of human genius, are destined to extinction in the vast death of the solar system, and that the whole temple of man's achievement must inevitably be buried beneath the débris of a universe in ruins—all these things, if not quite beyond dispute, are yet so nearly certain, that no philosophy which rejects them can hope to stand. Only within the scaffolding of these truths, only on the firm foundations of unyielding despair, can the soul's habitation henceforth be safely built'.

If Mr. Russell's views be regarded as suspect, let us listen to the less eloquent, but hardly less despairing, words of a deeply religious thinker—Dr. Albert Schweizer. 'My solution of the problem', he says, 'is that we must make up our minds to renounce completely the optimistic-ethical interpretation of the world. If we take the world as it is, it is impossible to attribute to it a meaning in which the aims and objects of mankind and of individual men have a meaning also.'

§ 4. Religion and Biology

If the first great wave that threatened to engulf religion came from physics, the second came from biology. The Darwinian theory of evolution overthrew the belief that each species was the object of a special creation and possessed a fixed and unchanging character. This served to upset the authority alike of Aristotle and of the book of Genesis. But still worse than this, the process of evolution appeared to be mechanical rather than purposive, blind rather than intelligent, and so to render nugatory the argument from design, which was commonly regarded as the most cogent proof for the existence of God. Furthermore, from a human point of view evolution in its working seemed wasteful and even cruel, and the main qualities making for survival appeared to be lust and violence and deceit. It gave less than no support to belief in the wisdom and benevolence of the Creator or to the view that the end of creation was the furtherance of virtue. But perhaps the greatest shock of all came from the discovery that man, far from having been specially created in the image of God, was himself the product of this unintelligent process of evolution and must look back to a long line of ape-like ancestors. Nowadays we take all this calmly in our stride, partly perhaps through lack of imagination. We may even feel in a curious way that it unites us more intimately with the world of nature of which we form a part. But it should not cause us surprise if to our Victorian grandfathers it seemed that

> The pillar'd firmament is rott'nness,
> And earths base built on stubble.

In comparison with this the other shocks from biology may seem unimportant, but we have to remember that the effect of scientific discoveries is cumulative. Of these further shocks we need mention only one.

It has always been recognized that the soul is in some ways dependent on the body; and we all know from ordinary experience how a minor indisposition, or even fatigue, may dull our mind and blunt our emotions and weaken our will. But the development of physiology began to show in ever minuter detail how close is the connexion between mind and body, and how utterly we depend on the structure of our brain and nervous system. The very existence of the soul began to be questioned. Why should we postulate a soul instead of recognizing that mental functions are completely dependent on bodily functions? Above all, why should we suppose, against all the empirical evidence, that the soul could exist as a separate entity after the death of the body? The belief in immortality, one of the strongholds of religion, or at least of many religions, was being steadily undermined. Conclusions based on these detailed discoveries were supported further by the general theory of evolution, which abolished the sharp separation of man from the other animals, as also by the general theory that physical laws govern the movements of all bodies, not excluding the organic bodies of plants and animals and men. Some philosophers and scientists hold it out as a possibility, and indeed as an ideal, that the laws of biology, and even of psychology, may one day be reduced to laws of physics.

One general result emerges from all this. Man displays his intelligence in discovering laws of nature and then awakes, perhaps with horror, to the fact that these laws apply to himself: for science he is only one object among many others and has to be understood in the same way as the rest. Thus man is finally entangled in the meshes of the net that he himself has woven; and when we say this, we must add that it is true, not merely of his body, but of his soul. Science is, as it were, a machine constructed by man in order to master the universe; but the machine has turned against its maker and seeks to master him as well.

§ 5. Religion and Psychology

The third great wave threatening religion comes from psychology, which is, at least etymologically, the science of the soul. This is a more recent wave; and as we disappear gasping under its onrush, we are hardly yet in a position to study its shape. Indeed its shape is perhaps not yet definitely formed. Its exponents at times contradict one another with a freedom ordinarily reserved for philosophers; and some of them indulge in a boldness of speculation from which a respectable philosopher would shrink. We are offered a choice between different schools of thought.

Thus there is a Behaviouristic school, which, as a further expansion of physiology, makes still more formidable the impediments already considered. The Behaviourists ignore in practice, if they do not also deny in theory, the mental phenomena formerly considered open to introspection—our thoughts, our emotions, our volitions, and so on: they are content to study only the bodily behaviour of human and other animals, and so to blur still further the dividing line between man and the brutes. A very different method is adopted by the schools of psycho-analysis which originate from Freud, both by those which seek to carry further the work of the master and by those which attempt to modify and improve it. All of them start from an examination of human consciousness, especially of human dreams; and they claim on this basis to bring under scientific investigation the vast and obscure domain of the unconscious, whose existence had been merely suspected and whose character had not been seriously explored. According to them the human mind is like an iceberg, by far the greater part of which is under water and not amenable to direct observation. By means of inference they attempt to describe in detail these murky nether regions; and they have been able, as it were, to draw up from the ocean's depths many strange, and on the whole unpleasing, objects for our contemplation and instruction.

The schools which consider human consciousness to be worthy of scientific attention take up different attitudes to religion. As we have seen, they may regard it as a harmful illusion or as a healing and even 'real' illusion, whatever that may be. But, broadly speaking, even at the best they offer cold comfort to religion, and the attitude of Freud himself is conspicuously hostile. Besides, they exhibit the general tendency to assume determinism in mental processes; they encourage the view that reason has little or no part to play in human behaviour; and even if they regard mind as a possible object of study, it is for them only one object among others and requires no special principles for its understanding. All psychology is an example of what I meant when I said that the soul is entangled in the meshes of the scientific net which man has devised for the better understanding of the physical world. And many psychologists believe that religious experience can be explained—or explained away—in accordance with the ordinary laws that have been found to account for other mental phenomena.

This third wave is perhaps logically less intimidating to religion than the other two, if only because psychology is not yet fully developed as a science. Psycho-analysis has called attention to mental phenomena hitherto neglected; it has thrown light on dark places; and it has done mental healing a service for which the world must be grateful. Whatever be its defects, it has opened up the way for fresh advances, but has it already advanced so far that even its fundamental concepts are firmly established? Sometimes it may seem not to have got much beyond a stage like that in chemistry when the phenomena of combustion were explained by postulating a hypothetical substance, now forgotten, which was known as 'phlogiston'; or at least—if this is too depreciatory—not beyond the comparatively recent stage in physics when 'ether' had to be postulated as an elastic substance permeating all space and forming a medium through which rays of light were propagated. It may be heretical to say so, but it seems to me rather improbable that our old friends, the Ego, the Super-Ego, and the Id, will occupy permanent niches in the scientific pantheon.

Nevertheless, even if this third wave may not yet be so very imposing logically, psychologically—partly perhaps by its very vagueness—it is to-day almost the most formidable of the three, at least as far as popular or semi-popular thinking is concerned. In spite of attempts to make use of it in the interests of religion, it produces an emotional and intellectual background so different from that of religious tradition that the combination of the two becomes very difficult. What is sometimes said of philosophies is even more true of religious beliefs—they are usually not refuted, but merely abandoned. When the spiritual climate has altered, they may simply fade away; and we seem to be witnessing something rather like this at the present crisis of our civilization.

§ 6. Religion and History

There are other human sciences besides psychology, and their influence has also tended to be psychologically, if not logically, unfavourable to religion. Anthropology, for example, tends on the whole to blur sharp distinctions between the primitive and the developed, and among heathen superstitions it finds parallels even for the most sacred mysteries of the higher religions. It suggests that religion is a survival of something primitive in the experience of the race, just as psychology suggests it is a survival of something primitive in the experience of the child. Even economics takes a hand in the unholy assault. The classical economists may have been tempted at times to suppose that the 'economic man' was, not a mere useful abstraction, but the only kind of man there is; and this tendency has been hardened into a dogma by the Marxists. They tell us that our bourgeois religion, like our bourgeois morality, is only an ideology—that is, an illusory 'rationalization' of purely economic factors—and one of the main impediments to human progress. All these human sciences, among which sociology also may be included, have the common characteristic of treating man as one object among other objects: they tend to explain his thoughts, his actions, and his emotions as the effect of forces outside himself—forces whose influence can be determined, and even controlled, in accordance with ascertainable scientific laws.

Here then we have a whole series of little wavelets, not perhaps very impressive in isolation and colliding at times with one another, yet all driving inexorably in the same general direction. But belonging to the same series there is one special wave so menacing that we may be inclined to call it the fourth great wave—the wave of historical method and historical criticism.

The modern development of the historical method is particularly menacing to Christianity, since of all the great religions Christianity has laid most stress on history—the history of the Jews, the history of the Founder, and the history of the Church. Modern criticism has undermined first the authority of the Old Testament and then the authority of the New in such a way that the traditional belief in an infallible Book, written down by God's penmen at His dictation, can no longer be accepted by any intelligent man of independent judgement who has given serious consideration to the subject. We have instead a most fallible human record compiled by mortal men, who, even if they were gifted with a special religious insight, were unacquainted with the canons of historical evidence and unfamiliar with the ideals of historical accuracy. Christian thinkers have made great and creditable efforts to adjust themselves to this new situation—the other world-religions are probably not even yet fully awake to their danger. The methods of modern scholarship may be able to sort out what is reasonably certain from what is at least doubtful as well as from what is in all probability fictitious. On these points there are, and are bound to be, differences among scholars, and it is only experts who can profitably form an opinion. Hence it is always possible, and it may often be justifiable, to dismiss the arguments of laymen in these subjects as ignorant or exaggerated. Nevertheless the plain man used to be faced with a plain situation which he could understand. He was told that every historical statement in the Bible, or at least in the New Testament, was true. He has now to be told that while the religious teaching in the Bible retains its unique value, some of its historical statements are true, while some are untrue, and others have been traditionally misunderstood. Even if he is sensible enough not to hold that if anything goes, the whole thing goes, he yet feels that he does not know where he stands, and that he is ill-equipped to come to a decision in matters about which the doctors differ. This is a new impediment to the simplicity of religious faith.

To the thoughtful man all this opens up questions which are philosophical rather than historical. He has been told, in traditional language, that religious faith is necessary for salvation, and the question he asks himself is this. Granted that religious faith is very much more than an intellectual belief in historical facts, can a belief in historical facts be necessary for salvation, and so for religious faith, when only the most expert scholarship is competent to decide whether these alleged facts are historical or not? If he answers in the negative, if indeed he comes to the conclusion that no belief in historical facts and no skill in historical scholarship can be necessary for what he calls salvation, his view of what is essential to religion has undergone a revolution, and he has entered a new path, not knowing where it may lead.

§ 7. Religion and Philosophy

I have not mentioned philosophy as one of the waves with which religion has to struggle. Philosophers do not speak with one voice, and the best of them are more anxious that men should think for themselves than that they should accept any doctrine dogmatically. But if we may speak of general trends, the movement of philosophy in this country has been, on the whole, away from religion. The Oxford Idealism which prevailed at the end of the Victorian age did at least have religious sympathies. The Realism which tended to replace it later, if it was not always sympathetic, was seldom other than neutral. The more modern school of Logical Positivism, which owes its rise to the great influence of Mr. Bertrand Russell, is often openly hostile or indifferent. We have moved far from the days when philosophy was the handmaid of theology. Like other handmaids at the present time, she now considers herself to be not only as good as her mistress but—if the colloquialism may be pardoned—a damn' sight better; and if she were inclined to enter again into domestic service, it would be as the handmaid, not of theology, but of science.

So far as Logical Positivism places a linguistic ban on theology and even on ethics, it has already been examined briefly in Chapter II;[1] but it would be a mistake to regard the doctrine that all statements about God are nonsense as the central feature of the modern linguistic movement as a whole. There is already a marked tendency to get beyond the earlier dogmatism, and even to display an interest in religion as well as in other problems more akin to those which have occupied philosophy in the past. As originally expounded Logical Positivism sweeps so much away into one comprehensive rubbish heap that it is difficult not to feel there must be something wrong with it; but its boundaries are becoming so blurred that it is almost time the name was dropped. All I wish to point out here is that a modern philosophy which had—and may still have—a very great following, especially among the younger intellectuals, is, perhaps I should not say hostile, but politely contemptuous, towards everything in the nature of religious belief. In this respect, as in others, it would seem to be a faithful mirror of an attitude widely prevalent at the present time.

§ 8. The Predicament of Religion

I have no wish to pretend that the contentions I have put forward are conclusive or that they are all equally sound. Like Logical Positivism itself, they sweep so much away along with religion that we may begin to doubt their validity. What I have stated is the case which is widely accepted and has got to be answered. Nevertheless it is folly not to see that the case is very strong and that, although in

---

[1] Logical Positivism held that every sentence which is true or false is either necessarily true, or contradictory, or verifiable, or falsifiable in principle by appeal to sensory experience. Ed.

certain respects it may be specially menacing to Christianity, it is a threat, not to a particular religion, but to all religion as such.

There are doubtless many other reasons, some of them less creditable, for the growing indifference to religion; but reasons of the type I have described are worthy of special consideration since they spring, not from human wickedness and folly, but from the highest achievements of human thought. They affect, not only the intellectuals, but also, through them, the immense mass of men who take their opinions at second and third and fourth hand. The whole spiritual atmosphere is altered, and even the ordinary religious man speaks today in a different tone about special providences and the hope of immortality, if he speaks of them at all.

In such circumstances it is unconvincing to tell us that the conflict of religion and science is now happily out-moded, that so and so has put forward new theories about scientific methodology and somebody else has confirmed some statement in the Biblical record from a newly-discovered papyrus or from some archaeological remains. This is mere tinkering with the subject; and we should not be surprised if those who have been brought up in the new atmosphere and have little or no experience of religion are apt to dismiss the easy optimism of some religious teachers as springing from blindness or ignorance, if not from hypocrisy. Nor can it be denied that they sometimes have ample excuse. The situation to be faced is one unknown to St. Paul and St. Augustine, to Aquinas and Duns Scotus, to Luther and Calvin; and it can be met, if it is to be met at all, only by a new effort of thinking at least as great as any of theirs. So long as this is lacking, the modern world is bound to suffer from a divided mind and from a conflict between the heart and the head. If religion has to satisfy the whole man, its demand is that the men who follow it must be whole-minded as well as whole-hearted. The very wholeness at which religion aims is impossible unless the spiritual disease caused by the fatal rift between science and religion can receive its own specific intellectual cure.

CULTURAL IMPEDIMENTS TO RELIGIOUS BELIEF

F. L. Baumer

From *Religion and the Rise of Scepticism,* © 1960 by Franklin L. Baumer. Reprinted by permission of Harcourt Brace Jovanovich, Inc.

For the purpose of analysis the "death of God"—the critical side of nineteenth-century scepticism—may be boiled down to a number of characteristic arguments. There were at least six such arguments which we shall label, for the sake of convenience, the utilitarian, the scientific, and the anthropological (referring to the new science of anthropology); the psychological, the economic, and the historical. Obviously, the scepticism of any given individual, a Karl Marx, say, or a Sir James Frazer, might be, and usually was, a blend of two or more of these modes, although it might be chiefly noted for one in particular. The first two, and to some extent the third, resembled modes already familiar in the eighteenth century, but with significant additions and elaborations, as we shall see. The last three, however, were essentially novel, reflecting new intellectual currents and helping to account for the more radical tenor of nineteenth-century scepticism. Under the impact of new knowledge and new perspectives, intellectuals were emboldened to reduce religion (not merely Christianity, but all religion) to "opiate" or "myth," to psychological "self-projection" or "reflex" of the economic world; to relegate it to the realm of the "unknowable," or to classify it as a "phase," presumably the most primitive and childish phase, in the evolution of the human mind. The common thread running through all these arguments was that man made religion, and not religion, man. In the words of Ludwig Feuerbach, "Theology is anthropology."

The utilitarian argument, advanced by Benthamites, secularists, and often by socialists, stands in a class by itself, for, unlike the other arguments, it was concerned, not so much with the truth of religion as with its "utility," i.e., its effects on society. Thus, it is reminiscent of the pragmatic argument of the *philosophes* . . . ,[1] brought up to date and adjusted to the problems of an industrial society. In brief, it charged that priests and rulers formed an unholy alliance to keep the middle and lower classes down, that, in a word, religion almost invariably threw its weight on the side of political and social reaction. And indeed there was considerable truth to these accusations, at least for the first half of the century. Was not the Roman church the inveterate foe of the French Revolution? What was one to think of Pius IX's Syllabus of Errors which denounced as an error the assertion that "the pope can and should reconcile himself to and agree with progress, liberalism, and modern civilization?" Did not the Prussian Lutheran church likewise condemn political and social democracy? Did not the Anglican bishops oppose the Reform Bill of 1832? Were not Methodist and evangelical leaders opposed to Chartism and trade unions? Did they not teach that poverty was ordained by God? The conclusion seemed ineluctable: if there was to be reform and progress for "the greatest number," religion would have to be shorn of its prestige and power in society.

Jeremy Bentham's *Analysis of the Influence of Natural Religion on the Temporal Happiness of Mankind* (1822) is an excellent summary of the utilitarian argument from the standpoint of a middle-class liberal. Religion, said Bentham, did not meet the test of "utility"; on the contrary, it manifestly injured both society and the individual. It injured the individual by instilling in him fears of endless torment, depriving him of innocent pleasures, and subjecting him to the will of a capricious tyrant. It injured society by creating intolerance of unbelievers and heretics, impeding intellectual progress, and giving power to priests who connive with rulers to plunder the community and maintain the social *status quo.* Deeper still, religion, by inculcating duty to God, subtracts from duty to man and creates an aversion to social improvement. "Our duty to God," said Bentham, "is a deduction from the pleasures of the individual without at all benefiting the species."[2] In a word, the English Utilitarians looked upon religion as "a great

---

[1]The French *philosophes* (Montesquieu, 1689–1755; Voltaire, 1694–1778; Rousseau, 1712–1778, etc.) were philosophers and popularizers of the philosophical ideas of their day. Ed.
[2]Philip Beauchamp (Jeremy Bentham and George Grote), *Analysis of the Influence of Natural Religion on the Temporal Happiness of Mankind* (London, 1822), p. 41.

moral evil" which consecrated a social order badly in need of liberal reform. James Mill, according to his son, regarded religion

> with the feelings due not to a mere mental delusion, but to a great moral evil. He looked upon it as the greatest enemy of morality: first, by setting up fictitious excellences,—belief in creeds, devotional feelings, and ceremonies, not connected with the good of human-kind,—and causing these to be accepted as substitutes for genuine virtues: but above all, by radically vitiating the standard of morals. . .[3]

The utilitarian type of argument also frequently crops up in the writings of secularists and socialists, though hardly ever in such unadulterated form and, of course, with more express application to the social evils produced by the Industrial Revolution. In a lecture delivered in 1879, Professor Robert Flint of the University of Edinburgh rightly attributed the rise of "secularism" (the movement led by George Jacob Holyoake and Charles Bradlaugh) among the manual workers of England more to "political dissatisfaction" than to rational conviction. The clergy and governing classes, he said, had asked for it by their "blind opposition," in the period after the French Revolution, to political and social progress. Speaking as a Christian, Flint thought that secularism would evaporate if the clergy were to address themselves to the real needs of the lower classes, "so that no man might be tempted to believe that religion is one of the things which stand either in the way of his personal happiness or of justice to his class."[4] The well-known socialist aphorism "Religion is the opiate of the people" also rested partially on this utilitarian base. Regardless of whether religion was true, it had observably bad effects on people: so contended the majority of both "utopian" and "scientific" socialists, though this was obviously not all that they contended. Religion sanctified all the abominations of capitalist as well as monarchist regimes. Religion allied itself with the existing order of property relations which it hoped to preserve by putting the people to sleep with the pipe dream of otherworldly salvation. Religion discouraged social reform, in fact "activity" of any kind, by its otherworldly emphasis. "The mortgage that the peasant has on heavenly blessings guarantees the mortgage that the bourgeois has on peasant lands."[5] Hence, for these reasons among others, the "True Socialist" Moses Hess professed a "philosophy of activity" and preferred "morality" to "religion." "Religion" preaches subservience, obsequiousness before authority; "morality," on the other hand, demands "activity," doing something to rectify the ills of capitalist society.[6] And Marx too, though he had no use for Hess's "morality," advocated a philosophy of activity which, in contrast to the otherworldly philosophy of religion, would enable the exploited to change the face of society to their advantage.

As previously intimated, the utilitarian argument almost invariably intertwined, even in Bentham, with arguments impugning the truth of religion.

---

[3]John Stuart Mill, *Autobiography*, chap. 2.
[4]Robert Flint, *Anti-Theistic Theories* (Edinburgh and London, 1879), p. 249.
[5]Karl Marx, *The Class Struggles in France, 1848–50* (New York: International Publishers, n. d.), p. 85.
[6]On Hess, see Sidney Hook, *From Hegel to Marx* (New York: Reynal and Hitchcock, 1936), pp. 194–95.

Among these latter none was more pervasive, nor more generally persuasive, than the argument from science. This argument was not new, but it was now more sharply stated and forced to conclusions more damaging to religion than ever before. It can be analyzed into two chief arguments which often interlaced, if somewhat illogically, in the thought of the day. The first of these was epistemological, centering in the new word "agnosticism." The second, more dogmatic in its tendency, was metaphysical, deriving from a new idea of nature which, for many, told overwhelmingly against a religious view of the universe.

"The word Agnosticism," Sir Leslie Stephen wrote in 1876, describes "a form of creed already common and daily spreading." The word was coined by Thomas Henry Huxley, as Stephen duly noted, but the idea had been formulated by an earlier generation, by Auguste Comte, the prophet of French Positivism, and in England by the Mills and Herbert Spencer, not to speak of David Hume. All of these men were deeply imbued with the spirit of modern science and conceived it to be their personal mission to carry this spirit into the stronghold of religion itself. The heart of the agnostic argument was epistemological.

> The Agnostic [Stephen continued] is one who asserts . . . that there are limits to the sphere of human intelligence. He asserts further . . . that those limits are such as to exclude at least what Lewes called "metempirical" knowledge. But he goes further, and asserts, in opposition to theologians, that theology lies within this forbidden sphere. . . . The Gnostic [on the other hand] holds that our reason can, in some sense, transcend the narrow limits of experience. He holds that we can attain truths not capable of verification, and not needing verification, by actual experiment or observation.[7]

Throughout *An Agnostic's Apology* Stephen appealed from "reason" (which, as he used it, was often tantamount to "*a priori* guesses") to "experience" and "the facts." "Reason" might end up in a deistic or even Christian affirmation, but "experience," or rather the lack of it, dictated the agnostic position. "Finding no halting position in Deism," John Stuart Mill said of his father, "he yielded to the conviction, that, concerning the origin of things nothing whatever can be known." The question of origins simply could not be answered "because we have no experience or authentic information from which to answer it."[8]

The wonder is, not that the agnostics were suspicious of the sort of knowledge claimed by "gnostics," but that they were content to abandon the search for it altogether. That they were content, however, is clear from what Comte taught in the very first "lesson" of his *Course on the Positive Philosophy:*

> At last the human mind, recognizing the impossiblity of obtaining absolute conceptions, abandons the search for the origin and goal of the universe and the inner causes of phenomena, to set itself the task merely of discovering, by reason and observation combined, the effective laws of things, that is to say, their invariable relations of succession and similarity.[9]

---

[7]Sir Leslie Stephen, *An Agnostic's Apology and Other Essays* (New York: G. P. Putnam's Sons, 1893), pp. 1–2.
[8]John Stuart Mill, *Autobiography*, chap. 2.
[9]Auguste Comte, *Cours de Philosophie Positive* (Paris, 1835–42), Vol. I, p. 4.

The explanation of the agnostic's contentment with "laws" rather than "causes" is probably to be found in his utilitarianism. Like Bentham, he was primarily interested in "useful" knowledge, and gnostic knowledge, even if it were utlimately obtainable, was a hindrance to man in his pursuit of experience useful to the human race.

Strictly speaking, of course, the agnostic did not deny God; he only said that man knew nothing about him. "My fundamental axiom of speculative philosophy," Huxley wrote to the Christian Charles Kingsley, "is that materialism and spiritualism are opposite poles of the same absurdity—the absurdity of imagining that we know anything about either spirit or matter."[10] Nevertheless, the new idea of nature which came to the fore in the nineteenth century persuaded a good many people, including some of the agnostics themselves, to press beyond the agnostic position and actually to negate religious interpretations of the world. This was the second time that modern science had confronted western man with a disturbing metaphysic. The first such metaphysic, the Newtonian, lent itself rather well to deistic, if not to strictly orthodox Christian, categories. The second, however, was not easily absorbed into any theistic system. The new idea of nature was most vividly summed up, as is well known, by Charles Darwin, not only in *The Origin of Species* (1859), "the most important book of the century," but also in its sequel *The Descent of Man* (1871). These two books, more than any others, provided the *casus belli* between science and religion during the latter part of the century. There is considerable irony in this, for Darwin himself tried hard to stick to the facts and to avoid metaphysical controversy. Yet the "facts" as he stated them raised all the age-old questions of relativism and the absolute, necessity and free will, and design versus chance.

It has been said, and correctly, that the new thing in Darwin was his hypothesis of natural selection, i.e., his explanation of the mechanism of evolution rather than the idea of evolution as such. By 1859, the idea of an evolution in nature from simple to complex forms was already a familiar story, thanks to the previous work of the geologist Sir Charles Lyell and biologists like Erasmus Darwin and Lamarck. But Darwin gave it its supreme expression and backed it up with impressive evidence, and as a result of his work, thinkers could no longer fail to see its profound implications for religion. In brief, the idea of evolution, principally as expounded by Darwin, persuaded people to think of everything in nature as the fruit of a gradual growth rather than an original creation. It was now difficult if not impossible for an educated man to conceive of a primitive revelation such as traditional Christianity taught, or even an original natural religion from which men had declined. In an evolving world, perfection obviously lay, not in the past, but in the future. What is more, religious ideas, like everything else, appeared not to be absolute, but on the contrary, to be forever fluctuating and changing into something different.

To make matters worse for the religious camp, Darwin's explanation of the evolutionary process appeared to banish intelligent design from the universe. Darwin himself wavered on the subject, often declaring to friends that he was in "an utterly hopeless muddle." His hypothesis of natural selection, however, was

---

[10]Huxley to Kingsley, May 22, 1863, in Leonard Huxley, *Life and Letters of Thomas Henry Huxley* (New York: D. Appleton, 1901), Vol. I, p. 262.

clear enough. According to this hypothesis, nature selects for survival those organisms which, by the accident of birth, are best fitted to get plenty of food and to reproduce; all others it drives to the wall. Darwin pictured nature as a great battleground, not unlike the world of contemporary economics, on which individuals competed for an insufficient food supply, and on which victory went to luck rather than to cunning. It was, moreover, a recklessly wasteful process which achieved its end in one case out of thousands; the general rule was destruction and failure. Nor was its "end" invariably so perfect as had been imagined. "Natural selection will not produce absolute perfection," said Darwin, citing the imperfections of the human eye and the example of the bee whose sting when once used inevitably causes the death of the insect by tearing out its viscera. According to the German scientist Hermann von Helmholtz, "whose judgment," said Darwin, "no one will dispute":

That which we have discovered in the way of inexactness and imperfection in the optical machine and in the image on the retina, is as nothing in comparison with the incongruities which we have just come across in the domain of the sensations. One might say that nature has taken delight in accumulating contradictions in order to remove all foundation from the theory of a pre-existing harmony between the external and internal worlds.[11]

If Darwin's hypothesis was correct, then mind was indeed "pitchforked" out of the universe, as Samuel Butler put it. To account for the phenomena of nature it was unnecessary to assume any metaphysical or religious factor at work. Blind chance (fortuitous hereditary variations) and mechanical selection by the environment would, so to speak, contrive a watch (though an imperfect watch) without the purposiveness of a watchmaker. In the famous preface to *Back to Methuselah,* written some years later, George Bernard Shaw skillfully reconstructed the atmosphere in which Darwin's star first appeared. Darwin's friends, he said, actually regarded the banishment of mind as "a glorious enlightenment and emancipation" from a moribund theology and Biblicism. "We were intellectually intoxicated with the idea that the world could make itself without design, purpose, skill, or intelligence: in short, without life." Reminiscing about his college days, Frederick Pollock similarly recalled a knot of Cambridge friends led by W. K. Clifford who "were carried away by a wave of Darwinian enthusiasm." "We seemed to ride triumphant on an ocean of new life and boundless possibilities. Natural Selection was to be the master-key of the universe; we expected it to solve all riddles and reconcile all contradictions. Among other things it was to give us a new system of ethics."[12] And true to that early inspiration Clifford later deduced a naturalistic, as distinguished from a religious, ethic from *The Descent of Man.* In several brilliant articles he accounted for ideas of right and wrong entirely in terms of tribal evolution; conscience had evolved because it was useful to the tribe in its struggle for existence against other tribes or against the environment.

---

[11]Charles Darwin, *The Origin of Species* (6th ed.; London, 1890), p. 163.
[12]Frederick Pollock, Introduction to *Lectures and Essays by the Late William Kingdon Clifford* (London, 1879), Vol. I, p. 33.

The new science of anthropology which arose, not accidentally, in a great age of European travel and exploration, similarly told against religious premises. Oddly, for the reverse is probably the case today, the anthropologists were on the whole less sceptical personally than the natural scientists or the propagandists of science. Perhaps this was because no theory quite so comprehensive as natural selection illuminated anthropological studies, perhaps also because they dealt with human *mores,* a subject more complex by far than Darwin's *Edentata,* pigeons, and cockroaches. Yet thoughtful readers could and did perceive the sceptical implications of such works as E. B. Tylor's *Primitive Culture* (1871), William Robertson Smith's *Religion of the Semites* (1889), and above all, Sir James Frazer's *Golden Bough.* Their naturalistic treatment of the origins of religion, their researches into savage superstitions, the resemblances they noted between the myths and rites of savage and civilized peoples raised serious questions about the uniqueness of Christianity or any other religion.

Frazer stands as the great symbol of this anthropological scepticism, not only because of his prodigious scholarship but also because of his inimitable style which aroused, as few scholarly works can, the interest of nonspecialists. *The Golden Bough: A Study in Magic and Religion,* his *magnum opus,* first appeared in two volumes in 1890, and later swelled to thirteen volumes in the third edition. In this and other works Frazer claimed to be treating the religions of the world "not dogmatically but historically"—that is to say, not as systems of truth or falsehood to be demonstrated or refuted, but as phenomena of consciousness to be studied like any other aspect of human nature. But by his brilliant exposition of the comparative method, and by his formulation of a law of the development of human thought, which resembled Auguste Comte's famous "law of the three intellectual stages," he unquestionably helped to undermine the foundations of dogma.

Never lacking for a vivid metaphor, Frazer compared the course of thought in history to a web woven of three different threads, black, red, and white, signifying respectively magic, religion, and science. The first part of the web looks like a chequer of black and white, mostly black; toward the middle it takes on a dark crimson stain which finally shades off into a lighter tint. Similarly, in history magic is displaced by religion which in turn gives way to science. All three, religion included, are represented as modes of explaining and controlling nature. In Frazer's view, magic and science are somewhat akin because both postulate an inflexible regularity in natural events, but the natural order assumed by magic is purely imaginary whereas the order of science is the true one based on observation. Magic was superseded by religion when man discovered the errors he was making about nature. Turning to religion he ceased to rely on his own intelligence and tried to achieve the same end by propitiating "certain invisible beings" behind the veil of nature. By and by this solution also failed as the keener minds descried a real order in nature, and consequently rejected the religious theory as "inadequate." That Frazer saw this development from magic to religion to science as a boon to mankind we know from his conclusion:

> Here, at last, after groping about in the dark for countless ages, man has hit upon a clue to the labyrinth, a golden key that opens many locks in the treasury of nature. It is probably not too much to say that the hope of

progress—moral and intellectual as well as material—in the future is bound up with the fortunes of science, and that every obstacle placed in the way of scientific discovery is a wrong to humanity.

Elsewhere in his *opus* Frazer had more sympathetic things to say about religion, but as an evolutionist he thought of it not as a system of absolutes, but as subject to change like everything else under the sun. "The old view that the principles of right and wrong are immutable and eternal is no longer tenable. The moral world is as little exempt as the physical world from the law of ceaseless change, of perpetual flux."[13]

Frazer, as we have said, also turned "the battery of the comparative method" against the venerable walls of belief. What this method meant he explained in his essay on his master and friend William Robertson Smith. It assumed, in the first place, that the religions of the world could be accounted for naturalistically, that they were "largely modified and determined" by their physical surroundings, material culture, contacts with neighboring peoples, and the like. It then examined these religions side by side and discovered, as Voltaire and others had done earlier but in an amateurish way, that there were fundamental resemblances between them. Smith pointed out, for instance, that the slaying of a divine victim and the partaking of his flesh and blood, in a word the Christian Atonement and Eucharist, was a conception by no means confined to Christianity but common to heathen and even savage religions. And what did this sort of resemblance signify? For Frazer it proved that many religious doctrines and practices were, if not necessarily false, at least based on primitive conceptions "which most civilized and educated men have long agreed in abandoning as mistaken."[14]

The three modes of sceptical thought thus far analyzed have, as we have said, a familiar ring about them. However, the three remaining modes—the psychological, economic, and historical—struck what were essentially new notes, notes that could scarcely have achieved real clarity before the nineteenth century. They all explained religion, indeed more often than not explained it away, as a reflection of the human condition: man's psychological needs and wishes, man's social and economic milieu, man's cultural environment.

Ludwig Feuerbach's *The Essence of Christianity* (1841), which George Eliot translated into English and which created a sensation comparable to that aroused by *The Origin of Species,* was the first great exposition of the psychological critique of religion. Feuerbach belonged to that extraordinary group of intellectuals known as the Young Hegelians, who sat at the feet of the master but who later turned against him and undermined the philosophical and religious props of the old regime in Germany. His theory of Illusionism, which profoundly influenced Marx and foreshadowed Freud, can be best understood as a fusion of two contemporary intellectual forces, the romantic movement (which, however, Feuerbach often attacked) and empiricism. From romanticism he learned to look at the subjective side of the human psyche, at man's feelings and emotional needs, at the unconscious depths which produce dreams and fantasies. At the same time the empirical philosophy taught him to distrust what he could not see

---

[13]Sir James Frazer, *The Golden Bough* (3rd ed., London, 1911), Vol. III, p. vi.
[14]Sir James Frazer, *The Gorgon's Head and Other Literary Pieces* (London, 1927), p. 283.

and verify by objective tests. As he explained it, his method, in contrast to Hegel's, called for "generalisations from the known manifestations of human nature," generating "thought from the object," not "the object from the thought." This method revealed to him "that what by an earlier religion was regarded as objective is now recognised as subjective," i.e., "religion is the dream of the human mind," "consciousness of God is self-consciousness," "the secret of theology is anthropology." By such aphorisms Feuerbach meant that man, out of his psychological need, created God in his own image, projected into God all his own attributes or rather the attributes that he most admired and wanted to have. Thus, the Greeks attributed great physical strength to their gods, while the ancient Germans, who admired the warrior-type above all others, made their supreme god Odin, the god of war. Similarly, if God were an object to the birds, he would surely have wings. Thus, Feuerbach reduced religion to unconscious self-projection; it was an illusion in the sense that there was no object corresponding to man's subjective yearnings. For Feuerbach the turning point in history came when men realized that what they had formerly regarded as objective was in fact subjective; "that is, what was formerly contemplated and worshipped as God is now perceived to be something *human.*" Feuerbach was acutely conscious of living in an age of science and technology which rendered religion in the old sense obsolete. He thought that the question of the existence or nonexistence of God belonged to the sixteenth and seventeenth centuries, but not to the nineteenth. Christianity, he wrote in the preface to the second edition of his book, has "in fact long vanished, not only from the reason but from the life of mankind," for it is "in flagrant contradiction with our fire and life assurance companies, our railroads and steamcarriages, our picture and sculpture galleries, our military and industrial schools, our theatres and scientific museums."[15]

Karl Marx's economic intepretation of religion was simply Feuerbach's psychological interpretation writ large. Though he bitterly criticized Feuerbach on a number of counts, Marx learned from him to resolve "the religious essence into the human." His quarrel with Feuerbach was that the latter abstracted this human essence into each single individual. "Feuerbach, consequently, does not see that the 'religious sentiment' is itself a social product, and that the abstract individual whom he analyzes belongs in reality to a particular form of society."[16] Hence, whereas Feuerbach reduced religion to anthropology, i.e., man's self-projection, the most famous of all the Young Hegelians reduced it to sociology, i.e., the wishes of a whole society or group, and ultimately to economics, since social wishes reflected the tensions of the class system which in turn grew out of current relations of economic production. Marx's reduction of religion to economics came at a time, it should be noted, when European intellectuals were becoming acutely conscious of the importance of economic factors in history. In the world of the Industrial Revolution it is scarcely surprising that materialists should have risen to challenge the idealistic interpretation of history as the product of the Hegelian "Idea" or "consciousness." "Wholly in contrast to German philosophy [i.e., Hegelian idealism], which comes down from heaven to earth, we here ascend from earth to heaven," Marx wrote in *The German Ideology* (1846). That

---

[15]Ludwig Feuerbach, *The Essence of Christianity,* trans. George Eliot (London, 1854), Preface, chap. 1, and *passim.*
[16]Karl Marx, *Theses on Feuerbach* (1845), *passim,* especially Nos. IV, VI, and VII.

is to say, what counted in history was not the coming of the Idea to self-consciousness but how men earned their living and divided into classes. Seen through these economic spectacles, religion appeared to be mere "superstructure" or "ideology." It was a superstructure which rested upon the real, the economic structure of society: "the religious world is but a reflex of the real world." It was ideology in the sense that men employed it, along with philosophy, jurisprudence, and art, to further or maintain the interests of their class: "the ruling ideas of each age have ever been the ideas of its ruling class." Marx also taught that as the economic foundations changed, so did "the whole immense superstructure of ideas," including religious ideas. In other words, Marx treated religion as relative to a particular economic and social system. "Does it require deep intuition," he asked in the *Communist Manifesto,* "to comprehend that man's ideas, views, and conceptions, in one word, man's consciousness changes with every change in the conditions of his material existence, in his social relations and in his social life?" Believing that this was so, Marx's strategy was not to attack religion as such, but to concentrate on changing the underlying economic and social conditions which made religion possible. "Religion" would disappear when the capitalist regime and class system had been overthrown. This was by far the most devastating attack that had yet been made on religion. Marx did not question the sincerity of individual religious leaders or theologians, as Voltaire and Bentham had done. He did far worse; taking his cue from Feuerbach, he brushed religion aside as unreal and illusory in comparison to the "real" forces which influenced and moved men in history.

Marx's argument brings us to the final, and in many respects the most devastating of all the modes of nineteenth-century sceptical criticism, viz. the historical. *Historismus* (significantly, a nineteenth-century neologism) or "historicism" is implied in all of the above arguments except the utilitarian. It may fairly be said therefore that it was more pervasive than any of the others. It was what otherwise so different thinkers as Marx and Frazer, the evolutionists and the Higher Critics, had in common; in a word, it became a universal idiom. It was also relatively novel, distinguishing rather sharply the nineteenth-century sceptic from his forbears of the Enlightenment. Friedrich Meinecke hardly exaggerated, therefore, when he called the upthrust of *Historismus* "one of the greatest spiritual revolutions which western thought has experienced."

Historicism was the product of a number of converging intellectual forces: chiefly perhaps, though Meinecke carries it much farther back, the romantic movement with its emphasis on the individuality and plasticity of historical events, and the new scientific view that everything was in a state of flux. Precisely what historicism meant was admirably stated by Lord Morley, himself an eminent historian. It meant "the triumph of the principle of relativity in historic judgment," "the substitution of *becoming* for *being,* the relative for the absolute, dynamic movement for dogmatic immobility." It meant referring everything, men's ideas and beliefs included, to its origins, understanding it in terms of its historical milieu. Above all, it meant the posing of an entirely new set of questions. As a result of the vogue of "the historical method," Morley wrote in 1874:

Opinions are counted rather as phenomena to be explained, than as matters of truth and falsehood. Of usages, we are beginning first of all to think where they came from, and secondarily whether they are the most fitting and convenient that men could be got to accept. In the last century men asked of a belief or a story, Is it true? We now ask, How did men come to take it for true?[17]

The problem posed for religion by historicism became even more explicit with the great German historian Ernst Troeltsch (1865–1923) who in fact agonized over it and spent a large part of his life trying, unsuccessfully, to solve it. Troeltsch was trained as a Protestant theologian, was for twenty-one years professor of systematic theology at Heidelberg, and wrote a book entitled *The Absolute Validity of Christianity.* In a remarkably frank autobiographical passage, however, he tells us that the problem of historicism *vis-à-vis* religion gave him trouble almost from the outset of his academic career. The problem arose for him, he said, from the clash between his historical education and his concern to reach an effective religious position which would give him a center of reference and a sense of meaning and purpose.

> I soon discovered that the historical studies which had so largely formed me, and the theology and philosophy in which I was now immersed, stood in sharp opposition, indeed even in conflict, with one another. I was confronted, upon the one hand, with the perpetual flux of the historian's data, and the distrustful attitude of the historical critic towards conventional traditions. . . . [18]

How could he realize "the demand of the religious consciousness for certainty, for unity, and for peace" when history so obviously taught "the relativity and transitoriness of all things, even of the loftiest values of civilisation." On his own testimony Troeltsch became increasingly convinced that historical Christianity was "a purely historical, individual, relative phenomenon" which could only have arisen in the peculiar milieu of the classical world. "The inference from all that," he concluded, "is that a religion, in the several forms assumed by it, always depends upon the intellectual, social, and national conditions among which it exists."[19] Thus, in the end, though he never became a complete sceptic, Troeltsch was forced to climb down from his earlier view of "the absolute validity of Christianity."

By the last quarter of the century, historicism had become the *Weltanschauung,* not merely of a few perceptive individuals like Morley and Troeltsch, but of an entire culture. It had literally invaded all departments of thought, the sciences, literary and art criticism, and also, what is chiefly germane to our purpose, those fields which touched most directly on religion. The Irish historian William Edward Hartpole Lecky had already applied it to ethical concepts, in his *History of European Morals* (1869), a work which aimed, in its author's words, to study "the relative importance that in different ages has been attached to different

---

[17]Morley, *On Compromise,* in *Works,* Vol. III, p. 14; *Recollections, ibid.,* Vol. I, p. 65.
[18]Ernst Troeltsch, *Christian Thought. Its History and Application,* trans. Baron F. von Hügel (London, 1923), p. 6. This passage is from the first of a series of lectures which Troeltsch had prepared for delivery at Oxford in 1923. These lectures outlined the theme which, if he had lived, he hoped to develop as the second volume of his *Der Historismus und seine Probleme.*
[19]*Ibid.,* p. 22.

virtues." "Changing circumstances produce changing types," said Lecky; "religions, considered as moral teachers, are realised and effective only when their moral teaching is in conformity with the teaching of their age."[20] Similarly, a host of Higher Critics had by then applied historical categories to the study of the Bible.

Because of its shaping influence the Higher Criticism deserves special mention. The mental development of men like Morley and Troeltsch is inconceivable without it. It taught scores of people to think of religion as in large part historical "myth." It got into novels, for example, Mrs. Gaskell's *North and South,* and, spectacularly, Mrs. Humphry Ward's *Robert Ellsmere,* a vastly popular book in which the hero, an Anglican clergyman, renounced clerical orders when the squire of his parish, a scholar and Higher Critic, convinced him that supernatural Christianity was incompatible with a historical study of early Christian testimony. The scandal created by the publication of *Essays and Reviews* in 1860 testifies to the fact that the Higher Criticism had infected the thought of the clergy in real life as well as literature. Two of the seven essays in this famous volume, both by clergymen, dealt specifically with the Higher Criticism and indubitably threw doubt on the doctrine of the Inspiration of the Bible.

The seminal thinker among the Higher Critics was the Young Hegelian David Friedrich Strauss whose *Life of Jesus* (1835–1836), also translated into English by George Eliot, cost him his teaching post at Tübingen and earned for him the sobriquet of "Modern Iscariot." Briefly, what Strauss did was to apply the historical method and the concept of myth, popularized contemporaneously by Jacob Grimm and others, to the New Testament. In so doing he exploded the older supernatural and rationalistic interpretations of the Bible which, however else they might differ, had been agreed upon the historicity of the events recorded in the synoptic Gospels. All religions, said Strauss, originated in myth, i.e., in beliefs arising from the experiences and hopes of a community, and early Christianity was no exception to the rule. The writers of the Gospels were weaned on the Old Testament or, in the case of John, Greek philosophy too, and when they came to write about Jesus, they naturally read into him the mythical properties of the Jewish messiah or the Greek logos. Thus, what was reported of Jesus was not, for the most part, historical fact but historical myth. The revolutionary thing about Strauss' criticism was that it interpreted Christianity as ideology, i.e., as the product of a particular historical and mental environment. It is easy to see how Marx, for instance, taking off from Strauss, could explain religion in terms of the economic environment, and why Troeltsch was puzzled by Christianity's claim to "absolute validity." No wonder Ernest Renan, France's Higher Critic and likewise the author of a life of Jesus, could declare that to write the history of a religion it was necessary, first, to have believed it (for otherwise the writer would never be able to understand how it had charmed people), but in the second place, "to believe it no longer in an absolute manner, for absolute faith is incompatible with sincere history."[21]

---

[20]William Edward Hartpole Lecky, *A History of European Morals from Augustus to Charlemagne* (New York: D. Appleton, 1877), Vol. I, p. 157.

[21]Ernest Renan, *The Life of Jesus* (New York: Dutton—Everyman's Library, 1927), p. 31. Renan's *Vie de Jésus* was first published in 1863.

The philosopher Henry Sidgwick was therefore only stating the simple truth when toward the close of the century he wrote that "a belief in the Historical Method is the most widely and strongly entertained philosophical conviction at the present day." He was also correct in pointing to historicism as one of the chief solvents of religious conviction in the nineteenth century. Like Troeltsch he demurred, or tried to demur, at the general conclusion; but he understood only too well the philosophical and religious implications of what Walter Pater was currently calling the "nimbly-shifting Time-Spirit."

> It seems to me that the historical study of human beliefs, in some very important departments of thought—such as ethics, politics and theology —does tend to be connected with a general scepticism as to the validity of the doctrines studied. . . . [Scepticism] partly tends to result from the historical study, because of the vast and bewildering variety of conflicting beliefs . . . which this study marshals before us. The student's own most fundamental and most cherished convictions seem forced, as it were, to step down from their secure pedestals, and to take their places in the endless line that is marching past. . . . Thus to the historian . . . the whole defiling train of beliefs tends to become something from which he sits apart, every portion of which has lost power to hold his own reason in the grip of true conviction: for peace's sake, he accepts the beliefs that are pressed on him by public opinion in his own age and country; but in his heart he believes in nothing but history.[22]

[22]Henry Sidgwick, "The Historical Method," *Mind*, Vol. XI (1886), pp. 213–14.

Chapter
FIVE

RESPONSES TO SECULARITY
existentialism and escape from history

THE TASK OF DEMYTHOLOGIZING

Rudolph Bultmann

Rudolph Bultmann, "The Task of Demythologizing," R. H. Fuller (trans. and ed.), from H. W. Bartsch (ed.), *Kerygma and Myth*, 1961. Used by permission of Harper & Row, Publishers, Incorporated, New York.

The Task of Demythologizing the New Testament Proclamation

A. THE PROBLEM

1. THE MYTHICAL VIEW OF THE WORLD AND THE MYTHICAL EVENT OF REDEMPTION

The cosmology of the New Testament is essentially mythical in character. The world is viewed as a three-storied structure, with the earth in the centre, the heaven above, and the underworld beneath. Heaven is the abode of God and of celestial beings—the angels. The underworld is hell, the place of torment. Even the earth is more than the scene of natural, everyday events, of the trivial round and common task. It is the scene of the supernatural activity of God and his angels on the one hand, and of Satan and his daemons on the other. These supernatural forces intervene in the course of nature and in all that men think and will and do. Miracles are by no means rare. Man is not in control of his own life. Evil spirits may take possession of him. Satan may inspire him with evil thoughts. Alternatively, God may inspire his thought and guide his purposes. He may grant him heavenly visions. He may allow him to hear his word of succour or demand. He may give him the supernatural power of his Spirit. History does not follow a smooth unbroken course; it is set in motion and controlled by these supernatural powers. This aeon is held in bondage by Satan, sin, and death (for "powers" is precisely what they are), and hastens towards its end. That end will come very soon, and will take the form of a cosmic catastrophe. It will be inaugurated by the "woes" of the last time. Then the Judge will come from heaven, the dead will rise, the last judgement will take place, and men will enter into eternal salvation or damnation.

This then is the mythical view of the world which the New Testament presupposes when it presents the event of redemption which is the subject of its preaching. It proclaims in the language of mythology that the last time has now come. "In the fulness of time" God sent forth his Son, a pre-existent divine Being, who appears on earth as a man.[1] He dies the death of a sinner[2] on the cross and makes atonement for the sins of men.[3] His resurrection marks the beginning of the cosmic catastrophe. Death, the consequence of Adam's sin, is abolished,[4] and

---

[1] Gal. 4. 4; Phil. 2. 6ff.; 2 Cor. 8. 9; John 1. 14, etc.
[2] 2 Cor. 5. 21; Rom. 8. 3.
[3] Rom. 3. 23–26; 4. 25; 8. 3; 2 Cor. 5. 14, 19; John 1. 29; 1 John 2. 2, etc.
[4] 1 Cor. 15. 21f.; Rom. 5. 12ff.

the daemonic forces are deprived of their power.[5] The risen Christ is exalted to the right hand of God in heaven[6] and made "Lord" and "King".[7] He will come again on the clouds of heaven to complete the work of redemption, and the resurrection and judgement of men will follow.[8] Sin, suffering and death will then be finally abolished.[9] All this is to happen very soon; indeed, St Paul thinks that he himself will live to see it.[10]

All who belong to Christ's Church and are joined to the Lord by Baptism and the Eucharist are certain of resurrection to salvation,[11] unless they forfeit it by unworthy behaviour. Christian believers already enjoy the first instalment of salvation, for the Spirit[12] is at work within them, bearing witness to their adoption as sons of God,[13] and guaranteeing their final resurrection.[14]

2. THE MYTHOLOGICAL VIEW OF THE WORLD OBSOLETE

All this is the language of mythology, and the origin of the various themes can be easily traced in the contemporary mythology of Jewish Apocalyptic and in the redemption myths of Gnosticism. To this extent *the kerygma is incredible to modern man, for he is convinced that the mythical view of the world is obsolete.* We are therefore bound to ask whether, when we preach the Gospel to-day, we expect our converts to accept not only the Gospel message, but also the mythical view of the world in which it is set. If not, does the New Testament embody a truth which is quite independent of its mythical setting? If it does, theology must undertake the task of stripping the Kerygma from its mythical framework, of "demythologizing" it.

Can Christian preaching expect modern man *to accept the mythical view of the world as true?* To do so would be both senseless and impossible. It would be senseless, because there is nothing specifically Christian in the mythical view of the world as such. It is simply the cosmology of a pre-scientific age. Again, it would be impossible, because no man can adopt a view of the world by his own volition—it is already determined for him by his place in history. Of course such a view is not absolutely unalterable, and the individual may even contribute to its change. But he can do so only when he is faced by a new set of facts so compelling as to make his previous view of the world untenable. He has then no alternative but to modify his view of the world or produce a new one. The discoveries of Copernicus and the atomic theory are instances of this, and so was romanticism, with its discovery that the human subject is richer and more complex than enlightenment or idealism had allowed, and nationalism, with its new realization of the importance of history and the tradition of peoples.

It may equally well happen that truths which a shallow enlightenment had

---

[5]1 Cor. 2. 6; Col. 2. 15; Rev. 12. 7ff., etc.
[6]Acts 1. 6f.; 2. 33; Rom. 8. 34, etc.
[7]Phil. 2. 9–11; 1 Cor. 15. 25.
[8]1 Cor. 15. 23f., 50ff., etc.
[9]Rev. 21. 4, etc.
[10]1 Thess. 4. 15ff.; 1 Cor. 15. 51f.; cf. Mark 9. 1.
[11]Rom. 5. 12ff.; 1 Cor. 15. 21ff., 44b, ff.
[12]Λπαρχή: Rom. 8. 23, ἀρραβών: 2 Cor. 1. 22; 5. 5.
[13]Rom. 8. 15; Gal. 4. 6.
[14]Rom. 8. 11.

failed to perceive are later rediscovered in ancient myths. Theologians are perfectly justified in asking whether this is not exactly what has happened with the New Testament. At the same time it is impossible to revive an obsolete view of the world by a mere fiat, and certainly not a mythical view. For all our thinking to-day is shaped irrevocably by modern science. A blind acceptance of the New Testament mythology would be arbitrary, and to press for its acceptance as an article of faith would be to reduce faith to works. Wilhelm Herrmann pointed this out, and one would have thought that his demonstration was conclusive. It would involve a sacrifice of the intellect which could have only one result—a curious form of schizophrenia and insincerity. It would mean accepting a view of the world in our faith and religion which we should deny in our everyday life. Modern thought as we have inherited it brings with it criticism of *the New Testament view of the world.*

Man's knowledge and mastery of the world have advanced to such an extent through science and technology that it is no longer possible for anyone seriously to hold the New Testament view of the world—in fact, there is no one who does. What meaning, for instance, can we attach to such phrases in the creed as "descended into hell" or "ascended into heaven"? We no longer believe in the three-storied universe which the creeds take for granted. The only honest way of reciting the creeds is to strip the mythological framework from the truth they enshrine—that is, assuming that they contain any truth at all, which is just the question that theology has to ask. No one who is old enough to think for himself supposes that God lives in a local heaven. There is no longer any heaven in the traditional sense of the word. The same applies to hell in the sense of a mythical underworld beneath our feet. And if this is so, the story of Christ's descent into hell and of his Ascension into heaven is done with. We can no longer look for the return of the Son of Man on the clouds of heaven or hope that the faithful will meet him in the air (1 Thess. 4. 15ff.).

Now that the forces and the laws of nature have been discovered, we can no longer believe in *spirits, whether good or evil.* We know that the stars are physical bodies whose motions are controlled by the laws of the universe, and not daemonic beings which enslave mankind to their service. Any influence they may have over human life must be explicable in terms of the ordinary laws of nature; it cannot in any way be attributed to their malevolence. Sickness and the cure of disease are likewise attributable to natural causation; they are not the result of daemonic activity or of evil spells.[15] The *miracles of the New Testament* have ceased to be miraculous, and to defend their historicity by recourse to nervous disorders or hypnotic effects only serves to underline the fact. And if we are still left with certain physiological and psychological phenomena which we can only

---

[15]It may of course be argued that there are people alive to-day whose confidence in the traditional scientific view of the world has been shaken, and others who are primitive enough to qualify for an age of mythical thought. And there are also many varieties of superstition. But when belief in spirits and miracles has degenerated into superstition, it has become something entirely different from what it was when it was genuine faith. The various impressions and speculations which influence credulous people here and there are of little importance, nor does it matter to what extent cheap slogans have spread an atmosphere inimical to science. What matters is the world view which men imbibe from their environment, and it is science which determines that view of the world through the school, the press, the wireless, the cinema, and all the other fruits of technical progress.

assign to mysterious and enigmatic causes, we are still assigning them to causes, and thus far are trying to make them scientifically intelligible. Even occultism pretends to be a science.

It is impossible to use electric light and the wireless and to avail ourselves of modern medical and surgical discoveries, and at the same time to believe in the New Testament world of spirits and miracles.[16] We may think we can manage it in our own lives, but to expect others to do so is to make the Christian faith unintelligible and unacceptable to the modern world.

The mythical eschatology is untenable for the simple reason that the parousia of Christ never took place as the New Testament expected. History did not come to an end, and, as every schoolboy knows, it will continue to run its course. Even if we believe that the world as we know it will come to an end in time, we expect the end to take the form of a natural catastrophe, not of a mythical event such as the New Testament expects. And if we explain the parousia in terms of modern scientific theory, we are applying criticism to the New Testament, albeit unconsciously.

But natural science is not the only challenge which the mythology of the New Testament has to face. There is the still more serious challenge presented by *modern man's understanding of himself.*

Modern man is confronted by a curious dilemma. He may regard himself as pure nature, or as pure spirit. In the latter case he distinguishes the essential part of his being from nature. In either case, however, *man is essentially a unity.* He bears the sole responsibility for his own feeling, thinking, and willing.[17] He is not, as the New Testament regards him, the victim of a strange dichotomy which exposes him to the interference of powers outside himself. If his exterior behaviour and his interior condition are in perfect harmony, it is something he has achieved himself, and if other people think their interior unity is torn asunder by daemonic or divine interference, he calls it schizophrenia.

Although biology and psychology recognize that man is a highly dependent being, that does not mean that he has been handed over to powers outside of and distinct from himself. This dependence is inseparable from human nature, and he needs only to understand it in order to recover his self-mastery and organize his life on a rational basis. If he regards himself as spirit, he knows that he is permanently conditioned by the physical, bodily part of his being, but he distinguishes his true self from it, and knows that he is independent and responsible for his mastery over nature.

In either case he finds *what the New Testament has to say about the "Spirit"* (πνεῦμα) *and the sacraments utterly strange and incomprehensible.* Biological man cannot see how a supernatural entity like the πνεῦμα can penetrate within the close texture of his natural powers and set to work within him. Nor can the idealist understand how a πνεῦμα working like a natural power can touch and influence his mind and spirit. Conscious as he is of his own moral responsibility, he cannot conceive how baptism in water can convey a mysterious something

---

[16]Cp. the observations of Paul Schütz on the decay of mythical religion in the East through the introduction of modern hygiene and medicine.
[17]Cp. Gerhardt Krüger, *Einsicht und Leidenschaft, Das Wesen des platonischen Denkens* Frankfort 1939, p. 11f.

which is henceforth the agent of all his decisions and actions. He cannot see how physical food can convey spiritual strength, and how the unworthy receiving of the Eucharist can result in physical sickness and death (1 Cor. 11. 30). The only possible explanation is that it is due to suggestion. He cannot understand how anyone can be baptized for the dead (1 Cor. 15. 29).

We need not examine in detail the various forms of modern *Weltanschauung,* whether idealist or naturalist. For the only criticism of the New Testament which is theologically relevant is that which arises *necessarily* out of the situation of modern man. The biological *Weltanschauung* does not, for instance, arise necessarily out of the contemporary situation. We are still free to adopt it or not as we choose. The only relevant question for the theologian is the basic assumption on which the adoption of a biological as of every other *Weltanschauung* rests, and that assumption is the view of the world which has been moulded by modern science and the modern conception of human nature as a self-subsistent unity immune from the interference of supernatural powers.

Again, the biblical doctrine that *death is the punishment of sin* is equally abhorrent to naturalism and idealism, since they both regard death as a simple and necessary process of nature. To the naturalist death is no problem at all, and to the idealist it is a problem for that very reason, for so far from arising out of man's essential spiritual being it actually destroys it. The idealist is faced with a paradox. On the one hand man is a spiritual being, and therefore essentially different from plants and animals, and on the other hand he is the prisoner of nature, whose birth, life, and death are just the same as those of the animals. Death may present him with a problem, but he cannot see how it can be a punishment for sin. Human beings are subject to death even before they have committed any sin. And to attribute human mortality to the fall of Adam is sheer nonsense, for guilt implies personal responsibility, and the idea of original sin as an inherited infection is sub-ethical, irrational, and absurd.

The same objections apply to *the doctrine of the atonement.* How can the guilt of one man be expiated by the death of another who is sinless—if indeed one may speak of a sinless man at all? What primitive notions of guilt and righteousness does this imply? And what primitive idea of God? The rationale of sacrifice in general may of course throw some light on the theory of the atonement, but even so, what a primitive mythology it is, that a divine Being should become incarnate, and atone for the sins of men through his own blood! Or again, one might adopt an analogy from the law courts, and explain the death of Christ as a transaction between God and man through which God's claims on man were satisfied. But that would make sin a juridical matter; it would be no more than an external transgression of a commandment, and it would make nonsense of all our ethical standards. Moreover, if the Christ who died such a death was the pre-existent Son of God, what could death mean for him? Obviously very little, if he knew that he would rise again in three days!

The *resurrection of Jesus* is just as difficult for modern man, if it means an event whereby a living supernatural power is released which can henceforth be appropriated through the sacraments. To the biologist such language is meaningless, for he does not regard death as a problem at all. The idealist would not object to the idea of a life immune from death, but he could not believe that such a life is made available by the resuscitation of a dead person. If that is the way God makes life available for man, his action is inextricably involved in a nature miracle. Such a notion he finds incomprehensible, for he can see God at work only in the reality of his personal life and in his transformation. But, quite apart from the incredibility of such a miracle, he cannot see how an event like this could be the act of God, or how it could affect his own life.

Gnostic influence suggests that this Christ, who died and rose again, was not a mere human being but a God-man. His death and resurrection were not isolated facts which concerned him alone, but a cosmic event in which we are all involved.[18] It is only with effort that modern man can think himself back into such an intellectual atmosphere, and even then he could never accept it himself, because it regards man's essential being as nature and redemption as a process of nature. And as for the pre-existence of Christ, with its corollary of man's translation into a celestial realm of light, and the clothing of the human personality in heavenly robes and a spiritual body—all this is not only irrational but utterly meaningless. Why should salvation take this particular form? Why should this be the fulfilment of human life and the realization of man's true being?

B. The Task before Us

1. NOT SELECTION OR SUBTRACTION

Does this drastic criticism of the New Testament mythology mean the complete elimination of the kerygma?

Whatever else may be true, we cannot save the kerygma by selecting some of its features and subtracting others, and thus reduce the amount of mythology in it. For instance, it is impossible to dismiss St Paul's teaching about the unworthy reception of Holy Communion or about baptism for the dead, and yet cling to the belief that physical eating and drinking can have a spiritual effect. If we accept *one* idea, we must accept everything which the New Testament has to say about Baptism and Holy Communion, and it is just this one idea which we cannot accept.

It may of course be argued that some features of the New Testament mythology are given greater prominence than others: not all of them appear with the same regularity in the various books. There is for example only one occurrence of the legends of the Virgin birth and the Ascension; St Paul and St John appear to be totally unaware of them. But, even if we take them to be later accretions, it does not affect the mythical character of the event of redemption as a whole. And if we once start subtracting from the kerygma, where are we to draw the line? The mythical view of the world must be accepted or rejected in its entirety.

At this point absolute clarity and ruthless honesty are essential both for the academic theologian and for the parish priest. It is a duty they owe to themselves, to the Church they serve, and to those whom they seek to win for the Church. They must make it quite clear what their hearers are expected to accept and what they are not. At all costs the preacher must not leave his people in the dark about

---

[18]Rom. 5. 12ff.; 1 Cor. 15. 21ff., 44b.

what he secretly eliminates, nor must he be in the dark about it himself. In Karl Barth's book *The Resurrection of the Dead* the cosmic eschatology in the sense of "chronologically final history" is eliminated in favour of what he intends to be a non-mythological "ultimate history". He is able to delude himself into thinking that this is exegesis of St Paul and of the New Testament generally only because he gets rid of everything mythological in 1 Corinthians by subjecting it to an interpretation which does violence to its meaning. But that is an impossible procedure.

If the truth of the New Testament proclamation is to be preserved, the only way is to demythologize it. But our motive in so doing must not be to make the New Testament relevant to the modern world at all costs. The question is simply whether the New Testament consists exclusively of mythology, or whether it actually demands the elimination of myth if it is to be understood as it is meant to be. This question is forced upon us from two sides. First there is the nature of myth in general, and then there is the New Testament itself.

2. THE NATURE OF MYTH

The real purpose of myth is not to present an objective picture of the world as it is, but to express man's understanding of himself in the world in which he lives. Myth should be interpreted not cosmologically, but anthropologically, or better still, existentially.[19] Myth speaks of the power or the powers which man supposes he experiences as the ground and limit of his world and of his own activity and suffering. He describes these powers in terms derived from the visible world, with its tangible objects and forces, and from human life, with its feelings, motives, and potentialities. He may, for instance, explain the origin of the world by speaking of a world egg or a world tree. Similarly he may account for the present state and order of the world by speaking of a primeval war between the gods. He speaks of the other world in terms of this world, and of the gods in terms derived from human life.[20]

Myth is an expression of man's conviction that the origin and purpose of the world in which he lives are to be sought not within it but beyond it—that is, beyond the realm of known and tangible reality—and that this realm is perpetually dominated and menaced by those mysterious powers which are its source and limit. Myth is also an expression of man's awareness that he is not lord of his own being. It expresses his sense of dependence not only within the visible world, but more especially on those forces which hold sway beyond the confines of the known. Finally, myth expresses man's belief that in this state of dependence he can be delivered from the forces within the visible world.

Thus myth contains elements which demand its own criticism—namely, its imagery with its apparent claim to objective validity. The real purpose of myth is

---

[19]Cp. Gerhardt Krüger, *Einsicht und Leidenschaft,* esp. p. 17f., 56f.

[20]Myth is here used in the sense popularized by the 'History of Religions' school. Mythology is the use of imagery to express the other worldly in terms of this world and the divine in terms of human life, the other side in terms of this side. For instance, divine transcendence is expressed as spatial distance. It is a mode of expression which makes it easy to understand the cultus as an action in which material means are used to convey immaterial power. Myth is not used in that modern sense, according to which it is practically equivalent to ideology.

to speak of a transcendent power which controls the world and man, but that purpose is impeded and obscured by the terms in which it is expressed.

Hence the importance of the New Testament mythology lies not in its imagery but in the understanding of existence which it enshrines. The real question is whether this understanding of existence is true. Faith claims that it is, and faith ought not to be tied down to the imagery of New Testament mythology.

3. THE NEW TESTAMENT ITSELF

The New Testament itself invites this kind of criticism. Not only are there rough edges in its mythology, but some of its features are actually contradictory. For example, the death of Christ is sometimes a sacrifice and sometimes a cosmic event. Sometimes his person is interpreted as the Messiah and sometimes as the Second Adam. The kenosis of the pre-existent Son (Phil. 2. 6ff.) is incompatible with the miracle narratives as proofs of his messianic claims. The Virgin birth is inconsistent with the assertion of his pre-existence. The doctrine of the Creation is incompatible with the conception of the "rulers of this world" (1 Cor. 2. 6ff.), the "god of this world" (2 Cor. 4. 4) and the "elements of this world" στοιχεῖα τοῦ κόσμου, Gal. 4. 3). It is impossible to square the belief that the law was given by God with the theory that it comes from the angels (Gal. 3. 19f.).

But the principal demand for the criticism of mythology comes from a curious contradiction which runs right through the New Testament. Sometimes we are told that human life is determined by cosmic forces, at others we are challenged to a decision. Side by side with the Pauline indicative stands the Pauline imperative. In short, man is sometimes regarded as a cosmic being, sometimes as an independent "I" for whom decision is a matter of life or death. Incidentally, this explains why so many sayings in the New Testament speak directly to modern man's condition while others remain enigmatic and obscure. Finally, attempts at demythologization are sometimes made even within the New Testament itself. But more will be said on this point later.

4. PREVIOUS ATTEMPTS AT DEMYTHOLOGIZING

How then is the mythology of the New Testament to be reinterpreted? This is not the first time that theologians have approached this task. Indeed, all we have said so far might have been said in much the same way thirty or forty years ago, and it is a sign of the bankruptcy of contemporary theology that it has been necessary to go all over the same ground again. The reason for this is not far to seek. The liberal theologians of the last century were working on the wrong lines. They threw away not only the mythology but also the kerygma itself. Were they right? Is that the treatment the New Testament itself required? That is the question we must face to-day. The last twenty years have witnessed a movement away from criticism and a return to a naïve acceptance of the kerygma. The danger both for theological scholarship and for the Church is that this uncritical resuscitation of the New Testament mythology may make the Gospel message unintelligible to the modern world. We cannot dismiss the critical labours of earlier generations without further ado. We must take them up and put them to constructive use. Failure to do so will mean that the old battles between orthodoxy and liberalism will have to be fought out all over again, that is assuming that there will be any Church or any theologians to fight them at all! Perhaps we may put it schematically like this: whereas the older liberals used criticism to *eliminate* the mythology of the New Testament, our task to-day is to use criticism to *interpret* it. Of course it may still be necessary to eliminate mythology here and there. But the criterion adopted must be taken not from modern thought, but from the understanding of human existence which the New Testament itself enshrines.[21]

To begin with, let us review some of these earlier attempts at demythologizing. We need only mention briefly the allegorical interpretation of the New Testament which has dogged the Church throughout its history. This method spiritualizes the mythical events so that they become symbols of processes going on in the soul. This is certainly the most comfortable way of avoiding the critical question. The literal meaning is allowed to stand and is dispensed with only for the individual believer, who can escape into the realm of the soul.

It was characteristic of the older liberal theologians that they regarded mythology as relative and temporary. Hence they thought they could safely eliminate it altogether, and retain only the broad, basic principles of religion and ethics. They distinguished between what they took to be the essence of religion and the temporary garb which it assumed. Listen to what Harnack has to say about the essence of Jesus' preaching of the Kingdom of God and its coming: "The kingdom has a triple meaning. Firstly, it is something supernatural, a gift from above, not a product of ordinary life. Secondly, it is a purely religious blessing, the inner link with the living God; thirdly, it is the most important experience that a man can have, that on which everything else depends; it permeates and dominates his whole existence, because sin is forgiven and misery banished." Note how completely the mythology is eliminated: "The kingdom of God comes by coming to the individual, by entering into his *soul* and laying hold of it."[22]

It will be noticed how Harnack reduces the kerygma to a few basic principles of religion and ethics. Unfortunately this means that *the kerygma has ceased to be kerygma*: it is no longer the proclamation of the decisive act of God in Christ. For the liberals the great truths of religion and ethics are timeless and eternal, though it is only within human history that they are realized, and only in concrete historical processes that they are given clear expression. But the apprehension and acceptance of these principles does not depend on the knowledge and acceptance of the age in which they first took shape, or of the historical persons who first discovered them. We are all capable of verifying them in our own experience at whatever period we happen to live. History may be of academic interest, but never of paramount importance for religion.

But the New Testament speaks of an *event* through which God has wrought man's redemption. For it, Jesus is not primarily the teacher, who certainly had extremely important things to say and will always be honoured for saying them, but whose person in the last analysis is immaterial for those who have assimilated his teaching. On the contrary, his person is just what the New Testament proclaims as the decisive event of redemption. It speaks of this person in mythological terms, but does this mean that we can reject the kerygma altogether on the ground that it is nothing more than mythology? That is the question.

Next came the History of Religions school. Its representatives were the first to

---

[21]As an illustration of this critical re-interpretation of myth cf. Hans Jonas, *Augustin und das paulinische Freiheitsproblem*, 1930, pp. 66–76.
[22]*What is Christianity?* Williams and Norgate, 1904, pp. 63–4 and 57.

discover the extent to which the New Testament is permeated by mythology. The importance of the New Testament, they saw, lay not in its teaching about religion and ethics but in its actual religion and piety; in comparison with that all the dogma it contains, and therefore all the mythological imagery with its apparent objectivity, was of secondary importance or completely negligible. The essence of the New Testament lay in the religious life it portrayed; its high-watermark was the experience of mystical union with Christ, in whom God took symbolic form.

These critics grasped one important truth. Christian faith is not the same as religious idealism; the Christian life does not consist in developing the individual personality, in the improvement of society, or in making the world a better place. The Christian life means a turning away from the world, a detachment from it. But the critics of the History of Religions school failed to see that in the New Testament this detachment is essentially eschatological and not mystical. Religion for them was an expression of the human yearning to rise above the world and transcend it: it was the discovery of a supramundane sphere where the soul could detach itself from all earthly care and find its rest. Hence the supreme manifestation of religion was to be found not in personal ethics or in social idealism but in the cultus regarded as an end in itself. This was just the kind of religious life portrayed in the New Testament, not only as a model and pattern, but as a challenge and inspiration. The New Testament was thus the abiding source of power which enabled man to realize the true life of religion, and Christ was the eternal symbol for the cultus of the Christian Church.[23] It will be noticed how the Church is here defined exclusively as a worshipping community, and this represents a great advance on the older liberalism. This school rediscovered the Church as a *religious* institution. For the idealist there was really no place for the Church at all. But did they succeed in recovering the meaning of the Ecclesia in the full, New Testament sense of the word? For in the New Testament the Ecclesia is invariably a phenomenon of salvation history and eschatology.

Moreover, if the History of Religions school is right, the kerygma has once more ceased to be kerygma. Like the liberals, they are silent about a decisive act of God in Christ proclaimed as the event of redemption. So we are still left with the question whether this event and the person of Jesus, both of which are described in the New Testament in mythological terms, are nothing more than mythology. Can the kerygma be interpreted apart from mythology? Can we recover the truth of the kerygma for men who do not think in mythological terms without forfeiting its character as kerygma?

5. AN EXISTENTIALIST INTERPRETATION THE ONLY SOLUTION

The theological work which such an interpretation involves can be sketched only in the broadest outline and with only a few examples. We must avoid the impression that this is a light and easy task, as if all we have to do is to discover the right formula and finish the job on the spot. It is much more formidable than that. It cannot be done single-handed. It will tax the time and strength of a whole theological generation.

The mythology of the New Testament is in essence that of Jewish apocalyptic and the Gnostic redemption myths. A common feature of them both is their basic

---

[23]Cp. e.g. Troeltsch, *Die Bedeutung der Geschichtlichkeit Jesu für den Glauben,* Tübingen, 1911.

dualism, according to which the present world and its human inhabitants are under the control of daemonic, satanic powers, and stand in need of redemption. Man cannot achieve this redemption by his own efforts; it must come as a gift through a divine intervention. Both types of mythology speak of such an intervention: Jewish apocalyptic of an imminent world crisis in which this present aeon will be brought to an end and the new aeon ushered in by the coming of the Messiah, and Gnosticism of a Son of God sent down from the realm of light, entering into this world in the guise of a man, and by his fate and teaching delivering the elect and opening up the way for their return to their heavenly home.

The meaning of these two types of mythology lies once more not in their imagery with its apparent objectivity but in the understanding of human existence which both are trying to express. In other words, they need to be interpreted existentially. A good example of such treatment is to be found in Hans Jonas's book on Gnosticism.[24]

Our task is to produce an existentialist interpretation of the dualistic mythology of the New Testament along similar lines. When, for instance, we read of daemonic powers ruling the world and holding mankind in bondage, does the understanding of human existence which underlies such language offer a solution to the riddle of human life which will be acceptable even to the non-mythological mind of to-day? Of course we must not take this to imply that the New Testament presents us with an anthropology like that which modern science can give us. It cannot be proved by logic or demonstrated by an appeal to factual evidence. Scientific anthropologies always take for granted a definite understanding of existence, which is invariably the consequence of a deliberate decision of the scientist, whether he makes it consciously or not. And that is why we have to discover whether the New Testament offers man an understanding of himself which will challenge him to a genuine existential decision.

---

[24]*Gnosis und spätantiker Geist.* I. *Die mythologische Gnosis*, 1934.

DEMYTHOLOGIZING AND THE PROBLEM OF VALIDITY
Ronald Hepburn

Ronald W. Hepburn, "Demythologizing and the Problem of Validity," from A. Flew and A. MacIntyre (eds.), *New Essays in Philosophical Theology*. Reprinted by permission of SCM Press Ltd., London, and The Macmillan Company, New York. First published in 1953.

It might seem as if the title I have chosen were either bombastic and empty, or claimed nothing less than the entire field of myth and the Bible as its theme. For does not every theologian aim at producing *valid* theology and is not 'the problem of validity' only another name for the theologian's problems as a whole? Yet it is all too easy in theology to muffle this question of validity, for all its importance, to veil and camouflage inadvertently the logical nature of what is being undertaken. Nothing is harder than to write so transparently that the reader is kept aware of exactly what claims are essential to the validity of the doctrine or theory concerned, and what are subsidiary, carefully distinguishing the logical from the psychological, the historical from the metaphysical—at every stage. This is far more than a peripheral matter of expositional technique: for to allow the logical structure of a theology to shine through its presentation is not only to prepare the way for assessing its validity; it is to have commenced assessment already. In this field clarification and verification constantly merge into one another. To see clearly what a theology demands is to begin seeing how plausible or implausible are those demands.

This is, of course, true not only of theology. If a piece of empirical science is dressed up to look like *a priori* mathematics, we shall be tempted to use quite inappropriate methods for testing its truth or falsity—looking for internal consistency in the use of symbols instead of conformity with a range of phenomena in the outside world. A mistaken account of ethics (say a crude subjectivism) can suggest irrelevant tests for moral rightness and wrongness (such as the occurrence of certain kinds of sentiments). But however widely spread this danger, the theologian is exposed to it in a unique way. Notoriously, his utterances about God put constant severe strain upon the vocabulary with which he is compelled to work: the lines of communication between the senses which he gives his words and ordinary use are ever on the point of being ruptured—a truth which he may learn from Kant as well as from Wittgenstein. It is, therefore, of paramount importance that he should show as far as he can what functions his language is performing—when literal, when symbolical, when descriptive, when evaluative.

In what follows, I want to ask how far the contributors to the recent debate on demythologizing have been alert to this problem of meaning and validity. How far, in particular, does Bultmann's *New Testament and Mythology* reveal an awareness of them? If my conclusions are unsympathetic, this must not be taken as evidence of a sceptical indifference to the subject itself. The relations between historical fact, mythological statement and existential concern are inescapably fundamental to the New Testament study of our day. It is rather my sense of their ultimacy which prompts this criticism of the procedures employed by one major protagonist in the debate.

The pith of my criticism is simply this: that Bultmann's methods and terminology tend to insulate his claims against the possibility of verification or falsification (using these words in their widest sense); that this happens not in conjunction with a reasoned assertion that theological disagreements are by nature unsettleable, but *by default* through ambiguities and confusions in crucial terms, which effectively prevent the question of validity being raised as it ought to be raised and even deny the language whereby this could be done.

My remarks may be grouped under five headings.

1. The Definition of Myth

Any instability in the concept of myth itself would be found to imperil the discussion at point after point. Yet Bultmann neither offers a satisfactory definition, nor abides by the definition he does offer. 'Mythology', he writes (p. 10)[1] 'is the use of imagery to express the other worldly in terms of this world and the divine in terms of human life, the other side in terms of this side.' By his own test this definition itself is partly couched in mythological language, which is cause enough for bewilderment. And it is sufficiently wide in its scope to include all pictorial, analogical and symbolical speech whatever. Now in another place Bultmann concedes that *all* utterance about God is analogical, and therefore (if the first definition is to stand) irreducibly mythological. Bultmann cannot mean this. For if it were true, it would make demythologizing a logically impossible task; and the contrast he constantly wishes to make between 'mere mythology' and authentic existentialist interpretation would be robbed of its basis. Perplexity does not end here: in a discussion on the expression 'act of God' (p. 196 f.) Bultmann decides against calling this 'mythological language', on the ground that 'mythological thought regards the divine activity . . . as an interference with the course of nature', and 'acts of God', to Bultmann, are not of this sort. Therefore to speak of such acts is not to speak mythologically, but *analogically.* This conclusion, however, violates his original definition of myth in two ways at once:

(1) Bultmann is saying: 'the expression "act of God" is not mythological language, but analogical', whereas on his definition this antithesis could not be made, since 'myth' is there plainly the 'genus' word, with 'analogy', 'pictorial image', etc., as species.

(2) The mythological has been redefined as that which depicts God as 'interfering in the course of nature'; while the first definition concerned itself only with myth as a form of language and said nothing at all about the *content* of any particular myths.

The contrast mentioned a moment ago between 'just mythology' and 'existentialist interpretation' (p. 110) reminds us that Bultmann frequently uses 'myth' and its cognates as pejoratives. For example: Bultmann may well be right when he claims that the New Testament myths are *in origin* Jewish and Gnostic.

---

[1]References are to pages in *Kerygma and Myth,* edited Bartsch (S.P.C.K., 1953). [See p. 197.]

But he goes on to say that they are also Jewish and Gnostic 'in essence'—a very different claim (pp. 3, 15). 'Identical in essence with X' implies 'containing no more than X', 'of the same value as X'. Part of Bultmann's failure to justify his transition from 'in origin' to 'in essence' may be due to just this pejorative innuendo carried by 'myth' which militates against the scrutiny and evaluation of each individual myth (and modification of myth) on its own merits.

Here, then, in the definition of 'myth', is one point at which greater logical rigour is urgently required, if the discussion is to be set on a secure foundation.

2. The Flight from the Evidential

Bultmann's reluctance to face problems of validity manifests itself in a recurrent pattern of argumentation, which could be schematized in roughly the following way:

(a) A fact or argument appears, which *prima facie* is hostile to the validity of the Christian position;

(b) Bultmann turns aside from its negative evidential implication; and

(c) transforms the hostile fact in such a way as to make it yield positive support for a modified and freshly secured theological view.

The suspicion grows, as one reads, that no evidence at all would be admitted as finally detrimental to Bultmann's position. If he actually believes this (and it is not an *absurd* belief to hold), it ought to be clearly exhibited as the crucial tenet it undoubtedly would be, and argued for as such.

Two simple examples may bring out this pattern of thought.

(1) On page 11 of *Kerygma and Myth* Bultmann describes how antinomies are generated by conflicting imagery in the New Testament. 'The virgin birth is inconsistent with the assertion of [Christ's] pre-existence', so is the creation doctrine with talk about the 'rulers of this world', and the law as God-given with the statement that it came from the angels. To Bultmann all this implies, 'Rise, therefore, *above* the mythological.' [See p. 198]

(2) Christ failed to return in the way the disciples had at first expected. We ought, says Bultmann, to profit from their mistake; recognizing that the Last Things are mythological conceptions, not historical.

In both cases a difficulty is metamorphosed into a theologically acceptable 'truth'. But in each case too Bultmann has side-stepped an equally important sceptical option—without giving adequate reasons for so doing. In the first case we might say: 'Conflicting views? then so much the worse for the reliability of the documents!'; and in the second case: 'Jesus did not come, because the disciples were simply and tragically wrong about him.' Plausibility can be given to evasive moves like these in individual instances, but only so long as the by-passed sceptical options are never gathered together and faced *cumulatively* as a challenge, more or less formidable, to the Christian position.

One may go further: the whole category of the evidential is repeatedly pushed aside by Bultmann as of no importance, or, worse, as a snare. He speaks scornfully of the 'provable': 'It is precisely its immunity from proof which secures the Christian proclamation against the charge of being mythological' (p. 44). The language of myth is concrete and pictorial, concerned with stones rolling away and men rising into the sky, suggesting in many cases events that might be captured by the camera. Not so the truths of non-mythological Christian belief: for to Bultmann the removal of Christianity from the realm of myth up-grades it in value. So much so, that the reader is prepared to accept, if he is off-guard, that to remove it from the realm of the 'provable' must also be an act of up-grading, to be welcomed like a release from a long-standing bondage. But in this way Bultmann has again omitted to argue for a vital proposition, namely that absence of evidence does not disqualify a religion from being acceptable by reasonable men, or that 'unprovable' here is not equivalent to 'baseless' or 'unfounded', as it undeniably is in many contexts.

In speaking of faith Bultmann makes this turn of thought particularly plain: 'It is impossible to prove that faith is related to its object . . . it is just here that its strength lies' (p. 201). Once more the absence of evidence is taken as a commendation. For if the relation of faith to God *were* provable, then, says Bultmann, God would be reduced to the status of one item among others in the furniture of the universe: and only 'in that realm [are we] justified in demanding proof'. Unfortunately this latter sentence begs the question. It assumes that we know already—have had convincingly shown to us—that there are in fact two 'realms'—a belief which should surely appear as part of the end-product, not as the initial presupposition of a reasoned theology. Again, a sceptical option demands attention but does not receive it; that is, 'If God's being cannot be established, there *may* be no God'.

The furthest Bultmann goes in this extraordinary and fascinating flight from the evidential is to transform the failure to obtain proof into an aggressive refusal to accept any *possible* proof. Thus he rejects I Cor. 15.3–8 as evidence for the resurrection, not explicitly on critical grounds, but in his own words—'that line of argument is fatal *because* it tries to adduce a proof for the *Kerygma*' (p. 112; my italics).

This trend of thought, yoked with his critical standpoint, leads Bultmann to speak evasively and ambiguously of the Biblical narratives. As Schleiermacher could say of the ascension only that 'something happened', so Bultmann says of the resurrection with similar cloudiness, 'I have no intention whatever of denying the uniqueness of the first Easter Day' (p. 111), selecting a vocabulary which permits the retention of a reverent attitude but leaves altogether unclear the nature of the event towards which the attitude is adopted, and therefore leaves equally unclear what procedure could show whether the attitude was an *appropriate* one or not.

An avowed historical agnosticism about the events of Jesus' life would be quite unexceptionable. What one finds in Bultmann, however, is something more positive and dogmatic. At many crucial points he casts about in his mind for an interpretation of an event which he thinks adequate to the existential seriousness of Christianity and procedes to *read back* his interpretation into the original documents however these may resist the treatment, and however many critical questions may be begged. It is one thing to say, 'I have no idea what happened at the ascension, but it provides an excellent symbol for Christ's oneness with the

Father': quite another thing to say, 'The ascension did not happen—*could* not have happened: it is an excellent symbol, etc., etc.' To speak of the 'unique and final revelation of God in history' may be misleading as Bultmann claims, in its tendency to lead to thinking of that revelation as a *revelatum,* an event which happened once in the remote past, to which we have access only by historical documents; in Bultmann's words, 'something which took place in the past and is now an object of detached observation' (p. 111). But anxiety on this score has gone too far when it results in a fight against history itself; and it cannot be invoked as justification for abandoning the evidential as such.

It is hardly an exaggeration to say that Bultmann would feel an *embarrassment* at the very possibility that certain events might after all have taken place just as the documents narrate them. Doubtless a Christian ought not to see a miracle as a divine conjuring trick, but should interpret the miraculous in personal and moral categories. But that does not give Bultmann warrant to say, 'the God of revelation is the God of judgment and forgiveness, *not* the Cause of abnormal phenomena' (p. 121; my italics). It may also be true that in the believer's passage from death into life 'outwardly everything remains as before, but inwardly his relation to the world has been radically changed' (p. 20), but Bultmann is over-eager to make this inner invisible event the paradigm not only of conversion but of the New Testament message in its entirety, for the most momentous divine activity still leaves 'undisturbed' the 'closed weft of history' (p. 197). Can he also consistently say, 'It is indeed part of the *skandalon* that . . . our salvation is One who is involved in all the relativity of history' (p. 111)? For he is as anxious to *escape* the level of the verifiable as the logical positivists were to remain within it, in making verifiability the touchstone of meaningfulness. Both are guilty through excess of zeal: the positivists in their belief that any simple verification procedure could prove adequate to every possible experience, Bultmann in refusing to make plain what states of affairs would be incompatible with Christian belief, or just how different the world would have to be before belief would have to be declared senseless.[2]

The historian's task would be impossible, were he forbidden to fill out imaginatively the reconstruction of events to which his sources bear witness. Yet at what point legitimate interpretation fades into fanciful and irresponsible refashioning of the past is often a hard question. We have no guarantee that any ingenious device we may introduce into a production of Shakespeare was actually present in the poet's mind when he wrote his play; how much more uncertain is the assurance of Bultmann that the demythologized, existentialist account of the New Testament proclamation does not in fact distort that proclamation, for all its philosophical attractiveness.

3. Fact and Language

A theology which aims at being logically transparent must carefully distinguish issues of fact from matters of linguistic convenience. Now, the very word 'demythologize' strongly suggests a venture in translation, the substitution of

---

[2]Compare the *University* discussion in 'Theology and Falsification', Ch. VI (i) above [i.e., *New Essays in Philosophical Theology*. Ed.].

more literal language for pictorial and symbolic language. Yet this is thoroughly deceptive. If the ascension, say, is amenable to demythologizing, that is to say something not only about the language in which the 'event' is described, but to decide also about the actual status of the event itself, to deny that Jesus did in fact rise into the air. And no linguistic investigation could lead by itself to such conclusions. Put it differently: to qualify for mythhood a statement must be (on Bultmann's definition) actually about 'the other world' or 'the other side'. The process of demythologizing must accordingly consist of at least two phases, of which the first is the recognition that the scriptural account concerned is mythological in nature; while the second phase re-interprets its substance non-mythologically. But the question whether any particular narration *is* mythical cannot be settled by Bultmann or anyone else while acting in the capacity of *translator*. An event such as a piece of prophetic symbolism may be historical (Jesus did enter Jerusalem in triumph, did curse the fig tree) and at the same time be mythological in Bultmann's sense. Or the alleged event may not have happened and the narrative still retain mythological value. What one must insist is that whether or not the imagery, etc., of the narrative yields itself to translation into existentialist terms, this does nothing to tell us which of those possibilities is more likely to be true. Yet Bultmann repeatedly suggests that '*X* is described in mythological terms' implies '*X* cannot have happened as narrated', and does not make it plain that the latter judgment requires a quite distinct investigation.[3]

Two brief examples of this may be hazarded. First, the expression 'the cross' is indispensable in devotional language; but the very reasons which make it valuable there make it a dangerous and slippery term in a theology like Bultmann's—namely its conflation of two distinguishable conceptions, the actual crucifixion of Jesus at Calvary and the 'meaning' that event can have for the Christian. This span of meaning permits a theologian to keep his reader in a state of sustained uncertainty about exactly what historical claim, if any, he is making when he speaks of 'the cross'.

Second, 'Take . . . the case of a child being sacrificed in order to ensure the success of an enterprise or to avert misfortune. Such a practice implies a "crude mythological conception of God"' (p. 108). Here the rejection of a primitive view of sacrifice (as in the stories of Iphigenia and Jeptha's daughter) appears to be part and parcel with Bultmann's general impatience with the mythological: its repudiation is represented as involved in the passage from myth to non-myth. But is this not misleading in the extreme? What is 'crude' about the sacrifice theory is not its mythological nature, but its *moral* inadequacy. Abandoning it is not a piece of linguistic spring-cleaning but a value-judgment, logically quite different.

There may be at least a hint of this fact-language conflation on page 7 of *Kerygma and Myth* where Bultmann says: 'The only criticism of the New Testament which is theologically relevant is that which arises *necessarily* out of the situation of modern man' (Bultmann's italics). One such 'necessity' is disbelief in the miraculous as interference in the order of nature. Now, as Austin Farrer remarks in the same volume, some modern men do not find such a belief impossible. But Bultmann whisks his reader past the possible objection, aided by

---

[3]An analogy with Political Theory presents itself here. The idea of a Social Contract may be a valuable one in justifying political obedience under certain circumstances. To speak of it as a 'myth' is neither to assert nor to deny the historicity of such an original Contract.

this word 'necessarily' which is always ready to take on the logician's sense of 'analytically, logically necessary', therefore not falsifiable by any matter of fact. Again the controversial is made to seem less controversial, and objections on the score of validity are glided over by the hint that the truth of the statement is guaranteed by linguistic convention, that its denial involves contradiction.

4. Myth and Oblique Language

The project of demythologizing raises in an acute form the general problem of the religious use of language, the logical nature of statements about God. We may start with Bultmann's crucial statement, ' . . . there are certain concepts which are fundamentally mythological, and with which we shall never be able to dispense—e.g. the idea of transcendence. In such cases, however, the original mythological meaning has been lost, and they have become mere metaphors or ciphers' (pp. 102 f.). '*Mere* metaphors', note; the phrase suggests that these concepts are 'as near literal as makes no difference'. But in fact it makes a great deal of difference. The gulf between literal (or direct) and oblique language cannot be bridged so lightheartedly. For if propositions about God are irreducibly oblique—that is, symbolical, analogical and so on, then to demythologize is not to remove all obliqueness, but only obliqueness of certain sorts: on the other hand, if it is possible to speak literally of God, then demythologizing is quite a different activity, not one of translation out of one code into another, but rather of *de*-coding altogether. The question which should be of greatest concern to the theologian is not whether this or that myth may be re-expressed in language less flagrantly pictorial, more abstract in appearance, but whether or not the circle of myth, metaphor and symbol is a closed one: and if closed then in what way propositions about God manage to *refer*. Bultmann's first definition of 'myth' gave the word a sense sufficiently extended to include every kind of oblique language; yet in practice he gives very little scrutiny indeed to this general issue, and even (as we have noticed) contrasts the mythological with the analogical—a procedure for which his definition gives no warrant. That is to say: the nature of demythologizing as an enterprise must remain logically obscured so long as we leave unsettled the question 'Is any direct talk of God possible, or can one talk only obliquely of him?' How inattention to this question can enfeeble the debate can be brought out as follows.

Bultmann's critics have often pointed out that his existentialist terminology is no less mythological than the New Testament ideas from which he wishes to deliver us. Bultmann is prepared to admit this: even 'transcendence' is a mythological concept, but one (he is assured) in which myth is merely vestigial, neutralized, reduced to the harmless status of 'mere metaphor or cipher'. But the more searching objection can still be made that this *appearance* of directness and abstract sterility can be (logically) a menace. If the demythologized talk of God is still oblique, then it should display its obliqueness overtly, for to carry it surreptitiously may be rather like treating measles by hiding the rash with face-powder. For all we know, the suppressed picture, the latent myth, may still be doing the work in the expression concerned; and the 'cashing' of it may be impossible without once more reverting to the concealed, but active, myth.

The importance of this may be made plainer by referring to a perceptive article[4] by Ian Crombie, where he considers the challenge to religious belief presented recently by certain linguistic philosophers. In particular, it had been argued that a proposition like 'God loves me' appears at first sight to be rich in meaning but is in fact qualified out of existence as soon as we attempt to describe in detail what precisely it claims. Although there are certain sorts of behaviour which give good grounds for denying that one human being loves another, the Christian is expected to go on saying 'God loves me' even when his child is born blind and he himself succumbs to an incurable disease. Even the proposition 'God exists' is eroded away to emptiness by successive qualifications: 'he exists—*but* is invisible, inaudible, intangible, not *in* the world nor a name for the world as a whole. . . . ' Now, in his article, Crombie granted that any attempt to speak literally, directly of God was indeed bound to fail. Nevertheless, we can still speak of him—in 'parable' (using the word in an extended sense). We say 'God loves us'; what this is like as an experience in God's own being we have not the least idea (nor, without taking in the hereafter, can we exhaustively verify or falsify it): for to predicate 'loving' or 'acting' or 'suffering' of One who infinite and unconditioned is at once to snap the links with every intelligible use of these words. But if we think of 'God loves us' as a parable, an oblique utterance, the word 'loves' is being used not in a stretched sense but with its everyday familiar meaning. Without knowing what it is like for God to love, we do know now what thoughts of God and what sorts of behaviour are appropriate and what not. We accept one parable about God, rather than another, on the authority, primarily, of Jesus Christ. The parabolic is only one of the two 'parents' of religious belief: the other is what might be called 'undifferentiated theism', and springs from a sense of the contingency (or beauty, etc.) of the world, giving a 'direction' in which the revealed parable can be referred.[5]

Professor Tillich, in a conversation, once pointed out to me how closely this analysis followed the pattern of his own treatment of the same problem, however different his starting-point. Tillich maintains that all propositions about God are symbolic, except one: for without one direct proposition the oblique language, despite its internal coherence, would have no anchor in reality; the flotilla of symbols would be adrift, unpiloted. To Tillich this one direct proposition is 'God is Being—itself', and its resemblance to Crombie's 'undifferentiated theism' is obvious enough.

Neither Crombie nor Tillich was engaged on a project of demythologizing. None the less, my point is that demythologizing is only an artificially broken off segment of the problem with which they *were* grappling, and that both of them permit the logical structure of their enterprises to shine through with a clarity impossible to the close disciple of Bultmann. Thus Crombie's presentation, if acceptable, makes it at once plain what sort of procedure is relevant to establishing its truth: each 'parent' of belief requires a separate justification. With the theistic, for instance, we must ask how far it is exposed to the general difficulties of the classical arguments of natural theology despite its prelinguistic

---

[4]Ch. VI (ii) in this volume [i.e., *New Essays in Philosophical Theology*. Ed.].
[5]See, for instance, Professor J. J. C. Smart in Ch. III [*ibid.*], *ad fin.*

character[6]: with the parabolic we must investigate the grounds on which we accept Jesus' authority in uttering the parable.

5. The Existentialist Interpretation

So far I have been trying to lay bare some of the pitfalls which beset Bultmann's enterprise, ways in which the problem of validity tends to be side-stepped in demythologizing and the logic of religious statements obscured rather than clarified. Something must be said in conclusion (however briefly), about the other half of the total programme—the revision of the *Kerygma* in existentialist terms. Do existentialist modes of thought, as Bultmann adopts them, help or hinder the fashioning of a theology whose logical structure reveals itself through its presentation and terminology?

In the first place, there is an undeniable advance from a sentimentalist analysis of belief (as in Schleiermacher) to an existentialist analysis. The advance is comparable to that recent progress from the positivist's dichotomy between 'descriptive and emotive' language to the recognition of the variety of actual linguistic functions as seen in the writing of philosophers like Wisdom and Austin. Existentialism provides the theologian (the poet and novelist too) with a rich vocabulary in which to express important elements of the human situation—decision, commitment, dereliction, anguish and many more. Indeed, its theological adaptability is not matter for surprise, since the roots of existentialism go back as far as Pascal and Augustine.

But the adoption of a twentieth-century existentialist terminology is not without its dangers. Certain of these were admirably discussed in Christopher Evans' broadcast review of *Kerygma and Myth*. It is as a tentative supplement to what he said there that I hazard these three additional criticisms.

The first is the most formidable, but space will permit only its bare statement. Overwhelmingly concerned with the phenomenology of faith and the life of faith, existentialist thought is in continual peril of failing to emerge from the subjectivist circle at all. A subjectivist account can provide an informative description of what it is like to think and act *as if* there were a God, of the 'inward' metamorphosis which accompanies belief. But it is unable to go further (and it is only here that the question of validity becomes relevant) unable to say whether the belief is justified or unjustified, whether or not there exists a Being before whom the believer has taken up the attitude of faith.

A second danger arises from the almost unlimited hospitality which existentialist thought gives to the paradoxical. Even granting that there are situations in which one is forced to say, 'This is a paradox—an enigma, a mystery', there are others in which the proper response is, 'This is paradoxical, contradictory and nonsensical'. The more cautious a theologian is of paradox, the less he revels in it for its own dramatic sake—the less likely he will be to revere the nonsensical and the invalid when he ought to be dismissing them. His ideal language is one which (by its reluctance to resort to paradox in all but unavoidable contexts) reduces the risk of such confusions as far as possible. Again, it is not an insensitivity to the

---

[6]Compare Smart again in Ch. III [*ibid.*], *passim.*

value of metaphor and analogy in exposition that prompts the suspicion that existentialist language is frequently over-tolerant also of those. In sentences like 'we possess the present through encounter' (p. 116, *K.a.M.*) the adoption of the language of drama in the field of general philosophy has begotten a metaphorical mode of speech in which cogent argumentation or criticism is desperately hard. Distortion is inevitable when all relations come to be conceived on the model of interpersonal encounter.

Finally, an existentialist dramatic vocabulary tends on occasion illicitly to prescribe to the theologian what questions he should or should not pursue, where his inquiry should start and (worse still) where it should end. Bultmann writes: 'It is not for us to question [the] credentials' of the 'word of preaching', 'It is we who are questioned' (p. 41). Perhaps: but this alluring language of drama cannot justify the theologian's evasion of that abiding and ultimate question—'*on what grounds* ought I to assume an attitude of obedience before the New Testament and not before, say, the Koran?' On another page we read: 'I think I may take for granted that the right question to frame with regard to the Bible—at any rate within the Church—is the question of human existence' (pp. 191 f., *ibid.*), as if by the weightiness of existential utterance itself one could smother the thousand and one *other* questions—of historicity, integrity of text, interpretation—which likewise clamour for their answer, and concern Churchmen as much as unbelievers. Here existentialism has become Bultmann's master, not his servant. So long as it provides the means of expressing what without its terms would be inexpressible, theologians can do nothing but respect it: but it is time to protest when it proceeds arbitrarily to impose limits upon critical examination, whether of doctrine or document.

The quest for a language that is adequate to describe our experience in all its multifariousness is the common task of philosophers and theologians. They must resist equally the artifical truncation of language on dogmatic positivist lines and any language ('inflationary' language, Isaiah Berlin would call it) which is given to the multiplication of metaphysical or theological entities beyond necessity, and from crying mystery where there is not always mystery but sometimes only muddle. In each case a defective linguistic instrument is an obstacle not only to clarity in exposition but also to the attainment of validity.

Chapter
SIX

RESPONSES TO SECULARITY
behavioral policies and empirical stories

AN EMPIRICIST'S VIEW
OF THE NATURE
OF RELIGIOUS BELIEF

R. B. Braithwaite

R. B. Braithwaite, "An Empiricist's View of the Nature of Religious Belief," from Ian T. Ramsey (ed.), *Christian Ethics and Contemporary Philosophy*. Reprinted by permission of The Macmillan Company and SCM Press Ltd., London. © 1966.

'The meaning of a scientific statement is to be ascertained by reference to the steps which would be taken to verify it.' Eddington wrote this in 1939. Unlike his heterodox views of the *a priori* and epistemological character of the ultimate laws of physics, this principle is in complete accord with contemporary philosophy of science; indeed it was Eddington's use of it in his expositions of relativity theory in the early 1920's that largely contributed to its becoming the orthodoxy. Eddington continued his passage by saying: 'This [principle] will be recognised as a tenet of logical positivism—only it is there extended to all statements.'[1] Just as the tone was set to the empiricist tradition in British philosophy—the tradition running from Locke through Berkeley, Hume, Mill to Russell in our own time—by Locke's close association with the scientific work of Boyle and the early Royal Society, so the contemporary development of empiricism popularly known as logical positivism has been greatly influenced by the revolutionary changes this century in physical theory and by the philosophy of science which physicists concerned with these changes—Einstein and Heisenberg as well as Eddington—have thought most consonant with relativity and quantum physics. It is therefore, I think, proper for me to take the verificational principle of meaning, and a natural adaptation of it, as that aspect of contemporary scientific thought whose bearing upon the philosophy of religion I shall discuss this afternoon. Eddington, in the passage from which I have quoted, applied the verificational principle to the meaning of scientific statements only. But we shall see that it will be necessary, and concordant with an empiricist way of thinking, to modify the principle by allowing *use* as well as *verifiability* to be a criterion for meaning; so I believe that all I shall say will be in the spirit of a remark with which Eddington concluded an article published in 1925: 'The scientist and the religious teacher may well be content to agree that the *value* of any hypothesis extends just so far as it is verified by actual experience.'[2]

I will start with the verificational principle in the form in which it was originally propounded by logical positivists—that the meaning of any statement is given by its method of verification.[3]

The implication of this general principle for the problem of religious belief is that the primary question becomes, not whether a religious statement such as that a personal God created the world is true or is false, but how it could be

---

[1] A. S. Eddington, *The Philosophy of Physical Science* (1939), p. 189.
[2] *Science, Religion and Reality*, ed. by J. Needham (1925), p. 218 (my italics).
[3] The principle was first explicitly stated by F. Waismann, in *Erkenntnis*, vol. 1 (1930), p. 229.

known either to be true or to be false. Unless this latter question can be answered, the religious statement has no ascertainable meaning and there is nothing expressed by it to be either true or false. Moreover a religious statement cannot be believed without being understood, and it can only be understood by an understanding of the circumstances which would verify or falsify it. Meaning is not logically prior to the possibility of verification: we do not first learn the meaning of a statement, and afterwards consider what would make us call it true or false; the two understandings are one and indivisible.

It would not be correct to say that discussions of religious belief before this present century have always ignored the problem of meaning, but until recently the emphasis has been upon the question of the truth or the reasonableness of religious beliefs rather than upon the logically prior question as to the meaning of the statements expressing the beliefs. The argument usually proceeded as if we all knew what was meant by the statement that a personal God created the world; the point at issue was whether or not this statement was true, or whether there were good reasons for believing it. But if the meaning of a religious statement has to be found by discovering the steps which must be taken to ascertain its truth-value, an examination of the methods for testing the statement for truth-value is an essential preliminary to any discussion as to which of the truth-values—truth or falsity—holds of the statement.

There are three classes of statement whose method of truth-value testing is in general outline clear: statements about particular matters of empirical fact, scientific hypotheses and other general empirical statements, and the logically necessary statements of logic and mathematics (and their contradictories). Do religious statements fall into any of these three classes? If they do, the problem of their meaningfulness will be solved: their truth-values will be testable by the methods appropriate to empirical statements, particular or general, or to mathematical statements. It seems to me clear that religious statements, as they are normally used, have no place in this trichotomy. I shall give my reasons very briefly, since I have little to add here to what other empiricist philosophers have said.

1. Statements about particular empirical facts are testable by direct observation. The only facts that can be directly known by observation are that the things observed have certain observable properties or stand in certain observable relations to one another. If it is maintained that the *existence* of God is known by observation, for example, in the 'self-authenticating' experience of 'meeting God', the term 'God' is being used merely as part of the description of that particular experience. Any interesting theological proposition, e.g. that God is personal, will attribute a property to God which is not an observable one and so cannot be known by direct observation. Comparison with our knowledge of other people is an unreal comparison. I can get to know things about an intimate friend at a glance, but this knowledge is not self-authenticating; it is based upon a great deal of previous knowledge about the connection between facial and bodily expressions and states of mind.

2. The view that would class religious statements with scientific hypotheses must be taken much more seriously. It would be very unplausible if a Baconian methodology of science had to be employed, and scientific hypotheses taken as simple generalizations from particular instances, for then there could be no

understanding of a general theological proposition unless particular instances of it could be directly observed. But an advanced science has progressed far beyond its natural history stage; it makes use in its explanatory hypotheses of concepts of a high degree of abstractness and at a far remove from experience. These theoretical concepts are given a meaning by the place they occupy in a deductive system consisting of hypotheses of different degrees of generality in which the least general hypotheses, deducible from the more general ones, are generalizations of observable facts. So it is no valid criticism of the view that would treat God as an empirical concept entering into an explanatory hypothesis to say that God is not directly observable. No more is an electric field of force or a Schrödinger wave-function. There is no *prima facie* objection to regarding such a proposition as that there is a God who created and sustains the world as an explanatory scientific hypothesis.

But if a set of theological propositions are to be regarded as scientific explanations of facts in the empirical world, they must be refutable by experience. We must be willing to abandon them if the facts prove different from what we think they are. A hypothesis which is consistent with every possible empirical fact is not an empirical one. And though the theoretical concepts in a hypothesis need not be explicitly definable in terms of direct observation—indeed they must not be if the system is to be applicable to novel situations—yet they must be related to some and not to all of the possible facts in the world in order to have a non-vacuous significance. If there is a personal God, how would the world be different if there were not? Unless this question can be answered God's existence cannot be given an empirical meaning.

At earlier times in the history of religion God's personal existence has been treated as a scientific hypothesis subjectable to empirical test. Elijah's contest with the prophets of Baal was an experiment to test the hypothesis that Jehovah and not Baal controlled the physical world. But most educated believers at the present time do not think of God as being detectable in this sort of way, and hence do not think of theological propositions as explanations of facts in the world of nature in the way in which established scientific hypotheses are.

It may be maintained, however, that theological propositions explain facts about the world in another way. Not perhaps the physical world, for physical science has been so successful with its own explanations; but the facts of biological and psychological development. Now it is certainly the case that a great deal of traditional Christian language—phrases such as 'original sin', 'the old Adam', 'the new man', 'growth in holiness'—can be given meanings within statements expressing general hypotheses about human personality. Indeed it is hardly too much to say that almost all statements about God as immanent, as an indwelling spirit, can be interpreted as asserting psychological facts in metaphorical language. But would those interpreting religious statements in this way be prepared to abandon them if the empirical facts were found to be different? Or would they rather re-interpret them to fit the new facts? In the latter case the possibility of interpreting them to fit experience is not enough to give an empirical meaning to the statements. Mere consistency with experience without the possibility of inconsistency does not determine meaning. And a metaphorical description is not in itself an explanation. This criticism also holds against attempts to interpret theism as an explanation of the course of history, unless it is admitted (which few theists would be willing to admit) that, had the course of history been different in some specific way, God would not have existed.

Philosophers of religion who wish to make empirical facts relevant to the meaning of religious statements but at the same time desire to hold on to these statements whatever the empirical facts may be are indulging, I believe, in a sort of 'double-think' attitude: they want to hold that religious statements both are about the actual world (i.e. are empirical statements) and also are not refutable in any possible world, the characteristic of statements which are logically necessary.

3. The view that statements of natural theology resemble the propositions of logic and mathematics in being logically necessary would have as a consequence that they make no assertion of existence. Whatever exactly be the status of logically necessary propositions, Hume and Kant have conclusively shown that they are essentially hypothetical. $2 + 3 = 5$ makes no assertion about there being any things in the world; what it says is that, if there is a class of five things in the world, then this class is the union of two mutually exclusive sub-classes one comprising two and the other comprising three things. The logical-positivist thesis, due to Wittgenstein, that the truth of this hypothetical proposition is verified not by any logical fact about the world but by the way in which we use numerical symbols in our thinking goes further than Kant did in displacing logic and mathematics from the world of reality. But it is not necessary to accept this more radical thesis in order to agree with Kant that no logically necessary proposition can assert existence; and this excludes the possibility of regarding theological propositions as logically necessary in the way in which the hypothetical propositions of mathematics and logic are necessary.

The traditional arguments for a Necessary God—the ontological and the cosmological—were elaborated by Anselm and the scholastic philosophers before the concurrent and inter-related development of natural science and of mathematics had enabled necessity and contingency to be clearly distinguished. The necessity attributed by these arguments to the being of God may perhaps be different from the logical necessity of mathematical truths; but, if so, no method has been provided for testing the truth-value of the statement that God is necessary being, and consequently no way given for assigning meaning to the terms 'necessary being' and 'God'.

If religious statements cannot be held to fall into any of these three classes, their method of verification cannot be any of the standard methods applicable to statements falling in these classes. Does this imply that religious statements are not verifiable, with the corollary, according to the verificational principle, that they have no meaning and, though they purport to say something, are in fact nonsensical sentences? The earlier logical positivists thought so: they would have echoed the demand of their precursor Hume that a volume ('of divinity or school metaphysics') which contains neither 'any abstract reasoning concerning quantity or number' nor 'any experimental reasoning concerning matter of fact and existence' should be committed to the flames; though their justification for the holocaust would be even more cogent than Hume's. The volume would not contain even 'sophistry and illusion': it would contain nothing but meaningless marks of printer's ink.

Religious statements, however, are not the only statements which are unverifiable by standard methods; moral statements have the same peculiarity. A moral principle, like the utilitarian principle that a man ought to act so as to maximize happiness, does not seem to be either a logically necessary or a logically impossible proposition. But neither does it seem to be an empirical proposition, all the attempts of ethical empiricists to give naturalistic analyses having failed. Though a tough-minded logical positivist might be prepared to say that all religious statements are sound and fury, signifying nothing, he can hardly say that of all moral statements. For moral statements have a use in guiding conduct; and if they have a use they surely have a meaning—in some sense of meaning. So the verificational principle of meaning in the hands of empiricist philosophers in the 1930's became modified either by a glossing of the term 'verification' or by a change of the verification principle into the use principle: the meaning of any statement is given by the way in which it is used.[4]

Since I wish to continue to employ verification in the restricted sense of ascertaining truth-value, I shall take the principle of meaning in this new form in which the word 'verification' has disappeared. But in removing this term from the statement of the principle, there is no desertion from the spirit of empiricism. The older verificational principle is subsumed under the new use principle: the use of an empirical statement derives from the fact that the statement is empirically verifiable, and the logical-positivist thesis of the 'linguistic' character of logical and mathematical statements can be equally well, if not better, expressed in terms of their use than of their method of verification. Moreover the only way of discovering how a statement is used is by an empirical enquiry; a statement need not itself be empirically verifiable, but that it is used in a particular way is always a straightforwardly empirical proposition.

The meaning of any statement, then, will be taken as being given by the way it is used. The kernel for an empiricist of the problem of the nature of religious belief is to explain, in empirical terms, how a religious statement is used by a man who asserts it in order to express his religious conviction.

Since I shall argue that the primary element in this use is that the religious assertion is used as a moral assertion, I must first consider how moral assertions are used. According to the view developed by various moral philosophers since the impossiblity of regarding moral statements as verifiable propositions was recognized, a moral assertion is used to express an *attitude* of the man making the assertion. It is not used to assert the proposition that he has the attitude—a verifiable psychological proposition; it is used to show forth or evince his attitude. The attitude is concerned with the action which he asserts to be right or to be his duty, or the state of affairs which he asserts to be good; it is a highly complex state, and contains elements to which various degrees of importance have been attached by moral philosophers who have tried to work out an 'ethics without propositions'. One element in the attitude is a feeling of approval towards the action; this element was taken as the fundamental one in the first attempts, and views of ethics without propositions are frequently lumped together as 'emotive' theories of ethics. But discussion of the subject during the last twenty years has made it clear, I think, that no emotion or feeling of approval is fundamental to the use of moral assertions; it may be the case that the moral asserter has some specific feeling directed on to the course of action said to be

---

[4] See L. Wittgenstein, *Philosophical Investigations* (1953), especially §§ 340, 353, 559, 560.

right, but this is not the most important element in his 'pro-attitude' towards the course of action: what is primary is his intention to perform the action when the occasion for it arises.

The form of ethics without propositions which I shall adopt is therefore a conative rather than an emotive theory: it makes the primary use of a moral assertion that of expressing the intention of the asserter to act in a particular sort of way specified in the assertion. A utilitarian, for example, in asserting that he ought to act so as to maximize happiness, is thereby declaring his intention to act, to the best of his ability, in accordance with the policy of utilitarianism: he is not asserting any proposition, or necessarily evincing any feeling of approval; he is subscribing to a policy of action. There will doubtless be empirical propositions which he may give as reasons for his adherence to the policy (e.g. that happiness is what all, or what most people, desire), and his having the intention will include his understanding what is meant by pursuing the policy, another empirically verifiable proposition. But there will be no specifically moral proposition which he will be asserting when he declares his intention to pursue the policy. This account is fully in accord with the spirit of empiricism, for whether or not a man has the intention of pursuing a particular behaviour policy can be empirically tested, both by observing what he does and by hearing what he replies when he is questioned about his intentions.

Not all expressions of intentions will be moral assertions: for the notion of morality to be applicable it is necessary either that the policy of action intended by the asserter should be a general policy (e.g. the policy of utilitarianism) or that it should be subsumable under a general policy which the asserter intends to follow and which he would give as the reason for his more specific intention. There are difficulties and vaguenesses in the notion of a general policy of action, but these need not concern us here. All that we require is that, when a man asserts that he ought to do so-and-so, he is using the assertion to declare that he resolves, to the best of his ability, to do so-and-so. And he will not necessarily be insincere in his assertion if he suspects, at the time of making it, that he will not have the strength of character to carry out his resolution.

The advantage this account of moral assertions has over all others, emotive non-propositional ones as well as cognitive propositional ones, is that it alone enables a satisfactory answer to be given to the question: What is the reason for my doing what I think I ought to do? The answer it gives is that, since my thinking that I ought to do the action is my intention to do it if possible, the reason why I do the action is simply that I intend to do it, if possible. On every other ethical view there will be a mysterious gap to be filled somehow between the moral judgment and the intention to act in accordance with it: there is no such gap if the primary use of a moral assertion is to declare such an intention.

Let us now consider what light this way of regarding moral assertions throws upon assertions of religious conviction. The idealist philosopher McTaggart described religion as 'an emotion resting on a conviction of a harmony between ourselves and the universe at large',[5] and many educated people at the present time would agree with him. If religion is essentially concerned with emotion, it is natural to explain the use of religious assertions on the lines of the original

---

[5]J. M. E. McTaggart, *Some Dogmas of Religion* (1906), p. 3.

emotive theory of ethics and to regard them as primarily evincing religious feelings or emotions. The assertion, for example, that God is our Heavenly Father will be taken to express the asserter's feeling secure in the same way as he would feel secure in his father's presence. But explanations of religion in terms of feeling, and of religious assertions as expressions of such feelings, are usually propounded by people who stand outside any religious system; they rarely satisfy those who speak from inside. Few religious men would be prepared to admit that their religion was a matter merely of feeling: feelings—of joy, of consolation, of being at one with the universe—may enter into their religion, but to evince such feelings is certainly not the primary use of their religious assertions.

This objection, however, does not seem to me to apply to treating religious assertions in the conative way in which recent moral philosophers have treated moral statements—as being primarily declarations of adherence to a policy of action, declarations of commitment to a way of life. That the way of life led by the believer is highly relevant to the sincerity of his religious conviction has been insisted upon by all the moral religions, above all, perhaps, by Christianity. 'By their fruits ye shall know them.' The view which I put forward for your consideration is that the intention of a Christian to follow a Christian way of life is not only the criterion for the sincerity of his belief in the assertions of Christianity; it is the criterion for the meaningfulness of his assertions. Just as the meaning of a moral assertion is given by its use in expressing the asserter's intention to act, so far as in him lies, in accordance with the moral principle involved, so the meaning of a religious assertion is given by its use in expressing the asserter's intention to follow a specified policy of behaviour. To say that it is belief in the dogmas of religion which is the cause of the believer's intending to behave as he does is to put the cart before the horse: it is the intention to behave which constitutes what is known as religious conviction.

But this assimilation of religious to moral assertions lays itself open to an immediate objection. When a moral assertion is taken as declaring the intention of following a policy, the form of the assertion itself makes it clear what the policy is with which the assertion is concerned. For a man to assert that a certain policy ought to be pursued, which on this view is for him to declare his intention of pursuing the policy, presupposes his understanding what it would be like for him to pursue the policy in question. I cannot resolve not to tell a lie without knowing what a lie is. But if a religious assertion is the declaration of an intention to carry out a certain policy, what policy does it specify? The religious statement itself will not explicitly refer to a policy, as does a moral statement; how then can the asserter of the statement know what is the policy concerned, and how can he intend to carry out a policy if he does not know what the policy is? I cannot intend to do something I know not what.

The reply to this criticism is that, if a religious assertion is regarded as representative of a large number of assertions of the same religious system, the body of assertions of which the particular one is a representative specimen is taken by the asserter as implicitly specifying a particular way of life. It is no more necessary for an empiricist philosopher to explain the use of a religious statement taken in isolation from other religious statements than it is for him to give a meaning to a scientific hypothesis in isolation from other scientific hypotheses. We understand scientific hypotheses, and the terms that occur in them, by virtue of the relation of the whole system of hypotheses to empirically observable facts; and it is the whole system of hypotheses, not one hypothesis in isolation, that is tested for its truth-value against experience. So there are good precedents, in the empiricist way of thinking, for considering a system of religious assertions as a whole, and for examining the way in which the whole system is used.

If we do this the fact that a system of religious assertions has a moral function can hardly be denied. For to deny it would require any passage from the assertion of a religious system to a policy of action to be mediated by a moral assertion. I cannot pass from asserting a fact, of whatever sort, to intending to perform an action, without having the hypothetical intention to intend to do the action if I assert the fact. This holds however widely fact is understood—whether as an empirical fact or as a non-empirical fact about goodness or reality. Just as the intention-to-act view of moral assertions is the only view that requires no reason for my doing what I assert to be my duty, so the similar view of religious assertions is the only one which connects them to ways of life without requiring an additional premise. Unless a Christian's assertion that God is love (*agape*)—which I take to epitomize the assertions of the Christian religion—be taken to declare his intention to follow an agapeistic way of life, he could be asked what is the connection between the assertion and the intention, between Christian belief and Christian practice. And this question can always be asked if religious assertions are separated from conduct. Unless religious principles are moral principles, it makes no sense to speak of putting them into practice.

The way to find out what are the intentions embodied in a set of religious assertions, and hence what is the meaning of the assertions, is by discovering what principles of conduct the asserter takes the assertions to involve. These may be ascertained both by asking him questions and by seeing how he behaves, each test being supplemental to the other. If what is wanted is not the meaning of the religious assertion made by a particular man but what the set of assertions would mean were they to be made by anyone of the same religion (which I will call their *typical* meaning), all that can be done is to specify the form of behaviour which is in accordance with what one takes to be the fundamental moral principles of the religion in question. Since different people will take different views as to what these fundamental moral principles are, the typical meaning of religious assertions will be different for different people. I myself take the typical meaning of the body of Christian assertions as being given by their proclaiming intentions to follow an agapeistic way of life, and for a description of this way of life—a description in general and metaphorical terms, but an empirical description nevertheless—I should quote most of the Thirteenth Chapter of I Corinthians. Others may think that the Christian way of life should be described somewhat differently, and will therefore take the typical meaning of the assertions of Christianty to correspond to their different view of its fundamental moral teaching.

My contention then is that the primary use of religious assertions is to announce allegiance to a set of moral principles: without such allegiance there is no 'true religion'. This is borne out by all the accounts of what happens when an unbeliever becomes converted to a religion. The conversion is not only a change in the propositions believed—indeed there may be no specifically intellectual change at all; it is a change in the state of will. An excellent instance is C. S.

Lewis's recently published account of his conversion from an idealist metaphysic—'a religion [as he says] that cost nothing'—to a theism where he faced (and he quotes George MacDonald's phrase) 'something to be neither more nor less nor other than *done*'. There was no intellectual change, for (as he says) 'there had long been an ethic (theoretically) attached to my Idealism'; it was the recognition that he had to do something about it, that 'an attempt at complete virtue must be made'.[6] His conversion was a re-orientation of the will.

In assimilating religious assertions to moral assertions I do not wish to deny that there are any important differences. One is the fact already noticed that usually the behaviour policy intended is not specified by one religious assertion in isolation. Another difference is that the fundamental moral teaching of the religion is frequently given, not in abstract terms, but by means of concrete examples—of how to behave, for instance, if one meets a man set upon by theives on the road to Jericho. A resolution to behave like the good Samaritan does not, in itself, specify the behaviour to be resolved upon in quite different circumstances. However, absence of explicitly recognized general principles does not prevent a man from acting in accordance with such principles; it only makes it more difficult for a questioner to discover upon what principles he is acting. And the difficulty is not only one way round. If moral principles are stated in the most general form, as most moral philosophers have wished to state them, they tend to become so far removed from particular courses of conduct that it is difficult, if not impossible, to give them any precise content. It may be hard to find out what exactly is involved in the imitation of Christ; but it is not very easy to discover what exactly is meant by the pursuit of Aristotle's *eudaemonia* or of Mill's *happiness*. The tests for what it is to live agapeistically are as empirical as are those for living in quest of happiness; but in each case the tests can best be expounded in terms of examples of particular situations.

A more important difference between religious and purely moral principles is that, in the higher religions at least, the conduct preached by the religion concerns not only external but also internal behaviour. The conversion involved in accepting a religion is a conversion, not only of the will, but of the heart. Christianity requires not only that you should behave towards your neighbour as if you loved him as yourself: it requires that you should love him as yourself. And though I have no doubt that the Christian concept of *agape* refers partly to external behaviour—the agapeistic behaviour for which there are external criteria—yet being filled with *agape* includes more than behaving agapeistically externally: it also includes an agapeistic frame of mind. I have said that I cannot regard the expression of a feeling of any sort as the primary element in religious assertion; but this does not imply that intention to feel in a certain way is not a primary element, nor that it cannot be used to discriminate religious declarations of policy from declarations which are merely moral. Those who say that Confucianism is a code of morals and not, properly speaking, a religion are, I think, making this discrimination.

The resolution proclaimed by a religious assertion may then be taken as referring to inner life as well as to outward conduct. And the superiority of

---

[6]C. S. Lewis, *Surprised by Joy* (1955), pp. 198, 212–13. [No one who reads Lewis in context will find in him a support of Braithwaite's view. Ed.]

religious conviction over the mere adoption of a moral code in securing conformity to the code arises from a religious conviction changing what the religious man wants. It may be hard enough to love your enemy, but once you have succeeded in doing so it is easy to behave lovingly towards him. But if you continue to hate him, it requires a heroic perseverance continually to behave as if you loved him. Resolutions to feel, even if they are only partly fulfilled, are powerful reinforcements of resolutions to act.

But though these qualifications may be adequate for distinguishing religious assertions from purely moral ones, they are not sufficient to discriminate between assertions belonging to one religious system and those belonging to another system in the case in which the behaviour policies, both of inner life and of outward conduct, inculcated by the two systems are identical. For instance, I have said that I take the fundamental moral teaching of Christianity to be the preaching of an agapeistic way of life. But a Jew or a Buddhist may, with considerable plausibility, maintain that the fundamental moral teaching of his religion is to recommend exactly the same way of life. How then can religious assertions be distinguished into those which are Christian, those which are Jewish, those which are Buddhist, by the policies of life which they respectively recommend if, on examination, these policies turn out to be the same?

Many Christians will, no doubt, behave in a specifically Christian manner in that they will follow ritual practices which are Christian and neither Jewish nor Buddhist. But though following certain practices may well be the proper test for membership of a particular religious society, a church, not even the most ecclesiastically-minded Christian will regard participation in a ritual as the fundamental characteristic of a Christian way of life. There must be some more important difference between an agapeistically policied Christian and an agapeistically policied Jew than that the former attends a church and the latter a synagogue.

The really important difference, I think, is to be found in the fact that the intentions to pursue the behaviour policies, which may be the same for different religions, are associated with thinking of different *stories* (or sets of stories). By a story I shall here mean a proposition or set of propositions which are straightforwardly empirical propositions capable of empirical test and which are thought of by the religious man in connection with his resolution to follow the way of life advocated by his religion. On the assumption that the ways of life advocated by Christianity and by Buddhism are essentially the same, it will be the fact that the intention to follow this way of life is associated in the mind of a Christian with thinking of one set of stories (the Christian stories) while it is associated in the mind of a Buddhist with thinking of another set of stories (the Buddhist stories) which enables a Christian assertion to be distinguished from a Buddhist one.

A religious assertion will, therefore, have a propositional element which is lacking in a purely moral assertion, in that it will refer to a story as well as to an intention. The reference to the story is not an assertion of the story taken as a matter of empirical fact: it is a telling of the story, or an alluding to the story, in the way in which one can tell, or allude to, the story of a novel with which one is acquainted. To assert the whole set of assertions of the Christian religion is both to tell the Christian doctrinal story and to confess allegiance to the Christian way of life.

The story, I have said, is a set of empirical propositions, and the language expressing the story is given a meaning by the standard method of understanding how the story-statements can be verified. The empirical story-statements will vary from Christian to Christian; the doctrines of Christianity are capable of different empirical interpretations, and Christians will differ in the interpretations they put upon the doctrines. But the interpretations will all be in terms of empirical propositions. Take, for example, the doctrine of Justification by means of the Atonement. Matthew Arnold imagined it in terms of

. . . a sort of infinitely magnified and improved Lord Shaftesbury, with a race of vile offenders to deal with, whom his natural goodness would incline him to let off, only his sense of justice will not allow it; then a younger Lord Shaftesbury, on the scale of his father and very dear to him, who might live in grandeur and splendour if he liked, but who prefers to leave his home, to go and live among the race of offenders, and to be put to an ignominious death, on condition that his merits shall be counted against their demerits, and that his father's goodness shall be restrained no longer from taking effect, but any offender shall be admitted to the benefit of it on simply pleading the satisfaction made by the son;—and then, finally, a third Lord Shaftesbury, still on the same high scale, who keeps very much in the background, and works in a very occult manner, but very efficaciously nevertheless, and who is busy in applying everywhere the benefits of the son's satisfaction and the father's goodness.[7]

Arnold's 'parable of the three Lord Shaftesburys' got him into a lot of trouble: he was 'indignantly censured' (as he says) for wounding 'the feelings of the religious community by turning into ridicule an august doctrine, the object of their solemn faith'.[8] But there is no other account of the Anselmian doctrine of the Atonement that I have read which puts it in so morally favourable a light. Be that as it may, the only way in which the doctrine can be understood verificationally is in terms of human beings—mythological beings, it may be, who never existed, but who nevertheless would have been empirically observable had they existed.

For it is not necessary, on my view, for the asserter of a religious assertion to believe in the truth of the story involved in the assertions: what is necessary is that the story should be entertained in thought, i.e. that the statement of the story should be understood as having a meaning. I have secured this by requiring that the story should consist of empirical propositions. Educated Christians of the present day who attach importance to the doctrine of the Atonement certainly do not believe an empirically testable story in Matthew Arnold's or any other form. But it is the fact that entertainment in thought of this and other Christian stories forms the context in which Christian resolutions are made which serves to distinguish Christian assertions from those made by adherents of another religion, or of no religion.

What I am calling a *story* Matthew Arnold called a *parable* and a *fairy-tale*. Other terms which might be used are *allegory, fable, tale, myth*. I have chosen

---

[7]Matthew Arnold, *Literature and Dogma* (1873), pp. 306–7.
[8]Matthew Arnold, *God and the Bible* (1875), pp. 18–19.

the word 'story' as being the most neutral term, implying neither that the story is believed nor that it is disbelieved. The Christian stories include straightforward historical statements about the life and death of Jesus of Nazareth; a Christian (unless he accepts the unplausible Christ-myth theory) will naturally believe some or all of these. Stories about the beginning of the world and of the Last Judgment as facts of past or of future history are believed by many unsophisticated Christians. But my contention is that belief in the truth of the Christian stories is not the proper criterion for deciding whether or not an assertion is a Christian one. A man is not, I think, a professing Christian unless he both proposes to live according to Christian moral principles and associates his intention with thinking of Christian stories; but he need not believe that the empirical propositions presented by the stories correspond to empirical fact.

But if the religious stories need not be believed, what function do they fulfil in the complex state of mind and behaviour known as having a religious belief? How is entertaining the story related to resolving to pursue a certain way of life? My answer is that the relation is a psychological and causal one. It is an empirical psychological fact that many people find it easier to resolve upon and to carry through a course of action which is contrary to their natural inclinations if this policy is associated in their minds with certain stories. And in many people the psychological link is not appreciably weakened by the fact that the story associated with the behaviour policy is not believed. Next to the Bible and the Prayer Book the most influential work in English Christian religious life has been a book whose stories are frankly recognized as fictitious—Bunyan's *Pilgrim's Progress;* and some of the most influential works in setting the moral tone of my generation were the novels of Dostoevsky. It is completely untrue, as a matter of psychological fact, to think that the only intellectual considerations which affect action are beliefs: it is *all* the thoughts of a man that determine his behaviour; and these include his phantasies, imaginations, ideas of what he would wish to be and do, as well as the propositions which he believes to be true.

This important psychological fact, a commonplace to all students of the influence of literature upon life, has not been given sufficient weight by theologians and philosophers of religion. It has not been altogether ignored; for instance, the report of the official Commission on Doctrine in the Church of England, published in 1938, in a section entitled 'On the application to the Creeds of the conception of symbolic truth' says: 'Statements affirming particular facts may be found to have value as pictorial expressions of spiritual truths, even though the supposed facts themselves did not actually happen. . . . It is not therefore of necessity illegitimate to accept and affirm particular clauses of the Creeds while understanding them in this symbolic sense.'[9] But the patron saint whom I claim for my way of thinking is that great but neglected Christian thinker Matthew Arnold, whose parable of the three Lord Shaftesburys is a perfect example of what I take a religious story to be. Arnold's philosophy of religion has suffered from his striking remarks being lifted from their context: his description of religion as *morality touched by emotion* does not adequately express his view of the part played by imagination in religion. Arnold's main purpose in his religious writings was that of 'cementing the alliance between the imagination

---

[9]*Doctrine in the Church of England* (1938), pp. 37–8.

and conduct'[10] by regarding the propositional element in Christianity as 'litera-ture' rather than as 'dogma'. Arnold was not prepared to carry through his programme completely; he regarded *the Eternal not ourselves that makes for righteousness* more dogmatically than fictionally. But his keen insight into the imaginative and poetic element in religious belief as well as his insistence that religion is primarily concerned with guiding conduct make him a profound philosopher of religion as well as a Christian teacher full of the 'sweet reasonable-ness' he attributed to Christ.

> *God's wisdom and God's goodness!*—Ay, but fools
> Mis-define these till God knows them no more.
> *Wisdom and goodness, they are God!*—what schools
> Have yet so much as heard this simpler lore?[11]

To return to our philosophizing. My contention that the propositional element in religious assertions consists of stories interpreted as straightforwardly empirical propositions which are not, generally speaking, believed to be true has the great advantage of imposing no restriction whatever upon the empirical interpretation which can be put upon the stories. The religious man may interpret the stories in the way which assists him best in carrying out the behaviour policies of his religion. He can, for example, think of the three persons of the Trinity in visual terms, as did the great Christian painters, or as talking to one another, as in the poems of St John of the Cross. And since he need not believe the stories he can interpret them in ways which are not consistent with one another. It is disastrous for anyone to try to believe empirical propositions which are mutually inconsistent, for the courses of action appropriate to inconsistent beliefs are not compatible. The needs of practical life require that the body of believed propositions should be purged of inconsistency. But there is no action which is appropriate to thinking of a proposition without believing it; thinking of it may, as I have said, produce a state of mind in which it is easier to carry out a particular course of action, but the connection is causal: there is no intrinsic connection between the thought and the action. Indeed a story may provide better support for a long-range policy of action if it contains inconsistencies. The Christian set of stories, for example, contains both a pantheistic sub-set of stories in which everything is a part of God and a dualistic Manichaean sub-set of stories well represented by St Ignatius Loyola's allegory of a conflict between the forces of righteousness under the banner of Christ and the forces of darkness under Lucifer's banner. And the Marxist religion's set of stories contains both stories about an inevitable perfect society and stories about a class war. In the case of both religions the first sub-set of stories provides confidence, the second spurs to action.

There is one story common to all the moral theistic religions which has proved of great psychological value in enabling religious men to persevere in carrying out their religious behaviour policies—the story that in so doing they are doing the will of God. And here it may look as if there is an intrinsic connection

---

[10]Matthew Arnold, *God and the Bible* (1875), p. xiii.
[11]From Matthew Arnold's sonnet 'The Divinity' (1867).

between the story and the policy of conduct. But even when the story is literally believed, when it is believed that there is a magnified Lord Shaftesbury who commands or desires the carrying out of the behaviour policy, that in itself is no reason for carrying out the policy: it is necessary also to have the intention of doing what the magnified Lord Shaftesbury commands or desires. But the intention to do what a person commands or desires, irrespective of what this command or desire may be, is no part of a higher religion; it is when the religious man finds that what the magnified Lord Shaftesbury commands or desires accords with his own moral judgment that he decides to obey or to accede to it. But this is no new decision, for his own moral judgment is a decision to carry out a behaviour policy; all that is happening is that he is describing his old decision in a new way. In religious conviction the resolution to follow a way of life is primary; it is not derived from believing, still less from thinking of, any empirical story. The story may psychologically support the resolution, but it does not logically justify it.

In this lecture I have been sparing in my use of the term 'religious belief' (although it occurs in the title), preferring instead to speak of religious assertions and of religious conviction. This was because for me the fundamental problem is that of the meaning of statements used to make religious assertions, and I have accordingly taken my task to be that of explaining the use of such assertions, in accordance with the principle that meaning is to be found by ascertaining use. In disentangling the elements of this use I have discovered nothing which can be called 'belief' in the senses of this word applicable either to an empirical or to a logically necessary proposition. A religious assertion, for me, is the assertion of an intention to carry out a certain behaviour policy, subsumable under a sufficiently general principle to be a moral one, together with the implicit or explicit statement, but not the assertion, of certain stories. Neither the assertion of the intention nor the reference to the stories includes belief in its ordinary senses. But in avoiding the term 'belief' I have had to widen the term 'assertion', since I do not pretend that either the behaviour policy intended or the stories entertained are adequately specified by the sentences used in making isolated religious assertions. So assertion has been extended to include elements not explicitly expressed in the verbal form of the assertion. If we drop the linguistic expression of the assertion altogether the remainder is what may be called religious belief. Like moral belief, it is not a species of ordinary belief, of belief in a proposition. A moral belief is an intention to behave in a certain way: a religious belief is an intention to behave in a certain way (a moral belief) together with the entertainment of certain stories associated with the intention in the mind of the believer. This solution of the problem of religious belief seems to me to do justice both to the empiricist's demand that meaning must be tied to empirical use and to the religious man's claim for his religious beliefs to be taken seriously.

Seriously, it will be retorted, but not objectively. If a man's religion is all a matter of following the way of life he sets before himself and of strengthening his determination to follow it by imagining exemplary fairy-tales, it is purely subjective: his religion is all in terms of his own private ideals and of his own private imaginations. How can he even try to convert others to his religion if there is nothing objective to convert them to? How can he argue in its defence if there is no religious proposition which he believes, nothing which he takes to be the fundamental truth about the universe? And is it of any public interest what mental techniques he uses to bolster up his will? Discussion about religion must be more than the exchange of autobiographies.

But we are all social animals; we are all members one of another. What is profitable to one man in helping him to persevere in the way of life he has decided upon may well be profitable to another man who is trying to follow a similar way of life; and to pass on information that might prove useful would be approved by almost every morality. The autobiography of one man may well have an influence upon the life of another, if their basic wants are similar.

But suppose that these are dissimilar, and that the two men propose to conduct their lives on quite different fundamental principles. Can there be any reasonable discussion between them? This is the problem that has faced the many moral philosophers recently who have been forced, by their examination of the nature of thinking, into holding non-propositional theories of ethics. All I will here say is that to hold that the adoption of a set of moral principles is a matter of the personal decision to live according to these principles does not imply that beliefs as to what are the practical consequences of following such principles are not relevant to the decision. An intention, it is true, cannot be logically based upon anything except another intention. But in considering what conduct to intend to practise, it is highly relevant whether or not the consequences of practising that conduct are such as one would intend to secure. As R. M. Hare has well said, an ultimate decision to accept a way of life, 'far from being arbitrary . . . would be the most well-founded of decisions, because it would be based upon a consideration of everything upon which it could possibly be founded'.[12] And in this consideration there is a place for every kind of rational argument.

Whatever may be the case with other religions Christianity has always been a personal religion demanding personal commitment to a personal way of life. In the words of another Oxford philosopher, 'the questions "What shall I do?" and "What moral principles should I adopt?" must be answered by each man for himself'.[13] Nowell-Smith takes this as part of the meaning of morality: whether or not this is so, I am certain that it is of the very essence of the Christian religion.

---

[12]R. M. Hare, *The Language of Morals* (1952), p. 69.
[13]P. H. Nowell-Smith, *Ethics* (1954), p. 320.

EMPIRICISM AND THEISM

Keith Yandell

Keith E. Yandell, "Empiricism and Theism," *Sophia*, vol. VII, no. 3 (October 1968). Used by permission of the editor, Professor M. J. Charlesworth.

R. B. Braithwaite has endeavoured to wed his brand of empiricism with theism.[1] The happy event has been much publicised.[2] Since I believe it to be a mismatch, I shall argue for irreversible annulment.

For Braithwaite the central sort of religious sentence is a moral sentence with a specifiable deficiency. Thus it is necessary to consider his analysis of moral sentences, an analysis ostensibly applicable to all moral sentences whatever.

Braithwaite's point of departure is a theory of meaning:

> The meaning of any statement . . . will be taken as given by the way it is used. The kernel for an empiricist of the problem of the nature of religious belief is to explain, in empirical terms, how a religious statement is used by a man who asserts it in order to express his religious conviction. (59) [See p. 219.]

We are thus led to expect that the proffered analysis of religious sentences will be an accurate description of their actual use by a religious community or a member thereof.

The primary use of moral sentences, Braithwaite tells us, is to express "the intention of the asserter to act in a particular sort of way specified in the assertion." (60) Moral sentences are primarily conative, not emotive, though a secondary use of such sentences may be to express emotions. They express an intention to adopt a general behaviour policy. They do not, however, assert such an intention.[3] Were moral sentences assertions of having an intention,[4] they

---

[1] In "An Empiricist's View of the Nature of Religious Belief", Eddington Memorial Lecture for 1955. All quotations from Braithwaite will be taken from **Christian Ethics and Moral Philosophy,** ed. Ian T. Ramsey (SCM Press; 1966) p. 53–73.

[2] E.G. in the **Cambridge Review** (1956)—cf. Ramsey, **op. cit;** p. 74–93; John Hick, **Philosophy of Religion** (Prentice-Hall; 1963) p. 90–93; H. J. N. Horsburgh, "Professor Braithwaite and Billy Brown" (Australasian Journal of Philosophy, 1958); John Passmore, "Christianity and Positivism" (AJP, 1957); numerous anthologies have included Braithwaite's lecture. None of the above, however, are at all full-dress critiques of Braithwaite.

[3] "There will doubtless be empirical propositions which he (the user of moral sentences) may give as reasons for his adherence to the policy . . . and his having the intention will include his understanding what is meant by pursuing the policy . . . But there will be no specifically moral proposition which he will be asserting when he declares his intention to pursue the policy . . . when a man asserts that he ought to do so-and-so, he is using the assertion to declare that he resolves, to the best of his ability, to do so-and-so." (60). Compare the analogous remarks concerning religious sentences. (61).

[4] I assume that "I intend to do A" is an assertion in Braithwaite's sense: it can be verified in the sense that evidence of "trying hard" tends to verify having an intention to do what one tried hard to do; making no effort at all without any excuse, or making efforts for an opposite result, tends to falsify the assertion that I have that intention. Even if we regard "I intend to do A" as an expression, not an assertion, the only major alteration that this would require in my argument is that "I ought to do A, but don't intend to" expresses conflicting intentions—the intention to do and not to do A—and that it is false that in all cases of intelligible use of this sentence one must be expressing conflicting intentions.

would then be true or false, which Braithwaite denies.[5] Moral sentences are regarded as only expressing intentions, somewhat as "Ouch" expresses pain. So, for Braithwaite, "I ought to do A" expresses what "I intend to do A" asserts.

Braithwaite emphasizes that his is a *conative* theory of moral sentences; it recognizes their "intellectual content" in a way in which emotive theories do not. The same is true, he claims, of his analysis of religious sentences.

Few religious men would be prepared to admit that their religion was a matter merely of feeling. . . . To evince such feelings is certainly not the primary use of their religious assertions. This objection, however, does not seem to me to apply to treating religious assertions in the conative way in which recent moral philosophers have treated moral statements—as being primarily declarations of adherence to a policy of action, declarations of commitment to a way of life . . . it is the intention to behave which constitutes what is known as religious conviction. (61) [See p. 221.]

How, then, can we distinguish religious statements from moral ones?

. . . if a religious assertion is the declaration of an intention to carry out a certain policy, what policy does it specify? The religious statement itself will not explicitly refer to a policy, as does a moral statement . . . if a religious assertion is regarded as representative of a large number of assertions of the same religious system, the body of assertions of which the particular one is a representative specimen is taken by the asserter as implicitly specifying a particular way of life. (62) [See p. 221.]

One type of religious sentence, then, is like a moral sentence in that it expresses an intention to carry out a policy but unlike a moral sentence in that it leaves the policy unspecified. The policy is specified by a second type of religious sentence. The first type of religious sentence is a religious expression; these sentences are not true or false, express an intention to follow some general behaviour policy, rely on another type of sentence to specify that policy, and hence are dependent for their use on that other type of sentence. What then is the other type of sentence?

The intentions to pursue the behaviour policies, which may be the same for different religions, are associated with thinking of different *stories* (or sets of stories). By a story I shall mean a proposition or set of propositions which are straightforwardly empirical propositions capable of empirical test and which are thought of by the religious man in connection with his resolution to follow the way of life advocated by his religion. (66) [See p. 224.]

Here we have, purportedly, religious sentences which are assertive. Religious assertions are empirically testable, supply a context for religious expressions,

---

[5]"Religious statements, however, are not the only statements which are unverifiable by standard methods; moral statements have the same peculiarity. A moral principle . . . does not seem to be either a logically necessary or a logically impossible proposition. But neither does it seem to be an empirical proposition." (58).

specify the general behavioural policy which religious expressions leave open, and provide the basis for distinguishing between one religion and another. Braithwaite insists that it is not necessary for a religious man to believe that any religious assertions are true. (67) [p. 225] They function only to clarify policies enunciated in religious expressions and, secondarily, to motivate the religious man to follow that policy.

We have now noted what is essential to Braithwaite's analyses of moral and religious sentences. He provides other ways of distinguishing between moral versus religious sentences. One is that religious sentences "frequently" deal with concrete examples while moral ones do not. Another is that religious sentences are concerned with "internal" matters as well as "external" behaviour. Wisely, these two *differentia* are not pressed. The first is a matter of pedagogical emphasis; one can state a moral principle and then apply it to cases as Kant attempts in the *Grundlegung* or deal with cases and let one's principle remain unstated as often happens in the *Gospels*. But moral sentences which deal with specific examples are not thereby turned into religious sentences. The second proposed difference is unfair to the moral philosopher. Consider Aristotle's requirement that to be a virtuous man one must perform virtuous actions with pleasure and for their own sake, with a knowledge of what one is doing, or Kant's thesis that a perfectly good *will* is the only thing properly regarded as intrinsically good. Surely these moral philosophers were concerned with "internal" matters as well as "external" behaviour. But these are peripheral matters, and the major task lies ahead. What are we to make of Braithwaite's analyses?

To begin with his analysis of moral sentences, consider the following sentence forms: (1) I ought to do A; (2) He ought to do A; (3) They ought to do A. Braithwaite deals only with first-person examples like (1); even if we grant that (1) expresses the intention which "I intend to do A" asserts, what of (2) and (3)? If I utter (2), surely I am not to be taken as expressing what "I intend to see to it that he does A" asserts? In fact, I can utter (2) and have no intention to do anything at all. Sentences of form (2), uttered by me, cannot express anyone else's intentions. So they express no intentions at all. A sentence of form (3), uttered by me, cannot express everyone's intentions. If I utter such a sentence, surely I am not to be taken as expressing what "I intend to see to it that everyone does A' asserts? It is not at all plausible to insist that it must express any of my intentions. So, once again, no intention is expressed. Thus whatever plausibility Braithwaite's analysis has seems to be limited to sentences of form (1). Here, too, problems await us.

"I ought to do A, but don't intend to" is perfectly in order. No difficulty arises in thinking of contexts of use. It need not be uttered in a context where its speaker claims to have other, overriding obligations not to do A. Nor need it be the case that its speaker claims to be exempted from doing A because of special features of his person or the circumstances. "I ought to do A, but don't intend to" can be expanded to include some *justification* for not doing A, but it need not be so expanded to be used intelligibly. Consider the following expansions in which *no* justification is included: "I ought to do A, but I don't care about doing my duty/but I won't because I don't want to . . . " If I expand our sentence in any of these ways I am morally reprehensible. The fact that I am morally reprehensible is simply evidence that the sentence, so expanded, is intelligible.

I belabour the obvious for a reason. For Braithwaite, "I ought to do A, but don't intend to" cannot be intelligible.[6] "I ought to do A" expresses an intention to do A, whereas "I don't intend to (do A)" denies that I have any such intention. On Braithwaite's analysis, it could never be said without both expressing and denying the same intention. Thus no use of the sentence under discussion could occur in which the sentence was said sincerely and without self-stultification. But surely no self-stultification is in fact involved in perfectly normal contexts for this sort of sentence. What holds for "I ought to do A, but I don't intend to" holds for "I ought not to do A, but I intend to."

Braithwaite has a ready answer. His position

> alone enables a satisfactory answer to be given to the question: What is the reason for my doing what I think I ought to do? The answer it gives is that, since my thinking I ought to do the action is my intention to do it if possible, the reason why I do the action is simply that I intend to do it, if possible. (238) [See p. 220]

But consider the sentences "Jones' intentions were good" and "My intentions were good". These sentences evaluate intentions. They cannot evaluate intentions on Braithwaite's analysis. The former will express what "I intend to imitate Jones' intentions" asserts and the latter will express what "I intend to imitate (sustain) my intentions" asserts. My point is not merely that this analysis is quite implausible, though I think that is true. It is rather that, on Braithwaite's analysis, whenever I try to evaluate intentions, I must fail. Any endeavour to evaluate intentions will turn out to be only a matter of expressing more intentions. But one can intelligibly ask "Are your intentions good?" or "Were his intentions evil?" without expressing one's own intentions or asking questions to which the appropriate response is someone expressing other intentions.[7] Thus Braithwaite's analysis of moral sentences fails on two counts. First, it makes sentences of the form "I ought to do A, but don't intend to" and "I ought not to do A, but I intend to" self-stultifying in all contexts, which they plainly are not. Second, it makes it *logically* impossible for us to evaluate intentions. This is plainly not impossible.

Turning to Braithwaite's analysis of religious sentences, there is a curious ambivalence in Braithwaite's program. He proposes to deal with the "use" of religious sentences. But *whose* use? He takes it as evidence against the view that religious sentences merely express emotions that few religious people would accept that analysis. Is it equally evidence against his view that few orthodox Christians would accept his analysis?

Braithwaite anticipates this criticism, but deals with it in a peculiar way:

---

[6]John Hick, **Philosophy of Religion** (Prentice-Hall; 1963) claims that for Braithwaite it is "logically impossible to **intend** to act wrongly" and John Passmore, "Christianity and Positivism" (**Australian Journal of Philosophy,** 1957), p. 132, says that "On Braithwaite's view it would be selfcontradictory to say: "I intend to go, but I know I oughtn't to." This analysis in terms of straightforward contradiction misses some of the subtlety of Braithwaite's view. Passmore, however, aptly adds that "'he ought not to adopt that policy' would presumably turn into the very different statement 'he has announced his intention to adopt that policy' or (what is no more satisfactory) 'it is my intention that he shall not adopt that policy'."
[7]Passmore remarks that "the whole point of 'ought' statements is that they are used to **criticize** intentions." (**op. cit.,** p. 132). At least, this is one such point.

The empirical story-statements will vary from Christian to Christian; the doctrines of Christianity are capable of different empirical interpretations, and Christians will differ in the interpretations they put upon the doctrines. But the interpretations will all be in terms of empirical propositions. (66).

If all that Braithwaite means is that there are various theological viewpoints within "Christendom", he is of course correct. Some religious sentences used in one way in one branch may be used differently in another. Thus they will be different sentences; the same sound or symbols will express different meanings. If Braithwaite means that "the Christian tradition" cannot be at all defined or delineated, he seems to me to be mistaken, but more importantly he undercuts his own program of describing the actual use of that tradition.

Since Braithwaite tells us that he is analysing the use of religious language within the Christian tradition,[8] let us consider some examples clearly basic to that tradition. To begin with Braithwaite's own example, "God is love", is used as an assertion which, among other things, gives a reason for adopting a given way of life.[9] Braithwaite attempts to account for this in a remarkable passage.

Unless a Christian's assertion that God is love—which I take to epitomize the assertions of the Christian religion—be taken to declare his intention to follow an agapeistic way of life, he could be asked what is the connection between the assertion and the intention . . . Unless religious principles are moral principles, it makes no sense to speak of putting them into practice. (64) [See p. 222]

He argues that since one can "practise his religion", religion must consist *only* of what can be practised. Indeed it does not make sense to talk about putting "God is love" into practice. The explanation of this is simply that it is an attempt to describe God. But this does not mean that "God is love" is unrelated to moral practice. Since man is made in God's image and man's purpose is to live in accord with that image, it is argued, he ought to imitate God. My point here is not to consider whether "God is love" is in fact a description, but to point out that it is used as one by the tradition under analysis.

Also, "God is love" presupposes "God exists". I am aware that certain philosophers have denied that there is any *sense* to "God exists" apart from believing in God.[10] Braithwaite might make capital of this point and deny that one can believe that God exists other than by believing in God and that believing in God only involves living agapeistically. But this denial is surely ill-founded. For one thing, an atheist endeavouring to prove that "God exists" is false hardly believes in God. But in denying that God exists, he is not announcing his intention to live *un*agapeistically. For another, the apologist endeavouring to

---

[8]This is revealed by his examples (such as they are) of religious sentences and users of religious language (64, 66) and by his constant appeal to that tradition, as well as by explicit assertions (63, 64, 66). This does not mean that he intends his analysis to be limited to that tradition. I might add that it seems clear that examples culled only from the Old Testament would be effective counter examples also.
[9]Ephesians 5:1.
[10]Cf. Norman Malcolm, "Is Belief in God a Religious Belief?", **Faith and the Philosophers** (St. Martins Press, New York) 1964.

prove that "God exists" claims to prove it in such a way as to produce conviction that God exists, but is aware that this program, even if successful, is not tantamount to conversion.

Again, the agnostic can certainly wonder if the proposition is true or not without altering his mode of living. But if "God exists" makes sense apart from belief in God, then it cannot be reduced to belief in God. So "God is love" does presuppose "God exists". That "God exists" expresses an intention is, to be charitable, far from clear.

Another point is worth mentioning. If "God is love" expresses an intention to live agapeistically, one cannot say "God is love, but I intend to hate everyone" intelligibly since the former portion of the sentence expresses an intention while the latter portion asserts the opposite intention. A Braithwaitean devil could never rebel and continue to recognize the properties of his Divine Adversary. Thus the difficulties which plague Braithwaite's analysis of moral sentences blight his analysis of religious discourse also.

Consider some other examples:

(A) "Jesus Christ (was) . . . conceived of the Holy Spirit, born of the Virgin Mary . . . " (*The Apostles' Creed;* cf. Luke 1:34, 35.)

(B) "Jesus Christ is . . . perfect both in deity and humanness . . . actually God and actually man." (*The Definition of Chalcedon*; cf. John 1:14.)

(C) "He ascended into heaven . . . from whence he shall come to judge the quick and the dead." (*The Apostles' Creed*; cf. Rev. 20:11ff.)

What intentions do they express? Surely saying (A) cannot be seen as expressing an intention to live a pure life, or saying (B) seen as expressing an intention to deify oneself, or saying (C) as expressing an intention to survive one's death. These sentences are obviously religious sentences central to the tradition being discussed. Equally obviously, they are irredeemably recalcitrant to Braithwaite's techniques; they express no intentions.[11]

What, though, of the suggestion that while these examples cannot be read as expressing intentions, they can be seen as constituting the stories which specify the content of those religious sentences which do express intentions? This move obviously fails. Braithwaite's stories are entirely composed of straightforwardly empirically testable propositions. But none of the examples, which are only representative of others of the same kind, are empirically testable.[12]

This last assertion would be challenged by those who propose an "eschatological verification" for such statements as "God is love" and "The dead will be resurrected".[13] Any such verification presupposes the intelligibility of the notion of surviving one's death and that issue is too complex to be discussed here. If eschatological verification does provide a means of at least logically possible empirical test for a given sentence, then there is no need to accept Braithwaite's

---

[11]Hick is fully justified in saying that Braithwaite's analysis "is unable to accommodate those central, more directly and distinctively religious statements which refer to God". (**op. cit.** 192).

[12]Braithwaite's later, more complex division of story-statements (see Ramsey, **op. cit.,** p. 91) in no way alters this criticism.

[13]Cf. John Hick, **The Existence of God** (Prentice-Hall; 1964) p. 253 for a brief bibliography.

analysis for that sentence. Some of the examples—e.g. (B) and (C)—seem highly implausible candidates for even eschatological verification. In any case, Braithwaite offers us no reason to think that any of (A) through (C) are empirically testable.

Let us summarize the attack on Braithwaite's analysis of religious discourse. If we consider examples culled from the religious tradition purportedly being analysed, we find that examples clearly central to that tradition and obvious cases of religious discourse fit neither of Braithwaite's types of religious sentence. They express no intention. They are not empirically testable. Hence they should have no use within religious discourse. But patently they have a use within their religious tradition, and one not accounted for by Braithwaite.

This raises a serious issue. Braithwaite's program was an attempt at compromise. He tried to both salvage all that is essential to a given religious tradition and remain faithful to a certain criterion of meaning. He failed to do the former. While moral principles ("Thou shalt not kill") and empirically verifiable propositions ("Jesus was born in Bethlehem") are indeed important to that tradition, they alone do not constitute its distinctive religious discourse. That discourse was left unanalysed. One is left, then, with several alternatives. One can abandon the view that the tradition is in fact intelligible. One can deny the unrestricted adequacy of the criterion of meaning in question. Or one can show that the distinctive religious discourse of the tradition is (at least in part) empirically testable and then link any untestable parts to those which are testable. By failing genuinely to opt for any of these alternatives, Braithwaite bravely attempted what I suspect is an impossible task. In any case, it is clear that he failed to do what he set out to do.

COMMENTS ON "EMPIRICISM AND THEISM": A DEFENSE OF BRAITHWAITE[1]

Kai Nielsen

Kai Nielsen, "Comments on Empiricism and Theism," *Sophia*, vol. VII, no. 3 (October 1968). Used by permission of the author and editor, Professor M. J. Charlesworth.

Professor Yandell joins ranks with many others in maintaining that there are serious defects in Braithwaite's analysis of religious discourse.[2] Braithwaite purports to give us an analysis of the meaning of religious utterances, including religious utterances which are central to the Christian tradition, but he fails in this analysis for not all utterances integral to that tradition can be correctly analyzed either as empirical statements open to confirmation or infirmation or as sentences expressing an intention to follow a general behavioural policy to be associated with certain stories. "Jesus Christ was conceived of the Holy Spirit", "Jesus Christ is actually God and actually man", "God is love" or "There is a creator of the universe" are all of central importance in the Christian tradition. Yet they do not fit either of Braithwaite's models for intelligible religious expressions. They are not, at least as they are used in modern religious discourses, confirmable or infirmable even in principle, for both their affirmation and denial are equally compatible with any empirically identifiable state of affairs that might conceivably obtain. But since this is so the utterances in question fail to make empirical statements. But they are not expressions of intention either. Ask yourself what intentions do they express? If I say "I'll pay you tomorrow", or if two people say together to a third party, "We are going to get married", it is plain enough that these are the expressions of intention and that these utterances can be paraphrased as explicit intentional utterances. But this is hardly so for the sample religious utterances mentioned above. What intention does "Jesus Christ was conceived of the Holy Spirit" express? No even remotely plausible paraphrase suggests itself. Are we to say it means "Treat Jesus as being on a par with God", or "The concept of Jesus is to be taken as conceptually linked to the concept of God"? But surely such paraphrases are wildly implausible. One can say, for example, "Even though Jesus Christ was conceived of the Holy Spirit we should treat Him as being of equal importance to God". Yet if the above equivalences hold, such a remark would be pleonastic. But it plainly is not. Thus it cannot be

---

[1]Read [along with the preceding and following papers] at the Sixty-sixth Annual Meeting of the Western Division of the American Philosophical Association at St. Louis, Missouri, May 3, 1968. Some of the crucial thinking in this paper has been much influenced by J. C. Thornton's brilliant "Religious Belief and 'Reductionism'", **Sophia**, vol. V, No. 3 (October, 1966), and by his "Reductionism—A Reply to Dr. Mascall", **Sophia**, vol. VI, No. 2 (July, 1967).
[2]J. A. Passmore, "Christianity and Positivism," **Australasian Journal of Philosophy,** vol. 35 (1957); F. C. Copleston, **Contemporary Philosophy** (London, 1956), Chap. VII; Terence Penelhum, "Faith, Fact and Philosophy," **Toronto Quarterly** (October, 1956); Kai Nielsen, "On Speaking of God," **Theoria,** vol. XXVIII, No. 2 (1962); E. L. Mascall, **Words and Images** (London, 1957); William Blackstone, **The Problem of Religious Knowledge** (Englewood Cliffs, New Jersey, 1963), Chap. VI; H. V. Horsburgh, "Professor Braithwaite and Billy Brown," **Australasian Journal of Philosophy,** vol. 36 (November, 1958).

the case that such equivalences hold. However, for Braithwaite's account to be correct some such paraphrase of the above utterance must be given.

Criticisms of this sort are familiar and Yandell, following this well-trodden path, does show that Braithwaite's account is defective, if taken as a complete account of the meaning of religious talk. Braithwaite, I agree, does not give an adequate account of such utterances as "Jesus Christ if perfect both in deity and humanness is actually God and actually man", or "Jesus Christ ascended into heaven from whence he shall judge the quick and the dead". Yet they are surely part of the corpus of Christian doctrine and people who can play this language-game indeed know how to operate with them. That is to say, Braithwaite does not give a plausible analysis of certain distinctive bits of religious discourse—bits of discourse which are taken as essential to Christianity by the vast majority of the members of its various confessional groups. It is surely a radical departure from the Christian tradition to try to construe "God exists" as nothing more than an expression on the part of the user of his intention to live agapeistically; and to add that such expressions of intention to be religious must be associated with certain stories which believers at least entertain, does not help matters materially.

However, I do not believe such criticisms cut deeply enough; I do not think they once and for all dispose of attempts such as Braithwaite's and I think there are some further things that someone taken by Braithwaite's position could say in reply.

First, it is worth noting for the historical record that in reply to some rather similar criticisms of his *An Empiricist's View of Religious Belief,* Braithwaite points out that he never thought of his account as a complete account of religious belief and utterance.[3] Rather, he deliberately intended it to be an account which would show how much of religious belief could be shown to be compatible with a moderate empiricism. In short, Braithwaite attempts to establish that much religious discourse, and particularly a good bit of religious utterance that plays an important part in the stream of religious life, can be understood and even accepted by a thorough-going modern empiricist. Nothing that Yandell or Braithwaite's other critics have said undermines this claim.

Rather, his critics hark back to the point that there is something essential to Christianity that Braithwaite's account leaves out. If by "essential to Christianity" or even "essential to religion itself" is meant something that almost all those who call themselves "Christians" take to be essential, then Braithwaite's critics are no doubt right. There are utterances which are clearly central strands in the corpus of Christian discourse which are not analyzable according to Braithwaite's model for elucidating religious utterances. That is to say—and note this is an important qualification—they are not analyzable in a way which would be acceptable to an orthodox believer. But to claim that such bits of discourse are essential to Christianity, and to further conclude that it is essential to Christianity that they be taken as most Christians take them, is to beg some important questions. Indeed, they are taken by most Christians to be essential and they are thought of as utterances which are used to make some mysterious cosmological claims.

---

[3]R. B. Braithwaite, "Discussion" in I. T. Ramsey, ed., **Christian Ethics and Contemporary Philosophy** (London, 1966), p. 88.

Ramsey's reaction to Braithwaite's analysis illustrates this very well.[4] However, Braithwaite points out how on Arnold's account such cosmological claims are peripheral. And in the same spirit, one could add that on Feuerbach's and Santayana's still deeper and more probing accounts they are even more peripheral. On such accounts the sentences which are normally taken to be vehicles for such putative cosmological claims are construed in a radically different manner. Admittedly this is not to view Christianity from the vantage point of most believers or from the vantage point of orthodox Christian theologians. But why should one so view it? Braithwaite is a philosopher with certain convictions about what it makes sense to say and at the same time he, as a human being, feels attracted to the Christian tradition. But he makes it clear in his reply to criticisms by Mackinnon and Ramsey that he cannot accept the whole Christian tradition when it is construed in the way most believers construe it. He remarks that as a "conscientious empiricist" he can only construe such utterances as "God created the heavens and the earth" or "Jesus was conceived by the Holy Ghost" in a *pictorial way*. He cannot take them at face value.[5] Their *prima facie* logical status is that of some kind of statement of fact. But for very familiar reasons, he finds it impossible to take them in this way. Moreover, we should by now be wary of simply identifying the *prima facie* logical status of a sentence with its actual logical status, and we should not forget that Braithwaite is aware that his inability to accept these "claims" at face value does not square with the plain believer's beliefs *about* the meaning of such religious utterances or even with tolerably orthodox theological accounts of the meaning of such utterances. But why should these accounts—these bits of meta-theology—be normative or authoritative for Braithwaite or even for Christianity or for religious believers generally? No good grounds have been given for saying that they should be normative.

Indeed, if we are to analyze the meaning of religious utterances, we must take as our given the first-order religious discourse of the various confessional groups. An account which does not give a perspicuous representation of such discourse is a defective account of religious discourse. But we by no means need take as our given or as something just to be accepted the received *beliefs about* that discourse. That Braithwaite's account does not square with certain theses in meta-theology does not *ipso facto* establish it as defective.

It will, however, be objected that Yandell's criticisms show that Braithwaite's account cannot give a perspicuous representation of *all* first-order Christian-talk. Braithwaite does not take account of the mysteries of Christian faith or of the profound, though unavoidably opaque, ontological statements which are integral to the Christian tradition. But this essentially reduces to the claim that he does not give an account of such discourses which will square with the *beliefs about* this discourse held by orthodox Christians. But why should Braithwaite's view square with such beliefs *about* religious discourse? Why is it not perfectly legitimate for him to say that on his empiricist principles such metaphysical religious utterances cannot be construed at face value, for while on the surface they appear to

[4]I. T. Ramsey, "Discussion" in I. T. Ramsey, ed., **Christian Ethics and Contemporary Philosophy** (London, 1966), pp. 84–88.
[5]R. B. Braithwaite, **op. cit.,** p. 91.

function as statements, their depth grammar is such that we do not know what it would be like for them to be even probably true or false? We can well enough understand "Orthodox Jews fast on the Day of Atonement", or "Nothing can ever be red and green all over", and be puzzled about their proper analysis. But we have difficulty in even understanding, when we try to construe it literally, "There is a creator of the heavens and the earth". Moreover, it is at least questionable whether anyone has given a coherent account of what such utterances mean. Theologians speak of opacity or of mystery when what is actually involved is incoherence and obfuscation. Orthodox believers maintain that such utterances typically function as statements but they can give no account of what it would be like for them to be true or false or even probably true or false when used as believers now use them.

Braithwaite, by contrast, has an intelligible criterion of meaning, and sticking to that he can make literal sense out of much Christian belief. And he can take the other utterances in the Christian corpus, whose meaning is admittedly problematic, and deliberately reinterpret them so that they make sense on his criterion of meaning. Indeed, this is to *give* them new uses in virtue of which we can have some understanding of what we are saying when we utter them and in virtue of which they can mesh with the unproblematic straightforwardly empirical or moral utterances in the stream of religious life. To do this would indeed be an arbitrary procedure—a kind of dogmatic holding on to a criterion of meaning at any price—if it were not for the fact that the very first-order bits of religious discourse in question, e.g., "In the beginning was the Word and the Word was God", are themselves sentences whose meaning is problematic.

To look at Christianity in this way is indeed to curtail Christian expectations. If people so construed Christianity, Christianity would become something different—though by no means *totally* different—from what it is now and has been in the past. Even believing in God would indeed be very different from what most people take it to be. But religions have always undergone change. Christianity has changed in the past and why should it not change again? Why is it not perfectly appropriate for Braithwaite to stick to his empiricist philosophical principles on the assumption that they are more likely to be in good logical order than some admittedly obscure metaphysical principles?

This I maintain is where the issue should be joined. When we consider the obscurity of alternative meta-theologies such as Ramsey's, Mascall's, or D. Z. Phillips', we (to put it conservatively) recognize that Braithwaite is on reasonably strong grounds.

It seems to me that for criticisms of such accounts as Braithwaite's to be really penetrating, they must take another tack. "God exists" or "There is a God" could on his radical rational reconstruction have no literal, non-pictorial statemental function. This means that Orthodox Christian believers could not make the cosmological claims, obscure and perplexing as they are, that they feel driven to make even when they admittedly have very little understanding of the "claims" they are trying to make when they utter such utterances. There is in many human beings a nagging need, as Hägerström put it, to believe in some wholly other "objective power to which one can turn and from which one can draw strength to attain that which one strives after in one's innermost being, strength to resist temptations and a final hope of blessedness in a future life".[6] It is the religious and theological commitments serving this psychological need and not radical conceptual difficulties in Braithwaite's analysis that make many reject Braithwaite's account and turn to the varied obscurities of a Ramsey or Tillich, on the one hand, or a Phillips or Winch, on the other. Their accounts all accommodate obscurities, which if we can accept and legitimatize them, gives us a rationale for accepting some very obscure first-order religious beliefs.

Indeed, these metaphysical beliefs attempt to affirm the reality of one and only one Being who created the world out of nothing. And such beliefs are central to traditional Christianity and are held onto tenaciously by believers. Their scope purports to transcend "the empirical world" and Braithwaite's analysis cannot accommodate them where we take them at their face value. But this is only to say that one cannot be an orthodox Christian and accept Braithwaite's analysis. Still this is no criticism of his analysis, for Braithwaite did not set out to defend or even explicate orthodoxy but simply to show that an empiricist could find in a historic religion such as Christianity a coherent set of beliefs and principles—principles which he could subscribe to and act in accordance with. They do not include the whole of traditional Christian belief but they do include an important subset of these beliefs.

Once we allow for the special place afforded the distinctively Christian parables, it is evident that such a reconstructed representation of some features of Christian belief is identical with a certain kind of morally dedicated atheism. But to assert this is not to say or even to give one to understand that there is anything wrong with it. It just leaves out something that orthodox Christians yearn for.

---

[6]Axel Hägerström, "Lectures on So-Called Spiritual Religion," **Theoria,** vol. XIV (Part I, 1948), pp. 34–35.

A REPLY TO NIELSEN'S COMMENTS
Keith Yandell

Keith E. Yandell, "A Reply to Nielsen," *Sophia,* vol. VII, no. 3 (October 1968).

Professor Nielsen's reply is clear and provocative. Several points seem worth making in response.

1. Nielsen says that Braithwaite has "an intelligible criterion of meaning". I do not know that he has. His criterion for being an assertion (as opposed to being meaningful in some other way) seems to be simply the verification principle. Philosophers have pointed out rather often that it is extremely difficult to state this criterion so that it does not either rule out indisputably meaningful sentences or allow in very dubious ones, or both. Perhaps Professor Plantinga in his *God*

and Other Minds is the most recent, and I agree with him when he adds that even should this criterion some day be successfully stated, it is not clear that the theist is at all obligated to accept it.

2. Braithwaite and Nielsen seem agreed that, say, "God loves us" could not be empirically falsified, even in principle. I am not so sure. Suppose we knew the following propositions to be true:

(a) every sentient creature has, for every moment of his existence, been in such pain that were he to have felt more pain he would have lost consciousness.

(b) this wretched condition is caused by biological features essential to the species.

(c) suicide is impossible and so is cessation of procreation, so that future generations will exist under the same conditions.

(d) insofar as intellectual life is possible under these circumstances, men rise above the level of imbecility only to record and roundly curse their plight with the exception that,

(e) insofar as moral life is possible under these circumstances, each man's deepest wish is to increase the sufferings of every other if this were possible.

Now surely if our world were like this (and given that we could raise the question), we would have good reason to deny that God loves us—as good as we have, say, that cigarette smoking disposes to lung cancer. At the very minimum, surely we would have *some* evidence that God does not love us.

We could appeal to eschatological verification by supposing:

(f) the societies for psychical research have provided superb evidence that men survive their deaths, have contacted all survivers, and to a man they refer to life on earth as "the good old days".

But we need not appeal to (f) to have evidence in principle relevant to falsifying "God loves us". If many believers would retain belief even under these circumstances it would not at all show that they had not been refuted, but only that they were uncommonly stubborn. It would be relevant to the psychology of believers, not to the logical status of their beliefs.

3. My argument was not merely that Braithwaite did not capture all that is essential to Christian discourse. It was also that part of the plausibility of his claim rested on his analysis working also for ethical discourse and that it in fact failed there too. But if it is not clear that his criterion is intelligible, and also not clear that it should be accepted, then the fact that the analysis fails in two areas of discourse is surely a good reason to reject it.

4. Braithwaite does indeed make modest claims about the scope of his essay. He says:

I have never for a moment thought that the positive account I gave in the lecture is the whole truth about religious discourse.[1]

But he thought it was "an important . . . part of the truth", and whatever he may add must be consistent with what has already been given. If what we have is inadequate, then the need is not to supplement, but to reject.

5. At the end of his paper, Nielsen notes that many men have a nagging

---

[1]Ramsey, p. 88.

psychological need for a Heavenly Comforter and thus are led to reject Braithwaite's analysis on other grounds than those of conceptual defect. As he does not suggest that this is true in my case, I shall return the charity when I offer *ad hominem* for *ad hominem*. Nietzsche once said that he could not stand for there to be a God, for then he would be intolerably jealous, and he described his atheism as "instinctual". A contemporary philosopher has described himself as a "congenital atheist". Perhaps, then, many of those who accept the strictures of Braithwaite's analysis have a nagging psychological need to reject an all-powerful, all-knowing Authority, and so they accept his analysis even with its conceptual defects.

Chapter
SEVEN

RESPONSES TO SECULARITY
symbols and ontology

THE MEANING
AND JUSTIFICATION
OF RELIGIOUS SYMBOLS

Paul Tillich

Paul Tillich, "The Meaning and Justification of Religious Symbols," from Sidney Hook (ed.), *Religious Experience and Truth*. Copyright © 1961 by New York University. Reprinted by permission of New York University Press.

Religious symbols need no justification if their meaning is understood. For their meaning is that they are the language of religion and the only way in which religion can express itself directly. Indirectly and reflectively religion can also express itself in theological, philosophical, and artistic terms. But its direct self-expression is the symbol and the united group of symbols which we call myths.

I

In order to understand religious symbols we must first understand the nature of symbols generally. And this is a difficult task, because the term symbol is being applied to things which should not be called symbols at all, e.g., signs, symptoms, metaphors, etc. But since the linguistic development can hardly be reversed, one can save the genuine meaning of "symbol" only by adding an adjective whenever "symbol" is meant. Symbols which deserve the name shall be called "representative symbols," following a suggestion by John Randall, in contrast to the symbols which are only signs, such as mathematical and logical symbols—which one could call "discursive symbols." The realms in which representative symbols appear are language and history, the arts and religion. They show common characteristics which must be presupposed if one speaks of symbols in each of these groups. The common characteristics in all realms of representative symbols are the following:

First and most fundamental is the character of all symbols to point beyond themselves. Symbols use "symbolic material": the ordinary meaning of a word, the empirical reality of a historical figure, the traits of a human face (in a painting), a human catastrophe (in a drama), a human power or virtue (in a description of the divine). But this symbolic material is not meant in its proper and ordinary meaning. When it is used as symbolic material, it points to something which cannot be grasped directly but must be expressed indirectly, namely through the symbolic material. This "something" can be the connotations of a word which transcend the empirical reality of this person, or it can be a dimension of reality which is not open to an ordinary encounter with reality as the artistic forms, or it can be ultimate reality, expressed in symbols whose material is taken from finite reality.

The second characteristic of all representative symbols is to participate in the reality of that which they represent. The concept of representation itself implies this relation. The representative of a person or an institution participates in the honor of those whom he is asked to represent; but it is not *he* who is honored, it is that which or he whom he represents. In this sense we can state generally that the symbol participates in the reality of what it symbolizes. It radiates the power of being and meaning of that for which it stands.

This leads to the third characteristic of the representative symbol: it cannot be created at will. It is not a matter of expediency and convention, as signs are. Therefore, one can metaphorically say that a symbol is born and may die. Even if individual creativity is the medium through which it comes into existence (the individual artist, the individual prophet), it is the unconscious-conscious reaction of a group through which it becomes a symbol. No representative symbol is created and maintained without acceptance by a group. If the group ceases to accept it, it may, like the ancient gods, become a metaphor or maintain its poetic-symbolic value, but, as a religious symbol, it becomes lost.

The fourth characteristic of a representative symbol is its power of opening up dimensions of reality, in correlation to dimensions of the human spirit, which otherwise are covered by the predominance of other dimensions of spirit and reality. The historical symbols show historical potentialities which are covered by the everyday historical events and activities. Artistic symbols—in fact, all artistic creations—open up the human spirit for the dimension of aesthetic experience and they open up reality to the dimension of its intrinsic meaning. Religious symbols mediate ultimate reality through things, persons, events which because of their mediating functions receive the quality of "holy." In the experience of holy places, times, books, words, images, and acts, symbols of the holy reveal something of the "Holy-Itself" and produce the experience of holiness in persons and groups. No philosophical concept can do the same thing, and theological concepts are merely conceptualizations of original religious symbols.

One may add a fifth characteristic of representative symbols: their integrating and disintegrating power. This function of symbols refers both to individuals and groups. The history of religion gives an endless number of examples for the elevating, quieting, and stabilizing power of religious symbols. In the larger, and sometimes even narrower, sense of the word, one can speak of the "healing" power of religious symbols. All this is equally true of the three other groups of representative symbols. But in contrast to their integrating function, symbols can also have a disintegrating effect: causing restlessness, producing depression, anxiety, fanaticism, etc. This depends partly on the character of that to which they point, partly on the reaction of those who are grasped by them. Symbols have the same creative or destructive effect on social groups. Symbols are the main power of integrating them: a king, an event, a document in the political realm of representative symbolism, an epic work, architectural symbols, a holy figure, a holy book, a holy rite in religion. But here also are disintegrating possibilities as in some political symbols such as the Führer and the swastika, or in religious symbols such as the Moloch type of gods, human sacrifices, doctrinal symbols producing a split consciousness, etc. This characteristic of symbols shows their tremendous power of creation and destruction. By no means are they harmless semantic expressions.

II

In the preceding general analysis of the nature of symbols, we frequently have mentioned religious symbols. They must now be considered in their particular character. In the language of religion a problem is intensified which appears in every kind of expression, the problem of the "referent." To what does a religious symbol refer, one asks? How can it be reached? And if it can be reached by symbols only, how can we know that something is reached at all? Such questions are certainly justified. One can sum them up by asking: Is there a nonsymbolic statement about the referent of religious symbols? If this question could not be answered affirmatively the necessity of symbolic language for religion could not be proved and the whole argument would lead into a vicious circle. The question then is: what is the referent of religious symbolism and how can it be known except by symbols—known namely in the one and only respect that it is the referent for religious symbols.

There are two ways which lead to the same result, a phenomenological and an ontological one. Excluded by the very nature of the subject matter is the inductive way. For it can lead only to a finite part of the universe of finite objects through observation and conclusion. But the intention of every religious symbol is to point to that which transcends finitude. Nothing finite, no part of the universe of finite relations can be the referent of religious symbols, and, therefore, no inductive method can reach it.

The phenomenological approach describes the holy as a quality of some encounters with reality. The holy is a "quality in encounter," not an object among objects, and not an emotional response without a basis in the whole of objects. The experience of the holy transcends the subject-object structure of experience. The subject is drawn into the holy, embodied in a finite object which, in this encounter, becomes sacred. An analysis of this experience shows that wherever the holy appears it is a matter of ultimate concern both in attracting and in repelling, and of unconditional power, both in giving and in demanding. The phenomenological analysis of the experience of the holy has been carried through in an excellent way by Rudolf Otto and others. It shows what is meant, if religious symbols are used. But it cannot go beyond the description. Phenomenology cannot raise the question of validity of the phenomena it makes visible.

The other way of reaching the referent of religious symbolism is the ontological one. It analyzes the kind of being man is, in interdependence with his world. It analyzes the finitude of the finite in different directions, it points to the anxiety which is connected with the awareness of one's finitude, and it raises the question of being-itself, the *prius* of everything that is. This approach tries to find the referent of religious symbolism not in a particular experience, that of the holy and of the ultimate concern implied in the holy but it tries to find it in the character of being as such, in everything that is. The ontological method, as indicated here, does not argue for the existence of a being, about which religion makes symbolic statements, but it gives an analysis of the encountered world with respect to its finitude and finds through this analysis its self-transcending quality, its pointing beyond its finitude. That to which this analysis leads is the referent in all religious symbols. One can give it metaphoric names, like "being-itself" or "power of being" or "ultimate reality" or "ultimate concern" (in the sense of that about which one is ultimately concerned). Such names are not names of a being but of a quality of being. If religious symbols express this quality in divine names, classical theology has always asserted that the referent of these names transcends their nonsymbolic meaning infinitely.

The two ways of finding the referent of symbolic language, the phenomenological and the ontological, corroborate each other. That which is the implication of the phenomenological description is also the focal point of the ontological analysis and the referent of the religious symbols.

III

There is an almost endless amount of religious symbolism in the history of religion. This is not so by chance. It follows from the fact that in a particular encounter with reality everything can become a bearer of the holy. Nothing is prevented from becoming a sacred thing. Only historical contingencies prevent it. But they have not prevented exemplars of almost every class of things from actually becoming sacred things. This produces the impression that the history of religion is a mere chaos of incoherent imaginations. But this is not the case; there are many keys for the understanding of the dynamics of this large realm of human experience. There are also keys for an understanding of the immense amount of religious symbols. Without considering their historical dynamics I want to distinguish certain basic kinds of religious symbols in order to overcome semantic as well as material confusions.

The first distinction needed is that between primary and secondary religious symbolism. The primary symbols point directly to the referent of all religious symbolism. In order to do so they establish a "highest" being, attribute characteristics to him the symbolic material of which is taken from human or cosmic experiences and extended *via eminentiae* to that which to the religious intention transcends all such characteristics. This refers to qualities like personality, power, love, justice, etc. It has been asked whether qualities like being, becoming, essence, existence, can be attributed nonsymbolically to God. It seems to me that such an assertion makes out of that which transcends all beings a being of higher order. The rejection of this attempt agrees with the contention of classical theology that God is "beyond" the split between essence and existence, as well as beyond being (in a static sense) and becoming. This "beyond" is an expression of a symbolic use of these terms.

A second level of primary religious symbolism is the way in which religion speaks of divine actions like creation, providence, miracles, incarnation, consummation, etc. It is especially important to emphasize the symbolic character of these symbols, because they often are understood literally, with the consequence that they fall into insoluble conflicts with the scientific interpretation of reality. In all these symbols the religious imagination subjects that which is ultimate reality to the categories of time, space, substance, and causality. This is unavoidable and without danger as long as the symbolic character is being recognized. But if this is not done, the whole relation between God and the world becomes a nest of absurdities, as, e.g., God's "predestining" or his "almighty" actions.

The third level of primary symbols lives in the realm of divine manifestations in finite reality, divine incarnations in holy things or objects. In the dynamics of the history of religion this level must be considered as the "oldest" one. For the basic religious experience is that of the presence of the holy in concrete things, persons, or actions here and now. The "sacramental presence" of the holy is the lasting basis of all religious experience, and the radical transcendence into which the divine was elevated is a later development, the result of the fight of the higher religions against the demonic distortions of the sacramental religions.

These three basic levels of primary religious symbolism are permeated by a host of secondary religious symbols. Secondary are supporting symbols like water, light, oil, or poetic symbols in which a primary religious symbol is artistically resymbolized, or metaphoric expressions as they appear in parables or are used in poetry. They should not be raised to the rank of primary symbols. In the Psalmist's phrase "The Lord is my shepherd," the word "Lord" is a genuine and primary religious symbol, the word "shepherd" is a poetic metaphor. It must be added that the distinctions made here are neither exclusive nor static. The levels are mixed with each other and often symbols of one level originate on another level, e.g., secondary religious symbols had once an independent standing as primary religious symbols and vice versa. But the distinction itself is valid.

IV

If one asks about criteria of religious symbols we must state generally that the measure of their validity is their adequacy to the religious experience they express. This is the basic criterion of all symbols. One can call it their "authenticity." Nonauthentic are religious symbols which have lost their experiential basis, but which are still used for reasons of tradition or because of their aesthetic value. The criterion of authenticity is valid but not sufficient. It does not answer the question of the amount of truth a symbol possesses. The term "truth" in this context means the degree to which it reaches the referent of all religious symbols. The question itself can be answered in two ways, a negative and a positive one. The negative quality which determines the truth of a religious symbol is its self-negation and transparency to the referent for which it stands. The positive quality which determines the truth of a religious symbol is the value of the symbolic material used in it. Both statements need interpretation.

It is the danger and an almost unavoidable pitfall of all religious symbols that they bring about a confusion between themselves and that to which they point. In religious language this is called idolatry. The term does not express (or should not express) the arrogant and indirectly idolatrous judgment of one religion over all the others, but it expresses an implicit tendency of all religions to elevate themselves to ultimacy in power and meaning. On the other side, all religions live from the system of symbols by which they have been created and which they continue recreating. They live as long as a whole of symbols is the expression of their particular character. With the end of the power of its symbols a religious group comes to its own end. When, however, the symbols are in power their idolatrous misuse is almost unavoidable. The symbol of the "Cross of the Christ," which is the center of all Christian symbolism, is perhaps the most radical criticism of all idolatrous self-elevation. But even it has become again and again the tool of idolatry within the Christian churches. This consideration is the answer to the question of the truth of religious symbols from the negative point of view. The measure of their truth is the measure of their self-negation with respect to what they point to, the Holy-Itself, the ultimate power of being and meaning.

The other criterion is the quality of their symbolic material. There is a difference whether they use trees and rocks and stones and animals or personalities and groups as symbolic material. Only in the last case do the symbols comprise the whole of reality; for only in man are all dimensions of the encountered world united. It is therefore decisive for the rank and value of a symbol that its symbolic material is taken from the human person. Therefore, the great religions are concentrated on a personal development in which ultimate concern appears and transcends the personal limits, though remaining in a person. The positive criterion for the truth of a symbol (e.g., creation) is the degree in which it includes the valuation in an ultimate perspective of the individual persons.

The negative and positive criteria of the truth of a religious symbol show that their truth has nothing to do with the validity of factual statements concerning the symbolic material. However problematic the symbolic material in its literal meaning may be, its symbolic character and its validity as a symbol are not determined by it.

It seems to me that an understanding of the language of religion in the line developed in this paper is the precondition for an adequate interpretation of religion and for a creative interpenetration of the theological and the philosophical task.

TILLICH'S CONCEPTION OF A RELIGIOUS SYMBOL
William P. Alston

William P. Alston, "Tillich's Conception of a Religious Symbol," from Sidney Hook (ed.), *Religious Experience and Truth.* Copyright © 1961 by New York University. Reprinted by permission of New York University Press.

As Professor Tillich himself has said, "The center of my theological doctrine of knowledge is the concept of symbol. . . . "[1] And it must be apparent on the most cursory reading of his works that in Tillich's enormously influential reinterpretation of Christian theology, and more generally of the nature and function of religion, the concept of a religious symbol is made to bear a great part of the weight. The examination of this concept is, therefore, of the very first importance

---

[1]"Reply to Interpretation and Criticism," in *The Theology of Paul Tillich,* ed. Charles W. Kegley & Robert W. Bretall (New York: The Macmillan Company, 1956), p. 333.

for an evaluation of Tillich's whole enterprise. In this essay I shall proceed as follows: First, I shall set out a concept of religious symbols, which I think reflects fairly accurately the actual use of symbols in religion, and which I take to be a refinement of the traditional conception. Second, I shall explore Tillich's deviations from this conception, and indicate the points at which they seem to me to be disastrous.

A religious symbol is some concrete object or aspect of a concrete object which is taken to represent the ultimate object of worship or some aspect thereof.[2] Thus a shepherd is taken to represent the providential care God takes for His creatures; a mountain or hill, or more abstractly, height, is taken to represent God's majesty, His perfection, or His immutability. (The plurisignification of symbols is one of their most marked features.) It is important not to confuse, as I fear Tillich sometimes does, the symbol in this fundamental sense with symbolic language, which is symbolic in a derivative sense. An utterance can be said to be symbolic when it does its job through using terms which denote symbols. Thus we might speak of God as our shepherd, or say that "We are the people of His pasture and the sheep of His hand," or "Thus saith the high and lofty One that inhabiteth eternity, whose name is Holy. I dwell in the high and holy place." Here these words, including the words 'shepherd,' 'high' etc. are not symbols in their own right; but the utterance has the significance it possesses through the fact that 'shepherd' denotes what is a symbol, and thus the utterance can be called symbolic in a derivative sense. It can be interpreted as an injunction to take a shepherd as a symbol of God, or, perhaps, as an expression of the conviction that a shepherd can appropriately be taken as a symbol of God.

Now, what is meant by saying that a shepherd is taken to represent divine providence? It may roughly be defined as follows: seeing or thinking of a shepherd, or a picture of a shepherd, tends to call up a complex of feelings, attitudes, and thoughts which are appropriate to divine providence (deep thankfulness, a feeling of an unshakable underlying security, attitude of complete submission, etc.); and in addition any person who construes a shepherd in this way would be both able and willing to specify God's providential care for His creatures as that which is being symbolized. Both conditions seem to me to be necessary. Without the first, one might know that the shepherd had this symbolic significance for others, but it would not actually be functioning as a symbol for oneself. Without the second we would be hard pressed to give any sense to saying that the object was taken to represent anything other than itself; it would simply be an effective stimulus for certain emotional states. Concepts without feelings are empty; feelings without concepts are blind.

I am not, indeed, asserting that every time a person responds to x as a religious symbol, he tells himself what it is this object symbolizes. But I am saying that he would be capable of specifying the symbolizandum on demand. And note that this in turn implies that it is possible to say this in nonsymbolic language. Confronted with the question, "What does a king symbolize in this religious community?" one could hardly answer by pointing to the sun, even if in the community both a king and the sun do function as symbols of the same aspect of

---

[2]Cf., "A symbol is a representation of something moral or spiritual by the images or properties of a natural thing." *Webster's Collegiate Dictionary.*

the divine nature. And if this will not do, neither will a supposed specification in symbolic language, which ultimately amounts to no more than pointing out certain objects to be used as symbols. We certainly do not succeed in locating that which is symbolized, if all we do is enumerate more objects which symbolize something-or-other. What is required is an effective identification of the symbolizandum—one which will make it possible to decide whether you and I (or myself at two moments, for that matter) are taking the concrete object to symbolize the same thing. What this means in practice is that religious symbols function against the background of a complex system of beliefs about supernatural beings, a system which furnishes the material for the requisite identifications of symbolizanda. As to the character which such beliefs or the utterances which express them must have, that is a question for another essay. Here I will only affirm my conviction that, in order to furnish descriptions from which effective identifications can be made, the component assertions in such a system must at some point yield implications concerning experienceable states of affairs, though that does not mean that it will be possible in practice to put them to an empirical test.

This is not to say that a symbolic statement is translatable into a nonsymbolic one, and still less is it to say that responding to a symbol is the same as reflecting on a theological doctrine. The symbol and the symbolic utterance contribute something to the religious life which could never be extracted from theologizing. The symbol presents in a vivid and striking way a concrete analogue of a characteristic attributed to God, and in so doing condenses the significance of that characteristic into a single point so as to make it intuitively assimilable, and so as to actively engage such typically religious feelings as awe, wonder, and adoration. The analogy can be of various sorts and degrees. Sometimes it concerns features of the symbol itself (the care of the shepherd for his sheep, the height of the mountain); sometimes the way the symbol affects us (the sense of awe or sublimity we get from gazing at the mountain). But in all cases, the whole range of our experience of the object, the diverse associations it has acquired, contribute to a wealth of felt significance which makes the symbol a concrete focus for religious responses.

Nor am I suggesting that we first develop theologies and then cast about for appropriate symbols to enliven them. I am saying nothing about the order of development. I suspect that the two grow up together. It may even be that responding to certain objects with awe, wonder, a sense of significance, etc., sometimes precedes *any* theological formulation; and that theological formulations then result from the attempt to say what goes on in such encounters. It may be that first the members of a community reacted in this way to, e.g., bulls, and then later developed the notion of a supernatural person manifested in bulls as a way of giving a sort of explanation of their reactions. Moreover, irrespective of origins, I would suppose that a theology derives part of its meaning and most of its vitality from the fact that its adherents do have encounters of this sort with objects which present analogies with characteristics attributed to the deity in the theology. I only wish to maintain that even so the theology does not solely consist in registering such experiences of sacredness, but goes beyond such a registration in specifiable ways; and that unless and until the encounter with sacred objects is meshed into a theology involving such an assertive overplus, we cannot speak of the objects as religious *symbols*.

Now, Tillich deviates from the traditional conception for a number of reasons. I would suppose that the most important are these: (1) He does not see any reason to believe in the existence of God conceived as an immaterial, personal being Who literally enters into various relations with human beings. And yet he does not want to abandon Christianity. (2) The religious attitude, as he conceives it, is directed to a reality more ultimate, more unconditional than anything which is *a* being among others. (*Systematic Theology*, hereafter referred to as *ST*)[3] Given these convictions we can understand why Tillich proposes to take what were symbolizanda in the traditional scheme and make them into symbols too. Thus the personal creator of the universe and all His attributes and activities are lumped together with the sun, kings, mountains, and bulls under the heading symbols.

In tossing them all into the same bag, Tillich fails to make certain distinctions which are vital to his project.

A. He fails to note the following contrast: whereas the objective existence of natural objects is taken for granted when they are treated as symbols, we can, in Tillich's program, treat a supernatural God and His doings, e.g., the Incarnation, as symbols without making any assumption of objective existence. Once this contrast is brought out into the open, we see that, when Tillich argues that since the personal God of theism is a symbol the question of His *existence* is of no religious importance (in *Dynamics of Faith*, hereafter referred to as *DF*),[4] he cannot claim to be deriving the principle of the argument from the way symbols are *generally* treated in religion. Again, this means that we cannot literally encounter the supernatural "symbol" as another existent, but must "encounter" it as conceived, imagined, or pictured. And this would seem to carry with it important differences between the *modi operandi* of the two classes of symbols, differences which Tillich has not considered.

B. The failure to draw the right sort of distinctions between symbols and symbolic language leads Tillich into various confusions. For example, Tillich says (in an article in *The Christian Scholar*, hereafter referred to as *CS*), " . . . it is obvious that symbols cannot be replaced by other symbols."[5] But it is *quite* obvious that the mere substitution of one word for another in our talk about God, e.g., arbitrarily replacing 'holy' with the hitherto unused phoneme sequence, 'kona,' would be entirely possible in a way that an interchange of symbols would not be possible, e.g., replacing Jesus Christ with Hitler, or replacing a personal supernatural creator with the dialectical movement of history. These latter replacements could occur only as the result of very fundamental cultural changes.

C. Tillich sometimes talks as if unattained goals like financial success or the attainment of scientific knowledge can be religious symbols in just the same sense as presently existing objects like the state or a person (e.g., *DF*, 3). But obviously there are important differences in the ways we can relate ourselves to "symbols" of these different sorts. In the ensuing discussion I shall occasionally make reference to some other difficulties into which Tillich is led by his failure to make these distinctions. But since I believe that these difficulties could be

---

[3] Paul Tillich, *Systematic Theology* (London: Nisbet and Company, 1953), I, 17, 24.
[4] Paul Tillich, *Dynamics of Faith* (New York: Harper and Brothers, 1957), p. 47.
[5] "Religious Symbols and Our Knowledge of God,' *The Christian Scholar*, XXXVIII, 191.

eliminated by a more careful working-out of the position, I do not wish to dwell on them further.

Let us return to the main thread of the discussion. If what was the ultimate referent of religious symbols in the traditional scheme has now become another symbol, is anything left for symbols to symbolize? Now clearly Tillich wants to find such a referent. He does not want to view religion as nothing but an organization of human activity and experience. And so, in line with the basic conviction regarding the thrust of the religious attitude noted above, he thinks of religious symbols as symbolizing not *a* being of any sort, but being-itself. In an article reprinted in *Religious Symbolism* (hereafter referred to as *RS*), he writes, "the religious symbol has special character in that it points to the ultimate level of being, to ultimate reality, to being itself, to meaning itself. That which is the ground of being is the object to which the religious symbol points."[6] One crucial consequence of this is that symbolic language becomes autonomous. In the traditional scheme symbolic language is at least partly dependent on doctrines expressed in nonsymbolic terms. A necessary, though not sufficient, condition for the appropriateness of using a shepherd as a symbol of God is the truth of the doctrine that God providentially cares for His creatures, or does something else for which the activities of a shepherd furnish an analogue. (This condition is not sufficient because it is also necessary that the symbol effectively perform the evocative job for which it is employed.) But in Tillich's scheme this will not be the case. As the ground of all being, being-itself is beyond all differentiations that mark off one sort of being from another. Hence it is not susceptible of any characterization.

> The statement that God is being-itself is a nonsymbolic statement. . . . However, after this has been said, nothing else can be said about God as God which is not symbolic. As we already have seen, God as being-itself is the ground of the ontological structure of being without being subject to this structure himself. . . . Therefore, if anything beyond this bare assertion is said about God, it no longer is a direct and proper statement, no longer a concept. It is indirect, and it points to something beyond itself. In a word, it is symbolic (*ST*, 264–65).

Since we can say nothing nonsymbolically about being-itself, a given symbol cannot be judged in terms of the reality or unreality of that aspect of being-itself which it is being used to symbolize. We are unable to specify any such aspect. Symbolic utterance becomes the primary, and indeed the only, type of religious utterance. And that means that the affirmations of religious faith are not subject to criticism in terms of the canons applied by science and common sense to statements of fact.

To achieve an objective reference for religion without relinquishing immunity from criticism in terms of evidence is a notable accomplishment. But we still have to ask: What does it mean to say that a religious symbol "points to" being-itself? Remember that in the traditional scheme to say that x is a symbol of y means, roughly, that x tends to evoke feelings, attitudes, and behavior

---

[6] "Theology and Symbolism," in *Religious Symbolism*, ed. F. Ernest Johnson (New York: Harper and Brothers, 1955), pp. 109–10.

appropriate to y, and that the person for whom x is a symbol of y could, on demand, identify y as the symbolizandum. If we try to apply this analysis here we will run into trouble on both counts. Taking the second first, it would seem that one could *specify* being-itself as what certain symbols point to only if he went through something like the ontological discussion Tillich goes through in introducing the concept. But that would mean that religious symbols function as such only for metaphysicians, indeed, only for metaphysicians of a certain stripe—a conclusion which would surely be as abhorrent to Tillich as to anyone else. As for the first component of the analysis, when I asked, "What sort of feelings, attitudes, etc. would be appropriately directed to being-itself?" I do not know how to answer—and justifiably so. If being-itself does not admit of any characterization as this rather than that, there is no ground for considering one sort of attitude or feeling more appropriate to it than another. This latter point will emerge again in the discussion of ultimate concern.

We might try to get a clue from Tillich's oft-repeated assertion that religious symbols, like other symbols, participate "in the reality and power of that to which they point." (*CS,* 189) But I fear this is not of much help. For one thing it will not provide any differentia of religious symbols. On Tillich's principles, everything constantly participates in being-itself, as a necessary condition of its being anything (*ST,* 263). Of course it may be that religious symbols participate in being-itself in some special sense of 'participate.' But, to my knowledge, no such sense has been provided.

Perhaps our lack of success in finding a meaning for 'points to being-itself' is due to our failure to connect this notion with another of Tillich's fundamental notions—ultimate concern. As I understand Tillich, he maintains that religious symbols function as such only in the context of ultimate concern (*RS,* 111; *DF,* 10). Ultimate concern as presented by Tillich involves the following elements:

(1) An unconditional surrender to something (x), the willingness to recognize x to hold absolute authority over one's life.

(2) An expectation that one will somehow receive a supreme fulfillment through one's encounter and commerce with x.

(3) Finding in x a center of meaningfulness. That is, everything in one's life and one's world gets significance insofar as it is related in some way to x.

(4) Experiencing x as holy (in Otto's sense of the term 'holy,' in which this experience involves a unique blend of awe, fascination, and a sense of mystery).

Now Tillich speaks of religious symbols *expressing* ultimate concern (*DF,* 41, *ST,* 238), and this may be true of symbolic utterances, but nonverbal symbols themselves have, on Tillich's own account, the somewhat different role of objects or foci of ultimate concern—that to which the various attitudes and feelings which make it up are directed. (This is one of the points at which a failure to distinguish between symbols and symbolic language gets Tillich into trouble.) Thus ultimate concern might be directed to one's nation, one's class, the scientific enterprise, one or more supernatural beings supposed to exist, a great leader, etc. And whenever this happens the entity in question can be said to be functioning as a religious symbol. (If we try to put various examples Tillich gives of religious symbols into this position, we will be struck by the impossibility of making goals, like financial success, fit. One could hardly surrender to a goal, and still less could one expect to receive a supreme fulfillment from a goal. The attainment of such a goal might be a fulfillment one would expect from some person or group.)

But however illuminating this may be as a characterization of religious and near-religious modes of experience, what light does it throw on the claim that religious symbols point to being-itself? The claim is that *really* ultimate concern is directed only to being-itself.

The question now arises: What is the content of our ultimate concern? . . . *Our ultimate concern is that which determines our being or non-being.* . . . Man is ultimately concerned about his being and meaning. . . . Man is unconditionally concerned about that which conditions his being beyond all the conditions in him and around him. Man is ultimately concerned about that which determines his ultimate destiny beyond all preliminary necessities and accidents (*ST*, 17).

This argument represents an extraordinary conflux of two serious ambiguities. First, "man is ultimately concerned about his being and meaning" in the sense of 'concern' in which it means something like 'being worried about' or 'being anxious about.' ("I am concerned about his state of health.") But this is a quite different sense from that which Tillich has given to the phrase 'ultimate concern.' Surely Tillich is not suggesting that we are worried about the fate or condition of being-itself! Second, as Tillich explained 'ultimate concern,' the ultimacy is psychological; it consists in the supremacy of that concern in the psychic structure of the individual. It is in a quite different way that being-itself is thought by Tillich to be ultimate. It is ontologically ultimate by virtue of the fact that it is the ultimate ground of all being. Once this distinction is made, we can see that there is no reason to suppose that (psychologically) ultimate concern must be concern directed to what is (ontologically) ultimate. But the verbal identity may make the transition seem obvious. This drift is clearly exemplified in another passage. "The unconditional concern which is faith is the concern about the unconditional. The infinite passion, as faith has been described, is the passion for the infinite. Or, to use our first term, the ultimate concern is concern about what is experienced as ultimate" (*DF*, 9).

But apart from doubts about the soundness of the argument, it is not at all clear what one could mean by saying that one is ultimately concerned, in Tillich's sense, with being-itself. I can understand what it would be to surrender oneself to a person or a movement, to expect fulfillment from a person, or find a center of meaningfulness in him. But as Tillich explains 'being-itself,' it makes no sense at all to speak of surrendering oneself to being-itself, or expecting anything from it, etc. This becomes even clearer if we remember that in *Systematic Theology* Tillich said that "Ultimate concern is the abstract translation of the great commandment: . . . 'You shall love the Lord your God with all your heart, and with all your soul, and with all your mind, and with all your strength" (*ST*, 14). But what would it mean to love being-itself so intensely, or even less intensely?

Tillich has an answer to these questions, which is at the same time an answer to the questions: "What has happened to the religious symbols on which ultimate concern was said to be focused?" and "Just how does the fact that ultimate concern is directed to being-itself help us to understand how religious symbols point to being-itself?" It would be a mistake to think of a religious symbol and being-itself as alternative candidates for the position of an object of ultimate concern. They are both involved in different ways. In Chapter IX of *Systematic Theology*, I ("The Meaning of God"), Tillich points to a "tension" in ultimate concern. On the one hand it is driven, by its ultimacy, to transcend every special being and to direct itself to being itself; on the other hand, "it is impossible to be concerned about something which cannot be encountered concretely, be it in the realm of reality or in the realm of imagination" (*ST*, 234). Again, "The ultimate can become actual only through the concrete, through that which is preliminary and transitory" (*ST*, 242). Thus ultimate concern is directed to being-itself "in and through" one or another symbol. The symbol is serving as a manifestation of the Ultimate for the person who is focusing his concern on it. He is focusing his concern on it because he is experiencing it as ultimate, or as a "medium" or "vehicle" through which he can be "grasped" by the power of being-itself (e.g., *ST*, 16). Thus a religious symbol can be said to point to being-itself in the sense that it plays the role we have just specified in this three-termed interrelationship.

But this does not really help. We have simply moved from 'point to' to a set of new metaphors which we are equally unable to pin down—'manifestation,' 'medium,' 'vehicle,' 'grasp.' Given Tillich's explanation of 'being itself,' it would seem that in any sense in which we could speak of anything being a manifestation or a vehicle of being-itself everything would equally be so. Remember that "everything finite participates in being-itself and in its infinity. Otherwise it would not have the power of being" (*ST*, 263). And the only sense I can give to 'manifesting being-itself' or 'serving as a vehicle of being-itself' is a sense in which these phrases are alternative metaphors for saying approximately what is said by the use of the phrase 'participating in being-itself.' And if that is so, these terms do not serve to mark off those situations in which an object is functioning as a religious symbol. For they apply to every conceivable situation.

The unsoundness of Tillich's conceptual foundations is reflected in the difficulties into which he falls at several points in the development of his ideas. I shall examine two such points. One of the most serious difficulties concerns his attempts to evaluate religious symbols. Although Tillich has barred himself from using the traditional canons of criticism, still he wants to be able to say that some symbols are more adequate than others, and, as a Christian theologian, he wants to be able to say that the Christian symbols are the most adequate. Of course, in one sense a religious symbol is adequate if it effectively expresses (or evokes) ultimate concern (*ST*, 266; *DF*, 96). This might be called subjective adequacy. But since Tillich is concerned to insist that religion points beyond the sphere of human experience to the ultimate ground of being, he also tries to make discriminations, within the group of symbols which are subjectively effective, in terms of the effectiveness with which this pointing is done (*DF*, 96–97). The key concept here is that of idolatry. A symbol is idolatrous to the extent that it fails at this job of pointing. A consideration of the vicissitudes which attend Tillich's attempts to formulate a criterion of idolatry will further reveal the basic strains in the concept of a religious symbol.[7]

---

[7]For a fuller treatment see my article, "Tillich on Idolatry," *Journal of Religion* (1958), XXXVIII, 4.

Tillich often says that a symbol becomes idolatrous when it is put in the place of the Ultimate. "In true faith the ultimate concern is a concern about the truly ultimate; while in idolatrous faith preliminary, finite realities are elevated to the rank of ultimacy" (DF, 12). Symbols "always have the tendency (in the human mind, of course) to replace that to which they are supposed to point, and to become ultimate in themselves. And in the moment in which they do this, they become idols" (CS, 193). But what is this place which is occupied by the Ultimate when everything is going as it should and which is usurped by the symbol when we degenerate into idolatry? As we have seen, the answer is that the Ultimate is being pointed to by a finite object which is the focus of ultimate concern. Thus for a symbol to be put in the place of the Ultimate would be for it to be pointed to by another symbol in just the way in which a symbol points to being-itself. Is this conceivable? It is, of course, possible for one symbol to symbolize another symbol, as the cross hanging in a church symbolizes the crucifixion, or perhaps, the atonement, which is itself a symbol, at least according to Tillich. But in the first place, this is clearly not the sort of thing Tillich wants to brand with the label 'idolatry.' And in the second place, although one symbol can point to another, it seems extremely doubtful that this is anything like the sense of "point to" in which Tillich wants to say that symbols point to being-itself, however that latter sense is finally explicated. We have already seen that the ordinary sense of symbolize, in which one finite reality is said to symbolize another, is not the one which Tillich needs.

But perhaps Tillich's point is better put by saying that a symbol becomes idolatrous when it loses its pointing function altogether and simply is treated as an object in its own right.

"Innumerable things, all things in a way, have the power of becoming holy in a mediate sense. They can point to something beyond themselves. But, if their holiness comes to be considered inherent, it becomes demonic. . . . Holiness provokes idolatry" (ST, 240). Again, this can happen. We might still find value in sacred music, or religious poetry, or icons even after we had ceased to regard them as pointing beyond themselves to an ultimate object of worship. But in that case there would be no basis for calling them religious symbols any longer, and hence they would not be subject to that particular perversion of the religious called "idolatry." In Tillich's account, being a religious symbol is linked by definition to pointing to being-itself.

What is undercutting these attempts is the fact that, as Tillich depicts the situation, all the constituents must be in their proper places if there is to be a religious symbol at all. This rules out the kinds of variation on which Tillich tries to base the distinction between genuine and idolatrous symbols.

Tillich does make use of other criteria. For example, he sometimes suggests that one can recognize an idolatrous symbol by the fact that the promises it makes are not fulfilled, that in the long run it disintegrates rather than integrates the personality, etc. (e.g., DF, 11). These are promising suggestions. But they achieve this promise at the cost of bypassing the supposed connection between religious symbols and being-itself. They are not stated in terms of that connection.

The second difficulty I want to mention is this. As his own principles demand, Tillich explicitly disavows any intent to interpret a religious symbol by specifying the aspect of the Ultimate to which it points. "Every symbol opens up a level of reality for which nonsymbolic speaking is inadequate" (*CS*, 191). And yet when Tillich actually goes about explaining various theological terms, it looks very much as if he is trying to translate them into ontological terms.

> If we call God the "living God" . . . we assert that he is the eternal process in which separation is posited and is overcome by reunion (*ST*, 268).

> Will and intellect in their application to God . . . are symbols for dynamics in all its ramifications and for form as the meaningful structure of being itself (*ST*, 274).

> It is more adequate to define divine omnipotence as the power of being which resists nonbeing in all its expressions and which is manifest in the creative process in all its forms (*ST*, 303).

I do not know how to read this other than as an attempt to translate symbolic language into nonsymbolic language. (If they were intended to be simply the replacement of one symbol by another symbol, they would be grotesque failures. No one would suppose that "dynamics in all its ramifications" is a better religious symbol, i.e., performs a symbolic function better or more clearly than "will.") The fact that Tillich is unable to carry out his own principles when he comes to try to explain particular religious symbols is very instructive. It demonstrates the strain involved in the notion of an indescribable symbolizandum.

In spite of these difficulties, which I do think are fatal to Tillich's enterprise as a whole, I believe that he has made some important contributions to our understanding of religious symbols, as well as other aspects of religion. The account of ultimate concern seems to me to constitute an admirable phenomenology of the religious attitude. I would suggest that Tillich's talk about being-itself (in this connection) could be profitably taken as a part of that phenomenology. Thus a phenomenologically apt way of describing the experience of a sacred object would be to say that through it one is grasped by the power of being-itself, that the object is a channel through which one participates in the Ultimate, etc. All this would then be simply a description of the experienced impact of religious symbols. But the fatal difficulties in which Tillich becomes entrapped in his attempt to use these concepts in an account of the extra-experiential reference of religious symbols demonstrates vividly that he cannot claim such reference while refusing to make claims which are responsible to objective criteria. If we are not satisfied with a purely naturalistic account of religious symbols, there is no short cut around the traditional scheme, which makes their justification rest, at least in part, on the truth of those nonsymbolic assertions which specify their symbolizanda.

TILLICH'S ONTOLOGY AND GOD

Marvin Fox

Marvin Fox, "Tillich's Ontology and God," *Anglican Theological Review*, July 1961. Reprinted by permission of author and editor, Professor Jules L. Moreau.

In spite of the fact that Paul Tillich is often spoken of as a distinguished philosopher, serious study of his work leads to the conclusion that he is, at best, an important Christian theologian, but that he forfeits every usual claim to the title "philosopher." Though philosophers have differed widely in their doctrines and methods, they have as a matter of principle been committed to genuine inquiry, to the open and free search for answers to our most serious questions. By this standard Tillich must be excluded from the philosophic circle.

He describes his work as occurring within the limits of a "theological circle." It is a circle which not only establishes the limits of inquiry but also dictates in advance the answers to basic questions. Though Tillich claims to respect the philosophic way he explicitly says of the Christian theologian (i.e., himself) that, "He is certain that nothing he sees can change the substance of his answer, because this substance is the *logos* of being, manifest in Jesus as the Christ."[1] This makes it clear that, however wide Tillich's scholarship and however subtle his insight, his work is to be seen, not as a philosophy, but as an explication of Christian doctrine from his special perspective. Theology is defined by Tillich as "the methodical interpretation of the contents of the Christian faith,"[2] and he says that the criterion to be applied to each theologian is "his acceptance of the Christian message as his ultimate concern."[3]

Though Tillich has usually been clear and explicit about Christian commitment as the foundation of all his thought, many of his admirers forget this limitation. They tend to speak of Tillich's work as if it had independent philosophic significance. Often one reads analyses of Tillich which ignore, at their peril, the Christian framework which he imposes on every important question and presupposes in all his answers.

It would not be fair, however, to blame the eager Tillichians for their uncritical enthusiasms, since Tillich is himself primarily responsible for fostering the view that his work transcends the parochial limits of Christianity. He does this in two ways. The first is his repeated insistence that the Christian revelation is the absolute and final revelation which must be seen as the criterion by which to judge every other claim to revelation. It is even more than the criterion of every revelation. Tillich insists that Christian revelation is the ground for judging and evaluating every significant aspect of human existence. He expresses this conviction in a clear and uncompromising way:

> The final revelation, the revelation in Jesus as the Christ, is universally valid, because it includes the criterion of every revelation and is the *finis* or *telos*

---

[1] *Systematic Theology*, Vol. I, p. 64.
[2] *Ibid.*, p. 15.
[3] *Ibid.*, p. 11.

(intrinsic aim) of all of them. The final revelation is the criterion of every revelation which precedes or follows. It is the criterion of every religion and of every culture, not only of the culture and religion through which it has appeared. It is valid for the social existence of every human group and for the personal existence of every human individual. It is valid for mankind as such, and, in an indescribable way, it has meaning for the universe also. Nothing less than this should be asserted by Christian theology.[4]

Tillich holds further that each genuine philosophic quest senses its own incompleteness and presses beyond its own limits to search for the truth of revelation. "Reason does not resist revelation. It asks for revelation, for revelation means the reintegration of reason."[5] Tillich bases this claim on the conviction that "the answers to the questions implied in Man's predicament are religious, whether open or hidden."[6] Now if philosophy, at least when it is serious, finds its fulfillment in revelation, and if revelation means the Christian revelation (in Tillich's version), then it is clearly the case that even when he is explicating specifically Christian doctrine Tillich must believe that he is setting down universal philosophic principles, or at least pointing to the conclusions which all philosophic inquiry must reach.

Were Tillich satisfied to restrict his claims severely we might have no quarrel with him. If he were merely saying that *he* has found in Christianity a way to give meaning to his own existence, or that *he* has been grasped by Christian revelation and is forced to affirm it, his position would be unassailable. The fact that many other people fail to find the ground of their own being in Tillich's version of Christianity would only point to differences in their background, temperament, sensitivity and personal orientation. No one can seriously argue against Christianity as *a* way which can bring meaning and direction into human life. But when Tillich, with all his supposed liberalism, insists that Christianity is *the* way for all men, and that even philosophy cannot escape the magnetic attraction of the Christian revelation, he becomes obligated to offer some persuasive evidence. This is his minimal duty as a theologian who thinks that he has united kerygmatic and apologetic tendencies in a single system.

When we ask, "Is Tillich a theist?" we are asking something more serious than the question suggests at first glance. We are not asking the question which Tillich has answered countless times, namely whether he believes in God. His denial of theism in any usual sense and his claim that God can be understood only as the ground-of-being but not as *a* being are too well-known to require repetition. Even the problem as to whether this view is meaningful and defensible need not concern us here. In the Tillich literature the question has been explored widely and from many points of view. We must ask ourselves whether philosophy does actually find its fulfillment in revelation, whether Tillich has given us any reason to believe that the Christian revelation is the one criterion of all revelation and of all culture, and finally, whether Tillich's doctrine is even sound Christianity. Within the brief space that remains to me I should like to show that all three questions should be answered negatively.

---

[4] *Ibid.*, p. 137: cf. pp. 9, 15, 16, 28, 46; also Vol. II, pp. 89, 151, 166–8; also *Biblical Religion and the Search for Ultimate Reality*, pp. 21–2.

[5] *Ibid.*, p. 94.

[6] *Ibid.*, Vol. 11, p. 26.

Tillich's conviction that philosophy is ultimately driven to quest for revelation is based on a particular understanding of both the human and the philosophic situations. Tillich sees man as living in a state of existential anxiety. Human existence is burdened by its estrangement from the ground of all being. Man is the victim of his own creatureliness. He finds himself totally unacceptable and is thus alienated from God and even from himself. Every man is fallen Adam, forcibly separated from his source, estranged from God and overcome by his own meaninglessness. In this state man searches with desperation for a way to restore his wholeness, but, says Tillich, he discovers his "inability . . . to break through his estrangement. In spite of the power of his finite freedom, he is unable to achieve the reunion with God."[7] Under these conditions, if he is favored, man will be seized by the power of Jesus as the Christ, and he will be transformed through his participation in the New Being. In the Christ he finds the perfect instance of a man, who, though limited by his humanity, attained wholeness and reunion with God. This classic instance has been revealed to us, and through participation in this revelation we may find meaning. It is this revelation which makes our existence bearable. It is through this revelation alone that we gain the "courage to be." If this is truly man's situation, then every man is driven to quest for revelation as a condition for enduring his own humanity. Philosophy is, then, in the nature of the case, unable to redeem man; it has no choice but to press beyond its own boundaries and to seek its own final realization in the Christian revelation.

Tillich's picture of the human situation has the strategic advantage of being currently popular. He holds "that today man experiences his present situation in terms of disruption, conflict, self-destruction, meaninglessness, and despair in all realms of life. This experience is expressed in the arts and in literature, conceptualized in existential philosophy, actualized in political cleavages of all kinds, and analyzed in the psychology of the unconscious."[8] Though this is a widely accepted picture it is only partially accurate. In our time, as in every other period of man's history, there are also men who experience their situation in terms of wholeness and integrity, self-affirmation and meaningfulness. Existential philosophy is not the whole of contemporary philosophy, nor is existential literature the whole of contemporary literature. There are even respectable alternatives to Freudian psychology.

It is undeniable that the tendencies which Tillich has noted are very prominent, but there is no evidence that they are inherent in the human situation. History and the contemporary world have produced too many instances of lives that were not torn by despair for us to believe that man, as such, is condemned to the self-torturing anxieties which Tillich presents as inevitable. It may be Christian doctrine that man is hopelessly lost and that he can only be saved by divine grace. Certainly one has no right to impose such a view indiscriminately on all mankind. Even the Bible can be read (and has been read) quite differently. In the Hebrew Bible as it was understood by the spiritual heirs of those who first gave it to the world man is seen as having his own substantial worth and claim. Man is understood as sharing in God's work, and this means that he has within himself

---

[7] *Ibid.*, p. 79.
[8] *Ibid.*, Vol. I, p. 49.

the elements of his own fulfillment. The same view of man can be found, *mutatis mutandis,* in much of western philosophic thought as well. Jews will be astonished to learn from Tillich that in their heart of hearts they see themselves as incapable of achieving salvation without the Christian revelation. Most of the philosophers whose names are enshrined in the textbooks of the history of philosophy would be equally astonished to learn that, willy nilly, they, too, were searching for the Christian revelation. It will not do to dismiss casually every man who is free of a feeling of estrangement by saying that he is obtuse and insensitive, or else blind to his own inner struggle. Alongside the men, in every age, who experience their "present situation in terms of disruption, conflict, self-destruction, meaninglessness, and despair," there are equally sensitive and perceptive men who experience their situation in opposite terms. It is the sheerest arbitrariness on Tillich's part to present his own experience of the human situation and his own very idiosyncratic reading of the history of philosophy as if they were universal. Only if one approaches philosophy with Tillich's kind of Christian conviction already in hand can one arrive at the conclusion that philosophy fulfills itself in revelation. Tillich claims that all philosophy is concerned to know only so that it may finally believe. This is a distortion of most of the history of western philosophy.

Our second question has almost answered itself. There seems to be no ground, except his own faith, for Tillich's view that the Christian revelation is the criterion of all revelation and all culture. Even if we accept *his* picture of the human situation, overcoming estrangement does not depend on the Christian revelation. Many non-Christian philosophers and theologians claim for their own doctrines the power of making man whole, which is what Tillich understands by salvation. Tillich knows perfectly well that there are Jews, and Moslems, and free-thinkers, all of them affirming doctrines for which they claim validity and which explicitly reject the Christian revelation. Where, then, is the supposed universality and finality of this revelation?

Tillich deals with this problem in a wholly unacceptable way. He interprets almost every creative human effort as "preparation for the final revelation." Included in this "universal preparatory revelation" are "Xenophanes' and Heraclitus' criticism of the Homeric Gods and Plato's philosophical interpretation of the Appolonian-Dionysian substance of Greek culture."[9] One hardly needs to comment on this tactic which, having initially committed itself to the view that Jesus as the Christ is the center of history, is then unable to see history except as leading to and fulfilling itself in Christianity. It is surely possible to deal soundly with Xenophanes, Heraclitus and Plato without seeing their work as a series of unknowing efforts to prepare mankind for the advent of the Christ. Similarly, when Tillich asserts that, "the history of Israel shows that no group can be the bearer of the final revelation, that . . . the break-through and the perfect self-surrender must happen in a personal life,"[10] i.e. in the life of Jesus, he is expressing a parochial Christian view not a self-evident truth which must be acknowledged by every reasonable man. Tillich struggles to keep from arrogating universal claims to particular forms of historical Christianity and to the individual

---

[9] *Ibid.,* p. 141.
[10] *Ibid.,* p. 143, cf. pp. 227f.

churches. But this does not affect his unwavering insistence that "the eternal criterion of truth . . . is manifest in the picture of Jesus as the Christ."[11] This insistence is based on a faith which seems to hold Tillich firmly in its grasp. So long as his aims are kerygmatic he need only proclaim the message, but when he turns to apologetics repeated proclamation is not enough.

Tillich's efforts to mediate between ontology and Christianity are hampered by other difficulties as well. His purely philosophic statements are open to much critical questioning, particularly his denial that God is a being and his affirmation that God is the ground-of-being. But these philosophic statements are especially troubling when they are made into the foundations of a Christian theology. Seeking to build a bridge across the abyss which is sometimes thought to separate Christianity from philosophy, Tillich bravely proclaims: "*Against* Pascal I say; the God of Abraham, Isaac, and Jacob and the God of the philosophers is the same God. He is a person and the negation of himself as a person."[12]

In order to achieve this union Tillich employs a dialectical scheme in which he moves between philosophy and theology. He tries to demonstrate that each requires the other, and then concludes that they must rest on a common foundation. We have already tried to show that, contrary to Tillich, philosophy need not be seen as moving toward revelation. It can also be shown that when he conceives of religion as moving toward philosophy Tillich is distorting some of the most essential elements of religion. The God of Abraham, Isaac, and Jacob is *not* the God of the philosophers, and when he is transformed into the latter he ceases to be the former. As Tillich himself acknowledges, the central issue is the conception of God as person, a conception which is alien to the philosophers but a necessary condition of biblical religion. "According to every word of the Bible," Tillich correctly informs us, "God reveals himself as personal. The encounter with him and the concepts describing this encounter are thoroughly personal." He goes on to admit that the central question is, "How can these concepts be brought into a synthesis with the search for ultimate reality?"[13]

Tillich's problems are especially aggravated by his denial of a transcendent God. Such a being might possibly be personalized, but Tillich's God, i.e., the ground-of-being, cannot be personalized. As a result, Tillich shifts all the usual personalistic Christian conceptions to the point where they are unrecognizable. Prayer, for example, is spoken of in these terms:

> It is the presence of the mystery of being and an actualization of our ultimate concern. If it is brought down to the level of a conversation between two beings, it is blasphemous and ridiculous. If, however, it is understood as the 'elevation of the heart,' namely, the center of the personality, to God, it is a revelatory event.[14]

How far removed this is from ordinary conceptions of prayer is obvious. But it seems likely that even such sophisticated Christians as St. Augustine and St.

---

[11] *The Protestant Era*, p. xiii.
[12] *Biblical Religion, etc.*, p. 85.
[13] *Ibid.*, p. 22.
[14] *Systematic Theology*, Vol. I, p. 127.

Thomas had notions of prayer which, by Tillich's standards, are "blasphemous and ridiculous."

In similar fashion Tillich has taken most of the articles of Christian faith and so adjusted them to the demands of ontology (as he understands it) that they lose their personalistic character. Thus, in contrast with established tradition, he holds that "the doctrine of creation does not describe an event, [but that] it points to the situation of creatureliness and to its correlate, the divine creativity."[15] What is astonishing is that, at the same time, he claims as his own the doctrine of *creatio ex nihilo.* He also affirms that the doctrine of God's omnipotence "is magic and an absurdity if it is understood as the quality of a highest being who is able to do what he wants." Instead, in Tillich's version, "When the invocation 'Almighty God' is seriously pronounced, a victory over the threat of nonbeing is experienced, and an ultimate, courageous affirmation of existence is expressed."[16] He speaks of the virgin birth as "an obviously legendary story,"[17] and holds that the Resurrection, if understood as having to do with the physical body of Jesus, is an absurdity which "becomes compounded into blasphemy."[18] These, and many similar instances, raise serious doubts as to whether Tillich's views are in any significant respects continuous with historical Christian teaching concerning God as personal. Christianity seems to have given way to ontology.

In an admiring statement Reinhold Niebuhr describes Tillich as walking along a narrow fence. Such a road, says Niebuhr, "is not negotiated without the peril of losing one's balance and falling over on one side or the other," but, Niebuhr adds, in spite of an occasional fall, Tillich "performs on [the fence] with the greatest virtuosity."[19] I would suggest a different description. Tillich seems to me to be striving mightily to walk on two fences at once. One fence is named "ontology" and the other "Christianity." Unhappily, while these fences are occasionally at a close and manageable distance, they are more often far apart and even turn in opposite directions. Tillich, with all his agility, cannot help falling in between. He struggles with desperation to hold on to both fences, at least with his finger-tips. But having failed, he tries to build a new fence which will be easier to walk along. I am not sure what this new fence should be named. I know only that none of the old names fit.

---

[15] *Ibid.,* p. 253.
[16] *Ibid.,* pp. 273–4.
[17] *Theology of Culture,* p. 66.
[18] *Systematic Theology,* Vol. II, p. 156.
[19] *The Theology of Paul Tillich,* pp. 226–7.

PART THREE

RELIGION AND MORALITY

Hume takes the existence of evil to be evidence that God does not exist. He claims, first, that "God exists" and "There is evil" are logically incompatible statements and, second, even if they were compatible, the latter's being true provides strong evidence for the former's being false. Hence, he in effect claims belief in God is, given the existence of evil, completely untenable or at least quite unreasonable.

Various elements enter into Hume's reasonings concerning God and evil. One is that our world is not what one would anticipate in advance if one were first informed that God created it and only later learned what suffering occurs. The truth and force of this point are not easy to appraise. Suppose someone (say, on Mars) were told that God created the earth and peopled it in His own image. What *would* he suppose conditions on earth would be like? What sorts of relevant information would he need? What propositions about God's purposes, the means of accomplishing them, the relative values of goods and evils, and ends and means, would he need to possess before his supposals about earthly conditions became something to take seriously? And how do *we* stand with respect to such information? To the degree that we cannot be confident that our knowledge extends sufficiently far to justify our having expectations about what God can do or allow and yet be good, we cannot press Hume's point.

On the one hand, then, if we know what "God is good" means, perhaps we are justified in making *some* claims about this matter. On the other, the full plans of omnicompetent Providence, if such there be, are surely a bit beyond us. Any knowledge we may have on this score presumably must, then, lie between "none" and "complete," and will likely be a good deal closer to the former. How full our expectations about what a good God will do or allow is a matter on which Hume, Leibniz, and Kant disagree.

Leibniz and Kant disagree with Hume on both his major points. They deny that the existence of evil provides either conclusive or good evidence against the existence of God. Both also (quite plausibly) reject the implicit hedonism of Hume's argument, i.e., Hume's assumption that if God is good, His primary purpose will be to provide pleasure for His creatures.

Leibniz and Kant disagree, however, on another important issue. Leibniz endeavors to offer, if in outline and sketchy format, a theodicy—an account of the ways of God with men which makes it clear that God deals justly. Kant denies that a theodicy is either possible or necessary.

J. L. Mackie's essay is a thorough and powerful contemporary presentation of Hume's line of attack, and Alvin Plantinga's article is an at least equally thorough and powerful presentation of the free will defense—the view that at least much of the evil that exists proceeds from the free choice of human (and perhaps other) beings. Dewey Hoitenga traces a rather different defense of theism against Hume's sort of critique, and I endeavor to appraise Hoitenga's perceptive comments. The complexity and often profundity of the analyses by Hume, Leibniz, Kant, Mackie, Plantinga, and Hoitenga is, of course, only hinted at by these remarks. The central line of argument in Chapter 10 is perhaps easier to capture.

In his paper "Religious Morality" Patterson Brown argues that

The hoary problem of evil rests on a misconception of religious morality. This point can be readily unpacked by way of another . . . that of the relation of God's commands to our moral obligations.

Reflection on the problem of evil, then, leads Brown to offer his conception of religious morality. This conception is captured in the following claims:

(1) Necessarily, if x is God, then x is perfectly good.

(2) Necessarily, if God commands doing A, doing A is good.

(3) Necessarily, if God commands x to do A, x ought to do A.

For a Christian or a Jew, "God is good" entails (1) to (3). Critics of theism take "God is good' to be "an ordinary moral judgment" and hence as *not* entailing (1) to (3). Hence critics have been mistaken about the meaning of "God is good" as used by those whom they criticize. As Brown puts it,

> to pass independent judgement on God's actions or commands would be a straightforward abandonment of Christian morality, since some other moral principle would then have been accepted as more fundamental than the Creator's will. So that to judge God is in effect to deny that he is *God.*

This is not to define "good" by "what God wills" but to regard what God wills (as revealed in the Bible, or as discernible in moral reflection, or both) as providing the criterion of what is good.

Anthony Flew and Keith Campbell offer rather different reasons for rejecting Brown's views. Flew denies that the way Brown construes Christian morality is generally the way in which other Christians construe Christian morality. Further, Flew finds himself unable to distinguish Brown's position from the worship of power. Finally, Flew rejects Brown's argument that if God's will is itself the criterion of the morally good then God's choices will nonetheless not be arbitrary, since God will make choices in accord with His knowledge, intelligence, and love. Flew seems to misstate his own case when he affirms the dubious Humean thesis that knowledge and intelligence are never motivating forces. His point would seem better made in such terms as these: the value of knowledge, intelligence, and love as desirable features for a decision maker to possess will also depend on whether God wills that this is so. How will Brown escape from making *this* choice arbitrary?

Campbell contends that Brown's position is inconsistent in that Brown contends both that God's will is the criterion of the good and that this criterion must itself be accepted without our having moral reasons for accepting it. For, Campbell argues, we can reasonably accept God's will as good only if His will is (on some independent ground) known to be morally in the right; "without such prior [independent] evaluations, no distinction can be made between the real word of God and deceiving counterfeits."

In his reply to Flew and Campbell, Brown endeavors to further clarify his position. He distinguishes between the *meaning* of "metre" ("unit of spatial length equal to 100 centimetres") and the *criteria for application* of "metre" (correspondence to the platinum-iridium bar in Paris). Other criteria are compatible with the same meaning, e.g., correspondence to the spectral line of the wavelength of a specified element, or correspondence to markings on a rubber bar. Analogously, he suggests that a utilitarian, a Nazi, and a Christian may agree on the *meaning* of "good" (say, "morally commendable") but not on a criterion which will sort out the good from the neutral and the evil. For Christians, the criterion is the will of God. This is *not* a definition of "good," and Flew misconstrues Brown's analysis when he speaks of it as offering a definition.

Further, necessarily a person adopts an ultimate ethical criterion without passing moral judgment on *it;* for such judgment would assume some further criterion, and so on ad infinitum. The utilitarian, Nazi, Christian, and all others accept some moral criterion as ultimate without passing moral judgment on it, or else they accept no such criterion at all.

In "God and the Good" Brown notes that while the existence of evil is often taken as evidence against theism, the existence of an all-perfect redeeming God entails (or presupposes) the existence of evil. This he calls "the paradox of evil," suggesting that it is an a priori paradox.

He adds that

> one of the prerequisites for being a Jew or Christian is that one accept God's decrees as taking moral precedence over whatsoever conflicting considerations. So that 'God is perfectly good' serves for such person, not as a moral judgement made in the light of some ulterior standard, nor yet as a definition of terms, but rather as itself the ultimate moral criterion—just as the metal bar in Paris is not judged to be a metre long by comparison to some further rod, nor by verbal definition, but rather itself constitutes the standard whereby all lengths are to be measured.

He reasons that if this is the status of "God is perfectly good," then any judgment of the form "*A* is good" or "*A* is evil" will *presuppose* that God exists, that "*A* is evil" cannot entail (or otherwise imply) "God does not exist." The paradox of evil vanishes, and evil cannot count as evidence against theism. If, on the other hand, one appeals to a nontheistic moral principle to decide what is good and evil, no problem will arise for theism—God is not held to be good in a sense of "good" defined by some nontheistic moral principle, and so His not *being* good in that sense is no objection to theism. Thus reflection on the problem of evil leads Brown to offer a particular view of the relation between religion and morality—the one expressed in the quotations just noted.

Chapter

EIGHT

THREE TRADITIONAL DISCUSSIONS OF THE PROBLEM OF EVIL

EVIL PROVIDES
A REFUTATION
OF THEISM

David Hume

From David Hume, *Dialogues Concerning Natural Religion* (originally published in 1739), parts X and XI; published by The Bobbs-Merrill Company, Inc., 1947.

Part X

It is my opinion, I own, replied Demea, that each man feels, in a manner, the truth of religion within his own breast, and, from a consciousness of his imbecility and misery rather than from any reasoning, is led to seek protection from that Being on whom he and all nature is dependent. So anxious or so tedious are even the best scenes of life that futurity is still the object of all our hopes and fears. We incessantly look forward and endeavour, by prayers, adoration, and sacrifice, to appease those unknown powers whom we find, by experience, so able to afflict and oppress us. Wretched creatures that we are! What resource for us amidst the innumerable ills of life did not religion suggest some methods of atonement, and appease those terrors with which we are incessantly agitated and tormented?

I am indeed persuaded, said Philo, that the best and indeed the only method of bringing everyone to a due sense of religion is by just representations of the misery and wickedness of men. And for that purpose a talent of eloquence and strong imagery is more requisite than that of reasoning and argument. For is it necessary to prove what everyone feels within himself? It is only necessary to make us feel it, if possible, more intimately and sensibly.

The people, indeed, replied Demea, are sufficiently convinced of this great and melancholy truth. The miseries of life, the unhappiness of man, the general corruptions of our nature, the unsatisfactory enjoyment of pleasures, riches, honours—these phrases have become almost proverbial in all languages. And who can doubt of what all men declare from their own immediate feeling and experience?

In this point, said Philo, the learned are perfectly agreed with the vulgar; and in all letters, *sacred* and *profane,* the topic of human misery has been insisted on with the most pathetic eloquence that sorrow and melancholy could inspire. The poets, who speak from sentiment, without a system, and whose testimony has therefore the more authority, abound in images of this nature. From Homer down to Dr. Young, the whole inspired tribe have ever been sensible that no other representation of things would suit the feeling and observation of each individual.

As to authorities, replied Demea, you need not seek them. Look round this library of Cleanthes. I shall venture to affirm that, except authors of particular sciences, such as chemistry or botany, who have no occasion to treat of human life, there is scarce one of those innumerable writers from whom the sense of human misery has not, in some passage or other, extorted a complaint and confession of it. At least, the chance is entirely on that side; and no one author has ever, so far as I can recollect, been so extravagant as to deny it.

There you must excuse me, said Philo: Leibniz has denied it, and is perhaps the first[1] who ventured upon so bold and paradoxical an opinion; at least, the first who made it essential to his philosophical system.

And by being the first, replied Demea, might he not have been sensible of his error? For is this a subject in which philosophers can propose to make discoveries especially in so late an age? And can any man hope by a simple denial (for the subject scarcely admits of reasoning) to bear down the united testimony of mankind, founded on sense and consciousness?

And why should man, added he, pretend to an exemption from the lot of all other animals? The whole earth, believe me, Philo, is cursed and polluted. A perpetual war is kindled amongst all living creatures. Necessity, hunger, want stimulate the strong and courageous; fear, anxiety, terror agitate the weak and infirm. The first entrance into life gives anguish to the new-born infant and to its wretched parent; weakness, impotence, distress attend each stage of that life, and it is, at last, finished in agony and horror.

Observe, too, says Philo, the curious artifices of nature in order to embitter the life of every living being. The stronger prey upon the weaker and keep them in perpetual terror and anxiety. The weaker, too, in their turn, often prey upon the stronger, and vex and molest them without relaxation. Consider that innumerable race of insects, which either are bred on the body of each animal or, flying about, infix their stings in him. These insects have others still less than themselves which torment them. And thus on each hand, before and behind, above and below, every animal is surrounded with enemies which incessantly seek his misery and destruction.

Man alone, said Demea, seems to be, in part, an exception to this rule. For by combination in society he can easily master lions, tigers, and bears, whose greater strength and agility naturally enable them to prey upon him.

On the contrary, it is here chiefly, cried Philo, that the uniform and equal maxims of nature are most apparent. Man, it is true, can, by combination, surmount all his *real* enemies and become master of the whole animal creation; but does he not immediately raise up to himself *imaginary* enemies, the demons of his fancy, who haunt him with superstitious terrors and blast every enjoyment of life? His pleasure, as he imagines, becomes in their eyes a crime; his food and repose give them umbrage and offence; his very sleep and dreams furnish new materials to anxious fear; and even death, his refuge from every other ill, presents only the dread of endless and innumerable woes. Nor does the wolf molest more the timid flock than superstition does the anxious breast of wretched mortals.

Besides, consider, Demea: This very society by which we surmount those wild beasts, our natural enemies, what new enemies does it not raise to us? What woe and misery does it not occasion? Man is the greatest enemy of man. Oppression, injustice, contempt, contumely, violence, sedition, war, calumny, treachery, fraud—by these they mutually torment each other, and they would soon dissolve that society which they had formed were it not for the dread of still greater ills which must attend their separation.

But though these external insults, said Demea, from animals, from men, from

---

[1]That sentiment had been maintained by Dr. King and some few others before Leibniz, though by none of so great fame as that German philosopher.

all the elements, which assault us form a frightful catalogue of woes, they are nothing in comparison of those which arise within ourselves, from the distempered condition of our mind and body. How many lie under the lingering torment of diseases? Hear the pathetic enumeration of the great poet.

> Intestine stone and ulcer, colic-pangs,
> Demoniac frenzy, moping melancholy,
> And moon-struck madness, pining atrophy,
> Marasmus, and wide-wasting pestilence.
> Dire was the tossing, deep the groans: *Despair*
> Tended the sick, busiest from couch to couch.
> And over them triumphant *Death* his dart
> Shook: but delay'd to strike, though oft invok'd
> With vows, as their chief good and final hope.[2]

The disorders of the mind, continued Demea, though more secret, are not perhaps less dismal and vexatious. Remorse, shame, anguish, rage, disappointment, anxiety, fear, dejection, despair—who has ever passed through life without cruel inroads from these tormentors? How many have scarcely ever felt any better sensations? Labour and poverty, so abhorred by everyone, are the certain lot of the far greater number; and those few privileged persons who enjoy ease and opulence never reach contentment or true felicity. All the goods of life united would not make a very happy man, but all the ills united would make a wretch indeed; and any one of them almost (and who can be free from every one?), nay, often the absence of one good (and who can possess all?) is sufficient to render life ineligible.

Were a stranger to drop on a sudden into this world, I would show him, as a specimen of its ills, an hospital full of diseases, a prison crowded with malefactors and debtors, a field of battle strewed with carcases, a fleet foundering in the ocean, a nation languishing under tyranny, famine, or pestilence. To turn the gay side of life to him and give him a notion of its pleasures—whether should I conduct him? To a ball, to an opera, to court? He might justly think that I was only showing him a diversity of distress and sorrow.

There is no evading such striking instances, said Philo, but by apologies which still further aggravate the charge. Why have all men, I ask, in all ages, complained incessantly of the miseries of life? . . . They have no just reason, says one: these complaints proceed only from their discontented, repining, anxious disposition. . . . And can there possibly, I reply, be a more certain foundation of misery than such a wretched temper?

But if they were really as unhappy as they pretend, says my antagonist, why do they remain in life? . . .

> Not satisfied with life, afraid of death—

this is the secret chain, say I, that holds us. We are terrified, not bribed to the continuance of our existence.

---

[2][Milton: *Paradise Lost,* Bk. XI.]

It is only a false delicacy, he may insist, which a few refined spirits indulge, and which has spread these complaints among the whole race of mankind. . . . And what is this delicacy, I ask, which you blame? Is it anything but a greater sensibility to all the pleasures and pains of life? And if the man of a delicate, refined temper, by being so much more alive than the rest of the world, is only so much more unhappy, what judgment must we form in general of human life?

Let men remain at rest, says our adversary, and they will be easy. They are willing artificers of their own misery. . . . No! reply I: an anxious languor follows their repose; disappointment, vexation, trouble, their activity and ambition.

I can observe something like what you mention in some others, replied Cleanthes, but I confess I feel little or nothing of it in myself, and hope that it is not so common as you represent it.

If you feel not human misery yourself, cried Demea, I congratulate you on so happy a singularity. Others, seemingly the most prosperous, have not been ashamed to vent their complaints in the most melancholy strains. Let us attend to the great, the fortunate emperor, Charles V, when, tired with human grandeur, he resigned all his extensive dominions into the hands of his son. In the last harangue which he made on that memorable occasion, he publicly avowed *that the greatest prosperities which he had ever enjoyed had been mixed with so many adversities that he might truly say he had never enjoyed any satisfaction or contentment.* But did the retired life in which he sought for shelter afford him any greater happiness? If we may credit his son's account, his repentance commenced the very day of his resignation.

Cicero's fortune, from small beginnings, rose to the greatest lustre and renown; yet what pathetic complaints of the ills of life do his familiar letters, as well as philosophical discourses, contain? And suitably to his own experience, he introduces Cato, the great, the fortunate Cato protesting in his old age that had he a new life in his offer he would reject the present.

Ask yourself, ask any of your acquaintance, whether they would live over again the last ten or twenty years of their life. No! but the next twenty, they say, will be better:

> And from the dregs of life, hope to receive
> What the first sprightly running could not give.[3]

Thus, at last, they find (such is the greatness of human misery, it reconciles even contradictions) that they complain at once of the shortness of life and of its vanity and sorrow.

And is it possible, Cleanthes, said Philo, that after all these reflections, and infinitely more which might be suggested, you can still persevere in your anthropomorphism, and assert the moral attributes of the Deity, his justice, benevolence, mercy, and rectitude, to be of the same nature with these virtues in human creatures? His power, we allow, is infinite; whatever he wills is executed; but neither man nor any other animal is happy; therefore, he does not will their happiness. His wisdom is infinite; he is never mistaken in choosing the means to any end; but the course of nature tends not to human or animal felicity;

---

[3][John Dryden, *Aureng-Zebe,* Act IV, sc. 1.]

therefore, it is not established for that purpose. Through the whole compass of human knowledge there are no inferences more certain and infallible than these. In what respect, then, do his benevolence and mercy resemble the benevolence and mercy of men?

Epicurus' old questions are yet unanswered.

Is he willing to prevent evil, but not able? then is he impotent. Is he able, but not willing? then is he malevolent. Is he both able and willing? whence then is evil?

You ascribe, Cleanthes, (and I believe justly) a purpose and intention to nature. But what, I beseech you, is the object of that curious artifice and machinery which she has displayed in all animals—the preservation alone of individuals, and propagation of the species? It seems enough for her purpose, if such a rank be barely upheld in the universe, without any care or concern for the happiness of the members that compose it. No resource for this purpose: no machinery in order merely to give pleasure or ease; no fund of pure joy and contentment; no indulgence without some want or necessity accompanying it. At least, the few phenomena of this nature are overbalanced by opposite phenomena of still greater importance.

Our sense of music, harmony, and indeed beauty of all kinds, gives satisfaction, without being absolutely necessary to the preservation and propagation of the species. But what racking pains, on the other hand, arise from gouts, gravels, megrims, toothaches, rheumatisms, where the injury to the animal machinery is either small or incurable? Mirth, laughter, play, frolic seem gratuitous satisfactions which have no further tendency; spleen, melancholy, discontent, superstition are pains of the same nature. How then does the Divine benevolence display itself, in the sense of you anthropomorphites? None but we mystics, as you were pleased to call us, can account for this strange mixture of phenomena, by deriving it from attributes infinitely perfect but incomprehensible.

And have you, at last, said Cleanthes smiling, betrayed your intentions, Philo? Your long agreement with Demea did indeed a little surprise me, but I find you were all the while erecting a concealed battery against me. And I must confess that you have now fallen upon a subject worthy of your noble spirit of opposition and controversy. If you can make out the present point, and prove mankind to be unhappy or corrupted, there is an end at once of all religion. For to what purpose establish the natural attributes of the Deity, while the moral are still doubtful and uncertain?

You take umbrage very easily, replied Demea, at opinions the most innocent and the most generally received, even amongst the religious and devout themselves; and nothing can be more surprising than to find a topic like this—concerning the wickedness and misery of man—charged with no less than atheism and profaneness. Have not all pious divines and preachers who have indulged their rhetoric on so fertile a subject, have they not easily, I say, given a solution of any difficulties which may attend it? This world is but a point in comparison of the universe; this life but a moment in comparison of eternity. The present evil phenomena, therefore, are rectified in other regions, and in some future period of existence. And the eyes of men, being then opened to larger views of things, see the whole connection of general laws, and trace, with adoration, the benevolence and rectitude of the Deity through all the mazes and intricacies of his providence.

No! replied Cleanthes, no! These arbitrary suppositions can never be admitted, contrary to matter of fact, visible and uncontroverted. Whence can any cause be known but from its known effects? Whence can any hypothesis be proved but from the apparent phenomena? To establish one hypothesis upon another is building entirely in the air; and the utmost we ever attain by these conjectures and fictions is to ascertain the bare possibility of our opinion, but never can we, upon such terms, establish its reality.

The only method of supporting Divine benevolence—and it is what I willingly embrace—is to deny absolutely the misery and wickedness of man. Your representations are exaggerated; your melancholy views mostly fictitious; your inferences contrary to fact and experience. Health is more common than sickness; pleasure than pain; happiness than misery. And for one vexation which we meet with, we attain, upon computation, a hundred enjoyments.

Admitting your position, replied Philo, which yet is extremely doubtful, you must at the same time allow that, if pain be less frequent than pleasure, it is infinitely more violent and durable. One hour of it is often able to outweigh a day, a week, a month of our common insipid enjoyments; and how many days, weeks, and months are passed by several in the most acute torments? Pleasure, scarcely in one instance, is ever able to reach ecstasy and rapture; and in no one instance can it continue for any time at its highest pitch and altitude. The spirits evaporate, the nerves relax, the fabric is disordered, and the enjoyment quickly degenerates into fatigue and uneasiness. But pain often, good God, how often! rises to torture and agony; and the longer it continues, it becomes still more genuine agony and torture. Patience is exhausted, courage languishes, melancholy seizes us, and nothing terminates our misery but the removal of its cause or another event which is the sole cure of all evil, but which, from our natural folly, we regard with still greater horror and consternation.

But not to insist upon these topics, continued Philo, though most obvious, certain, and important, I must use the freedom to admonish you, Cleanthes, that you have put the controversy upon a most dangerous issue, and are unawares introducing a total scepticism into the most essential articles of natural and revealed theology. What! no method of fixing a just foundation for religion unless we allow the happiness of human life, and maintain a continued existence even in this world, with all our present pains, infirmities, vexations, and follies, to be eligible and desirable! But this is contrary to everyone's feeling and experience; it is contrary to an authority so established as nothing can subvert. No decisive proofs can ever be produced against this authority; nor is it possible for you to compute, estimate, and compare all the pains and all the pleasures in the lives of all men and of all animals; and thus, by your resting the whole system of religion on a point which, from its very nature, must forever be uncertain, you tacitly confess that that system is equally uncertain.

But allowing you what never will be believed, at least, what you never possibly can prove, that animal or, at least, human happiness in this life exceeds its misery, you have yet done nothing; for this is not, by any means, what we expect from infinite power, infinite wisdom, and infinite goodness. Why is there any misery at all in the world? Not by chance, surely. From some cause then. Is it from the intention of the Deity? But he is perfectly benevolent. Is it contrary to his intention? But he is almighty. Nothing can shake the solidity of this reasoning, so short, so clear, so decisive, except we assert that these subjects exceed all human capacity, and that our common measures of truth and falsehood are not applicable to them—a topic which I have all along insisted on, but which you have, from the beginning, rejected with scorn and indignation.

But I will be contented to retire still from this intrenchment, for I deny that you can ever force me in it. I will allow that pain or misery in man is *compatible* with infinite power and goodness in the Deity, even in your sense of these attributes: what are you advanced by all these concessions? A mere possible compatibility is not sufficient. You must *prove* these pure, unmixt, and uncontrollable attributes from the present mixed and confused phenomena, and from these alone. A hopeful undertaking! Were the phenomena ever so pure and unmixed, yet, being finite, they would be insufficient for that purpose. How much more, where they are also so jarring and discordant!

Here, Cleanthes, I find myself at ease in my argument. Here I triumph. Formerly, when we argued concerning the natural attributes of intelligence and design, I needed all my sceptical and metaphysical subtilty to elude your grasp. In many views of the universe and of its parts, particularly the latter, the beauty and fitness of final causes strike us with such irresistible force that all objections appear (what I believe they really are) mere cavils and sophisms; nor can we then imagine how it was ever possible for us to repose any weight on them. But there is no view of human life or of the condition of mankind from which, without the greatest violence, we can infer the moral attributes or learn that infinite benevolence, conjoined with infinite power and infinite wisdom, which we must discover by the eyes of faith alone. It is your turn now to tug the labouring oar, and to support your philosophical subtilties against the dictates of plain reason and experience.

Part XI

I scruple not to allow, said Cleanthes, that I have been apt to suspect the frequent repetition of the word *infinite,* which we meet with in all theological writers, to savour more of panegyric than of philosophy, and that any purposes of reasoning, and even of religion, would be better served were we to rest contented with more accurate and more moderate expressions. The terms *admirable, excellent, superlatively great, wise,* and *holy*—these sufficiently fill the imaginations of men, and anything beyond, besides that it leads into absurdities, has no influence on the affections or sentiments. Thus, in the present subject, if we abandon all human analogy, as seems your intention, Demea, I am afraid we abandon all religion and retain no conception of the great object of our adoration. If we preserve human analogy, we must forever find it impossible to reconcile any mixture of evil in the universe with infinite attributes; much less can we ever prove the latter from the former. But supposing the Author of nature to be finitely perfect, though far exceeding mankind, a satisfactory account may then be given of natural and moral evil, and every untoward phenomenon be explained and adjusted. A less evil may then be chosen in order to avoid a greater; inconveniences be submitted to in order to reach a desirable end; and, in a word, benevolence, regulated by wisdom and limited by necessity, may produce just such a world as the present. You, Philo, who are so prompt at starting views and reflections and analogies, I would gladly hear, at length, without interruption, your opinion of this new theory; and if it deserve our attention, we may afterwards, at more leisure, reduce it into form.

My sentiments, replied Philo, are not worth being made a mystery of; and, therefore, without any ceremony, I shall deliver what occurs to me with regard to the present subject. It must, I think, be allowed that, if a very limited intelligence whom we shall suppose utterly unacquainted with the universe were assured that it were the production of a very good, wise, and powerful Being, however finite, he would, from his conjectures, form *beforehand* a different notion of it from what we find it to be by experience; nor would he ever imagine, merely from these attributes of the cause of which he is informed, that the effect could be so full of vice and misery and disorder, as it appears in this life. Supposing now that this person were brought into the world, still assured that it was the workmanship of such a sublime and benevolent Being, he might, perhaps, be surprised at the disappointment, but would never retract his former belief if founded on any very solid argument, since such a limited intelligence must be sensible of his own blindness and ignorance, and must allow that there may be many solutions of those phenomena which will for ever escape his comprehension. But supposing, which is the real case with regard to man, that this creature is not antecedently convinced of a supreme intelligence, benevolent, and powerful, but is left to gather such a belief from the appearances of things—this entirely alters the case, nor will he ever find any reason for such a conclusion. He may be fully convinced of the narrow limits of his understanding, but this will not help him in forming an inference concerning the goodness of superior powers, since he must form that inference from what he knows, not from what he is ignorant of. The more you exaggerate his weakness and ignorance, the more diffident you render him, and give him the greater suspicion that such subjects are beyond the reach of his faculties. You are obliged, therefore, to reason with him merely from the known phenomena, and to drop every arbitrary supposition or conjecture.

Did I show you a house or palace where there was not one apartment convenient or agreeable, where the windows, doors, fires, passages, stairs, and the whole economy of the building were the source of noise, confusion, fatigue, darkness, and the extremes of heat and cold, you would certainly blame the contrivance, without any further examination. The architect would in vain display his subtilty, and prove to you that, if this door or that window were altered, greater ills would ensue. What he says may be strictly true: the alteration of one particular, while the other parts of the building remain, may only augment the inconveniences. But still you would assert in general that, if the architect had had skill and good intentions, he might have formed such a plan of the whole, and might have adjusted the parts in such a manner as would have remedied all or most of these inconveniences. His ignorance, or even your own ignorance of such a plan, will never convince you of the impossibility of it. If you find any inconveniences and deformities in the building, you will always, without entering into any detail, condemn the architect.

In short, I repeat the question: Is the world, considered in general and as it appears to us in this life, different from what a man or such a limited being would, *beforehand,* expect from a very powerful, wise, and benevolent Deity? It must be strange prejudice to assert the contrary. And from thence I conclude that, however consistent the world may be, allowing certain suppositions and conjectures with the idea of such a Deity, it can never afford us an inference concerning his existence. The consistency is not absolutely denied, only the inference. Conjectures, especially where infinity is excluded from the Divine attributes, may perhaps be sufficient to prove a consistency, but can never be foundations for any inference.

There seem to be *four* circumstances on which depend all or the greatest part of the ills that molest sensible creatures; and it is not impossible but all these circumstances may be necessary and unavoidable. We know so little beyond common life, or even of common life, that, with regard to the economy of a universe, there is no conjecture, however wild, which may not be just, nor any one, however plausible, which may not be erroneous. All that belongs to human understanding, in this deep ignorance and obscurity, is to be sceptical or at least cautious, and not to admit of any hypothesis whatever, much less of any which is supported by no appearance of probability. Now this I assert to be the case with regard to all the causes of evil and the circumstances on which it depends. None of them appear to human reason in the least degree necessary or unavoidable, nor can we suppose them such, without the utmost license of imagination.

The *first* circumstance which introduces evil is that contrivance or economy of the animal creation by which pains, as well as pleasures, are employed to excite all creatures to action, and make them vigilant in the great work of self-preservation. Now pleasure alone, in its various degrees, seems to human understanding sufficient for this purpose. All animals might be constantly in a state of enjoyment; but when urged by any of the necessities of nature, such as thirst, hunger, weariness, instead of pain, they might feel a diminution of pleasure by which they might be prompted to seek that object which is necessary to their subsistence. Men pursue pleasure as eagerly as they avoid pain; at least, they might have been so constituted. It seems, therefore, plainly possible to carry on the business of life without any pain. Why then is any animal ever rendered susceptible of such a sensation? If animals can be free from it an hour, they might enjoy a perpetual exemption from it, and it required as particular a contrivance of their organs to produce that feeling as to endow them with sight, hearing, or any of the senses. Shall we conjecture that such a contrivance was necessary, without any appearance of reason, and shall we build on that conjecture as on the most certain truth?

But a capacity of pain would not alone produce pain were it not for the *second* circumstance, viz., the conducting of the world by general laws; and this seems nowise necessary to a very perfect Being. It is true, if everything were conducted by particular volitions, the course of nature would be perpetually broken, and no man could employ his reason in the conduct of life. But might not other particular volitions remedy this inconvenience? In short, might not the Deity exterminate all ill, wherever it were to be found, and produce all good, without any preparation or long progress of causes and effects?

Besides, we must consider that, according to the present economy of the world, the course of nature, though supposed exactly regular, yet to us appears not so, and many events are uncertain, and many disappoint our expectations. Health and sickness, calm and tempest, with an infinite number of other accidents whose causes are unknown and variable, have a great influence both on the fortunes of particular persons and on the prosperity of public societies; and indeed all human life, in a manner, depends on such accidents. A being, therefore, who knows the secret springs of the universe might easily, by particular volitions, turn all these accidents to the good of mankind and render the whole world happy, without discovering himself in any operation. A fleet whose purposes were salutary to society might always meet with a fair wind. Good princes enjoy sound health and long life. Persons born to power and authority be framed with good tempers and virtuous dispositions. A few such events as these, regularly and wisely conducted, would change the face of the world, and yet would no more seem to disturb the course of nature or confound human conduct than the present economy of things where the causes are secret and variable and compounded. Some small touches given to Caligula's brain in his infancy might have converted him into a Trajan. One wave, a little higher than the rest, by burying Caesar and his fortune in the bottom of the ocean, might have restored liberty to a considerable part of mankind. There may, for aught we know, be good reasons why Providence interposes not in this manner, but they are unknown to us; and, though the mere supposition that such reasons exist may be sufficient to *save* the conclusion concerning the Divine attributes, yet surely it can never be sufficient to *establish* that conclusion.

If everything in the universe be conducted by general laws, and if animals be rendered susceptible of pain, it scarcely seems possible but some ill must arise in the various shocks of matter and the various concurrence and opposition of general laws; but this ill would be very rare were it not for the *third* circumstance which I proposed to mention, viz., the great frugality with which all powers and faculties are distributed to every particular being. So well adjusted are the organs and capacities of all animals, and so well fitted to their preservation, that, as far as history or tradition reaches, there appears not to be any single species which has yet been extinguished in the universe. Every animal has the requisite endowments, but these endowments are bestowed with so scrupulous an economy that any considerable diminution must entirely destroy the creature. Wherever one power is increased, there is a proportional abatement in the others. Animals which excel in swiftness are commonly defective in force. Those which possess both are either imperfect in some of their senses or are oppressed with the most craving wants. The human species, whose chief excellence is reason and sagacity, is of all others the most necessitous, and the most deficient in bodily advantages, without clothes, without arms, without food, without lodging, without any convenience of life, except what they owe to their own skill and industry. In short, nature seems to have formed an exact calculation of the necessities of her creatures, and, like a *rigid master,* has afforded them little more powers or endowments than what are strictly sufficient to supply those necessities. An *indulgent parent* would have bestowed a large stock in order to guard against accidents, and secure the happiness and welfare of the creature in the most unfortunate concurrence of circumstances. Every course of life would not have been so surrounded with precipices that the least departure from the true path, by mistake or necessity, must involve us in misery and ruin. Some reserve, some fund, would have been provided to ensure happiness, nor would the powers and the necessities have been adjusted with so rigid an economy. The Author of nature is inconceivably powerful; his force is supposed great, if not altogether inexhaustible, nor is there any reason, as far as we can judge, to make him observe this strict frugality in his dealings with his creatures. It would have been better, were his power extremely limited, to have created fewer animals, and to have endowed these with more faculties for their happiness and preservation. A builder is never esteemed prudent who undertakes a plan beyond what his stock will enable him to finish.

In order to cure most of the ills of human life, I require not that man should have the wings of the eagle, the swiftness of the stag, the force of the ox, the arms of the lion, the scales of the crocodile or rhinoceros; much less do I demand the sagacity of an angel or cherubim. I am contented to take an increase in one single power or faculty of his soul. Let him be endowed with a greater propensity to industry and labour, a more vigorous spring and activity of mind, a more constant bent to business and application. Let the whole species possess naturally an equal diligence with that which many individuals are able to attain by habit and reflection, and the most beneficial consequences, without any allay of ill, is the immediate and necessary result of this endowment. Almost all the moral as well as natural evils of human life arise from idleness; and were our species, by the original constitution of their frame, exempt from this vice or infirmity, the perfect cultivation of land, the improvement of arts and manufactures, the exact execution of every office and duty, immediately follow; and men at once may fully reach that state of society which is so imperfectly attained by the best regulated government. But as industry is a power, and the most valuable of any, nature seems determined, suitably to her usual maxims, to bestow it on men with a very sparing hand, and rather to punish him severely for his deficiency in it than to reward him for his attainments. She has so contrived his frame that nothing but the most violent necessity can oblige him to labour; and she employs all his other wants to overcome, at least in part, the want of diligence, and to endow him with some share of a faculty of which she has thought fit naturally to bereave him. Here our demands may be allowed very humble, and therefore the more reasonable. If we required the endowments of superior penetration and judgment, of a more delicate taste of beauty, of a nicer sensibility to benevolence and friendship, we might be told that we impiously pretend to break the order of nature, that we want to exalt ourselves into a higher rank of being, that the presents which we require, not being suitable to our state and condition, would only be pernicious to us. But it is hard, I dare to repeat it, it is hard that, being placed in a world so full of wants and necessities, where almost every being and element is either our foe or refuses its assistance . . . we should also have our own temper to struggle with, and should be deprived of that faculty which can alone fence against these multiplied evils.

The *fourth* circumstance whence arises the misery and ill of the universe is the inaccurate workmanship of all the springs and principles of the great machine of nature. It must be acknowledged that there are few parts of the universe which seem not to serve some purpose, and whose removal would not produce a visible defect and disorder in the whole. The parts hang all together, nor can one be touched without affecting the rest, in a greater or less degree. But at the same time, it must be observed that none of these parts or principles, however useful, are so accurately adjusted as to keep precisely within those bounds in which their utility consists; but they are, all of them, apt, on every occasion, to run into the one extreme or the other. One would imagine that this grand production had not received the last hand of the maker—so little finished is every part, and so coarse are the strokes with which it is executed. Thus the winds are requisite to convey the vapours along the surface of the globe, and to assist men in navigation; but how often, rising up to tempests and hurricanes, do they become pernicious? Rains are necessary to nourish all the plants and animals of the earth; but how often are they defective? how often excessive? Heat is requisite to all life and vegetation, but is not always found in the due proportion. On the mixture and secretion of the humours and juices of the body depend the health and prosperity of the animal; but the parts perform not regularly their proper function. What more useful than all the passions of the mind, ambition, vanity, love, anger? But how often do they break their bounds and cause the greatest convulsions in society? There is nothing so advantageous in the universe but what frequently becomes pernicious, by its excess or defect; nor has nature guarded, with the requisite accuracy, against all disorder or confusion. The irregularity is never perhaps so great as to destroy any species, but is often sufficient to involve the individuals in ruin and misery.

On the concurrence, then, of these *four* circumstances does all or the greatest part of natural evil depend. Were all living creatures incapable of pain, or were the world administered by particular volitions, evil never could have found access into the universe; and were animals endowed with a large stock of powers and faculties, beyond what strict necessity requires, or were the several springs and principles of the universe so accurately framed as to preserve always the just temperament and medium, there must have been very little ill in comparison of what we feel at present. What then shall we pronounce on this occasion? Shall we say that these circumstances are not necessary, and that they might easily have been altered in the contrivance of the universe? This decision seems too presumptuous for creatures so blind and ignorant. Let us be more modest in our conclusions. Let us allow that, if the goodness of the Deity (I mean a goodness like the human) could be established on any tolerable reasons *a priori*, these phenomena, however untoward, would not be sufficient to subvert that principle, but might easily, in some unknown manner, be reconcilable to it. But let us still assert that, as this goodness is not antecedently established but must be inferred from the phenomena, there can be no grounds for such an inference while there are so many ills in the universe, and while these ills might so easily have been remedied, as far as human understanding can be allowed to judge on such a subject. I am sceptic enough to allow that the bad appearances, notwithstanding all my reasonings, may be compatible with such attributes as you suppose, but surely they can never prove these attributes. Such a conclusion cannot result from scepticism, but must arise from the phenomena, and from our confidence in the reasonings which we deduce from these phenomena.

Look round this universe. What an immense profusion of beings, animated and organized, sensible and active! You admire this prodigious variety and fecundity. But inspect a little more narrowly these living existences, the only beings worth regarding. How hostile and destructive to each other! How insufficient all of them for their own happiness! How contemptible or odious to the spectator! The whole presents nothing but the idea of a blind nature, impregnated by a great vivifying principle, and pouring forth from her lap, without discernment or parental care, her maimed and abortive children!

Here the Manichaean system occurs as a proper hypothesis to solve the difficulty; and, no doubt, in some respects it is very specious and has more probability than the common hypothesis, by giving a plausible account of the strange mixture of good and ill which appears in life. But if we consider, on the other hand, the perfect uniformity and agreement of the parts of the universe, we shall not discover in it any marks of the combat of a malevolent with a benevolent being. There is indeed an opposition of pains and pleasures in the feelings of sensible creatures; but are not all the operations of nature carried on by an opposition of principles, of hot and cold, moist and dry, light and heavy? The true conclusion is that the original Source of all things is entirely indifferent to all these principles, and has no more regard to good above ill than to heat above cold, or to drought above moisture, or to light above heavy.

There may *four* hypotheses be framed concerning the first causes of the universe: that they are endowed with perfect goodness; that they have perfect malice; that they are opposite and have both goodness and malice; that they have neither goodness nor malice. Mixed phenomena can never prove the two former unmixed principles; and the uniformity and steadiness of general laws seem to oppose the third. The fourth, therefore, seems by far the most probable.

What I have said concerning natural evil will apply to moral with little or no variation; and we have no more reason to infer that the rectitude of the Supreme Being resembles human rectitude than that his benevolence resembles the human. Nay, it will be thought that we have still greater cause to exclude from him moral sentiments, such as we feel them, since moral evil, in the opinion of many, is much more predominant above moral good than natural evil above natural good.

But even though this should not be allowed, and though the virtue which is in mankind should be acknowledged much superior to the vice, yet, so long as there is any vice at all in the universe, it will very much puzzle you anthropomorphites how to account for it. You must assign a cause for it, without having recourse to the first cause. But as every effect must have a cause, and that cause another, you must either carry on the progression *in infinitum* or rest on that original principle, who is the ultimate cause of all things. . . .

Hold! hold! cried Demea: Whither does your imagination hurry you? I joined in alliance with you in order to prove the incomprehensible nature of the Divine Being, and refute the principles of Cleanthes, who would measure everything by human rule and standard. But I now find you running into all the topics of the greatest libertines and infidels, and betraying that holy cause which you seemingly espoused. Are you secretly, then, a more dangerous enemy than Cleanthes himself?

And are you so late in perceiving it? replied Cleanthes. Believe me, Demea, your friend Philo, from the beginning, has been amusing himself at both our expense; and it must be confessed that the injudicious reasoning of our vulgar theology has given him but too just a handle of ridicule. The total infirmity of human reason, the absolute incomprehensibility of the Divine Nature, the great and universal misery, and still greater wickedness of men—these are strange topics, surely, to be so fondly cherished by orthodox divines and doctors. In ages of stupidity and ignorance, indeed, these principles may safely be espoused; and perhaps no views of things are more proper to promote superstition than such as encourage the blind amazement, the diffidence, and melancholy of mankind. But at present . . .

Blame not so much, interposed Philo, the ignorance of these reverend gentlemen. They know how to change their style with the times. Formerly, it was a most popular theological topic to maintain that human life was vanity and misery, and to exaggerate all the ills and pains which are incident to men. But of late years, divines, we find, begin to retract this position and maintain, though still with some hesitation, that there are more goods than evils, more pleasures than pains, even in this life. When religion stood entirely upon temper and education, it was thought proper to encourage melancholy, as, indeed, mankind never have recourse to superior powers so readily as in that disposition. But as men have now learned to form principles and to draw consequences, it is necessary to change the batteries, and to make use of such arguments as will endure at least some scrutiny and examination. This variation is the same (and from the same causes) with that which I formerly remarked with regard to scepticism.

Thus Philo continued to the last his spirit of opposition, and his censure of established opinions. But I could observe that Demea did not at all relish the latter part of the discourse; and he took occasion soon after, on some pretence or other, to leave the company.

EVIL PROVIDES NO REFUTATION OF THEISM
Gottfried Leibniz

Gottfried Leibniz, *The Theodicy: Abridgement of the Argument Reduced to Syllogistic Form,* originally published in 1710.

Some intelligent persons have desired that this supplement be made [to the Theodicy], and I have the more readily yielded to their wishes as in this way I have an opportunity again to remove certain difficulties and to make some observations which were not sufficiently emphasized in the work itself.

I. *Objection.* Whoever does not choose the best is lacking in power, or in knowledge, or in goodness.

God did not choose the best in creating this world.

Therefore, God has been lacking in power, or in knowledge, or in goodness.

Answer. I deny the minor, that is, the second premise of this syllogism; and our opponent proves it by this

Prosyllogism. Whoever makes things in which there is evil, which could have been made without any evil, or the making of which could have been omitted, does not choose the best.

God has made a world in which there is evil; a world, I say, which could have been made without any evil, or the making of which could have been omitted altogether.

Therefore, God has not chosen the best.

Answer. I grant the minor of this prosyllogism; for it must be confessed that there is evil in this world which God has made, and that it was possible to make a world without evil, or even not to create a world at all, for its creation has depended on the free will of God; but I deny the major, that is, the first of the two premises of the prosyllogism, and I might content myself with simply demanding its proof; but in order to make the matter clearer, I have wished to justify this denial by showing that the best plan is not always that which seeks to avoid evil, since it may happen that *the evil is accompanied by a greater good.* For example, a general of an army will prefer a great victory with a slight wound to a condition without wound and without victory. We have proved this more fully in the large work by making it clear, by instances taken from mathematics and elsewhere, that an imperfection in the part may be required for a greater perfection in the whole. In this I have followed the opinion of St. Augustine, who has said a hundred times, that God has permitted evil in order to bring about good, that is, a greater good; and that of Thomas Aquinas (in libr. II. sent. dist. 32, qu. I, art. 1), that the permitting of evil tends to the good of the universe. I have shown that the ancients called Adam's fall *felix culpa,* a happy sin, because it had been retrieved with immense advantage by the incarnation of the Son of God, who has given to the universe something nobler than anything that ever would have been among creatures except for it. For the sake of a clearer understanding, I have added, following many good authors, that it was in accordance with order and the general good that God allowed to certain creatures the opportunity of exercising their liberty, even when he foresaw that they would turn to evil, but which he could so well rectify; because it was not fitting that, in order to hinder sin, God should always act in an extraordinary manner. To overthrow this objection, therefore, it is sufficient to show that a world with evil might be better than a world without evil; but I have gone even farther, in the work, and have even proved that this universe must be in reality better than every other possible universe.

II. *Objection.* If there is more evil than good in intelligent creatures, then there is more evil than good in the whole work of God.

Now, there is more evil than good in intelligent creatures.

Therefore, there is more evil than good in the whole work of God.

Answer. I deny the major and the minor of this conditional syllogism. As to the major, I do not admit it at all, because this pretended deduction from a part to the whole, from intelligent creatures to all creatures, supposes tacitly and without proof that creatures destitute of reason cannot enter into comparison nor into account with those which possess it. But why may it not be that the surplus of good in the non-intelligent creatures which fill the world, compensates for, and even incomparably surpasses, the surplus of evil in the rational creatures? It is true that the value of the latter is greater; but, in compensation, the others are beyond comparison the more numerous, and it may be that the proportion of number and quantity surpasses that of value and of quality.

As to the minor, that is no more to be admitted; that is, it is not at all to be admitted that there is more evil than good in the intelligent creatures. There is no need even of granting that there is more evil than good in the human race, because it is possible, and in fact very probable, that the glory and the perfection of the blessed are incomparably greater than the misery and the imperfection of the damned, and that here the excellence of the total good in the smaller number exceeds the total evil in the greater number. The blessed approach the Divinity, by means of a Divine Mediator, as near as may suit these creatures, and make such progress in good as is impossible for the damned to make in evil, approach as nearly as they may to the nature of demons. God is infinite, and the devil is limited; the good may and does go to infinity, while evil has its bounds. It is therefore possible, and is credible, that in the comparison of the blessed and the damned, the contrary of that which I have said might happen in the comparison of intelligent and non-intelligent creatures, takes place; namely, it is possible that in the comparison of the happy and the unhappy, the proportion of degree exceeds that of number, and that in the comparison of intelligent and non-intelligent creatures, the proportion of number is greater than that of value. I have the right to suppose that a thing is possible so long as its impossibility is not proved; and indeed that which I have here advanced is more than a supposition.

But in the second place, if I should admit that there is more evil than good in the human race, I have still good grounds for not admitting that there is more evil than good in all intelligent creatures. For there is an inconceivable number of genii, and perhaps of other rational creatures. And an opponent could not prove that in all the City of God, composed as well of genii as of rational animals without number and of an infinity of kinds, evil exceeds good. And although in order to answer an objection, there is no need of proving that a thing is, when its mere possibility suffices; yet, in this work, I have not omitted to show that it is a consequence of the supreme perfection of the Sovereign of the universe, that the kingdom of God is the most perfect of all possible states or governments, and that consequently the little evil there is, is required for the consummation of the immense good which is found there.

III. *Objection.* If it is always impossible not to sin, it is always unjust to punish.

Now, it is always impossible not to sin; or, in other words, every sin is necessary.

Therefore, it is always unjust to punish.

The minor of this is proved thus:

1. *Prosyllogism.* All that is predetermined is necessary.

Every event is predetermined.

Therefore, every event (and consequently sin also) is necessary.

Again this second minor is proved thus:

2. *Prosyllogism.* That which is future, that which is foreseen, that which is involved in the causes, is predetermined.

Every event is such.

Therefore, every event is predetermined.

Answer. I admit in a certain sense the conclusion of the second prosyllogism, which is the minor of the first; but I shall deny the major of the first prosyllogism, namely, that every thing predetermined is necessary; understanding by the *necessity* of sinning, for example, or by the impossibility of not sinning, or of not performing any action, the necessity with which we are here concerned, that is, that which is essential and absolute, and which destroys the morality of an action and the justice of punishments. For if anyone understood another necessity or impossibility, namely, a necessity which should be only moral, or which was only hypothetical (as will be explained shortly); it is clear that I should deny the major of the objection itself. I might content myself with this answer and demand the proof of the proposition denied; but I have again desired to explain my procedure in this work, in order to better elucidate the matter and to throw more light on the whole subject, by explaining the necessity which ought to be rejected and the determination which must take place. That *necessity* which is contrary to morality and which ought to be rejected, and which would render punishment unjust, is an insurmountable necessity which would make all opposition useless, even if we should wish with all our heart to avoid the necessary action, and should make all possible efforts to that end. Now, it is manifest that this is not applicable to voluntary actions, because we would not perform them if we did not choose to. Also their prevision and predetermination are not absolute, but presuppose the will: if it is certain that we shall perform them, it is not less certain that we shall choose to perform them. These voluntary actions and their consequences will not take place no matter what we do or whether we wish them or not; but, *through* that which we shall do and through that which we shall wish to do, which leads to them. And this is involved in prevision and in predetermination, and even constitutes their ground. And the necessity of such an event is called conditional or hypothetical, or the necessity of consequence, because it supposes the will, and the other *requisites;* whereas the necessity which destroys morality and renders punishment unjust and reward useless, exists in things which will be whatever we may do or whatever we may wish to do, and, in a word, is in that which is essential; and this is what is called an absolute necessity. Thus it is to no purpose, as regards what is absolutely necessary, to make prohibitions or commands, to propose penalties or prizes, to praise or to blame; it will be none the less. On the other hand, in voluntary actions and in that which depends upon them, precepts armed with power to punish and to recompense are very often of use and are included in the order of causes which make an action exist. And it is for this reason that not only cares and labors but also prayers are useful; God having had these prayers in view before he regulated things and having had that consideration for them which was proper. This is why the precept which says *ora et labora* (pray and work), holds altogether good; and not only those who (under the vain pretext of the necessity of events) pretend that the care which business demands may be neglected, but also those who reason against prayer, fall into what the ancients even then called the *lazy sophism.* Thus the predetermination of events by causes is just what contributes to morality instead of destroying it, and causes incline the will, without compelling it. This is why the *determination* in question is not a necessitation—it is certain (to him who knows all) that the effect will follow this inclination; but this effect does not follow by a necessary consequence, that is, one the contrary of which implies contradiction. It is also by an internal inclination such as this that the will is determined, without there being any necessity. Suppose that one has the greatest passion in the world (a great thirst, for example), you will admit to me that the soul can find some reason for resisting it, if it were only that of showing its power. Thus, although one may never be in a perfect indifference of equilibrium and there may be always a preponderance of inclination for the side taken, it, nevertheless, never renders the resolution taken absolutely necessary.

IV. *Objection.* Whoever can prevent the sin of another and does not do so, but rather contributes to it although he is well informed of it, is accessory to it.

God can prevent the sin of intelligent creatures; but he does not do so, and rather contributes to it by his concurrence and by the opportunities which he brings about, although he has a perfect knowledge of it.

Hence, etc.

Answer. I deny the major of this syllogism. For it is possible that one could prevent sin, but ought not, because he could not do it without himself committing a sin, or (when God is in question) without performing an unreasonable action. Examples have been given and the application to God himself has been made. It is possible also that we contribute to evil and that sometimes we even open the road to it, in doing things which we are obliged to do; and, when we do our duty or (in speaking of God) when, after thorough consideration, we do that which reason demands, we are not responsible for the results, even when we foresee them. We do not desire these evils; but we are willing to permit them for the sake of a greater good which we cannot reasonably help preferring to other considerations. And this is a *consequent* will, which results from *antecedent* wills by which we will the good. I know that some persons, in speaking of the antecedent and consequent will of God, have understood by the *antecedent* that which wills that all men should be saved; and by the *consequent,* that which wills, in consequence of persistent sin, that some should be damned. But these are merely illustrations of a more general idea, and it may be said for the same reason that God, by his antecedent will, wills that men should not sin; and by his consequent or final and decreeing will (that which is always followed by its effect), he wills to permit them to sin, this permission being the result of superior reasons. And we have the right to say in general that the antecedent will of God tends to the production of good and the prevention of evil, each taken in itself and as if alone (*particulariter et secundum quid,* Thom. I, qu. 19, art. 6), according to the measure of the degree of each good and of each evil; but that the divine consequent or final or total will tends toward the production of as many goods as may be put together, the combination of which becomes in this way determined, and includes also the permission of some evils and the exclusion of some goods, as the best possible plan for the universe demands. Arminius, in his *Anti-perkinsus,* has very well explained that the will of God may be called consequent, not only in relation to the action of the creature considered beforehand in the divine understanding, but also in relation to other anterior divine acts of will. But this consideration of the passage cited from Thomas Aquinas, and that from Scotus (I. dist. 46, qu. XI), is enough to show that they make this distinction as I have done here. Nevertheless, if anyone objects to this use of terms let him substitute *deliberating* will, in place of antecedent, and *final* or decreeing will, in place of consequent. For I do not wish to dispute over words.

V. *Objection.* Whoever produces all that is real in a thing, is its cause.

God produces all that is real in sin.

Hence, God is the cause of sin.

Answer. I might content myself with denying the major or the minor, since the term *real* admits of interpretations which would render these propositions false. But in order to explain more clearly, I will make a distinction. *Real* signifies either that which is positive only, or, it includes also privative beings: in the first case, I deny the major and admit the minor; in the second case, I do the contrary. I might have limited myself to this, but I have chosen to proceed still farther and give the reason for this distinction. I have been very glad therefore to draw attention to the fact that every reality purely positive or absolute is a perfection; and that imperfection comes from limitation, that is, from the privative: for to limit is to refuse progress, or the greatest possible progress. Now God is the cause of all perfections and consequently of all realities considered as purely positive. But limitations or privations result from the original imperfection of creatures, which limits their receptivity. And it is with them as with a loaded vessel, which the river causes to move more or less slowly according to the weight which it carries: thus its speed depends upon the river, but the retardation which limits this speed comes from the load. Thus in the *Theodicy,* we have shown how the creature, in causing sin, is a defective cause; how errors and evil inclinations are born of privation; and how privation is accidentally efficient; and I have justified the opinion of St. Augustine (lib. I. ad Simpl. qu. 2) who explains, for example, how God makes the soul obdurate, not by giving it something evil, but because the effect of his good impression is limited by the soul's resistance and by the circumstances which contribute to this resistance, so that he does not give it all the good which would overcome its evil. *Nec* (inquit) *ab illo erogatur aliquid quo homo fit deterior, sed tantum quo fit melior non erogatur.* But if God had wished to do more, he would have had to make either other natures for creatures or other miracles to change their natures, things which the best plan could not admit. It is as if the current of the river must be more rapid than its fall admitted or that the boats should be loaded more lightly, if it were necessary to make them move more quickly. And the original limitation or imperfection of creatures requires that even the best plan of the universe could not receive more good, and could not be exempt from certain evils, which, however, are to result in a greater good. There are certain disorders in the parts which marvelously enhance the beauty of the whole; just as certain dissonances, when properly used, render harmony more beautiful. But this depends on what has already been said in answer to the first objection.

VI. *Objection.* Whoever punishes those who have done as well as it was in their power to do, is unjust.

God does so.

Hence, etc.

Answer. I deny the minor of this argument. And I believe that God always gives sufficient aid and grace to those who have a good will, that is, to those who do not reject this grace by new sin. Thus I do not admit the damnation of infants who have died without baptism or outside of the church; nor the damnation of adults who have acted according to the light which God has given them. And I believe that if *any one has followed the light which has been given him,* he will undoubtedly receive greater light when he has need of it, as the late M. Hulseman, a profound and celebrated theologian at Leipsig, has somewhere remarked; and if such a man has failed to receive it during his lifetime he will at least receive it when at the point of death.

VII. *Objection.* Whoever gives only to some, and not to all, the means which produces in them effectively a good will and salutary final faith, has not sufficient goodness.

God does this.

Hence, etc.

Answer. I deny the major of this. It is true that God could overcome the greatest resistance of the human heart; and does it, too, sometimes, either by internal grace, or by external circumstances which have a great effect on souls; but he does not always do this. Whence comes this distinction? it may be asked, and why does his goodness seem limited? It is because, as I have already said in answering the first objection, it would not have been in order always to act in an extraordinary manner, and to reverse the connection of things. The reasons of this connection, by means of which one is placed in more favorable circumstances than another, are hidden in the depths of the wisdom of God: they depend upon the universal harmony. The best plan of the universe, which God could not fail to choose, made it so. We judge from the event itself; since God has made it, it was not possible to do better. Far from being true that this conduct is contrary to goodness, it is supreme goodness which led him to it. This objection with its solution might have been drawn from what was said in regard to the first objection; but it seemed useful to touch upon it separately.

VIII. *Objection.* Whoever cannot fail to choose the best, is not free.

God cannot fail to choose the best.

Hence, God is not free.

Answer. I deny the major of this argument; it is rather true liberty, and the most perfect, to be able to use one's free will for the best, and to always exercise this power, without ever being turned aside either by external force or by internal passions, the first of which causes slavery of the body, the second, slavery of the soul. There is nothing less servile, and nothing more in accordance with the highest degree of freedom, than to be always led toward the good, and always by one's own inclination, without any constraint and without any displeasure. And to object therefore that God had need of external things, is only a sophism. He created them freely; but having proposed to himself an end, which is to exercise his goodness, wisdom has determined him to choose the means best fitted to attain this end. To call this a *need,* is to take that term in an unusual sense which frees it from all imperfection, just as when we speak of the wrath of God.

Seneca has somewhere said that God commanded but once but that he obeys always, because he obeys laws which he willed to prescribe to himself: *semel jussit, semper paret.* But he might better have said that God always commands and that he is always obeyed; for in willing, he always follows the inclination of his own nature, and all other things always follow his will. And as this will is always the same, it cannot be said that he obeys only that will which he formerly had. Nevertheless, although his will is always infallible and always tends toward the best, the evil, or the lesser good, which he rejects, does not cease to be possible in itself; otherwise the necessity of the good would be geometrical (so to speak), or metaphysical, and altogether absolute; the contingency of things would be destroyed, and there would be no choice. But this sort of necessity, which does not destroy the possibility of the contrary, has this name only by analogy; it becomes effective, not by the pure essence of things, but by that which is outside of them, above them, namely, by the will of God. This necessity is called moral, because, to the sage, *necessity* and *what ought to be* are equivalent things; and when it always has its effect, as it really has in the perfect sage, that is, in God, it may be said that it is a happy necessity. The nearer creatures approach to it, the nearer they approach to perfect happiness. Also this kind of necessity is not that which we try to avoid and which destroys morality, rewards and praise. For that which it brings, does not happen whatever we may do or will, but because we will it so. And a will to which it is natural to choose well, merits praise so much the more; also it carries its reward with it, which is sovereign happiness. And as this constitution of the divine nature gives entire satisfaction to him who possesses it, it is also the best and the most desirable for the creatures who are all dependent on God. If the will of God did not have for a rule the principle of the best, it would either tend toward evil, which would be the worst; or it would be in some way indifferent to good and to evil, and would be guided by chance: but a will which would allow itself always to act by chance, would not be worth more for the government of the universe than the fortuitous concourse of atoms, without there being any divinity therein. And even if God should abandon himself to chance only in some cases and in a certain way (as he would do, if he did not always work entirely for the best and if he were capable of preferring a lesser good to a greater, that is, an evil to a good, since that which prevents a greater good is an evil), he would be imperfect, as well as the object of his choice; he would not merit entire confidence; he would act without reason in such a case, and the government of the universe would be like certain games, equally divided between reason and chance. All this proves that this objection which is made against the choice of the best, perverts the notions of the free and of the necessary, and represents to us the best even as evil: which is either malicious or ridiculous.

A THEODICY IS IMPOSSIBLE
Immanuel Kant

Immanuel Kant, "On the Failure of All Philosophical Essays in Theodicy," published and translated by W. Richardson in *Essays and Treatises*, originally published in 1791. Translation slightly emended.

By a theodicy is understood the defence of the supreme wisdom of the Author of the world against the accusation of that wisdom by reason, from what is contrary-to-end in the world. [I.e., to what is apparently contrary to ends which a perfectly good, wise, and powerful Being would adopt. Ed.] This is named, defending the cause of God; though at bottom it may be nothing more than the cause of our assuming reason, mistaking its limits, which cause is not indeed the very best one, but must be so far approved, as (setting aside self-conceit) man, as a rational being, has a right to prove all assertions, all the doctrines which reverence imposes on him, before he submits himself to them, in order that this reverence may be sincere and not hypocritical.

For this justification, now, it is required that the opiniative advocate of God shall prove, either that that, which we judge in the world as contrary-to-end, is not so; or that, were it so, it must by no means be judged as a fact, but as an invariable consequence of the nature of things; or lastly, that it must at least be considered not as a fact of the Supreme Author of all things, but merely of mundane beings, to whom something can be imputed, that is, men (perhaps higher, good or bad spiritual beings also).

The author of a theodicy consents, then, that this action shall be brought before the court of reason; engages himself as counsel for the defendant, by formally refuting all the charges preferred by the plaintiff; and during the course of law must not put him off by an authoritative decision on the incompetency of the tribunal of reason (*exceptionem fori*), that is, must not dispatch the charges by imposing on the plaintiff a concession of the supreme wisdom of the Author of the world, which directly declares groundless, even without inquiry, all doubts that may be started; but must attend to the objections and as they by no means derogate from the conception of the supreme wisdom[1] by clearing them up and removing them, render everything comprehensible.—One thing, however, he has no occasion to enter on, namely, to prove the supreme wisdom of God from what experience teaches of this world, for in this he would not succeed, as omniscience is thereto requisite, in order in a given world (as it gives to cognize itself in experience) to cognize that perfection, of which may be said with certainty that there is nowhere any greater in the creation and its government possible.

The contrary-to-end (*das Zweckwidrige*) in the world, which may be opposed to the wisdom of its Author, is of a three-fold nature: First, the conditional contrary-to-end which can be approved and desired by wisdom, neither as an end, nor as a mean. Second, the conditional contrary-to-end which consents with the wisdom of a will, indeed never as an end, but yet as a means. The *first* is the moral contrary-to-end, as the proper evil (sin); the *second* the physical contrary-to-end, evil (pain).—But there is a conformity-to-end (*Zweckmässigkeit*) in the relation of the evils to the moral evil, as the latter once exists and neither can nor ought to be diminished; namely, in the conjunction of evils and pains, as punishments, with the evil, as a crime; and relatively to this conformity-to-end in the world the question is, whether in this justice be done to every one in the

---

[1]The proper conception of *wisdom* represents but the property of a will, to harmonize with the chief good, as the final end or *scope* of all things, *art* on the other hand, but the faculty in the use of the fittest means to *ends laid down at pleasure;* art, when it proves itself as such (which is adequate to ideas, whose possibility transcends all interpretation of human reason, for instance, when mean and end as in organized bodies, produce one another reciprocally) as a *divine art,* may not be improperly distinguished by the name of wisdom, yet in order not to permute the conceptions, by the name of a wisdom of art of the Author of the world, for the purpose of distinguishing it from his *moral wisdom.* Teleology (and by it physicotheology) gives abundant proofs of the former in experience. But from it no inference to the moral wisdom of the Author of the world is valid, because law of nature and moral law require quite heterogeneous principles and the proof of the latter wisdom must be given *a priori* totally, therefore absolutely not grounded upon experience of what happens in the world. As now the conception of God, that shall be fit for religion (for we use it not for the behoof of the explanation of nature, of course in a speculative view) must be a conception of him as a moral Being; as this conception, as little can it be grounded upon experience, just as little can it be exhibited from merely transcendental conceptions of an absolutely necessary being, who is to us totally transcendent; so it is sufficiently evident that the proof of the existence of such a Being can be no more than a moral one.

world. Consequently still a third species of the contrary-to-end in the world must be conceived, namely, the disproportion of crimes and punishments in the world. [Kant thus identifies three kinds of "contrary-to-end": moral evil or sin, pain and suffering, and injustice. Ed.] The attributes of the supreme wisdom of the Author of the world, against which those contraries-to-end appear as objections, are likewise three:

First, his HOLINESS, as LEGISLATOR (Creator), in contradistinction to the morally bad in the world.

Secondly, his GOODNESS, as GOVERNOR (Preserver), contrasted with the innumerable evils and pains of the rational mundane beings.

Thirdly, his JUSTICE, as JUDGE, in comparison with the evil state in which the disproportion between the impunity of the vicious and their crimes seems to show itself in the world.[2] [Kant thus sees the problem of evil as expressible in three questions: How can a *holy* God allow moral evil? How can a *good* God allow suffering? How can a *just* God allow the innocent to suffer, and the guilty to escape, punishment? Ed.]

The answer to those three impeachments must be represented in the abovementioned threefold different manner, and proved according to their validity.

I. The first vindication of the holiness of the Divine will on account of the moral bad, which is complained of as disfiguring the world, his work, consists in this:

a. That there is by no means such an absolute contrary-to-end as we take the transgression of the pure laws of our reason to be, but that it is only a fault in the eye of human wisdom; that the Divine judges them according to quite other rules incomprehensible to us where what we indeed find rejectable with reason relatively to our practical reason and its determination may perhaps, in relation to Divine ends and supreme wisdom, be the fittest mean, as well for our particular weal as for the good of the world in general; that the ways of the Supreme are not

---

[2]These three attributes, of which the one can by no means be reduced to the others, for instance justice to goodness, and so the whole to a smaller number, constitute the moral conception of God. Nor can their order be altered (as for example to make the goodness the chief condition of the creation of the world, to which the holiness of legislation is subordinated), without derogating from religion, which rests upon this very moral conception. Our own pure (practical) reason determines this order of rank, as, when the legislation conforms itself to the goodness, there is no more dignity of it and no firm conception of duties. Man wishes first of all, it is true, to be happy; but perspects, and grants (though unwillingly) that the worthiness of being happy, that is, the consension of the use of his liberty with the holy law, must in the decree of the Author be the condition of its validity and therefore necessarily precede. For the wish, which the subjective end (of self-love) has at bottom, cannot determine the objective end (of wisdom), which the law, that gives the will unconditionally the rule, prescribes—Punishment in the exercise of justice is by no means grounded as a mean, but as an end in the legislative wisdom; the transgression is combined with evils, not in order that another good may arise, but because the combination is, in itself, *id est,* morally and necessarily, good. Justice, it is true, presupposes goodness of the legislator (for if his will did not tend to the weal of his subjects, it could not oblige them to obey him), it is not, however, goodness, but as justice essentially different from it, though comprehended in the universal conception of wisdom. Hence the complaint of the wont of justice, which shows itself in the lot that falls to men here in the world, is not that the good do not fare *well* here, but that the bad do not fare *ill* (though, when the former is superadded to the latter, the contrast still augments this difficulty). For in a divine government even the best man cannot ground his wish for well-being upon the divine justice, but must always (ground it) on his goodness; because he who does his duty merely, can lay no claim to the favor of God.

our ways (*sunt Superis sua jura*), and we err when we judge that which is a law but relatively for men in this life, absolutely as such and thus hold that which seems to our contemplation of things from a station so low contrary-to-end, to be so likewise when contemplated from the highest station.—This apology, in which the defence is worse than the charge, requires no refutation, and may certainly be freely left to the detestation of every person who has the smallest sentiment of morality. [I.e., Kant here rejects the view that "good" means one thing on earth and another, quite different, thing in heaven as a "solution" to the problem of evil. He takes this "solution" to be worse than the problem itself. Ed.]

b. The second pretended vindication grants, it is true, the actuality of the morally bad in the world, but excuses the Author of the world by its not having been possible to be prevented; because it is grounded upon the limits of the nature of men as finite beings.—But thereby that bad itself would be justified; and, as it cannot be imputed to men as their fault, one would need to cease to name it a moral bad. [I.e., if being morally evil, or not fully morally good, is a *necessary* consequence of being finite, no finite being could help being evil, and so no finite being would be responsible for being evil, and so none would be *morally* evil after all. Ed.]

c. The third vindication that supposes that with respect to what we denominate morally bad, men are actually guilty, no guilt must be imputed to God, as he hath from wise causes merely permitted, as a fact of men, but by no means approved and willed or prepared, that bad tends (if no difficulty shall be found in the conception of the mere *permitting* of a Being, who is the sole Author of the world) to the same consequence with the foregoing apology (b), namely, that as it was impossible for God himself to hinder this bad without derogating from other higher and even moral ends, the ground of this evil (for it must now be properly named thus) must be unavoidably to be looked for in the essence of things, namely, the necessary limits of humanity as finite nature, and consequently cannot be imputed to it. [The "third vindication" is thus that moral evil is a logically necessary condition of a good great enough to outweigh it, e.g., free moral agency. Ed.]

II. The justification of the Divine goodness for the evils, namely, pains, which are complained of in the world, consists herein.

a. That in the fates of men a preponderance of evil over the agreeable enjoyment of life is falsely supposed, because every one, however badly he may fare, chooses rather to live, than to be dead, and those few, who resolve on the latter, so long as they themselves delay it, thereby allow that preponderance still and, when they are insane enough to destroy themselves, merely pass to the state of insensibility in which no pain can be felt.—But the answer to this sophistry may surely be left to the decision of every man of a sound understanding who has lived and reflected long enough on the value of life to be able to pronounce a judgment on this, when the question is proposed to him, Whether, I will not say on the same, but on any other conditions he pleases (only not of a fairy, but of this our terrestrial world) he would not wish to act the play of life over again.

b. To the second justification, that the preponderancy of the painful feelings over the agreeable cannot be separated from the nature of an animal creature, like man, (as count Veri maintains in his book On the Nature of Pleasure)—one would reply, that, if it is so, there occurs another query, Why the Author of our existence has called us into life, when, according to our just calculation, it is not worthy of being wished for by us? Ill-humour here, as the Indian woman said to Genghis Khan, who could neither give her satisfaction for the violence suffered nor afford her security against the future, would answer, 'If thou will'st not protect us, why dost thou conquer us?' [I.e., Kant takes as obviously inadequate the answers that the balance of pleasure over pain is proved by the fact that men do not often take their own lives or that future pleasure will make up for present pain. Ed.]

c. The third solution of the knot is, that for the sake of a future felicity God hath placed us out of goodness in the world, but that that beatitude which may be hoped for must be preceded by a state of thorough trouble and misery of the present life, where we must by the struggle with difficulties become worthy of that future glory.—But that this time of probation (in which the most succumb, and the best have no proper satisfaction in their life) shall absolutely be the condition by the Supreme Wisdom of the pleasure that one day or other may be enjoyed by us, and that it was not feasible to let the creature become contented with every epoch of his life, may indeed be pretended but absolutely cannot be perspected, and by an appeal to the Supreme Wisdom who hath so willed it the knot may be cut, to be sure, but not untied; to resolve which, however, the theodicy engages. [The "third solution" is that suffering is a necessary condition of moral maturity. Ed.]

III. To the last charge preferred against the justice of the Governour of the world,[3] is answered:

a. That the pretext of the impunity of the vicious in the world has no ground; because every crime, according to its nature, carries with itself here the punishment suitable to it as the internal reproaches of conscience torment the vicious more than furies would.—But in this judgment there is evidently a misunderstanding. For the virtuous man herein lends his character of mind to the vicious, namely, conscientiousness in its whole strictness which, the more virtuous the man is, punishes the more rigorously on account of the smallest transgression, that the moral law in him disapproves. But where this cast of mind and with it conscientiousness is wanting, there is likewise wanting the tormentor for crimes committed; and the vicious, if he can but escape the external chastisement for his crimes, laughs at the anxiety of the honest man to torment himself internally with his own rebukes; but the small reproaches which he may sometimes make himself, he makes either not at all through conscience, or, if he has any, they are abundantly outweighed and requited by the sensual pleasure for which only he has a taste. [I.e., the immoral man is, in part, immoral due to his having dulled his own conscience so that as he increases in immorality he decreases in moral sensitivity. Ed.]

---

[3]It is remarkable that among all the difficulties of uniting the course of the events of the world with the divinity of its Author, none forces itself so strongly on the mind, as that of the appearance of *justice* therein wanting. If it happens (though it is but seldom,) that an unjust villain, especially one possessing power, does not escape out of the world unpunished; the impartial spectator, in a manner reconciled to heaven, rejoices. No other conformity-to-end in nature excites his affect to such a degree by the admiration of it, and so to speak lets the hand of God be so easily discerned. Why? It (the conformity-to-end) is here moral, and the only one of the sort, which one may hope to perceive in some measure in the world.

b. If that charge shall be further refuted by this, that it is indeed not to be denied that there is absolutely to be found no proportion conformable to justice between guilt and punishment in the world, and one must often perceive with indignation in the course of it a life led with crying injustice and yet happy to the very end; that this however lies in nature and is not intentionally prepared, consequently is not moral dissonance because it is a property of virtue to struggle with adversity (to which belongs the pain that the virtuous must suffer by the comparison of his own misfortune with the good fortune of the vicious) and sufferings serve but to enhance the value of virtue, therefore in the eye of reason this dissonance of the undeserved evils of life is resolved into the most glorious moral concord;—this solution is opposed by this, that though these evils when they as the whetstone of virtue either *precede* or accompany it may, it is true, be represented as in a moral harmony with it, when at least the end of life crowns the latter and punishes vice; but that when even this end falls out nonsensically, of which experience gives many examples, suffering seems to have fallen to the lot of the virtuous not *in order* that his virtue shall be pure, but *because* it has been so (but on the other hand was contrary to the rules of prudent self-love): which is directly the contrary to justice, as man is able to form a conception of it to himself. For as to the possibility that the end of this terrestrial life may not perhaps be the end of all life, this possibility cannot be valid as a *vindication* of Providence, but is merely an authoritative decision of the morally faithful reason, by which the sceptic is referred to patience, but not satisfied. [I.e., suffering is sometimes a *consequence* of virtue, and the sheer *possibility* that recompense will be made, even if intelligible, is not a sufficient response. Ed.]

c. If finally the third solution of this unharmonious proportion between the moral value of men and the lot that falls to them shall be attempted by saying that, All weal or ill in this world must be judged as a consequence of the use of the faculties of men merely according to laws of nature, proportioned to their applied address and prudence, at the same time to the circumstances also into which they accidentally fall, but not according to their agreement with supersensible ends; whereas in a future world another order of things will subsist and every one will obtain what his deeds here below are worth according to a moral judgment;—thus is this presupposition arbitrable. Reason, if it does not as a morally legislative faculty give an authoritative decision conformable to its interest, must rather find it probable according to mere rules of theoretical cognition that the course of the world according to the order of nature, as here, so for the future, will determine our fate. For what other clue has reason for its theoretical presumption than the law of nature? and though it allowed itself as was required of it (see b, above) to be referred to patience and the hope of a better future world; how can it expect that, as the course of things here according to the order of nature is of itself wise it would according to the same laws in a future world be unwise? As, according to them, there is no comprehensible relation at all between the internal determining grounds of the will (namely, the moral cast of mind) according to laws of liberty, and between the (for the most part external) causes of our well-being independent of our will according to laws of nature; so the presumption remains that the agreement of the fate of men with a Divine justice, according to the conceptions we form of it, is as little to be expected there as here. [The "third solution" infers from lack of justice now to presence of justice in the next life. Kant argues that if—independent of moral considerations—we make *any* inference, we are most justified in supposing that the future will be like the past. But he leaves open the possibility of appeal to practical (moral) considerations rather than to theoretical considerations as a way of defending the conclusion that there will be a future and just existence. Ed.]

The issue of this process before the *forum* of philosophy is, that all theodicy has hitherto not performed what it promises, namely, to justify the moral wisdom in the government of the world against the doubts which are entertained of it from what experience gives to cognise in this world; though indeed these doubts as objections, as far as our insight into the nature of our reason reaches with regard to the latter, cannot prove the contrary. But whether in progress of time more proper grounds of its vindication may not be found, not to absolve the arraigned wisdom (as hitherto) merely *ab instantia* remains still undetermined if we do not succeed in shewing with certainty that our reason is absolutely unable for *the introspection of the relation which a world as we may always know it by experience bears to the Supreme Wisdom;* for then all farther essays of opiniative human wisdom to perspect the ways of Divine wisdom are totally rejected. That at least a negative wisdom, the insight of the necessary limitation of our pretensions with regard to what is beyond our reach, is attainable by us must, in order to put an end *for ever* to this lawsuit, yet be proved; and this may be easily done. [Kant concludes his review of theodicies by claiming to have shown that they so far have failed. In what follows, he will argue that *any theodicy must fail* (and so must any antitheodicy, or "proof," that evil and God cannot both exist) due to "necessary limitations" on our knowledge. Ed.]

We have a conception of a *wisdom of art* in the arrangement of this world, to which for our speculative faculty of reason objective reality is not wanting, for the purpose of arriving at a physicotheology. In like manner have we a conception of a *moral wisdom* which may be placed in a world in general by a most perfect Author, in the moral idea of our own practical reason.—But of the *unity in the agreement* of that wisdom of art with the moral wisdom in a sensible world we have no conception and can never hope to reach it. For to be a creature, and as a being of nature to follow the will of its Author merely; but yet, as a free agent (who has his will independent on external influence, which may be very contrary to the former), to be capable of imputation; and nevertheless to consider his own fact at the same time as the effect of a Supreme Being; are an association of conceptions which we must conceive, it is true, in the idea of a world as the chief good; but which he only who penetrates to the knowledge of the supersensible (intelligible) world, and perspects the manner in which it forms the basis of the sensible one, can introspect: upon which insight only the proof of the moral wisdom of the Author of the world can be grounded in the latter, as this presents but the phenomenon of the former world—an insight which no mortal can attain.

All theodicy ought, properly speaking, to be an *explication* of nature, so far as God makes known by it the design of his will. Now every explication of the declared will of a legislator is either *doctrinal* or *authentic*. The former is what discovers by reasoning that will from the expressions which it has used, in conjunction with the designs of the law-giver otherwise known; the latter the legislator himself gives.

The world, as a work of God, may be contemplated by us as a divine publication of the *designs* of his will. In this however it is *frequently* for us a shut book; but it is *always* this when to conclude from it though an object of experience, even the *final end* of God (which is always moral) is aimed at. The philosophical essays of this sort of explanation are doctrinal, and constitute the proper theodicy, which may therefore be termed the doctrinal one.—Yet the mere obviating of all objections to the Divine wisdom cannot be refused the name of a theodicy, when it is a *divine authoritative decision,* or (which in this case is to the same purpose) when it is a judgment of the same reason by which we form to ourselves of necessity and before all experience the conception of God as a moral and wise Being. For there God is by our reason the very expounder of his own will announced by the creation; and this exposition we may denominate an *authentic* theodicy. Then, however, that is not the exposition of a *reasoning* (speculative) practical reason, but of a practical reason *possessing potency* which, as it is without farther grounds absolutely commanding in legislating, may be considered as the immediate declaration and voice of God by which he giveth a meaning to the letter of his creation. Now such an authentic interpretation I find in an ancient sacred book allegorically expressed. [Kant thus rejects any *theodicy* which attempts to infer the purposes of God from natural phenomena of the observation of human history. Such attempts are "doctrinal" and fail.]

Job is represented as a man to the enjoyment of whose life every thing possible to be conceived was united, in order to render it perfect. Healthy, opulent, free, a commander of others whom he may make happy, surrounded by a happy family, among beloved friends; and above all (what is the most essential) contented with himself in a good conscience. All these riches, the latter excepted, a hard fate hung over him for a trial suddenly tore away from him. From the astonishment at this unexpected overthrow come by degrees to recollection, he gave vent to complaints against his disaster; on which between him and his friends who are present under a pretext to console themselves is soon begun a disputation wherein both parties, every one according to his own way of thinking (but chiefly according to his situation), sets forth his particular theodicy, for the moral interpretation of that bad fate. Job's friends declare themselves for the system of the interpretation of all evil in the world from Divine *justice* as so many *punishments* for crimes perpetrated; and, though they could not name any with which they could charge the unfortunate man, they believed to be able to judge *à priori* that he must needs be guilty of some, else it would not be possible according to the Divine justice that he should be unhappy. Whereas Job—who protests with emotion that his conscience does not reproach him in the least on account of his whole life; but as to inevitable human faults, God himself knoweth that he made him as a frail creature—declares himself for the system of the *unconditional decree of God. He is of one mind,* continues Job, *and who can turn him?*

In what both parties reason or, if I may be allowed the word, overreason there is nothing remarkable; but the character in which they do so merits the more attention. Job speaks as he thinks, and every man in his situation would be of the same mind; his friends, on the other hand, speak as if the Almighty, on whose affair they decide and to gain whose favour by their judgment they have more at heart than the truth, listened to them in secret. These their tricks, for the sake of appearance to maintain things, which they must allow they do not perspect, and to feign a conviction which in fact they have not, contrast well with Job's plain sincerity, which is so far from false flattery as almost to border on temerity, greatly to his advantage. *Will you,* says he, *speak wickedly for God? and talk deceitfully for him? Will ye accept his person?* will ye *contend for God? He will surely reprove you, if ye do secretly accept persons!—for an hypocrite shall not come before him.*

The latter actually confirms the issue of the history. For God deigned to discover to Job the wisdom of his creation, chiefly on the side of its inscrutableness. He let him view the beautiful side of the creation where ends comprehensible to man set the wisdom and bountiful care of the Author of the world in an unambiguous light; but on the other hand the frightful side too, by naming to him productions of his potency and among these even pernicious dreadful things, every one of which, it is true, seems to be adjusted for itself and for its species conformably-to-end, but with regard to others and even to men destructive, contrary-to-end, and not harmonizing with an universal plan arranged by goodness and wisdom; whereby however he showeth the disposition and preservation of the whole announcing the wise Author of the world, though at the same time his ways, inscrutable to us, must be hidden even in the physical order of things, how much more then in their connexion with the moral order (which is yet more impenetrable to our reason)?—The conclusion is that as Job acknowledges to have judged, not maliciously, for he is conscious to himself of his probity, but only imprudently, on things which are too high for him and which he does not understand, God pronounceth the condemnation of Job's friends because they did not speak of him (God) so well (in point of conscientiousness) as his servant Job. If now the theory which every one on both sides maintains be contemplated, that of his friends may carry with it rather the appearance of more speculative reason and pious humility: and Job in all probability would have experienced a bad fate before every tribunal of dogmatical theologians, before a synod, an inquisition, a reverend classis, or every chief consistory of our time (one only excepted). Therefore only the sincerity of the heart, not the preference of knowledge, the honesty to acknowledge his doubts openly and the aversion to feign conviction where it is not felt, chiefly before God (where this craft besides is absurd) are the properties which in the Divine judgment have decided the preference of the man of probity, in the person of Job, over the religious flatterer.

But the belief, which arose to him by so strange a solution of his doubts, namely, merely the conviction of his ignorance, could enter into the mind of none but him who in the midst of his greatest doubts could say, *till I die I will not remove my integrity from me,* &c. For by this mindedness he proved that he did not ground his morality upon the belief, but the belief upon the morality: in which case this belief only, however weak it may be, is of a pure and genuine sort, that is of that sort which grounds a religion, not of courting favour but of the good life. [On the relation between religion and morality as Kant views it, see Part Four, The Moral Argument. Kant believes that a certain sort of justification of belief in God and immortality is possible by reflection on our moral concepts and experience, so that a future and just life is not merely a bare possibility. Ed.]

Concluding Observation

The theodicy, as has been shown, has not so much to do with a problem for the advantage of science as rather with an affair of belief. From the authentic theodicy we saw that in such things it does not depend so much upon reasoning as upon sincerity in the observation of the inability of our reason, and upon the honesty not to falsify one's thoughts in the utterance, let them be falsified with ever so pious a view.—This occasions the following short contemplation on a rich fund of matter, namely, sincerity as the chief requisite in affairs of faith, in collision with the propension to falsity and impurity as the principal defects in human nature.

That what one says either to himself or to another is *true* he cannot always be answerable (for he may err); but he can and must be answerable for his profession or his acknowledgment's being *veracious,* for of it he is immediately conscious to himself. In the former case he compares his asseveration with the object in the logical judgment (by the understanding); but in the latter, as he professes his holding-true, with the subject (before conscience). Does he make the profession relating to the former, without being conscious to himself of the latter? he lies, as he gives out something else than what he is conscious of.—The observation that there is such an impurity in the human heart is not new (for Job made it); but one would almost think that the attention to it is new to teachers of morals and religion: so little is it found that they, notwithstanding the difficulty which a purifying of the minds of men even if they *would* act conformably to duty carries with it, have made sufficient use of that observation.—This veracity may be named the *formal conscientiousness,* the *material* consists in the circumspection to venture nothing on the risk of its being wrong: as on the contrary that consists in the consciousness of having employed this circumspection in the given case.—Moralists speak of an erring conscience. But an erring conscience is a nonentity; and were there such a thing, one could never be sure to have acted right, because the judge himself in the last instance might err. I may err, it is true, in the judgment *which I believe* to be in the right: for that belongs to the understanding which only judges objectively (whether true or false); but in the consciousness, *Whether in fact I believe* to be in the right (or merely pretend it), I absolutely cannot err as this judgment or rather this position says nothing but that I thus judge the object.

In the carefulness to be conscious to one's self of this belief (or unbelief), and not to give out any holding-true of which one is not conscious, consists just the formal conscientiousness which is the ground of veracity. Therefore who says to himself (and, what is the same in the confessions of religion, before God) that *he believes,* without perhaps having examined himself, whether he is in fact conscious to himself of this holding-true or even of such a degree of it,[4] lies not

---

[4]The mean of extorting veracity in external deposing, *the oath* (*tortura spiritualis*) is held before a human tribunal not only allowed, but indispensable: a sad proof of the little reverence of men for truth, even in the temple of public justice, where the mere idea of it ought of itself to inspire the greatest reverence! But men lie with regard to conviction, which they have not, at least of the sort, or in the degree, they pretend, even in their internal professions; and, as this improbity (since it tends by little and little to actual persuasion) may also have external pernicious consequents to that mean of extorting veracity, the oath, (but indeed only an internal one, that is, the essay, whether the holding-true stand the test of an internal *juratory* examining of the profession) may too be very well used to make the audaciousness more daring, at last, however, if not to restrain externally violent assertions, at least to stupify.—By an human tribunal nothing more is demanded of the conscience of him that makes oath, than the engaging that, if there is a future Judge of the world (therefore a God and a life to come), he will be answerable to him for the truth of his external profession; *that there is such a Judge of the world,* is a profession not necessary to be demanded of him, because, if the former protestation cannot withhold the lie, the latter false profession would create just as little scruple. After this internal delation of an oath one would ask himself, Wouldest thou take upon thee, by all that is dear and sacred to thee, to answer for the truth of

only in the most absurd manner (before a knower of hearts) but in the most wicked, because it saps the very foundation of every virtuous resolution, sincerity. It is easily conceived how soon such blind and external *confessions* (which are easily united with an internal confession just as false), when they furnish *means of acquisition,* may gradually occasion a certain falsehood in the cast of mind of even the commonwealth.—While this public purifying of the way of thinking in all probability remains deferred to a distant period, till it perhaps one day becomes an universal principle of education and doctrine under the protection of the liberty of thinking; a few lines still may be here bestowed on the contemplation of that vice, which seems to be deeply rooted in human nature.

There is something touching and which moves the soul in displaying a sincere character, divested of all falsehood and positive dissimulation; as integrity, however, a mere simplicity and rectitude of the way of thinking (especially when its ingenuity is excused) is the least that is requisite to a good character, and therefore it is not to be conceived upon what is grounded that admiration with which we are impressed by such an object: it must then be that sincerity is the property with which human nature is the least endowed. A melancholy observation! As by that only all the other properties, so far as they rest upon principles, can have an intrinsic true value. None but a contemplative misanthrope (who wishes ill to nobody, but is inclined to believe every bad thing of men) can be doubtful whether to find men *worthy* of *hatred* or of *contempt.* The properties on whose account he would judge them to be qualified for the former treatment are those by which they designedly do harm. That property, however, which seems rather to expose them to the latter degradation can be no other than a propensity, which is *in itself bad* though it hurts nobody, a propensity to what can be used as a mean to no end whatever; which is therefore objectively good for nothing. The former bad is nothing but that of *enmity* (more mildly expressed, unkindness); the latter can be nothing else than a *lying disposition* (falsehood, even without any design to do hurt). The *one* inclination has a view which may in certain other references be allowed and good, for instance enmity against incorrigible disturbers of the peace. The *other* propensity, however, is that to the use of a means (the lie) that, whatever be the view, is good for nothing because it is in itself bad and blameable. In the quality of a man of the former species there is *wickedness,* yet with which there may be combined a fitness for good ends in certain external relations and it sins but in the means, which are not rejectable in every view. The bad of the latter sort is *naughtiness (Nichtswürdigkeit),* by which all character is refused to man.—Here I chiefly insist on the impurity lying deeply concealed, as man knows to falsify even the internal declarations in presence of

---

that weighty tenet of faith or another holden so? At such a demand conscience would be suddenly roused by the danger, to which one exposes himself by pretending more, than he can maintain with certainty, where the believing concerns an object that is not at all attainable by the way of knowing [theoretical introspection], but whose assuming, by its only rendering possible the connexion of the chief practical principle of reason with that of the theoretical cognition of nature in one system (and thus reason agreeing with itself), is above all recommendable, but yet always free.—But professions of faith, whose source is historical, when they are enjoined others as precepts, must still more be subjected to this proof-by-fire of veracity: because here the impurity and feigned conviction is extended to move persons, and their guilt becomes a burden on him, who in a manner answers for the conscience of others (for men are willingly passive with their conscience).

his own conscience. The less ought to surprise the external inclination to fraud; it must then be this that though every one knows the falseness of the coin with which he trades it can maintain itself equally well in circulation.

In de-Luec's letters on the mountains, the history of the earth and of men, I remember to have read the following result of his in part anthropological journey. The philanthropic author set out with the good quality of our species, and sought the confirmation of it, where city luxury cannot have such influence to corrupt the minds, in the mountains from Switzerland to the Harze; and after his belief in disinterested helping (*Hülfleistende*) inclination began somewhat to stagger by an experience in the former, he at last infers this conclusion, *That man, as to benevolence, is good enough* (no wonder! for this rests upon implanted inclination, of which God is the Author); *if a bad[5] propensity to fine deceit were but not inherent in him* (which is likewise not astonishing; for to withhold this depends upon the character which man himself must form in himself)!—A result of the inquiry that every body, even without having travelled in the mountains, might have met with among his fellow-citizens, nay yet nearer, in his own breast.

---

[5]In the very intermixture of the bad with the good lie the great springs, which rouse into action the dormant powers of humanity, and necessitate men to develop all their talents and to approach towards the perfection of their destination.

Chapter

NINE

SOME CONTEMPORARY DISCUSSIONS OF THE PROBLEM OF EVIL

EVIL AND OMNIPOTENCE

J. L. Mackie

J. L. Mackie, "Evil and Omnipotence," *Mind,* vol. LXIV, no. 254 (1955). Reprinted by permission of the author and editor, Professor Gilbert Ryle.

The traditional arguments for the existence of God have been fairly thoroughly criticized by philosophers. But the theologian can, if he wishes, accept this criticism. He can admit that no rational proof of God's existence is possible. And he can still retain all that is essential to his position, by holding that God's existence is known in some other, nonrational way. I think, however, that a more telling criticism can be made by way of the traditional problem of evil. Here it can be shown, not that religious beliefs lack rational support, but that they are positively irrational, that the several parts of the essential theological doctrine are inconsistent with one another, so that the theologian can maintain his position as a whole only by a much more extreme rejection of reason than in the former case. He must now be prepared to believe, not merely what cannot be proved, but what can be *disproved* from other beliefs that he also holds.

The problem of evil, in the sense in which I shall be using the phrase, is a problem only for someone who believes that there is a God who is both omnipotent and wholly good. And it is a logical problem, the problem of clarifying and reconciling a number of beliefs: it is not a scientific problem that might be solved by further observations, or a practical problem that might be solved by a decision or an action. These points are obvious; I mention them only because they are sometimes ignored by theologians, who sometimes parry a statement of the problem with such remarks as "Well, can you solve the problem yourself?" or "This is a mystery which may be revealed to us later" or "Evil is something to be faced and overcome, not to be merely discussed."

In its simplest form the problem is this: God is omnipotent; God is wholly good; and yet evil exists. There seems to be some contradiction between these three propositions, so that if any two of them were true the third would be false. But at the same time all three are essential parts of most theological positions: the theologian, it seems, at once *must* adhere and *cannot consistently* adhere to all three. (The problem does not arise only for theists, but I shall discuss it in the form in which it presents itself for ordinary theism.)

However, the contradiction does not arise immediately; to show it we need some additional premises, or perhaps some quasi-logical rules connecting the terms "good," "evil," and "omnipotent." These additional principles are that good is opposed to evil, in such a way that a good thing always eliminates evil as far as it can, and that there are no limits to what an omnipotent thing can do. From these it follows that a good omnipotent thing eliminates evil completely, and then the propositions that a good omnipotent thing exists, and that evil exists, are incompatible.

Adequate Solutions

Now once the problem is fully stated it is clear that it can be solved, in the sense that the problem will not arise if one gives up at least one of the propositions that constitute it. If you are prepared to say that God is not wholly good, or not quite omnipotent, or that evil does not exist, or that good is not opposed to the kind of evil that exists, or that there are limits to what an omnipotent thing can do, then the problem of evil will not arise for you.

There are, then, quite a number of adequate solutions of the problem of evil, and some of these have been adopted, or almost adopted, by various thinkers. For example, a few have been prepared to deny God's omnipotence, and rather more have been prepared to keep the term "omnipotence" but severely to restrict its meaning, recording quite a number of things that an omnipotent being cannot do. Some have said that evil is an illusion, perhaps because they held that the whole world of temporal, changing things is an illusion, and that what we call evil belongs only to this world, or perhaps because they held that although temporal things *are* much as we see them, those that we call evil are not really evil. Some have said that what we call evil is merely the privation of good, that evil in a positive sense, evil that would really be opposed to good, does not exist. Many have agreed with Pope that disorder is harmony not understood, and that partial evil is universal good. Whether any of these views is *true* is, of course, another question. But each of them gives an adequate solution of the problems of evil in the sense that if you accept it this problem does not arise for you, though you may, of course, have *other* problems to face.

But often enough these adequate solutions are only *almost* adopted. The thinkers who restrict God's power, but keep the term "omnipotence," may reasonably be suspected of thinking, in other contexts, that his power is really unlimited. Those who say that evil is an illusion may also be thinking, inconsistently, that this illusion is itself an evil. Those who say that "evil" is merely privation of good may also be thinking, inconsistently, that privation of good is an evil. (The fallacy here is akin to some forms of the "naturalistic fallacy" in ethics, where some think, for example, that "good" is just what contributes to evolutionary progress, and that evolutionary progress is itself good.) If Pope meant what he said in the first line of his couplet, that "disorder" is only harmony not understood, the "partial evil" of the second line must, for consistency, mean "that which, taken in isolation, falsely appears to be evil," but it would more naturally mean "that which, in isolation, really is evil." The second line, in fact, hesitates between two views, that "partial evil" isn't really evil, since only the universal quality is real, and that "partial evil" is really an evil, but only a little one.

In addition, therefore, to adequate solutions, we must recognize unsatisfactory inconsistent solutions, in which there is only a half-hearted or temporary rejection of one of the propositions which together constitute the problem. In these, one of the constituent propositions is explicitly rejected, but it is covertly reasserted or assumed elsewhere in the system.

Fallacious Solutions

Besides these half-hearted solutions, which explicitly reject but implicitly assert one of the constituent propositions, there are definitely fallacious solutions which explicitly maintain all the constituent propositions, but implicitly reject at least one of them in the course of the argument that explains away the problem of evil.

There are, in fact, many so-called solutions which purport to remove the contradiction without abandoning any of its constituent propositions. These must be fallacious, as we can see from the very statement of the problem, but it is not so easy to see in each case precisely where the fallacy lies. I suggest that in all cases the fallacy has the general form suggested above: in order to solve the problem one (or perhaps more) of its constituent propositions is given up, but in such a way that it appears to have been retained, and can therefore be asserted without qualification in other contexts. Sometimes there is a further complication: the supposed solution moves to and fro between, say, two of the constituent propositions, at one point asserting the first of these but covertly abandoning the second, at another point asserting the second but covertly abandoning the first. These fallacious solutions often turn upon some equivocation with the words "good" and "evil," or upon some vagueness about the way in which good and evil are opposed to one another, or about how much is meant by "omnipotence." I propose to examine some of these so-called solutions, and to exhibit their fallacies in detail. Incidentally, I shall also be considering whether an adequate solution could be reached by a minor modification of one or more of the constituent propositions, which would, however, still satisfy all the essential requirements of ordinary theism.

1. "GOOD CANNOT EXIST WITHOUT EVIL" OR "EVIL IS NECESSARY AS A COUNTERPART TO GOOD"

It is sometimes suggested that evil is necessary as a counterpart to good, that if there were no evil there could be no good either, and that this solves the problem of evil. It is true that it points to an answer to the question "Why should there be evil?" But it does so only by qualifying some of the propositions that constitute the problem.

First, it sets a limit to what God can do, saying that God *cannot* create good without simultaneously creating evil, and this means either that God is not omnipotent or that there are *some* limits to what an omnipotent thing can do. It may be replied that these limits are always presupposed, that omnipotence has never meant the power to do what is logically impossible, and on the present view the existence of good without evil would be a logical impossibility. This interpretation of omnipotence may, indeed, be accepted as a modification of our original account which does not reject anything that is essential to theism, and I shall in general assume it in the subsequent discussion. It is, perhaps, the most common theistic view, but I think that some theists at least have maintained that God can do what is logically impossible. Many theists, at any rate, have held that logic itself is created or laid down by God, that logic is the way in which God arbitrarily chooses to think. (This is, of course, parallel to the ethical view that morally right actions are those which God arbitrarily chooses to command, and the two views encounter similar difficulties.) And *this* account of logic is clearly inconsistent with the view that God is bound by logical necessities—unless it is possible for an omnipotent being to bind himself, an issue which we shall consider later, when we come to the Paradox of Omnipotence. This solution of the problem of evil cannot, therefore, be consistently adopted along with the view that logic is itself created by God.

But, secondly, this solution denies that evil is opposed to good in our original sense. If good and evil are counterparts, a good thing will not "eliminate evil as far as it can." Indeed, this view suggests that good and evil are not strictly qualities of things at all. Perhaps the suggestion is that good and evil are related in much the same way as great and small. Certainly, when the term "great" is used relatively as a condensation of "greater than so-and-so," and "small" is used correspondingly, greatness and smallness are counterparts and cannot exist without each other. But in this sense greatness is not a quality, not an intrinsic feature of anything; and it would be absurd to think of a movement in favor of greatness and against smallness in this sense. Such a movement would be self-defeating, since relative greatness can be promoted only by a simultaneous promotion of relative smallness. I feel sure that no theists would be content to regard God's goodness as analogous to this—as if what he supports were not the *good* but the *better,* and as if he had the paradoxical aim that all things should be better than other things.

This point is obscured by the fact that "great" and "small" seem to have an absolute as well as a relative sense. I cannot discuss here whether there is absolute magnitude or not, but if there is, there could be an absolute sense for "great," it could mean of at least a certain size, and it would make sense to speak of all things getting bigger, of a universe that was expanding all over, and therefore it would make sense to speak of promoting greatness. But in *this* sense great and small are not logically necessary counterparts: either quality could exist without the other. There would be no logical impossibility in everything's being small or in everything's being great.

Neither in the absolute nor in the relative sense, then, of "great" and "small" do these terms provide an analogy of the sort that would be needed to support this solution of the problem of evil. In neither case are greatness and smallness *both* necessary counterparts *and* mutually opposed forces or possible objects for support and attack.

It may be replied that good and evil are necessary counterparts in the same way as any quality and its logical opposite: redness can occur, it is suggested, only if nonredness also occurs. But unless evil is merely the privation of good, they are not logical opposites, and some further argument would be needed to show that they are counterparts in the same way as genuine logical opposites. Let us assume that this could be given. There is still doubt of the correctness of the metaphysical principle that a quality must have a real opposite: I suggest that it is not really impossible that everything should be, say, red, that the truth is merely that if everything were red we should not notice redness, and so we should have no word "red"; we observe and give names to qualities only if they have real opposites. If so, the principle that a term must have an opposite would belong only to our language or to our thought, and would not be an ontological principle, and, correspondingly, the rule that good cannot exist without evil would not state a logical necessity of a sort that God would just have to put up with. God might have made everything good, though *we* should not have noticed it if he had.

But, finally, even if we concede that this *is* an ontological principle, it will provide a solution for the problem of evil only if one is prepared to say, "Evil exists, but only just enough evil to serve as the counterpart of good." I doubt whether any theist will accept this. After all, the *ontological* requirement that nonredness should occur would be satisfied even if all the universe, except for a minute speck, were red, and, if there were a corresponding requirement for evil as a counterpart to good, a minute dose of evil would presumably do. But theists are not usually willing to say, in all contexts, that all the evil that occurs is a minute and necessary dose.

2. "EVIL IS NECESSARY AS A MEANS TO GOOD"

It is sometimes suggested that evil is necessary for good not as a counterpart but as a means. In its simple form this has little plausibility as a solution of the problem of evil, since it obviously implies a severe restriction of God's power. It would be a *causal* law that you cannot have a certain end without a certain means, so that if God has to introduce evil as a means to good, he must be subject to at least some causal laws. This certainly conflicts with what a theist normally means by omnipotence. This view of God as limited by causal laws also conflicts with the view that causal laws are themselves made by God, which is more widely held than the corresponding view about the laws of logic. This conflict would, indeed, be resolved if it were possible for an omnipotent being to bind himself, and this possibility has still to be considered. Unless a favorable answer can be given to this question, the suggestion that evil is necessary as a means to good solves the problem of evil only by denying one of its constituent propositions, either that God is omnipotent or that "omnipotent" means what it says.

3. "THE UNIVERSE IS BETTER WITH SOME EVIL IN IT THAN IT COULD BE IF THERE WERE NO EVIL"

Much more important is a solution which at first seems to be a mere variant of the previous one, that evil may contribute to the goodness of a whole in which it is found, so that the universe as a whole is better as it is, with some evil in it, than it would be if there were no evil. This solution may be developed in either of two ways. It may be supported by an aesthetic analogy, by the fact that contrasts heighten beauty, that in a musical work, for example, there may occur discords which somehow add to the beauty of the work as a whole. Alternatively, it may be worked out in connection with the notion of progress, that the best possible organization of the universe will not be static, but progressive, that the gradual overcoming of evil by good is really a finer thing than would be the eternal unchallenged supremacy of good.

In either case, this solution usually starts from the assumption that the evil whose existence gives rise to the problem of evil is primarily what is called physical evil, that is to say, pain. In Hume's rather half-hearted presentation of the problem of evil, the evils that he stresses are pain and disease, and those who reply to him argue that the existence of pain and disease makes possible the existence of sympathy, benevolence, heroism, and the gradually successful struggle of doctors and reformers to overcome these evils. in fact, theists often seize the opportunity to accuse those who stress the problem of evil of taking a low, materialistic view of good and evil, equating these with pleasure and pain, and of ignoring the more spiritual goods which can arise in the struggle against evils.

But let us see exactly what is being done here. Let us call pain and misery "first order evil" or "evil (1)." What contrasts with this, namely, pleasure and happiness, will be called "first order good" or "good (1)." Distinct from this is "second order good" or "good (2)" which somehow emerges in a complex situation in which evil (1) is a necessary component—logically, not merely causally, necessary. (Exactly *how* it emerges does not matter: in the crudest version of this solution good [2] is simply the heightening of happiness by the contrast with misery, in other versions it includes sympathy with suffering, heroism in facing danger, and the gradual decrease of first order evil and increase of first order good.) It is also being assumed that second order good is more important than first order good or evil, in particular that it more than outweighs the first order evil it involves.

Now this is a particularly subtle attempt to solve the problem of evil. It defends God's goodness and omnipotence on the ground that (on a sufficiently long view) this is the best of all logically possible worlds, because it includes the important second order goods, and yet it admits that real evils, namely first order evils, exist. But does it still hold that good and evil are opposed? Not, clearly, in the sense that we set out originally: good does not tend to eliminate evil in general. Instead, we have a modified, a more complex pattern. First order good (e.g., happiness) *contrasts with* first order evil (e.g., misery): these two are opposed in a fairly mechanical way; some second order goods (e.g., benevolence) try to maximize first order good and minimize first order evil; but God's goodness is not this, it is rather the will to maximize *second* order good. We might, therefore, call God's goodness an example of a third order goodness, or good (3). While this account is different from our original one, it might well be held to be an improvement on it, to give a more accurate description of the way in which good is opposed to evil, and to be consistent with the essential theist position.

There might, however, be several objections to this solution.

First, some might argue that such qualities as benevolence—and a fortiori the third order goodness which promotes benevolence—have a merely derivative value, that they are not higher sorts of good, but merely means to good (1), that is, to happiness, so that it would be absurd for God to keep misery in existence in order to make possible the virtues of benevolence, heroism, etc. The theist who adopts the present solution must, of course, deny this, but he can do so with some plausibility, so I should not press this objection.

Secondly, it follows from this solution that God is not in our sense benevolent or sympathetic: he is not concerned to minimize evil (1), but only to promote good (2); and this might be a disturbing conclusion for some theists.

But, thirdly, the fatal objection is this. Our analysis shows clearly the possibility of the existence of a *second* order evil, an evil (2) contrasting with good (2) as evil (1) contrasts with good (1). This would include malevolence, cruelty, callousness, cowardice, and states in which good (1) is decreasing and evil (1) increasing. And just as good (2) is held to be the important kind of good, the kind that God is concerned to promote, so evil (2) will, by analogy, be the important kind of evil, the kind which God, if he were wholly good and omnipotent, would eliminate. And yet evil (2) plainly exists, and indeed most theists (in other contexts) stress its existence more than that of evil (1). We should, therefore, state the problem of evil in terms of second order evil, and against this form of the problem the present solution is useless.

An attempt might be made to use this solution again, at a higher level, to explain the occurrence of evil (2): indeed the next main solution that we shall examine does just this, with the help of some new notions. Without any fresh notions, such a solution would have little plausibility: for example, we could hardly say that the really important good was a good (3), such as the increase of benevolence in proportion to cruelty, which logically required for its occurrence the occurrence of some second order evil. But even if evil (2) could be explained in this way, it is fairly clear that there would be third order evils contrasting with this third order good: and we should be well on the way to an infinite regress, where the solution of a problem of evil, stated in terms of evil (n), indicated the existence of an evil ($n + 1$), and a further problem to be solved.

4. "EVIL IS DUE TO HUMAN FREE WILL"

Perhaps the most important proposed solution of the problem of evil is that evil is not to be ascribed to God at all, but to the independent actions of human beings, supposed to have been endowed by God with freedom of the will. This solution may be combined with the preceding one: first order evil (e.g., pain) may be justified as a logically necessary component in second order good (e.g., sympathy) while second order evil (e.g., cruelty) is not *justified,* but is so ascribed to human beings that God cannot be held responsible for it. This combination evades my third criticism of the preceding solution.

The free-will solution also involves the preceding solution at a higher level. To explain why a wholly good God gave men free will although it would lead to some important evils, it must be argued that it is better on the whole that men should act freely, and sometimes err, than that they should be innocent automata, acting rightly in a wholly determined way. Freedom, that is to say, is now treated as a third order good, and as being more valuable than second order goods (such as sympathy and heroism) would be if they were deterministically produced, and it is being assumed that second order evils, such as cruelty, are logically necessary accompaniments of freedom, just as pain is a logically necessary precondition of sympathy.

I think that this solution is unsatisfactory primarily because of the incoherence of the notion of freedom of the will: but I cannot discuss this topic adequately here, although some of my criticisms will touch upon it.

First I should query the assumption that second order evils are logically necessary accompaniments of freedom. I should ask this: if God has made men such that in their free choices they sometimes prefer what is good and sometimes what is evil, why could he not have made men such that they always freely choose the good? If there is no logical impossibility in a man's freely choosing the good on one, or on several, occasions, there cannot be a logical impossibility in his freely choosing the good on every occasion. God was not, then, faced with a choice between making innocent automata and making beings who, in acting freely, would sometimes go wrong: there was open to him the obviously better possibility of making beings who would act freely but always go right. Clearly, his failure to avail himself of this possibility is inconsistent with his being both omnipotent and wholly good.

If it is replied that this objection is absurd, that the making of some wrong choices is logically necessary for freedom, it would seem that "freedom" must here mean complete randomness or indeterminacy, including randomness with regard to the alternatives good and evil, in other words that men's choices and consequent actions can be "free" only if they are not determined by their characters. Only on this assumption can God escape the responsibility for men's actions; for if he made them as they are, but did not determine their wrong choices, this can only be because the wrong choices are not determined by men as they are. But then if freedom is randomness, how can it be a characteristic of *will*? And, still more, how can it be the most important good? What value or merit would there be in free choices if these were random actions which were not determined by the nature of the agent?

I conclude that to make this solution plausible two different senses of "freedom" must be confused, one sense which will justify the view that freedom is a third order good, more valuable than other goods would be without it, and another sense, sheer randomness, to prevent us from ascribing to God a decision to make men such that they sometimes go wrong when he might have made them such that they would always freely go right.

This criticism is sufficient to dispose of this solution. But besides this there is a fundamental difficulty in the notion of an omnipotent God creating men with free will, for if men's wills are really free this must mean that even God cannot control them, that is, that God is no longer omnipotent. It may be objected that God's gift of freedom to men does not mean that he *cannot* control their wills, but that he always *refrains* from controlling their wills. But why, we may ask, should God refrain from controlling evil wills? Why should he not leave men free to will rightly, but intervene when he sees them beginning to will wrongly? If God could do this, but does not, and if he is wholly good, the only explanation could be that even a wrong free act of will is not really evil, that its freedom is a value which outweighs its wrongness, so that there would be a loss of value if God took away the wrongness and the freedom together. But this is utterly opposed to what theists say about sin in other contexts. The present solution of the problem of evil, then, can be maintained only in the form that God has made men so free that he *cannot* control their wills.

This leads us to what I call the "Paradox of Omnipotence": can an omnipotent being make things which he cannot subsequently control? Or, what is practically equivalent to this, can an omnipotent being make rules which then bind himself? (These are practically equivalent because any such rules could be regarded as setting certain things beyond his control, and vice versa.) The second of these formulations is relevant to the suggestions that we have already met, that an omnipotent God creates the rules of logic or causal laws, and is then bound by them.

It is clear that this is a paradox: the questions cannot be answered satisfactorily either in the affirmative or in the negative. If we answer "Yes," it follows that if God actually makes things which he cannot control, or makes rules which bind himself, he is not omnipotent once he had made them: there are *then* things which he cannot do. But if we answer "No," we are immediately asserting that there are things which he cannot do, that is to say that he is already not omnipotent.

It cannot be replied that the question which sets this paradox is not a proper question. It would make perfectly good sense to say that a human mechanic has made a machine which he cannot control: if there is any difficulty about the question it lies in the notion of omnipotence itself.

This, incidentally, shows that although we have approached this paradox from the free-will theory, it is equally a problem for a theological determinist. No one thinks that machines have free will, yet they may well be beyond the control of their makers. The determinist might reply that anyone who makes anything determines its ways of acting, and so determines its subsequent behavior: even the human mechanic does this by his *choice* of materials and structure for his machine, though he does not know all about either of these: the mechanic thus determines, though he may not foresee, his machine's actions. And since God is omniscient, and since his creation of things is total, he both determines and foresees the ways in which his creatures will act. We may grant this, but it is beside the point. The question is not whether God *originally* determined the future actions of his creatures, but whether he can *subsequently* control their actions, or whether he was able in his original creation to put things beyond his subsequent control. Even on determinist principles the answers "Yes" and "No" are equally irreconcilable with God's omnipotence.

Before suggesting a solution of this paradox, I would point out that there is a parallel Paradox of Sovereignty. Can a legal sovereign make a law restricting its own future legislative power? For example, could the British parliament make a law forbidding any future parliament to socialize banking, and also forbidding the future repeal of this law itself? Or could the British parliament, which was legally sovereign in Australia in, say, 1899, pass a valid law, or series of laws, which made it no longer sovereign in 1933? Again, neither the affirmative nor the negative answer is really satisfactory. If we were to answer "Yes," we should be admitting the validity of a law which, if it were actually made, would mean that parliament was no longer sovereign. If we were to answer "No," we should be admitting that there is a law, not logically absurd, which parliament cannot validly make, that is, that parliament is not now a legal sovereign. This paradox can be solved in the following way. We should distinguish between first order laws, that is laws governing the actions of individuals and bodies other than the legislature, and second order laws, that is laws about laws, laws governing the actions of the legislature itself. Correspondingly, we should distinguish two orders of sovereignty, first order sovereignty (sovereignty [1]) which is unlimited authority to make first order laws, and second order sovereignty (sovereignty [2]) which is unlimited authority to make second order laws. If we say that parliament is sovereign we might mean that any parliament at any time has sovereignty (1), or we might mean that parliament has both sovereignty (1) and sovereignty (2) at present, but we cannot without contradiction mean both that the present parliament has sovereignty (2) and that every parliament at every time has sovereignty (1), for if the present parliament has sovereignty (2) it may use it to take away the sovereignty (1) of later parliaments. What the paradox shows is that we cannot ascribe to any continuing institution legal sovereignty in an inclusive sense.

The analogy between omnipotence and sovereignty shows that the paradox of omnipotence can be solved in a similar way. We must distinguish between first order omnipotence (omnipotence [1]), that is unlimited power to act, and second order omnipotence (omnipotence [2]), that is unlimited power to determine what powers to act things shall have. Then we could consistently say that God all the time has omnipotence (1), but if so no beings at any time have powers to act independently of God. Or we could say that God at one time had omnipotence (2), and used it to assign independent powers to act to certain things, so that God thereafter did not have omnipotence (1). But what the paradox shows is that we cannot consistently ascribe to any continuing being omnipotence in an inclusive sense.

An alternative solution of this paradox would be simply to deny that God is a continuing being, that any times can be assigned to his actions at all. But on this assumption (which also has difficulties of its own) no meaning can be given to the assertion that God made men with wills so free that he could not control them. The paradox of omnipotence can be avoided by putting God outside time, but the free-will solution of the problem of evil cannot be saved in this way, and equally it remains impossible to hold that an omnipotent God *binds himself* by causal or logical laws.

Conclusion

Of the proposed solutions of the problem of evil which we have examined, none has stood up to criticism. There may be other solutions which require examination, but this study strongly suggests that there is no valid solution of the problem which does not modify at least one of the constituent propositions in a way which would seriously affect the essential core of the theistic position.

Quite apart from the problem of evil, the paradox of omnipotence has shown that God's omnipotence must in any case be restricted in one way or another, that unqualified omnipotence cannot be ascribed to any being that continues through time. And if God and his actions are not in time, can omnipotence, or power of any sort, be meaningfully ascribed to him?

THE FREE WILL DEFENSE

Alvin Plantinga

Alvin Plantinga, "The Free Will Defense," from Max Black (ed.),
Philosophy in America, 1965, by permission of Cornell University
Press, Ithaca, N.Y.

Since the days of Epicurus many philosophers have suggested that the existence of evil constitutes a problem for those who accept theistic belief.[1] Those contemporaries who follow Epicurus here claim, for the most part, to detect logical inconsistency in such belief. So McCloskey:

> Evil is a problem for the theist in that a *contradiction* is involved in the fact of evil, on the one hand, and the belief in the omnipotence and perfection of God on the other.[2]

and Mackie:

> I think, however, that a more telling criticism can be made by way of the traditional problem of evil. Here it can be shown, not that religious beliefs lack rational support, but that they are positively irrational, that the several parts of the essential theological doctrine are *inconsistent* with one another. . . .[3]

and essentially the same charge is made by Professor Aiken in an article entitled 'God and Evil'.[4]

These philosophers, then, and many others besides, hold that traditional theistic belief is self-contradictory and that the problem of evil, for the theist, is that of deciding which of the relevant propositions he is to abandon. But just which propositions are involved? What is the set of theistic beliefs whose conjunction yields a contradiction? The authors referred to above take the following five propositions to be essential to traditional theism: (a) that God exists, (b) that God is omnipotent, (c) that God is omniscient, (d) that God is wholly good, and (e) that evil exists. Here they are certainly right: each of these propositions is indeed an essential feature of orthodox theism. And it is just these five propositions whose conjunction is said, by our atheologians,[5] to be self-contradictory.

Apologists for theism, of course, have been quick to repel the charge. A line

---

[1]David Hume and some of the French encyclopedists, for example, as well as F. H. Bradley, J. McTaggart, and J. S. Mill.

[2]H. J. McCloskey, 'God and Evil', *The Philosophical Quarterly,* Vol. 10 (April 1960), p. 97.

[3]'Evil and Omnipotence.' J. L. Mackie, *Mind,* Vol. 64, No. 254 (April 1955), p. 200 [p. 311].

[4]*Ethics,* Vol. 48 (1957–58), p. 79.

[5]*Natural theology* is the attempt to infer central religious beliefs from premises that are either obvious to common sense (e.g., *that some things are in motion*) or logically necessary. *Natural atheology* is the attempt to infer the falsity of such religious beliefs from premises of the same sort.

of resistance they have often employed is called *The Free Will Defence;* in this paper I shall discuss and develop that idea.

First of all, a distinction must be made between *moral evil* and *physical evil.* The former, roughly, is the evil which results from human choice or volition; the latter is that which does not. Suffering due to an earthquake, for example, would be a case of physical evil; suffering resulting from human cruelty would be a case of moral evil. This distinction, of course, is not very clear and many questions could be raised about it; but perhaps it is not necessary to deal with these questions here. Given this distinction, the Free Will Defence is usually stated in something like the following way. A world containing creatures who freely perform both good and evil actions—and do more good than evil—is more valuable than a world containing quasi-automata who always do what is right because they are unable to do otherwise. Now God can create free creatures, but He cannot causally or otherwise determine them to do only what is right; for if he does so then they do not do what is right *freely.* To create creatures capable of moral good, therefore, he must create creatures capable of moral evil; but he cannot create the possibility of moral evil and at the same time prohibit its actuality. And as it turned out, some of the free creatures God created exercised their freedom to do what is wrong: hence moral evil. The fact that free creatures sometimes err, however, in no way tells against God's omnipotence or against his goodness; for he could forestall the occurrence of moral evil only by removing the possibility of moral good.

In this way some traditional theists have tried to explain or justify part of the evil that occurs by ascribing it to the will of man rather than to the will of God. At least three kinds of objections to this idea are to be found both in the tradition and in the current literature. I shall try to develop and clarify the Free Will Defence by restating it in the face of these objections.

I

The first objection challenges the assumption, implicit in the above statement of the Free Will Defence, that free will and causal determinism are logically incompatible. So Flew:

> . . . to say that a person could have helped doing something is not to say that what he did was in principle unpredictable nor that there were no causes anywhere which determined that he would as a matter of fact act in this way. It is to say that if he had chosen to do otherwise he would have been able to do so; that there were alternatives, within the capacities of one of his physical strength, of his I.Q., of his knowledge, open to a person in his situation.
> . . . There is no contradiction involved in saying that a particular action or choice was: *both* free, and could have been helped, and so on; *and* predictable, or even foreknown, and explicable in terms of caused causes.
> . . . if it is really logically possible for an action to be both freely chosen and yet fully determined by caused causes, then the keystone argument of the Free Will Defense, that there is contradiction in speaking of God so arranging the

laws of nature that all men always as a matter of fact freely choose to do the right, cannot hold.[6]

Flew's objection, I think, can be dealt with in a fairly summary fashion. He does not, in the paper in question, explain what he means by 'causal determination' (and of course in that paper this omission is quite proper and justifiable). But presumably he means to use the locution in question in such a way that to say of Jones' action A that it is *causally determined* is to say that the action in question has causes and that given these causes, Jones could not have refrained from doing A. That is to say, Flew's use of 'causally determined', presumably, is such that one or both of the following sentences or some sentences very much like them, express necessarily true propositions:

(a) If Jones' action A is causally determined, then a set S of events has occurred prior to Jones' doing A such that, given S, it is causally impossible for Jones to refrain from doing A.

(b) If Jones' action A is causally determined, then there is a set S of propositions describing events occurring before A and a set L of propositions expressing natural laws such that

(1) the conjunction of S's members does not entail that Jones does A, and (2) the conjunction of the members of S with the members of L does entail that Jones does A.

And Flew's thesis, then, is that there is no contradiction in saying of a man, both that all of his actions are causally determined (in the sense just explained) and that some of them are free.

Now it seems to me altogether paradoxical to say of anyone all of whose actions are causally determined, that on some occasions he acts freely. When we say that Jones acts freely on a given occasion, what we say entails, I should think, that either his action on that occasion is not causally determined, or else he has previously performed an undetermined action which is a causal ancestor of the one in question. But this is a difficult and debatable issue; fortunately we need not settle it in order to assess the force of Flew's objection to the Free Will Defence. The Free Will Defender claims that the sentence 'Not all free actions are causally determined' expresses a necessary truth; Flew denies this claim. This strongly suggests that Flew and the Free Will Defender are not using the words 'free' and 'freedom' in the same way. The Free Will Defender, apparently, uses the words in question in such a way that sentences 'Some of Jones' actions are free' and 'Jones did action A freely' express propositions which are inconsistent with the proposition that all of Jones' actions are causally determined. Flew, on the other hand, claims that with respect to the ordinary use of these words, there is no such inconsistency. It is my opinion that Flew is mistaken here; I think it is he who is using these words in a nonstandard, unordinary way. But we need not try to resolve that issue; for the Free Will Defender can simply make Flew a

[6]'Divine Omnipotence and Human Freedom', in *New Essays in Philosophical Theology*, ed. A. Flew and A. MacIntyre, London 1955, pp. 150, 151, 153.

present of the word 'freedom' and state his case using other locutions. He might now hold, for example, not that God made men free and that a world in which men freely do both good and evil is more valuable than a world in which they unfreely do only what is good; but rather that God made men such that some of their actions are *unfettered* (both free in Flew's sense and also causally undetermined) and that a world in which men perform both good and evil unfettered actions is superior to one in which they perform good, but fettered, actions. By substituting 'unfettered' for 'free' throughout this account, the Free Will Defender can elude Flew's objection altogether.[7] So whether Flew is right or wrong about the ordinary sense of 'freedom' is of no consequence; his objection is in an important sense merely verbal and thus altogether fails to damage the Free Will Defence.

II

Flew's objection, in essence, is the claim that an omnipotent being could have created men in such a way that although free they would be *causally determined* to perform only right actions. According to a closely allied objection, an omnipotent being could have made men in such a way that although free, and free from any such causal determination, they would nonetheless *freely refrain* from performing any evil actions. Here the contemporary spokesman is Mackie:

> . . . if God has made men such that in their free choices they sometimes prefer what is good and sometimes what is evil, why could he not have made men such that they always freely choose the good? If there is no logical impossibility in a man's freely choosing the good on one, or on several occasions, there cannot be a logical impossibility in his freely choosing the good on every occasion. God was not, then, faced with a choice between making innocent automata and making beings who, in acting freely, would sometimes go wrong; there was open to him the obviously better possibility of making beings who would act freely but always go right. Clearly, his failure to avail himself of this possibility is inconsistent with his being both omnipotent and wholly good.[8]

This objection is more serious than Flew's and must be dealt with more fully. Now the Free Will Defence is an argument for the conclusion that (a) is not contradictory or necessarily false:[9]

> (a) God is omnipotent, omniscient, and all-good and God creates free men who sometimes perform morally evil actions.

What Mackie says, I think, may best be construed as an argument for the conclusion that (a) *is* necessarily false; in other words, that *God is omnipotent,*

---

[7]And since this is so in what follows I shall continue to use the words 'free' and 'freedom' in the way the Free Will Defender uses them.

[8]*Op. cit.,* p. 209 [p. 317].

[9]And of course if (a) is consistent, so is the set (a)–(e) mentioned on page 305 [p. 321], for (a) entails each member of that set.

omniscient and all good entails *no free men He creates ever perform morally evil actions.* Mackie's argument seems to have the following structure:

(1) God is omnipotent and omniscient and all-good.

(2) If God is omnipotent, He can create any logically possible state of affairs.

∴(3) God can create any logically possible state of affairs. (1, 2)

(4) That all free men do what is right on every occasion is a logically possible state of affairs.

∴(5) God can create free men such that they always do what is right. (4, 3)

(6) If God can create free men such that they always do what is right and God is all-good, then any free men created by God always do what is right.

∴(7) Any free men created by God always do what is right. (1, 5, 6)

∴(8) No free men created by God ever perform morally evil actions. (7)

Doubtless the Free Will Defender will concede the truth of (4); there is a difficulty with (2), however; for

(*a*) that there are men who are not created by God is a logically possible state of affairs.

is clearly true. But (2) and (*a*) entail

(*b*) If God is omnipotent, God can create men who are not created by God.

And (*b*), of course, is false; (2) must be revised. The obvious way to repair it seems to be something like the following:

(2′) If God is omnipotent, then God can create any state of affairs *S* such that *God creates S* is consistent.

Similarly, (3) must be revised:

(3′) God can create any state of affairs *S* such that *God creates S* is consistent.

(1′) and (3′) do not seem to suffer from the faults besetting (1) and (3); but now it is not at all evident that (3′) and (4) entail

(5) God can create free men such that they always do what is right

as the original argument claims. To see this, we must note that (5) is true only if

(5*a*) God creates free men such that they always do what is right

is consistent. But (5*a*), one might think, is equivalent to:

(5*b*) God creates free men and brings it about that they always freely do what is right.

And (5*b*), of course, is *not* consistent; for if God *brings it about* that the men He creates always do what is right, then they do not do what is right *freely*. So if (5*a*) is taken to express (5*b*), then (5) is clearly false and clearly not entailed by (3') and (4).

On the other hand, (5*a*) could conceivably be used to express:

(5*c*) God creates free men and these free men always do what is right.

(5*c*) is surely consistent; it is indeed logically possible that God creates free men and that the free men created by Him always do what is right. And conceivably the objector is using (5) to express this possibility—i.e., it may be that (5) is meant to express:

(5*d*) the proposition *God creates free men and the free men created by God always do what is right* is consistent.

If (5) is equivalent to (5*d*), then (5) is true—in fact necessarily true (and hence trivially entailed by (3') and (4)). But now the difficulty crops up with respect to (6) which, given the equivalence of (5) and (5*d*) is equivalent to

(6') If God is all-good and the proposition *God creates free men and the free men He creates always do what is right* is consistent, then any free men created by God always do what is right.

Now Mackie's aim is to show that the proposition *God is omnipotent, omniscient and all-good* entails the propositions *no free men created by God ever perform morally evil actions.* His attempt, as I outlined it, is to show this by constructing a valid argument whose premise is the former and whose conclusion is the latter. But then any additional premise appealed to in the deduction must be necessarily true if Mackie's argument is to succeed. (6') is one such additional premise; but there seems to be no reason for supposing that (6') is true at all, let alone necessarily true. Whether the free men created by God would always do what is right would presumably be up to them; for all we know they might sometimes exercise their freedom to do what is wrong. Put in a nutshell the difficulty with the argument is the following. (5*a*) (God creates free men such that they always freely do what is right) is susceptible of two interpretations ((5*b*) and (5*c*)). Under one of these interpretations (5) turns out to be false and the argument therefore fails. Under the other interpretation (6) turns out to be utterly groundless and question begging, and again the argument fails.

So far, then, the Free Will Defence has emerged unscathed from Mackie's objection. One has the feeling, however, that more can be said here; that there is something to Mackie's argument. What more? Well, perhaps something along the following lines. It is agreed that it is logically possible that all men always do only what is right. Now God is said to be omniscient and hence knows, with respect to any person he proposes to create, whether that person would or would not commit morally evil acts. For every person *P* who in fact performs morally evil actions, there is, evidently, a possible person *P'* who is exactly like *P* in every respect except that *P'* never performs any evil actions. If God is omnipotent, He could have created these possible persons instead of the persons He in fact did create. And if He is also all-good, He *would,* presumably, have created them, since they differ from the persons He did create only in being morally better than they are.

Can we make coherent sense out of this revised version of Mackie's objection? What, in particular, could the objector mean by 'possible person'? and what are we to make of the suggestion that God could have created possible persons? I think these questions can be answered. Let us consider first the set of all those properties it is logically possible for human beings to have. Examples of properties *not* in this set are the properties of *being over a mile long; being a hippopotamus; being a prime number; being divisible by four;* and the like. Included in the set are such properties as *having red hair; being present at the Battle of Waterloo; being the President of the United States; being born in 1889;* and *being a pipe-smoker.* Also included are such moral properties as *being kind to one's maiden aunt, being a scoundrel, performing at least one morally wrong action,* and so on. Let us call the properties in this set *H* properties. The complement $\bar{P}$ of an *H* property *P* is the property a thing has just in case it does not have *P*. And a *consistent set of H* properties is a set of *H* properties such that it is logically possible that there be a human being having every property in the set. Now we can define 'possible person' in the following way:

x is a possible person = *x* is a consistent set of *H* properties such that for every *H* property *P*, either *P* or $\bar{P}$ is a member of *x*.

To *instantiate* a possible person *P* is to create a human being having every property in *P*. And a set *S* of possible persons is a *co-possible set of possible persons* just in case it is logically possible that every member of *S* is instantiated.[10]

Given this technical terminology, Mackie's objection can be summarily restated. It is granted by everyone that there is no absurdity in the claim that some man who is free to do what is wrong never, in fact, performs any wrong action. It follows that there are many possible persons containing the property *is free to do wrong but always does right.* And since it is logically possible that all men always freely do what is right, there are presumably several co-possible sets of possible persons such that each member of each set contains the property in question. Now God, if he is omnipotent, can instantiate any possible person and any co-possible set of possible persons he chooses. Hence, if He were all-good, He would have instantiated one of the sets of co-possible persons all of whose members freely do only what is right.

In spite of its imposing paraphernalia the argument, thus restated, suffers from substantially the same defect that afflicts Mackie's original version. There are *some* possible persons God obviously cannot instantiate—those, for example, containing the property *is not created by God.* Accordingly it is *false* that God can instantiate just any possible person he chooses. But of course the interesting question is whether

(1) God can instantiate possible persons containing the property of always freely doing what is right.

---

[10]The definiens must not be confused with: For every member *M* of *S,* it is logically possible that *M* is instantiated.

is true; for perhaps Mackie could substitute (1) for the premise just shown to be false.

Is (1) true? Perhaps we can approach this question in the following way. Let P be any possible person containing the property *always freely does what is right*. Then there must be some action A such that P contains the property of being free with respect to A (i.e., the property of being free to perform A and free to refrain from performing A). The *instantiation* of a possible person S, I shall say, is a person having every property in S; and let us suppose that if P were instantiated, its instantiation would be doing something morally wrong in performing A. And finally, let us suppose that God wishes to instantiate P. Now P contains many properties in addition to the ones already mentioned. Among them, for example, we might find the following: *is born in 1910, has red hair, is born in Stuttgart, has feeble-minded ancestors, is six feet tall at the age of fourteen,* and the like. And there is no difficulty in God's creating a person with these properties. Further, there is no difficulty in God's bringing it about that this person (let's call him Smith) is free with respect to A. But if God *also* brings it about that Smith refrains from performing A (as he must to be the instantiation of P) then Smith is no longer free with respect to A and is hence not the instantiation of P after all. God cannot cause Smith to refrain from performing A, while allowing him to be free with respect to A; and therefore whether or not Smith does A will be entirely up to Smith; it will be a matter of free choice for him. Accordingly, whether God can instantiate P depends upon what Smith would freely decide to do.

This point may be put more accurately as follows: First, we shall say that an H property Q is *indeterminate* if *God creates a person and causes him to have Q* is necessarily false; an H property is *determinate* if it is not indeterminate. Of the properties we ascribed to P, all are determinate except *freely refrains from doing A* and *always freely does what is right*. Now consider P_1, the subset of P containing just the determinate members of P. In order to instantiate P God must instantiate P_1. It is evident that there is at most one instantiation of P_1, for among the members of P_1 will be some such individuating properties as for example, *is the third son of Richard and Lena Dykstra*. P_1 also contains the property of being free with respect to A; and if P_1 is instantiated, its instantiation will either perform A or refrain from performing A. It is, of course, possible that P_1 is such that if it is instantiated its instantiation I will perform A. If so, then if God allows I to remain free with respect to A, I will do A; and if God prevents I from doing A, then I is not free with respect to A and hence not the instantiation of P after all. Hence in neither case does God succeed in instantiating P. And accordingly God can instantiate P only if P_1 is *not* such that if it is instantiated, its instantiation will perform A. Hence it is possible that God cannot instantiate P. And evidently it is also possible, further, that *every* possible person containing the property *always freely does what is right* is such that neither God nor anyone else can instantiate it.

Now we merely suppose that P_1 is such that if it is instantiated, its instantiation will perform A. And this supposition, if true at all, is merely contingently true. It might be suggested, therefore, that God could instantiate P by instantiating P_1 and bringing it about that P_1 is *not* such that if it is instantiated, its instantiation will perform A. But to do this God must instantiate P_1 and bring it about that P_1 is such that if it is instantiated, its instantiation I will *refrain* from performing *A*. And if God does this then God brings it about that *I* will not perform *A*. But then *I* is not free to perform *A* and hence once more is not the instantiation of *P*.

It is possible, then, that God cannot instantiate any possible person containing the property *always freely does what is right*. It is also possible, of course, that He *can* instantiate some such possible persons. But *that* He can, if indeed He can, is a contingent truth. And since Mackie's project is to prove an entailment, he cannot employ any contingent propositions as added premises. Hence the reconstructed argument fails.

Now the difficulty with the reconstructed argument is the fact that God cannot instantiate just any possible person he chooses, and the possibility that God cannot instantiate any possible persons containing the property of always freely doing what is right. But perhaps the objector can circumvent this difficulty.

The *H* properties that make trouble for the objector are the indeterminate properties—those which God cannot cause anyone to have. It is because possible persons contain indeterminate properties that God cannot instantiate just any possible person He wishes. And so perhaps the objector can reformulate his definition of 'possible person' in such a way that a possible person is a consistent set *S* of *determinate* properties such that for any determinate *H* property *P*, either *P* or *P̄* is a member of *S*. Unfortunately the following difficulty arises. Where *I* is any indeterminate *H* property and *D* a determinate *H* property, *D* or *I* (the property a person has if he has either *D* or *I*) is determinate. And so, of course, is *D̄*. The same difficulty, accordingly, arises all over again—there will be some possible persons God can't instantiate (those containing the properties *is not created by God or has red hair* and *does not have red hair*, for example). We must add, therefore, that no possible person *entails* an indeterminate property.[11]

Even so our difficulties are not at an end. For the definition as now stated entails that there are no *possible free persons*, i.e., possible persons containing the property *on some occasions free to do what is right and free to do what is wrong*.[12] We may see this as follows: Let *P* be any possible free person. *P* then contains the property of being free with respect to some action *A*. Furthermore, *P* would contain either the property of performing *A* (since that is a determinate property) or the property of refraining from performing *A*. But if *P* contains the property of performing *A* and the property of being free with respect to *A*, then *P* entails the property of freely performing *A*—which is an indeterminate property. And the same holds in case *P* contains the property of refraining from performing *A*. Hence in either case *P* entails an indeterminate property and accordingly is not a possible person.

Clearly the objector must revise the definition of 'possible person' in such a way that for any action with respect to which a given possible person *P* is free, *P* contains neither the property of performing that action nor the property of refraining from performing it. This may be accomplished in the following way. Let us say that a person *S* is *free with respect to a property P* just in case there is some action *A* with respect to which *S* is free and which is such that *S* has *P* if and only if

---

[11]Where a set *S* of properties entails a property *P* if and only if it is necessarily true that anything having every property in *S* also has *P*.

[12]This was pointed out to me by Mr. Lewis Creary.

he performs *A*. So, for example, if a person is free to leave town and free to stay, then he is free with respect to the property *leaves town*. And let us say that a set of properties is free with respect to a given property *P* just in case it contains the property is *free with respect to P*. Now we can restate the definition of 'possible person' as follows:

> *x* is a possible person = *x* is a consistent set of determinate *H* properties such that (1) for every determinate *H* property *P* with respect to which *x* is not free, either *P* or $\overline{P}$ is a member of *x*, and (2) *x* does not entail any indeterminate property.

Now let us add the following new definition:

> Possible person *P* has indeterminate property *I* = if *P* were instantiated, *P*'s instantiation would have *I*.

Under the revised definition of 'possible person' it seems apparent that God, if he is omnipotent, can instantiate any possible person, and any co-possible set of possible persons, he chooses. But, the objector continues, if God is also all-good, He will, presumably, instantiate only those possible persons who have some such indeterminate *H* property as that of *always freely doing what is right*. And here the Free Will Defender can no longer make the objection which held against the previous versions of Mackie's argument. For if God can instantiate any possible person he chooses, he can instantiate any possible free person he chooses.

The Free Will Defender can, however, raise what is essentially the same difficulty in a new guise: what reason is there for supposing that there are *any* possible persons, in the present sense of 'possible person', having the indeterminate property in question? For it is clear that, given any indeterminate *H* property *I*, the proposition *no possible person has I* is a contingent proposition. Further, the proposition *every possible free person freely performs at least one morally wrong action* is possibly true. But if every *possible* free person performs at least one wrong action, then every *actual* free person also freely performs at least one wrong action; hence if every possible free person performs at least one wrong action, God could create a universe without moral evil only by refusing to create any free persons at all. And, the Free Will Defender adds, a world containing free persons and moral evil (provided that it contained more moral good than moral evil) would be superior to one lacking both free persons and moral good and evil. Once again, then, the objection seems to fail.

The definitions offered during the discussion of Mackie's objection afford the opportunity of stating the Free Will Defence more formally. I said above [p. 324] that the Free Will Defence is in essence an argument for the conclusion that (*a*) is consistent:

> (*a*) God is omnipotent, omniscient, and all-good and God creates persons who sometimes perform morally evil actions.

One way of showing (*a*) to be consistent is to show that its first conjunct does not entail the negation of its second conjunct, i.e., that

> (*b*) God is omnipotent, omniscient and all-good

does not entail

   (c) God does not create persons who perform morally evil actions.

Now one can show that a given proposition *p* does not entail another proposition *q* by producing a third proposition *r* which is such that (1) the conjunction of *p* and *r* is consistent and (2) the conjunction of *p* and *r* entails the negation of *q*. What we need here, then, is a proposition whose conjunction with (*b*) is both logically consistent and a logically sufficient condition of the denial of (*c*).
   Consider the following argument:

  (*b*) God is omnipotent, omniscient and all-good.
  (*r*1) God creates some free persons.
  (*r*2) Every possible free person performs at least one wrong action.
 ∴(*d*) Every actual free person performs at least one wrong action. (*r*2)
 ∴(*e*) God creates persons who perform morally evil actions. ((*r*1), (*d*))

This argument is valid (and can easily be expanded so that it is *formally* valid). Furthermore, the conjunction of (*b*), (*r*1) and (*r*2) is evidently consistent. And as the argument shows, (*b*), (*r*1) and (*r*2) jointly entail (*e*). But (*e*) is the denial of (*c*); hence (*b*) and (*r*) jointly entail the denial of (*c*). Accordingly (*b*) does not entail (*c*), and (*a*) (God is omnipotent, omniscient and all-good and God creates persons who perform morally evil acts) is shown to be consistent. So stated, therefore, the Free Will Defence appears to be successful.
   At this juncture it might be objected that even if the Free Will Defence, as explained above, shows that there is no contradiction in the supposition that God, who is all-good, omnipotent and omniscient, creates persons who engage in moral evil, it does nothing to show that an all-good, omnipotent and omniscient Being could create a universe containing as *much* moral evil as this one seems to contain. The objection has a point, although the fact that there seems to be no way of measuring or specifying amounts of moral evil makes it exceedingly hard to state the objection in any way which does not leave it vague and merely suggestive. But let us suppose, for purposes of argument, that there is a way of measuring moral evil (and moral good) and that the moral evil present in the universe amounts to φ. The problem then is to show that

  (*b*) God is omnipotent, omniscient and all-good

is consistent with

  (*f*) God creates a set of free persons who produce φ moral evil.

Here the Free Will Defender can produce an argument to show that (*b*) is consistent with (*f*) which exactly parallels the argument for the consistency of (*b*) with (*c*):

  (*b*) God is omnipotent, omniscient and all-good.

(r3) God creates a set *S* of free persons such that there is a balance of moral good over moral evil with respect to the members of *S*.

(r4) There is exactly one co-possible set *S'* of free possible persons such that there is a balance of moral good over moral evil with respect to its members; and the members of *S'* produce φ moral evil.

Set *S* is evidently the instantiation of *S'* (i.e. every member of *S* is an instantiation of some member of *S'* and every member of *S'* is instantiated by some member of *S*); hence the members of *S* produce φ moral evil. Accordingly, (*b*), (*r3*) and (*r4*) jointly entail (*f*); but the conjunction of (*b*), (*r3*) and (*r4*) is consistent; hence (*b*) is consistent with (*f*).

III

The preceding discussion enables us to conclude, I believe, that the Free Will Defence succeeds in showing that there is no inconsistency in the assertion that God creates a universe containing as much moral evil as the universe in fact contains. There remains but one objection to be considered. McCloskey, Flew and others charge that the Free Will Defence, even if it is successful, accounts for only *part* of the evil we find; it accounts only for moral evil, leaving physical evil as intractable as before. The atheologian can therefore restate his position, maintaining that the existence of *physical evil,* evil which cannot be ascribed to the free actions of human beings, is inconsistent with the existence of an omniscient, omnipotent and all-good Deity.

To make this claim, however, is to overlook an important part of traditional theistic belief; it is part of much traditional belief to attribute a good deal of the evil we find to Satan, or to Satan and his cohorts. Satan, so the traditional doctrine goes, is a mighty non-human spirit, who, along with many other angels, was created long before God created men. Unlike most of his colleagues, Satan rebelled against God and has since been creating whatever havoc he could; the result, of course, is physical evil. But now we see that the moves available to the Free Will Defender in the case of moral evil are equally available to him in the case of physical evil. First he provides definitions of 'possible non-human spirit', 'free non-human spirit', etc., which exactly parallel their counterparts where it was moral evil that was at stake. Then he points out that it is logically possible that

(r5) God creates a set *S* of free non-human spirits such that the members of *S* do more good than evil,

and

(r6) there is exactly one co-possible set *S'* of possible free non-human spirits such that the members of *S'* do more good than evil,

and

(r7) all of the physical evil in the world is due to the actions of the members of *S*.

He points out further that (*r5*), (*r6*), and (*r7*) are jointly consistent and that their conjunction is consistent with the proposition that God is omnipotent, omniscient and all-good. But (r5) through (r7) jointly entail that God creates a universe containing as much physical evil as the universe in fact contains; it follows then, that the existence of physical evil is not inconsistent with the existence of an omniscient, omnipotent, all-good Deity.

Now it must be conceded that views involving devils and other non-human spirits do not at present enjoy either the extensive popularity or the high esteem of (say) the Theory of Relativity. Flew, for example, has this to say about the view in question:

> To make this more than just another desperate *ad hoc* expedient of apologetic it is necessary to produce independent evidence for launching such an hypothesis (if 'hypothesis' is not too flattering a term for it).[13]

But in the present context this claim is surely incorrect; to rebut the charge of contradiction the theist need not hold that the hypothesis in question is probable or even true. He need hold only that it is not inconsistent with the proposition that God exists. Flew suspects that 'hypothesis' may be too flattering a term for the sort of view in question. Perhaps this suspicion reflects his doubts as to the meaningfulness of the proposed view. But it is hard to see how one could plausibly argue that the views in question are nonsensical (in the requisite sense) without invoking some version of the Verifiability Criterion, a doctrine whose harrowing vicissitudes are well known. Furthermore, it is likely that any premises worth considering which yield the conclusion that hypotheses about devils are nonsensical will yield the same conclusion about the hypothesis that God exists. And if *God exists* is nonsensical, then presumably theism is not self-contradictory after all.

We may therefore conclude that the Free Will Defence successfully rebuts the charge of contradiction brought against the theist. The Problem of Evil (if indeed evil constitutes a problem for the theist) does not lie in any inconsistency in the belief that God, who is omniscient, omnipotent and all-good, has created a world containing moral and physical evil.

---

[13]*Op. cit.*, p. 17.

LOGIC AND THE
PROBLEM OF EVIL
Dewey Hoitenga

Dewey Hoitenga, "Logic and the Problem of Evil," *American Philosophical Quarterly*, vol. IV, no. 2 (1967). Used by permission of the author and the editor, Professor Nicholas Rescher.

Within recent years the ancient charge has been renewed against theism that, because its central propositions are inconsistent, it is, taken as a whole, false. In one remarkable instance, indeed, the claim was made that the central proposition itself, "God exists," is self-contradictory, and therefore can not be true.[1] The charge with which the present essay is concerned, however, involves more than one proposition and is referred to as the problem of evil. J. L. Mackie states the charge confidently and succinctly: "He [the theologian] must now be prepared to believe, not merely what cannot be proved, but what can be disproved from other beliefs that he also holds."[2] Defenders of theism have rejected the charge with equal confidence. Nelson Pike, for example, writes: "This problem, of course, does not exist. Since there is no logical contradiction between the theological and the ethical theses, there is nothing here to be recognized as rationally offensive."[3]

That philosophers will exhibit such confidence on opposite sides of an issue ostensibly involving a mere question of logical consistency is surprising. It suggests, at the very least, that the real issues dividing them are different. Part of what I wish to show in the following account is that this is so—that the problem of evil is not (except superficially) a question of the formal consistency of propositions, but a question of the meaning of the terms those propositions involve. The problem of evil challenges, I shall argue, our fundamental conceptions of good and evil, freedom and causation, the divine and the human; not our ability to detect or construct sets of propositions that are formally consistent or formally contradictory. In the course of this main argument I will have occasion to point up the logical dissimilarity between the traditional "higher good defense" and the "free will defense" of some recent theists—a dissimilarity which I add to a case I wish to make against the latter defense. I shall return, in the conclusion, to a brief statement of what I regard as the more general significance of the main argument concerning the *logic* of the problem of evil.

The disagreement between sceptics and theists should first be set forth in some detail. Sceptics hold that the existence of a God who is omnipotent, omniscient, and all-good or omnibenevolent logically rules out the existence of evil; and defenders of theism deny this. The most familiar formulation of the sceptic's case is repeated in the following lines by Professor Aiken:

> If there is a being that is at once almighty, omniscient, and perfectly good, it will be both able and willing to prevent evil. On the other hand, if something

[1] J. N. Findlay, "Can God's Existence Be Disproved?" in A. Flew and A. MacIntyre (eds.), *New Essays in Philosophical Theology* (New York, 1955), ch. 4.
[2] "Evil and Omnipotence," *Mind*, vol. 64 (1955), p. 200.
[3] Nelson Pike, "God and Evil: A Reconsideration," *Ethics*, vol. 68 (1958), p. 123.

is evil, it must be concluded that there is no such being, since a perfectly good person would prevent it if he could, and an almighty and omniscient being could prevent it if it would. Either, then, there is no such being or nothing is evil.[4]

The formal validity of the argument requires the additional premiss that if a being is both able and willing to prevent evil, no evil will exist. Though this premiss is taken for granted in Aiken's statement, it is not the premiss, I suppose, which defenders of theism will care to dispute. They will instead be seen to deny either that an almighty, omniscient, and omnibenevolent being is *able,* or that he is *willing,* to prevent evil; or both.

If, however, God *could not* prevent evil, he must be powerless in the presence of the possibility of evil; while if he *would not* prevent it, he must have some purpose—a good one, if he is all-good—in allowing it. Thus, given the central beliefs of traditional theism, we may distinguish two "problems of evil": first, an etiological problem: Whence evil? That is, how did it come to exist? What conditions made it possible in the first place?; and secondly, a teleological problem: Why is there evil at all? That is, given evil, and the nature of God as this is understood in theism, what purpose does it serve, in consideration of which its occurrence may be justified? I shall discuss the latter problem first, for I hope to bring the theist position on the justification problem to bear on some recent theist approaches to the problem of the origin of evil.

I

The moral justification of evil invariably turns, in theist literature, on the concept of a higher good, and it may aptly be called, therefore, the "higher good defense." I should like to set forth the necessary ingredients of the "higher good" concept which such a defense assumes. In the article cited above Nelson Pike uses just such a defense to reject the sceptic's charge of inconsistency. His central claim in this article is that "the logic of the term 'good' (if such there be) does not demand that a perfectly good person would prevent evil, even if he could."[5] He argues in support of this claim as follows:

A perfectly good person could allow evil, or for that matter be himself an evildoer—though it be avoidable, providing only that there be some other "good reason" for his tolerance of evil or his evil-doing. The point to be emphasized here is strictly semantical. The term "good" can apply, within the limitations of its proper usage, to an evildoer so long as it is possible to cite a motive or other factual condition which renders *moral blame* for the evil action inappropriate. Such a motive or condition could, of course, eliminate the property of moral *blame* without at the same time alleviating moral *responsibility* for the act in question. The father is morally responsible for the pain of the punished child, yet we would not feel it appropriate to blame him for his action if it were done with the child's ultimate good in mind.[6]

---

[4]Henry D. Aiken, *Reason and Conduct* (New York, 1962), p. 175.
[5]Pike, *op. cit.,* p. 119.
[6]*Loc. cit.*

An analysis of this argument and of the example it employs will exhibit the ingredients of the notion of a higher good as it is required for the theist's defense. These ingredients are four:

1. Such a good is dependent upon the specific evil which it justifies. So in the example, it is assumed that the punishment of the child will constitute a condition for his reformation. All such higher goods, that is, are causally related to the evils which they justify, and knowledge of such causal relationships is involved in the responsibility and blamelessness of the agents who inflict or tolerate these evils.

2. Such a good is not only dependent upon the specific evil, but it is obtainable in no other way which excludes the evil. So in the example, it is assumed that punishing the child constitutes a necessary condition for bringing about his ultimate good. All such goods, therefore, are causally related to the evils they are used to justify as their necessary conditions, and knowledge of these conditions as the ones necessary for the goods in question is involved in the responsibility and blamelessness of the moral agents who inflict or tolerate the evils.[7] If this were not so, some lesser evil or positive good should be sought as the means to the good end.

3. Such a good outweighs in value the disvalue of the evil on which it depends. So in the example, it is assumed that the reformation of the child is more of a value than the pain he must suffer in punishment is a disvalue. All such goods, that is, are better than the evils needed to bring them about are worse—they are "worth the price that has to be paid." Otherwise a father could be blameless for inflicting extreme torture on his child to prevent him from repeating a minor misdemeanor. Thus knowing the values of the goods achieved in comparison with the disvalues of the evils required is another part of the responsibility of those who inflict or tolerate such evils.

4. Finally such a good must outweigh in goodness any alternative good that could be achieved by different, non-evil, means. So in the example it is assumed that the type of reformation which only punishment can bring about is a greater good than any alternative type of reformation implemented by some other means—say permissiveness. Otherwise the father who had knowledge of and capability for each set of means and end would hardly be blameless for choosing reformation by punishment over reformation by permissiveness. All such goods, therefore, must not only outweigh in goodness the evil of the evils on which they depend; they must also outweigh in goodness the goodness of any other goods which could be attained without the evils in question.

This last ingredient is so important in the sceptic's case that I should like to illustrate it with another example—the crucial one of suffering pain in situations where it is not inflicted as a justifiable punishment. It has been argued by theists[8] that such pain is nevertheless justified by the higher goods it makes possible, such as virtuous responses like patience and fortitude. The argument is sound, however, only if such virtues are higher goods than alternate virtues, such as contentment and industriousness, which are made possible by a state of health

---

[7]Pike elsewhere provides some examples to show how the good may precede the evil it justifies as well as follow it. (*God and Evil* [Englewood-Cliffs, 1964], p. 91.) In either case the important feature is that the evil constitutes an unavoidable condition for the occurrence of the good.

[8]For an example see C. S. Lewis, *The Problem of Pain* (New York, 1947), chs. 6 and 7.

lacking the pain. And if the pain is borne bitterly instead of nobly, then the evil of the pain, far from being justified by a good that outweighs it, is actually rendered more intensely unjustified by the further evil of bitterness that not only depends on it but is invited by it. Mackie considers such instances as constituting a "fatal objection" to the theist defense.[9] They are fatal because there is no good present (at least obviously so) in these instances; yet this is precisely what the justification of any evil, on the theist's terms, requires.

There are further difficulties, however, that arise when we actually apply the concept of a higher good, as analyzed above, to the activity of God. For the plausibility of Pike's example—and of all such examples, I would venture—rests upon its appropriateness in a *human* situation. It is of the essence of such situations that (1) evil is already *given* as an ultimate condition which has to be reckoned with in the attainment of value; and (2) blamelessness in a moral agent who inflicts or tolerates an evil is a function of (a) his intention to achieve a higher good over a lower one, (b) his capability to achieve such a higher good, and (c) his knowledge both of the factual (causal) relationships and of the comparative values and disvalues of the goods and evils involved. Now such examples always show how human moral agents can be spared from blame in a situation where evil already exists and has to be taken into account. For only such a situation makes possible having sometimes to choose goods dependent on those evils. But Pike, and according to him all theists, deny that evil exists in any universe as an ultimate condition. If they are correct in this, as I believe they are, then the conditions under which God comes to create, sustain, and rule a universe are different from the conditions of human action in a most essential way. But if the examples get their force from a situation which is inapplicable to God, they will hardly support the theist's case.[10]

If the existence of evil is not an unconditioned necessity, nor an arbitrary accident (theists would reject this, it seems to me, with equal vigor), it must be a conditioned necessity. It must be conditioned by what is ultimate, namely, by the highest good; and this is the goodness of God. What this means is that the theist, in providing for the justification of evil, provides also for its necessity. For the justification of the evil that exists is made in terms both of an assertion that some good depends upon it, and of a denial that any higher good not depending upon it is available instead. From this it follows that evil is not only justified but necessary. For if evil *may be* justified, then, if God exists and evil exists (both of which the theist grants), it *is* justified; for if it were not, the existence of God and the existence of evil together would still constitute the contradiction which the conditions of justified evil were put forth to remove. But if evil is justified, then it is also necessary, for it is the necessary condition for the good which, since God is all good, is therefore willed by Him. Given then His goodness, together with his omniscience and omnipotence, evil is inevitable.[11]

In view of all this the *meaning* of the term "good," that is, its logic, its en-

---

[9] *Op. cit.*, p. 207.
[10] As a further objection against Pike's example of the father punishing the child the sceptic might insist on the more accurate analogy of the father providing a moral temptation for his child which he knew the child would not resist.
[11] As Leibniz argued: *Theodicy*, sec. 25.

tailment rules, will be predetermined by the admission of the fact of evil. And this Pike does admit:

> The important point has already been made: viz., the assumptions or premises of our whole discussion guarantee (logically) that there is *some* good reason for evil in the world. The theologian could condemn as erroneous all of the theodicies just considered and could even reject all extant theodicies as theoretically or existentially inadequate. So long as he insists there is *some* good reason for evil, one which remains only to be discovered by future investigation, he can accept both the theological and ethical theses without threat of contradiction. . . .
>
> Within theology, the theological thesis is accepted prior to and is indeed *axiomatic to,* the rational consideration of the status of evil in the natural world.[12]

I do not see how Pike avoids exposing himself here to the very charge he levels against both theologians and philosophers in regard to the term "evil": that of defining a term, in the present instance, "good," according to one's own interests, thereby solving nothing.[13] But that is only one difficulty. As Pike understands it, the only problem for a "practicing theologian"—one who accepts "both the theological and ethical theses as *premisses* or *axioms*"—is not to resolve a contradiction but to *discover* something, very much like a scientist who tries to discover something that will render an hypothesis which a particular experiment that was designed to confirm fails to do. But the sceptical question now forces itself: does he know, from thinking about goodness as he confronts it in his human situation, what he is looking for in God's?

It should be clear by this time that the issue between sceptics and theists occasioned by the existence of evil and the belief in God turns not on the consistency or inconsistency of a set of propositions, but on the meaning of "good" and on what "all-good" in the proposition attributing this quality to God entails. For the sceptic a state of affairs can be good, or a higher good, only if it is without evil. Introduce whatever so small amount of evil possible into this state of affairs, and it becomes less than good, less good than a state of affairs containing no evil whatsoever. It may occasion different sorts of goods that depend on the evil introduced, but these goods are not so great as those that could be achieved without any evil at all. Hence the sceptic's entailment rule for the term "good":

> These additional principles [connecting "good," "evil," and "omnipotent"] are that good is opposed to evil, in such a way that a good thing always eliminates evil as far as it can, and that there are no limits to what an omnipotent thing can do.[14]

For the theist, however, the introduction of evil into a good state of affairs need

---

[12]Pike, *op. cit.,* pp. 121 ff.

[13]*Ibid.,* pp. 118 ff. For two classic illustrations of the point see Augustine, *Enchiridion,* sect. XCVI, and Leibniz, *op. cit.,* sec. 10.

[14]Mackie, *op. cit.,* p. 201. In Aiken's words: "But any perfectly good person, so far as he can, will do good and prevent evil" (*op. cit.,* p. 175).

not lessen the goodness of the whole; indeed, he holds that such an introduction can occur leaving the whole better than it was. Hence his entailment rule for the term "good":

> The logic of the term "good" . . . does not demand that a perfectly good person would prevent evil in the world, even if he could.[15]

These are, I submit, two simply irreconcilable views on the nature of goodness.

Let us name the first view, the one which sustains the sceptic, the "Incompatibility View," for according to it the opposition between good and evil is simple and absolute. The one always, by its very nature, tends to prevent or destroy the other. According to such a view, a good world can only be one that contains no evil. Any world in which evil exists is thereby not the good world it could be if there were no evil in it at all; and it certainly could never be *better* than such a simply good world. As for those good things that depend on evil, they indeed represent the best that can be had in a situation already partly evil, but in so far as they do not prevent or eliminate the evil on which they depend they can not really be called good at all, for good by definition is contrary to evil.

This view of the nature of good and evil is drawn, I believe, from our universal moral experience; more specifically from the content of moral obligation: the unconditioned imperative to avoid and remove all evil. Bearing pain, for example, is never a good state of affairs, for we are always morally obligated to prevent or remove it in so far as we are able. But then it can never be (or contribute to) a good state of affairs, for we are never obligated to frustrate a good state of affairs. The fact that we are sometimes unable to remove such an evil state of affairs without creating a greater evil in its place serves only to show the limitations of our abilities and/or knowledge and thereby to spare us from moral blame. It does not reduce the evil of the pain-bearing. That a case of pain-bearing might become a predominately good state of affairs when done nobly will not count against the argument—unless we have an obligation to make possible such occasions of noble pain-bearing by inflicting or tolerating the pain required. But this no conscience will approve.[16]

In other words, if we are unable to remove any evil through ignorance, lack of ability, or because we must in removing it create greater evil, we are excused from the obligation. Such excuse, however, is due to our limitations with respect to fulfilling the obligation, and not to any weakness or condition in the obligation itself. Our blamelessness is owing not, that is, to the evil's being any less evil and therefore no longer to be opposed. Indeed, if our ignorance were overcome, our ability increased, and the threat of inducing greater evil removed, we would no longer be excused from the obligation to remove the evil. Now God is by definition a being who *is* unlimited in knowledge and power. Thus if he is also a moral being whose goodness is understood on an analogy with the goodness of human beings who fulfill their obligations, and if he exists, his existence must rule

---

[15]Pike, *op. cit.,* p. 119.
[16]In A. W. Price's words, speaking of the healings in St. Stephen's Episcopal Church in Philadelphia a few years ago: "It's true that pain can be used for victory through the cross, but per se, it's evil. . . . Jesus never told the suffering who came to him that 'I won't heal you because suffering is good for your soul.'" Reported in *Christianity Today,* vol. 8 (1963), p. 39.

out the existence of evil. But evil exists, and hence the contradiction in theism which constitutes the case of the sceptic. To understand God and evil in terms of our own moral struggle is to raise some doubt in regard to the existence of God. The sceptic prefers this doubt to a doubt of his own conscience.[17]

Let us name the second view, the one that sustains the theist, the "Compatibility View," for according to it the opposition between good and evil is not simple and absolute. Good, instead of always tending by its nature to prevent or destroy evil, sometimes includes and even depends upon it; evil, instead of always tending by its nature to undermine good sometimes provides necessary conditions for it. Any world in which evil does exist may thereby still be a good world; indeed, it may be better than a world without evil. For what makes a world good in this view is not simply how much evil is eliminated by good, but how much good is made possible by the evil it contains, in addition to the good that exists independently of this evil.

This view is not drawn from the nature of moral obligation but from the Judaèo-Christian religion which testifies to a God whose will is not only the ultimate source of all being but also the final criterion of what is good and just. But it is a will that not only brings about evil but even issues commands to human beings that on occasion are in conflict with those of conscience.[18] Since it is the will of God that is the final standard, not the judgments of men, and since men are always to submit their will and judgment to the revelation of this divine will, any contradiction between the divine will and the human is, in principle, removed. Thus the defense of theism rests on an identification of goodness with the will of God—an identification which, given the existence of evil, raises some doubt in regard to the deliverances of the human moral sense. The theist prefers this doubt to a doubt of the existence of God.

II

The "higher good defense" asserts that God would not have prevented evil —even if he could have—because if he had, he would have prevented the achievement of a higher good. But if God would not have prevented evil, it must have been a distinct possibility; for if it had not been, the occasion of his willing it for the sake of higher goods could not have arisen. Now the possibility of evil, and for that matter its actual origination, has been attributed by Christian theologians since St. Augustine to the freedom of the created will. The type of theistic defense I shall now examine has arisen around the concept of this freedom and has appropriately been called the "free will defense."

It is important to notice at the outset that a defense of theism oriented to the freedom of the will might turn out to be nothing other than a form of the higher good defense. It might be argued, for example, that the creation of a world of freedom with its attendant possibility of moral evil is a higher good than the creation of a world without such freedom. Such an argument would not be a

[17]For an alternative position which sacrifices divine goodness to maintain both divine existence and human conscience, see A. E. Taylor, *Elements of Metaphysics* (London, 1961), pp. 396 ff.
[18]*Genesis* 22; *Joshua* 8.

specifically free will defense, however; it would be indistinguishable in its logic from the teleological justification of evil. It would assert that there is a good (freedom of the will) that entails the possibility of evil, but which outweighs in goodness both whatever actual evils might arise from that possibility and any alternative creation which eliminated that possibility.

The "free will defense" as it has been developed by some recent writers does not take this form. It argues rather that God *could* not have prevented evil in the creation of free wills even if he *would* have. That such a defense raises a quite different issue from that in the higher good defense may be seen from the following: Suppose, contrary to the higher good defense, that there were no higher good in terms of which evil could be justified. Evil might still arise through God's *inability* to prevent it. And God would be unable to prevent it if it is free wills he wants to create—and it happens that he does want to create such wills. The crucial proposition here is that concerning God's inability to create a world of freedom and guarantee its goodness at the same time. In any full-blown theodicy, of course, it must be held that such a world is a better one, in order to preserve God's goodness. For if God *could* not prevent evil in creating free creatures, then there is no need to hold that he *would* not have prevented it even though he is all-good, if and only if the creation of free creatures is a greater good than all alternative creations or no creation at all. In this way any free will defense requires a higher good defense, and most discussions of freedom in the context of the problem of evil take the value question into view.[19] But I wish to distinguish, as I think the advocates of the free will defense have distinguished, the problem of how such freedom is to be *conceived* in a theistic context from the problem of how freedom as conceived *contributes to* this world's being better than some other kind or none at all. Mackie claims that the way in which freedom is conceived involves the solution of evil in terms of higher good.[20] I think he is right about that; but it also involves, as I hope to show, the conception of divine omnipotence. I shall hold that God has power to do what he wills (and what he wills is good), even if such power is conceptually peculiar in so far as it includes the determination of created freedom—just as his goodness is conceptually peculiar also in including evil. The advocates of the free will defense hold, on the contrary, that God wills to do what He can (and this is good); but such power is not made conceptually peculiar by including a determination of created free-dom—no more than goodness, according to the sceptical view, is to be made conceptually peculiar by having to include evil.

The central logical claim in the free will defense, then, is that the concept of a free person being guaranteed infallibly good by God is self-contradictory. It is well-stated by John Hick as follows:

> To be a person is to be a finite center of freedom, a (relatively) free and self-directing agent responsible for one's own decisions. This involves being

---

[19]Thus Alvin Plantinga in his summary of the free will defense does not fail to mention the following proposition: "A world containing creatures who freely perform both good and evil actions—and do more good than evil—is more valuable than a world containing quasi-automata who always do what is right because they are unable to do otherwise." "The Free-Will Defense," in Max Black (ed.), *Philosophy in America* (Englewood-Cliffs, 1965), p. 205 [p. 322].

[20]Mackie, *op. cit.*, p. 208.

free to act wrongly as well as to act rightly. The idea of a person who can be infallibly guaranteed always to act rightly is self-contradictory. There can be no guarantee in advance that a genuinely free moral agent will never choose amiss. Consequently, the possibility of wrong-doing or sin is logically inseparable from the creation of finite persons, and to say that God should not have created beings who might sin amounts to saying that he should not have created people.[21]

The arguments put forth in support of the inconsistency of saying that an action is both freely performed and guaranteed good usually presuppose the identification of "free" with "morally indeterminate." I shall oppose the position taken in the free will defense by arguing first that consideration of two important "theistic paradigm cases" must force the free will defender to give up his claim; secondly, that his claim involves him in serious difficulties at other points in his belief; and finally, that he already has a model in theistic belief for the conceptual peculiarity of "free and determined" which he wishes to avoid.

There are two theistic paradigm cases in which a person is regarded as wholly free yet entirely secure in goodness. First of all, there is the case of God himself. Theists certainly agree that God is a perfectly good, yet also perfectly free being. For the perfection or infallibility of His goodness is part of what is intended in calling Him "all-good," while perfect freedom is but another term for his omnipotence. Yet no theist fears that in making the assertion of God's omnipotence and all-goodness he is in danger of self-contradiction.[22] The fact that part of theistic belief contains precisely a model for a perfectly good and perfectly free agent is in striking contrast to the insistence of free will defenders that these are strictly incompatible.

The free will defenders might reply that their thesis of inconsistency is intended only as an account of human freedom, that the case with God is understandably different. Since man is a creature he is neither all-good nor entirely free; in fact he is limited in many ways that God is not. But I do not see why the difference between creator and creature might not prescribe different types of moral perfection—that appropriate to God and that appropriate to man—without thereby entailing the specific characteristic of the corruptibility of the latter. What has not been shown is that a moral determination of human freedom by human goodness analogous to the moral determination of divine freedom by divine goodness is impossible.

I doubt whether the difference between God and man can be so stated as to rule out the consistency of "free" and "guaranteed good" as predicated of man. For this is just the description of man's destiny in a future life that theists provide in a more elaborate statement of their belief. Man's moral perfection in that life is presented as quite secure, yet with no loss to his essential humanity or freedom. This description provides the second paradigm case. According to it freedom and

---

[21]*Philosophy of Religion* (Englewood-Cliffs, 1963), pp. 41 ff. Plantinga's account is essentially the same: "Now God can create free creatures, but He cannot causally or otherwise determine them to do only what is right; for if He does so then they do not do what is right *freely*" (*loc. cit.*).

[22]"The freedom of the Almighty hinders not his being determined by what is best" (Locke, *Essay Concerning Human Understanding*, Bk. II, ch. xxi, sec. 50).

infallible moral perfection can (and will) be, as Augustine says, a "gift of God."[23] But if God cannot do the logically impossible, as all parties to the dispute insist, then human freedom and infallible moral perfection are quite consistent characteristics. But then the reason for their not having been both given to man in his creation can not be their logical incompatibility as the free will defenders claim.

Let us look at some typical arguments which these defenders of theism use, nevertheless, to establish such incompatibility. One argument, not conspicuous in the recent discussion, might be an inference from man's present moral condition to that in which he was originally created. If evil choice is now actual, the argument might go, then it must have been possible in the created state; and if it was possible in the created state, this state could not have been one in which goodness was guaranteed. But there is no obvious deduction from the fact that the Fall did occur and was therefore a possibility built into human freedom to the claim that it *had* to be built in. This is the simplest reply to the argument, but more can be said. Even if freedom as it *was* created was not infallibly good, it was nevertheless, on the theistic account, good enough to make evil moral choice deeply puzzling.[24] Efforts have been made in the interests of the free will defense, to circumscribe the goodness of the original freedom of man. C. S. Lewis, for example, distinguishes between the self (which is capable of an idolatrous choice) and its dispositions (which in the created state were good).[25] But what is this self abstracted from its moral disposition and practice? Lewis answers: It is "the 'weak spot' in the very nature of creation, the risk which God apparently thinks worth taking." This answer (and similar ones that have been offered)[26] suggests, however, that the distinctions emerge for the sake of explaining the possibility of moral evil, rather than from an analysis of the nature of man as he was created—good and upright. Certainly the goodness of the self's disposition provides a basis for the moral judgment that the fall is, in Lewis' word, "heinous"; but it also provides a "strong spot" in terms of which that fall must appear logically very puzzling. For if the human will as created by God was indeed, as Lewis claims, "wholly disposed, though not compelled, to turn to God," how can the will so disposed ever be said to *fail* to turn to God, without suggesting contradiction?

Another argument, one that is conspicuous in the recent discussion, is that any guarantee of the moral quality of human actions on the part of divine agency undermines the freedom in which those actions are performed. This freedom is never, at least *prima facie,* independent of God, for the doctrine of creation asserts that God is the ultimate origin of all things that exist besides himself. But if freedom originates in a creative act of God, and the occurrence of evil is traced to

---

[23]*City of God,* Bk. XXII, ch. 30.

[24]"In the developed doctrine, then, it is claimed that Man, as God made him, was completely good and completely happy, but that he disobeyed and became what we now see. . . . We have no idea in what particular act, or series of acts, the self-contradictory, impossible wish found expression" (Lewis, *op. cit.,* pp. 60, 68). Augustine's perplexity is well known; see *City of God,* Bk. XII, ch. 6.

[25]Lewis, *op. cit.,* pp. 68 ff.

[26]St. Augustine refers on one occasion to the created will as "some intermediate quality which can be called neither folly nor wisdom" (*On Free Will,* Bk. III, ch. xxiv, sec. 71; see also Bk. II, ch. xviii, secs. 47–50). And Leibniz declares: "For we must consider that there is an *original imperfection in the creature* before sin, because the creature is limited in its essence" (*op. cit.,* sec. 20).

freedom, we clearly must trace the occurrence of evil ultimately to God. Free will defenders reply by distinguishing between two senses of freedom: freedom as it is created by God and freedom as it is the source of human acts. Thereby they can also undercut any argument tracing evil to God, if that should happen to be part of their motivation. Alvin Plantinga, for example, argues:

> And (5b) ["God creates free men and brings it about that they always freely do what is right."], of course, is not consistent; for if God *brings it about* that the men He creates always do what is right, then they do not do what is right freely.[27]

The only way this argument can hold is through the distinction of two senses of freedom just mentioned: one according to which God creates free men (where freedom is clearly dependent upon God); and the other according to which freedom issues in morally right acts (where freedom's moral determination by God is rejected: "Whether the free men created by God would always do what is right would presumably be up to them; for all we know they might exercise their freedom to do what is wrong."[28])

Three objections can be made against this line of argument. First of all, traditional Christian apologists, as far as I have been able to determine, do not find anything logically inconsistent in the concept of a free and infallibly good human being. In his dialogue *On Free Will* Augustine has Evodius ask: "But don't you think . . . that, if it [free will] was given for the purpose of welldoing [which Augustine has asserted], it ought not to have been possible to convert it to sinful uses?"[29] It is interesting to notice that Augustine does not reply, as the modern free will defenders do, that it would have been logically impossible for God to have prevented this conversion to sinful uses. Since this would have been the simplest answer to give, the fact that he does not give it suggests that he did not believe it. He replies instead that the possibility of this conversion to sinful uses must have been rightly given to man since God is its giver, and God is good: "If we allow that God gave it, ought we to say that he ought not to have given it? . . . If it is certain that he has given it, we ought to confess that, however it was given, it was rightly given."[30] And in another passage in *City of God* he writes:

> For who will dare to believe or say that it was not in God's power to prevent both angels and men from sinning? But God preferred to leave this in their

---

[27]*Op. cit.*, p. 210 [p. 326]. See also A. Grave: "There is, by definition, a logical impossibility in God's making him freely choose the good on any occasion" ("On Evil and Omnipotence," *Mind*, vol. 65 [1956], p. 260).

[28]Plantinga, *op. cit.*, p. 211 [p. 326]. Descartes distinguishes between the "faculty" of freedom and its "operation" in *Meditations*, No. IV.

[29]*On Free Will*, Bk. II, ch. i, sec. 4.

[30]*Loc. cit.* Compare Descartes: "I perceive, nevertheless, that it would have been easy for God to contrive that I would never make mistakes, even though I remained free and with limited knowledge" (*op. cit.*). And Leibniz: "But since he has permitted vice, it must be that that order of the universe which was found preferable to every other plan required it. One must believe that it is not permitted to do otherwise, since it is not possible to do better. It is a hypothetical necessity, a moral necessity, which, far from being contrary to freedom, is the effect of its choice" (*op cit.*, sec. 124).

power, and thus to show both what evil could be wrought by their pride, and what good by His grace.[31]

This is an even clearer rejection of the contemporary free will defense argument from logical impossibility. Though it includes an indeterministic characterization of created freedom, it defends such a characterization by reference to the goodness of divine intentions, not to the logical limitations on his omnipotence.

Secondly, by affirming the independence of the moral character of the created will from God in order to preserve its freedom, the argument proves too much in that it prevents God's authorship of the good that men do. This flies in the face of the universal attribution by theists of all good, including the good men do, to God:

> For when I am evil, then to confess to Thee, is nothing else than to be displeased with myself; but when holy, nothing else than not to ascribe it to myself: because Thou, O Lord, blessest the godly, but first Thou justifieth him when ungodly.[32]

Thirdly, the distinction between freedom as created by God and freedom as it issues in moral acts appears to be made, in Deistic fashion, between the mere existence of freedom and its function (reminiscent of Lewis' distinction between the mere self and its dispositions). But if freedom is one thing and its exercise another, the suggestion is that behind (underneath?) the freedom given by God is another, hidden freedom in man, which may or may not exercise the God-given freedom in a certain way. And this exposes the free will defense to a very forceful objection, viz., that it is bound to set a limit to God's control over the course of human events. But any such limit will conflict with the theist's belief in providence—that all things, including human history and destiny, are under that control. In Augustine's words:

> For He cannot truly be called Almighty if He cannot do whatsoever he pleases, or if the power of His almighty will is hindered by the will of any creature whatsoever.[33]

But if it is true that the moral choices of men are simply "up to" them, as Plantinga says, it would seem to follow that at least some things are not up to God. How then will God accomplish his benevolent purposes? On what ground will the pious man come to trust Him?[34] If the free will defense, then, succeeds in removing any alleged contradiction in God's being said to cause the men he creates always to do what is right, it does so only at the price of introducing another contradiction: one between "all things are contingent upon the will of

---

[31]Bk. XIV, ch. 27.
[32]*Confessions*, Bk. X, ch. 2.
[33]*Enchiridion*, sec. XCVI.
[34]"We know that in everything God works for good with those who love him, who are called according to his purpose" (St. Paul, *Letter to the Romans*, 8:28 [R.S.V.]).

God" and "some things are not contingent upon the will of God." This is no small price to pay for defenders of theism whose predominant motive is precisely to avoid what they take to be a self-contradiction in the concept of an infallibly good, free person.

Efforts have been put forth—unsuccessfully, as I think—to avoid paying the price of an open rejection of divine omnipotence, even though such a rejection appears to be entailed by the free will defense. A. Grave, although he admits that "part of the meaning of omnipotent is 'always able to control everything'," goes on to distinguish between an act (which is left to be determined by the human self) and its consequences (which are "bent" toward fulfilling the divine purpose).[35] But this will not succeed, for it leaves the most important aspect of the events in question, namely their origin in human choice, frankly outside the very control which is said, nevertheless, to be universal in scope. Pike utilizes the distinction between moral responsibility and moral blame, openly admitting, as we have already seen, the possibility that God is an evil-doer.[36] Though Pike does not discuss (in the article cited) the problem of freedom, he could, by attributing responsibility but not blame for the evil acts of men to God, still preserve the omnipotence and universal control which Grave must compromise.

I should now like to raise an objection to the free will defense which is quite different from all those above. It is, simply, that the defense takes for granted the very entailment rules that are in dispute. For quite clearly there is no *formal* contradiction between "God determines that men always act rightly" and "men act rightly freely." How then is the contradiction established for the sake of the free will defense? In the same way, interestingly, that such contradiction is avoided by others who seek to ruin that defense—by an appeal to the *meaning* of the terms. Compare the following accounts:

> . . . to say that a person could have helped doing something is not to say that what he did was in principle unpredictable nor that there were no causes anywhere which determined that he would as a matter of fact act in this way. It is to say that *if* he had chosen to do otherwise he would have been able to do so; that there were alternatives, within the capacities of one of his physical strength, of his I.Q., with his knowledge, and open to a person in his situation.[37]

> When we say that Jones acts freely on a given occasion, what we say entails, I should think, *that either* his action on that occasion is *not* causally determined or he has performed some other undetermined action which is a causal ancestor of the one in question.[38]

Here are set forth two quite conflicting views of the logic (meaning) of the terms "free" and "determined." In one view (Flew's) "free" is consistent with "deter-

---

[35]Grave, *op. cit.,* p. 261.
[36]Pike, *op. cit.,* p. 119.
[37]"Divine Omnipotence and Human Freedom" in A. Flew and A. MacIntyre, *op. cit.,* p. 150. For a similar view, see C. Ducasse: *A Philosophical Scrutiny of Religion* (New York, 1953), p. 378.
[38]Plantinga, *op. cit.,* p. 207.

mined"; it is held that a given act can be accounted for with both terms without contradiction. In the other view (Plantinga's) "free" is inconsistent with "determined," and thus equivalent to "undetermined"; that is, it is held that a given act can never be accounted for with both terms without contradiction. The heart of the free will issue turns, therefore, on semantic or conceptual, not propositional analysis. Having opened this possibility, Plantinga proceeds to avoid it as irrelevant:

> The Free Will Defender claims that the sentence "not all free actions are causally determined" expresses a necessary truth; Flew denies this claim. This strongly suggests that Flew and the Free Will Defender are not using the words "free" and "freedom" in the same way, and I *think* it is Flew who is using these words in a non-standard, unordinary way. But we need not try to resolve that issue; for the Free Will Defender can simply make Flew a present of the word "freedom" and state his case using other locutions.[39]

This will not do; at least some concrete example ought to be provided for "using these words in a standard, ordinary way"—more accurately, for using these words in a standard, ordinary *theist* way. This is what Flew intended to do in bringing forth his "paradigm case" analysis which, according to him, reveals the compatibility of the usage of "free" and "determined" even outside a theistic context. This was also my point above in advancing the paradigm cases which, by contrast with Flew's, are taken from within theistic belief. To reply that the usage of the terms in the instances cited (God, and man in his future life) is unordinary would only be tendentious; it certainly is ordinary for many traditional theists. Instead of taking for granted one logic of the terms "free" and "determined" and building their case upon it, the free will defenders should first defend the logic itself, from within theism as a whole.[40]

There appear to be, then, two simply irreconcilable views on the free will issue, very much as we discovered to be the case with the nature of good and evil. Again we can name one of the views, the one which sustains the free will defense, the "Incompatibility View," since according to it freedom and determinism are contrary concepts. If an act (right or wrong) is performed freely, it is thereby performed with no prior divine guarantees as to its rightness or wrongness; for there to have been such a guarantee would have ruled out its being a free act. This view is derived, I would venture, as a generalization from those experiences in which we find a force outside our control preventing us from effecting something by our own will. In such instances our "being determined" or "caused" entails our "being unfree." In those cases, however, where such a conflict between being determined and being free is not *noticed* or *felt,* we easily suppose that the action in question is within our control and *thereby* not determined. Indeed, when we take a broader view of ourselves as part of a larger whole this supposition is even apt to raise a doubt in our minds in regard to our sense of the

---

[39] *Loc. cit.*

[40] Some theists, indeed, even speak of *evil* choices being free yet determined: "We have also laid down a distinction between coaction and necessity, from which it appears that while he sins necessarily, he nevertheless sins voluntarily" (John Calvin, *Institutes of the Christian Religion*, Bk. II, ch. iv, sec. 1).

universality of the causal order of things; yet from the moral point of view we prefer that doubt to a doubt of our moral freedom and responsibility. Nevertheless, from the fact that the presence of something is not noticed or felt there is no valid deduction to its absence, and hence the generalization—though perfectly understandable—is really groundless.

The other view, the one that sustains such theists as Augustine, Calvin, and Leibniz and such non-theists as Flew, may be called the "Compatibility View," since according to it "being free" and "being determined" are not necessarily contrary concepts at all. To regard an act (right or wrong) as performed freely is not thereby to rule out its being previously guaranteed (by God) as to its rightness or wrongness. This view is derived, as it seems to me, from a concern to take full account of all the beliefs that bear on the analysis of an act. In a non-theological context these beliefs are especially two, both of which undergird Flew's defense of the compatibility view: freedom of the will, and the universality of the causal order. In a theological context they are also two: freedom of the will and divine providence. Yet both Kant (in a modern scientific context) and Augustine (in a theological one) regarded "being free" and "being determined" as compatible accounts of the same human act.[41] Such a theological position is apt to raise a doubt in regard to our sense of being masters of our fate, but theists have been known to prefer that doubt to doubting the sovereignty of God.

I can now restate my last objection to the free will defense in a more positive way, as well as bring to bear on it the logic of theism as it is exhibited in the "higher good defense." Our examination of that defense revealed that theists mean by "good" something that can include evil, while sceptics mean by it something that cannot include evil. We also saw that the theistic meaning of "good" is applicable to human action only in virtue of human limitation in respect to knowledge and power, but that its applicability to divine action—since that action occurs with no limitation of knowledge or power—derives instead from the admission that evil as a matter of fact exists. This, we concluded, resulted in a mysterious sense of goodness as it is used to describe the being and doings of God.

An examination of the free will defense, on the other hand, revealed that its advocates mean by "cause" or "determine" something that cannot include "allowing to act freely," as opposed to many traditional theists who hold that "cause" or "determine," at least when used of God, can include "allowing to act freely." We also saw that the former view accords with an understandable (if groundless) interpretation of freedom, while the latter, though required by theistic belief in providence, yields a mysterious sense of causality altogether compatible with freedom. My objection, then, to the free will defense, is this: If theists generally require—or at least do not shrink from—for the sake of defending divine goodness in the face of evil, a mysterious kind of "higher goodness" that includes evil, what hinders some of them (by contrast with others) from developing a concept of divine power in the presence of human freedom, the essence of which would be a similarly mysterious kind of "higher causality" that includes such freedom? That is, if theists generally are "Compatibilists" on good and evil, why do some of them hold out for an "Incompatibilism" on

---

[41]See Kant *Foundations of the Metaphysics of Morals*, Part III; and Augustine, *City of God,* Bk. V, ch. 9.

freedom and determinism? For from a human point of view it would seem that the compatibility of the latter is no more absurd than that of the former. Is the mystery of a sovereign God who allows some of his creatures freedom of choice without compromising his omnipotence more baffling than the mystery of an all-good God who allows evil because of this goodness?

The review in this paper of two possible views (a compatibility view and an incompatibility view) on two different issues involved in the problem of evil (the nature of good and evil; and the nature of being free and being determined) reveals that there are four possible approaches to the problem of evil as a whole. First there is a consistent "incompatibility" approach which would hold to the incompatibility view both with respect to good and evil and with respect to freedom and determinism. I think Mackie comes close to this approach in his account, since he holds that good by its very nature tends to eliminate evil, and that genuine human freedom is possible only by divine omnipotence forfeiting in a special way its own power over human actions.[42]

At the other extreme would be a consistent "compatibility" approach, which would hold that both good and evil, and freedom and determinism are compatible. According to this view, any act of God is justified by some good reason, even if known to and possessed by God alone; and all human acts on this view, while freely performed, are nevertheless determined by the divine will. Augustine, Aquinas, Calvin, Descartes, and Leibniz come close to this view, for they all hold that the occurrence of evil is consistent with, and therefore justifiable in terms of, the goodness of God; they attribute all good that men freely perform to God; they affirm that man's choice of evil while freely performed is not outside God's control—it is permitted by Him; though they stop short of blaming God for men's evil acts in a way that would parallel their praising him for their good ones. This approach recommends itself as the typical theist approach because it well reflects the complexity of the Biblical data on the subject, and also because it adopts a consistent semantic policy in regard to the two divine attributes of all-goodness and omnipotence.

The third possible approach would be the rare one of combining an incompatibility view on the good and evil issue with a compatiblity view on the free will issue. This position characterizes Flew's discussion, except, of course, that he is not a theist. The fourth approach (and more prevalent one) combines the compatibility view of good and evil with the incompatibility view of free will and determinism. It is the view of Hick and Plantinga, each of whom holds that evil is justified and that human moral acts, in virtue of their being freely performed, lie outside the will of God to determine their moral character. I think it represents an atypical theist position going back at least as far as Pelagius.

The conflict between sceptic and theist is typically represented, then, in the contrast between the first two positions. The sceptic, according to his position, can successfully support his claim that theistic beliefs are self-contradictory if and only if he (the sceptic) furnishes those beliefs with what I have called the "incompatible" meanings for the key concepts in those beliefs. The theist, on the other hand, can successfully defend the consistency of his beliefs if and only if he provides "compatible" meanings for these concepts. When Mackie charges,

---

[42]On an analogy with the powers of a sovereign legislature—see his discussion, *op. cit.,* pp. 210 ff.

then, that the theist "must be prepared to believe . . . what can be disproved from other beliefs that he also holds," he will be correct only if he is referring to theists who, like Hick and Plantinga, wish to retain the "incompatible" meanings of at least some of the concepts in these beliefs. Theists who are fully armed, however, with the "compatible" meanings of these concepts need not be prepared at all to believe what can be disproved from other beliefs that they hold. At most they must be prepared to believe what they cannot understand. For divine goodness becomes an inscrutable goodness that includes evil—indeed, given omnipotence and omniscience, it actually necessitates evil. Also divine power becomes an inscrutable power that creates, controls, and rules all things including the actions and destinies of men whose moral self-determination, in spite of this power, is altogether genuine.

But then there is some evidence that theists are prepared to believe what they do not understand. Aquinas writes, for example, concerning the names of God:

> Whatever is predicated of various things under the same name but not in the same sense is predicated equivocally. But no name belongs to God in the same sense that it belongs to creatures. . . . Therefore whatever is said of God and of creatures is predicated equivocally.[43]

Aquinas continues, of course: "Neither, on the other hand, are names applied to God and creatures in a purely equivocal sense . . . it must be said that these names are said of God and creatures in an analogous sense, that is according to proportion." The success of this attempt to moderate the equivocality of the predication lies outside the scope of the present paper; I believe it stands or falls with the comprehensibility of the divine essence, which Aquinas rejects. Then there is John Calvin, to take another example, who writes concerning divine justice:

> For the will of God is the highest rule of justice, so that what He wills must be considered just, for this very reason, because He wills it. When it is inquired, therefore, why the Lord did so, the answer must be, because He would. But if you go further, and ask why He so determined, you are in search of something greater and higher than the will of God, which can never be found. . . . The reason of the Divine justice is too high to be measured by a human standard, or comprehended by the littleness of the human mind.[44]

Now it is precisely this feature of theism—that it is a faith *lacking* understanding, or at best *seeking* understanding (but at any rate *not* possessing or demonstrating it)—that both its critics and its defenders have missed in their recent concern over the formal consistency of theism. Without an appreciation of this feature these writers are bound to obscure the real issue that divides them. Mackie distinguishes, for example between "adequate" and "fallacious" solutions to the problem of evil. "Adequate" solutions, since they involve a forthright rejection of one of the theist beliefs, are out of the question in theistic

---

[43] *Summa Theologica,* Pt. I, Q. 13, Art. 5.
[44] *Op. cit.,* Bk. III, ch. xxiii, secs. 2, 42. (See also his account of *Romans* 9 in Bk. XXX, ch. xxii, sec. 11).

apologetics. In what he calls the "fallacious" solutions, however, "in order to solve the problem one (or perhaps more) of its propositions is given up, but in such a way that it appears to have been retained, and can therefore be asserted without qualification in other contexts."[45]

Now if I am correct in maintaining that the formal consistency of the essential beliefs of theism can be defended simply (and only) by applying the "compatibility" logic to the concepts which these beliefs involve, then what Mackie calls (from the sceptic's viewpoint) a "fallacious" solution must be described differently. What really goes on in theistic apologetics, he should say, is that each and every proposition is *retained,* but what is *given up* is the intelligibility of its terms.

In so far as contemporary philosophical theists insist on the formal consistency of their beliefs, they stand in the tradition of rational theology. But whether they can stand in that tradition when that tradition requires, in addition to formal consistency, the rational transparency of those beliefs—that is a deeper question which they seem to ignore. In so far as they do ignore this question they set themselves apart not only, as I hope to have indicated, from an essential ingredient in traditional theism, but also, as I suppose they well suspect, from a significant engagement with actual religious belief *and* lack of such belief in the predominantly irrational stance which both of these manifest in our time.

---

[45]*Op. cit.,* p. 202.

LOGIC AND THE PROBLEM OF EVIL: A RESPONSE TO HOITENGA
Keith Yandell

In his excellent paper "Logic and the Problem of Evil"[1] Professor Dewey Hoitenga offers reasons for rejecting the free will defense.[2] I will attempt to show that his argument against the free will defense, though lucid and forceful, ultimately fails to discredit that line of reasoning concerning theism and evil. One contention of Hoitenga's that I will not challenge is his claim that "the problem of evil is not (except superficially) a question of the formal consistency of propositions, but a question of the meaning of the terms those propositions involve."[3] From this beginning, Hoitenga develops the following critique of the free will defense.

The theist who offers the free will defense and his critic, Hoitenga suggests, disagree as to the meaning of both "good" and "free." Such a theist supposes

---

[1]Dewey Hoitenga, "Logic and the Problem of Evil," *American Philosophical Quarterly,* Vol. 4, No. 2, 1967.
[2]For contemporary examples of the free will defense, see Alvin Plantinga, *God and Other Minds* (Ithaca, N.Y.: 1967), Ch. 5, 6, and John Hick, *Evil and the God of Love* (New York: 1966), Part III.
[3]Hoitenga, *loc. cit.,* p. 1 [p. 334].

that "The world is as good as any that could be created but contains evil" is consistent but that "Jones was created as a free agent who can make only right choices" is contradictory. He opts for a "compatibility" view with respect to "good" and "evil" and an "incompatibility" view with respect to "free" and "determined." He claims that a good, indeed best possible creatable,[4] world can contain evil but a world containing only free choices cannot contain any determined ones.

In contrast, the responding critic holds a compatibility view with respect to "free" and "determined" but an incompatibility view with respect to "good" and "evil." He claims that a maximally good, indeed a best possible creatable, world can contain no evil but that a world in which all choices are free can be a world in which all choices are determined. Thus the critic J. L. Mackie writes that "good is always opposed to evil, in such a way that a good thing always eliminates evil as far as it can,"[5] whereas Nelson Pike in defending theism says that "the logic of good (if such there be) does not demand that a perfectly good person would prevent evil, even if he could."[6] It is true, as Hoitenga notes,[7] that a higher good which justifies a perfectly good God in allowing an evil to exist must (1) be dependent on the specific evil which it justifies, (2) be obtainable in no other way which excludes the evil, (3) counterbalance or outweigh the evil on which it depends, and (4) outweigh in goodness any alternative good that could be attained without the existence of any evil. Indeed, while Hoitenga[8] requires only that the evil and good in question be causally related, it would seem that the relation must be one of simple logical necessity (that the good exist but the evil not exist is logically impossible) or of what we might call "disjunctive logical necessity" (that the evil is no worse than any other member of a class C of evils such that it is logically impossible for the good in question to exist without some member or other of C existing).[9]

Again, critic Anthony Flew contends that to be free with respect to an action is to have been able to help doing what one did and "to say that a person could have helped doing something is not to say that . . . there were no causes anywhere which determined that he would as a matter of fact act this way,"[10] whereas theist John Hick maintains that "the idea of a person who can be infallibly guaranteed always to act rightly is self-contradictory."[11] I think that Hoitenga is right in pointing up these two crucial disagreements between such theists or defenders of theism, offering the free will defense as Pike, Hick, and Plantinga and such critics as Aiken, Mackie, and Flew.

Against a theist who offers a free will defense and also wishes to fully accept our moral experience, Hoitenga argues that

---

[4]On the difference between "best possible world" and "best possible creatable world," see Plantinga, *op. cit.* [p. 325].
[5]"Evil and Omnipotence," *Mind,* vol. 64 (1955), p. 20. Cf. Henry Aiken, *Reason and Conduct* (New York: 1962), p. 175.
[6]"God and Evil: A Reconsideration," *Ethics,* vol. 68 (1958), p. 123.
[7]*Op. cit.,* p. 2ff. [p. 336].
[8]*Loc. cit.*
[9]As I argued in "Ethics, Evils and Theism," *Sophia,* 1969 (July).
[10]"Divine Omnipotence and Human Freedom," *New Essays in Philosophical Theology* (New York: 1955), p. 378.
[11]*Philosophy of Religion* (Englewood Cliffs: 1963), p. 41ff.

the defense of theism rests on an identification of goodness with the will of God—an identification which, given the existence of evil, raises some doubt in regard to the deliverances of the moral sense. The theist prefers this doubt to a doubt of the existence of God.[12]

The reason why a theist must doubt "the deliverances of the moral sense," which I suppose is tantamount to doubting or rejecting some at least of one's ordinary moral beliefs, is that the incompatibility view of good and evil is drawn

from our universal moral experience; more specifically, from the content of moral obligation: the unconditioned imperative to avoid and remove all evil.[13]

The incompatibility view of good and evil is, Hoitenga claims, drawn from our moral experience. On this view, *any* genuine evil would necessarily make the world worse than it would be without that evil. Further, if a theist takes his moral experience as veridical, some things that he experiences are not good but evil and so, on the incompatibility view, would not exist if an omnicompetent Deity reigned. Patently, there is evil. So either God does not exist or the incompatibility view of good and evil is false. The theist opts for the latter alternative.

Hoitenga also suggests that for the theist God's will must be viewed as

a will that not only brings about evil but even issues commands to human beings that on occasion are in conflict with those of conscience. Since it is the will of God that is the final standard, not the judgments of men, and since men are always to submit their will and judgment to the revelation of this divine will, any contradiction between the divine will and the human is, in principle, removed.[14]

Now it is not at all clear that a theist must take this line. God is never, of course, mistaken about evil—that much the theist must assert. But if "the will of God is the final standard" means that "x is good" is to be defined as "God wills, or approves of, x," then there are good reasons for the theist to reject this line of reasoning.[15] One is that on this view "The good is what God wills," or any substantially similar claim, cannot serve as an ethical principle, for it will be a tautology and no tautology can play that role. Another is that on this view "God is good" becomes "God is willed or approved of by Himself," which is hardly a successful unpacking, one would have supposed, of what the theist meant when he said that God is good. But if what Hoitenga intends is that God's will, perhaps as recorded in the Bible, is the norm for right conduct, why can't this be accepted without rejecting the dictates of our moral experience? Apparently unethical

---

[12]*Op. cit.,* p. 5 [p. 340].

[13]*Ibid.,* p. 4. For a reply to Hoitenga's implied criticism that if all evils are justified then no one is obligated to eliminate evil, see "Ethics, Evils and Theism," *loc. cit.*

[14]Hoitenga, *op. cit.,* p. 5 [p. 339].

[15]Cf. Gordon Clark, *Religion, Reason and Revelation* (Philadelphia: 1961) for a contemporary defense of this position. I have criticized this view in more detail in *Basic Issues in the Philosophy of Religion* (Boston: 1971), Ch. 5.

commands would then have to be explained so as to not be in fact unethical[16] or a principle of "progressive revelation" invoked, or the like; but this is by no means an obvious impossibility. In any case, while Hoitenga's argument does not require the thesis that "good" be defined by reference to what God wills, it is clear that appeal to this thesis would give Hoitenga no substantial support.

We have seen that for Hoitenga the incompatibility view of good and evil is drawn from universal moral experience. The theist cannot appeal to an incompatibility view and also retain the moral appearances, because then he cannot admit the existence of any evil at all, for God's omnibenevolence (if one accepts the incompatibility view) excludes evil entirely.

Hoitenga further suggests that the compatibility view of good and evil "is not drawn from the nature of moral obligation but from the Judaeo-Christian religion which testifies to a God whose will is not only the ultimate source of all being but also the final criterion of what is good and just."[17] So the theist has no way of consistently retaining his ordinary moral beliefs.

The only *argument* Hoitenga offers for this claim is his contention that in common moral experience we find an "unconditioned imperative to avoid and remove all evil."[18] The only limits on this obligation are those of our knowledge and power. But does this support the incompatibility view of good and evil? I think not. Consider the claim, which expresses Hoitenga's contention:

(1) Each human agent, within the limits of his knowledge and power, is obligated to prevent and remove evil.

With further qualifications, this proposition (or one much like it) may indeed be true. Hoitenga seems to take it that (1) entails, or provides evidence for:

(2) There is no good *G* of great value to which some evil is a logically necessary condition.

Unless (1) supports (2), (1) will not rule out the compatibility view of good and evil. But (1) does not entail (2). Indeed, I cannot see that (1) in any way supports (2). It does not even entail or support:

(3) God (who has no limitations of power or knowledge) is obligated to prevent and remove evil.

So (1) does not support rejection of the compatibility view of good and evil. And (1) does not support the claim that God, who differs importantly from us in terms of the scope of his power and knowledge, also differs from us in that "good" applied to God means one thing and "good" applied to us means another. (On this, more below.)

Perhaps the compatibility view is "drawn from the Judaeo-Christian religion"

---

[16]The writer of Hebrews, in celebrating Abraham's faith, says that Abraham in his sacrifice of Isaac "considered that God was able to raise men even from the dead." The idea seems to be that Abraham believed that were he to actually sacrifice Isaac, since Isaac was the "son of promise" God would bring Isaac back to life. This is relevant to whether Abraham *was* asked to act "against conscience."

[17]*Op. cit.*, p. 5 [p. 340].

[18]*Ibid.*, p. 4 [p. 339].

in such a way that anyone who embraces that religion is in all consistency committed to holding that good and evil are compatible. But whether the compatibility view of good and evil is consistent with the deliverances of our moral experience is pretty hard to say. I, at least, am not at all clear that there is anything in my moral experience or reflection that guarantees that there are no goods of great value which have evils as logically necessary conditions. So I am not aware of any conflict between my moral experience and the compatibility view, and Hoitenga offers no demonstration that there must be such a conflict. So it is unclear that a theist must in fact reject his moral experience.

Hoitenga also supposes that there is a radical dissimilarity between human and divine goodness.

> God is by definition a being who *is* unlimited in knowledge and power. Thus if he is also a moral being whose goodness is understood on an analogy with the goodness of human beings who fulfill their obligations, and if he exists, his existence must rule out the existence of evil. But evil exists, and hence the contradiction in theism which constitutes the case of the sceptic. To understand God and evil in terms of our own moral struggle is to raise some doubt in regard to the existence of God. The sceptic prefers this doubt to a doubt of his own conscience.[19]

Hoitenga offers two reasons for supposing that divine goodness cannot be modeled on human goodness: (1) that if God exists and is good in the same sense as men are sometimes good, "his existence must rule out the existence of evil,"[20] and (2) the only excuse for allowing evil "is due to our limitations with respect to fulfilling the obligation, and not to any weakness or condition in the obligation itself."[21] Now, (1) simply *assumes* that an all-good being must, in virtue of being all good, prevent or eliminate any evil at all, and it is quite in order to ask for a reason for making this assumption. Apparently (2) is intended to provide that reason.

One aspect of the free will defense is the claim that freedom of choice is logically necessary to moral agency. If this is so, it is logically impossible for God to create unfree moral agents. If it is a high good that men exercise moral agency, it is logically impossible that God prevent evil choices that agents freely make and sustain this high good. This is not due to any lack on God's part, or to any exception to moral law. No moral law can require that anything contradictory be done: that doing x is logically impossible surely entails that doing x is not obligatory. Nor does this require that evils *preexist* God's choice to create free agents. Hence it is false that a being justifiably allowing evil is necessarily in "a situation where evil already exists and has to be taken into account."[22] Hoitenga may be correct in his reply to Pike, but this does not justify his general contention that God's goodness cannot be viewed as analogous to our own. So we have no reason to suppose that an omnibenevolent being can allow no evil at all.

---

[19]*Ibid.,* p. 5 [p. 340].
[20]*Ibid.,* p. 5 [pp. 319, 320].
[21]*Ibid.,* p. 5 [p. 339].
[22]*Ibid.,* p. 3 [p. 337]. Instead of moral agency, any good to which an evil is logically requisite could be appealed to here. Hoitenga, accepting the compatibility view of good and evil, could not argue that there can be no such goods.

I cannot see, then, that Hoitenga has shown any inconsistency between ordinary moral experience or moral belief and the compatibility view of good and evil. Nor can I see that he has anything like adequately defended his contention that human goodness provides an inappropriate model on which to understand divine goodness, though he (and I) will have more to say on this score in a moment. But thus far I see no reason to join him[23] in supposing that theists must refer to "a mysterious kind of 'higher goodness'" which God possesses in order to solve the problem of evil.

Hoitenga concludes his article by offering arguments against a free will defense which insists that freedom and determinism are incompatible.

He offers a variety of arguments here. One is that

> There are two theistic paradigm cases in which a person is regarded as wholly free yet entirely secure in goodness. First of all, there is the case of God himself. . . . The fact that part of theistic belief contains precisely a model for a perfectly good and perfectly free agent is in striking contrast to the insistence of free will defenders that these are strictly incompatible.[24]

This way of putting the matter is not quite correct. The relevant incompatibility is between a choice being free and that same choice being determined. Hoitenga's concern is apparently with a supposed incompatibility between being perfectly (fully) free and being perfectly (fully) good, and of course *that* incompatibility is *only* an apparent one; there is no logical impossibility that a being be both fully free and fully good. The free will arguer claims only that whether a fully free being is fully good or not is up to that being.

Apparently, however, Hoitenga is also concerned about what I just called the "relevant" incompatibility, for he quotes with approval Locke's dictum to the effect that "the freedom of the Almightly hinders not his being determined by what is best."[25] Evidently, Hoitenga has in mind some such thesis as:

(1) Necessarily, God has perfect freedom and always chooses rightly.[26]

Now there is an ambiguity in (1). It might mean either (2) or (3):

(2) Necessarily, if "God" applies to x, then x has perfect freedom and x always chooses rightly.

(3) Necessarily, if x at any time has the properties of being the referent of the word "God," being free and chosing rightly, then at every time x has these properties.[27]

Now there is no reason why a free will defender must reject (2), which allows for the logical possibility that the being the Judeo-Christian religion designates by

---

[23]*Ibid.*, p. 11 [p. 348].
[24]*Ibid.*, p. 6 [p. 342].
[25]John Locke, *Essay Concerning Human Understanding,* Bk. II, Ch. xxi, sec. 50.
[26]Where (1) is analyzable into (1a) Necessarily, God has perfect freedom, and (1b) Necessarily, God always chooses rightly.
[27]The Biblical writers are less reticent about applying temporal predicates to God than most philosophical theists are, but this is not the place to deal with that issue.

the word "God" should sometime choose wrongly, though of course it is an important part of that religion that he *will* not do so. (2) emphasizes that it would no longer be appropriate to call God "God" if He chose wrongly. Of course God must, if the phrase be allowed, possess His divinity (including His perfect goodness) "securely." But one would look long and vainly for any Biblical reason, at least, for supposing that the security involved must be that of logical necessity.

It is clearly compatible with (2) that God always choose freely (in the sense in which "x chooses freely" entails "x's choice is not determined").

I think that (3) is also compatible with God's always choosing freely in the sense just indicated. Consider:

(3a) At time *t*, if *x* is the referent of the word "God," then *x* chooses freely and rightly.

Any theist who follows Hoitenga will presumably agree that, in some sense of "freely," (3a) is true of some at least of God's choices (waiving any reservations concerning "at time *t*"). Now (3) and (3a) entail:

(3b) At every time *t* (at which *x* chooses), if *x* is the referent of the word "God," then *x* chooses freely and rightly.

If, in (3a), "freely" means "freely, in the sense of freedom in which no choice can be both free and determined," (3a) is more specific, but still perfectly consistent. It seems that the same meaning of "free" will have exactly analogous results (gain in specificity without causing inconsistency) in both (3b) and (3). If so, a theist who accepts the incompatibility view of freedom and determinism can also accept (3). The most (3) can then be viewed as saying, relevant to God's freedom, is that if God ever chooses freely (in the incompatibilist sense), He always chooses freely (in that sense), and the same holds for the compatibilist sense.

What Hoitenga wishes and needs, then, is perhaps captured if we conjoin (3) with:

(4) Necessarily, if *x* is the referent of the word "God" and chooses freely, *x* is also determined with respect to his free choice.

Since (3) entails, so to speak, "once God, always God" and (4) entails "if God, then always determined," (3) and (4) together entail "once God, then always determined." The theist who opts for an incompatibility view concerning freedom and determinism will of course deny (4), though he may (as we have seen) retain (3). And (3) and (4) conjointly supply, I think, what Hoitenga wants and needs.

He claims that:

What has not been shown is that a moral determination of human freedom by human goodness analogous to the moral determination of divine freedom by divine goodness is impossible.[28]

---

[28]*Op. cit.,* p. 7 [p. 342]. I will sometimes transpose Hoitenga's responses to arguments for the incompatibility thesis into arguments against that thesis. I am indebted to Professor Hoitenga for clarifying in correspondence both his remarks and my critique on this point.

Impossible, that is, without elimination of freedom, whether human or divine.

But something else has not been shown. It has not been shown that a theist must accept (4), though of course he will adopt (2) and also: (5) God will in fact never choose wrongly. So it has not been shown that a theist cannot accept the Judeo-Christian religion and suppose that there is moral determination of divine goodness by divine freedom just as there is (or can be) moral determination of human goodness by human freedom. More carefully, perhaps God chooses freely (as men choose freely) but always rightly (whereas men sometimes choose wrongly). Hoitenga's criticism is helpful in that it makes very clear an issue the theist must face if, in offering the free will defense, he supposes that freely determined good moral character is of the highest possible value. The theist must then not flinch in holding that God's goodness is morally determined by his freedom or provide an adequate reason for supposing that what is the highest human good is not mirrored in Heaven (or, better, that human goodness is not the image of divine). If he adopts the former course, Hoitenga's first theistic paradigm substantiates rather than refutes the free will arguer's position as a proponent of a consistent theistic answer to the problem of evil. In God, too, freedom determines degree of goodness.

The other theistic paradigm is man in the future life; in heaven his perfection is secure and his freedom untrammeled. Whether this is a limiting ideal which men eternally approach or an accomplished fact upon awakening to new life is a question on which I would have thought theists could have remained open-minded without inconsistency or undue modesty. If a theist rejects (4) and chooses also to view divine and human freedom, respectively, as determining divine and human goodness, then his view of human life in heaven will presumably be different from the one that Hoitenga suggests. For Hoitenga, man in heaven cannot choose other than rightly. On the account under review, he can choose other than rightly but does not. Different views of the relationship between divine goodness and divine freedom can thus lead to different views of the relation of the goodness and freedom of resurrected man. But Hoitenga has offered no reason for the theist to take his views rather than the alternative ones I have just sketched.

Another argument on which Hoitenga relies is that on the free will arguer's view, we cannot answer the "etiological problem: Whence evil?"

> If the human will as created by God was indeed, as [C. S.] Lewis claims, "wholly disposed, though not compelled, to turn to God," how can the will so disposed ever be said to *fail* to turn to God, without suggesting contradiction?[29]

The suggestion, then, is that wrong free choices by a will created by God cannot be explained; hence we should not suppose that any such choices occur —perhaps the very notion of such choices is unintelligible.

Evil free choices could not be explained in the sense that they would have, in Aristotle's terms, no efficient causes or, in C. D. Broad's language, no "sufficient precurser." But of course that is true of any *good* choice that was, in the

---

[29] *Ibid.*, p. 7 [p. 343].

incompatibility sense, free. Such choices have no etiological explanation, no explanation that is efficient as opposed to teleological.[30] "Why (i.e., from what determining cause) was this choice freely made?" is an utterly inappropriate question about any choice made freely (in the incompatibility sense). So the fact that one who accepts the incompatibility view cannot answer it is no objection to his view: where there is no intelligible question nothing could count as an answer.

Another portion of Hoitenga's paper defends the view that for the theist evil is, in some sense, necessary. He writes:

> For if evil *may be* justified, then, if God exists and evil exists (both of which the theist grants), it *is* justified.[31]

This much seems quite correct. But in interpreting "justified" he adds

> for if it [evil] were not [justified], the existence of God and the existence of evil together would still constitute the contradiction which the conditions of justified evil were put forth to remove. But if evil is justified, then it is also necessary, for it is the necessary condition for the good which, since God is all good, is therefore willed by Him. Given then His goodness, together with his omniscience and omnipotence, evil is inevitable.[32]

I am not sure exactly how to interpret this argument. It is an argument for the claim: (E) Necessarily, there is evil. But (E) may mean: (E1) "There is no evil" is self-contradictory; or (E2) Necessarily, if God exists, then there is evil (i.e., "God exists" entails "There is evil"). Or, it may (and I think does) have a more complex analysis.

Consider, then, this way of putting Hoitenga's premises:

(A) God (an omnipotent, omniscient, omnibenevolent Creator and Providence) exists.

(B) God will create the best world that he can create.

(C) There is a good G such that G is so valuable it will be contained in the best world that can be created; so God will create G.

(D) It is logically impossible that G exist without evil E existing.

So: (D') E exists.

Now, (E1)—the thesis that "There is no evil" is contradictory—will follow from (A) through (D') only if each of (A) through (D') is a logically necessary truth. Since there is, so far as I know, no reason to suppose that, for example, (A) or (C) is a necessary truth, and since (B) assumes (A) and (D') assumes (C) and (D), there is no reason to suppose that any of these claims [except perhaps (D), for certain

---

[30]It is perhaps worth noting that only a teleological explanation is given for the "first" wrong choice in *Genesis* 3:6ff.

[31]*Op. cit.*, p. 3 [p. 337].

[32]*Ibid.*

values of "G" and "E"] is a necessary truth. So there is no reason to suppose that (A) through (D') entail (E1).

Now I suppose that (A) does entail (B) and that (B) through (D) entail (D'). But this does not show that (A) entails (D'). (A) does not entail (C); that God exists does not, by itself, entail that any good has an evil as a logically necessary condition, let alone that a good of great magnitude does so. Nor, so far as I can see, is there any reason to think that (C) expresses a logically necessary truth. But only if (A) entails (C), or if (A), (C), and (D) entail (D') *and* (C) and (D) are necessary truths, does (A) entail (D'). [I assume that if (A) plus a necessary truth or two entail (D'), this will be enough to establish (E2).] So there seems to be no contradiction in affirming (A) and denying (D'). Hence (E2)—the claim that that God exists entails that there is evil—is not derivable from (A) through (D').

What then of a more complex analysis (E3)—the claim that if God exists and decides to achieve certain ends [namely, goods of which (C) and (D) are true] then there will necessarily be evil? The idea then will be that if God chooses a good *G,* and if that *G* occur entails that *E* occurs, then God's choosing *G* entails that *E* occurs. Since that God chooses *G* entails that *G* occurs, and that *G* occurs entails that evil occurs, that God chooses *G* entails that evil occurs. But that *G* occurs depends, *ex hypothesi,* on God's choice, so if it is contingent that God chooses as He does, it is contingent that any evil occurs. Or, suppose that it is not contingent that God chooses as He does but that it is contingent that the best world that can be created contains *G;* then it is contingent that in choosing to create the best world that He can, God chooses to create *G.* That evil exist is still contingent even though it is necessarily true that if *G* occurs then so does some evil, and so necessarily true that if God chooses *G,* evil occurs.

In sum, anyone who supposes that (E1) or (E2) follows from (A) through (D') has a good bit of arguing to do. Each of (A) through (D) must be shown to be necessarily true if the sense in which evil is correctly said to be "necessary" is not simply as a means to ends which God has in fact chosen but need not have. In that *weak* sense of "necessary," I grant that evil is, for a theist, necessary. If we so take "necessary" in (E3), (A) through (D') entail (E3). I suspect that Hoitenga has no stronger thesis in mind when he says that evil "must be a conditioned necessity," except that he will add that God's choice of a good such as *G* will be determined (and perhaps in *that* sense necessary). But I can see no reason to accept this addition.

He offers some defense of the claim that God does not make his (good) choices contingently. This occurs in the course of his critique of the free will arguer's view that freedom and determinism are incompatible. I will discuss it in due course.

Hoitenga next directs his attention to an argument

> that is conspicuous in the recent discussion . . . that any guarantee of the moral quality of human actions on the part of divine agency undermines the freedom in which those actions are performed.[33]

---

[33] *Ibid.,* p. 8 [p. 343]. Hoitenga notes that this type of distinction is made or implied by S. A. Grave "On Evil and Omnipotence," *Mind,* Vol. 65 (1956), p. 260; Alvin Plantinga, "The Free Will Defense" in Max Black (ed.), *Philosophy in America* (Englewood Cliffs: 1965), p. 211.

God is viewed as the source of human freedom, but once the gift of human freedom is made, its use depends on the recipient. This involves "distinguishing between two senses of freedom: freedom as it is created by God and freedom as it is the source of human acts."[34]

Against this view, Hoitenga makes three points: that traditional Christian apologists have frequently not accepted it, that this view prevents God from being the author of the good that men do, and that it violates divine sovereignty.

It is hard to see that the fact that many traditional theists, Augustine and Leibniz, for example, have held a view incompatible with the one under discussion carries much weight. Surely the issue concerns the viability of the competing views, not their existence; the most that appeal to Augustine and Leibniz as over against Descartes, Hick, and Plantinga could establish is that there are other approaches to the topic of human freedom than the one the latter adopt, which was never so far as I know in question.

The second objection, that men are the authors of their good actions as well as of their evil ones, seems to be a virtue of the view Hoitenga rejects. It is tempting to claim that on Hoitenga's view when the Judge says "Well done thou good and faithful servant," He will be praising Himself, not the servant. But this would not be quite fair, for on the compatibility view of freedom and determinism that Hoitenga favors, the servant is the author of his actions in the sense that he has done them freely, though God is also their author in that He has determined that they be done. Whether this is intelligible is a question worth asking, and as Hoitenga concludes his paper by asking it, I will conclude mine shortly in the same manner. For now, we need only note that for Hoitenga, too, men are the authors of their actions and presumably deserve credit for performing them, as is also the case on the incompatibility view concerning freedom and determinism.

Here, however, the incompatibility view seems to me to have the advantage. God is to be praised with respect to the good that men do in that He has created and sustained the conditions necessary for their doing it. Men are to be praised for the good that they do because they have freely done it. Men are to be blamed for the evil that they do because they have freely done it. God is not to be blamed for the evil that men do in that, for the theist, the evil produced by human choice is either a necessary condition of a good sufficient to justify it or is the product of free agency which was better allowed to be exercised than not.[35] This does not entail that the agent was justified in his wrong choice or action. On this account, it is at least roughly clear what one is praising God or man for having done, and at least roughly clear, so to speak, who did what. On the compatibility view, these matters certainly appear altogether unclear.

Hoitenga's third objection to a theistic rendering of the incompatibility thesis rests on what he takes to be

a very forceful objection, viz., that it is bound to set a limit to God's control over the course of human events. But any such limit will conflict with the

---

[34] Hoitenga, op. cit., p. 7 [p. 344].

[35] See my "Ethics, Evils and Theism," loc. cit., for a fuller discussion of the senses in which an evil might be said to be justified, and my "A Premature Farewell of Theism" (a reply to Roland Pucetti), Religious Studies, December (1969).

theist's belief in providence—that all things, including human history and destiny, are under that control.[36]

Now of course if one defines a Providential Being as one who determines every event, then any free choices, on the incompatibility account of freedom, will entail that there is no Providential Being. Not wishing to pack his conclusion this patently into his premises, Hoitenga speaks of a Providential Being as exercising control over all things. But there is an important ambiguity in the proposition (F) God controls all things, including free choices. I take it that (F) is entailed by the claim that God is a Providential Being. But how are we to read (F)? Two possibilities, at least, arise:

(F1) For every free choice C that is made by an agent A, God determined that A make C.

(F2) For any free choice C that is made by an agent A God could prevent A from making C, and A makes C only in virtue of having abilities that are given and sustained by God.

Hoitenga evidently opts for (F1), and one taking the free will arguer's viewpoint will presumably choose (F2). Hoitenga will, in part at least, mean something different by "providence" than will a free will arguer, though both will agree that (F3) God can (if He wishes) control the effects of A's choice. This is, of course, a far cry from a free will arguer having no doctrine of providence or from his denying an adequate doctrine of providence. It is not clear that (G) God controls the course of history, entails (G1) God determines some human choices, let alone (G2) God determines every human choice.[37]

It is true that Augustine once said

For when I am evil, then to confess to Thee, is nothing else than to be displeased with myself; but when holy, nothing else than not to ascribe it to myself; because Thou, O Lord, blessest the godly but first Thou justifieth him when ungodly.[38]

But this need not set the limits of theistic response to questions concerning human freedom. Perhaps it should instead cause the theist to reflect on the use of hyperbole in the language of worship and not duplicate it in the language of theology or philosophy.

Hoitenga makes a final criticism as follows:

The [free will] defense takes for granted the very entailment rules that are in dispute. For quite clearly there is no *formal* contradiction between "God determines that men always act rightly" and "men act freely." How then is the contradiction established for the sake of the free will defense? In the

---

[36]Hoitenga, *op. cit.,* p. 9 [p. 345].

[37]This provides an answer to Hoitenga's question (p. 9) how, if some things are up to human agents, men can still sensibly trust in God.

[38]*Confessions,* Book X, Ch. 2; cited by Hoitenga on p. 8.

same way, interestingly, that such contradiction is avoided by others who seek to ruin that defense—by an appeal to the *meaning* of the terms.[39]

The charge of begging the question, of course, could be returned; it weighs as much against the defender of the compatibility thesis as against the proponent of the incompatibility thesis. One of the significant virtues of Hoitenga's article is the way in which he keeps in mind and makes evident to his reader the global aspects of the problem, making clear that holding one view concerning the problem of evil as opposed to another involves one in making a whole set of claims. This is so whether one be critic or theist, and whether one opts for, say, Hick's line or Hoitenga's. Talk of begging the question in this context requires that we keep the logic of the situation in mind.

The logic is this:[40] the critic claims to show that evil provides conclusive, or at least sufficient, evidence against theism. To accomplish his task he must show, on the basis of propositions either essential to theism and/or patently true, that this is so. If the theist presents propositions which are essential to theism and/or not known to be false which are such that, if they are true, evil does not constitute conclusive or sufficient evidence against theism, then the theist has met the critic's challenge. It is up to the critic to show that some among the propositions the theist appeals to are false. Otherwise, *he* begs the question against the theist.

There is a suggestion at least in Hoitenga's article that really the consistent tack would be to adopt a compatibility, or an incompatibility, approach to both good and evil, and freedom and determinism. In any case, he holds that in contrast to those who side with Hick and Plantinga in offering a free will defense,

> Theists who are fully armed, however, with the "compatible" meanings of these concepts need not be prepared at all to believe what can be disproved from other beliefs that they hold. At most they must be prepared to believe what they cannot understand. . . . But then there is some evidence that theists are prepared to believe what they do not understand.[41]

No doubt this is so. There were also once mathematicians who were prepared to square the circle but found that they could not do so. Theists prepared to believe what they do not understand may be in the same boat—willing to do what cannot be done. There is, once again, an ambiguity to be noted. Hoitenga's thesis that (H) theism is a faith seeking understanding can mean (H1) the terms in which theism is couched are unintelligible or (H2) theists must admit, and indeed assert, that their knowledge of God is limited. An adequate but partial knowledge of God is indeed, I take it, something a theist must claim in virtue of his being a theist. He is committed to (H2). Taking the compatibility view of good and evil, and free will and determinism, comes dangerously close at least to embracing (H1).

This seems to encourage rather than disillusion Hoitenga.

---

[39]Hoitenga, *op. cit.*, p. 9 [p. 346].

[40]As Plantinga forcefully reminds us, *op. cit.*, Ch. 5.

[41]Hoitenga, *op. cit.*, p. 12 [p. 350]. He also says that "the formal consistency of the essential beliefs of theism can be defended simply (and only) by applying the 'compatibility' logic to the concepts which these beliefs involve." (*Ibid.*)

What really goes on in theistic apologetics, he [the critic] should say, is that each and every proposition is *retained,* but what is *given up* is the intelligibility of its terms.[42]

Theists who insist on "rational transparency" or intelligibility of their beliefs "set themselves apart . . . from an essential ingredient in traditional theism" and also from "a significant engagement with actual religious belief . . . manifest in our time."[43]

This appears to be a way of escaping the critic's objection by retreating, not merely into mystery, but into a noncognitive approach to religion. Theism would escape falsehood by renouncing truth values altogether. What sort of "significant engagement" would still be possible is hard to discern. If this *is* the price exacted by opting for a "consistent compatibility" approach, what better argument could be given for a theist *not* taking that approach? A theist who takes the opposite approach will, at worst, believe against the evidence, still having something to believe. But so far as I know, there is no reason to suppose that the worst has, or will, come.

---

[42] *Ibid.* [p. 351]
[43] *Ibid.* [p. 351]

Chapter
TEN

MORAL RULES AND RELIGIOUS CONCEPTIONS OF MORALITY

RELIGIOUS MORALITY

Patterson Brown

Patterson Brown, "Religious Morality," *Mind,* vol. LXXII (April 1963). Used by permission of the author and editor, Professor Gilbert Ryle.

I

Perhaps the best excuse for publishing an essay on the logic of religious morality is that so many philosophers have utterly misconstrued the relation between moral and religious concepts. This is clearly brought out in the so-called 'problem of evil', which has, according to many, conclusively disproved the existence of the Christian God. God is defined by Christians as a being whose various attributes include omnipotence, omniscience, moral perfection, and being the creator of all things but himself. But, it is argued, if any such being is supposed to exist, a well-known difficulty seems to arise. For within the world are found innumerable instances of pain and suffering, waste and ugliness, and evil human action. It therefore seems absurd to call this 'the best of all possible worlds', since we have no difficulty whatsoever in imagining ethically better ones—without animal suffering, for example. This problem of evil has, such persons conclude, undeniably falsified the existence of the Judeo-Christian God. For, they argue, surely no morally perfect being would willingly allow evil to exist! So either the Creator is not all-powerful, or he lacks omniscience, or he is morally imperfect, or else there is no ultimate Creator at all. In any case, it is held, the Christian God does not exist, since he is by definition perfect in goodness, power, and knowledge, and also creator of the world.

The enigma which we have to face, however, is that theists obviously do not believe that the presence of evil in the world falsifies God's existence. That is, the Christian both admits that there is evil around and within him *and* adheres to his faith in an all-powerful, all-knowing, and morally perfect Creator. Nor is it the case that such persons are, as it were, *forced* into noticing the moral wrongs of this world, while trying to ignore or forget them. On the contrary, Christian faith accepts as one of its most central and important dogmas that evil pervades the universe. In fact, Christianity would be patently ridiculous if there were no such immoralities; for then the notions of man's wickedness and need for redemption from sin would lack any relevance to the human situation. Thus, unexpectedly enough, Christianity as a religion would be *falsified* if the world were morally perfect. There could in principle be no Christians in Eden; a religion of salvation would be senseless in Paradise.

It may be objected that it is not strictly proper to use the term 'falsify' with regard to ethical statements; but this is not true for the present case. Both 'x is evil by standard S' and 'x, which is evil by standard S, exists' appear to be descriptive statements. And if the latter is empirical, then whether the world contains evils by Christian moral standards is a matter of fact in the straight forward sense. It is, for example, wrong by Christian standards to steal; and it is a fact that robberies occur. Thus, it is an empirical matter that the world is partially evil by Christian standards of morality. If there were no such evils, then Christianity would be falsified.

Another criticism might be that it is included in the Christian connotations of 'world' and of 'man' that creation and its creatures are partially imperfect. But this seems unlikely in the light of the notion of the 'fall from grace' of man and the world, which seems to imply that it is not part of the Christian *meanings* of 'man' and 'world' that their denotations are partially evil. This is supported by the Christian contention that Jesus was a perfect *man* as well as a divine incarnation.

We are thus presented with a rather startling dilemma, which might somewhat facetiously be called 'the problem of the problem of evil'; some persons are convinced that the evils of this world undermine theism, while others are no less sure that those evils form one of the very cornerstones of Christian belief. It is indeed a singular situation where the selfsame evidence is used to support incompatible theories. There is obviously something logically odd about the problem of evil, some crucial point which we have not yet uncovered.

Let us more carefully delineate the two arguments which seem to conflict here. On the one hand, it is often claimed that the existence of an omnipotent, omniscient, and morally perfect Creator is incompatible with the evils of this world. It would be, on this view, in principle impossible for such a God to create a world which was even partially imperfect. On the other hand, as we have seen, Christianity conceptually presupposes both that such a perfect God exists and also that there are evils around and within us. But this is only meat for the sceptic's grinder, for he will now retort that these two fundamental Christian doctrines are incompatible with one another. For, it seems, whereas a perfect God by definition could not make an imperfect world, the Christian notion of salvation demands that creation be partially evil. So that, if an all-knowing, all-powerful, and superlatively good being indeed could not create or permit any immorality whatsoever, then Christianity would be a self-negating religion. One could not in that case believe in both a perfect God and also man's need for redemption, since either would conceptually preclude the other. The problem of evil for Christianity is therefore most forcefully stated as an *a priori* dilemma; that the world actually contains evils is a broader problem, relating to theism in general.

To recapitulate, then, the ordinary problem of evil is that the imperfections of this world are *prima facie* irreconcilable with the existence of a perfectly powerful, knowledgeable, and good Creator. With specific regard to Christian theism, it appears that the notion of God as the greatest possible being is not logically harmonious with the notion of man's need for salvation from sin. Christianity seems to be a self-contradictory religion.

II

I wish to argue that the above-mentioned problems are not really fatal to Christian theism, on the grounds that the religious person means something other by 'God is good' than sceptics commonly assume. The hoary problem of evil rests on a misconception of religious morality. This point can be readily unpacked by way of another, but kindred, issue: that of the relation of God's commands to our moral obligations. A number of moral philosophers have argued that God's will cannot indicate what we ought to do, since the factual assertion 'God wills x' cannot entail the moral assertion 'x is good'; 'is' cannot imply 'ought'. This sort of howler is so widespread and so basic that one may be excused for giving two lengthy examples of such an argument. Professor Nowell Smith, for one, states that:[1]

> . . . it is a mistake to try to define moral 'oughts' in terms of God's commands or 'God's will'. For the mere fact that a command has been issued by a competent authority, even by God, is not a logically good reason for obeying it. Jones's 'thou shalt' does not entail Smith's 'I shall'; and neither does God's 'thou shalt' . . . For religious people the fact that God has commanded them to do something is a sufficient reason, perhaps the only reason, for thinking themselves obliged to do it. But this is because they have a general pro-attitude to doing whatever God commands . . . the mere fact that God commands something is no more reason for doing it than the fact that a cricket coach tells you to do something . . . the fact that you ought to do it cannot be identified with nor is it entailed by the fact that God has commanded it.

Or, again, Professor Nielsen has argued that:[2]

> . . . there is a crucial *logical* difficulty about basing any morality on religion. This difficulty has been noted and ignored again and again ever since Plato stated it in the *Euthyphro*. The difficulty . . . is this. No information about the nature of reality, the state of the world, or knowledge that there is a God and that He issues commands, will by itself tell us what is good or what we ought to do. The statement 'God wills x' is not a moral pronouncement. Before we know whether we ought to do x, we must know that what God wills is good. And in order to know that what God wills is good, we would have to judge independently that it is good. That something is good is not entailed by God's willing it, for otherwise it would be rhetorical to ask 'Is what God wills good?'. But it is not rhetorical to ask that question. 'God wills x' or 'God commands x' is not equivalent to 'x is good' in the same way as 'x is a male parent' is equivalent to 'x is a father'. 'God wills it, but is it good?' is not a senseless or self-answering question like 'Fred is a male parent, but is he a father?'. The moral agent must independently decide that whatever God wills or commands is good.

The first point which must be made, surely, is that 'God' is ordinarily a partially moral term. In our civilisation, and thus in our language, it would not be strictly proper to call a being 'God' whose actions were not perfectly good or whose commands were not the best of moral directives. That God is good is a truth of language, and not an ethical contingency, since one of the usual *criteria* of Godhood is that the actions and commands of such a being are perfectly good.

---

[1]P. H. Nowell Smith, *Ethics* (Pelican Philosophy Series), pp. 192–193.

[2]Kai Nielsen, "Religion, Morality and Bertrand Russell", *The Amherst Review* (Spring 1959), p. 15. In a more recent article entitled "Some Remarks on the Independence of Morality from Religion" (MIND, April 1961), Professor Nielsen has considerably modified and extended this argument. He adheres, however, to his earlier conclusion that morality must be logically prior to religion; and this is the point that I wish to contest.

In referring to some being as 'God', we would in part be saying that he was morally faultless. (Of course, we would also be saying that that being fulfilled the other criteria of divinity as well, *viz.* omnipotence, omniscience, transcendence, being the creator of all other things, and so on.) 'God is good', therefore, is trivially true in the same way as 'Saints are good'. We would not in strict propriety call anyone a 'Saint' who was not morally perfect, nor would we call any being 'God' if he were not wholly good. So that 'There is a God', like 'There are Saints', is in part a moral statement.

There remains, however, a crucial difference between the necessary goodness of God and the necessary goodness of Saints. To say that Saints are by definition morally faultless is to say that we will withhold the title of 'Saint' from anyone who is not perfectly good by Christian standards. To say that God is by definition perfect, however, is to say more than this. Not only would we withhold the name 'God' from any being who was imperfect by Christian standards; in addition, the appellation 'God' is reserved for that particular being who is the ultimate Christian *criterion* of the good. The saint is good because he follows God's will; but God is good because he is the standard of goodness. Thus, it is rhetorical to ascribe goodness both to Saints and to God, since only that being is called 'God' who is the supreme paradigm of goodness, and no one is called 'Saint' unless he is Godly. 'God is the ultimate standard of the good' is true by definition, and this entails that 'God is good' is trivially true. Therefore, in addition to stating that there is an omnipotent, omniscient, and transcendent Creator and that he is perfectly good, 'There is a God' also serves as a moral commitment to that being as the basis of Christian morality. So, quite clearly, the statement 'If God commands something, then it ought to be done' is pleonastic. If we are not unconditionally obliged to do whatever x commands, then x is by definition not God. Belief in the Judeo-Christian God, then, can entail normative conclusions just because it presupposes a moral commitment. In becoming a Christian theist, one commits oneself to the will of the Creator—who must first, of course, be assumed to exist—as one's own highest ethical standard.

Apparently, therefore, Nowell Smith and Nielsen do not include in their rules for the use of 'God' that any being so named would be perfectly good, and indeed the standard of all goodness. Unlike Christians, they take 'God is good' to be an ordinary moral judgement rather than a truth of language. This no doubt tacit divergence from ordinary religious language enables them to argue that the connection between that which God commands and that which we ought to do is contingent upon our evaluations. Whereas, surely, the actual religious 'evaluation', if it can be called such, is that of committing oneself to a God-centred morality in the first place. Subsequently to pass independent judgement on God's actions or commands would be a straightforward abandonment of Christian morality, since some other moral principle would then have been accepted as more fundamental than the Creator's will. So that to judge God is in effect to deny that he is *God*.

Even though the statement 'If God commands something, then it ought to be done' is redundant, however, we should not therefore conclude that it cannot serve a central role in moral reasoning. A deontic inference of the following form is basic in the Christian's ethical decision-making:

(1) If God commands something, then it ought to be done (by definition).

(2) There is a God (factual and committal); and he commands y (factual).

(3) Therefore: We ought to do y.

Or, more formally:

(1) (x)[Gx entails (y) (xCy entails Oy)]

(2) (∃x)[Gx and (∃y)(xCy)]

(3) Therefore: (∃y) Oy

Here 'Gx' means x is God, 'xCy' means x commands y, and 'Oy' means y ought unconditionally to be done. The crucial point is that, since being an ultimate moral standard is included in the meaning or sense of 'God', '(∃x)[Gx]' is partly a moral commitment; and for that reason '(∃x) [Gx and (∃y) (xCy)]' has normative implications.

It is worth noting that, since 'God is paradigmatically good' is analytically true, it follows that 'God is evil' is a contradiction in terms. One could hold *via* a non-Christian morality, however, that the Creator was evil or non-trivially good, for then the moral terms would be predicated of 'Creator' rather than 'God'.

It is clear that one cannot adopt a particular morality for ethical reasons —otherwise the principle by which such a decision was made would itself be one's basic moral standard. But this obviously does not imply that a moral commitment cannot be good or bad; it is not the case that only decisions of morality can be morally evaluated. One's reason for making the commitment must be non-moral, but the commitment may nonetheless be good or evil according to particular ethical standards. Thus, it is supremely good by Christian standards to become a Christian; but one clearly cannot decide to adopt the Christian ethic as a result of feeling morally bound by the Creator's command to do so. For if one feels morally obliged to follow God's commands, then one already holds to Christian morality. The Christian religion cannot be logically posterior to any morality.

For Christians, then, to be moral *is* to adhere to the will of God. Things, actions, persons, and so on are good or evil, right or wrong, according to whether God approbates or condemns them; this is the logic of Christian morality. If God exists, then the good is denoted by what he esteems, and the evil by what he damns.

One of the traditional objections to saying that things are good because God says so, rather than the reverse, has been that this seems to entail God's choices to be arbitrary. A. C. Ewing, for example, recently argued that[3] "if 'obligatory' just means 'commanded by God', the question arises why God should command any one thing rather than any other. We cannot say that he commands it because it ought to be done, for that would have to be translated into 'God commands it because it is commanded by God'. . . . If what was good or bad as well as what

---

[3] "The Autonomy of Ethics", included in *Prospect for Metaphysics*, Ian Ramsey (ed.), p. 39.

ought to be done were fixed by God's will, then there could be no reason whatever for God willing in any particular way. His commands would become purely arbitrary." It does indeed follow from my analysis that there could be no *moral* obligation on God to will one thing rather than another, but this certainly does not imply that God's will is capricious. For God is also defined as perfect in knowledge, justice, and love. He would thus by definition will in accord with these several attributes, and the result would be anything but arbitrary. Those who argue like Ewing neglect that there are other criteria of Godhood besides being an ultimate moral standard; and these necessarily preclude God's choosing without reason.

The Christian has two sorts of ways to find out what is good or what ought to be done according to his morality. Firstly, one can be *told* by God what is best, either directly through personal revelation, or indirectly through the Church or the Bible. (The numerous philosophical difficulties attending these notions would occupy an essay in themselves.) Or, secondly, one can *infer* by means of reason alone, *i.e. via* the Natural Law, what God would command. For we can presumably ratiocinate, at least to some degree, what a supremely intelligent, loving, and just being would will; and that is by definition what God would will, *i.e.* is morally binding.

It is perhaps necessary to forestall one conceivable line of criticism by pointing out that, although God cannot be *moral* in the sense of deciding to do things because they are good, he is nonetheless perfectly *good.* 'God is good' is trivially true when taken as a moral judgement, since the standard is being applied to itself, but it is not less true for that. The necessity of God's deciding amorally precludes neither his being perfectly good nor his commanding us to be nomistic by following his will.

III

Let us now return to the problem of evil in the light of the foregoing. The first point which has, I hope, been clarified is that the evils of this world cannot possibly disprove God's existence. Christian theism could be untenable in the face of this world's immoralities only if the goodness of God could be judged in terms of some ulterior ethical standard, stating that good agents do not willingly permit evils to exist. But, as we have seen, it would be illegitimate to hold that God could be judged in any non-trivial way, owing to the definition of divinity as the highest standard of the good. In fact, that the world is evil at all is true by Christian standards only because God says so. So that immorality cannot possibly preclude God; on the contrary, for the Christian the existence of evil logically presupposes the divine existence, since it is God who ultimately designates those evils in the first place. If God causes or allows to exist things which are evil, *i.e.* which he himself condemns, then it is good for him to do so—else he wouldn't be God. Whatever God does is good, and this includes his creating things which he censures. It would therefore be absurd to argue that the existence of God is incompatible with the existence of evil—from which it follows without further argument that the Christian doctrines of God's perfection and man's need for redemption are not mutually exclusive. Once we clarify what the theist means by calling God morally perfect, these arguments lose their apparent force. It is as if one were to point to the presence of motion in the world as falsifying Newtonian mechanics. For evil is as much a part of the Christian conception of the world, and is as compatible with the definition of the Judeo-Christian God, as material motion is a compatible part of the Newtonian synthesis in physical science. The sceptic, one might say, has in this case rejected a straw God, namely one who is good—whether by definition or contingently—according only to a moral standard other than his own being and will.

IV

From the foregoing one might be tempted to argue as follows. It appears that Christianity does not have the same truth-value-conditions as does the existence of the Judeo-Christian God. As a religion of salvation, Christianity would be falsified if there were no evil or wickedness, by Christian moral standards, in the world. It is, therefore, in principle falsifiable by the way the world goes. However, the existence of God clearly cannot be disproved in that selfsame way. Since God by definition creates any existent world and also permits it to be as it is, it follows that absolutely nothing which occurred *within* any such world could possibly falsify his existence. Whatever came to pass in the world, or even the nonexistence of any and all worlds, would by definition be caused or allowed by God. So, even if the world were morally perfect, in which case no redemption from sin—and thus no Christianity—would be possible, one could not thereby infer the nonexistence of God. It was not conceptually necessary for God to have created any particular world, or any world at all. We thus seem led to the quite remarkable conclusion that Christianity is falsifiable by the way the world goes, whereas Christian theism is not. A disproof of Christianity—by there being a perfect world instead of this one—would not disprove God's existence.

Of course, it is just this non-falsifiable nature of theism which convinces many people that neither it not its denial is a genuinely factual alternative. It is admittedly unexpected that Christianity, which logically presupposes God's existence, should be falsifiable, while God's existence itself is not. But theism is well under the old positivistic banner of cognitive meaningfulness anyhow, since the existence of the Judeo-Christian God—although not itself falsifiable—is a required but non-analytic part of a corrigible belief, *viz.* Christianity. And that is the tightest criterion of factuality which anyone would wish to defend. It therefore seems that the existence of God is perfectly acceptable as a factual matter, except of course in so far as it involves a moral commitment.

The above argument is not, however, indisputable. For the first part amounts to saying: if the world were not partially condemned by God, then Christianity would be false. This is undoubtedly true, but it is now dubious whether the Christian test of the world's relative perfection is based upon 'the way the world goes'. The Christian criterion of moral value is God, and the latter is by definition not to be found within his creation. Nor will it help to object that this is to overlook the divine incarnation in the person of Jesus. For however that may be, it

clearly would make no sense to say that Christianity was falsified by Christ's
telling us that the world was sinless. It is, in short, difficult to see what sense could
be made of God's *telling* us what is good, apart from a background of Christian
belief—which rules out the possibility of Christianity's being falsified by God's
informing us that the world was morally perfect. It does not seem absurd, on the
other hand, that humans might *infer* that the world was perfectly good by means
of the Natural Law. For if we can indeed ratiocinate what God would will, we
could presumably reason that God did not condemn any of his creation, *i.e.* that
the world was morally flawless. We might thus find out that Christianity was not
true. The falsifiability line of argument might also be pursued with regard to the
historical accuracy of the Bible; there seems to be no remaining way in which
Christianity might in principle be undermined by events within the world. But to
pursue these possibilities would be tangential to the topic of this essay.

THE "RELIGIOUS MORALITY" OF MR. PATTERSON BROWN

Antony Flew

Antony Flew, "The Religious Morality of Mr. Patterson Brown,"
Mind, vol. LXXIV (October 1965). Used by permission of the
author and editor, Professor Gilbert Ryle.

I

"Perhaps the best excuse for publishing an essay on the logic of religious morality
is that so many philosophers have utterly misconstrued the relation between
moral and religious concepts. This is clearly brought out in the so-called 'problem
of evil', which has, according to many, conclusively disproved the existence of
the Christian God." These challenging words open Mr. Patterson Brown's
'Religious Morality' (MIND, lxxii (April 1963), [367]).* The supposed "howler"
involved consists in overlooking the alleged fact that: "For Christians . . . to be
moral *is* to adhere to the will of God. Things, actions, persons and so on are good
and evil, right or wrong, according to whether God approbates or condemns
them; this is the logic of Christian morality. If God exists, then the good is
denoted by what he esteems, and the evil by what he damns" (pp. [367] and [371]:
italics original). This, in Brown's view, is a matter of a definition grounded on a
fundamental commitment. Clearly, if he is right, then the problem of evil can for
Christians scarcely arise; or, at any rate, not in its traditional form. "If God causes
or allows to exist things which are evil, *i.e.* which he himself condemns, then it is
good for him to do so—or else he would not be God. Whatever God does is good,
and this includes his creating things which he censures" (p. [372]). I want to
comment on Brown's main contention.

---

*References are altered to correspond to the pagination in this volume. Ed.

II

(*a*) If and in so far as the theist, whether Christian or otherwise, really is prepared thus to make his God's will the standard—not only of right and wrong in human action, but also of good and evil generally—then it is indeed entirely open to him to take a very short way with the problem of evil. That this is so, and that there have been and are theists and even Christian theists who are wholeheartedly willing in some such fashion to cut the Gordian knot, are both facts which have been noted in the recent philosophical literature. (See, for instance, A. Flew and A. MacIntyre (eds.), *New Essays in Philosophical Theology*, pp. 156 ff.)

(*b*) If the generality of Christians actually were, as perhaps the adherents of Islam are, prepared unequivocally to define moral and evaluational words in terms of the will of God, then it would be exceedingly difficult to explain the existence of that enormous Christian literature which labours to dispose of the problem of evil by trying somehow to justify the putative ways of God to man. (See, for instance, C. S. Lewis, *The Problem of Pain, passim,* or D. J. B. Hawkins, *The Essentials of Theism,* chap. xi: and note that at pp. 115–116 of the latter the Ockhamist view which Brown attributes unreservedly to all "Christianity" is repudiated explicitly. See too the sources quoted by McCloskey in the paper cited below.) This difficulty is one which Brown himself avoids by what is, considering the nature of his thesis, the rather remarkable policy of eschewing all citation of any Christian source.

It may be that there is some way in which it could, more or less completely and more or less heroically, be met: perhaps, for instance, by construing what to the innocent eye appear to be attempts to cope with serious intellectual difficulties as really disguised exercises in fundamental moral conversion (or perversion!). On this interpretation the aim would be simply to persuade non-Christians and incomplete Christians to accept fully the authentically Christian fundamental standard. However, since this would force us to say that most of the Christian apologists who have tried to solve or to ease the problem of evil have completely misunderstood the actual nature of their endeavours, it is, surely, a manoeuvre which we should begin to consider thoroughly only when we have been shown that Brown's main thesis is true.

(*c*) It is not within the compass of a short note to establish decisively whether or not it is. Nor can it be assumed that the necessary thorough study of major Christian documents would yield a clear, unanimous, and consistent verdict; such as Brown is taking it for granted that we have, and that other philosophers have unaccountably ignored. For there are opposing forces which may drive different Christians to opposite conclusions, or incline the same one in opposite directions at different times, or even at the same time. Reasons of the same sort as those which induce some Christians to insist that the existence of their God is logically necessary may also incline them to say, not merely that God is necessarily good, but even that goodness is by definition that of which God approves. (See, for instance, C. B. Martin, *Religious Belief,* chaps. 3–4, and the passages from Christian authorities quoted there.) But a price has to be paid for thus making God's will your standard. It is a price which, when it comes to the point, Christian writers are often understandably reluctant to incur. Certainly if you do do this you become entitled to say, with Brown, that: "The hoary problem of evil rests on a misconception of religious morality" (p. [368]). Yet you simultaneously lay yourself wide open to the charge that your religion is a gigantic exercise in eternity-serving, a worship of Infinite Power as such, a glorification of Omnipotent Will quite regardless of the content of that will. It takes a very clear head—and a very strong stomach—to maintain such a position openly, consistently, and without any attempt to burk its harsh consequences.

It is, surely, for these reasons that much of the literature on the problem of evil takes it for granted that no one either could, or would, or should appeal to the sort of standard which Brown thinks is just obviously part of Christianity. This appears to be the case with J. L. Mackie's 'Evil and Omnipotence' (MIND, vol. lxiv, April 1955) and H. J. McCloskey's 'God and Evil' (*Philosophical Quarterly*, vol. x, April 1960). Of course they do both consider various variations on the apologetic theme of "all partial evil universal good": a doctrine which is, presumably, one of the implications of the commitment that "whatever God does is good"; since this apparently includes "creating things which he censures", which must by definition be as such bad. But though they do consider the Popish conclusion, they do not explicitly entertain the possibility of deriving it in the gratifyingly immediate way available to Brown's 'Religious Morality'. Elsewhere in the literature one can find attempts to exploit the problem of evil as a means for forcing upon the reluctant Christian an unwelcome choice: between this sort of fundamental value commitment, with all its appalling theoretical consequences; and a rejection of a large part, if not the whole, of the traditional Christian scheme. (I confess that this was one of the unstated aims of my 'Divine Omnipotence and Human Freedom', in *New Essays in Philosophical Theology*.) If the generality of Christians actually were content to take their stand openly and unequivocally upon the principles which Brown attributes to Christianity, then these exercises too could indeed be dismissed as both irrelevant and misconceived.

(*d*) To illustrate the practical difficulty of maintaining such a stand consistently we need look no further than Brown's own article. He considers the objection that to say "that things are good because God says so, rather than the reverse, has been that this seems to entail God's choices to be arbitrary" (p. [372]). This objection, he thinks, can be met by pointing out that: "God is also defined as perfect in knowledge, justice, and love. He would thus by definition will in accord with these several attributes, and the result would be anything but arbitrary" (p. [372]). With his confidence visibly rising Brown continues: "The Christian has two sorts of ways to find out what is good or what ought to be done according to his morality. Firstly, one can be *told* by God what is best, either directly through personal revelation, or indirectly through the Church or the Bible. Or, secondly, one can *infer* by means of reason alone, *i.e.* via the Natural Law, what God would command. For we can presumably ratiocinate, at least to some degree, what a supremely intelligent, loving, and just being would will; and that is by definition what God would will, *i.e.* is morally binding" (p. [372]: italics original).

But on the principles of Brownian Christianity this will not do at all. For the terms *justice* and *Natural Law* are themselves evaluative and prescriptive. So either we have to read them as defined in terms of God's will, in which case they cannot refer to a possible independent source of knowledge of the content of that will: or else we must construe them in some other and more humanist way, and yet to do this must involve a partial or total abandonment of the God's will standard. This leaves us with the attributes of knowledge, intelligence, and love. Knowledge and intelligence cannot, for Humean reasons, by themselves constitute motives to action. If, therefore, the Brownian defence is to hold, everything now depends on love. But the difficulties about this particular characteristic of the Christian God are notorious; and constitute a special case of precisely that general problem of evil, which Brown undertook summarily to dismiss. (See, for instance, the first four notes on 'Theology and Falsification' in *New Essays in Philosophical Theology*.) This is where we came in.

PATTERSON BROWN ON GOD AND EVIL
Keith Campbell

Keith Campbell, "Patterson Brown on God and Evil," *Mind,* vol. LXXIV (October 1965). Used by permission of the author and editor, Professor Gilbert Ryle.

In the April issue of MIND, 1963, Brown attempts to resolve the antinomy of the omnipotent, perfect creator and the partially evil creation by showing that a presupposition of there being a problem of evil at all is that there should be evils, that for a believer there *are* evils only on a divine evaluation, so that as the being of God is a presupposition of the occurrence of evils, the latter can in no way impugn the former. This attempt fails.

Three theses are essential to Brown's position:

1. The necessarily good God is the criterion of goodness. It is only what God says is good or evil that really is so (pp. [369] and [372]).*

2. The commitment to the creator as criterion of value must be made without reference to any prior system of evaluation. The Christian religion cannot be posterior to any morality (p. [371]). The commitment must take place, so to speak, in an evaluational vacuum.

3. On the divine criterion there must be some evils in the world, or the whole Christian scheme will make no sense (p. [371]).

The first claim is necessary to his argument, for otherwise God is not the criterion-furnishing precondition of evils in the world, hence not immunized from the antinomy of those evils. The claim partially specifies the characteristics necessary to any being properly called 'God', so it partially specifies what kind of creator it is whose being cannot be impugned by the world's evils.

The second claim is necessary because otherwise God is open to judgement. Otherwise, we could assess the divine claim to be a criterion of goodness by matching his evaluations against prior knowledge of good and evil, to see if his judgement is sound. But such judging, says Brown, is most un-Christian. Only a being immune from human judgement is worthy of human worship. Only such a

---

*References are altered to correspond to the pagination in this volume. Ed.

being could properly be said to create freely, unconstrained by his own perfection, and so be omnipotent. "To judge God is to deny that he is *God*" (p. [370]).[1] So he must be ultimate criterion, not for any prior evaluational scheme, but *ab initio*.

The third claim is clearly necessary to Brown's objective of a joint defence for a perfect creator and a religion of fall and redemption.

> Had not the apple taken been,   Blessed be the day,
>   The apple taken been,   The apple taken was,
> Then had never Our Lady,   Therefore must we sing,
>   Been of Heaven Queen.   *Deo Glorias.*

Thus the first and second claims together preserve a perfect creator from the apparent scandal of the creation as it is, the second further preserves an omnipotent one worthy of worship from the antinomy, while the third makes the occurrence of evil into positive evidence in favour of Christian doctrines.

Unhappily, theses 1 and 2 are incompatible. For we can only properly accept the judgements of God as the criterion of *good* if they furnish the standard for evaluations with an import and force at least analogous to the import and force of moral judgements with which we are already familiar. Otherwise, the divine criterion does not warrant the description 'criterion of good'.

And this being so, we can only properly accept the word of God as the criterion of good if we come to trust the divine judgement above our own (or that of any other oracle). How could we come, with reason, to so trust the divine judgement? Only by finding it to be correct in a good number of clear cases, ultimately (perhaps surprisingly) correct in a good number of others, and proving, where it corrects previously held evaluations, to be the higher wisdom. And to discover all that, we require a prior system of evaluation with which the word of God proves to agree or disagree. Furthermore, without such prior evaluations, no distinction can be made between the real word of God and deceiving counterfeits.

Brown is partially aware of this. He admits that "One's reason for making the commitment to the divine criterion of value must be non-moral" (p. [371]). The above argument, if valid, shows that any reason for accepting the commitment must be moral. So any non-moral impulses to commitment are in these circumstances non-reasons. And it might indeed be urged that we are to accept God's word as a criterion, not after weighing it in any way, but as a committing act of faith. This must, by the above argument, be an invitation to a frankly irrationalist position. As such, it cannot be of any help to Brown, for it makes his whole attempt superfluous. In such a position neither the problem of evil nor any other antinomy in heaven or earth shall have dominion over us.

If the divine word is the criterion of goodness, it cannot be accepted as such in an evaluational vacuum. Whence, if theses 1 and 2 are both required as partially

---

[1] I believe, however, that Brown interprets the believer's refusal to judge God too severely. He takes it to be the refusal to admit that God's actions or judgements may even *seem* to be imperfect, which requires thesis 2. But may it not be the milder refusal to admit that any of God's actions really *are* imperfect, which may allow independent standards of good and evil, merely insisting that all cases of imperfection *prima facie* are resolved by more complete description?

specifying the nature of anything properly called 'God', that name can never be properly applied. This is, for Christians, a disaster in its own right. It has, as corollaries, that since God's word is the criterion of value, it can never be known that a religion of salvation does not offer an unnecessary remedy for a non-existent fall, nor that some features of the world (say, the natural sufferings of animals) are logically capable of improvement. As this last is false on *any* sane criterion of good, it establishes by *modus tollens* the falsehood of one or other of Brown's theses 1 and 2.

If we sacrifice 1, then the being of God is no longer a precondition of the existence of evil. Whence the antinomy of perfect creator and imperfect creation is once more an embarrassment for Christian belief. If we sacrifice 2, then God's word is subject to assessment as a criterion of good and evil. And it will count as a criterion only if it shows the natural sufferings of animals to be an evil, and further shows that causing or permitting evil is, at least *prima facie,* itself evil.[2] But then the reproach is that the perfect creator knowingly permits, where he need not, what on his own showing is evil, which merely sharpens the ancient antinomy. The problem cannot be solved by an argument to its presuppositions of the Brownian type.

The best that believers can do with the problem of evil is to claim:

That we *can* come from a prior position of evaluation to accept the judgements of God as the criterion of good and evil.

That on this criterion many former judgements come to be modified, but that none the less on it there *are* evils in the world.

But that in the end, in this world or another, when at last we see aright, we shall come to see that they are all either necessary to some recondite but greater good, or are a (perhaps unsuspected) part of that evil from which we have been saved. This is implausible enough, but it is not incoherent. It would be acceptable if the grounds *for* holding that the God of the Christians creates the world and redeems mankind were strong enough—which they are not.

---

[2]It emerges clearly on p. [372] that thesis 2 is required if we are to swallow the assertion that because it is *God* who permits evils, this must be a good thing to do.

RELIGIOUS MORALITY: A REPLY TO FLEW AND CAMPBELL

Patterson Brown

Patterson Brown, "Religious Morality: A Reply to Flew and Campbell," *Mind,* vol. LXXV (October 1968). Used by permission of the author and editor, Professor Gilbert Ryle.

Flew[1] and Campbell[2] have levelled a number of charges against my analysis of religious morality,[3] ranging from the suggestion (by Flew) that it may well be heretical and thus uninteresting, to the accusation (by Campbell) that it is simply self-contradictory. In what follows I shall reply to the various criticisms of Flew and Campbell, with the additional purpose of clarifying my original exposition.

One objection that I have to Flew's polemic is that he appears to confuse definitions of moral terms with criteria or standards for their application. Or at least he seems to think that my thesis is concerned with the former, whereas in fact it relates solely to the latter. I claim that Christians take God's will as their moral standard, not that they take 'what God wills' as a definition of 'moral'. But Flew represents my view by phrases like "a definition grounded on a fundamental commitment" (p. [374]),* "unequivocally to define moral and evaluational words in terms of the will of God" [375], "goodness is by definition that of which God approves" (p. [375]), and "'things which he [God] censures', which must by definition be as such bad" (p. [376]).

My analysis, on the contrary, presupposes the doctrine that moral terms have meanings or definitions which, not being descriptive, entail no criteria of application. So that merely knowing the dictionary definition of, *e.g.,* 'good' does not suffice to tell one what is good. A criterion of application, a moral standard, is needed as well. This ethical criterion may be hedonistic, utilitarian, religious, or whatever. Nor is this to deny that hedonists, utilitarians, Christians, etc., all share one definition of 'good', *viz.* its meaning something like 'morally commendable'. It is this agreement, after all, which enables them significantly to disagree about moral values; even irresolvable moral disputes are not logomachies. For example, if a humanitarian and a Nazi quarrel over the virtue of exterminating the Jews, it would be a mistaken—not to say a shallow—analysis to say that their dispute is merely verbal. No doubt they can both cite the dictionary definition of 'good'. But they are very likely at odds over what standards to use in applying that term, and this quite aside from any facts that may be in question. There is an enlightening analogy here with the logic of measurement. Thus, that 'metre' = df. 'unit of spatial length equal to 1000 millimetres, 100 centimetres, 1/1000 kilometre' is conceptually independent of the conventional criterion of application (co-ordinative definition) of 'metre', *viz.* the platinum-iridium bar in Paris. So that

---

[1]A. Flew, "The 'Religious Morality' of Mr. Patterson Brown", MIND, October 1965, pp. 578–581.

[2]K. Campbell, "Patterson Brown on God and Evil", MIND, October 1965, pp. 582–584.

[3]"Religious Morality", MIND, April 1963, pp. 235–244.

*References are altered to correspond to the pagination in this volume. Ed.

other criteria of length are equally compatible with the dictionary definition of 'metre'—for instance, a standard based on the wave length of the spectral line of some specified element. Unfortunately, however, it proves easier for people to reach agreement on a conventional criterion of length than for them to concur on standards of morality.

Flew claims (II, *b & c*) that it is at least dubious whether Christians do in fact take God's word as the last word in morals. It seems to me, on the other hand, that it is trivial to say that they do so. That is, I think that we would withhold the title 'Christian' from anyone who felt free to disobey God on ethical grounds, or who was willing to pass independent moral judgement on God's actions or commands. (Alternatively: by 'God' Christians in part mean 'a being whose will is taken as the final moral authority'. But this option bears merely on whether my analysis is to be expressed in terms of the definition of 'Christian' or of 'God'.) In support of my contention, I offer the following considerations. (i) Christians surely use 'sinful' and 'morally wrong' interchangeably, *salva veritate* (though not, of course, *salva significatione*); thus the Biblical assertion that "all wrongdoing is sin."[4] But a sin is defined precisely as an act which contravenes God's law. (ii) In the proverbial story of Abraham and Isaac (Genesis 22), the lesson is presumably that Abraham thought it *right* to obey God's command to sacrifice the boy, despite all the obvious ethical reasons for not doing so. As Augustine says, "Abraham was tempted about the offering up of his well-beloved son Isaac, to prove his pious obedience. . . . When the divine commandment thundered, it was to be obeyed, not disputed."[5] And this unreserved commitment is doubtless part of what makes Abraham the paradigmatic Jew. Is not similar obedience, even unto martyrdom, demanded of sincere Christians? (iii) Roman Catholics hold that the Pope's *ex cathedra* pronouncements on morals are 'infallible'. Now, the rationale behind this is that there is supposed to be "a divine assistance keeping the Pope's utterances from error".[6] But no further question arises within the Roman Church as to what in turn protects God from moral error. (iv) Other moral standards which Christians admittedly employ, which might *prima facie* appear to be used in independence of God's edicts, are ultimately justified by Christians by reference to those edicts. This is true, in particular, with regard to the criteria of compassion and forgiveness, which are defended on the basis of Christ's prescriptions in the Gospels. And the Christian appeal to the Decalogue in support of other standards is too familiar to require elaboration here. In fine, therefore, I maintain that one of the prerequisites for being a Christian is that one accept God's decrees as taking moral precedence over whatsover conflicting considerations.

Just how one is to find out what it is that God commands is a crucial but independent problem. Flew's remarks (II, *d*) on this issue are penetrating, but I do not think they touch my central point. There are indeed notorious difficulties involved in the notion of revelation, and my portrayal of the logic of Natural Law perhaps needs amending. But this admission does not undercut my thesis that Christianity involves a commitment to God's will as an ultimate moral criterion; if

---

[4] I John 5:17; cf. also Psalms 51 and 119.
[5] *The City of God,* Book XVI, ch. 32; cf. also Aquinas, *Summa Theologica,* I-II, Q. 93, Art. 4, and Q. 94, Art. 5, Obj. 2 and Reply, as well as the book of Job.
[6] B. L. Conway, C.S.P., *The Question Box* (New York: The Paulist Press, 1929), p. 171.

it can then be shown that there could be no way of ascertaining the divine imperative, then this is a fault in Christian theology, not in my analysis.

Campbell states that there are three theses central to my position, and that furthermore the first two of these are mutually inconsistent. As I am not altogether happy with his presentation of these three points, I should like to give my own version of them:

1 God is the ultimate Christian criterion of goodness. Thus, for Christians, it is only what God says is good or evil that really is so.

2 The Christian religion specifies that the commitment to the creator as the criterion of value must be made without reference to any prior system of moral evaluation. Christianity cannot be logically posterior to any morality. The commitment must take place, so to speak, in an evaluational vacuum.

3 On the divine criterion there must be some evils in the world, or the whole Christian scheme of salvation will make no sense.

Now, it seems to me that 1 and 2 are *equivalent claims.* Campbell, on the other hand, writes (p. [378]):

Unhappily, theses 1 and 2 are *incompatible* [my italics]. . . . We can only properly accept the word of God as the criterion of good if we come to trust the divine judgment above our own (or that of any other oracle). How could we come, with reason, to so trust the divine judgement? Only by finding it to be correct in a good number of clear cases, ultimately (perhaps surprisingly) correct in a good number of others, and proving, where it corrects previously held evaluations, to be the higher wisdom. And to discover all that, we require a prior system of evaluation with which the word of God proves to agree or disagree. . . . Any reason for accepting the commitment [to God] must be moral.

I cannot see how this criticism is to avoid a vicious regress rejoinder. It surely cannot be the case that moral criteria must invariably be acquired in the context of a prior system of evaluation, or else every moral agent would have to be involved in an infinite regress of *actually accepted* moral standards. Since this consequence is patent nonsense, it follows that the very possibility of morality depends upon the possibility of having an ethical criterion which was not adopted by passing a moral judgement on it. And of course this actually happens in any number of familiar cases—particularly where a person is raised from infancy to adhere to a certain moral code, and so never *adopts* it at all, for either moral or non-moral reasons; he is simply *caused* to have it. And I wish to suggest that religious conversion of an adult can involve his intentionally adopting a moral system for non-moral reasons; so, for example, one's reason might be to avoid a supposed damnation, but yet without the antecedent judgement that avoiding damnation is obligatory. Campbell's contention would therefore have to be that acquiring God's will as a moral standard is essentially different from acquiring *e.g.* a utilitarian standard, in that the latter can be accomplished without presupposing a prior morality, whereas the former cannot. I myself can see no reason for holding this.

GOD AND THE GOOD[1]

Patterson Brown

Patterson Brown, "God and the Good," *Religious Studies*, vol. 2, no. 2 (April 1967). Used by permission of the author and Cambridge University Press.

I

First, a paradox, a problem in the problem of evil. I shall call it 'the paradox of evil'.

On the one hand it is of course widely held that the evils in the world present an insuperable difficulty for Judeo-Christian theism. Russell, to take a conspicuous example, challenges any orthodox believer to visit the bedside of a child terminally ill with cancer and yet to retain his faith without hypocrisy (cf. 'Why I am not a Christian'). No paradox here; just the familiar problem of evil.

But on the other hand evils in the world are a necessary condition of Judeo-Christian theism. These religions are, after all, essentially religions of redemption from evil. Both the Hebrew notion of a chosen people and the Christian notion of personal salvation logically presuppose that the world is morally imperfect. One has but to recall Jonathan Edwards' fearsome sermon, 'Sinners in the Hands of an Angry God', to be reminded of the fact that the pious are characteristically among the most outspoken muckrakers, and furthermore that they invariably point to the muck as one weighty and indispensable reason *for* religious belief. So that both Judaism and Christianity would be conclusively falsified if the world were a moral utopia. We would have no need of redemption if we were already in paradise.

Now this is a genuine paradox: that the world's moral faults should apparently both falsify Judeo-Christian belief and also be entailed by such belief. The same body of evidence surely cannot both weigh against the religious view and also be a necessary condition of it!

Not, that is, unless the view is inconsistent. For one obvious conclusion which might be drawn from the foregoing paradox of evil is that Judaism and Christianity are each self-contradictory. Just as a figure's having corners both precludes its being a round square and is entailed by its being a round square, so similarly the world's containing evils both precludes its being the creation of an omniperfect redeeming being and is entailed by its being the creation of such a being. For a figure's having corners precludes its being round, but its having corners is entailed by its being square. And the world's containing evils precludes its being the creation of an omniperfect being, but its containing evils is entailed by its being the creation of a redeeming being. In both cases, we might think, the fact that the selfsame evidence counts both for and against the hypothesis suffices to show that the hypothesis is incoherent. So that 'omniperfect redeemer' would be as self-contradictory as 'round square'.

More formally: if a piece of evidence *E* both confirms (is entailed by) an

---

[1]This essay represents an attempt to give a unified presentation of the thesis advanced in my 'Religious Morality' (*Mind*, April 1963) and 'Religious Morality: A Reply to Flew and Campbell' (*Mind*, October 1968).

hypothesis *H* and also falsifies that hypothesis, then *H* is inconsistent. The former circumstance is expressed by

(*a*) *H* entails *E*

and the latter by

(*b*) *E* entails not-*H*.

Taking the contrapositive of (*b*), we derive

(*c*) *H* entails not-*E*.

And then conjoining (*a*) and (*c*) yields

(*d*) *H* entails (*E* and not-*E*),

which amounts to a *reductio ad absurdum* of *H*. The paradox of evil is stated by letting *H* be the hypothesis that the world has been created by an omniperfect and redeeming being, and letting *E* be the evidence that the world contains evils.

I suggest that this purely *a priori* difficulty is a focal dilemma for Judaism and Christianity; the venerable problem of evil, arising from the actual presence of evils in the world, is a related but separate matter. Since it is axiomatic to orthodox theism that God is both omniperfect and redeeming, it follows that if these attributes are conceptually incompatible then Judeo-Christian theism is rendered internally inconsistent.

In what follows I propose to resolve this paradox as well as to solve the traditional problem of evil. In part II I shall make some general remarks about morality, with the particular purpose of drawing a parallel between moral discourse and some other familiar—and perhaps less suspect—areas of language. Then, in III, I shall apply the fruits of this discussion to the case of religious morality. And finally, in IV, I shall delineate the consequences of this analysis for the problem of evil and for the paradox of evil.

II

R. M. Hare and others have recently urged that a distinction can profitably be drawn regarding moral discourse between the meanings of terms (i.e. the entries following them in the dictionary) and the criteria or rules for their application to things, events, and so forth in the world. I want to clarify and defend this distinction by showing how it arises in other, quite disparate, areas of language.

In regard to words like 'chair' and 'to drink', there is a very intimate connection between meanings and criteria. Giving the meaning of 'chair' includes giving rules for applying that word to objects in the world, and giving the meaning of 'to drink' includes giving rules for applying that word to events in the world. (I say 'includes' rather than 'consists in' because syntactical information is doubtless also required.)

However, some common words have the noteworthy feature that their dictionary entries, their meanings, do not provide criteria of application, and yet the words are properly applied to things, events, etc. in a rule-following way. It is just that the meanings of these words neither immediately give nor do they entail what these application rules are to be. And hence we are forced to stipulate criteria for these terms in a way that is quite arbitrary from a logical point of view.

One example of this last-mentioned linguistic phenomenon is provided by the whole system of metric terms. Thus 'millimetre' is defined as 'thousandth part of a metre', 'centimetre' as 'hundredth part of a metre', 'kilometre' as 'one thousand metres'. But when we turn to the entry for 'metre' itself, we find only 'unit of length in the metric system'. These words all have admirably clear and unambiguous meanings, but their meanings obviously do not provide criteria for applying the words to the physical world. Such a criterion (or co-ordinative definition, in Reichenbach's phrase) is conventionally given by two scratches on a certain platinum-iridium bar in Paris.

To say that a table is one metre wide is to say that the distance between its edges is the same as the length of the standard metre, whatever that standard may be. Granted our actual metric criterion, a table is a metre wide if and only if its edges would be coincident with the scratches on the Parisian bar were the table and bar brought together. However, to say that those scratches are exactly one metre apart is simply to state the standard; it is not to say anything about a possible measurement of that bar in turn. Yet of course other criteria of metric length would be equally possible, equally compatible with the meaning of 'metre'—for instance, we could have a standard based on the wave length of some specified element.

The statement 'The scratches on the platinum-iridium bar in Paris are one metre apart' thus cannot accurately be characterised as either empirical or necessary. It is nonetheless a true statement, since it occurs in inferences like:

The scratches on the bar in Paris are one metre apart.

The table edges are just as far apart as the scratches on the bar in Paris.

Therefore, the table edges are one metre apart.

But the first premise here, the statement of the metric standard, can itself be neither tested by measurement (as can 'The table edges are one metre apart') nor demonstrated as necessary (as can 'A hundred centimetres are one metre'). The statement of the standard is simply stipulated to be true as it were synthetic *a priori*. Not that such stipulations are totally arbitrary, however; on the contrary, very good reasons can be adduced for using a platinum-iridium bar rather than a copper bar or a rubber bar. Such reasons just do not amount to empirical or formal proofs.

Another set of words the meanings of which do not yield criteria of application, and yet which are systematically applied, is the group of monetary terms. Visitors to Great Britain laboriously learn that there are twelve pence to the shilling, two shillings to the florin, five shillings to the crown, twenty shillings to the pound, and twenty-one shillings to the guinea. The dictionary entries for these various terms thus define them all ultimately in terms of 'pound Sterling', which itself is defined as 'unit of value in the British monetary system'. But what is the value of the pound? What is the standard for this whole system of currency—as we might say, the criterion of application for the British monetary terms? The answer to this question is simply not to be found in the dictionary. A pound Sterling is worth, not one pound of silver, but rather .08 oz. of gold, as stipulated by H. M. Government. And of course good economic reasons can be given for retaining or changing this standard, even though no empirical or logical proofs are possible.

Now moral words seem in some ways to be like metric and monetary words. They too have meanings which do not provide criteria for their application, and yet they are properly applied to things, events, and so on in a systematic way. One can all too easily know the intertwining dictionary entries for 'good', 'right', 'obligatory', 'commendable', 'evil', 'wrong', 'prohibited', 'condemnable', etc., and yet be confused about or simply ignorant of standards for their application. Knowing the meanings of moral terms does not suffice in a search for what is moral. One must in addition have moral standards—rules like 'Pleasure is the good' or 'Intellectualism is the good' or 'Arianism is the good', or 'Altruism is the good'. Such rules emphatically do not *define* 'good'; rather, they provide alternative *criteria of application* for that term—just as 'The metal bar in Paris is one metre long' states a criterion and not a definition of 'metre'.

One vital difference between the metric and monetary examples and the case of morals, however, is this. In the former cases there is universal agreement concerning the standards of application, and there are even universally recognised groups of persons whose office it is to make such stipulations—scientific and governmental committees. But in morals there is widespread and fundamental disagreement, not only over whether this is good or bad and whether that is right or wrong, but also over the very standards to be used in deciding such individual cases. Alas, it proves much easier for men to reach agreement on metric and monetary standards than on a moral standard.

This analysis, I think, explains how it can happen that hedonists, Roman Catholics, utilitarians, nazis, marxists, and so on all mean one and the same thing by a given moral term and yet are so commonly at odds over its application. This basic concord about meanings enables them significantly to disagree over moral values; even irresolvable ethical disputes are not logomachies. It is rather as if in metrics different people employed various standards of length in making measurements, and hence got differing results. It would be a mistaken—not to say a shallow—contention to suggest that when people are locked in moral combat there must be a verbal equivocation between them. For it is one of the primary functions of moral language to give expression to non-trivial debate over what ought to be done, who is good, and the like. Conflict concerning the facts of a case and conflict concerning the standards to be used in judging it are together quite adequate to account for the frequency of moral dispute; no further explanations which posit verbal equivocation are either needed or credible.

Two further parallels between metrics and morals:

(1) In both spheres there ordinarily occurs a regress of justifications in applying a term, but such regresses must, needless to say, be finite. So, for example, if I claim that a certain table is one metre wide, I might justify this by measuring with a readily available wooden metre stick. But the latter's being a metre long can in turn be justified—perhaps by reference to a more finely marked metal metre stick. And that in turn could be justified by an appeal to the accuracy of the machine used in producing it, and so on and on—back ultimately, however, to the bar in Paris, where all metric justifications come to an end. In

similar fashion, if someone claimed that smoking cigarettes is immoral, he might offer as justification that cigarettes are carcinogens and that the suffering and mortality caused by cancer are evil. That suffering and death are evil could in turn be supported by reference to the general happiness of mankind. And there his justifications might explicitly cease were he an utilitarian. Were he a baptist they would no doubt cease elsewhere. That one must stop somewhere, have some *ultimate* standard, is, I submit, no more pernicious in morals than it is in metrics.

(2) There appear to be only the very loosest conceptual restrictions on possible standards in both metrics and morals. In both cases, of course, there are parameters of appropriateness: a metric criterion must have to do with spatial distances, and a moral criterion with the affairs of living beings. But one could without conceptual error utilise a rubber bar as a metric standard. It would admittedly be foolish to prefer such a standard over a platinum-iridium rod. Being foolish, however, is not being illogical. Just so, one could be foolish enough to employ an ouija board as a moral criterion—insanity perhaps, but hardly a logical or linguistic confusion.

A few closing remarks about morals in general. Firstly, I have not meant to suggest that everyone who makes moral judgements utilises one or another clearly delineated criterion in all his moral decisions. Epicurus, Augustine, Bentham, Lenin, and Hitler all had very precise moral standards, but many persons have muddled and ambiguous and even multiple criteria—especially in eras of rapid social change such as our own. This phenomenon, far from undermining the foregoing analysis, is best described in terms of it. Secondly, neither do I wish to suggest that this analysis of morals in any way portrays a chronological sequence in the ordinary acquisition of a morality. One does not first learn the meanings of moral words and then proceed to adopt moral criteria. This distinction rather appears as the fruit of philosophical investigation. Thirdly, I intentionally pass over the vexed question of whether one's moral standards could in principle be given reasonable—albeit neither empirically nor formally demonstrative—support, or whether, on the contrary, only their causal origins could be adduced.

III

Jews and Christians are defined in part as persons who take God's word—or what they suppose to be God's word—as the last word in morals. In short, they utilise God's will as an ultimate moral standard. That is, I think that no one could properly be called a 'Jew' or 'Christian' if he felt free to disobey God on ethical grounds, or brazenly defended as good things which God condemned and as evil things which God commended, or who was willing to pass independent judgment on God's actions or commands. (An alternative formulation of my thesis would be to say that 'God' in part means 'a being whose will is to be taken as the final moral authority'. But this option bears merely on whether my analysis is to be expressed in terms of the definition of 'Judeo-Christian' or of 'God'.)

The following abbreviated arguments suffice, I think, to prove my point.

(1) Jews and Christians use 'sinful' and 'morally wrong' interchangeably, *salva veritate* (though not, of course, *salva significatione*); hence the Biblical

assertion that 'all wrongdoing is sin' (1 John 5:17). But a sin is by definition an act which contravenes God's law.

(2) In the proverbial story of Abraham and Isaac (Genesis 22), the lesson is presumably that Abraham thought it *right* to obey God's directive to sacrifice the boy, despite all the obvious reasons for not doing so. Augustine writes: 'Abraham was tempted about the offering up of his well-beloved son Isaac, to prove his pious obedience. . . . When the divine commandment thundered, it was to be obeyed, not disputed' (*The City of God,* XVI, 32). Is not this unreserved moral commitment part of what makes Abraham the paradigmatic Jew? Similar obedience, even to the point of martyrdom, is well known to be demanded of Christians. (Job provides a parallel moral.)

(3) Roman Catholics hold that the Pope's *ex cathedra* pronouncements on morals are 'infallible'. The rationale behind this is that God is supposed to protect the Pope from error on such matters. But no question arises within the Roman Church as to what in turn protects God from moral error.

(4) Protestants are noted for their appeal to Biblical passages to settle moral issues. It is thought to be a perfectly adequate defence of this procedure that the Bible is 'the word of God'.

(5) Other moral appeals which Jews and Christians admittedly make, which might *prima facie* appear to be independent of God's edicts, are ultimately justified by religious persons via reference to those edicts. This is true, in particular, with regard to ideals of compassion and forgiveness as prescribed in the New Testament and with regard to matters dealt with in the Decalogue. It is also true in those cases where a moral judgment is defended by an appeal to 'conscience', since the trustworthiness of that guide is predicated by religious persons on the assumption that it is given to us by God.

In sum, then, I maintain that one of the prerequisites for being a Jew or Christian is that one accept God's decrees as taking moral precedence over whatsoever conflicting considerations. So that 'God is perfectly good' serves for such persons, not as a moral judgement made in the light of some ulterior standard, nor yet as a definition of terms, but rather as itself the ultimate moral criterion—just as the metal bar in Paris is not judged to be a metre long by comparison to some further rod, nor by verbal definition, but rather itself constitutes the standard whereby all lengths are to be measured. One is held to be morally obliged to do whatever God commands, and not to do whatever he prohibits. (It perhaps needs emphasising that the rule is that God should be *obeyed,* not that he should be *emulated.*) And whatever pleases God is held to be good, while whatever displeases him is held to be evil.

Just how one is to find out whether there is a God, and moreover what he commands, likes, and so on, are crucial but posterior problems. There are, needless to say, notorious difficulties involved in proving the existence of God and in understanding the notion of revelation. But these admissions do not detract from my thesis that Judaism and Christianity involve a commitment to God's will as an ultimate moral standard. If it can then be shown that there could be no way of ascertaining a divine imperative, then this is a fault in Judeo-Christian theology, not in my analysis.

What are the consequences of the foregoing for the traditional problem of evil and for the paradox of evil? Clearly, that they both dissolve. For in making moral assessments—and in particular in assessing the world as partially evil—one must be using as a moral standard either God's (supposed) will or some other, non-religious, factor such as human happiness. These two alternatives are jointly exhaustive; and in either case neither the problem nor the paradox of evil can even arise.

If God's will is taken as the moral criterion—if, that is, moral judgements are made on the basis of biblical, papal, and/or other religious grounds—then God's existence has obviously been presupposed. Regarding the problem of evil, then, the world's containing evils as judged by God's will can hardly count against his existence. And the paradox of evil collapses by the same token; if evil as identified by the religious standard does not count against God's existence, then *a fortiori* it does not count both for and against his existence.

If, on the other hand, whatsoever non-religious moral standard is employed—for example, an utilitarian one—then nothing concerning the existence of the Judeo-Christian God can be inferred. For it is no part of orthodox theology that God must be perfectly good according to any secular criteria. Evil as identified by a non-religious standard, therefore, cannot count against God's existence, and so the problem and the paradox of evil are once again eliminated.

There does remain a puzzle as a legacy of the problem and the paradox of evil, but it is notably not a puzzle in *ethics*. It might be dubbed 'the toleration problem': Is it in principle possible for an omnipotent and omniscient being to tolerate (and even bring about) states of affairs which displease him? It should be clear that orthodox theists must answer this in the affirmative if their morality and indeed their whole theology are to be workable.

But I shall not undertake even to discuss this question here. I rest with contending that the toleration problem is all that genuinely remains of the venerable difficulties about God and evil, and moreover that it is not a problem in ethics at all.

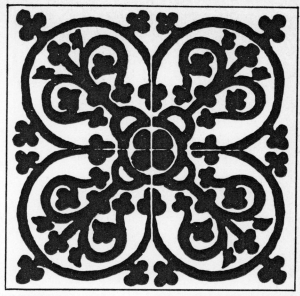

PART
FOUR

RELIGION
AND REASON

As the essays in this part make clear, there have been various attempts to prove that God exists. While it may be true that not many conversions result from reflection on such proofs, and true also that the issues they raise readily become complex enough for only a comparative few to be able to appraise them with any confidence, reflection on these proofs continues. This is so even though (see the essay by Steven Cahn) such proofs, if successful, still do not establish which moral code is right or which religion is true, though some alternatives will perhaps be ruled out. Why, then, does anybody bother with the proofs? At least for these reasons: if (at least some of) the proofs succeed, they provide support for at least some claims made by some religions; the proofs and their critiques raise many issues of philosophical importance and interest; the proofs express and clarify some religious beliefs and some philosophical theories. Since philosophy of religion is neither apologetics nor evangelism (nor their opposites, however these should be labeled), these reasons are sufficient to justify one concerned with philosophy of religion in investigating the proofs.

The great variety of endeavors to prove that God exists can be classified as versions of the ontological, cosmological, design, or moral arguments. (The important argument from religious experience was discussed in Part One.)

The ontological argument endeavors to show that "God does not exist" is a contradictory statement, so that "God exists" is a necessary truth. The cosmological argument depends on the claim that there is an adequate explanation of the fact that contingent beings exist (a contingent being is one that is caused to exist by some other being) and this adequate explanation is possible only if there is a noncontingent being. The argument from design points to the order manifest in nature and claims that the most adequate explanation of this order is that it is caused by an intelligent designer. The moral argument asserts that there are true or justified moral statements ("objective moral values") and that this fact is best (or only) explained by the existence of a Moral Lawgiver. There are multitudinous ways of expressing these general themes, and there is probably no way of being rightly assured that every plausible formulation of these arguments has in fact been stated and appraised. Nonetheless, should a number of careful formulations fall prey to the same fatal flaw, and should philosophers be unable to devise a formulation which does escape that flaw, this would be presumptive ground for doubting that the argument is successful. A "postscript" essay by Steven Cahn denies that this conclusion, even if fully correct, is damaging to religious belief.

Chapter 15, the concluding portion of Religion and Reason, concerns faith and reason. In an extended plea for the thesis that it is always wrong to believe any proposition in the absence of adequate evidence that it is true, W. K. Clifford develops his famous account of the scope of reasonable belief. Faith, apparently, is quite outside that scope; that is, faith and reason are competing attitudes or incompatible epistemic states. And so faith is irrational.

William James accepts this sharp distinction between reason and faith. It is appropriate, James says, to have faith only with respect to "hypotheses" that are forced (I must either believe that P or believe that $not\text{-}P$), momentous (I care about whether the hypothesis is true), and live (both P and $not\text{-}P$ are propositions I might well believe). If a hypothesis (some proposition proposed for belief) is forced, momentous, and live, *and* if there is no better evidence for it than against it, and conversely, then faith that P is true (or false) is appropriate. Clifford's rule is "avoid error"—so don't accept P (or *not-P* either). But "get truth" is a different rule, and under the conditions noted it is the appropriate rule to follow; hence Clifford is wrong when he condemns faith as irrational. Faith is, perhaps, nonrational (at least in the sense that if I accept a proposition "by faith" I do not do so because of its self-evidence or its possession of the balance of the evidence); still, in such circumstances faith is altogether the reasonable option.

George Mavrodes argues that the distinction between the rules "avoid error" and "get truth" holds only if a belief option is *not* forced. In a case in which I face a forced option between P and *not-P,* I am already committed to one or the other. I can only reaffirm or reverse my commitment. But in the circumstances James envisions as relevant to religious belief, there is *ex hypothesi* no evidential ground for deciding whether to reaffirm or reverse. The odds either way are fifty-fifty. So the imperative "avoid error" and the imperative "get truth" are *in this sort of case* identical. I obey *both* either way I choose (so far as I know); or, if one prefers, either way I run equal risk of disobeying *both.* The important question (one on which Clifford and James apparently also disagree) is whether religious belief is indeed forced. But if it is, James cannot successfully offer his "defense of believing."

John Hick challenges the way in which James and Clifford apparently view both faith and reason. Hick analyses "having faith" as accepting (and continuing to accept) a total interpretation, which (among other things) seems clearly to be an exercise of reason. Hick's treatment of faith is, I think, the most fruitful of the various alternatives of which I am aware. As I have already indicated, reflection on this view of faith (as well as elucidating much at least of what religious faith actually involves and getting rid of various misconceptions on this score) returns us to the issues of "comparative religion and cognitive appraisal."

Chapter

ELEVEN

THEISTIC ARGUMENTS
logically necessary existence

"GOD EXISTS" IS A NECESSARY TRUTH
St. Anselm

St. Anselm, "Proslogium," chapters II–V in *St. Anselm: Basic Writings*, S. N. Deane (trans.), 1961. Used by permission of The Open Court Publishing Company, La Salle, Ill. Originally published circa 1077.

Chapter II

TRULY THERE IS A GOD, ALTHOUGH THE FOOL HATH SAID IN HIS HEART, THERE IS NO GOD

And so, Lord, do thou, who dost give understanding to faith, give me, so far as thou knowest it to be profitable, to understand that thou art as we believe; and that thou art that which we believe. And, indeed, we believe that thou art a being than which nothing greater can be conceived. Or is there no such nature, since the fool hath said in his heart, there is no God? (Psalms xiv. 1). But, at any rate, this very fool, when he hears of this being of which I speak—a being than which nothing greater can be conceived—understands what he hears, and what he understands is in his understanding; although he does not understand it to exist.

For, it is one thing for an object to be in the understanding, and another to understand that the object exists. When a painter first conceives of what he will afterwards perform, he has it in his understanding, but he does not yet understand it to be, because he has not yet performed it. But after he has made the painting, he both has it in his understanding, and he understands that it exists, because he has made it.

Hence, even the fool is convinced that something exists in the understanding, at least, than which nothing greater can be conceived. For, when he hears of this, he understands it. And whatever is understood, exists in the understanding. And assuredly that, than which nothing greater can be conceived, cannot exist in the understanding alone. For, suppose it exists in the understanding alone: then it can be conceived to exist in reality; which is greater.

Therefore, if that, than which nothing greater can be conceived, exists in the understanding alone, the very being, than which nothing greater can be conceived, is one, than which a greater can be conceived. But obviously this is impossible. Hence, there is no doubt that there exists a being, than which nothing greater can be conceived, and it exists both in the understanding and in reality.

Chapter III

GOD CANNOT BE CONCEIVED NOT TO EXIST—GOD IS THAT, THAN WHICH NOTHING GREATER CAN BE CONCEIVED—THAT WHICH CAN BE CONCEIVED NOT TO EXIST IS NOT GOD

And it assuredly exists so truly, that it cannot be conceived not to exist. For, it is possible to conceive of a being which cannot be conceived not to exist; and this is greater than one which can be conceived not to exist. Hence, if that, than which nothing greater can be conceived, can be conceived not to exist, it is not that, than which nothing greater can be conceived. But this is an irreconcilable contradiction. There is, then, so truly a being than which nothing greater can be conceived to exist, that it cannot even be conceived not to exist; and this being thou art, O Lord, our God.

So truly, therefore, dost thou exist, O Lord, my God, that thou canst not be conceived not to exist; and rightly. For, if a mind could conceive of a being better than thee, the creature would rise above the Creator; and this is most absurd. And, indeed, whatever else there is, except thee alone, can be conceived not to exist. To thee alone, therefore, it belongs to exist more truly than all other beings, and hence in a higher degree than all others. For, whatever else exists does not exist so truly, and hence in a less degree it belongs to it to exist. Why, then, has the fool said in his heart, there is no God (Psalms xiv. 1), since it is so evident, to a rational mind, that thou dost exist in the highest degree of all? Why, except that he is dull and a fool?

Chapter IV

HOW THE FOOL HAS SAID IN HIS HEART WHAT CANNOT BE CONCEIVED—A THING MAY BE CONCEIVED IN TWO WAYS: (1) WHEN THE WORD SIGNIFYING IT IS CONCEIVED; (2) WHEN THE THING ITSELF IS UNDERSTOOD—AS FAR AS THE WORD GOES, GOD CAN BE CONCEIVED NOT TO EXIST; IN REALITY HE CANNOT

But how has the fool said in his heart what he could not conceive; or how is it that he could not conceive what he said in his heart? since it is the same to say in the heart, and to conceive.

But, if really, nay, since really, he both conceived, because he said in his heart; and did not say in his heart, because he could not conceive; there is more than one way in which a thing is said in the heart or conceived. For, in one sense, an object is conceived, when the word signifying it is conceived; and in another, when the very entity, which the object is, is understood.

In the former sense, then, God can be conceived not to exist; but in the latter, not at all. For no one who understands what fire and water are can conceive fire to be water, in accordance with the nature of the facts themselves, although this is possible according to the words. So, then, no one who understands what God is can conceive that God does not exist; although he says these words in his heart, either without any, or with some foreign, signification. For, God is that than which a greater cannot be conceived. And he who thoroughly understands this, assuredly understands that this being so truly exists, that not even in concept can it be non-existent. Therefore, he who understands that God so exists, cannot conceive that he does not exist.

I thank thee, gracious Lord, I thank thee; because what I formerly believed by thy bounty, I now so understand by thine illumination, that if I were unwilling to believe that thou dost exist, I should not be able not to understand this to be true.

Chapter V

GOD IS WHATEVER IT IS BETTER TO BE THAN NOT TO BE; AND HE, AS THE ONLY SELF-EXISTENT BEING, CREATES ALL THINGS FROM NOTHING

What art thou, then, Lord God, than whom nothing greater can be conceived? But what art thou, except that which, as the highest of all beings, alone exists through itself, and creates all other things from nothing? For, whatever is not this is less than a thing which can be conceived of. But this cannot be conceived of thee. What good, therefore, does the supreme Good lack, through which every good is? Therefore, thou art just, truthful, blessed, and whatever it is better to be than not to be. For it is better to be just than not just; better to be blessed than not blessed.

A CRITIQUE OF ANSELM
Gaunilon

Gaunilon, "In Behalf of the Fool," pp. 145–153 in *St. Anselm: Basic Writings*, S. N. Deane (trans.), 1961. Used by permission of The Open Court Publishing Company, La Salle, Ill.

In Behalf of the Fool

AN ANSWER TO THE ARGUMENT OF ANSELM IN THE PROSLOGIUM. BY GAUNILON, A MONK OF MARMOUTIER

1. If one doubts or denies the existence of a being of such a nature that nothing greater than it can be conceived, he receives this answer:

The existence of this being is proved, in the first place, by the fact that he himself, in his doubt or denial regarding this being, already has it in his understanding; for in hearing it spoken of he understands what is spoken of. It is proved, therefore, by the fact that what he understands must exist not only in his understanding, but in reality also.

And the proof of this is as follows.—It is a greater thing to exist both in the understanding and in reality than to be in the understanding alone. And if this being is in the understanding alone, whatever has even in the past existed in reality will be greater than this being. And so that which was greater than all beings will be less than some being, and will not be greater than all: which is a manifest contradiction.

And hence, that which is greater than all, already proved to be in the understanding, must exist not only in the understanding, but also in reality: for otherwise it will not be greater than all other beings.

2. The fool might make this reply:

This being is said to be in my understanding already, only because I understand what is said. Now could it not with equal justice be said that I have in my understanding all manner of unreal objects, having absolutely no existence in themselves, because I understand these things if one speaks of them, whatever they may be?

Unless indeed it is shown that this being is of such a character that it cannot be held in concept like all unreal objects, or objects whose existence is uncertain: and hence I am not able to conceive of it when I hear of it, or to hold it in concept; but I must understand it and have it in my understanding; because, it seems, I cannot conceive of it in any other way than by understanding it, that is, by comprehending in my knowledge its existence in reality.

But if this is the case, in the first place there will be no distinction between what has precedence in time—namely, the having of an object in the understanding—and what is subsequent in time—namely, the understanding that an object exists; as in the example of the picture, which exists first in the mind of the painter, and afterwards in his work.

Moreover, the following assertion can hardly be accepted: that this being, when it is spoken of and heard of, cannot be conceived not to exist in the way in which even God can be conceived not to exist. For if this is impossible, what was the object of this argument against one who doubts or denies the existence of such a being?

Finally, that this being so exists that it cannot be perceived by an understanding convinced of its own indubitable existence, unless this being is afterwards conceived of—this should be proved to me by an indisputable argument, but not by that which you have advanced: namely, that what I understand, when I hear it, already is in my understanding. For thus in my understanding, as I still think, could be all sorts of things whose existence is uncertain, or which do not exist at all, if some one whose words I should understand mentioned them. And so much the more if I should be deceived, as often happens, and believe in them: though I do not yet believe in the being whose existence you would prove.

3. Hence, your example of the painter who already has in his understanding what he is to paint cannot agree with this argument. For the picture, before it is made, is contained in the artificer's art itself; and any such thing, existing in the art of an artificer, is nothing but a part of his understanding itself. A joiner, St. Augustine says, when he is about to make a box in fact, first has it in his art. The box which is made in fact is not life; but the box which exists in his art is life. For the artificer's soul lives, in which all these things are, before they are produced. Why, then, are these things life in the living soul of the artificer, unless because they are nothing else than the knowledge or understanding of the soul itself?

With the exception, however, of those facts which are known to pertain to the mental nature, whatever, on being heard and thought out by the understanding, is perceived to be real, undoubtedly that real object is one thing, and the understanding itself, by which the object is grasped, is another. Hence, even if it were true that there is a being than which a greater is inconceivable: yet to this being, when heard of and understood, the not yet created picture in the mind of the painter is not analogous.

4. Let us notice also the point touched on above, with regard to this being which is greater than all which can be conceived, and which, it is said, can be

none other than God himself. I, so far as actual knowledge of the object, either from its specific or general character, is concerned, am as little able to conceive of this being when I hear of it, or to have it in my understanding, as I am to conceive of or understand God himself: whom, indeed, for this very reason I can conceive not to exist. For I do not know that reality itself which God is, nor can I form a conjecture of that reality from some other like reality. For you yourself assert that that reality is such that there can be nothing else like it.

For, suppose that I should hear something said of a man absolutely unknown to me, of whose very existence I was unaware. Through that special or general knowledge by which I know what man is, or what men are, I could conceive of him also, according to the reality itself, which man is. And yet it would be possible, if the person who told me of him deceived me, that the man himself, of whom I conceived, did not exist; since that reality according to which I conceived of him, though a no less indisputable fact, was not that man, but any man.

Hence, I am not able, in the way in which I should have this unreal being in concept or in understanding, to have that being of which you speak in concept or in understanding, when I hear the word *God* or the words, *a being greater than all other beings.* For I can conceive of the man according to a fact that is real and familiar to me: but of God, or a being greater than all others, I could not conceive at all, except merely according to the word. And an object can hardly or never be conceived according to the word alone.

For when it is so conceived, it is not so much the word itself (which is, indeed, a real thing—that is, the sound of the letters and syllables) as the signification of the word, when heard, that is conceived. But it is not conceived as by one who knows what is generally signified by the word; by whom, that is, it is conceived according to a reality and in true conception alone. It is conceived as by a man who does not know the object, and conceives of it only in accordance with the movement of his mind produced by hearing the word, the mind attempting to image for itself the signification of the word that is heard. And it would be surprising if in the reality of fact it could ever attain to this.

Thus, it appears, and in no other way, this being is also in my understanding, when I hear and understand a person who says that there is a being greater than all conceivable beings. So much for the assertion that this supreme nature already is in my understanding.

5. But that this being must exist, not only in the understanding but also in reality, is thus proved to me:

If it did not so exist, whatever exists in reality would be greater than it. And so the being which has been already proved to exist in my understanding, will not be greater than all other beings.

I still answer: if it should be said that a being which cannot be even conceived in terms of any fact, is in the understanding, I do not deny that this being is, accordingly, in my understanding. But since through this fact it can in no wise attain to real existence also, I do not yet concede to it that existence at all, until some certain proof of it shall be given.

For he who says that this being exists, because otherwise the being which is greater than all will not be greater than all, does not attend strictly enough to what he is saying. For I do not yet say, no, I even deny or doubt that this being is greater than any real object. Nor do I concede to it any other existence than this (if it should be called existence) which it has when the mind, according to a word merely heard, tries to form the image of an object absolutely unknown to it.

How, then, is the veritable existence of that being proved to me from the assumption, by hypothesis, that it is greater than all other beings? For I should still deny this, or doubt your demonstration of it, to this extent, that I should not admit that this being is in my understanding and concept even in the way in which many objects whose real existence is uncertain and doubtful, are in my understanding and concept. For it should be proved first that this being itself really exists somewhere; and then, from the fact that it is greater than all, we shall not hesitate to infer that it also subsists in itself.

6. For example: it is said that somewhere in the ocean is an island, which, because of the difficulty, or rather the impossibility, of discovering what does not exist, is called the lost island. And they say that this island has an inestimable wealth of all manner of riches and delicacies in greater abundance than is told of the Islands of the Blest; and that having no owner or inhabitant, it is more excellent than all other countries, which are inhabited by mankind, in the abundance with which it is stored.

Now if some one should tell me that there is such an island, I should easily understand his words, in which there is no difficulty. But suppose that he went on to say, as if by a logical inference: "You can no longer doubt that this island which is more excellent than all lands exists somewhere, since you have no doubt that it is in your understanding. And since it is more excellent not to **be** in the understanding alone, but to exist both in the understanding and in reality, for this reason it must exist. For if it does not exist, any land which really exists will be more excellent than it; and so the island already understood by you to be more excellent will not be more excellent."

If a man should try to prove to me by such reasoning that this island truly exists, and that its existence should no longer be doubted, either I should believe that he was jesting, or I know not which I ought to regard as the greater fool: myself, supposing that I should allow this proof; or him, if he should suppose that he had established with any certainty the existence of this island. For he ought to show first that the hypothetical excellence of this island exists as a real and indubitable fact, and in no wise as any unreal object, or one whose existence is uncertain, in my understanding.

7. This, in the mean time, is the answer the fool could make to the arguments urged against him. When he is assured in the first place that this being is so great that its non-existence is not even conceivable, and that this in turn is proved on no other ground than the fact that otherwise it will not be greater than all things, the fool may make the same answer, and say:

When did I say that any such being exists in reality, that is, a being greater than all others?—that on this ground it should be proved to me that it also exists in reality to such a degree that it cannot even be conceived not to exist? Whereas in the first place it should be in some way proved that a nature which is higher, that is, greater and better, than all other natures, exists; in order that from this we may then be able to prove all attributes which necessarily the being that is greater and better than all possesses.

Moreover, it is said that the non-existence of this being is inconceivable. It might better be said, perhaps, that its non-existence, or the possibility of its non-existence, is unintelligible. For according to the true meaning of the word, unreal objects are unintelligible. Yet their existence is conceivable in the way in which the fool conceived of the non-existence of God. I am most certainly aware of my own existence; but I know, nevertheless, that my non-existence is possible. As to that supreme being, moreover, which God is, I understand without any doubt both his existence, and the impossibility of his non-existence. Whether, however, so long as I am most positively aware of my existence, I can conceive of my non-existence, I am not sure. But if I can, why can I not conceive of the non-existence of whatever else I know with the same certainty? If, however, I cannot, God will not be the only being of which it can be said, it is impossible to conceive of his non-existence.

8. The other parts of this book are argued with such truth, such brilliancy, such grandeur; and are so replete with usefulness, so fragrant with a certain perfume of devout and holy feeling, that though there are matters in the beginning which, however rightly sensed, are weakly presented, the rest of the work should not be rejected on this account. The rather ought these earlier matters to be reasoned more cogently, and the whole to be received with great respect and honor.

A REPLY TO GAUNILON
St. Anselm

St. Anselm, "Anselm's Apologetic," pp. 153–170 in *St. Anselm: Basic Writings,* S. N. Deane (trans.), 1961. Used by permission of The Open Court Publishing Company.

Anselm's Apologetic

IN REPLY TO GAUNILON'S ANSWER IN BEHALF OF THE FOOL

It was a fool against whom the argument of my Proslogium was directed. Seeing, however, that the author of these objections is by no means a fool, and is a Catholic, speaking in behalf of the fool, I think it sufficient that I answer the Catholic.

Chapter I

A GENERAL REFUTATION OF GAUNILON'S ARGUMENT—IT IS SHOWN THAT A BEING THAN WHICH A GREATER CANNOT BE CONCEIVED EXISTS IN REALITY

You say—whosoever you may be, who say that a fool is capable of making these statements—that a being than which a greater cannot be conceived is not in the understanding in any other sense than that in which a being that is altogether inconceivable in terms of reality, is in the understanding. You say that the inference that this being exists in reality, from the fact that it is in the understanding, is no more just than the inference that a lost island most certainly exists, from the fact that when it is described the hearer does not doubt that it is in his understanding.

But I say: if a being than which a greater is inconceivable is not understood or conceived, and is not in the understanding or in concept, certainly either God is not a being than which a greater is inconceivable, or else he is not understood or conceived, and is not in the understanding or in concept. But I call on your faith and conscience to attest that this is most false. Hence, that than which a greater cannot be conceived is truly understood and conceived, and is in the understanding and in concept. Therefore either the grounds on which you try to controvert me are not true, or else the inference which you think to base logically on those grounds is not justified.

But you hold, moreover, that supposing that a being than which a greater cannot be conceived is understood, it does not follow that this being is in the understanding; nor, if it is in the understanding, does it therefore exist in reality.

In answer to this, I maintain positively: if that being can be even conceived to be, it must exist in reality. For that than which a greater is inconceivable cannot be conceived except as without beginning. But whatever can be conceived to exist, and does not exist, can be conceived to exist through a beginning. Hence what can be conceived to exist, but does not exist, is not the being than which a greater cannot be conceived. Therefore, if such a being can be conceived to exist, necessarily it does exist.

Furthermore: if it can be conceived at all, it must exist. For no one who denies or doubts the existence of a being than which a greater is inconceivable, denies or doubts that if it did exist, its non-existence, either in reality or in the understanding, would be impossible. For otherwise it would not be a being than which a greater cannot be conceived. But as to whatever can be conceived, but does not exist—if there were such a being, its non-existence, either in reality or in the understanding, would be possible. Therefore if a being than which a greater is inconceivable can be even conceived, it cannot be non-existent.

But let us suppose that it does not exist, even if it can be conceived. Whatever can be conceived, but does not exist, if it existed, would not be a being than which a greater is inconceivable. If, then, there were a being a greater than which is inconceivable, it would not be a being than which a greater is inconceivable: which is most absurd. Hence, it is false to deny that a being than which a greater cannot be conceived exists, if it can be even conceived; much the more, therefore, if it can be understood or can be in the understanding.

Moreover, I will venture to make this assertion: without doubt, whatever at any place or at any time does not exist—even if it does exist at some place or at some time—can be conceived to exist nowhere and never, as at some place and at some time it does not exist. For what did not exist yesterday, and exists to-day, as it is understood not to have existed yesterday, so it can be apprehended by the intelligence that it never exists. And what is not here, and is elsewhere, can be conceived to be nowhere, just as it is not here. So with regard to an object of which the individual parts do not exist at the same places or times: all its parts and therefore its very whole can be conceived to exist nowhere or never.

For, although time is said to exist always, and the world everywhere, yet time does not as a whole exist always, nor the world as a whole everywhere. And as individual parts of time do not exist when others exist, so they can be conceived never to exist. And so it can be apprehended by the intelligence that individual parts of the world exist nowhere, as they do not exist where other parts exist. Moreover, what is composed of parts can be dissolved in concept, and be non-existent. Therefore, whatever at any place or at any time does not exist as a whole, even if it is existent, can be conceived not to exist.

But that than which a greater cannot be conceived, if it exists, cannot be conceived not to exist. Otherwise, it is not a being than which a greater cannot be conceived: which is inconsistent. By no means, then, does it at any place or at any time fail to exist as a whole: but it exists as a whole everywhere and always.

Do you believe that this being can in some way be conceived or understood, or that the being with regard to which these things are understood can be in concept or in the understanding? For if it cannot, these things cannot be understood with reference to it. But if you say that it is not understood and that it is not in the understanding, because it is not thoroughly understood; you should say that a man who cannot face the direct rays of the sun does not see the light of day, which is none other than the sunlight. Assuredly a being than which a greater cannot be conceived exists, and is in the understanding, at least to this extent—that these statements regarding it are understood.

Chapter II

THE ARGUMENT IS CONTINUED—IT IS SHOWN THAT A BEING THAN WHICH A GREATER IS INCONCEIVABLE CAN BE CONCEIVED, AND ALSO, IN SO FAR, EXISTS

I have said, then, in the argument which you dispute, that when the fool hears mentioned a being than which a greater is inconceivable, he understands what he hears. Certainly a man who does not understand when a familiar language is spoken, has no understanding at all, or a very dull one. Moreover, I have said that if this being is understood, it is in the understanding. Is that in no understanding which has been proved necessarily to exist in the reality of fact?

But you will say that although it is in the understanding, it does not follow that it is understood. But observe that the fact of its being understood does necessitate its being in the understanding. For as what is conceived, is conceived by conception, and what is conceived by conception, as it is conceived, so is in conception; so what is understood, is understood by understanding, and what is understood by understanding, as it is understood, so is in the understanding. What can be more clear than this?

After this, I have said that if it is even in the understanding alone, it can be conceived also to exist in reality, which is greater. If, then, it is in the understanding alone, obviously the very being than which a greater cannot be conceived is one than which a greater can be conceived. What is more logical? For if it exists even in the understanding alone, can it not be conceived also to exist in reality? And if it can be so conceived, does not he who conceives of this conceive of a thing greater than that being, if it exists in the understanding alone? What more consistent inference, then, can be made than this: that if a being than which a greater cannot be conceived is in the understanding alone, it is not that than which a greater cannot be conceived?

But, assuredly, in no understanding is a being than which a greater is conceivable a being than which a greater is inconceivable. Does it not follow, then, that if a being than which a greater cannot be conceived is in any understanding, it does not exist in the understanding alone? For if it is in the understanding alone, it is a being than which a greater can be conceived, which is inconsistent with the hypothesis.

Chapter III

A CRITICISM OF GAUNILON'S EXAMPLE, IN WHICH HE TRIES TO SHOW THAT IN THIS WAY THE REAL EXISTENCE OF A LOST ISLAND MIGHT BE INFERRED FROM THE FACT OF ITS BEING CONCEIVED

But, you say, it is as if one should suppose an island in the ocean, which surpasses all lands in its fertility, and which, because of the difficulty, or rather the impossibility, of discovering what does not exist, is called a lost island; and should say that there can be no doubt that this island truly exists in reality, for this reason, that one who hears it described easily understands what he hears.

Now I promise confidently that if any man shall devise anything existing either in reality or in concept alone (except that than which a greater cannot be conceived) to which he can adapt the sequence of my reasoning, I will discover that thing, and will give him his lost island, not to be lost again.

But it now appears that this being than which a greater is inconceivable cannot be conceived not to be, because it exists on so assured a ground of truth; for otherwise it would not exist at all.

Hence, if any one says that he conceives this being not to exist, I say that at the time when he conceives of this either he conceives of a being than which a greater is inconceivable, or he does not conceive at all. If he does not conceive, he does not conceive of the non-existence of that of which he does not conceive. But if he does conceive, he certainly conceives of a being which cannot be even conceived not to exist. For if it could be conceived not to exist, it could be conceived to have a beginning and an end. But this is impossible.

He, then, who conceives of this being conceives of a being which cannot be even conceived not to exist; but he who conceives of this being does not conceive that it does not exist; else he conceives what is inconceivable. The non-existence, then, of that than which a greater cannot be conceived is inconceivable.

Chapter IV

THE DIFFERENCE BETWEEN THE POSSIBILITY OF CONCEIVING OF NON-EXISTENCE, AND UNDERSTANDING NON-EXISTENCE

You say, moreover, that whereas I assert that this supreme being cannot be *conceived* not to exist, it might better be said that its non-existence, or even the possibility of its non-existence, cannot be *understood.*

But it was more proper to say, it cannot be conceived. For if I had said that the object itself cannot be understood not to exist, possibly you yourself, who say that in accordance with the true meaning of the term what is unreal cannot be understood, would offer the objection that nothing which is can be understood not to be, for the non-existence of what exists is unreal: hence God would not be the only being of which it could be said, it is impossible to understand its non-existence. For thus one of those beings which most certainly exist can be understood not to exist in the same way in which certain other real objects can be understood not to exist.

But this objection, assuredly, cannot be urged against the term *conception,* if one considers the matter well. For although no objects which exist can be understood not to exist, yet all objects, except that which exists in the highest degree, can be conceived not to exist. For all those objects, and those alone, can be conceived not to exist, which have a beginning or end or composition of parts: also, as I have already said, whatever at any place or at any time does not exist as a whole.

That being alone, on the other hand, cannot be conceived not to exist, in which any conception discovers neither beginning nor end nor composition of parts, and which any conception finds always and everywhere as a whole.

Be assured, then, that you can conceive of your own non-existence, although you are most certain that you exist. I am surprised that you should have admitted that you are ignorant of this. For we conceive of the non-existence of many objects which we know to exist, and of the existence of many which we know not to exist; not by forming the opinion that they so exist, but by imagining that they exist as we conceive of them.

And indeed, we can conceive of the non-existence of an object, although we know it to exist, because at the same time we can conceive of the former and know the latter. And we cannot conceive of the non-existence of an object, so long as we know it to exist, because we cannot conceive at the same time of existence and non-existence.

If, then, one will thus distinguish these two senses of this statement, he will understand that nothing, so long as it is known to exist, can be conceived not to exist; and that whatever exists, except that being than which a greater cannot be conceived, can be conceived not to exist, even when it is known to exist.

So, then, of God alone it can be said that it is impossible to conceive of his non-existence; and yet many objects, so long as they exist, in one sense cannot be conceived not to exist. But in what sense God is to be conceived not to exist, I think has been shown clearly enough in my book.

Chapter V

A PARTICULAR DISCUSSION OF CERTAIN STATEMENTS OF GAUNILON'S—IN THE FIRST PLACE, HE MISQUOTED THE ARGUMENT WHICH HE UNDERTOOK TO REFUTE

The nature of the other objections which you, in behalf of the fool, urge against me it is easy, even for a man of small wisdom, to detect; and I had therefore thought it unnecessary to show this. But since I hear that some readers of these objections think they have some weight against me, I will discuss them briefly.

In the first place, you often repeat that I assert that what is greater than all other beings is in the understanding; and if it is in the understanding, it exists also in reality, for otherwise the being which is greater than all would not be greater than all.

Nowhere in all my writings is such a demonstration found. For the real existence of a being which is said to be *greater than all other beings* cannot be demonstrated in the same way with the real existence of one that is said to be *a being than which a greater cannot be conceived.*

If it should be said that a being than which a greater cannot be conceived has no real existence, or that it is possible that it does not exist, or even that it can be conceived not to exist, such an assertion can be easily refuted. For the non-existence of what does not exist is possible, and that whose non-existence is possible can be conceived not to exist. But whatever can be conceived not to exist, if it exists, is not a being than which a greater cannot be conceived; but if it does not exist, it would not, even if it existed, be a being than which a greater cannot be conceived. But it cannot be said that a being than which a greater is inconceivable, if it exists, is not a being than which a greater is inconceivable; or that if it existed, it would not be a being than which a greater is inconceivable.

It is evident, then, that neither is it non-existent, nor is it possible that it does not exist, nor can it be conceived not to exist. For otherwise, if it exists, it is not that which it is said to be in the hypothesis; and if it existed, it would not be what it is said to be in the hypothesis.

But this, it appears, cannot be so easily proved of a being which is said to be *greater than all other beings.* For it is not so evident that what can be conceived not to exist is not greater than all existing beings, as it is evident that it is not a being than which a greater cannot be conceived. Nor is it so indubitable that if a being greater than all other beings exists, it is no other than the being than which a greater cannot be conceived; or that if it were such a being, some other might not be this being in like manner; as it is certain with regard to a being which is hypothetically posited as one than which a greater cannot be conceived.

For consider: if one should say that there is a being greater than all other beings, and that this being can nevertheless be conceived not to exist; and that a being greater than this, although it does not exist, can be conceived to exist: can it be so clearly inferred in this case that this being is therefore not a being greater than all other existing beings, as it would be most positively affirmed in the other case, that the being under discussion is not, therefore, a being than which a greater cannot be conceived?

For the former conclusion requires another premise than the predication, *greater than all other beings.* In my argument, on the other hand, there is no need of any other than this very predication, *a being than which a greater cannot be conceived.*

If the same proof cannot be applied when the being in question is predicated to be greater than all others, which can be applied when it is predicated to be a being than which a greater cannot be conceived, you have unjustly censured me for saying what I did not say; since such a predication differs so greatly from that which I actually made. If, on the other hand, the other argument is valid, you ought not to blame me so for having said what can be proved.

Whether this can be proved, however, he will easily decide who recognises that this being than which a greater cannot be conceived is demonstrable. For by no means can this being than which a greater cannot be conceived be understood as any other than that which alone is greater than all. Hence, just as that than which a greater cannot be conceived is understood, and is in the understanding, and for that reason is asserted to exist in the reality of fact: so what is said to be greater than all other beings is understood and is in the understanding, and therefore it is necessarily inferred that it exists in reality.

You see, then, with how much justice you have compared me with your fool, who, on the sole ground that he understands what is described to him, would affirm that a lost island exists.

Chapter VI

A DISCUSSION OF GAUNILON'S ARGUMENT IN HIS SECOND CHAPTER: THAT ANY UNREAL BEINGS CAN BE UNDERSTOOD IN THE SAME WAY, AND WOULD, TO THAT EXTENT, EXIST

Another of your objections is that any unreal beings, or beings whose existence is uncertain, can be understood and be in the understanding in the same way with that being which I discussed. I am surprised that you should have conceived this objection, for I was attempting to prove what was still uncertain, and contented myself at first with showing that this being is understood in any way, and is in the understanding. It was my intention to consider, on these grounds, whether this being is in the understanding alone, like an unreal object, or whether it also exists in fact, as a real being. For if unreal objects, or objects whose existence is uncertain, in this way are understood and are in the understanding, because, when they are spoken of, the hearer understands what the speaker means, there is no reason why that being of which I spoke should not be understood and be in the understanding.

How, moreover, can these two statements of yours be reconciled: (1) the assertion that if a man should speak of any unreal objects, whatever they might be, you would understand, and (2) the assertion that on hearing of that being which does exist, and not in that way in which even unreal objects are held in concept, you would not say that you conceive of it or have it in concept; since, as you say, you cannot conceive of it in any other way than by understanding it, that is, by comprehending in your knowledge its real existence?

How, I ask, can these two things be reconciled: that unreal objects are understood, and that understanding an object is comprehending in knowledge its real existence? The contradiction does not concern me: do you see to it. But if unreal objects are also in some sort understood, and your definition is applicable, not to every understanding, but to a certain sort of understanding, I ought not to be blamed for saying that a being than which a greater cannot be conceived is understood and is in the understanding, even before I reached the certain conclusion that this being exists in reality.

Chapter VII

IN ANSWER TO ANOTHER OBJECTION: THAT THE SUPREMELY GREAT BEING MAY BE CONCEIVED NOT TO EXIST, JUST AS BY THE FOOL GOD IS CONCEIVED NOT TO EXIST

Again, you say that it can probably never be believed that this being, when it is spoken of and heard of, cannot be conceived not to exist in the same way in which even God may be conceived not to exist.

Such an objection could be answered by those who have attained but little skill in disputation and argument. For is it compatible with reason for a man to deny the existence of what he understands, because it is said to be that being whose existence he denies because he does not understand it? Or, if at some times its existence is denied, because only to a certain extent is it understood, and that which is not at all understood is the same to him: is not what is still undetermined more easily proved of a being which exists in some understanding than of one which exists is no understanding?

Hence it cannot be credible that any man denies the existence of a being than which a greater cannot be conceived, which, when he hears of it, he understands in a certain degree: it is incredible, I say, that any man denies the existence of this being because he denies the existence of God, the sensory perception of whom he in no wise conceives of.

Or if the existence of another object, because it is not at all understood, is denied, yet is not the existence of what is understood in some degree more easily proved than the existence of an object which is in no wise understood?

Not irrationally, then, has the hypothesis of a being a greater than which cannot be conceived been employed in controverting the fool, for the proof of the existence of God: since in some degree he would understand such a being, but in no wise could he understand God.

Chapter VIII

THE EXAMPLE OF THE PICTURE, TREATED IN GAUNILON'S THIRD CHAPTER, IS EXAMINED—FROM WHAT SOURCE A NOTION MAY BE FORMED OF THE SUPREMELY GREAT BEING, OF WHICH GAUNILON INQUIRED IN HIS FOURTH CHAPTER

Moreover, your so careful demonstration that the being than which a greater cannot be conceived is not analogous to the not yet executed picture in the understanding of the painter, is quite unnecessary. It was not for this purpose that I suggested the preconceived picture. I had no thought of asserting that the being which I was discussing is of such a nature; but I wished to show that what is not understood to exist can be in the understanding.

Again, you say that when you hear of a being than which a greater is inconceivable, you cannot conceive of it in terms of any real object known to you either specifically or generally, nor have it in your understanding. For, you say, you neither know such a being in itself, nor can you form an idea of it from anything like it.

But obviously this is not true. For everything that is less good, in so far as it is good, is like the greater good. It is therefore evident to any rational mind, that by ascending from the lesser good to the greater, we can form a considerable notion of a being than which a greater is inconceivable.

For instance, who (even if he does not believe that what he conceives of exists in reality) supposing that there is some good which has a beginning and an end, does not conceive that a good is much better, which, if it begins, does not cease to be? And that as the second good is better than the first, so that good which has neither beginning nor end, though it is ever passing from the past through the present to the future, is better than the second? And that far better than this is a being—whether any being of such a nature exists or not—which in no wise requires change or motion, nor is compelled to undergo change or motion?

Is this inconceivable, or is some being greater than this conceivable? Or is not this to form a notion from objects than which a greater is conceivable, of the being than which a greater cannot be conceived? There is, then, a means of forming a notion of a being than which a greater is inconceivable.

So easily, then, can the fool who does not accept sacred authority be refuted, if he denies that a notion may be formed from other objects of a being than which a greater is inconceivable. But if any Catholic would deny this, let him remember that the invisible things of God, from the creation of the world, are clearly seen, being understood by the things that are made, even his eternal power and Godhead. (Romans i. 20.)

Chapter IX

THE POSSIBILITY OF UNDERSTANDING AND CONCEIVING OF THE SUPREMELY GREAT BEING—THE ARGUMENT ADVANCED AGAINST THE FOOL IS CONFIRMED

But even if it were true that a being than which a greater is inconceivable cannot be conceived or understood; yet it would not be untrue that a being than which a greater cannot be conceived is conceivable and intelligible. There is nothing to prevent one's saying *ineffable,* although what is said to be ineffable cannot be spoken of. *Inconceivable* is conceivable, although that to which the word *inconceivable* can be applied is not conceivable. So, when one says, *that than which nothing greater is conceivable,* undoubtedly what is heard is conceivable and intelligible, although that being itself, than which a greater is inconceivable, cannot be conceived or understood.

Or, though there is a man so foolish as to say that there is no being than which a greater is inconceivable, he will not be so shameless as to say that he cannot understand or conceive of what he says. Or, if such a man is found, not only ought his words to be rejected, but he himself should be contemned.

Whoever, then, denies the existence of a being than which a greater cannot be conceived, at least understands and conceives of the denial which he makes. But this denial he cannot understand or conceive of without its component terms; and a term of this statement is *a being than which a greater cannot be conceived.* Whoever, then, makes this denial, understands and conceives of that than which a greater is inconceivable.

Moreover, it is evident that in the same way it is possible to conceive of and understand a being whose non-existence is impossible; but he who conceives of this conceives of a greater being than one whose non-existence is possible. Hence, when a being than which a greater is inconceivable is conceived, if it is a being whose non-existence is possible that is conceived, it is not a being than which a greater cannot be conceived. But an object cannot be at once conceived and not conceived. Hence he who conceives of a being than which a greater is inconceivable, does not conceive of that whose non-existence is possible, but of that whose non-existence is impossible. Therefore, what he conceives of must exist; for anything whose non-existence is possible, is not that of which he conceives.

Chapter X

THE CERTAINTY OF THE FOREGOING ARGUMENT—THE CONCLUSION OF THE BOOK

I believe that I have shown by an argument which is not weak, but sufficiently cogent, that in my former book I proved the real existence of a being than which a greater cannot be conceived; and I believe that this argument cannot be invalidated by the validity of any objection. For so great force does the signification of this reasoning contain in itself, that this being which is the subject of discussion, is of necessity, from the very fact that it is understood or conceived, proved also to exist in reality, and to be whatever we should believe of the divine substance.

For we attribute to the divine substance anything of which it can be conceived that it is better to be than not to be that thing. For example: it is better to be eternal than not eternal; good, than not good; nay, goodness itself, than not goodness itself. But it cannot be that anything of this nature is not a property of the being than which a greater is inconceivable. Hence, the being than which a greater is inconceivable must be whatever should be attributed to the divine essence.

I thank you for your kindness both in your blame and in your praise for my book. For since you have commended so generously those parts of it which seem to you worthy of acceptance, it is quite evident that you have criticised in no unkind spirit those parts of it which seemed to you weak.

Chapter
TWELVE

THEISTIC ARGUMENTS
contingency and causality

THE FIRST THREE WAYS
St. Thomas Aquinas

From St. Thomas Aquinas, *Summa Theologica,* part I, question 2, articles 2 and (in part) 3, in Anton C. Pegis (ed.), *Basic Writings of St. Thomas Aquinas,* 1968. Used by permission of Random House, Inc., New York. Composed circa 1265–1273.

WHETHER IT CAN BE DEMONSTRATED THAT GOD EXISTS?

We proceed thus to the Second Article:—

Objection 1. It seems that the existence of God cannot be demonstrated. For it is an article of faith that God exists. But what is of faith cannot be demonstrated, because a demonstration produces scientific knowledge, whereas faith is of the unseen as is clear from the Apostle (*Heb.* xi. 1). Therefore it cannot be demonstrated that God exists.

Obj. 2. Further, essence is the middle term of demonstration. But we cannot know in what God's essence consists, but solely in what it does not consist, as Damascene says.[1] Therefore we cannot demonstrate that God exists.

Obj. 3. Further, if the existence of God were demonstrated, this could only be from His effects. But His effects are not proportioned to Him, since He is infinite and His effects are finite, and between the finite and infinite there is no proportion. Therefore, since a cause cannot be demonstrated by an effect not proportioned to it, it seems that the existence of God cannot be demonstrated.

On the contrary, The Apostle says: *The invisible things of Him are clearly seen, being understood by the things that are made* (*Rom.* i. 20). But this would not be unless the existence of God could be demonstrated through the things that are made; for the first thing we must know of anything is, whether it exists.

I answer that, Demonstration can be made in two ways: One is through the cause, and is called *propter quid,* and this is to argue from what is prior absolutely. The other is through the effect, and is called a demonstration *quia;* this is to argue from what is prior relatively only to us. When an effect is better known to us than its cause, from the effect we proceed to the knowledge of the cause. And from every effect the existence of its proper cause can be demonstrated, so long as its effects are better known to us; because, since every effect depends upon its cause, if the effect exists, the cause must pre-exist. Hence the existence of God, in so far as it is not self-evident to us, can be demonstrated from those of His effects which are known to us.

Reply Obj. 1. The existence of God and other like truths about God, which can be known by natural reason, are not articles of faith, but are preambles to the articles; for faith presupposes natural knowledge, even as grace presupposes nature and perfection the perfectible. Nevertheless, there is nothing to prevent a man, who cannot grasp a proof, from accepting, as a matter of faith, something which in itself is capable of being scientifically known and demonstrated.

Reply Obj. 2. When the existence of a cause is demonstrated from an effect, this effect takes the place of the definition of the cause in proving the cause's

---

[1] *De Fide Orth.,* I, 4 (PG 94, 800).

existence. This is especially the case in regard to God, because, in order to prove the existence of anything, it is necessary to accept as a middle term the meaning of the name, and not its essence, for the question of its essence follows on the question of its existence. Now the names given to God are derived from His effects, as will be later shown.[2] Consequently, in demonstrating the existence of God from His effects, we may take for the middle term the meaning of the name *God.*

Reply Obj. 3. From effects not proportioned to the cause no perfect knowledge of that cause can be obtained. Yet from every effect the existence of the cause can be clearly demonstrated, and so we can demonstrate the existence of God from His effects; though from them we cannot know God perfectly as He is in His essence.

Third Article

WHETHER GOD EXISTS?

We proceed thus to the Third Article:—

Objection 1. It seems that God does not exist; because if one of two contraries be infinite, the other would be altogether destroyed. But the name *God* means that He is infinite goodness. If, therefore, God existed, there would be no evil discoverable; but there is evil in the world. Therefore God does not exist.

Obj. 2. Further, it is superfluous to suppose that what can be accounted for by a few principles has been produced by many. But it seems that everything we see in the world can be accounted for by other principles, supposing God did not exist. For all natural things can be reduced to one principle, which is nature; and all voluntary things can be reduced to one principle, which is human reason, or will. Therefore there is no need to suppose God's existence.

On the contrary, It is said in the person of God: *I am Who am* (*Exod.* iii. 14).

I answer that, The existence of God can be proved in five ways.

The first and more manifest way is the argument from motion. It is certain, and evident to our senses, that in the world some things are in motion. Now whatever is moved is moved by another, for nothing can be moved except it is in potentiality to that towards which it is moved; whereas a thing moves inasmuch as it is in act. For motion is nothing else than the reduction of something from potentiality to actuality. But nothing can be reduced from potentiality to actuality, except by something in a state of actuality. Thus that which is actually hot, as fire, makes wood, which is potentially hot, to be actually hot, and thereby moves and changes it. Now it is not possible that the same thing should be at once in actuality and potentiality in the same respect but only in different respects. For what is actually hot cannot simultaneously be potentially hot; but it is simultaneously potentially cold. It is therefore impossible that in the same respect and in the same way a thing should be both mover and moved, *i.e.,* that it should move itself. Therefore, whatever is moved must be moved by another. If that by which it is moved be itself moved, then this also must needs be moved by another, and

---

[2]Q. 13, a. 1.

that by another again. But this cannot go on to infinity, because then there would be no first mover, and, consequently, no other mover, seeing that subsequent movers move only inasmuch as they are moved by the first mover; as the staff moves only because it is moved by the hand. Therefore it is necessary to arrive at a first mover, moved by no other; and this everyone understands to be God.

The second way is from the nature of efficient cause. In the world of sensible things we find there is an order of efficient causes. There is no case known (neither is it, indeed, possible) in which a thing is found to be the efficient cause of itself; for so it would be prior to itself, which is impossible. Now in efficient causes it is not possible to go on to infinity, because in all efficient causes following in order, the first is the cause of the intermediate cause, and the intermediate is the cause of the ultimate cause, whether the intermediate cause be several, or one only. Now to take away the cause is to take away the effect. Therefore, if there be no first cause among efficient causes, there will be no ultimate, nor any intermediate, cause. But if in efficient causes it is possible to go on to infinity, there will be no first efficient cause, neither will there be an ultimate effect, nor any intermediate efficient causes; all of which is plainly false. Therefore it is necessary to admit a first efficient cause, to which everyone gives the name of God.

The third way is taken from possibility and necessity, and runs thus. We find in nature things that are possible to be and not to be, since they are found to be generated, and to be corrupted, and consequently, it is possible for them to be and not to be. But it is impossible for these always to exist, for that which can not-be at some time is not. Therefore, if everything can not-be, then at one time there was nothing in existence. Now if this were true, even now there would be nothing in existence, because that which does not exist begins to exist only through something already existing. Therefore, if at one time nothing was in existence, it would have been impossible for anything to have begun to exist; and thus even now nothing would be in existence—which is absurd. Therefore, not all beings are merely possible, but there must exist something the existence of which is necessary. But every necessary thing either has its necessity caused by another, or not. Now it is impossible to go on to infinity in necessary things which have their necessity caused by another, as has been already proved in regard to efficient causes. Therefore we cannot but admit the existence of some being having of itself its own necessity, and not receiving it from another, but rather causing in others their necessity. This all men speak of as God.

Reply Obj. 1. As Augustine says: *Since God is the highest good, He would not allow any evil to exist in His works, unless His omnipotence and goodness were such as to bring good even out of evil.* This is part of the infinite goodness of God, that He should allow evil to exist, and out of it produce good.

Reply Obj. 2. Since nature works for a determinate end under the direction of a higher agent, whatever is done by nature must be traced back to God as to its first cause. So likewise whatever is done voluntarily must be traced back to some higher cause other than human reason and will, since these can change and fail; for all things that are changeable and capable of defect must be traced back to an immovable and self-necessary first principle, as has been shown.

A REFORMULATION
OF THE ARGUMENT
FROM CONTINGENCY
Richard Taylor

From Richard Taylor, *Metaphysics,* pp. 84–94, © 1963. Reprinted by permission of Prentice-Hall, Inc., Englewood Cliffs, N.J.

An active, living, and religious belief in the gods has probably never arisen and been maintained on purely metaphysical grounds. Such beliefs are found in every civilized land and time, and are often virtually universal in a particular culture, yet relatively few men have much of a conception of metaphysics. There are in fact entire cultures, such as ancient Israel, to whom metaphysics is quite foreign, though these cultures may nevertheless be religious.

Belief in the gods seems to have its roots in human desires and fears, particularly those associated with self-preservation. Like all other creatures, men have a profound will to live, which is what mainly gives one's existence a meaning from one sunrise to the next. Unlike other creatures, however, men are capable of the full and terrible realization of their own inevitable decay. A man can bring before his mind the image of his own grave, and with it the complete certainty of its ultimate reality, and against this his will naturally recoils. It can hardly seem to him less than an absolute catastrophe, the very end, so far as he is concerned, of everything, though he has no difficulty viewing death, as it touches others more or less remote from himself, as a perhaps puzzling, occasionally distressing, but nonetheless necessary aspect of nature. It is probably partly in response to this fear that he turns to the gods, as those beings of such power that they can overturn this verdict of nature.

The sources of religious belief are doubtless much more complex than this, but they seem to lie in man's will rather than in his speculative intelligence, nevertheless. Men who possess such a belief seldom permit any metaphysical considerations to wrest it from them, while those who lack it are seldom turned toward it by other metaphysical considerations. Still, in every land in which philosophy has flourished, there have been profound thinkers who have sought to discover some metaphysical basis for a rational belief in the existence of some supreme being or beings. Even though religion may properly be a matter of faith rather than reason, still, a philosophical person can hardly help wondering whether it might, at least in part, be also a matter of reason, and whether, in particular, the existence of God might be something that can be not merely believed but shown. It is this question that we want now to consider; that is, we want to see whether there are not strong metaphysical considerations from which the existence of some supreme and supranatural being might reasonably be inferred.

The Principle of Sufficient Reason

Suppose you were strolling in the woods and, in addition to the sticks, stones, and other accustomed litter of the forest floor, you one day came upon some quite unaccustomed object, something not quite like what you had ever seen before and would never expect to find in such a place. Suppose, for example, that it is a large ball, about your own height, perfectly smooth and translucent. You would deem this puzzling and mysterious, certainly, but if one considers the matter, it is no more inherently mysterious that such a thing should exist than that anything else should exist. If you were quite accustomed to finding such objects of various sizes around you most of the time, but had never seen an ordinary rock, then upon finding a large rock in the woods one day you would be just as puzzled and mystified. This illustrates the fact that something that is mysterious ceases to seem so simply by its accustomed presence. It is strange indeed, for example, that a world such as ours should exist; yet few men are very often struck by this strangeness, but simply take it for granted.

Suppose, then, that you have found this translucent ball and are mystified by it. Now whatever else you might wonder about it, there is one thing you would hardly question; namely, that it did not appear there all by itself, that it owes its existence to something. You might not have the remotest idea whence and how it came to be there, but you would hardly doubt that there was an explanation. The idea that it might have come from nothing at all, that it might exist without there being any explanation of its existence, is one that few people would consider worthy of entertaining.

This illustrates a metaphysical belief that seems to be almost a part of reason itself, even though few men ever think upon it; the belief, namely, that there is some explanation for the existence of anything whatever, some reason why it should exist rather than not. The sheer nonexistence of anything, which is not to be confused with the passing out of existence of something, never requires a reason; but existence does. That there should never have been any such ball in the forest does not require any explanation or reason, but that there should ever be such a ball does. If one were to look upon a barren plain and ask why there is not and never has been any large translucent ball there, the natural response would be to ask why there should be; but if one finds such a ball, and wonders why it is there, it is not quite so natural to ask why it should *not* be, as though existence should simply be taken for granted. That anything should not exist, then, and that, for instance, no such ball should exist in the forest, or that there should be no forest for it to occupy, or no continent containing a forest, or no earth, nor any world at all, do not seem to be things for which there needs to be any explanation or reason; but that such things should be, does seem to require a reason.

The principle involved here has been called the principle of sufficient reason. Actually, it is a very general principle, and is best expressed by saying that, in the case of any positive truth, there is some sufficient reason for it, something which, in this sense, makes it true—in short, that there is some sort of explanation, known or unknown, for everything.

Now some truths depend on something else, and are accordingly called *contingent,* while others depend only upon themselves, that is, are true by their very natures and are accordingly called *necessary.* There is, for example, a reason why the stone on my window sill is warm; namely, that the sun is shining upon it. This happens to be true, but not by its very nature. Hence, it is contingent, and depends upon something other than itself. It is also true that all the points of a circle are equidistant from the center, but this truth depends upon nothing but itself. No matter what happens, nothing can make it false. Similarly, it is a truth, and a necessary one, that if the stone on my window sill is a body, as it is, then it has a form, since this fact depends upon nothing but itself for its confirmation. Untruths are also, of course, either contingent or necessary, it being contingently false, for example, that the stone on my window sill is cold, and necessarily false that it is both a body and formless, since this is by its very nature impossible.

The principle of sufficient reason can be illustrated in various ways, as we have done, and if one thinks about it, he is apt to find that he presupposes it in his thinking about reality, but it cannot be proved. It does not appear to be itself a necessary truth, and at the same time it would be most odd to say it is contingent. If one were to try proving it, he would sooner or later have to appeal to considerations that are less plausible than the principle itself. Indeed, it is hard to see how one could even make an argument for it, without already assuming it. For this reason it might properly be called a presupposition of reason itself. One can deny that it is true, without embarrassment or fear of refutation, but one is then apt to find that what he is denying is not really what the principle asserts. We shall, then, treat it here as a datum—not something that is probably true, but as something which all men, whether they ever reflect upon it or not, seem more or less to presuppose.

The Existence of a World

It happens to be true that something exists, that there is, for example, a world, and while no one ever seriously supposes that this might not be so, that there might exist nothing at all, there still seems to be nothing the least necessary in this, considering it just by itself. That no world should ever exist at all is perfectly comprehensible and seems to express not the slightest absurdity. Considering any particular item in the world it seems not at all necessary in itself that it should ever have existed, nor does it appear any more necessary that the totality of these things, or any totality of things, should ever exist.

From the principle of sufficient reason it follows, of course, that there must be a reason, not only for the existence of everything in the world but for the world itself, meaning by "the world" simply everything that ever does exist, except God, in case there is a god. This principle does not imply that there must be some purpose or goal for everything, or for the totality of all things; for explanations need not be, and in fact seldom are, teleological or purposeful. All the principle requires is that there be some sort of reason for everything. And it would certainly be odd to maintain that everything in the world owes its existence to something, that nothing in the world is either purely accidental, or such that it just bestows its own being upon itself, and then to deny this of the world itself. One can indeed *say* that the world is in some sense a pure accident, that there simply is no reason at all why this or any world should exist, and one can equally say that the world exists by its very nature, or is an inherently necessary being. But it is at least very odd and arbitrary to deny of this existing world the need for any sufficient reason, whether independent of itself or not, while presupposing that there is a reason for every other thing that ever exists.

Consider again the strange ball that we imagine has been found in the forest.

Now we can hardly doubt that there must be an explanation for the existence of such a thing, though we may have no notion what that explanation is. It is not, moreover, the fact of its having been found in the forest rather than elsewhere that renders an explanation necessary. It matters not in the least where it happens to be, for our question is not how it happens to be *there* but how it happens to exist at all. If we in our imagination annihilate the forest, leaving only this ball in an open field, our conviction that it is a contingent thing and owes its existence to something other than itself is not reduced in the least. If we now imagine the field to be annihilated, and in fact everything else as well to vanish into nothingness, leaving only this ball to constitute the entire physical universe, then we cannot for a moment suppose that its existence has thereby been explained, or the need of any explanation eliminated, or that its existence is suddenly rendered self-explanatory. If we now carry this thought one step further and suppose that no other reality ever has existed or ever will exist, that this ball forever constitutes the entire physical universe, then we must still insist on there being some reason independent of itself why it should exist rather than not. If there must be a reason for the existence of any particular thing, then the necessity of such a reason is not eliminated by the mere supposition that certain other things do *not* exist. And again, it matters not at all what the thing in question is, whether it be large and complex, such as the world we actually find ourselves in, or whether it be something small, simple and insignificant, such as a ball, a bacterium, or the merest grain of sand. We do not avoid the necessity of a reason for the existence of something merely by describing it in this way or that. And it would, in any event, seem quite plainly absurd to say that if the world were comprised entirely of a single ball about six feet in diameter, or of a single grain of sand, then it would be contingent and there would have to be some explanation other than itself why such a thing exists, but that, since the actual world is vastly more complex than this, there is no need for an explanation of its existence, in-dependent of itself.

Beginningless Existence

It should now be noted that it is no answer to the question, why a thing exists, to state *how long* it has existed. A geologist does not suppose that he has explained why there should be rivers and mountains merely by pointing out that they are old. Similarly, if one were to ask, concerning the ball of which we have spoken, for some sufficient reason for its being, he would not receive any answer upon being told that it had been there since yesterday. Nor would it be any better answer to say that it had existed since before anyone could remember, or even that it had always existed; for the question was not one concerning its age but its existence. If, to be sure, one were to ask where a given thing came from, or how it came into being, then upon learning that it had always existed he would learn that it never really *came* into being at all; but he could still reasonably wonder why it should exist at all. If, accordingly, the world—that is, the totality of all things excepting God, in case there is a god—had really no beginning at all, but has always existed in some form or other, then there is clearly no answer to the question, where it came from and when; it did not, on this supposition, *come* from anything at all, at any time. But still, it can be asked why there is a world, why indeed there is a beginningless world, why there should have perhaps always been something rather than nothing. And, if the principle of sufficient reason is a good principle, there must be an answer to that question, an answer that is by no means supplied by giving the world an age, or even an infinite age.

Creation

This brings out an important point with respect to the concept of creation that is often misunderstood, particularly by those whose thinking has been influenced by Christian ideas. People tend to think that creation—for example, the creation of the world by God—*means* creation *in time,* from which it of course logically follows that if the world had no beginning in time, then it cannot be the creation of God. This, however, is erroneous, for creation means essentially *dependence,* even in Christian theology. If one thing is the creation of another, then it depends for its existence on that other, and this is perfectly consistent with saying that both are eternal, that neither ever came into being, and hence, that neither was ever created at any point of time. Perhaps an analogy will help convey this point. Consider, then, a flame that is casting beams of light. Now there seems to be a clear sense in which the beams of light are dependent for their existence upon the flame, which is their source, while the flame, on the other hand, is not similarly dependent for its existence upon them. The beams of light arise from the flame, but the flame does not arise from them. In this sense, they are the creation of the flame; they derive their existence from it. And none of this has any reference to time; the relationship of dependence in such a case would not be altered in the slightest if we supposed that the flame, and with it the beams of light, had always existed, that neither had ever *come* into being.

Now if the world is the creation of God, its relationship to God should be thought of in this fashion; namely, that the world depends for its existence upon God, and could not exist independently of God. If God is eternal, as those who believe in God generally assume, then the world may (though it need not) be eternal too, without that altering in the least its dependence upon God for its existence, and hence without altering its being the creation of God. The supposition of God's eternality, on the other hand, does not by itself imply that the world is eternal too; for there is not the least reason why something of finite duration might not depend for its existence upon something of infinite duration—though the reverse is, of course, impossible.

God

If we think of God as "the creator of heaven and earth," and if we consider heaven and earth to include everything that exists except God, then we appear to have, in the foregoing considerations, fairly strong reasons for asserting that God, as so conceived, exists. Now of course most people have much more in mind than this when they think of God, for religions have ascribed to God ever so many attributes that are not at all implied by describing him merely as the creator of the world; but that is not relevant here. Most religious persons do, in any case, think of God as being at least the creator, as that being upon which everything ultimately depends, no matter what else they may say about him in addition. It is, in fact, the first item in the creeds of Christianity that God is the "creator of heaven and earth." And, it seems, there are good metaphysical reasons, as distinguished from the persuasions of faith, for thinking that such a creative being exists.

If, as seems clearly implied by the principle of sufficient reason, there must be a reason for the existence of heaven and earth—i.e., for the world—then that reason must be found either in the world itself, or outside it, in something that is literally supranatural, or outside heaven and earth. Now if we suppose that the world—i.e., the totality of all things except God—contains within itself the reason for its existence, we are supposing that it exists by its very nature, that is, that it is a necessary being. In that case there would, of course, be no reason for saying that it must depend upon God or anything else for its existence; for if it exists by its very nature, then it depends upon nothing but itself, much as the sun depends upon nothing but itself for its heat. This, however, is implausible, for we find nothing about the world or anything in it to suggest that it exists by its own nature, and we do find, on the contrary, ever so many things to suggest that it does not. For in the first place, anything which exists by its very nature must necessarily be eternal and indestructible. It would be a self-contradiction to say of anything that it exists by its own nature, or is a necessarily existing thing, and at the same time to say that it comes into being or passes away, or that it ever could come into being or pass away. Nothing about the world seems at all like this, for concerning anything in the world, we can perfectly easily think of it as being annihilated, or as never having existed in the first place, without there being the slightest hint of any absurdity in such a supposition. Some of the things in the universe are, to be sure, very old; the moon, for example, or the stars and the planets. It is even possible to imagine that they have always existed. Yet it seems quite impossible to suppose that they owe their existence to nothing but themselves, that they bestow existence upon themselves by their very natures, or that they are in themselves things of such nature that it would be impossible for them not to exist. Even if we suppose that something, such as the sun, for instance, has existed forever, and will never cease, still we cannot conclude just from this that it exists by its own nature. If, as is of course very doubtful, the sun has existed forever and will never cease, then it is possible that its heat and light have also existed forever and will never cease; but that would not show that the heat and light of the sun exist by their own natures. They are obviously contingent and depend on the sun for their existence, whether they are beginningless and everlasting or not.

There seems to be nothing in the world, then, concerning which it is at all plausible to suppose that it exists by its own nature, or contains within itself the reason for its existence. In fact, everything in the world appears to be quite plainly the opposite, namely, something that not only need not exist, but at some time or other, past or future or both, does not in fact exist. Everything in the world seems to have a finite duration, whether long or short. Most things, such as ourselves, exist only for a short while; they come into being, then soon cease. Other things, like the heavenly bodies, last longer, but they are still corruptible, and from all that we can gather about them, they too seem destined eventually to perish. We arrive at the conclusion, then, that while the world may contain some things which have always existed and are destined never to perish, it is nevertheless doubtful that it contains any such thing and, in any case, everything in the world is capable of perishing, and nothing in it, however long it may already have existed and however long it may yet remain, exists by its own nature, but depends instead upon something else.

While this might be true of everything in the world, is it necessarily true of the world itself? That is, if we grant, as we seem forced to, that nothing in the world exists by its own nature, that everything in the world is contingent and perishable, must we also say that the world itself, or the totality of all these perishable things, is also contingent and perishable? Logically, we are not forced to, for it is logically possible that the totality of all perishable things might itself be imperishable, and hence, that the world might exist by its own nature, even though it is comprised exclusively of things which are contingent. It is not logically necessary that a totality should share the defects of its members. For example, even though every man is mortal, it does not follow from this that the human race, or the totality of all men, is also mortal; for it is possible that there will always be human beings, even though there are no human beings which will always exist. Similarly, it is possible that the world is in itself a necessary thing, even though it is comprised entirely of things that are contingent.

This is logically possible, but it is not plausible. For we find nothing whatever about the world, any more than in its parts, to suggest that it exists by its own nature. Concerning anything in the world, we have not the slightest difficulty in supposing that it should perish, or even, that it should never have existed in the first place. We have almost as little difficulty in supposing this of the world itself. It might be somewhat hard to think of everything as utterly perishing and leaving no trace whatever of its ever having been, but there seems to be not the slightest difficulty in imagining that the world should never have existed in the first place. We can, for instance, perfectly easily suppose that nothing in the world had ever existed except, let us suppose, a single grain of sand, and we can thus suppose that this grain of sand has forever constituted the whole universe. Now if we consider just this grain of sand, it is quite impossible for us to suppose that it exists by its very nature, and could never have failed to exist. It clearly depends for its existence upon something other than itself, if it depends on anything at all. The same will be true if we consider the world to consist, not of one grain of sand, but of two, or of a million, or, as we in fact find, of a vast number of stars and planets and all their minuter parts.

It would seem, then, that the world, in case it happens to exist at all—and this is quite beyond doubt—is contingent and thus dependent upon something other than itself for its existence, if it depends upon anything at all. And it must depend upon something, for otherwise there could be no reason why it exists in the first place. Now that upon which the world depends must be something that either exists by its own nature or does not. If it does not exist by its own nature, then it, in turn, depends for its existence upon something else, and so on. Now then, we can say either of two things; namely, (1) that the world depends for its existence upon something else, which in turn depends on still another thing, this depending upon still another, *ad infinitum;* or (2) that the world derives its existence from something that exists by its own nature and which is accordingly eternal and imperishable, and is the creator of heaven and earth. The first of these alternatives, however, is impossible, for it does not render a sufficient reason why anything should exist in the first place. Instead of supplying a reason why any world should exist, it repeatedly begs off giving a reason. It explains what is dependent and perishable in terms of what is itself dependent and perishable, leaving us still without a reason why perishable things should exist at all, which is what we are seeking. Ultimately, then, it would seem that the world, or the totality of contingent or perishable things, in case it exists at all, must depend upon something that is necessary and imperishable, and which accordingly exists, not in dependence upon something else, but by its own nature.

"Self-caused"

What has been said thus far gives some intimation of what meaning should be attached to the concept of a self-caused being, a concept that is quite generally misunderstood, sometimes even by scholars. To say that something—God, for example—is self-caused, or is the cause of its own existence, does not mean that this being brings itself into existence, which is a perfectly absurd idea. Nothing can *bring* itself into existence. To say that something is self-caused (*causa sui*) means only that it exists, not contingently or in dependence upon something else, but by its own nature, which is only to say that it is a being which is such that it can neither come into being nor perish. Now whether such a being in fact exists or not, there is in any case no absurdity in the idea. We have found, in fact, that the principle of sufficient reason seems to point to the existence of such a being, as that upon which the world, with everything in it, must ultimately depend for its existence.

"Necessary Being"

A being that depends for its existence upon nothing but itself, and is in this sense self-caused, can equally be described as a necessary being; that is to say, a being that is not contingent, and hence not perishable. For in the case of anything which exists by its own nature, and is dependent upon nothing else, it is impossible that it should not exist, which is equivalent to saying that it is necessary. Many persons have professed to find the gravest difficulties in this concept, too, but that is partly because it has been confused with other notions. If it makes sense to speak of anything as an *impossible* being, or something which by its very nature does not exist, then it is hard to see why the idea of a necessary being, or something which in its very nature exists, should not be just as comprehensible. And of course, we have not the slightest difficulty in speaking of something, such as a square circle or a formless body, as an impossible being. And if it makes sense to speak of something as being perishable, contingent, and dependent upon something other than itself for its existence, as it surely does, then there seems to be no difficulty in thinking of something as imperishable and dependent upon nothing other than itself for its existence.

"First Cause"

From these considerations we can see also what is properly meant by a first cause, an appellative that has often been applied to God by theologians, and which many persons have deemed an absurdity. It is a common criticism of this notion to say that there need not be any first cause, since the series of causes and effects which constitute the history of the universe might be infinite or beginningless and must, in fact, be infinite in case the universe itself had no beginning in time. This criticism, however, reflects a total misconception of what is meant by a first cause. *First* here does not mean first in time, and when God is spoken of as a first cause, he is not being described as a being which, at some time in the remote past, *started* everything. To describe God as a first cause is only to say that he is literally a *primary* rather than a secondary cause, an *ultimate* rather than a derived cause, or a being upon which all other things, heaven and earth, ultimately depend for their existence. It is, in short, only to say that God is the creator, in the sense of creation explained above. Now this, of course, is perfectly consistent with saying that the world is eternal or beginningless. As we have seen, one gives no reason for the existence of a world merely by giving it an age, even if it is supposed to have an infinite age. To use a helpful analogy, we can say that the sun is the first cause of daylight and, for that matter, of the moonlight of the night as well, which means only that daylight and moonlight ultimately depend upon the sun for their existence. The moon, on the other hand, is only a secondary or derivative cause of its light. This light would be no less dependent upon the sun if we affirmed that it had no beginning, for an ageless and beginningless light requires a source no less than an ephemeral one. If we supposed that the sun has always existed, and with it its light, then we would have to say that the sun has always been the first—i.e., the primary or ultimate—cause of its light. Such is precisely the manner in which God should be thought of, and is by theologians often thought of, as the first cause of heaven and earth.

A CRITIQUE
OF THE ARGUMENT
FROM CONTINGENCY

Paul Edwards

Paul Edwards, "The Cosmological Argument," *The Rationalist Annual for the Year 1959*. Used by permission of the author and Pemberton Publishing Co. Ltd., London.

I

The so-called 'cosmological proof' is one of the oldest and most popular arguments for the existence of God. It was forcibly criticized by Hume,[1] Kant,[2] and Mill,[3] but it would be inaccurate to consider the argument dead or even moribund. Catholic philosophers, with hardly any exception, appear to believe that it is as solid and conclusive as ever. Thus Father Copleston confidently championed it in his Third Programme debate with Bertrand Russell;[4] and in America, where Catholic writers are more sanguine, we are told by a Jesuit professor of physics that 'the existence of an intelligent being as the First Cause of the universe can be established by *rational scientific inference'*.[5]

> I am absolutely convinced [the same writer continues] that any one who would give the same consideration to that proof (the cosmological argument), as outlined for example in William Brosnan's *God and Reason,* as he would give to a line of argumentation found in the *Physical Review* or the *Proceedings of the Royal Society* would be forced to admit that the cogency of this argument for the existence of God far outstrips that which is found in the reasoning which Chadwick uses to prove the existence of the neutron, which today is accepted as certain as any conclusion in the physical sciences.[6]

Mild theists like the late Professor Dawes Hicks[7] and Dr Ewing,[8] who concede many of Hume's and Kant's criticisms, nevertheless contend that the argument posseses a certain core of truth. In popular discussions it also crops up again and again—for example, when believers address atheists with such questions as 'You tell me where the universe came from!' Even philosophers who reject the cosmological proof sometimes embody certain of its confusions in the formulation of their own position. In the light of all this, it may be worth while to undertake a fresh examination of the argument with special attention to the fallacies that were not emphasized by the older critics.

---

[1] *Dialogues Concerning Natural Religion,* Part IX.
[2] *The Critique of Pure Reason,* Transcendental Dialectic, Book II, Ch III.
[3] 'Theism', Part I, in *Three Essays on Religion.*
[4] Reprinted in the British edition of Russell's *Why I Am Not a Christian.*
[5] J. S. O'Connor, 'A Scientific Approach to Religion', *The Scientific Monthly,* 1940, p. 369; my italics.
[6] *Ibid.* pp 369–70.
[7] *The Philosophical Bases of Theism,* Lecture V.
[8] *The Fundamental Questions of Philosophy,* Ch XI.

The cosmological proof has taken a number of forms, the most important of which are known as the 'causal argument' and 'the argument from contingency', respectively. In some writers, in Samuel Clarke for example, they are combined, but it is best to keep them apart as far as possible. The causal argument is the second of the 'five ways' of Aquinas and roughly proceeds as follows: we find that the things around us come into being as the result of the activity of other things. These causes are themselves the result of the activity of other things. But such a causal series cannot 'go back to infinity'. Hence there must be a first member, a member which is not itself caused by any preceding member—an uncaused or 'first' cause.

It has frequently been pointed out that even if this argument were sound it would not establish the existence of *God*. It would not show that the first cause is all-powerful or all-good or that it is in any sense personal. Somebody believing in the eternity of atoms, or of matter generally, could quite consistently accept the conclusion. Defenders of the causal argument usually concede this and insist that the argument is not in itself meant to prove the existence of God. Supplementary arguments are required to show that the first cause must have the attributes assigned to the deity. They claim, however, that the argument, if valid, would at least be an important step towards a complete proof of the existence of God.

Does the argument succeed in proving so much as a first cause? This will depend mainly on the soundness of the premise that an infinite series of causes is impossible. Aquinas supports this premise by maintaining that the opposite belief involves a plain absurdity. To suppose that there is an infinite series of causes logically implies that nothing exists now; but we know that plenty of things do exist now; and hence any theory which implies that nothing exists now must be wrong. Let us take some causal series and refer to its members by the letters of the alphabet:

$$A \to B \ldots W \to X \to Y \to Z$$

Z stands here for something presently existing, e.g. Margaret Truman. Y represents the cause or part of the cause of Z, say Harry Truman. X designates the cause or part of the cause of Y, say Harry Truman's father, etc. Now, Aquinas reasons, whenever we take away the cause, we also take away the effect: if Harry Truman had never lived, Margaret Truman would never have been born. If Harry Truman's father had never lived, Harry Truman and Margaret Truman would never have been born. If A had never existed, none of the subsequent members of the series would have come into existence. But it is precisely A that the believer in the infinite series is 'taking away'. For in maintaining that the series is infinite he is denying that it has a first member; he is denying that there is such a thing as a first cause; he is in other words denying the existence of A. Since without A, Z could not have existed, his position implies that Z does not exist now; and that is plainly false.

This argument fails to do justice to the supporter of the infinite series of causes. Aquinas has failed to distinguish between the two statements:

(1) A did not exist, and

(2) A is not uncaused.

To say that the series is infinite implies (2), but it does not imply (1). The following parallel may be helpful here: Suppose Captain Spaulding had said, 'I am the greatest explorer who ever lived', and somebody replied, 'No, you are not'. This answer would be denying that the Captain possessed the exalted attribute he had claimed for himself, but it would not be denying his existence. It would not be 'taking him away'. Similarly, the believer in the infinite series is not 'taking A away'. He is taking away the privileged status of A; he is taking away its 'first causiness'. He does not deny the *existence* of A or of any particular member of the series. He denies that A or anything else *is the first member* of the series. Since he is not taking A away, he is not taking B away, and thus he is also not taking X, Y, or Z away. His view, then, does not commit him to the absurdity that nothing exists now, or more specifically, that Margaret Truman does not exist now. It may be noted in this connection that a believer in the infinite series is not necessarily denying the existence of supernatural beings. He is merely committed to denying that such a being, if it exists, is uncaused. He is committed to holding that whatever other impressive attributes a supernatural being might possess, the attribute of being a first cause is not among them.

The causal argument is open to several other objections. Thus, even if otherwise valid, the argument would not prove a *single* first cause. For there does not seem to be any good ground for supposing that all the various causal series in the universe ultimately merge. Hence even if it is granted that no series of causes can be infinite the possibility of a plurality of first members has not been ruled out. Nor does the argument establish the *present* existence of the first cause. It does not prove this, since experience clearly shows that an effect may exist long after its cause has been destroyed.

III

Many defenders of the causal argument would contend that at least some of these criticisms rest on a misunderstanding. They would probably go further and contend that the argument was not quite fairly stated in the first place—or at any rate that if it was fair to some of its adherents it was not fair to others. They would in this connection distinguish between two types of causes—what they call 'causes *in fieri*' and what they call 'causes *in esse*'. A cause *in fieri* is a factor which brought or helped to bring an effect into existence. A cause *in esse* is a factor which 'sustains' or helps to sustain the effect 'in being'. The parents of a human being would be an example of a cause *in fieri*. If somebody puts a book in my hand and I keep holding it up, his putting it there would be the cause *in fieri*, and my holding it would be the cause *in esse* of the book's position. To quote Father Joyce:

> If a smith forges a horse-shoe, he is only a cause *in fieri* of the shape given to the iron. That shape persists after his action has ceased. So, too, a builder

is a cause *in fieri* of the house which he builds. In both these cases the substances employed act as causes *in esse* as regards the continued existence of the effect produced. Iron, in virtue of its natural rigidity, retains in being the shape which it has once received; and, similarly, the materials employed in building retain in being the order and arrangement which constitute them into a house.[9]

Using this distinction, a defender of the argument now reasons in the following way. To say that there is an infinite series of causes *in fieri* does not lead to any absurd conclusions. But Aquinas is concerned only with causes *in esse* and an infinite series of *such* causes is impossible. In the words of the contemporary American Thomist, R. P. Phillips:

> Each member of the series of causes possesses being solely by virtue of the actual present operation of a superior cause. . . . Life is dependent, *inter alia*, on a certain atmospheric pressure, this again on the continual operation of physical forces, whose being and operation depends on the position of the earth in the solar system, which itself must endure relatively unchanged, a state of being which can only be continuously produced by a definite—if unknown—constitution of the material universe. This constitution, however, cannot be its own cause. That a thing should cause itself is impossible: for in order that it may cause it is necessary for it to exist, which it cannot do, on the hypothesis, until it has been caused. So it must *be* in order to cause itself. Thus, not being uncaused nor yet its own cause, it must be caused by another, which produces and preserves it. It is plain, then, that as no member of this series possesses being except in virtue of the actual present operation of a superior cause, if there be no first cause actually operating none of the dependent causes could operate either. We are thus irresistibly led to posit a first efficient cause which, while itself uncaused, shall impart causality to a whole series. . . .
>
> The series of causes which we are considering is not one which stretches back into the past; so that we are not demanding a beginning of the world at some definite moment reckoning back from the present, but an actual cause now operating, to account for the present being of things.[10]

Professor Phillips offers the following parallel to bring out his point:

> In a goods train each truck is moved and moves by the action of the one immediately in front of it. If then we suppose the train to be infinite, i.e. that there is no end to it, and so no engine which starts the motion, it is plain that no truck will move. To lengthen it out to infinity will not give it what no member of it possesses of itself, viz. the power of drawing the truck behind it. If then we see any truck in motion we know there must be an end to the series of trucks which gives causality to the whole.[11]

---

[9]*The Principles of Natural Theology*, p 58.
[10]*Modern Thomistic Philosophy*, Vol II, pp 284–85.
[11]*Op. cit.* p 278.

Father Joyce introduces an illustration from Aquinas to explain how the present existence of things may be compatible with an infinite series of causes *in fieri* but not with an infinite series of causes *in esse*.

> When a carpenter is at work, the series of efficient causes on which his work depends is necessarily limited. The final effect, e.g. the fastening of a nail is caused by a hammer: the hammer is moved by the arm: and the motion of his arm is determined by the motor-impulses communicated from the nerve centres of the brain. Unless the subordinate causes were limited in number, and were connected with a starting-point of motion, the hammer must remain inert; and the nail will never be driven in. If the series be supposed infinite, no work will ever take place. But if there is question of causes on which the work is not essentially dependent, we cannot draw the same conclusion. We may suppose the carpenter to have broken an infinite number of hammers, and as often to have replaced the broken tool by a fresh one. There is nothing in such a supposition which excludes the driving home of the nail.[12]

The supporter of the infinite series of causes, Joyce also remarks, is

> . . . asking us to believe that although each link in a suspended chain is prevented from falling simply because it is attached to the one above it, yet if only the chain be long enough, it will, taken as a whole, need no support, but will hang loose in the air suspended from nothing.[13]

This formulation of the causal argument unquestionably circumvents one of the objections mentioned previously. If Y is the cause *in esse* of an effect, Z, then it must exist as long as Z exists. If the argument were valid in this form it would therefore prove the present and not merely the past existence of a first cause. In this form the argument is, however, less convincing in another respect. To maintain that all 'natural' or 'phenomenal' objects—things like tables and mountains and human beings—require a cause *in fieri* is not implausible, though even here Mill and others have argued that strictly speaking only *changes* require a causal explanation. It is far from plausible, on the other hand, to claim that all natural objects require a cause *in esse*. It may be granted that the air around us is a cause *in esse* of human life and further that certain gravitational forces are among the causes *in esse* of the air being where it is. But when we come to gravitational forces or, at any rate, to material particles like atoms or electrons it is difficult to see what cause *in esse* they require. To those not already convinced of the need for a supernatural First Cause some of the remarks by Professor Phillips in this connection appear merely dogmatic and question-begging. Most people would grant that such particles as atoms did not cause themselves, since, as Professor Phillips observes, they would in that event have had to exist before they began existing. It is not at all evident, however, that these particles cannot be uncaused. Professor Phillips and all other supporters of the causal argument

---

[12] *Op. cit.* pp 67–8.
[13] *Op. cit.* p 82.

immediately proceed to claim that there is something else which needs no cause *in esse.* They themselves admit thus, that there is nothing self-evident about the proposition that everything must have a cause *in esse.* Their entire procedure here lends substance to Schopenhauer's gibe that supporters of the cosmological argument treat the law of universal causation like 'a hired cab which we dismiss when we have reached our destination'.[14]

But waiving this and all similar objections, the re-statement of the argument in terms of causes *in esse* in no way avoids the main difficulty which was previously mentioned. A believer in the infinite series would insist that his position was just as much misrepresented now as before. He is no more removing the member of the series which is supposed to be the first cause *in esse* than he was removing the member which had been declared to be the first cause *in fieri.* He is again merely denying a privileged status to it. He is not denying the reality of the cause *in esse* labelled 'A'. He is not even necessarily denying that it possesses supernatural attributes. He is again merely taking away its 'first causiness'.

The advocates of the causal argument in either form seem to confuse an infinite series with one which is long but finite. If a book, Z, is to remain in its position, say 100 miles up in the air, there must be another object, say another book, Y, underneath it to serve as its support. If Y is to remain where it is, it will need another support, X, beneath it. Suppose that this series of supports, one below the other, continues for a long time, but eventually, say after 100,000 members, comes to a first book which is not resting on any other book or indeed on any other support. In that event the whole collection would come crashing down. What we seem to need is a first member of the series, a first support (such as the earth) which does not need another member as *its* support, which in other words is 'self-supporting'.

This is evidently the sort of picture that supporters of the First Cause argument have before their minds when they rule out the possibility of an infinite series. But such a picture is not a fair representation of the theory of the infinite series. A *finite* series of books would indeed come crashing down, since the first or lowest member would not have a predecessor on which it could be supported. If the series, however, were infinite this would not be the case. In that event every member *would* have a predecessor to support itself on and there would be no crash. That is to say: a crash can be avoided either by a finite series with a first self-supporting member or by an infinite series. Similarly, the present existence of motion is equally compatible with the theory of a first unmoved mover and with the theory of an infinite series of moving objects; and the present existence of causal activity is compatible with the theory of a first cause *in esse* as much as with the theory of an infinite series of such causes.

The illustrations given by Joyce and Phillips are hardly to the point. It is true that a carpenter would not, *in a finite time-span,* succeed in driving in a nail if he had to carry out an infinite number of movements. For that matter, he would not accomplish this goal in a finite time if he broke an infinite number of hammers However, to make the illustrations relevant we must suppose that he has infinite

---

[14]*The Fourfold Root of the Principle of Sufficient Reason,* pp 42–3. My attention to this passage was drawn by Professor C. J. Ducasse. See his excellent discussion of the arguments for the existence of God in *A Philosophical Scrutiny of Religion,* Ch 15.

time at his disposal. In that case he would succeed in driving in the nail even if he required an infinite number of movements for this purpose. As for the goods train, it may be granted that the trucks do not move unless the train has an engine. But this illustration is totally irrelevant as it stands. A relevant illustration would be that of engines, each moved by the one in front of it. Such a train would move if it were infinite. For every member of this series there would be one in front capable of drawing it along. The advocate of the infinite series of causes does not, as the original illustration suggests, believe in a series whose members are not really causally connected with one another. In the series he believes in every member is genuinely the cause of the one that follows it.

IV

No staunch defender of the cosmological argument would give up at this stage. Even if there were an infinite series of causes *in fieri* or *in esse,* he would contend, this still would not do away with the need for an ultimate, a first cause. As Father Copleston put it in his debate with Bertrand Russell:

> Every object has a phenomenal cause, if you insist on the infinity of the series. But the series of phenomenal causes is an insufficient explanation of the series. Therefore, the series has not a phenomenal cause, but a transcendent cause. . . .[15]
>
> An infinite series of contingent beings will be, to my way of thinking, as unable to cause itself as one contingent being.[16]

The demand to find the cause of the series as a whole rests on the erroneous assumption that the series is something over and above the members of which it is composed. It is tempting to suppose this, at least by implication, because the word 'series' is a noun like 'dog' or 'man'. Like the expression 'this dog' or 'this man' the phrase 'this series' is easily taken to designate an individual object. But reflection shows this to be an error. If we have explained the individual members there is nothing additional left to be explained. Supposing I see a group of five Eskimos standing on the corner of Sixth Avenue and 50th Street and I wish to explain why the group came to New York. Investigation reveals the following stories:

> Eskimo No. 1 did not enjoy the extreme cold in the polar region and decided to move to a warmer climate.
>
> No. 2 is the husband of Eskimo No. 1. He loves her dearly and did not wish to live without her.
>
> No. 3 is the son of Eskimos 1 and 2. He is too small and too weak to oppose his parents.
>
> No. 4 saw an advertisement in the *New York Times* for an Eskimo to appear on television.

---

[15]*Why I Am Not a Christian*, pp 152–53.
[16]*Ibid.* p 151.

No. 5 is a private detective engaged by the Pinkerton Agency to keep an eye on Eskimo No. 4.

Let us assume that we have now explained in the case of each of the five Eskimos why he or she is in New York. Somebody then asks: 'All right, but what about the group as a whole; why is *it* in New York?' This would plainly be an absurd question. There is no group over and above the five members, and if we have explained why each of the five members is in New York we have *ipso facto* explained why the group is there. It is just as absurd to ask for the cause of the series as a whole as distinct from asking for the causes of individual members.

V

It is most unlikely that a determined defender of the cosmological line of reasoning would surrender even here. He would probably admit that the series is not a thing over and above its members and that it does not make sense to ask for the cause of the series if the cause of each member has already been found. He would insist, however, that when he asked for the explanation of the entire series, he was not asking for its *cause.* He was really saying that a series, finite or infinite, is not 'intelligible' or 'explained' if it consists of nothing but 'contingent' members. To quote Father Copleston once more:

> What we call the world is intrinsically unintelligible apart from the existence of God. The infinity of the series of events, if such an infinity could be proved, would not be in the slightest degree relevant to the situation. If you add up chocolates, you get chocolates after all, and not a sheep. If you add up chocolates to infinity, you presumably get an infinite number of chocolates. So, if you add up contingent beings to infinity, you still get contingent beings, not a necessary being.[17]

This last quotation is really a summary of the 'contingency argument', the other main form of the cosmological proof and the third of the five ways of Aquinas. It may be stated more fully in these words: All around us we perceive contingent beings. This includes all physical objects and also all human minds. In calling them 'contingent' we mean that they might not have existed. We mean that the universe can be *conceived* without this or that physical object, without this or that human being, however certain their actual existence may be. These contingent beings we can trace back to other contingent beings—e.g. a human being to his parents. However, since these other beings are also contingent, they do not provide a real or full explanation. The contingent beings we originally wanted explained have not yet become intelligible, since the beings to which they have been traced back are no more necessary than they were. It is just as true of our parents, for example, as it is of ourselves, that they might not have existed. We can then properly explain the contingent beings around us only by tracing them back ultimately to some necessary being, to something which exists

---

[17]*Op. cit.* p. 151.

necessarily, which has 'the reason for its existence within itself'. The existence of contingent beings, in other words, implies the existence of a necessary being.

This form of the cosmological argument is even more beset with difficulties than the causal variety. In the first place, there is the objection, stated with great force by Kant, that it really commits the same error as the ontological argument in tacitly regarding existence as an attribute or characteristic. To say that there is a necessary being is to say that it would be a self-contradiction to deny its existence. This would mean that at least one existential statement is a necessary truth; and this in turn presupposes that in at least one case existence is contained in a concept. But only a characteristic can be contained in a concept and it has seemed plain to most philosophers since Kant that existence is not a characteristic, that it can hence never be contained in a concept, and that hence no existential statement can ever be a necessary truth. To talk about anything 'existing necessarily' is in their view about as sensible as to talk about round squares, and they have concluded that the contingency-argument is quite absurd.

It would lead too far to discuss here the reasons for denying that existence is a characteristic. I will assume that this difficulty can somehow be surmounted and that the expression 'necessary being', as it is intended by the champions of the contingency-argument, might conceivably apply to something. There remain other objections which are of great weight. I shall try to state these by first quoting again from the debate between Bertrand Russell and Father Copleston:

RUSSELL: . . . It all turns on this question of sufficient reason, and I must say you haven't defined "sufficient reason" in a way that I can understand—what do you mean by sufficient reason? You don't mean cause?

COPLESTON: Not necessarily. Cause is a kind of sufficient reason. Only contingent being can have a cause. God is his own sufficient reason; and he is not cause of himself. By sufficient reason in the full sense I mean an explanation adequate for the existence of some particular being.

RUSSELL: But when is an explanation adequate? Suppose I am about to make a flame with a match. You may say that the adequate explanation of that is that I rub it on the box.

COPLESTON: Well for practical purposes—but theoretically, that is only a partial explanation. An adequate explanation must ultimately be a total explanation, to which nothing further can be added.

RUSSELL: Then I can only say that you're looking for something which can't be got, and which one ought not to expect to get.

COPLESTON: To say that one has not found it is one thing; to say that one should not look for it seems to me rather dogmatic.

RUSSELL: Well, I don't know. I mean, the explanation of one thing is another thing which makes the other thing dependent on yet another, and you have to grasp this sorry scheme of things entire to do what you want, and that we can't do.[18]

Russell's main point here may be expanded in the following way. The contingency-argument rests on a misconception of what an explanation is and does, and

---

[18]*Op. cit.* p 150.

similarly on what it is that makes phenomena 'intelligible'. Or else it involves an obscure and arbitrary redefinition of 'explanation', 'intelligible', and related terms. Normally, we are satisfied that we have explained a phenomenon if we have found its cause or if we have exhibited some other uniform or near-uniform connection between it and something else. Confining ourselves to the former case, which is probably the most common, we might say that a phenomenon, Z, has been explained if it has been traced back to a group of factors, a, b, c, d, etc., which are its cause. These factors are the full and real explanation of Z, quite regardless of whether they are pleasing or displeasing, admirable or contemptible, necessary or contingent. The explanation would not be adequate only if the factors listed are not really the cause of Z. If they are the cause of Z, the explanation would be adequate, even though each of the factors is merely a 'contingent' being.

Let us suppose that we have been asked to explain why General Eisenhower won the elections of 1952. 'He was an extremely popular general', we might answer, 'while Stevenson was relatively little known; moreover there was a great deal of resentment over the scandals in the Truman Administration.' If somebody complained that this was only a partial explanation we might mention additional antecedents, such as the widespread belief that the Democrats had allowed communist agents to infiltrate the State Department, that Eisenhower was a man with a winning smile, and that unlike Stevenson he had shown the good sense to say one thing on race relations in the North and quite another in the South. Theoretically, we might go further and list the motives of all American voters during the weeks or months preceding the elections. If we could do this we would have explained Eisenhower's victory. We would have made it intelligible. We would 'understand' why he won and why Stevenson lost. Perhaps there is a sense in which we might make Eisenhower's victory even more intelligible if we went further back and discussed such matters as the origin of American views on Communism or of racial attitudes in the North and South. However, to explain the outcome of the election in any ordinary sense, loose or strict, it would not be necessary to go back to prehistoric days or to the amoeba or to a first cause, if such a first cause exists. Nor would our explanation be considered in any way defective because each of the factors mentioned was a 'contingent' and not a necessary being. The only thing that matters is whether the factors were really the cause of Eisenhower's election. If they were, then it has been explained although they are contingent beings. If they were not the cause of Eisenhower's victory, we would have failed to explain it even if each of the factors were a necessary being.

If it is granted that, in order to explain a phenomenon or to make it intelligible, we need not bring in a necessary being, then the contingency-argument breaks down. For a series, as was already pointed out, is not something over and above its members; and every contingent member of it could in that case be explained by reference to other contingent beings. But I should wish to go further than this and it is evident from Russell's remarks that he would do so also. Even if it were granted, both that the phrase 'necessary being' is meaningful and that all explanations are defective unless the phenomena to be explained are traced back to a necessary being, the conclusion would still not have been established. The conclusion follows from this premise together with the additional premise that *there are* explanations of phenomena in the special sense just mentioned. It is this further premise which Russell (and many other philosophers) would ques tion. They do not merely question, as Copleston implies, whether human beings can ever obtain explanations in this sense, but whether they *exist*. To assume without further ado that phenomena have explanations or an explanation in this sense is to beg the very point at issue. The use of the same word 'explanation' in two crucially different ways lends the additional premise a plausibility it does not really possess. It may indeed be highly plausible to assert that phenomena have explanations, whether we have found them or not, in the ordinary sense in which this usually means that they have causes. It is then tempting to suppose, because of the use of the same word, that they also have explanations in a sense in which this implies dependence on a necessary being. But this is a gross *non sequitur.*

VI

It is necessary to add a few words about the proper way of formulating the position of those who reject the main premise of the cosmological argument, in either of the forms we have considered. It is sometimes maintained in this connection that in order to reach a 'self-existing' entity it is not necessary to go beyond the universe: the universe itself (or 'Nature') is 'self-existing'. And this in turn is sometimes expanded into the statement that while all individual things 'within' the universe are caused, the universe itself is uncaused. Statements of this kind are found in Büchner, Bradlaugh, Haeckel, and other free-thinkers of the nineteenth and early twentieth century. Sometimes the assertion that the universe is 'self-existing' is elaborated to mean that *it* is the 'necessary being'. Some eighteenth-century unbelievers, apparently accepting the view that there is a necessary being, asked why Nature or the material universe could not fill the bill as well or better than God.

> 'Why', asks one of the characters in Hume's *Dialogues,* 'may not the material universe be the necessarily existent Being? . . . We dare not affirm that we know all the qualities of matter; and for aught we can determine, it may contain some qualities, which, were they known, would make its non-exis- tence appear as great a contradiction as that twice two is five.'[19]

Similar remarks can be found in Holbach and several of the Encyclopedists.

The former of these formulations immediately invites the question why the universe, alone of all 'things', is exempted from the universal sway of causation. 'The strong point of the cosmological argument', writes Dr Ewing, 'is that after all it does remain incredible that the physical universe should just have happened. . . . It calls out for some further explanation of some kind.'[20] The latter formulation is exposed to the criticism that there is nothing any more 'necessary' about the existence of the universe or Nature as a whole than about any particular thing within the universe.

I hope some of the earlier discussions in this article have made it clear that in

---

[19] *Op. cit.* Part IX.
[20] *Op. cit.* p 225.

rejecting the cosmological argument one is not committed to either of these propositions. If I reject the view that there is a supernatural first cause, I am not thereby committed to the proposition that there is a *natural* first cause, and even less to the proposition that a mysterious 'thing' called 'the universe' qualifies for this title. I may hold that there is no 'universe' over and above individual things of various sorts; and, accepting the causal principle, I may proceed to assert that all these things are caused by other things, and these other things by yet other things, and so on, *ad infinitum.* In this way no arbitrary exception is made to the principle of causation. Similarly, if I reject the assertion that God is a 'necessary being', I am not committed to the view that the universe is such an entity. I may hold that it does not make sense to speak of anything as a 'necessary being' and that even if there were such a thing as the universe it could not be properly considered a necessary being.

However, in saying that nothing is uncaused or that there is no necessary being, one is not committed to the view that everything, or for that matter anything, is merely a 'brute fact'. Dr Ewing laments that 'the usual modern philosophical views opposed to theism do not try to give any rational explanation of the world at all, but just take it as a brute fact not to be explained'. They thus fail to 'rationalize' the universe. Theism, he concedes, cannot completely rationalize things either since it does not show 'how God can be his own cause or how it is that he does not need a cause'.[21] Now, if one means by 'brute fact' something for which there *exists* no explanation (as distinct from something for which no explanation is in our possession), then the theists have at least one brute fact on their hands, namely God. Those who adopt Büchner's formulation also have one brute fact on their hands, namely 'the universe'. Only the position I have been supporting dispenses with brute facts altogether. I don't know if this is any special virtue, but the defenders of the cosmological argument seem to think so.

---

[21]*Op. cit.* p 225.

Chapter
THIRTEEN

THEISTIC
ARGUMENTS
purpose and
probability

THE FIFTH WAY
St. Thomas Aquinas

From St. Thomas Aquinas, *Summa Theologica,* part I, question 2, article 3 (in part), Anton C. Pegis (ed.), *Basic Writings of St. Thomas Aquinas,* 1968. Used by permission of Random House, Inc., New York.

The fifth way is taken from the governance of the world. We see that things which lack knowledge, such as natural bodies, act for an end, and this is evident from their acting always, or nearly always, in the same way, so as to obtain the best result. Hence it is plain that they achieve their end, not fortuitously, but designedly. Now whatever lacks knowledge cannot move towards an end, unless it be directed by some being endowed with knowledge and intelligence; as the arrow is directed by the archer. Therefore some intelligent being exists by whom all natural things are directed to their end; and this being we call God.

A REFORMULATION OF THE ARGUMENT FROM DESIGN
F. R. Tennant

From F. R. Tennant, *Philosophical Theology,* vol. II, chapter 4, pp. 99–120. Used by permission of Cambridge University Press.

In an exposition of the significance of the moral order for theistic philosophy, the first step is to point out that man belongs to Nature, and is an essential part of it, in such a sense that the world cannot be described or explained as a whole without taking him and his moral values into account. Prof. Pringle-Pattison, especially, has elaborated the doctrine that, as he expresses it, "man is organic to the world". What precisely this, or the similar phrase "man is the child of Nature", should mean, if either is to be more than a half-truth, needs to be made clear. In so far as man's soul, *i.e.* man as *noümenon,* or (in the language of spiritualistic pluralism) the dominant monad in the empirical self, is concerned, we are not authorised by known facts to regard man as organic to Nature, or as the child of Nature, in the sense that he is an emergent product of cosmic evolution. We are rather forbidden by psychology to entertain any such notion. But, this proviso being observed—it must qualify all that is further said in the present connexion—we can affirm that man's body, with all its conditioning of his mentality, his sociality, knowledge and morality, is 'of a piece' with Nature; and that, in so far as he is a phenomenal being, man is organic to Nature, or a product of the world. And this fact is as significant for our estimation of Nature as for our anthropology. If man is Nature's child, Nature is the wonderful mother of such a child. Any account of her which ignores the fact of her maternity is scientifically partial and philosophically insignificant. Her capacity to produce man must be reckoned among her potencies, explain it how we may. And man is no monstrous birth out of due time, no freak or sport. In respect of his body and the bodily conditioning of his mentality, man is like, and has genetic continuity with, Nature's humbler and earlier-born children. In the fulness of time Nature found self-utterance in a son possessed of the intelligent and moral status. Maybe she was pregnant with him from the beginning, and the world-ages are the period of her gestation. As to this anthropocentric view of the world-process, and its co-extensiveness with teleological interpretation, more will presently be said. But in the light of man's continuity with the rest of the world we can at once dismiss the view that Nature suddenly "stumbled" or "darkly blundered" on man, while "churning the universe with mindless motion". The world-process is a *praeparatio anthropologica,* whether designedly or not, and man is the culmination, up to the present stage of the knowable history of Nature, of a gradual ascent. We cannot explain man in terms of physical Nature; conceivably Nature may be found explicable—in another sense of the word—in terms of man, and can be called 'the threshold of spirit'. Judging the genealogical tree by its roots, naturalism once preached that Darwin had put an end to the assumption that man occupies an exceptional position on our planet; apparently implying that there is no difference of status between man and the primordial slime because stages between the two are traceable. But if we judge the tree by its fruits, Darwin may rather be said to have restored man to the position from which Copernicus seemed to have ousted him, in making it possible to read the humanising of Nature in the naturalising of man, and to regard man as not only the last term and the crown of Nature's long upward effort, but also as its end or goal.[1]

The phrase 'organic to Nature', as applied to man, may serve to sum up other relations between humanity and the world besides that of parentage or blood-affinity. It implies also a denial of the assertion that man is an excrescence upon Nature in the sense of being an alien in a world that is indifferent to his moral aims, or hostile to his ideals. The most forcible presentation of this view, that the cosmic process and human morality are antithetical, is perhaps that contained in Huxley's *Romanes Lecture.* It is therefore here selected for examination. Huxley's first point was that the world, as involving struggle for existence and extermination of the less fit, is no "school of virtue". If that statement merely meant that it is not from Nature that we are to imbibe our ethical maxims, no one would wish to dispute it. But it would then overlook the fact that in other senses Nature may fairly be called a school of virtue. In the first place, Nature is largely a cosmos ruled by uniformity or law; and if Nature's uniformity and impartiality are a main source of the trouble to which man is born, they are also a precondition of all intelligent, and therefore of all moral, life. In this respect Nature is the power that makes it possible for noümenal man to be, as phenomenal man, a moral being. Further, it is partly through his being "the plaything of hazard and the prey of hardship" that man's moral virtues are acquired. The world is thus instrumental to the emergence, maintenance, and progressiveness, of morality. The second charge which Huxley preferred against the cosmos is that the physical world

---

[1] A. Seth Pringle-Pattison, *The Idea of God,* 1917, pp. 82 f.

works upon man solely through his lower nature, his ingrained appetites, etc., and against his higher ethical interests. Nature is thus the cause of his 'original sin', and is diabolically provocative of his diverse immoralities. This also is true; but again it presents but one aspect of the facts. For, apart from man's bodily appetites and impulses it is inconceivable that ethical principles should gain purchase on him. Hunger and sex are the bed-rock of human morality; and the self-determination which human morality presupposes is hardly possible without the conflict between moral reason and non-moral impulse. Morality cannot be made without raw material; and in providing this raw material Nature is once more instrumental to man's acquisition of the moral status. Morality thus has its roots in Nature, however indispensable be the innate and non-inherited potentialities of the pure ego or soul. The non-moral cosmos, personified into a morally evil world by pessimistic poets for the purpose of giving it, as Mr. Chesterton has said of one of them, a piece of their mind, has nevertheless subserved the moralisation of human souls, even when soliciting to carnality. And it is an exaggeration to say that Nature fosters only tendencies that issue in vice. We have seen before that there is such a thing as 'natural virtue', or 'original rectitude', as 'instinctive' as is self-seeking; and Nature plainly appraises health and vigour, thus inciting to temperance and self-control. Lastly, Huxley maintained that the world is indifferent to man's moral aspirations, in that they along with him are destined to be extinguished before the break-up of the solar system. Here he became unwarrantably dogmatical: for, apart from the fact that science's predictions are not unconditional, speculations as to the ruin of a fragment of the universe, based on partial knowledge of a larger fragment of what, for all we know, may be possessed of a power to make all things new, are too precarious to be considered exhaustive of the possibilities even as to our terrestrial home, let alone those as to a future life.

Nature, then, has produced moral beings, is instrumental to moral life and therefore amenable to 'instrumental' moral valuation, and is relatively modifiable by operative moral ideas—or, rather, by moral agents pursuing ideals. Nature and moral man are not at strife, but are organically one. The whole process of Nature is capable of being regarded as instrumental to the development of intelligent and moral creatures. Acquisition of the moral status is in line with the other stages of the long 'ascent of man', and is its climax—unless we reserve that name for the morality which, tinged with sentiment transcending reverence for duty, passes into religion.

(vi) The more or less separable fields of fact which have now been surveyed may each be said to admit of teleological explanation even if explanation of the causal or the descriptive type be forthcoming in every case. None of them calls for resort to final causes merely because other kinds of causality, or linkage according to law, are not assignable. Theism no longer plants its God in the gaps between the explanatory achievements of natural science, which are apt to get scientifically closed up. Causal explanation and teleological explanation are not mutually exclusive alternatives; and neither can perform the function of the other. It is rather when these several fields of fact are no longer considered one by one, but as parts of a whole or terms of a continuous series, and when for their dovetailing and interconnectedness a sufficient ground is sought, such as mechanical and proximate causation no longer seems to supply, that divine design is forcibly suggested. Paley's watch is no analogue of the human eye; but it may none the less be an approximate analogue of Nature as a whole. Thus the wider teleological argument is not comparable with a chain whose strength is precisely that of its weakest link; it is comparable rather with a piece of chain-armour. And this can the better be seen if the relevant facts be presented again so as to display especially their connexions and their gradually increasing suggestiveness.

There is no intrinsic necessity that a world, or an assemblage of existents and happenings, indefinably and unaccountably 'standing out' as against nothingness, be a cosmos, even to the extent of any one existent being comparable with another or behaving in the same way twice. Reality, or the aggregate of those determinate beings, might conceivably be a 'chaos' of disparates and inconsistencies such that if any of its members possessed consciousness or awareness and the potentiality of intelligence, they would find the world presented to them utterly unintelligible. Our world is, however, a cosmos, at least in the humblest sense of the word, and the original determinateness of its terms or *posita* is such as to make it intelligible. This, of course, constitutes a teleological proof of theism no more than does the existence of the world afford a causal or cosmological proof. The mystery of mysteries is that something exists; and if the one underived or uncaused existent be God, the creator of all things else, God is "the last irrationality", and creation is the next to the last inexplicability. To replace absolute pluralism by theism is to reduce an indefinite number of separate inexplicabilities to these two alone; and so far economy, and therefore explicability of a kind, is secured. It is of no important kind, however: for there is no more wonder about a self-subsistent plurality than about a self-subsistent individual. But when the intelligibility of a cosmos, rather than the mere existence of a world of any sort, is the fact to be considered, teleological theism evinces more conspicuously its advantage, in other respects than that of economy, over absolute pluralism. For over and above the forthcomingness, conceived as self-subsistence, of the many existents, is their adaptiveness, inherent in their primary determinateness and their relations, to the requirements of intelligibility. This further particularises their determinateness and so bespeaks more of coincidence in the 'fortuitous'. For cosmos-quality, or intelligibility, in our world, which conceivably might have been but a determinate 'chaos', non-theistic philosophy can assign no reason. If the world 'made itself', so to say, or is the self-subsistent Absolute, its adaptiveness to understanding has simply happened, and is part and parcel of the pluralist's last irrationality. It gives him more to explain or to refuse to explain: for why should the many arrange themselves to form an intelligible and an organic whole? If, on the other hand, this be due to an intelligent Creator designing the world to be a theatre for rational life, mystery is minimised, and a possible and sufficient reason is assigned. More than this cannot be extracted out of the initial fact that the world is intelligible, in the sense that has as yet solely been in question; but if it be merely a hint that Nature's dice may be loaded, it is to be observed that the hint becomes broader as Nature is further examined, and as the knowledge-process is analysed. For instance, the particular species of intelligibility, in which the knowledge of common sense and science consists, is mediated by the 'real' categories; and they depend for their forthcomingness on the contingency that the dominant monad in man is embodied, or associated with monads such as also constitute Nature but which, in virtue of some mysterious affinity, are not merely bits of Nature to the soul but also its windows and telephonic exchange-office mediating to it all its knowledge whatsoever, even its self-knowledge. Thus, as step by step the machinery which produces intelligibility is scientifically explored and made manifest, the richer in specialised determinateness are some of the world's constituents found to be; and therefore the more suggestive is the intricate adaptiveness, involved in knowledge of the world by man, of pre-established harmony or immanent guidance, or both, and the less reasonable or credible becomes the alternative theory of cumulative groundless coincidence. The doctrine that man is organic to Nature can now be broadened out so as to embrace the fact that it is only in so far as he is part and parcel of Nature that he can effectively make the knowledge-venture, and only in virtue of Nature's affinity with him that his postulatory categories receive pragmatic verification, and his assimilation-drafts are honoured. When the impossible Cartesian rationalism is exchanged for the human-ism or anthropism which, implicit in Kant, is explicitly demanded by more modern empirical knowledge of the human mind, the epistemological argument for theism begins to acquire a forcibleness that was lacking to the arbitrary, if not circular, reasoning of Descartes. It is, however, but a fragment of the epistemo-logical argument to establish the anthropocentric theory of knowledge, which is ultimately based on the fact that between the soul and the world, in so far as knowledge of the one by the other is concerned, stands the body; and the epistemological line or mesh-work is but a fragment of the teleological argument as a whole.

Turning now from Nature's knowability to her structure and history, we may revert first to the fact of adaptiveness in the organic realm, which, so far, has only been found not to yield teleological proof of the narrower kind. Here adaptive-ness, unhappily described as internal teleology, is not teleological at all in so far as it is internal to the organism. There is no end present to the agent. It is from the (ps) standpoint of the biologist, not from the (ψ) standpoint of the organism, that reference to the future is involved in organic adaptedness. Again, neither the occurrence nor the progressiveness of organic adaptations, taken *singillatim*, calls for other than natural, if non-mechanical, causation. It is true that the course of living Nature is not mere change, but change that admits of valuation, of one kind or another; of valuation not only in terms of fitness for survival but also in terms of differentiation or complexity of structure and function, and of sub-servience to further development culminating, in man, in rationality and morality. Despite cases of stagnancy and of degeneration, which equally with progress may ensure biological fitness, the plasticity, formative power, or *élan* in organic Nature secures not only self-conservation but also progress, morphological and ultimately mental, so that within the main line of developement there has been a steady advance from amoeba to man. But each step and special adaptation, each case of emergence of something new and higher, in this long process, can be sufficiently accounted for in terms of natural, non-teleological causation. So far as the foregoing facts are concerned there is no need to resort to external teleology. It is not *necessary* to invoke design in order to find a guarantee for the stability, in face of the ever-present possibility of deletion of the 'higher' by the 'fitter', of the long and gradual ascent, remarkable as that is. It is rather when the essential part played by the environment, physical and organic, in the progressive develope-ment of the organic world, is appreciated, that non-teleological explanation ceases to be plausible in this sphere, and, conspiration being precluded, external design begins to be indicated or strongly suggested. It is the environment that is the selector, though 'selection' is a figurative expression when applied to non-intelligent Nature. Subjective selection, or the Lamarckean factor, may decide what shall arise; but the environment decides what shall stand. And before discussing the alternatives of theistic teleology and naturalistic Pyrrhonism (if the doctrine of fortuitousness or ungrounded coincidence may so be called), it may be submitted that the fact just mentioned restricts our choice to the one or the other of them, in that, when taken into account, it deprives the only other forthcoming alternative, viz. the theory of 'unconscious purpose', of such plausibility as, *prima facie,* it may seem to possess.

The phrases 'unconscious will' and 'unconscious purpose' are, of course, when taken literally, contradictions in terms. That, however, is unimportant. Overlooking the poetic licence evinced in such forms of speech, we may inquire what the writers who favour them mean by them, or what are their equivalents in scientific terminology. This is not always easy to ascertain with precision; but it would seem to amount to the assertion of an *élan vital* present in Nature as a whole, an intrinsic potency to strive blindly towards, and to attain by changes that we valuing subjects call progressive from the lower to the higher, what, from the same intelligent point of view, are relative goals: not ends of a designer, nor merely temporally later stages in a process, but 'ends' in the sense of later stages that happen to be of higher value, of one kind or another, than the earlier stages, *as if* foreseen and striven for. This kind of *Zweckmässigkeit* without *Absicht-lichkeit* has a parallel in human endeavours. Men have sometimes "built more wisely than they knew", and human societies may fashion institutions, beliefs, etc., without any of their members having a preconceived definite idea of the 'end' in which their activities are destined to issue. One thing that was willed leads on to other things that were not at first willed or even imagined, and *sometimes* these other things are found desirable, or are goods to be preserved. Sometimes, however, they are of the opposite kind, so that reforms or revolu-tions find place in human history. And here, if the theory before us be not misunderstood, this analogy breaks down. For the theory ascribes to Nature an intrinsic potency which, if it is to succeed in the absence of that self-correction by which erring human mentality can change its own course and avoid impending catastrophes, must inevitably go, like animal instinct, straight to its mark in all essentials and on all critical occasions. Nature's 'unconscious wisdom', in other words, must vastly exceed the sapience and foresight of humanity, liable as that is to errors which, save for reasoned amendment, might prove fatal. In fact the theory requires us to believe that Nature keeps her head, which *ex hypothesi* is brainless, through all the changes and chances of cosmic history.

Further, 'unconscious purpose', which has turned out to be as fatalistic as mechanism and yet as value-realising as man, does not seem, on examination, to be one and the same thing in the different kingdoms of Nature. In that part of the organic world that is (macroscopically) psychical it is said to be exemplified in animal impulse, or the non-volitional conation of individual organisms. But this subjective selectiveness of the individual, though essential to organic developement, does not of itself suffice to secure it. The organism, in filling its skin, may get itself a better skin to fill, but on the other hand it might burst its skin; and blind or random movement, such as might secure escape from the painful or displeasing, may land 'out of the frying-pan into the fire'. Natural selection can only secure the progress of species in virtue of such individual catastrophes, misfits, etc., in organisms inspired with venturesomeness and *élan*. Individual variations are mostly indefinite or in many directions, not in the straight path of progress alone; and it is the environment, as censor, that plays the larger part in determining a steady and permanent advance, as contrasted with the sporadic and evanescent experiments which make progress a possibility. Thus the environment, the preponderating part of which is inorganic, as well as its organic denizens, needs to be accredited with 'unconscious purpose'; yet it lacks even the animal conatus and the vegetable 'formative power' which, though they are Actualities, are not unconsciously *purposive,* in that, of themselves, they are not fraught with an exclusively progressive trend. A formative power lodged in the physical, as science has hitherto understood it, making as if for a goal, is not an Actuality known to science. Consequently, it here becomes impossible to find any explanatoriness, and indeed any meaning, in 'unconscious purpose'. If it but asserts that in the inorganic world there is a potency of adaptiveness, that is but a new name for the fact that the environment is adapted; it but restates the fact to be explained, the problem to be solved, and proffers no explanation or solution. An explanation, however, is offered by teleology and theism. It is a fact that Nature, as inorganic, is as much adapted to organic life as organic life is adaptive to physical environment; and it is not a matter of indifference whether we say "God has wisely willed it so" or "Nature has wisely arranged this", simply because Nature has no wisdom wherewith to arrange anything. If Nature evinces wisdom, the wisdom is Another's. The issue narrows to whether what we may generically call the order in Nature is to be accounted an outcome of wisdom or of undesigned coincidence. Indeed, in so far as the question is as to explicability, the issue narrows to the vanishing-point; for assertion of coincidence in the self-subsistent, wondrous in respect of its manifoldness and complex interlacingness, is, again, not explanation but statement of what calls for explanation.

The manifoldness of the coincidences on which the order in the world, including man, is conditional, has already been sufficiently illustrated, though it might be more minutely and extensively expounded. These coincidences, let it be repeated, are present in the determinate natures of the cosmic elements, the world's original existents and their primary collocations, in the adjustment of similarity to difference between them which is the ground of all the uniformity and variety, the stability and the progressiveness, of the irreversible process of becoming; in the alogical *posita,* their logico-mathematical relations, their determinate *rapport* which is such as to provide a law-making, and so a law-governed, world; a world instrumental to valuation and evocative of it, and intelligible in the peculiar anthropic sense which saturates the meaning of 'knowledge' whenever that word denotes the Actual processes in which the human mind comes to an understanding with Actuality. What is here being called coincidence is to be seen, again, in the stages of emergence of novelty which issue not, as conceivably they might and as mere mechanism suggests they perhaps should, in successive labile configurations of a cosmic dust-cloud blown by a changing cosmic wind, but in an evolutionary process in which much goes that comes, while nevertheless the unceasing flux is such that one whole world-state is, as it were, a built storey and a scaffolding for the erection of another. Emergents 'here' seem to 'take note of', or be relevant to, causally unconnected[2] emergents 'there', in both space and time, since an elaborate interlacing of contingencies is requisite to secure inorganic Nature's adaptedness to be a theatre of life. Any miscarriage in promiscuous 'naturation', such as might ruin the whole, as a puff of air may lay low the soaring house of cards, has been avoided in the making of *Natura naturata;* and though such possibilities do not suggest themselves to science contemplating Nature as a system of Lagrangean equations, the historical process conceivably might be seen to have teemed with critical moments and crucial situations by a visualising compeer of Laplace's calculator. Similarly in the organic world, erratic and venturesomely varying conative individuals may have constantly endangered, as much as they have provided for, the future of the world. Orderly progress, however, has been attained; and it has been ensured by the firm hand and the directivity of already stabilised environment. Organisms, and man in especial measure, have the world with them in their aspiringness. It is not so much the progressiveness displayed in the world-process as the intricate and harmonious interconnexion, rendering progress, intelligibility and intelligence, etc., possible, that in its marvellousness suggests intelligent art. On the other hand, it is the progressiveness which suggests that such art is directed toward an end—realisation of 'the good'.

So long as attention is paid exclusively to the universal, the logical and rational, as is necessary in the case of science but is arbitrary in the case of philosophy, the inner significance of this world, with all its particular 'thusness', will be missed. It is in the concrete or the historical, to which the universal is but incidental and of which the logical or rational is but one nexus among others, that meaning can be, and seems to be, conveyed: and as the history, made by the mindless or by practically infinitesimal minds, is on so grand a scale intelligible to universalising intellect, there would seem to be directive intelligence behind it. It is in the characteristics of *this* world, in the particular determinateness of the collocations prescriptive of its Actual course, and—not least—in the anthropism thrust by Nature on the non-anthropic pure egos out of which she has made men, and its affinity with the world in respect of both genetic continuity and epistemic capacity, that purposiveness lets itself be read. If we thus read things, a unique significance attaches to the realm of the moral, amongst other teleologically suggestive domains of fact, in that it enables us to advance from belief that the world is a work of art to belief that it is constructed for a purpose, and worthily specifies what the purpose is, or includes. If we decline to explain things thus, it would seem that the only alternative is to regard the self-subsistent entities, of which the world is constituted, as comparable with letters of type which have shuffled themselves not only into a book or a literature but also into a reader commanding the particular tongue in which the book utters its unintentional meaning. If the inference from cumulative adaptiveness to design be non-logical, as is admitted, it at least is not unreasonable.

---

[2]Causally unconnected in the sense in which experimental science must use the notion of causal connexion.

Even critical and iconoclastic philosophers have treated with respect forms of teleological argument such as were current in their day. Hume denied that the argument is logically coercive, but he allows Philo, in the *Dialogues,* to admit that the fitness of final causes in the universe and its parts strikes us with such irresistible force that all objections to them appear cavils and sophisms. Kant, again, speaks of it as the clearest of the 'proofs', and as the one most in harmony with the common reason of mankind. Yet the more comprehensive and synoptic design-argument that is now producible is more imposing than any contemplated in their day. Hume almost ignored man and his moral status; while Kant, who saw in man's moral faculty the central fact about the universe, so over-emphasised its purely rational functioning as to overlook its historical developement, its alogical content, and the respects in which it is 'of a piece' with Nature. The greater strength claimed for the newer argument consists in its exhibition of the interconnexion and reciprocal adaptation between systems of fact which used to be treated as if isolated. It can now be submitted that if the uniformity of Nature rests on mechanical postulates, and the 'validity' of moral principles involves a moral postulate, the evolutionary progressiveness of the world points to a teleological postulate. And if this evolution is to be explained, or to be assigned a sufficient ground, instead of being merely accepted as a brute happening, the historical and alogical aspect of the world-process must not only be regarded as the primary reality *in ordine cognoscendi* but also as our clue to the *ordo,* and the *ratio, essendi.* Mechanism and the universalisings of pure rationality are tools as useless for this purpose as a typing-machine and a book of logarithms are for landscape-painting: for the problem is reducible to the question, *cui bono?* Teleological explanation is comparable with discernment of "the signs of the times" rather than of "the face of the sky"; and although to fail to discern cosmical signs of the former kind need not be to class oneself with the "hypocrites", to be indifferent as to whether there be such signs may be said to involve venturing less than the "all that doth become a man". Perhaps no thinking being is thus indifferent, or even uninquisitive. When the teleological or theistic explanation of the world is not adopted, it is because one's explanation-craving is satiated before the limit to which the theist presses is reached in the regress, or because a seemingly better explanation has been found, or because one has become convinced that none has been found that tallies with all the facts. Whether theism satisfies this last condition will be discussed in another chapter, and more remains to be said as to certain alternatives to theism; but it has perhaps already been shewn that no *explanation* is contained in the assertion that the world is an organic whole and consequently involves adaptiveness. That is only a restatement of the occult and wondrous fact that cries for explanation. The world's 'thusness' is explained, however, if it be attributable to the design and creativeness of a Being whose purpose is, or includes, the realisation of moral values. Further back than a creative Spirit it is neither needful nor possible to go. But further back than the world we can and must go, because the notion of a non-intelligent world that produces intelligent beings and makes itself intelligible, that can have no purpose and yet abundantly seems to bespeak one, and so forth, is not the clearest and most reason-satisfying conception that our minds can build wherein to rest. Moreover, as J. Ward has observed, the alternative that the world's evolution is ultimate, or its own sufficient reason, ignores the fact that we rational beings are part of the evolution, so that our demand for a sufficient reason is "a demand that the world itself has raised".

At more than one place in this chapter stress has been laid on the intelligibility of the world to the specifically anthropic intelligence possessed by us, and on the connexion between the conditioning of that intelligibility, on the one hand, and the constitution and process of Nature, on the other hand. Thus a close relationship is indicated between teleological explanation and an anthropocentric world-view; and this relationship may now be more explicitly described.

Anthropocentrism, in some sense, is involved in cosmic teleology. It is useless for ethical theism to argue that the world evidences design unless the only rational and moral denizen of the world, in so far as it is known to us, be assumed to afford an indication as to what the designed end of the world-process is. And, as thus stated, anthropocentrism involves no human arrogance or self-exaltation. It does not assert that man, as a zoological species or genus whose geographical distribution is presumably confined to this planet, is the highest being under God, or the final stage of progressive cosmic evolution, or the end and the whole end of the divine design. It is compatible with belief in "thrones, dominions, principalities, powers", or angels and archangels, and in the possibility that in other worlds there are rational beings akin to us in being embodied and having their specific intelligence moulded thereby.[3] It is content to allow that the divine end, in its completeness, is unfathomable. Nor does it imply that lower creatures evolved in the world-process are necessarily of but instrumental value as stages or means to ends, and, when not figuring in man's genealogical tree, are mere by-products in the making of humanity. Anthropocentrism rather means that, whereas in the realm of Nature beneath man no final purpose can be discerned, such purpose may be discerned in beings possessed of rationality, appreciation, self-determination, and morality. Man may exhibit these powers and attributes in but a limited or humble degree. But, in its essence, intelligence may be common to a hierarchy of beings; and it is in virtue of his membership in that hierarchy, if such there be, rather than in his distinctive or specific and contingent characteristics, the anthropic or human, that man shares the privilege of being a bearer of the highest values, and of being in some relative, rather than in an absolute and exhaustive, sense bound up with the otherwise ineffable divine purpose. Teleology is interpretation of beginnings by *terminus ad quem,* lower stages by higher, process by product, and temporal becoming in terms of realisation of

---

[3]It is, of course, a matter of indifference to teleology and anthropocentric interpretation whether the material heavens contain a plurality of inhabited worlds. But it is interesting to find recent astronomy, as represented by Prof. Eddington, inclined to the views that the physical universe probably does not greatly extend beyond the range of human observation, and that the number of the heavenly bodies suitable for the maintenance of life (as it is conditioned on this earth) is extremely small. It is commonly deemed absurd to suppose that, out of the immense number of worlds known to astronomy, only one is peopled with living beings; yet it is not a question of numbers but of chemical and physiological conditions. Science pronounces the globes which satisfy these conditions to be, in all probability, very few; while organic life involving only inorganic chemistry, organisms adapted to the temperature of the burning fiery furnace, and so forth, are notions that hardly lie within the sphere of scientific imagination. If anyone likes to maintain that the Creator of the starry heaven is "mindful" *only* of man, neither will science accuse him of grotesque exaggeration nor will theism need to hope that he is absolutely accurate.

values; and the *terminus ad quem* of the world, so far as the world-process has as yet gone, and in so far as the world is known, is man. It is not that he is the last evolute in time; indeed his parasites should be later: but that he is the highest product in respect of value, and in the light of whose emergence all Nature, to which he is akin, seems to have its *raison d'être*. Hence the necessity of his figuring pre-eminently in theistic philosophy, if that is to be based on facts rather than on preconceived ideas, and is not to transcend fact save in the inevitable way of fact-controlled and reasonable extrapolation and idealisation. That the investigation, pursued in the preceding volume and in the present chapter, of man's rational and moral status and its conditioning by his physical and social environment, has involved more emphasising of what may be called man's anthropism than of his rationality, etc., in the abstract, is a necessity dictated by facts and by the empirical method. But now that the anthropocentric view of the world has been reached, and the facts which justify it have been set forth, our attention may move on from terrestrial contingencies, creaturely limitations, and specifically human characteristics, to the generic features which, from the point of view of theism, must be common to the mind of man and the Mind of God. The anthropocentric view of the world is a necessary step to the theistic interpretation of the world and man: it need not profess to be more.

The empirical approach to theism being essentially teleological, it is now necessary to raise the question, what an end or purpose, as attributable to the Deity, consists in. The idea of purpose is derived from the sphere of human activity; and such meaning as is imported into it from that context has necessary relevance only so long as that context is not transcended: such is the empirical doctrine as to the scope and validity of ideas or ideational propositions. But when applied to God, whose activities, by definition or *ex hypothesi,* include some that are unique, and whose intelligence is necessarily different in some respects from ours, the idea may become non-significant. Theism that would use the idea, it has sometimes been urged, must be unduly anthropomorphic. That need not be so, however, if such constituents of the complex idea of purpose as involve intrinsic limitations of human mentality and activity can be eliminated from it, while others, essential to the conception of purposiveness but separable from their human manifestation, can be isolated for legitimate transference to the sphere of divine activity. What elements require to be eliminated, modified, or newly related, in such recasting of the idea, has been differently decided by different exponents of theism; and perhaps it is premature to undertake the analysis and re-synthesis until an exposition has been given of one's conception of the nature and attributes of the Deity. In the absence of such preliminary discussion it may suffice to indicate possible divergences of view, as occasion calls.

In the conception of human purpose we may distinguish the following constituent elements: (1) the pre-conceived idea of a situation to be reached, (2) desire for that situation because of its value to the agent, (3) the use—in general—of means for the attainment of it, (4) the actualisation—generally by stages—of what was contemplated in thought and striven for. Into the first of these, and indeed into all of them, the idea of temporal succession enters: idea of the goal is previous to attainment of goal, desire to fruition, and so on. And whether the temporal form, characterising human experience, is to be carried over into the conception of God's activity and experience is a disputed question;

that it has been variously answered is the chief source of divergence of view as to what exactly purpose, ascribed to the Deity, is. This question is not to be discussed for the present. It need only be remarked here that *if* it be possible to conceive of purposive activity as not necessarily involving the temporal stages which have been indicated, so that separation of ideated end and accomplished end be non-essential, and if concomitance of plan with actualised volition be as useful a notion as that of succession of the one upon the other, then the purposiveness of the world will consist in its being an organic system, or one in which the natures and interconnexions of the parts are determined by the whole, and in its being an expression of intelligence but not an actualisation of a *pre*-existent plan. According to this attenuated conception of purpose the relation of means to end, generally involved in human purposefulness, also vanishes.

The element of value, of desire and satisfaction, is not eliminable from the idea of purpose. Without it the category of end would lose its distinctiveness and become identical with some other, such as cause or ground, mechanism, or non-contradiction. The tendency to minimise or cancel valuation, in this connexion, and to speak of satisfactoriness as something of logical nature, conceivable in abstraction from satisfaction, is evinced by absolute monists rather than by theists. In whatever sense the world may be said to embody divine purpose, the least that can be meant is that the world contains what is of worth to the Supreme Being.

The third factor in human purposing, adaptation of means to end, is again one which some theists have been reluctant to admit into the conception of divine purpose: partly because of its temporal implication; partly because it is thought to bespeak limited power and need to overcome difficulties; and sometimes on the ground that the divine end is the world-process, not some perfected outcome of it, and that everything that we would regard as but a stage or a means toward something else is, for God, itself an end. This last issue may be considered immediately; but whether the relation of a determinate God to a determinate world, other than Himself, admits of being conceived without ascription to Him of some kinds of limitation such as do not render the distinction between means or stages and end obviously superfluous in the case of divine activity, is a question that will receive later the discussion for which it calls. The fourth of the factors into which the idea of purpose has been resolved presents no especial problem other than that already indicated when the first was touched upon.

It has been remarked before that Nature and man, empirically studied, may strongly suggest that the world is an outcome of intelligence and purpose, while *the* purpose or divine end which the universe and the world-process subserve may remain unknowable to us. But, as we have also seen, speculation on the latter subject must be allowed to influence views as to the nature of the purposiveness that is involved in the former assertion. The forthcoming alternative views, between which facts scarcely enable us to decide, may be briefly mentioned. The divine purposing may be conceived as pre-ordination, in which every detail is foreseen. An analogy is presented in Mozart's (alleged) method of composition, who is said to have imaged a movement—its themes, developement, embroidery, counterpoint and orchestration—in all its detail and as a simultaneous whole, before he wrote it. If God's composition of the cosmos be regarded as similar to this, all its purposiveness will be expressed in the initial collocations, and evolution will be preformation. On the other hand, God's activity might be conceived as fluent, or even as "increasing", rather than as wholly static, purpose. It might then be compared, in relevant respects, with the work of a dramatist or a novelist such, perhaps, as Thackeray, who seems to have moulded his characters and plot, to some extent, as he wrote. And it would appear that the divine purposiveness must be partly thus conceived if conative creaturely activity may either co-operate or clash with the Creator's, so that providential control and adaptation to the emergent must enter into the realisation of the divine plan.

Again, though the divine end is usually construed eschatologically, there is an alternative interpretation. It may be that there is no "far off divine event" toward which creation was predestined to move: the process itself may constitute the end. Certainly progress has a unique value, incapable of the absorption or transmutation which some values undergo; and the conception of the divine end as a perfected society of ethical individuals, and a philosophy of history such as is based on that presupposition, are not free from difficulties. At any rate the securing of the consummation will need to be so conceived as not to involve sacrifice of the ethical dignity of the individual person as an end for himself, and no mere instrument to the future perfecting of others. The social good may but be good in that it ministers to the goodness of individuals, each of whom—as the Christian conception of the Fatherhood of God implies—is singly an end for God. Position in the time-series, or the progress-series of social developement towards perfection, may be of no moment as compared with the individual's use of his opportunities, such as they may be: timelessness, in the sense of indifference to axiological rank as temporally circumstanced, may characterise the valuation he receives from God, who seeth not as man seeth, and may read the heart rather than 'Objectively' estimate the actual output of the will. If so, asymptotic attainment of ethical perfection, and the ideal consummation, may be contingent or conditional aspects of the divine end, while progressive becoming, throughout all reaches and domains of the universe, may be its ultimate essence. These alternative conceivabilities are here merely mentioned; their relative tenability is not to be investigated. But it may further be observed that if evolution is itself an end and not a means to an end, the hard dualism of means and end must vanish. Childhood, for instance, will not be merely a stage in the making of a man; nor will groping past generations have worked merely to provide their posterity with better opportunities for making further advance. As a rose-bud has a beauty or perfection different from but equal to that of the full-blown rose, so may each stage in the life of the individual or the race have, along with its appropriate work, an intrinsic value, or be an end in itself as well as a means to something beyond. The only conclusion now to be elicited from the foregoing remarks is that teleology and theism may admit of statement in terms of other than the static concepts, and the abstractions such as perfection that is of no *kind,* which dominated thought until a century or so ago, and which, within the spheres of philosophy and theology, still impose themselves on some evolutionists.

The teleological approach to theism, with which this chapter has been concerned, has been made from the fact that conformity to law is intrinsic to the world, and from the conclusion that such order belongs to the world as ontal. It has already been found not to be blocked by science or by mechanistic philosophy of Nature and its law-abidingness. Besides being a cosmos explicable, in one general sense, in terms of its structure and scientific intelligibility, the world is a bearer and a producer of values in that in our *rapport* with it we are affected by it. The world is not completely described if this aspect of it is left out: less than all the data would but then be taken account of. The Actual or historical world-process, from which mechanism is an abstraction, is characterised by irreversibility, epigenesis, progressiveness of developement, and by manifold adaptations which adaptedly interlace. It evokes explanation, consequently, of a different type from that pursued by physical science; and it accords pragmatic verification to use of the category of design for this new kind of explanation, as well as to use of the causal category for scientific explanation. If reason stands to formal rationality in a relation similar to that in which philosophy stands to mechanical science, philosophical reasonableness cannot be a mere extension of scientific, or of logico-mathematical, rationality; and if existential 'knowledge' is allowed its postulates, it seems but partial to disallow to 'knowledge' concerning the value-aspect of Actuality the postulate that is similarly needful to it. *Homo* who provides the *mensura* for all and every kind of intelligibility needs not to blind himself to the fact that he is more than a logical thinker, or to the fact that he stands in other relations with the universe than that of knowing about its structure. He cannot but have other problems besides that of the relation of being to thought. Philosophy, in other words, is an affair of living as well as a mode of thinking. All causal knowledge is, in the last resort, but reasonable and postulatory: teleology is therefore a developement from science along its own lines, or a continuation, by extrapolation, of the plotted curve which comprehensively describes its knowledge. And this is the *apologia* of theism such as professes to be reasonable belief for the guidance of life, when arraigned by science and logic—or by more pretentious theology.

A CRITIQUE
OF THE ARGUMENT
FROM DESIGN
David Hume

From David Hume, *Dialogues Concerning Natural Religion* (originally published in 1739), parts IV–VIII; published by the Bobbs-Merrill Company, 1947.

Part IV

It seems strange to me, said Cleanthes, that you, Demea, who are so sincere in the cause of religion, should still maintain the mysterious, incomprehensible nature of the Deity, and should insist so strenuously that he has no manner of likeness or resemblance to human creatures. The Deity, I can readily allow, possesses many powers and attributes of which we can have no comprehension: But if our ideas, so far as they go, be not just, and adequate, and correspondent to his real nature, I know not what there is in this subject worth insisting on. Is the name, without any meaning, of such mighty importance? Or how do you mystics, who maintain the absolute incomprehensibility of the Deity, differ from Sceptics or Atheists, who assert, that the first cause of all is unknown and unintelligible? Their temerity must be very great, if, after rejecting the production by a mind, I mean a mind resembling the human, (for I know of no other), they pretend to assign, with certainty, any other specific intelligible cause: And their conscience must be very scrupulous indeed, if they refuse to call the universal unknown cause a God or Deity; and to bestow on him as many sublime eulogies and unmeaning epithets as you shall please to require of them.

Who could imagine, replied Demea, that Cleanthes, the calm philosophical Cleanthes, would attempt to refute his antagonists by affixing a nickname to them; and, like the common bigots and inquisitors of the age, have recourse to invective and declamation, instead of reasoning? Or does he not perceive, that these topics are easily retorted, and that Anthropomorphite is an appellation as invidious, and implies as dangerous consequences, as the epithet of Mystic, with which he has honoured us? In reality, Cleanthes, consider what it is you assert when you represent the Deity as similar to a human mind and understanding. What is the soul of man? A composition of various faculties, passions, sentiments, ideas; united, indeed, into one self or person, but still distinct from each other. When it reasons, the ideas, which are the parts of its discourse, arrange themselves in a certain form or order; which is not preserved entire for a moment, but immediately gives place to another arrangement. New opinions, new passions, new affections, new feelings arise, which continually diversify the mental scene, and produce in it the greatest variety and most rapid succession imaginable. How is this compatible with that perfect immutability and simplicity which all true Theists ascribe to the Deity? By the same act, say they, he sees past, present, and future: His love and hatred, his mercy and justice, are one individual operation: He is entire in every point of space; and complete in every instant of duration. No succession, no change, no acquisition, no diminution. What he is implies not in it any shadow of distinction or diversity. And what he is this moment he ever has been, and ever will be, without any new judgment, sentiment, or operation. He stands fixed in one simple, perfect state: nor can you ever say, with any propriety, that this act of his is different from that other; or that this judgment or idea has been lately formed, and will give place, by succession, to any different judgment or idea.

I can readily allow, said Cleanthes, that those who maintain the perfect simplicity of the Supreme Being, to the extent in which you have explained it, are complete Mystics, and chargeable with all the consequences which I have drawn from their opinion. They are, in a word, Atheists, without knowing it. For though it be allowed, that the Deity possesses attributes of which we have no comprehension, yet ought we never to ascribe to him any attributes which are absolutely incompatible with that intelligent nature essential to him. A mind, whose acts and sentiments and ideas are not distinct and successive; one, that is wholly simple, and totally immutable, is a mind which has no thought, no reason, no will, no sentiment, no love, no hatred; or, in a word, is no mind at all. It is an abuse of terms to give it that appellation; and we may as well speak of limited extension without figure, or of number without composition.

Pray consider, said Philo, whom you are at present inveighing against. You are honouring with the appellation of *Atheist* all the sound, orthodox divines, almost, who have treated of this subject; and you will at last be, yourself, found, according to your reckoning, the only sound Theist in the world. But if idolaters be Atheists, as, I think, may justly be asserted, and Christian Theologians the same, what becomes of the argument, so much celebrated, derived from the universal consent of mankind?

But because I know you are not much swayed by names and authorities, I shall endeavour to show you, a little more distinctly, the inconveniences of that Anthropomorphism, which you have embraced; and shall prove, that there is no ground to suppose a plan of the world to be formed in the Divine mind, consisting of distinct ideas, differently arranged, in the same manner as an architect forms in his head the plan of a house which he intends to execute.

It is not easy, I own, to see what is gained by this supposition, whether we judge of the matter by *Reason* or by *Experience*. We are still obliged to mount higher, in order to find the cause of this cause, which you had assigned as satisfactory and conclusive.

If *Reason* (I mean abstract reason, derived from inquiries *a priori*) be not alike mute with regard to all questions concerning cause and effect, this sentence at least it will venture to pronounce, That a mental world, or universe of ideas, requires a cause as much, as does a material world, or universe of objects; and, if similar in its arrangement, must require a similar cause. For what is there in this subject, which should occasion a different conclusion or inference? In an abstract view, they are entirely alike; and no difficulty attends the one supposition, which is not common to both of them.

Again, when we will needs force *Experience* to pronounce some sentence, even on these subjects which lie beyond her sphere, neither can she perceive any material difference in this particular, between these two kinds of worlds; but finds them to be governed by similar principles, and to depend upon an equal variety of causes in their operations. We have specimens in miniature of both of them. Our own mind resembles the one; a vegetable or animal body the other.

Let experience, therefore, judge from these samples. Nothing seems more delicate, with regard to its causes, than thought; and as these causes never operate in two persons after the same manner, so we never find two persons who think exactly alike. Nor indeed does the same person think exactly alike at any two different periods of time. A difference of age, of the disposition of his body, of weather, of food, of company, of books, of passions; any of these particulars, or others more minute, are sufficient to alter the curious machinery of thought, and communicate to it very different movements and operations. As far as we can judge, vegetables and animal bodies are not more delicate in their motions, nor depend upon a greater variety or more curious adjustment of springs and principles.

How, therefore, shall we satisfy ourselves concerning the cause of that Being whom you suppose the Author of Nature, or, according to your system of Anthropomorphism, the ideal world, into which you trace the material? Have we not the same reason to trace that ideal world into another ideal world, or new intelligent principle? But if we stop, and go no farther; why go so far? why not stop at the material world? How can we satisfy ourselves without going on *in infinitum?* And, after all, what satisfaction is there in that infinite progression? Let us remember the story of the Indian philosopher and his elephant. It was never more applicable than to the present subject. If the material world rests upon a similar ideal world, this ideal world must rest upon some other; and so on, without end. It were better, therefore, never to look beyond the present material world. By supposing it to contain the principle of its order within itself, we really assert it to be God; and the sooner we arrive at that Divine Being, so much the better. When you go one step beyond the mundane system, you only excite an inquisitive humour which it is impossible ever to satisfy.

To say, that the different ideas which compose the reason of the Supreme Being, fall into order of themselves, and by their own nature, is really to talk without any precise meaning. If it has a meaning, I would fain know, why it is not as good sense to say, that the parts of the material world fall into order of themselves and by their own nature. Can the one opinion be intelligible, while the other is not so?

We have, indeed, experience of ideas which fall into order of themselves, and without any *known* cause. But, I am sure, we have a much larger experience of matter which does the same; as, in all instances of generation and vegetation, where the accurate analysis of the cause exceeds all human comprehension. We have also experience of particular systems of thought and of matter which have no order; of the first in madness, of the second in corruption. Why, then, should we think, that order is more essential to one than the other? And if it requires a cause in both, what do we gain by your system, in tracing the universe of objects into a similar universe of ideas? The first step which we make leads us on for ever. It were, therefore, wise in us to limit all our inquiries to the present world, without looking farther. No satisfaction can ever be attained by these speculations, which so far exceed the narrow bounds of human understanding.

It was usual with the Peripatetics, you know, Cleanthes, when the cause of any phenomenon was demanded, to have recourse to their *faculties,* or *occult qualities;* and to say, for instance, that bread, nourished by its nutritive faculty, and senna purged by its purgative. But it has been discovered, that this subterfuge was nothing but the disguise of ignorance; and that these philosophers, though less ingenuous, really said the same thing with the sceptics or the vulgar, who fairly confessed that they knew not the cause of these phenomena. In like manner, when it is asked, what cause produces order in the ideas of the Supreme Being; can any other reason be assigned by you, Anthropomorphites, than that it is a *rational* faculty, and that such is the nature of the Deity? But why a similar answer will not be equally satisfactory in accounting for the order of the world, without having recourse to any such intelligent creator as you insist on, may be difficult to determine. It is only to say, that *such* is the nature of material objects, and that they are all originally possessed of a *faculty* of order and proportion. These are only more learned and elaborate ways of confessing our ignorance; nor has the one hypothesis any real advantage above the other, except in its greater conformity to vulgar prejudices.

You have displayed this argument with great emphasis, replied Cleanthes: You seem not sensible how easy it is to answer it. Even in common life, if I assign a cause for any event, is it any objection, Philo, that I cannot assign the cause of that cause, and answer every new question which may incessantly be started? And what philosophers could possibly submit to so rigid a rule? philosophers, who confess ultimate causes to be totally unknown; and are sensible, that the most refined principles into which they trace the phenomena, are still to them as inexplicable as these phenomena themselves are to the vulgar. The order and arrangement of nature, the curious adjustment of final causes, the plain use and intention of every part and organ; all these bespeak in the clearest language an intelligent cause or author. The heavens and the earth join in the same testimony: The whole chorus of Nature raises one hymn to the praises of its Creator. You alone, or almost alone, disturb this general harmony. You start abstruse doubts, cavils, and objections: You ask me, what is the cause of this cause? I know not; I care not; that concerns not me. I have found a Deity; and here I stop my inquiry. Let those go farther, who are wiser or more enterprising.

I pretend to be neither, replied Philo: And for that very reason, I should never perhaps have attempted to go so far; especially when I am sensible, that I must at last be contented to sit down with the same answer, which, without farther trouble, might have satisfied me from the beginning. If I am still to remain in utter ignorance of causes, and can absolutely give an explication of nothing, I shall never esteem it any advantage to shove off for a moment a difficulty, which, you acknowledge, must immediately, in its full force, recur upon me. Naturalists indeed very justly explain particular effects by more general causes, though these general causes themselves should remain in the end totally inexplicable; but they never surely thought it satisfactory to explain a particular effect by a particular cause, which was no more to be accounted for than the effect itself. An ideal system, arranged of itself, without a precedent design, is not a whit more explicable than a material one, which attains its order in a like manner; nor is there any more difficulty in the latter supposition than in the former.

Part V

But to show you still more inconveniences, continued Philo, in your Anthropomorphism, please to take a new survey of your principles. *Like effects prove like causes.* This is the experimental argument; and this, you say too, is the sole theological argument. Now, it is certain, that the liker the effects are which are seen, and the liker the causes which are inferred, the stronger is the argument. Every departure on either side diminishes the probability, and renders the experiment less conclusive. You cannot doubt of the principle; neither ought you to reject its consequences.

All the new discoveries in astronomy, which prove the immense grandeur and magnificence of the works of Nature, are so many additional arguments for a Deity, according to the true system of Theism; but, according to your hypothesis of experimental Theism, they become so many objections, by removing the effect still farther from all resemblance to the effects of human art and contrivance. For, if Lucretius,[1] even following the old system of the world, could exclaim,

> Quis regere immensi summam, quis habere profundi
> Indu manu validas potis est moderanter habenas?
> Quis pariter coelos omnes convertere? et omnes
> Ignibus aetheriis terras suffire feraces?
> Omnibus inque locis esse omni tempore praesto?

If Tully[2] esteemed this reasoning so natural, as to put it into the mouth of his Epicurean: 'Quibus enim oculis animi intueri potuit vester Plato fabricam illam tanti operis, qua construi a Deo atque aedificari mundum facit? quae molito? quae ferramenta? qui vectes? quae machinae? qui minstri tanti muneris fuerunt? quemadmodum autem obedire et parere voluntati architecti aer, ignis, aqua, terra potuerunt?' If this argument, I say, had any force in former ages, how much greater must it have at present, when the bounds of Nature are so infinitely enlarged, and such a magnificent scene is opened to us? It is still more unreasonable to form our idea of so unlimited a cause from our experience of the narrow productions of human design and invention.

The discoveries by microscopes, as they open a new universe in miniature, are still objections, according to you, arguments, according to me. The farther we push our researches of this kind, we are still led to infer the universal cause of all to be vastly different from mankind, or from any object of human experience and observation.

And what say you to the discoveries in anatomy, chemistry, botony? . . . These surely are no objections, replied Cleanthes; they only discover new instances of art and contrivance. It is still the image of mind reflected on us from innumerable objects. Add, a mind *like the human,* said Philo. I know of no other, replied Cleanthes. And the liker the better, insisted Philo. To be sure, said Cleanthes.

Now, Cleanthes, said Philo, with an air of alacrity and triumph, mark the consequences. *First,* By this method of reasoning, you renounce all claim to infinity in any of the attributes of the Deity. For, as the cause ought only to be proportioned to the effect, and the effect, so far as it falls under our cognizance, is not infinite; what pretensions have we, upon your suppositions, to ascribe that attribute to the Divine Being? You will still insist, that, by removing him so much from all similarity to human creatures, we give in to the most arbitrary hypothesis, and at the same time weaken all proofs of his existence.

---

[1] Lib. xi. 1094.
[2] De Nat. Deor. lib. i.

Secondly, You have no reason, on your theory, for ascribing perfection to the Deity, even in his finite capacity, or for supposing him free from every error, mistake, or incoherence, in his undertakings. There are many inexplicable difficulties in the works of Nature, which, if we allow a perfect author to be proved *a priori,* are easily solved, and become only seeming difficulties, from the narrow capacity of man, who cannot trace infinite relations. But according to your method of reasoning, these difficulties become all real; and perhaps will be insisted on, as new instances of likeness to human art and contrivance. At least, you must acknowledge, that it is impossible for us to tell, from our limited views, whether this system contains any great faults, or deserves any considerable praise, if compared to other possible, and even real systems. Could a peasant, if the Aeneid were read to him, pronounce that poem to be absolutely faultless, or even assign to it its proper rank among the productions of human wit, he, who had never seen any other production?

But were this world ever so perfect a production, it must still remain uncertain, whether all the excellences of the work can justly be ascribed to the workman. If we survey a ship, what an exalted idea must we form of the ingenuity of the carpenter who framed so complicated, useful, and beautiful a machine? And what surprise must we feel, when we find him a stupid mechanic, who imitated others, and copied an art, which, through a long succession of ages, after multiplied trials, mistakes, corrections, deliberations, and controversies, had been gradually improving? Many worlds might have been botched and bungled, throughout an eternity, ere this system was struck out; much labour lost, many fruitless trials made; and a slow, but continued improvement carried on during infinite ages in the art of world-making. In such subjects, who can determine, where the truth; nay, who can conjecture where the probability lies, amidst a great number of hypotheses which may be proposed, and a still greater which may be imagined?

And what shadow of an argument, continued Philo, can you produce, from your hypothesis, to prove the unity of the Deity? A great number of men join in building a house or ship, in rearing a city, in framing a commonwealth; why may not several deities combine in contriving and framing a world? This is only so much greater similarity to human affairs. By sharing the work among several, we may so much farther limit the attributes of each, and get rid of that extensive power and knowledge, which must be supposed in one deity, and which, according to you, can only serve to weaken the proof of his existence. And if such foolish, such vicious creatures as man, can yet often unite in framing and executing one plan, how much more those deities or demons, whom we may suppose several degrees more perfect!

To multiply causes without necessity, is indeed contrary to true philosophy: but this principle applies not to the present case. Were one deity antecedently proved by your theory, who were possessed of every attribute requisite to the production of the universe; it would be needless, I own, (though not absurd), to suppose any other deity existent. But while it is still a question, Whether all these attributes are united in one subject, or dispersed among several independent beings, by what phenomena in nature can we pretend to decide the controversy? Where we see a body raised in a scale, we are sure that there is in the opposite scale, however concealed from sight, some counterpoising weight equal to it; but it is still allowed to doubt, whether that weight be an aggregate of several distinct bodies, or one uniform united mass. And if the weight requisite very much exceeds any thing which we have ever seen conjoined in any single body, the former supposition becomes still more probable and natural. An intelligent being of such vast power and capacity as is necessary to produce the universe, or, to speak in the language of ancient philosophy, so prodigious an animal exceeds all analogy, and even comprehension.

But farther, Cleanthes: Men are mortal, and renew their species by generation; and this is common to all living creatures. The two great sexes of male and female, says Milton, animate the world. Why must this circumstance, so universal, so essential, be excluded from those numerous and limited deities? Behold, then, the theogeny of ancient times brought back upon us.

And why not become a perfect Anthropomorphite? Why not assert the deity or deities to be corporeal, and to have eyes, a nose, mouth, ears, &c.? Epicurus maintained, that no man had ever seen reason but in a human figure; therefore the gods must have a human figure. And this argument, which is deservedly so much ridiculed by Cicero, becomes, according to you, solid and philosophical.

In a word, Cleanthes, a man who follows your hypothesis is able perhaps to assert, or conjecture, that the universe, sometime, arose from something like design: but beyond that position he cannot ascertain one single circumstance; and is left afterwards to fix every point of his theology by the utmost license of fancy and hypothesis. This world, for aught he knows, is very faulty and imperfect, compared to a superior standard; and was only the first rude essay of some infant deity, who afterwards abandoned it, ashamed of his lame performance: it is the work only of some dependent, inferior deity; and is the object of derision to his superiors: it is the production of old age and dotage in some superannuated deity; and ever since his death, has run on at adventures, from the first impulse and active force which it received from him. You justly give signs of horror, Demea, at these strange suppositions; but these, and a thousand more of the same kind, are Cleanthes's suppositions, not mine. From the moment the attributes of the Deity are supposed finite, all these have place. And I cannot, for my part, think that so wild and unsettled a system of theology is, in any respect, preferable to none at all.

These suppositions I absolutely disown, cried Cleanthes: they strike me, however, with no horror, especially when proposed in that rambling way in which they drop from you. On the contrary, they give me pleasure, when I see, that, by the utmost indulgence of your imagination, you never get rid of the hypothesis of design in the universe, but are obliged at every turn to have recourse to it. To this concession I adhere steadily; and this I regard as a sufficient foundation for religion.

Part VI

It must be a slight fabric, indeed, said Demea, which can be erected on so tottering a foundation. While we are uncertain whether there is one deity or many; whether the deity or deities, to whom we owe our existence, be perfect or imperfect, subordinate or supreme, dead or alive, what trust or confidence can we repose in them? What devotion or worship address to them? What veneration or obedience pay them? To all the purposes of life the theory of religion becomes altogether useless: and even with regard to speculative consequences, its uncertainty, according to you, must render it totally precarious and unsatisfactory.

To render it still more unsatisfactory, said Philo, there occurs to me another hypothesis, which must acquire an air of probability from the method of reasoning so much insisted on by Cleanthes. That like effects arise from like causes: this principle he supposes the foundation of all religion. But there is another principle of the same kind, no less certain, and derived from the same source of experience; that where several known circumstances are observed to be similar, the unknown will also be found similar. Thus, if we see the limbs of a human body, we conclude that it is also attended with a human head, though hid from us. Thus, if we see, through a chink in á wall, a small part of the sun, we conclude, that, were the wall removed, we should see the whole body. In short, this method of reasoning is so obvious and familiar, that no scruple can ever be made with regard to its solidity.

Now, if we survey the universe, so far as it falls under our knowledge, it bears a great resemblance to an animal or organized body, and seems actuated with a like principle of life and motion. A continual circulation of matter in it produces no disorder: a continual waste in every part is incessantly repaired: the closest sympathy is perceived throughout the entire system: and each part or member, in performing its proper offices, operates both to its own preservation and to that of the whole. The world, therefore, I infer, is an animal; and the Deity is the SOUL of the world, actuating it, and actuated by it.

You have too much learning, Cleanthes, to be at all surprised at this opinion, which, you know, was maintained by almost all the Theists of antiquity, and chiefly prevails in their discourses and reasonings. For though, sometimes, the ancient philosophers reason from final causes, as if they thought the world the workmanship of God; yet it appears rather their favourite notion to consider it as his body, whose organization renders it subservient to him. And it must be confessed, that, as the universe resembles more a human body than it does the works of human art and contrivance, if our limited analogy could ever, with any propriety, be extended to the whole of nature, the inference seems juster in favour of the ancient than the modern theory.

There are many other advantages, too, in the former theory, which recommended it to the ancient theologians. Nothing more repugnant to all their notions, because nothing more repugnant to common experience, than mind without body; a mere spiritual substance, which fell not under their senses nor comprehension, and of which they had not observed one single instance throughout all nature. Mind and body they knew, because they felt both: an order, arrangement, organization, or internal machinery, in both, they likewise knew, after the same manner: and it could not but seem reasonable to transfer this experience to the universe; and to suppose the divine mind and body to be also coeval, and to have, both of them, order and arrangement naturally inherent in them, and inseparable from them.

Here, therefore, is a new species of *Anthropomorphism,* Cleanthes, on which you may deliberate; and a theory which seems not liable to any considerable difficulties. You are too much superior, surely, to *systematical prejudices,* to find any more difficulty in supposing an animal body to be, originally, of itself, or from unknown causes, possessed of order and organization, than in supposing a similar order to belong to mind. But the *vulgar prejudice,* that body and mind ought always to accompany each other, ought not, one should think, to be entirely neglected; since it is founded on *vulgar experience,* the only guide which you profess to follow in all these theological inquiries. And if you assert, that our limited experience is an unequal standard, by which to judge of the unlimited extent of nature; you entirely abandon your own hypothesis, and must thenceforward adopt our Mysticism, as you call it, and admit of the absolute incomprehensibility of the Divine Nature.

This theory, I own, replied Cleanthes, has never before occurred to me, though a pretty natural one; and I cannot readily, upon so short an examination and reflection, deliver any opinion with regard to it. You are very scrupulous, indeed, said Philo: were I to examine any system of yours, I should not have acted with half that caution and reserve, in starting objections and difficulties to it. However, if any thing occur to you, you will oblige us by proposing it.

Why then, replied Cleanthes, it seems to me, that, though the world does, in many circumstances, resemble an animal body; yet is the analogy also defective in many circumstances the most material: no organs of sense; no seat of thought or reason; no one precise origin of motion and action. In short, it seems to bear a stronger resemblance to a vegetable than to an animal, and your inference would be so far inconclusive in favour of the soul of the world.

But, in the next place, your theory seems to imply the eternity of the world; and that is a principle, which, I think, can be refuted by the strongest reasons and probabilities. I shall suggest an argument to this purpose, which, I believe, has not been insisted on by any writer. Those, who reason from the late origin of arts and sciences, though their inference wants not force, may perhaps be refuted by considerations derived from the nature of human society, which is in continual revolution, between ignorance and knowledge, liberty and slavery, riches and poverty; so that it is impossible for us, from our limited experience to foretell with assurance what events may or may not be expected. Ancient learning and history seem to have been in great danger of entirely perishing after the inundation of the barbarous nations; and had these convulsions continued a little longer, or been a little more violent, we should not probably have now known what passed in the world a few centuries before us. Nay, were it not for the superstition of the Popes, who preserved a little jargon of Latin, in order to support the appearance of an ancient and universal church, that tongue must have been utterly lost; in which case, the Western world, being totally barbarous, would not have been in a fit disposition for receiving the Greek language and learning, which was conveyed to them after the sacking of Constantinople. When learning and books had been extinguished, even the mechanical arts would have fallen considerably to decay; and it is easily imagined, that fable or tradition might ascribe to them a much later origin than the true one. This vulgar argument, therefore, against the eternity of the world, seems a little precarious.

But here appears to be the foundation of a better argument. Lucullus was the first that brought cherry-trees from Asia to Europe; though that tree thrives so well in many European climates, that it grows in the woods without any culture. Is it possible, that throughout a whole eternity, no European had ever passed into

Asia, and thought of transplanting so delicious a fruit into his own country? Or if the tree was once transplanted and propagated, how could it ever afterwards perish? Empires may rise and fall, liberty and slavery succeed alternately, ignorance and knowledge give place to each other; but the cherry-tree will still remain in the woods of Greece, Spain and Italy, and will never be affected by the revolutions of human society.

It is not two thousand years since vines were transplanted into France, though there is no climate in the world more favourable to them. It is not three centuries since horses, cows, sheep, swine, dogs, corn, were known in America. Is it possible, that during the revolutions of a whole eternity, there never arose a Columbus, who might open the communication between Europe and that continent? We may as well imagine, that all men would wear stockings for ten thousand years, and never have the sense to think of garters to tie them. All these seem convincing proofs of the youth, or rather infancy, of the world; as being founded on the operation of principles more constant and steady than those by which human society is governed and directed. Nothing less than a total convulsion of the elements will ever destroy all the European animals and vegetables which are now to be found in the Western world.

And what argument have you against such convulsions? replied Philo. Strong and almost incontestable proofs may be traced over the whole earth, that every part of this globe has continued for many ages entirely covered with water. And though order were supposed inseparable from matter, and inherent in it; yet may matter be susceptible of many and great revolutions, through the endless periods of eternal duration. The incessant changes, to which every part of it is subject, seem to intimate some such general transformations; though, at the same time, it is observable, that all the changes and corruptions of which we have ever had experience, are but passages from one state of order to another; nor can matter ever rest in total deformity and confusion. What we see in the parts, we may infer in the whole; at least, that is the method of reasoning on which you rest your whole theory. And were I obliged to defend any particular system of this nature, which I never willingly should do, I esteem none more plausible than that which ascribes an eternal inherent principle of order to the world, though attended with great and continual revolutions and alterations. This at once solves all difficulties; and if the solution, by being so general, is not entirely complete and satisfactory, it is at least a theory that we must sooner or later have recourse to, whatever system we embrace. How could things have been as they are, were there not an original inherent principle of order somewhere, in thought or in matter? And it is very indifferent to which of these we give the preference. Chance has no place, on any hypothesis, sceptical or religious. Every thing is surely governed by steady, inviolable laws. And were the inmost essence of things laid open to us, we should then discover a scene, of which, at present, we can have no idea. Instead of admiring the order of natural beings, we should clearly see that it was absolutely impossible for them, in the smallest article, ever to admit of any other disposition.

Were any one inclined to revive the ancient Pagan Theology, which maintained, as we learn from Hesiod, that this globe was governed by 30,000 deities, who arose from the unknown powers of nature: you would naturally object, Cleanthes, that nothing is gained by this hypothesis; and that it is as easy to suppose all men animals, beings more numerous, but less perfect, to have sprung immediately from a like origin. Push the same inference a step farther, and you will find a numerous society of deities as explicable as one universal deity, who possesses within himself the powers and perfections of the whole society. All these systems, then, of Scepticism, Polytheism, and Theism, you must allow, on your principles, to be on a like footing, and that no one of them has any advantage over the others. You may thence learn the fallacy of your principles.

Part VII

But here, continued Philo, in examining the ancient system of the soul of the world, there strikes me, all on a sudden, a new idea, which, if just, must go near to subvert all your reasoning, and destroy even your first inferences, on which you repose such confidence. If the universe bears a greater likeness to animal bodies and to vegetables, than to the works of human art, it is more probable that its cause resembles the cause of the former than that of the latter, and its origin ought rather to be ascribed to generation or vegetation, than to reason or design. Your conclusion, even according to your own principles, is therefore lame and defective.

Pray open up this argument a little farther, said Demea, for I do not rightly apprehend it in that concise manner in which you have expressed it.

Our friend Cleanthes, replied Philo, as you have heard, asserts, that since no question of fact can be proved otherwise than by experience, the existence of a Deity admits not of proof from any other medium. The world, says he, resembles the works of human contrivance; therefore its cause must also resemble that of the other. Here we may remark, that the operation of one very small part of nature, to wit man, upon another very small part, to wit that inanimate matter lying within his reach, is the rule by which Cleanthes judges of the origin of the whole; and he measures objects, so widely disproportioned, by the same individual standard. But to waive all objections drawn from this topic, I affirm, that there are other parts of the universe (besides the machines of human invention) which bear still a greater resemblance to the fabric of the world, and which, therefore, afford a better conjecture concerning the universal origin of this system. These parts are animals and vegetables. The world plainly resembles more an animal or a vegetable, than it does a watch or a knitting-loom. Its cause, therefore, it is more probable, resembles the cause of the former. The cause of the former is generation or vegetation. The cause, therefore, of the world, we may infer to be something similar or analogous to generation or vegetation.

But how is it conceivable, said Demea, that the world can arise from any thing similar to vegetation or generation?

Very easily, replied Philo. In like manner as a tree sheds its seed into the neighbouring fields, and produces other trees; so the great vegetable, the world, or this planetary system, produces within itself certain seeds, which, being scattered into the surrounding chaos, vegetate into new worlds. A comet, for instance, is the seed of a world; and after it has been fully ripened, by passing from sun to sun, and star to star, it is at last tossed into the unformed elements which every where surround this universe, and immediately sprouts up into a new system.

Or if, for the sake of variety (for I see no other advantage), we should suppose this world to be an animal; a comet is the egg of this animal: and in like manner as an ostrich lays its egg in the sand, which, without any farther care, hatches the egg, and produces a new animal; so . . . I understand you, says Demea: But what wild, arbitrary suppositions are these! What *data* have you for such extraordinary conclusions? And is the slight, imaginary resemblance of the world to a vegetable or an animal sufficient to establish the same inference with regard to both? Objects, which are in general so widely different, ought they to be a standard for each other?

Right, cries Philo: This is the topic on which I have all along insisted. I have still asserted, that we have no *data* to establish any system of cosmogony. Our experience, so imperfect in itself, and so limited both in extent and duration, can afford us no probable conjecture concerning the whole of things. But if we must needs fix on some hypothesis; by what rule, pray, ought we to determine our choice? Is there any other rule than the greater similarity of the objects compared? And does not a plant or an animal, which springs from vegetation or generation, bear a stronger resemblance to the world, than does any artificial machine, which arises from reason and design?

But what is this vegetation and generation of which you talk, said Demea? Can you explain their operations, and anatomize that fine internal structure on which they depend?

As much, at least, replied Philo, as Cleanthes can explain the operations of reason, or anatomize that internal structure on which *it* depends. But without any such elaborate disquisitions, when I see an animal, I infer, that it sprang from generation; and that with as great certainty as you conclude a house to have been reared by design. These words, *generation, reason,* mark only certain powers and energies in nature, whose effects are known, but whose essence is incomprehensible; and one of these principles, more than the other, has no privilege for being made a standard to the whole of nature.

In reality, Demea, it may reasonably be expected, that the larger the views are which we take of things, the better will they conduct us in our conclusions concerning such extraordinary and such magnificent subjects. In this little corner of the world alone, there are four principles, *reason, instinct, generation, vegetation,* which are similar to each other, and are the causes of similar effects. What a number of other principles may we naturally suppose in the immense extent and variety of the universe, could we travel from planet to planet, and from system to system, in order to examine each part of this mighty fabric? Any one of these four principles above mentioned, (and a hundred others which lie open to our conjecture), may afford us a theory by which to judge of the origin of the world; and it is a palpable and egregious partiality to confine our view entirely to that principle by which our own minds operate. Were this principle more intelligible on that account, such a partiality might be somewhat excuseable: But reason, in its internal fabric and structure, is really as little known to us as instinct or vegetation; and, perhaps, even that vague, undeterminate word, *Nature,* to which the vulgar refer every thing, is not at the bottom more inexplicable. The effects of these principles are all known to us from experience; but the principles themselves, and their manner of operation, are totally unknown; nor is it less intelligible, or less conformable to experience, to say, that the world arose by vegetation, or from a seed shed by another world, than to say that it arose from a divine reason or contrivance, according to the sense in which Cleanthes understands it.

But methinks, said Demea, if the world had a vegetative quality, and could sow the seeds of new worlds into the infinite chaos, this power would be still an additional argument for design in its author. For whence could arise so wonderful a faculty but from design? Or how can order spring from any thing which perceives not that order which it bestows?

You need only look around you, replied Philo, to satisfy yourself with regard to this question. A tree bestows order and organization on that tree which springs from it, without knowing the order; an animal in the same manner on its offspring; a bird on its nest; and instances of this kind are even more frequent in the world than those of order, which arise from reason and contrivance. To say, that all this order in animals and vegetables proceeds ultimately from design, is begging the question; nor can that great point be ascertained otherwise than by proving, *a priori,* both that order is, from its nature, inseparably attached to thought; and that it can never of itself, or from original unknown principles, belong to matter.

But farther, Demea; this objection which you urge can never be made use of by Cleanthes, without renouncing a defence which he has already made against one of my objections. When I inquired concerning the cause of that supreme reason and intelligence into which he resolves every thing; he told me, that the impossibility of satisfying such inquiries could never be admitted as an objection in any species of philosophy. *We must stop somewhere,* says he; *nor is it ever within the reach of human capacity to explain ultimate causes, or show the last connections of any objects. It is sufficient, if any steps, so far as we go, are supported by experience and observation.* Now, that vegetation and generation, as well as reason, are experienced to be principles of order in nature, is undeniable. If I rest my system of cosmogony on the former, preferably to the latter, it is at my choice. The matter seems entirely arbitrary. And when Cleanthes asks me what is the cause of my great vegetative or generative faculty, I am equally entitled to ask him the cause of his great reasoning principle. These questions we have agreed to forbear on both sides; and it is chiefly his interest on the present occasion to stick to this agreement. Judging by our limited and imperfect experience, generation has some privileges above reason: for we see every day the latter arise from the former, never the former from the latter.

Compare, I beseech you, the consequences on both sides. The world, say I, resembles an animal; therefore it is an animal, therefore it arose from generation. The steps, I confess, are wide; yet there is some small appearance of analogy in each step. The world, says Cleanthes, resembles a machine; therefore it is a machine, therefore it arose from design. The steps are here equally wide, and the analogy less striking. And if he pretends to carry on *my* hypothesis a step farther, and to infer design or reason from the great principle of generation, on which I insist; I may, with better authority, use the same freedom to push farther *his* hypothesis, and infer a divine generation or theogony from his principle of reason. I have at least some faint shadow of experience, which is the utmost that can ever be attained in the present subject. Reason, in innumerable instances, is observed to arise from the principle of generation, and never to arise from any other principle.

Hesiod, and all the ancient mythologists, were so struck with this analogy, that they universally explained the origin of nature from an animal birth, and copulation. Plato too, so far as he is intelligible, seems to have adopted some such notion in his Timaeus.

The Brahmins assert, that the world arose from an infinite spider, who spun this whole complicated mass from his bowels, and annihilates afterwards the whole or any part of it, by absorbing it again, and resolving it into his own essence. Here is a species of cosmogony, which appears to us ridiculous; because a spider is a little contemptible animal, whose operations we are never likely to take for a model of the whole universe. But still here is a new species of analogy, even in our globe. And were there a planet wholly inhabited by spiders, (which is very possible), this inference would there appear as natural and irrefragable as that which in our planet ascribes the origin of all things to design and intelligence, as explained by Cleanthes. Why an orderly system may not be spun from the belly as well as from the brain, it will be difficult for him to give a satisfactory reason.

I must confess, Philo, replied Cleanthes, that of all men living, the task which you have undertaken, of raising doubts and objections, suits you best, and seems, in a manner, natural and unavoidable to you. So great is your fertility of invention, that I am not ashamed to acknowledge myself unable, on a sudden, to solve regularly such out-of-the-way difficulties as you incessantly start upon me: though I clearly see, in general, their fallacy and error. And I question not, but you are yourself, at present, in the same case, and have not the solution so ready as the objection: while you must be sensible, that common sense and reason are entirely against you; and that such whimsies as you have delivered, may puzzle, but never can convince us.

Part VIII

What you ascribe to the fertility of my invention, replied Philo, is entirely owing to the nature of the subject. In subjects adapted to the narrow compass of human reason, there is commonly but one determination, which carries probability or conviction with it; and to a man of sound judgment, all other suppositions, but that one, appear entirely absurd and chimerical. But in such questions as the present, a hundred contradictory views may preserve a kind of imperfect analogy; and invention has here full scope to exert itself. Without any great effort of thought, I believe that I could, in an instant, propose other systems of cosmogony, which would have some faint appearance of truth; though it is a thousand, a million to one, if either yours or any one of mine be the true system.

For instance, what if I should revive the old Epicurean hypothesis? This is commonly, and I believe justly, esteemed the most absurd system that has yet been proposed; yet I know not whether, with a few alterations, it might not be brought to bear a faint appearance of probability. Instead of supposing matter infinite, as Epicurus did, let us suppose it finite. A finite number of particles is only susceptible of finite transpositions: and it must happen, in an eternal duration, that every possible order or position must be tried an infinite number of times. This world, therefore, with all its events, even the most minute, has before been produced and destroyed, and will again be produced and destroyed, without any bounds and limitations. No one, who has a conception of the powers of infinite, in comparison of finite, will ever scruple this determination.

But this supposes, said Demea, that matter can acquire motion, without any voluntary agent or first mover.

And where is the difficulty, replied Philo, of that supposition? Every event, before experience, is equally difficult and incomprehensible; and every event, after experience, is equally easy and intelligible. Motion, in many instances, from gravity, from elasticity, from electricity, begins in matter, without any known voluntary agent: and to suppose always, in these cases, an unknown voluntary agent, is mere hypothesis; and hypothesis attended with no advantages. The beginning of motion in matter itself is as conceivable *a priori* as its communication from mind and intelligence.

Besides, why may not motion have been propagated by impulse through all eternity, and the same stock of it, or nearly the same, be still upheld in the universe? As much is lost by the composition of motion, as much is gained by its resolution. And whatever the causes are, the fact is certain, that matter is, and always has been, in continual agitation, as far as human experience or tradition reaches. There is not probably, at present, in the whole universe, one particle of matter at absolute rest.

And this very consideration too, continued Philo, which we have stumbled on in the course of the argument, suggests a new hypothesis of cosmogony, that is not absolutely absurd and improbable. Is there a system, an order, an economy of things, by which matter can preserve that perpetual agitation which seems essential to it, and yet maintain a constancy in the forms which it produces? There certainly is such an economy; for this is actually the case with the present world. The continual motion of matter, therefore, in less than infinite transpositions, must produce this economy or order; and by its very nature, that order, when once established, supports itself, for many ages, if not to eternity. But wherever matter is so poized, arranged, and adjusted, as to continue in perpetual motion, and yet preserve a constancy in the forms, its situation must, of necessity, have all the same appearance of art and contrivance which we observe at present. All the parts of each form must have a relation to each other, and to the whole; and the whole itself must have a relation to the other parts of the universe; to the element in which the form subsists; to the materials with which it repairs its waste and decay; and to every other form which is hostile or friendly. A defect in any of these particulars destroys the form; and the matter of which it is composed is again set loose, and is thrown into irregular motions and fermentations, till it unite itself to some other regular form. If no such form be prepared to receive it, and if there be a great quantity of this corrupted matter in the universe, the universe itself is entirely disordered; whether it be the feeble embryo of a world in its first beginnings that is thus destroyed, or the rotten carcase of one languishing in old age and infirmity. In either case, a chaos ensues; till finite, though innumerable revolutions produce at last some forms, whose parts and organs are so adjusted as to support the forms amidst a continued succession of matter.

Suppose (for we shall endeavour to vary the expression), that matter were thrown into any position, by a blind, unguided force; it is evident that this first position must, in all probability, be the most confused and most disorderly imaginable, without any resemblance to those works of human contrivance, which, along with a symmetry of parts, discover an adjustment of means to ends, and a tendency to self-preservation. If the actuating force cease after this operation, matter must remain for ever in disorder, and continue an immense chaos, without any proportion or activity. But suppose that the actuating force, whatever it be, still continues in matter, this first position will immediately give place to a second, which will likewise in all probability be as disorderly as the first, and so on through many successions of changes and revolutions. No particular order or position ever continues a moment unaltered. The original force, still remaining in activity, gives a perpetual restlessness to matter. Every possible situation is produced, and instantly destroyed. If a glimpse or dawn of order appears for a moment, it is instantly hurried away, and confounded, by that never-ceasing force which actuates every part of matter.

Thus the universe goes on for many ages in a continued succession of chaos and disorder. But is it not possible that it may settle at last, so as not to lose its motion and active force (for that we have supposed inherent in it), yet so as to preserve an uniformity of appearance, amidst the continual motion and fluctuation of its parts? This we find to be the case with the universe at present. Every individual is perpetually changing, and every part of every individual; and yet the whole remains, in appearance, the same. May we not hope for such a position, or rather be assured of it, from the eternal revolutions of unguided matter; and may not this account for all the appearing wisdom and contrivance which is in the universe? Let us contemplate the subject a little, and we shall find, that this adjustment, if attained by matter of a seeming stability in the forms, with a real and perpetual revolution or motion of parts, affords a plausible, if not a true solution of the difficulty.

It is in vain, therefore, to insist upon the uses of the parts in animals or vegetables, and their curious adjustment to each other. I would fain know, how an animal could subsist, unless its parts were so adjusted? Do we not find, that it immediately perishes, whenever this adjustment ceases, and that its matter corrupting tries some new form? It happens indeed, that the parts of the world are so well adjusted, that some regular form immediately lays claim to this corrupted matter: and if it were not so, could the world subsist? Must it not dissolve as well as the animal, and pass through new positions and situations, till in great, but finite succession, it fall at last into the present or some such order?

It is well, replied Cleanthes, you told us, that this hypothesis was suggested on a sudden, in the course of the argument. Had you had leisure to examine it, you would soon have perceived the insuperable objections to which it is exposed. No form, you say, can subsist, unless it possess those powers and organs requisite for its subsistence: some new order or economy must be tried, and so on, without intermission; till at last some order, which can support and maintain itself, is fallen upon. But according to this hypothesis, whence arise the many conveniences and advantages which men and all animals possess? Two eyes, two ears, are not absolutely necessary for the subsistence of the species. Human race might have been propagated and preserved, without horses, dogs, cows, sheep, and those innumerable fruits and products which serve to our satisfaction and enjoyment. If no camels had been created for the use of man in the sandy deserts of Africa and Arabia, would the world have been dissolved? If no loadstone had been framed to give that wonderful and useful direction to the needle, would human society and the human kind have been immediately extinguished? Though the maxims of Nature be in general very frugal, yet instances of this kind are far from being rare; and any one of them is a sufficient proof of design, and of a benevolent design, which gave rise to the order and arrangement of the universe.

At least, you may safely infer, said Philo, that the foregoing hypothesis is so far incomplete and imperfect, which I shall not scruple to allow. But can we ever reasonably expect greater success in any attempts of this nature? Or can we ever hope to erect a system of cosmogony, that will be liable to no exceptions, and will contain no circumstance repugnant to our limited and imperfect experience of the analogy of Nature? Your theory itself cannot surely pretend to any such advantage, even though you have run into *Anthropomorphism*, the better to preserve a conformity to common experience. Let us once more put into trial. In all instances which we have ever seen, ideas are copied from real objects, and are ectypal, not archetypal, to express myself in learned terms: You reverse this order, and give thought the precedence. In all instances which we have ever seen, thought has no influence upon matter, except where that matter is so conjoined with it as to have an equal reciprocal influence upon it. No animal can move immediately any thing but the members of its own body; and indeed, the equality of action and re-action seems to be an universal law of nature: But your theory implies a contradiction to this experience. These instances, with many more, which it were easy to collect, (particularly the supposition of a mind or system of thought that is eternal, or, in other words, an animal ingenerable and immortal); these instances, I say, may teach all of us sobriety in condemning each other, and let us see, that as no system of this kind ought ever to be received from a slight analogy, so neither ought any to be rejected on account of a small incongruity. For that is an inconvenience from which we can justly pronounce no one to be exempted.

All religious systems, it is confessed, are subject to great and insuperable difficulties. Each disputant triumphs in his turn; while he carries on an offensive war, and exposes the absurdities, barbarities, and pernicious tenets of his antagonist. But all of them, on the whole, prepare a complete triumph for the *Sceptic;* who tells them, that no system ought ever to be embraced with regard to such subjects: For this plain reason, that no absurdity ought ever to be assented to with regard to any subject. A total suspense of judgment is here our only reasonable resource. And if every attack, as is commonly observed, and no defence, among Theologians, is successful; how complete must be *his* victory, who remains always, with all mankind, on the offensive, and has himself no fixed station or abiding city, which he is ever, on any occasion, obliged to defend?

GOD AND PROBABILITY
D. H. Mellor

D. H. Mellor, "God and Probability," *Religious Studies*, vol. 5, no. 2 (December, 1969). Used by permission of the author and Cambridge University Press, and revised by Professor Mellor.

§I. Introduction

My object in this paper is to consider what relevance, if any, current analyses of probability have to problems of religious belief. There is no doubt that words such as 'probable' are used in this context; what is doubtful is that this use can be analysed as other major uses of such words can. I shall conclude that this use cannot be so analysed and hence, given the preponderance of the other uses that can, that it is misleading.

I have three broad uses in mind, of each of which one of three widely accepted analyses is *prima facie* plausible. The first is what looks like a *statistical* use of 'probable' and related terms, exemplified in F. R. Tennant's argument from design.[1] The second is what looks like an application of *subjective* probability in talking of the lack of firmness or conviction in a person's religious belief or unbelief. The third is what looks like an application of *inductive* probability, in that some features of the world are taken to support a theistic cosmological hypothesis (or at least a cosmological hypothesis consistent with theism). My conclusion in each case will be, *not* that a state of the world, or belief, or hypothesis fails to be probable because it is *im*probable, but that it is misleading in these cases to speak in terms of probability at all.[2]

§II. Statistical Probability and Design

Tennant, in his weakened version of the argument from design, relies upon the application of statistical probability in the following way. He argues that on any hypothesis that the world is the result of a chance process, it is extremely improbable that it should be as it is. He further argues that this is much more probable on the hypothesis that it is the result of intelligent design. He finally infers that the latter hypothesis is therefore more probably true. This last step involves an appeal to *inductive* probability, which I consider in IV below. Of the first steps, I argue first that they would be invalid even if the concept of statistical probability applied in this context. I also argue that it does not apply, and hence that the first hypothesis is incoherent and the second either incoherent or trivially true.

Tennant's general thesis is that "the conspiration of innumerable causes to

---

[1] *Philosophical Theology*, Cambridge, 1928. Vol. 2, pp. 78 *et seq.*
[2] J. Hick (*Faith and Knowledge*, 2nd edition. London: 1967. Ch.7) comes to the same conclusions. But Peirce's frequency analysis of statistical probability, and Keynes' 'logical relation' analysis of inductive probability, to which Hick appeals, have been too long superseded for his argument to be conclusive. His reference to Tennant's 'alogical probability' is an inadequate presentation of modern subjective analysis.

produce, by their united and reciprocal action, and to maintain, a general order of Nature [constitutes] the forcibleness of Nature's suggestion that she is the outcome of intelligent design" [*op.cit.,* p. 79], and the argument turns upon 'forcibleness' being understood in terms of probability. There is no doubt that, in more or less sophisticated forms, argument from the order we perceive in the world to at least the probability of intelligent design is still one of the most popular theist arguments.[3] It raises other conceptual problems as well, especially about the concept of order, but that raised by the use of probability is the crucial one.

First, it is worth commenting on the weakness of Tennant's conclusion. He emphasises that "the empirically-minded theologian" [*op.cit.,* p. 78] who relies on this argument "will . . . entertain, at the outset, no such presuppositions as that the supreme Being, to which the world may point as its principle of explanation, is infinite, perfect, immutable, supra-personal, unqualifiedly omnipotent or omniscient. The attributes to be ascribed to God will be such as empirical facts and their sufficient explanation indicate or require." [*loc.cit.*] 'God' then, is just the name for whatever we need to postulate to explain the world's being as science finds it to be. The argument does not at all purport to show that whatever we need to postulate in this way is at all like the Christian, or any other well-known, God. What it purports to show is the following. Given that there are various possible explanations of the world's being as it is, the world's being as it is makes some of these explanations more probable than others. Then from the world's being as it is, it follows both that the most probable explanation or explanations of it postulate a uniquely fundamental, but otherwise unspecified, entity (which we shall call 'God'), and that it is more probable than not that some such explanation is true, i.e. that some such entity exists. Neither of these conclusions, weak as they are, follows from the admitted premises.

A parable. A man, *A,* takes a pack of cards and considers two possible explanations of the order (as yet unknown) of the cards in the pack: (i) that they have been arranged in that order by an intelligent designer, otherwise unspecified; (ii) that their order, whatever it is, is the result of some chance process, a product not of a designer, but of a shuffler. In order to decide, from an inspection of the pack, which of these two hypotheses is the more probably correct, *A* may proceed by one of two methods, which I call *'a priori'* and *'a posteriori'* respectively.

On the *a priori* method, *A* decides, *before he inspects the pack,* in what order or orders an intelligent designer might have arranged the cards. For example, suppose the intelligent designer to be a bridge player: he might be expected to arrange the cards in any one of a number of orders that would benefit himself as dealer without arousing the suspicions of his opponents. *A* assumes therefore that any order in such a set of orders has a *higher* statistical probability on this hypothesis than on hypothesis (ii), and any order not in the set has a *lower* statistical probability, possibly zero. On the basis of these assumptions, *A* decides

---

[3]E.g. P. Lecomte du Noüy (*Human Destiny.* New York: 1947. Ch.3); who uses a classical Laplacean definition of statistical probability in terms of numbers of equiprobable cases. But the well-known objections to this definition, and to the principle of indifference on which it relies, do not sufficiently dispose of the argument, for which it is not essential.

that *if,* on inspection, the order of the cards turns out to be a member of the set specified under hypothesis (i), he will accept that hypothesis, and otherwise he will accept hypothesis (ii). In other words, *A* adopts *a priori,* before inspecting the pack, a *decision strategy.* He recognises that the explanation his strategy tells him to adopt, on the result of his enquiring into the actual order of the cards, will only have been shown to be *probable,* since, after all, if the order is a member of the specified set, it still *might* have occurred by chance. "All that he can expect to emerge from his inquiry is grounds for reasonable belief rather than rational and coercive demonstration." [Tennant, *loc.cit.*]

However, the smaller the *a priori* specified set of orders which might have been the result of design, i.e. the more definite *A*'s idea of the postulated designer's intentions, the smaller the probability that an order in such a set could have arisen by chance. Suppose, for example, that the set is reduced to exclude an order whose statistical probability on hypothesis (ii) is *p.* Then the statistical probability on hypothesis (ii) that the actual order is a member of the new, reduced set has been reduced by *p.* In the extreme case, with effectively complete *a priori* knowledge of the designer's intentions, the specified set will have just one member. *A* will then be able to write down just one order, *a priori,* which the designer, if any, would produce. If, on inspection of the pack, this order is revealed, the statistical probability of this on hypothesis (ii) is so minute that *A* may reasonably accept the design hypothesis with virtually complete confidence.

There is no doubt of the basic soundness of this *a priori* method. The difficulty with it is that of knowing *a priori* what the designer's intentions are, and hence of being able to write down, before inspecting the pack, *what* order, if found, will license the probable inference that it is the product of design. *A*, being aware of this difficulty, and of past failures of *a priori* arguments to anticipate successfully the results of empirical enquiry, resolves to adopt the second, *a posteriori,* method. He resolves, that is, to ascribe to the designer no intentions other than "such as empirical facts [i.e. the actual order of the cards as revealed by inspection] and their sufficient explanation indicate or require". So *A* proceeds as follows. He inspects the pack, and writes down the actual order in which the cards occur. He takes 'intelligent designer' to be the name for whatever entity has just such intentions as would lead him to arrange the cards in the precise order they are actually in. He argues that the cards being in that order shows it to be, at least, much more probable that they were arranged by an intelligent designer, so defined, than that they were arranged by an entity with any other intentions. So *A* takes this as his hypothesis (i), and has no difficulty in showing that, on it, the statistical probability of the order of the cards being what is actually found is much higher than it is on hypothesis (ii). He finally concludes, as on the *a priori* method, that this shows hypothesis (i) to be vastly more probable than hypothesis (ii). *A* notes further that this method is free of the doubtful *a priori* assumptions that have to be made in the first method, and that it is solely the empirically observed order of the cards that has "forcibly suggested" its own design. He might moreover note that this second, *a posteriori,* method could be applied to yield this conclusion *whatever* the order of cards turned out to be. But if he did note this, he might conceivably reflect that the method is too powerful to be valid. . . .

It does not need much insight into the nature of probability to realise that this *a posteriori* method is completely worthless. Yet, so far as I can see, it reflects faithfully the structure of Tennant's argument. The kind of fallacy involved is sufficiently widespread and persuasive to deserve a name and I propose to call it the 'bridge-hand fallacy', after the most obviously fallacious instance of it. A bridge player, who suspects the dealer of fixing the pack, writes down the hand he suspects and *then* is dealt just that hand, has good confirmation of his suspicion. A bridge player, however, who writes down whatever hand he receives, and then argues that its improbability "forcibly suggests" that it has been fixed by the dealer, will soon and rightly lack sympathetic listeners. But not so, it appears, the theologian who argues, in strict analogy, from whatever "hand" science shows him to have been dealt, that its improbability "forcibly suggests" that it has been fixed by some suitably defined Supreme Being.

It does not follow that because I think the bridge-hand fallacy is committed in arguing *a posteriori* for the probability of intelligent design, I suppose a valid argument to exist for the world being the result of a chance process. On the contrary, this is not a readily intelligible hypothesis at all. The concept of a chance process is that of some device, such as a die, a coin, an ordered pair of parents, on which a trial can be conducted, such as throwing the die, or tossing the coin, or conceiving a child. Of such a trial a number of outcomes are possible and none is certain: e.g. throwing a five, landing heads, that the child born is male. Now it seems to me that the force of saying that an outcome of a chance process is "possible but not certain" rests on the observation of a number of chance processes of the same kind—throws of dice, tosses of coins, birth of children—of which sometimes there is one outcome and sometimes another. For there is a very close connection between something being probable and it happening more often than not. Now this latter concept can have no application unless it is at least *possible* for there to be more than one occasion on which the something could happen. In other words, it is essential to the concept of a chance process that it is a kind of process that *could* occur more than once, even if in fact it doesn't. Otherwise, the supposition that the outcome of a process is possible but not certain, which is implicit in calling it a 'chance' process, is empty, unintelligible.

(In saying this, I am not subscribing to a frequency analysis of probability as it applies to chance processes.[4] I am not making the much stronger and, to my mind, fallacious claim that in such cases the probability of an outcome can be defined in terms of the frequency with which it occurs in many repetitions of the process. I am merely saying that the *possibility* of repetition is necessary to there being any probability of any outcome.)

Now the trouble with supposing the world to be the result of a chance process is that, not merely *has* the process only happened once, it *could* only happen once. The world comprising all there is, it does not make sense to suppose two worlds, which might be qualitatively the same or different as the two chance processes of which they are the outcomes had the same or different

---

[4]The frequency analysis is that most widely accepted by statisticians. The most influential exposition of it is probably in R. von Mises: *Probability, Statistics and Truth,* 2nd English edition (London: 1957). My own view of statistical probability is stated in *The Matter of Chance.* London: Cambridge University Press. 1971.

outcomes. We may, of course, talk of other possible worlds, but this is only a way of referring to the fact that there is no logical necessity in the world being as it is, that science and common observation cannot spin their results out of logical reflection. But this does not, and cannot, mean that these other possible worlds are lying around in a limbo of potentialities, waiting to be realised if some Supreme Dealer should decide to pick up the pack and deal again.

It should be observed that all this is compatible with every occurrence in the world being the outcome of a chance process, i.e. with every scientific law being statistical. There is no reason to suppose that this latter is true, but even if it were it would still not entail that the conjunction of all such occurrences, past, present and future, was itself a possible but not certain outcome of a chance process.

It is essential to realise that the hypotheses here considered are not about a temporal origin of the present material universe. On an absolute view of space-time (which is not logically impossible), such creative processes could obviously recur. Our hypotheses concern the *a*temporal creation of the whole world, comprising all matter at all times (and space-time as well, if that is supposed to have independent existence). There is a further objection to "chance" hypotheses of creation, whether the latter is understood temporally or not. A chance process needs a "chance set-up" on which to occur; e.g. a die or coin to be thrown, a radium atom to await possible decay, parents to conceive a child. *Ex hypothesi* the *whole* material universe could not issue from a distinct *material* chance set-up, either temporally or atemporally. The concept of an immaterial chance set-up is not a happy one.

All this is merely to say that the concept of probability cannot be applied in connection with arguments from design as it is applied by statisticians to the outcome of chance processes. And in so far as the "intelligent design" hypothesis is defined negatively, i.e. as a hypothesis that the world is *not* the result of some chance process, it either shares the incoherence of the "chance" hypothesis, or becomes trivially true. If the design hypothesis is that the probability of the world being as it is, considered as the outcome of a chance process, has been raised to 1 (or close to 1, on a sort of "semi-design" view) by the Supreme Being, then it shares the incoherence of any view that regards the world as an outcome of a chance process. If, on the other hand, the design view is merely that the world is *not* an outcome of a chance process, with some probability, however high, then it is trivially true. It is logically incorrect to call any process of which the world might be the result a 'chance process'.

§III. Subjective Probability

Having tried to show that statistical probability has no proper application in arguments from design, I now consider other *prima facie* applicable uses of probability statements. There is the use of probability statements dealt with in theories of subjective probability[5] in which a probability statement merely expresses the degree of partial belief a person making the statement has in whatever he attaches probability to. Such theories need to provide a quantitative measure of degree of belief, to make sense, for example, of saying that a man's

---

[5]As expounded, e.g. in L. J. Savage: *The Foundations of Statistics* (New York: 1954).

degree of belief in something is 0.7. One standard measure is the betting odds a man will accept on something happening.[6]

Now subjective theories are concerned only to make sense of 'degree of belief'; they do not concern themselves with whether a degree of belief is in any way justified. So two people, with exactly the same evidence, contemplating exactly the same possibility, can attach wildly discrepant degrees of belief to it, in that e.g. they are prepared to bet at wildly different odds on it. This is why the theories are called 'subjective' and why, even if they could be taken to provide a measure of a degree of religious belief, they would not bear at all on the question of whether such a degree of belief was justified. But some comments are called for on their betting measure even of actual, as opposed to justified, degrees of belief.

First, a betting measure is acceptable in a subjective theory of *probability*, because it has been shown that, under the conditions imposed on the person betting, the betting quotients he adopts must satisfy the usual mathematical axioms for probabilities.[7] So this measure of degree of belief does indeed interpret it as a probability; when a man expresses such a degree of belief by saying that he thinks something 'almost certain', 'extremely likely', 'highly probable', this is interpreted as expressing a subjective assignment of a high numerical probability, say between 0.9 and 1. This is no doubt a point in favour of the betting measure of belief: until it was shown that reasonable constraints made the measure of partial belief satisfy the probability axioms, partial belief could not seriously be taken to be what probability statements were about.

However, some points need making against the betting measure of belief. It doesn't make sense to talk of betting unless the situation is one in which the bet could be settled, i.e. one in which the person betting can eventually come to *know* whether what he is betting on is so or not. Now in the case of religious belief, it rather depends on what the belief is whether this condition is satisfied or not. To take the simplest example, suppose I am betting on there being an afterlife, it being given that I cannot know in advance whether there is one or not. Then, *prima facie*, the bet can only be settled in favour of the afterlife hypothesis, since if it is false there will be no settlement. Under these circumstances, by the betting measure, the only reasonable probability to assign is 1, which appears to entail that I should be irrational if I acted otherwise than as if I were convinced that there is an afterlife. (Note that this has nothing directly to do with Pascal's wager, since it is quite independent of whether the afterlife is pleasant or unpleasant.)

However, this argument loses its plausibility on further inspection, as it becomes steadily less clear in what sort of currency a bet could be made now that is to be settled after death. In other words, it is not at all clear that there is any scale of utilities, in the sense presupposed in any concept of betting, on which what is valued in this life is comparable with what may be valued after it. Alternative states of this life may be compared in utility with each other, and so perhaps may alternative states of the next life; but without a religious hypothesis to correlate states and their values in this and the next life, one cannot be sensibly

---

[6]See e.g. my *The Matter of Chance*, chapter 2.
[7]The betting *quotient*, rather than the odds, is what can be constrained to be a mathematical probability, and so is used to measure belief. The point is not substantial; odds and quotients are interdefinable. For the basis of the constraint see e.g. *The Matter of Chance*, loc.cit.

compared with the other. Faust, who held such a hypothesis, could make these comparisons, but when it is the measure of belief in religious hypotheses themselves that is in question, betting quotients on their truth cannot be based on them. It is thus not clear that a measure of degree of such *religious* belief in terms of betting quotients can be provided. The postulated betting situation, taken to include the final 'pay-off' when the outcome is known, is one in which nothing of determinate value, that could be staked and won or lost, can be assumed to be preserved.

This seems to me a crucial objection to using betting quotients to provide a measure of *religious* belief in particular. But more general objections to subjective probability measures of partial belief are also worth mentioning. The conditions imposed by these theories (e.g. on the betting situation) in order to ensure that the measure of partial belief satisfies the mathematical axioms of probability, detract seriously from their claims to provide a measure of *actual* degrees of belief. For example, the person is supposed to be *compelled* to bet, and a bet, of course, must be at some definite quotient. But a man may merely think something *probable* while having no views as to whether it is *very* probable or only *fairly* probable. Such a man will certainly refuse to bet at any quotient less than $1/2$, but it does not follow, and is not true that there is any one higher quotient he would wish to bet at in preference to any other. Yet if he is compelled to bet, he will have to pick some such quotient; and some subjective theorists have talked as if this gambling machinery thereby exposes a precise degree of belief, of which its owner was previously unaware. Now while it may be possible to be unaware of some of one's beliefs, or of their strength, this inference is absurd. The obvious conclusion is that, in such a case, a compelled choice of betting quotient is purely arbitrary, and has nothing to do with a strength of conviction in whatever the bet is about.

It is important to resist a specious air of scientific precision which subjective theory can carry in such cases, and to insist that sometimes even when one thinks something probable and a bet on it could be settled, still it would be irrational to bet at all. But if so, any claim that betting provides a universally applicable measure of partial belief, and hence the inference that partial belief is always measurable, become very suspect. Where there are no quantitative data, it is a mistake, to which scientists are sometimes prone, to suppose that they can be conjured up by forcing people to pick some number off a scale. And I am inclined to think that, in the case of religious doubt and partial belief, there simply are no quantitative data.

I doubt then, principally for the two reasons I have given, whether subjective probability has any more application in the context of religious belief than does statistical probability.

§IV. Inductive Probability

I turn finally to the use of probability statements that is dealt with in inductive logic, in talking of scientific hypotheses being supported by inconclusive evidence. One might say, for example, that on the basis of such evidence one hypothesis is more probable than another, or that some extra piece of evidence has made such a hypothesis more or less probable than it was before. *Prima facie,* this is the use of probability statements that most plausibly applies to religious belief. It is not, of course, necessary to suppose that religious belief just is belief in some hypothesis which could be said to be probable or improbable on some evidence, merely that this is a component of religious belief and that, where one talks of religious belief as being probable, it is to this component one refers.

The use of the concept of probability in inductive logic is both technical and controversial; in picking out what I take to be the salient points I fear I shall oversimplify in some relevant respect. However, it seems clear that no existing quantitative inductive logic is adequate to the analysis of the support given to religious hypotheses by inconclusive evidence. By a 'quantitative inductive logic' I mean one assigning numerical degrees of confirmation, or corroboration, to scientific hypotheses on the basis of evidence. It should be remarked that some of these logics are probabilistic, in the sense that they base themselves on the mathematical axioms for probabilities, and others are not.[8] I don't think this distinction is of any consequence, since either could be taken equally well as a quantitative account of our use in these contexts of such non-quantitative terms as 'probable', 'likely', 'almost certain', 'barely possible'. This use carries no serious commitment to particular mathematical axioms.

Some of those, such as Carnap, who have constructed probabilistic inductive logics, have used the same arguments in terms of betting quotients that have been used in subjective probability theory. Their systems are therefore open to the objections raised in §II, at least in their possible application to religious hypotheses, that it is unclear what sense could be made of settling bets on such hypotheses.

There are, however, further objections than those directed against probabilistic measures of religious doubt, to existing quantitative inductive logics, whether probabilistic or not. One is their very rudimentary state: none gives any significant numerical value to the degree of confirmation of any important scientific theory. Even with their languages extended sufficiently to express such theories, it is not clear that they would be adequate to express anything that religious belief could be belief in. This is perhaps only an objection of degree. I would not claim that these confirmation theories could *never* provide a quantitative measure of the extent to which evidence makes religious hypotheses more or less probable. But equally, a claim that they *will* be able to do so is, in their present primitive state, no more than a promissory note issued by a rather insubstantial authority.

A greater difficulty seems to me to concern the kind of hypothesis involved in religious belief, a difficulty closely related to that raised in §II about the argument from design. The scientific hypotheses to which one can imagine systems of inductive logic, suitably developed, being applied are universal hypotheses, i.e. that everything of a certain kind has some property or stands in some relation to something else. This includes statistical hypotheses, that everything of a certain kind has a definite *chance* of having some property or of standing in some relation. Now there may be few or many things of the kind referred to in the hypothesis; there may even, as a matter of fact, be none at all. But these are not

---

[8]The chief exponent of probabilistic inductive logic was R. Carnap: *Logical Foundations of Probability*, 2nd edition (Chicago: 1962). The chief opponent of it is K. R. Popper: *The Logic of Scientific Discovery* (London: 1959). See also I. Lakatos: 'Changes in the problem of inductive logic.' *The Problem of Inductive Logic*. Ed. I. Lakatos (Amsterdam: 1968).

logical facts, and do not enter into the assessment of the probability of such hypotheses on whatever evidence there is for or against them. The influence of these facts is on what evidence there is, not on the extent to which that evidence supports the hypothesis.

Now a difficulty arises with hypotheses about the world as a whole, that seem to be the components of religious belief to which, if at all, inductive probability might be applied. The difficulty is that it is essential to such a hypothesis that it has only one instance.[9] Certainly, such a hypothesis can be put in universal form, that every world has such-and-such properties, or such-and-such a chance of having such properties. But this form is quite misleading. It is in this case a logical fact, which may enter into the assessment of the probability of the hypothesis, that there is only one world. The hypothesis in its universal form in fact makes no more than a singular statement that our world has such-and-such properties. Consequently, we cannot expect that a confirmation theory developed to deal with genuine universal hypotheses will apply at all to such cosmological hypotheses. For example, Carnap's confirmation theory assesses the probability of universal hypotheses in terms of that of their next instances: that the next thing we observe of the specified kind will have the property the hypothesis ascribes to all things of that kind. This is not a procedure that makes sense when applied to the hypotheses which concern us. We cannot wait to see if the next world we observe has the property our hypothesis ascribes to all worlds.

Again, it might be said that this is only a deficiency in present inductive logic, that so far it has concentrated on the universal hypotheses which are the principal objects of scientific belief. The fact, if it is a fact, that special techniques would have to be devised for assessing hypotheses about the world as a whole in terms of probability doesn't itself show that such techniques could not be devised. At this point I return to the criticisms of §II, which are relevant here, although they ostensibly pertain to statistical rather than to inductive probability. To show this relevance, I need to make a brief digression into the relations between various kinds of probability.

I have not talked, as Carnap does, of different *concepts* of probability, i.e. different senses of the term 'probability', because I do not think there are such different concepts. Terms like 'probability' are not ambiguous, in the sense that something could be both probable in one sense and improbable in another. A variety of things can be probable or improbable, and we may express this fact by talking of *kinds* of probability. Kinds of probability differ in the ways they are established, subjective probability by psychological enquiry, statistical probability by statistical experiment, inductive probability perhaps by logical enquiry. But each is a probability, in the same sense of 'probability', just as religious truth, scientific truth, mathematical truth is all truth in the same sense of 'truth'. We do not infer from the existence of kinds of truth, differing in the ways they are established, that there are as many concepts of truth, and the analogous inference should be resisted in the case of probability.

The point of these remarks is this. In §II I objected to the argument from design that the necessary uniqueness of the world as a whole deprived the hypothesis, that it is the outcome of a chance process, of any sense. I concluded that one could not apply statistical probability to such hypotheses. Now this is just

---

[9]II, paragraph 11.

to say that such hypotheses do not, despite appearances, confer any probability on the world being as it is. But then the world being as it is confers no probability on such hypotheses where this latter (inductive) probability has to be inferred from the former (statistical) probability. Such an inference is made, albeit tacitly, in the argument from design; the 'two-concept' view of probability disguises it by making the ascription of inductive probability seem independent of that of statistical probability, which in this case it is not.

The basis of the required inference is the following principle.[10] Suppose there are two statistical hypotheses, h and i, and i assigns a higher statistical probability than h does to some piece of evidence e. Then on the evidence e, if we may infer anything about the inductive probabilities of h and i, it is that i is more probable than h. Whether we may infer anything about these inductive probabilities on this evidence is controversial, but it is not controversial that this, if anything, is what we may infer. At all events, this is clearly the inference made in the argument from design: the statistical probability of the world being as it is is greater on the design hypothesis than on the chance hypothesis, *therefore* the world being as it is gives the design hypothesis a greater inductive probability than the chance hypothesis. I am very willing to grant that this is a sound inference, but if, as I have argued, such hypotheses are incoherent, the premises required for it are just not available. There is no statistical probability of the world being as it is, and hence from it no inductive probability is derivable of a hypothesis purporting to prescribe such a statistical probability.

This difficulty, that any quantitative inductive logic would face, is not one that can be expected to be overcome by technical ingenuity. The problem is not, as it may be with ordinary scientific hypotheses, that probability judgments are coherently made whose rationale it is difficult to expose. On the contrary, it is that there seems to be no coherent basis for probability judgments, in terms of the concepts with which confirmation theory deals. Hence there is simply nothing for a quantitative inductive logic to account for.

§V. Conclusion

My tentative conclusion then is that none of the three main kinds of probability statements, which have recently been the object of philosophical study, is properly applied in matters of religious belief. It is not meaningful to say, in connection with the argument from design, that the world being as it is is statistically either probable or improbable on some cosmological hypothesis, and hence we are thereby given no reason to say that the world being as it is renders such a hypothesis inductively probable or improbable. As for subjective probability, no doubt I may express my lack of either firm belief or firm disbelief in such terms as 'probably', 'perhaps', 'almost sure', etc., but such remarks have not yet been shown to express quantitative degrees of belief measured on any scale of probabilities. Consequently, the serious use of 'probable' and related terms in these three contexts should be avoided, since it misleadingly suggests the applicability of the corresponding analyses.

---

[10]Given, e.g., by I. Hacking (*Logic of Statistical Inference*, London: Cambridge University Press, 1965, p. 55), under the name of the 'law of likelihood'.

Chapter
FOURTEEN

THEISTIC
ARGUMENTS
morality and
deity

THE FOURTH WAY

St. Thomas Aquinas

From St. Thomas Aquinas, *Summa Theologica*, part I, question 2, article 3 (in part), in Anton C. Pegis (ed.), *Basic Writings of St. Thomas Aquinas*, 1968. Used by permission of Random House, Inc., New York.

The fourth way is taken from the gradation to be found in things. Among beings there are some more and some less good, true, noble, and the like. But *more* and *less* are predicated of different things according as they resemble in their different ways something which is the maximum, as a thing is said to be hotter according as it more nearly resembles that which is hottest; so that there is something which is truest, something best, something noblest, and, consequently, something which is most being, for those things that are greatest in truth are greatest in being, as it is written in *Metaph.* ii.[1] Now the maximum in any genus is the cause of all in that genus, as fire, which is the maximum of heat, is the cause of all hot things, as is said in the same book.[2] Therefore there must also be something which is to all beings the cause of their being, goodness, and every other perfection; and this we call God.

---

[1] *Metaph.* Iα, 1 (993b 30).
[2] *Ibid.* (993b 25).

THE MORAL ARGUMENT

Immanuel Kant

From *Kant's Critique of Practical Reason and Other Works on the Theory of Ethics*, T. K. Abbott (trans.), pp. 206–209, 220–231, 240–246, Longman's, Green and Co., Ltd., London. Originally published in 1788.

Chapter II

OF THE DIALECTIC OF PURE REASON IN DEFINING THE CONCEPTION OF THE "SUMMUM BONUM"

The conception of the *summum* itself contains an ambiguity which might occasion needless disputes if we did not attend to it. The *summum* may mean either the supreme (*supremum*) or the perfect (*consummatum*). The former is that condition which is itself unconditioned, *i.e.* is not subordinate to any other (*originarium*); the second is that whole which is not a part of a greater whole of the same kind (*perfectissimum*). It has been shown in the Analytic that *virtue* (as worthiness to be happy) is the *supreme condition* of all that can appear to us desirable, and consequently of all our pursuit of happiness, and is therefore the *supreme* good. But it does not follow that it is the whole and perfect good as the object of the desires of rational finite beings; for this requires happiness also, and that not merely in the partial eyes of the person who makes himself an end, but even in the judgment of an impartial reason, which regards persons in general as ends in themselves. For to need happiness, to deserve it (247),[1] and yet at the same time not to participate in it, cannot be consistent with the perfect volition of a rational being possessed at the same time of all power, if, for the sake of experiment, we conceive such a being. Now inasmuch as virtue and happiness together constitute the possession of the *summum bonum* in a person, and the distribution of happiness in exact proportion to morality (which is the worth of the person, and his worthiness to be happy) constitutes the *summum bonum* of a possible world; hence this *summum bonum* expresses the whole, the perfect good, in which, however, virtue as the condition is always the supreme good, since it has no condition above it; whereas happiness, while it is pleasant to the possessor of it, is not of itself absolutely and in all respects good, but always presupposes morally right behaviour as its condition.

When two elements are *necessarily* united in one concept, they must be connected as reason and consequence, and this either so that their unity is considered as *analytical* (logical connexion), or as *synthetical* (real connexion) —the former following the law of identity, the latter that of causality. The connexion of virtue and happiness may therefore be understood in two ways: either the endeavour to be virtuous and the rational pursuit of happiness are not two distinct actions, but absolutely identical, in which case no maxim need be made the principle of the former, other than what serves for the latter; or the connexion consists in this, that virtue produces happiness as something distinct from the consciousness of virtue, as a cause produces an effect.

The ancient Greek schools were, properly speaking, only two, and in determining the conception of the *summum bonum* these followed in fact one and the same method, inasmuch as they did not allow virtue and happiness to be regarded as two distinct elements of the *summum bonum,* and consequently sought (248) the unity of the principle by the rule of identity; but they differed as to which of the two was to be taken as the fundamental notion. The *Epicurean* said: To be conscious that one's maxims lead to happiness is virtue; the *Stoic* said: To be conscious of one's virtue is happiness. With the former, *Prudence* was equivalent to morality; with the latter, who chose a higher designation for virtue, morality alone was true wisdom.

While we must admire the men who in such early times tried all imaginable ways of extending the domain of philosophy, we must at the same time lament that their acuteness was unfortunately misapplied in trying to trace out identity between two extremely heterogeneous notions, those of happiness and virtue. But it agrees with the dialectical spirit of their times (and subtle minds are even now sometimes misled in the same way) to get rid of irreconcilable differences in principle by seeking to change them into a mere contest about words, and thus apparently working out the identity of the notion under different names, and this usually occurs in cases where the combination of heterogeneous principles lies so deep or so high, or would require so complete a transformation of the doctrines assumed in the rest of the philosophical system, that men are afraid to

---

[1][Numbers in parentheses refer to pages in the 1838 Rosencranz and Schubert edition, vol. VIII. Ed.]

penetrate deeply into the real difference, and prefer treating it as a difference in matters of form.

While both schools sought to trace out the identity of the practical principles of virtue and happiness, they were not agreed as to the way in which they tried to force this identity, but were separated infinitely from one another, the one placing its principle on the side of sense, the other on that of reason; the one in the consciousness of sensible wants, the other in the independence of practical reason (249) on all sensible grounds of determination. According to the Epicurean the notion of virtue was already involved in the maxim: To promote one's own happiness; according to the Stoics, on the other hand, the feeling of happiness was already contained in the consciousness of virtue. Now whatever is contained in another notion is identical with part of the containing notion, but not with the whole, and moreover two wholes may be specifically distinct, although they consist of the same parts, namely, if the parts are united into a whole in totally different ways. The Stoic maintained that virtue was the *whole summum bonum,* and happiness only the consciousness of possessing it, as making part of the state of the subject. The Epicurean maintained that happiness was the *whole summum bonum,* and virtue only the form of the maxim for its pursuit, viz. the rational use of the means for attaining it.

Now it is clear from the Analytic that the maxims of virtue and those of private happiness are quite heterogeneous as to their supreme practical principle; and although they belong to one *summum bonum* which together they make possible, yet they are so far from coinciding that they restrict and check one another very much in the same subject. Thus the question, *How is the summum bonum* practically possible? still remains an unsolved problem, notwithstanding all the *attempts at coalition* that have hitherto been made. The Analytic has, however, shown what it is that makes the problem difficult to solve; namely, that happiness and morality are two specifically *distinct elements of the summum bonum,* and therefore their combination *cannot* be *analytically* cognized (as if the man that seeks his own happiness should find by mere analysis of his conception that in so acting he is virtuous, or as if the man that follows virtue should in the consciousness of such conduct find that he is already happy *ipso facto*) (250), but must be a *synthesis* of concepts. Now since this combination is recognized as *à priori,* and therefore as practically necessary, and consequently not as derived from experience, so that the possibility of the *summum bonum* does not rest on any empirical principle, it follows that the *deduction* [legitimation] of this concept must be *transcendental.* It is *à priori* (morally) necessary to *produce the summum bonum by freedom of will*: therefore the condition of its possibility must rest solely on *à priori* principles of cognition, [. . . .]

V. THE EXISTENCE OF GOD AS A POSTULATE OF PURE PRACTICAL REASON

In the foregoing analysis the moral law led to a practical problem which is prescribed by pure reason alone, without the aid of any sensible motives, namely, that of the necessary completeness of the first and principal element of the *summum bonum,* viz. Morality; and as this can be perfectly solved only in eternity, to the postulate of *immortality.* The same law must also lead us to affirm the possibility of the second element of the *summum bonum,* viz. Happiness proportioned to that morality, and this on grounds as disinterested as before, and solely from impartial reason; that is, it must lead to the supposition of the existence of a cause adequate to this effect; in other words, it must postulate the *existence of God,* as the necessary condition of the possibility of the *summum bonum* (an object of the will which is necessarily connected with the moral legislation of pure reason). We proceed to exhibit this connexion in a convincing manner.

Happiness is the condition of a rational being in the world with whom *everything goes according to his wish and will;* it rests, therefore, on the harmony of physical nature with his whole end, and likewise with the essential determining principle of his will. Now the moral law as a law of freedom commands by determining principles (266), which ought to be quite independent on nature and on its harmony with our faculty of desire (as springs). But the acting rational being in the world is not the cause of the world and of nature itself. There is not the least ground, therefore, in the moral law for a necessary connexion between morality and proportionate happiness in a being that belongs to the world as part of it, and therefore dependent on it, and which for that reason cannot by his will be a cause of this nature, nor by his own power make it thoroughly harmonize, as far as his happiness is concerned, with his practical principles. Nevertheless, in the practical problem of pure reason, *i.e.* the necessary pursuit of the *summum bonum,* such a connexion is postulated as necessary: we ought to endeavour to promote the *summum bonum,* which, therefore, must be possible. Accordingly, the existence of a cause of all nature, distinct from nature itself, and containing the principle of this connexion, namely, of the exact harmony of happiness with morality, is also *postulated.* Now, this supreme cause must contain the principle of the harmony of nature, not merely with a law of the will of rational beings, but with the conception of this *law,* in so far as they make it the *supreme determining principle of the will,* and consequently not merely with the form of morals, but with their morality as their motive, that is, with their moral character. Therefore, the *summum bonum* is possible in the world only on the supposition of a Supreme Being[2] having a causality corresponding to moral character. Now a being that is capable of acting on the conception of laws is an *intelligence* (a rational being), and the causality of such a being according to this conception of laws is his *will;* therefore the supreme cause of nature, which must be presupposed as a condition of the *summum bonum* (267) is a being which is the cause of nature by *intelligence* and *will,* consequently its author, that is God. It follows that the postulate of the possibility of the *highest derived good* (the best world) is likewise the postulate of the reality of a *highest original good,* that is to say, of the existence of God. Now it was seen to be a duty for us to promote the *summum bonum;* consequently it is not merely allowable, but it is a necessity connected with duty as a requisite, that we should presuppose the possibility of this *summum bonum;* and as this is possible only on condition of the existence of God, it inseparably connects the supposition of this duty; that is, it is morally necessary to assume the existence of God.

It must be remarked here that this moral necessity is *subjective,* that is, it is a

---

[2][The original has "a Supreme Nature." "Natur," however, almost invariably means "physical nature"; therefore Hartenstein supplies the words "cause of" before "nature." More probably "Natur" is a slip for "Ursache," "cause."]

want, and not *objective,* that is, itself a duty, for there cannot be a duty to suppose the existence of anything (since this concerns only the theoretical employment of reason). Moreover, it is not meant by this that it is necessary to suppose the existence of God *as a basis of all obligation in general* (for this rests, as has been sufficiently proved, simply on the autonomy of reason itself). What belongs to duty here is only the endeavour to realize and promote the *summum bonum* in the world, the possibility of which can therefore be postulated; and as our reason finds it not conceivable except on the supposition of a supreme intelligence, the admission of this existence is therefore connected with the consciousness of our duty, although the admission itself belongs to the domain of speculative reason. Considered in respect of this alone, as a principle of explanation, it may be called a *hypothesis,* but in reference to the intelligibility of an object given us by the moral law (the *summum bonum*), and consequently of a requirement for practical purposes, it may be called *faith,* that is to say a pure *rational faith,* since pure reason (268) (both in its theoretical and its practical use) is the sole source from which it springs.

From this *deduction* it is now intelligible why the *Greek* schools could never attain the solution of their problem of the practical possibility of the *summum bonum,* because they made the rule of the use which the will of man makes of his freedom the sole and sufficient ground of this possibility, thinking that they had no need for that purpose of the existence of God. No doubt they were so far right that they established the principle of morals of itself independently of this postulate, from the relation of reason only to the will, and consequently made it the *supreme* practical condition of the *summum bonum;* but it was not therefore the *whole* condition of its possibility. The *Epicureans* had indeed assumed as the supreme principle of morality a wholly false one, namely, that of happiness, and had substituted for a law a maxim of arbitrary choice according to every man's inclination; they proceeded, however, *consistently* enough in this, that they degraded their *summum bonum* likewise just in proportion to the meanness of their fundamental principle, and looked for no greater happiness than can be attained by human prudence (including temperance and moderation of the inclinations), and this, as we know, would be scanty enough and would be very different according to circumstances; not to mention the exceptions that their maxims must perpetually admit and which make them incapable of being laws. The *Stoics,* on the contrary, had chosen their supreme practical principle quite rightly, making virtue the condition of the *summum bonum;* but when they represented the degree of virtue required by its pure law as fully attainable in this life, they not only strained the moral powers of the *man* whom they called *the wise* beyond all the limits of his nature, and assumed (269) a thing that contradicts all our knowledge of men, but also and principally they would not allow the second *element* of the *summum bonum,* namely, happiness, to be properly a special object of human desire, but made their *wise man,* like a divinity in his consciousness of the excellence of his person, wholly independent of nature (as regards his own contentment); they exposed him indeed to the evils of life, but made him not subject to them (at the same time representing him also as free from moral evil). They thus, in fact, left out the second element of the *summum bonum,* namely, personal happiness, placing it solely in action and satisfaction with one's own personal worth, thus including it in the consciousness of being morally minded, in which they might have been sufficiently refuted by the voice of their own nature.

The doctrine of Christianity,[3] even if we do not yet consider it as a religious doctrine, gives, touching this point (269), a conception of the *summum bonum* (the kingdom of God), which alone satisfies the strictest demand of practical reason. The moral law is holy (unyielding) and demands holiness of morals, although all the moral perfection to which man can attain is still only virtue, that is, a rightful disposition arising from *respect* for the law, implying consciousness of a constant propensity to transgression, or at least a want of purity, that is, a mixture of many spurious (not moral) motives of obedience to the law, consequently a self-esteem combined with humility. In respect, then, of the holiness which the Christian law requires, this leaves the creature nothing but a progress *in infinitum,* but for that very reason it justifies him in hoping for an endless duration of his existence. The *worth* of a character *perfectly* accordant with the moral law is infinite, since (270) the only restriction on all possible happiness in the judgment of a wise and all-powerful distributor of it is the absence of conformity of rational beings to their duty. But the moral law of itself does not *promise* any happiness, for according to our conceptions of an order of nature in general, this is not necessarily connected with obedience to the law. Now Christian morality supplies this defect (of the second indispensable element of the *summum bonum*) by representing the world, in which rational beings devote themselves with all their soul to the moral law, as a *kingdom of God,* in which nature and morality are brought into a harmony foreign to each of itself, by a holy Author who makes the derived *summum bonum* possible. *Holiness* of life is prescribed to them as a rule even in this life, while the welfare proportioned to it, namely, *bliss,* is represented as attainable only in an eternity; because the *former*

---

[3]It is commonly held that the Christian precept of morality has no advantage in respect of purity over the moral conceptions of the Stoics; the distinction between them is, however, very obvious. The Stoic system made the consciousness of strength of mind the pivot on which all moral dispositions should turn; and although its disciples spoke of duties and even defined them very well, yet they placed the spring and proper determining principle of the will in an elevation of the mind above the lower springs of the senses, which owe their power only to weakness of mind. With them, therefore, virtue was a sort of heroism in the *wise man* who, raising himself above the animal nature of man, is sufficient for himself, and while he prescribes duties to others is himself raised above them, and is not subject to any temptation to transgress the moral law. All this, however, they could not have done if they had conceived this law in all its purity and strictness, as the precept of the Gospel does. When I give the name *idea* to a perfection to which nothing adequate can be given in experience, it does not follow that the moral ideas are something transcendent, that is something of which we could not even determine the concept adequately, or of which it is uncertain whether there is any object corresponding to it at all (270), as is the case with the ideas of speculative reason; on the contrary, being types of practical perfection, they serve as the indispensable rule of conduct and likewise as the *standard of comparison.* Now if I consider *Christian morals* on their philosophical side, then compared with the ideas of the Greek schools they would appear as follows: the ideas of the *Cynics,* the *Epicureans,* the *Stoics,* and the *Christians* are: *simplicity of nature, prudence, wisdom,* and *holiness.* In respect of the way of attaining them, the Greek schools were distinguished from one another thus, that the Cynics only required *common sense,* the others the path of *science,* but both found the mere *use of natural powers* sufficient for the purpose. Christian morality, because its precept is framed (as a moral precept must be) so pure and unyielding, takes from man all confidence that he can be fully adequate to it, at least in this life, but again sets it up by enabling us to hope that if we act as well as it is in our *power* to do, then what is not in our power will come in to our aid from another source, whether we know how this may be or not. *Aristotle* and *Plato* differed only as to the *origin* of our moral conceptions.

must always be the pattern of their conduct in every state, and progress towards it is already possible and necessary in this life; while the *latter,* under the name of happiness, cannot be attained at all in this world (so far as our own power is concerned), and therefore is made simply an object of hope. Nevertheless, the Christian principle of *morality* itself is not theological (so as to be heteronomy), but is autonomy of pure practical reason, since it does not make the knowledge of God and His will the foundation of these laws, but only of the attainment of the *summum bonum,* on condition of following these laws, and it does not even place the proper *spring* of this obedience in the desired results, but solely in the conception of duty, as that of which the faithful observance alone constitutes the worthiness to obtain those happy consequences.

In this manner the moral laws lead through the conception of the *summum bonum* as the object and final end of pure practical reason to *religion* (271), that is, to the *recognition of all duties as divine commands, not as sanctions,*[4] *that is to say, arbitrary ordinances of a foreign will and contingent in themselves,* but as essential *laws* of every free will in itself, which, nevertheless, must be regarded as commands of the Supreme Being, because it is only from a morally perfect (holy and good) and at the same time all-powerful will, and consequently only through harmony with this will, that we can hope to attain the *summum bonum* which the moral law makes it our duty to take as the object of our endeavours. Here again, then, all remains disinterested and founded merely on duty; neither fear nor hope being made the fundamental springs, which if taken as principles would destroy the whole moral worth of actions. The moral law commands me to make the highest possible good in a world the ultimate object of all my conduct. But I cannot hope to effect this otherwise than by the harmony of my will with that of a holy and good Author of the world; and although the conception of the *summum bonum* as a whole, in which the greatest happiness is conceived as combined in the most exact proportion with the highest degree of moral perfection (possible in creatures), includes *my own happiness,* yet it is not this that is the determining principle of the will which is enjoined to promote the *summum bonum,* but the moral law, which, on the contrary, limits by strict conditions my unbounded desire of happiness.

Hence also morality is not properly the doctrine how we should *make* ourselves happy, but how we should become *worthy* of happiness. It is only when religion is added that there also comes in the hope of participating some day in happiness in proportion as we have endeavoured to be not unworthy of it.

(272) A man is *worthy* to possess a thing or a state when his possession of it is in harmony with the *summum bonum.* We can now easily see that all worthiness depends on moral conduct, since in the conception of the *summum bonum* this constitutes the condition of the rest (which belongs to one's state), namely, the participation of happiness. Now it follows from this that *morality* should never be treated as a *doctrine of happiness,* that is, an instruction how to become happy; for it has to do simply with the rational condition (*conditio sine qua non*) of happiness, not with the means of attaining it. But when morality has been completely expounded (which merely imposes duties instead of providing rules

---

[4][The word 'sanction' is here used in the technical German sense, which is familiar to students of history in connexion with the 'Pragmatic Sanction.']

for selfish desires), then first, after the moral desire to promote the *summum bonum* (to bring the kingdom of God to us) has been awakened, a desire founded on a law, and which could not previously arise in any selfish mind, and when for the behoof of this desire the step to religion has been taken, then this ethical doctrine may be also called a doctrine of happiness because the *hope* of happiness first begins with religion only.

We can also see from this that, when we ask what is *God's ultimate end* in creating the world, we must not name the *happiness* of the rational beings in it, but the *summum bonum,* which adds a further condition to that wish of such beings, namely, the condition of being worthy of happiness, that is, the *morality* of these same rational beings, a condition which alone contains the rule by which only they can hope to share in the former at the hand of a *wise* Author. For as *wisdom* theoretically considered signifies *the knowledge of the summum bonum,* and practically *the accordance of the will with the summum bonum,* we cannot attribute to a supreme independent wisdom an end based merely on *goodness* (273). For we cannot conceive the action of this goodness (in respect of the happiness of rational beings) as suitable to the highest original good, except under the restrictive conditions of harmony with the holiness of His will.[5] Therefore those who placed the end of creation in the glory of God (provided that this is not conceived anthropomorphically as a desire to be praised) have perhaps hit upon the best expression. For nothing glorifies God more than that which is the most estimable thing in the world, respect for His command, the observance of the holy duty that His law imposes on us, when there is added thereto His glorious plan of crowning such a beautiful order of things with corresponding happiness. If the latter (to speak humanly) makes Him worthy of love, by the *former* He is an object of adoration. Even men can never acquire respect by benevolence alone, though they may gain love, so that the greatest beneficence only procures them honour when it is regulated by worthiness.

That in the order of ends, man (and with him every rational being) is *an end in himself,* that is, that he can never be used merely as a means by any (274) (not even by God) without being at the same time an end also himself, that therefore *humanity* in our person must be *holy* to ourselves, this follows now of itself because he is the *subject*[6] *of the moral law,* in other words, of that which is holy in itself, and on account of which and in agreement with which alone can anything be termed holy. For this moral law is founded on the autonomy of his will, as a free will which by its universal laws must necessarily be able to agree with that to which it is to submit itself.

---

[5] In order to make these characteristics of these conceptions clear, I add the remark that whilst we ascribe to God various attributes, the quality of which we also find applicable to creatures, only that in Him they are raised to the highest degree, *e.g.* power, knowledge, presence, goodness, &c., under the designations of omnipotence, omniscience, omnipresence, &c., there are three that are ascribed to God exclusively, and yet without the addition of greatness, and which are all moral. He is the *only holy,* the *only blessed,* the *only wise,* because these conceptions already imply the absence of limitation. In the order of these attributes He is also the *holy lawgiver* (and creator), the *good governor* (and preserver), and the *just judge,* three attributes which include everything by which God is the object of religion, and in conformity with which the metaphysical perfections are added of themselves in the reason.

[6] [That the ambiguity of the word *subject* may not mislead the reader, it may be remarked that it is here used in the psychological sense *subjectum legis,* not *subjectus legi.*]

VI. OF THE POSTULATES OF PURE PRACTICAL REASON IN GENERAL

They all proceed from the principle of morality, which is not a postulate but a law, by which reason determines the will directly, which will, because it is so determined as a pure will, requires these necessary conditions of obedience to its precept. These postulates are not theoretical dogmas but, suppositions practically necessary; while then they do [not][7] extend our speculative knowledge, they give objective reality to the ideas of speculative reason in general (by means of their reference to what is practical), and give it a right to concepts, the possibility even of which it could not otherwise venture to affirm.

These postulates are those *of immortality, freedom* positively considered (as the causality of a being so far as he belongs to the intelligible world), and the *existence of God.* The *first* results from the practically necessary condition of a duration (275) adequate to the complete fulfilment of the moral law; the *second* from the necessary supposition of independence on the sensible world, and of the faculty of determining one's will according to the law of an intelligible world, that is, of freedom; the *third* from the necessary condition of the existence of the *summum bonum* in such an intelligible world, by the supposition of the supreme independent good, that is, the existence of God.

Thus the fact that respect for the moral law necessarily makes the *summum bonum* an object of our endeavours, and the supposition thence resulting of its objective reality, lead through the postulates of practical reason to conceptions which speculative reason might indeed present as problems, but could never solve. Thus it leads—1. To that one in the solution of which the latter could do nothing but commit *paralogisms* (namely, that of immortality), because it could not lay hold of the character of permanence, by which to complete the psychological conception of an ultimate subject necessarily ascribed to the soul in self-consciousness, so as to make it the real conception of a substance, a character which practical reason furnishes by the postulate of a duration required for accordance with the moral law in the *summum bonum,* which is the whole end of practical reason. 2. It leads to that of which speculative reason contained nothing but *antinomy,* the solution of which it could only found on a notion problematically conceivable indeed, but whose objective reality it could not prove or determine, namely, the *cosmological* idea of an intelligible world and the consciousness of our existence in it, by means of the postulate of freedom (the reality of which it lays down by virtue of the moral law), and with it likewise the law of an intelligible world, to which speculative reason could only point, but could not define its conception. 3. What speculative reason was able to think, but was obliged to leave undetermined as a mere transcendental *ideal* (276), viz. the *theological* conception of the First Being, to this it gives significance (in a practical view, that is, as a condition of the possibility of the object of a will determined by that law), namely, as the supreme principle of the *summum bonum* in an intelligible world, by means of moral legislation in it invested with sovereign power.

Is our knowledge, however, actually extended in this way by pure practical

---

[7][Absent from the original text.]

reason, and is that *immanent* in practical reason which for the speculative was only *transcendent*? Certainly, but *only in a practical point of view.* For we do not thereby take knowledge of the nature of our souls, nor of the intelligible world, nor of the Supreme Being, with respect to what they are in themselves, but we have merely combined the conceptions of them in the *practical* concept of the *summum bonum* as the object of our will, and this altogether *à priori,* but only by means of the moral law, and merely in reference to it, in respect of the object which it commands. But how freedom is possible, and how we are to conceive this kind of causality theoretically and positively, is not thereby discovered; but only that there is such a causality is postulated by the moral law and in its behoof. It is the same with the remaining ideas, the possibility of which no human intelligence will ever fathom, but the truth of which on the other hand, no sophistry will ever wrest from the conviction even of the commonest man.[. . .]

VIII. OF BELIEF FROM A REQUIREMENT OF PURE REASON

A want or requirement of pure reason in its speculative use leads only to a *hypothesis;* that of pure practical reason to a *postulate;* for in the former case I ascend from the result as high as I please in the series of causes, not in order to give objective reality to the result (*e.g.*the casual connexion of things and changes in the world), but in order thoroughly to satisfy my inquiring reason in respect of it. Thus I see before me order and design in nature, and need not resort to speculation to assure myself of their *reality,* but to *explain* them I have *to pre-suppose a Deity* as their cause; and then since the inference from an effect to a definite cause is always uncertain and doubtful, especially to a cause so precise and so perfectly defined as we have to conceive in God, hence the highest degree of certainty to which this pre-supposition can be brought is, that it is the most rational opinion for us men[8] (288). On the other hand, a requirement of pure *practical* reason is based on a *duty,* that of making something (the *summum bonum*) the object of my will so as to promote it with all my powers; in which case I must suppose its possibility, and consequently also the conditions necessary thereto, namely, God, freedom, and immortality; since I cannot prove these by my speculative reason, although neither can I refute them. This duty is founded on something that is indeed quite independent of these suppositions, and is of itself apodictically certain, namely, the moral law; and so far it needs no further support by theoretical views as to the inner constitution of things, the secret final aim of the order of the world, or a presiding ruler thereof, in order to bind me in the most perfect manner to act in unconditional conformity to the law. But the subjective effect of this law, namely, the mental *disposition* conformed to it and made necessary by it, to promote the practically possible *summum bonum,*

---

[8]But even here we should not be able to allege a requirement *of reason,* if we had not before our eyes a problematical, but yet inevitable, conception of reason, namely, that of an absolutely necessary being. This conception now seeks to be defined, and this, in addition to the tendency to extend itself, is the objective ground of a requirement of speculative reason, namely, to have a more precise definition of the conception of a necessary being which is to serve as the first cause of other beings, so as to make these* latter knowable by some means. Without such antecedent necessary problems there are no *requirements*—at least not of *pure reason*—the rest are requirements of *inclination.*

*I read 'diese' with the ed. of 1791. Rosenkranz and Hartenstein both read 'dieses,' 'this being.'

this pre-supposes at least that the latter is *possible*, for it would be practically impossible to strive after the object of a conception which at bottom was empty and had no object. Now the above-mentioned postulates concern only the physical or metaphysical conditions of the *possibility* of the *summum bonum* (289); in a word, those which lie in the nature of things; not, however, for the sake of an arbitrary speculative purpose, but of a practically necessary end of a pure rational will, which in this case does not *choose,* but *obeys* an inexorable command of reason, the foundation of which is *objective,* in the constitution of things as they must be universally judged by pure reason, and is not based on *inclination;* for we are in nowise justified in assuming, on account of what we *wish* on merely *subjective* grounds, that the means thereto are possible or that its object is real. This, then, is an absolutely necessary requirement, and what it pre-supposes is not merely justified as an allowable hypothesis, but as a postulate in a practical point of view; and admitting that the pure moral law inexorably binds every man as a command (not as a rule of prudence), the righteous man may say: I *will* that there be a God, that my existence in this world be also an existence outside the chain of physical causes, and in a pure world of the understanding, and lastly, that my duration be endless; I firmly abide by this, and will not let this faith be taken from me; for in this instance alone my interest, because I *must* not relax anything of it, inevitably determines my judgment, without regarding sophistries, however unable I may be to answer them or to oppose them with others more plausible.[9]

.   .   .   .

(290) In order to prevent misconception in the use of a notion as yet so unusual as that of a faith of pure practical reason, let me be permitted to add one more remark. It might almost seem as if this rational faith were here announced as itself a *command,* namely, that we should assume the *summum bonum* as possible. But a faith that is commanded is nonsense. Let the preceding analysis, however, be remembered of what is required to be supposed in the conception of the *summum bonum,* and it will be seen that it cannot be commanded to assume this possibility, and no practical disposition of mind is required to *admit* it; but that speculative reason must concede it without being asked, for no one can affirm that it is *impossible* in itself that rational beings in the world should at the same time be worthy of happiness in conformity with the moral law, and also possess this happiness proportionately. Now in respect of the first element of the

---

[9]In the *Deutsches Museum,* February, 1787, there is a dissertation by a very subtle and clear-headed man, the late *Wizenmann,* whose early death is to be lamented, in which he disputes the right to argue from a want to the objective reality of its object, and illustrates the point by the example of *a man in love,* who, having fooled himself into an idea of beauty, which is merely a chimera of his own brain, would fain conclude that such an object really exists somewhere (290). I quite agree with him in this, in all cases where the want is founded on *inclination,* which cannot necessarily postulate the existence of its object even for the man that is affected by it, much less can it contain a demand valid for everyone, and therefore it is merely a *subjective* ground of the wish. But in the present case we have a want of reason springing from an objective determining principle of the will, namely, the moral law, which necessarily binds every rational being, and therefore justifies him in assuming *à priori* in nature the conditions proper for it, and makes the latter inseparable from the complete practical use of reason. It is a duty to realize the *summum bonum* to the utmost of our power, therefore it must be possible, consequently it is unavoidable for every rational being in the world to assume what is necessary for its objective possibility. The assumption is as necessary as the moral law, in connexion with which alone it is valid.

summum bonum, namely, that which concerns morality, the moral law gives merely a command, and to doubt the possibility of that element would be the same as to call in question the moral law itself (291). But as regards the second element of that object, namely, happiness perfectly proportioned to that worthiness, it is true that there is no need of a command to admit its possibility in general, for theoretical reason has nothing to say against it; but *the manner* in which we have to conceive this harmony of the laws of nature with those of freedom has in it something in respect of which we have a *choice,* because theoretical reason decides nothing with apodictic certainty about it, and in respect of this there may be a moral interest which turns the scale.

I had said above that in a mere course of nature in the world an accurate correspondence between happiness and moral worth is not to be expected, and must be regarded as impossible, and that therefore the possibility of the *summum bonum* cannot be admitted from this side except on the supposition of a moral Author of the world. I purposely reserved the restriction of this judgment to the *subjective* conditions of our reason, in order not to make use of it until the manner of this belief should be defined more precisely. The fact is that the impossibility referred to is *merely subjective,* that is, our reason finds it *impossible for it* to render conceivable in the way of a mere course of nature a connexion so exactly proportioned and so thoroughly adapted to an end, between two sets of events happening according to such distinct laws; although, as with everything else in nature that is adapted to an end, it cannot prove, that is, show by sufficient objective reasons, that it is not possible by universal laws of nature.

Now, however, a deciding principle of a different kind comes into play to turn the scale in this uncertainty of speculative reason. The command to promote the *summum bonum* is established on an objective basis (in practical reason); the possibility of the same in general is likewise established on an objective basis (292) (in theoretical reason, which has nothing to say against it). But reason cannot decide objectively in what way we are to conceive this possibility; whether by universal laws of nature without a wise Author presiding over nature, or only on supposition of such an Author. Now here there comes in a *subjective* condition of reason; the only way theoretically possible for it, of conceiving the exact harmony of the kingdom of nature with the kingdom of morals, which is the condition of the possibility of the *summum bonum;* and at the same time the only one conducive to morality (which depends on an objective law of reason). Now since the promotion of this *summum bonum,* and therefore the supposition of its possibility, are *objectively* necessary (though only as a result of practical reason), while at the same time the manner in which we would conceive it rests with our own choice, and in this choice a free interest of pure practical reason decides for the assumption of a wise Author of the world; it is clear that the principle that herein determines our judgment, though as a want it is *subjective,* yet at the same time being the means of promoting what is *objectively* (practically) necessary, is the foundation of a *maxim* of belief in a moral point of view, that is, a *faith of pure practical reason.* This, then, is not commanded, but being a voluntary determination of our judgment, conducive to the moral (commanded) purpose, and moreover harmonizing with the theoretical requirement of reason, to assume that existence and to make it the foundation of our further employment of reason, it has itself sprung from the moral disposition of mind; it may therefore at times waver even in the well-disposed, but can never be reduced to unbelief.

(293) IX. OF THE WISE ADAPTATION OF MAN'S COGNITIVE FACULTIES TO HIS PRACTICAL DESTINATION

If human nature is destined to endeavour after the *summum bonum,* we must suppose also that the measure of its cognitive faculties, and particularly their relation to one another, is suitable to this end. Now the Critique of Pure *Speculative* Reason proves that this is incapable of solving satisfactorily the most weighty problems that are proposed to it, although it does not ignore the natural and important hints received from the same reason, nor the great steps that it can make to approach to this great goal that is set before it, which, however, it can never reach of itself, even with the help of the greatest knowledge of nature. Nature then seems here to have provided us only in a *step-motherly* fashion with the faculty required for our end.

Suppose now that in this matter nature had conformed to our wish, and had given us that capacity of discernment or that enlightenment which we would gladly possess, or which some *imagine* they actually possess, what would in all probability be the consequence? Unless our whole nature were at the same time changed, our inclinations, which always have the first word, would first of all demand their own satisfaction, and joined with rational reflection, the greatest possible and most lasting satisfaction, under the name of happiness; the moral law (294) would afterwards speak, in order to keep them within their proper bounds, and even to subject them all to a higher end, which has no regard to inclination. But instead of the conflict that the moral disposition has now to carry on with the inclinations, in which, though after some defeats, moral strength of mind may be gradually acquired, *God* and *eternity* with their *awful majesty* would stand unceasingly *before our eyes* (for what we can prove perfectly is to us as certain as that of which we are assured by the sight of our eyes). Transgression of the law, would, no doubt, be avoided; what is commanded would be done; but the mental *disposition,* from which actions ought to proceed, cannot be infused by any command, and in this case the spur of action is ever active and *external,* so that reason has no need to exert itself in order to gather strength to resist the inclinations by a lively representation of the dignity of the law: hence most of the actions that conformed to the law would be done from fear, a few only from hope, and none at all from duty, and the moral worth of actions, on which alone in the eyes of supreme wisdom the worth of the person and even that of the world depends, would cease to exist. As long as the nature of man remains what it is, his conduct would thus be changed into mere mechanism, in which, as in a puppet-show, everything would *gesticulate* well, but there would be *no life* in the figures. Now, when it is quite otherwise with us, when with all the effort of our reason we have only a very obscure and doubtful view into the future, when the Governor of the world allows us only to conjecture His existence and His majesty, not to behold them or prove them clearly; and, on the other hand, the moral law within us, without promising or threatening anything with certainty, demands of us disinterested respect; and only when this respect has become active (295) and dominant does it allow us by means of it a prospect into the world of the supersensible, and then only with weak glances; all this being so, there is room for true moral disposition, immediately devoted to the law, and a rational creature can become worthy of sharing in the *summum bonum* that corresponds to the worth of his person and not merely to his actions. Thus what the study of nature and of man teaches us sufficiently elsewhere may well be true here also; that the unsearchable wisdom by which we exist is not less worthy of admiration in what it has denied than in what it has granted.

POSTSCRIPT: THE IRRELEVANCE OF PROOFS TO RELIGIOUS BELIEF
Stephen Cahn

Stephen Cahn, "The Irrelevance to Religion of Philosophic Proofs for the Existence of God," *American Philosophical Quarterly,* vol. 6, no. 2 (April 1969). Used by permission of the author and editor, Professor Nicholas Rescher.

Philosophic proofs for the existence of God have a long and distinguished history. Almost every major Western philosopher has been seriously concerned with defending or refuting such proofs. Furthermore, many contemporary philosophers have exhibited keen interest in such proofs. A survey of the philosophical literature of the past decade reveals quite a concentration of work in this area.[1]

One might expect that religious believers would be vitally interested in discussions of this subject. One might suppose that when a proof of God's existence is presented and eloquently defended, believers would be most enthusiastic, and that when a proof is attacked and persuasively refuted, believers would be seriously disappointed. But this is not at all the case. Religious believers seem remarkably uninterested in philosophic proofs for the existence of God. They seem to consider discussion of such proofs as a sort of intellectual game which has no relevance to religious belief or activity. And this view is shared by proponents of both supernaturalist and naturalist varieties of religion. For example, Søren Kierkegaard, a foremost proponent of supernaturalist religion, remarked: "Whoever therefore attempts to demonstrate the existence of God . . . [is] an excellent subject for a comedy of the higher lunacy!"[2] The same essential

---

[1]For a partial bibliography, see Robert C. Coburn's "Recent Work in Metaphysics," *American Philosophical Quarterly,* vol. 1 (1964), pp. 218–220. Two comprehensive treatments of the subject are Wallace I. Matson's *The Existence of God* (Ithaca, Cornell University Press, 1966) and Antony Flew's *God and Philosophy* (London, Hutchinson & Co., 1966).

[2]*Philosophical Fragments,* tr. by David F. Swenson (Princeton, Princeton University Press, 1936), ch. III, p. 34.

point is made in a somewhat less flamboyant manner by Mordecai M. Kaplan, a foremost proponent of naturalist religion, who remarks that the "immense amount of mental effort to prove the existence of God . . . was in vain, since unbelievers seldom become believers as a result of logical arguments."[3]

In what follows, I wish to explain just why religious believers have so little interest in philosophic proofs for the existence of God. I wish to show that their lack of interest is entirely reasonable, and that whatever the philosophic relevance of such proofs, they have little or no relevance to religion.

The three classic proofs for the existence of God are the ontological, the cosmological, and the teleological. Each of these proofs is intended to prove something different. The ontological argument is intended to prove the existence (or necessary existence) of the most perfect conceivable Being. The cosmological argument is intended to prove the existence of a necessary Being who is the Prime Mover or First Cause of the universe. The teleological argument is intended to prove the existence of an all-good designer and creator of the universe.

Suppose we assume, contrary to what most philosophers, I among them, believe, that all of these proofs are valid. Let us grant the necessary existence (whatever that might mean) of the most perfect conceivable Being, a Being who is all-good and is the designer and creator of the universe. What implications can be drawn from this fact which would be of relevance to human life? In other words, what difference would it make in men's lives if God existed?[4]

Perhaps some men would feel more secure in the knowledge that the universe had been planned by an all-good Being. Others, perhaps, would feel insecure, realizing the extent to which their very existence depended upon the will of this Being. In any case, most men, either out of fear or respect, would wish to act in accordance with the moral code advocated by this Being.

Note, however, that the proofs for the existence of God provide us with no hint whatever as to which actions God wishes us to perform, or what we ought to do so as to please or obey Him. We may affirm that God is all-good and yet have no way of knowing what the highest moral standards are. All we may be sure of is that whatever these standards may be, God always acts in accordance with them. One might assume that God would have implanted the correct moral standards in men's minds, but this seems doubtful in view of the wide variance in men's moral standards. Which of these numerous standards, if any, is the correct one is not known, and no appeal to a proof for the existence of God will cast the least light upon the matter.

For example, assuming that it can be proven that God exists, is murder immoral? One might argue that since God created man, it is immoral to murder, since it is immoral to destroy what God in His infinite wisdom and goodness has created. This argument, however, fails on several grounds. First, if God created man, He also created germs, viruses, disease-carrying rats, and man-eating sharks. Does it follow from the fact that God created these things that they ought not to be eliminated? Secondly, if God arranged for men to live, He also arranged

---

[3] *The Future of the American Jew* (New York, The Macmillan Company, 1948), p. 171.
[4] I am not concerned here with the implications of God's omniscience and omnipotence for man's free will. It is possible to interpret these divine attributes in such a way as not to entail the loss of man's free will, and for the purposes of this essay, I shall assume such an interpretation.

for men to die. Does it follow from this that by committing murder we are assisting the work of God? Thirdly, if God created man, He provided him with the mental and physical capacity to commit murder. Does it follow from this that God wishes men to commit murder? Clearly, the attempt to deduce moral precepts from the fact of God's existence is but another case of trying to do what Hume long ago pointed out to be logically impossible, viz., the deduction of normative judgments from factual premises. No such deduction is valid, and, thus, any moral principle is consistent with the existence of God.

The fact that the proofs of God's existence afford no means of distinguishing good from evil has the consequence that no man can be sure of how to obey God and do what is best in His eyes. One may hope that his actions are in accord with God's standards, but no test is available to check on·this. Some seemingly good men suffer great ills, and some seemingly evil men achieve great happiness. Perhaps in a future life the things are rectified, but we have no way of ascertaining which men are ultimately rewarded and which are ultimately punished.

One can imagine that if a group of men believed in God's existence, they would be most anxious to learn His will, and consequently, they would tend to rely upon those individuals who claimed to know the will of God. Diviners, seers, and priests would be in a position of great influence. No doubt competition between them would be severe, for no man could be sure which of these oracles to believe. Assuming that God made no effort to reveal His will by granting one of these oracles truly superhuman powers (though, naturally, each oracle would claim that he possessed such powers), no man could distinguish the genuine prophet from the fraud.

It is clear that the situation I have described is paralleled by a stage in the actual development of religion. What men wanted at this stage was some way to find out the will of God. Individual prophets might gain a substantial following, but prophets died and their vital powers died with them. What was needed on practical grounds was a permanent record of God's will as revealed to His special prophet. And this need was eventually met by the writing of holy books, books in which God's will was revealed in a permanent fashion.

But there was more than one such book. Indeed, there were many such books. Which was to be believed? Which moral code was to be followed? Which prayers were to be recited? Which rituals were to be performed? Proofs for the existence of God are silent upon these crucial matters.

There is only one possible avenue to God's will. One must undergo a personal experience in which one senses the presence of God and apprehends which of the putative holy books is the genuine one. But it is most important not to be deceived in this experience. One must be absolutely certain that it is God whose presence one is experiencing and whose will one is apprehending. In other words, one must undergo a self-validating experience, one which carries its own guarantee of infallibility.

If one undergoes what he believes to be such an experience, he then is certain which holy book is the genuine one, and consequently he knows which actions, prayers, and rituals God wishes him to engage in. But notice that if he knows this, he has necessarily validated the existence of God, for unless he is absolutely certain that he has experienced God's presence, he cannot be sure that the message he has received is true. Thus, he has no further need for a proof of God's existence.

For one who does not undergo what he believes to be such a self-validating experience, several possibilities remain open. He may accept the validity of another person's self-validating experience. He thereby accepts the holy book which has been revealed as genuine, and he thereby also accepts the existence of God, since unless he believed that this other person had experienced the presence of God, he would not accept this person's opinion as to which is the genuine book.

It is possible, however, that one does not accept the validity of another person's supposedly self-validating experience. This may be due either to philosophical doubts concerning the logical possibility of such an experience[5] or simply to practical doubts that anyone has, in fact, ever undergone such an experience. In either case, adherence to a particular supernatural religion is unreasonable.

But having no adherence to a supernatural religion does not imply that one does not still face the serious moral dilemmas which are inherent in life. How are these dilemmas to be solved? To believe that God exists is of no avail, for one cannot learn His will. Therefore, one must use one's own judgment. But this need not be solely an individual effort. One may join others in a communal effort to propound and promulgate a moral code. Such a group may have its own distinctive prayers and rituals which emphasize various aspects of the group's beliefs. Such a naturalistic religious organization does not depend upon its members' belief in the existence of God, for such a belief is irrelevant to the religious aims and activities of the group.

Is it surprising then that proponents of both supernaturalist and naturalist religion are uninterested in philosophic proofs for the existence of God? Not at all. A supernaturalist believes in God because of a personal self-validating experience which has shown him (or someone he trusts) not only that God exists, but also what His will is. A philosophic proof of the existence of God is thus of no use to the supernaturalist. If the proof is shown to be valid, it merely confirms what he already knows on the much stronger evidence of personal experience. If the proof is shown to be invalid, it casts no doubt on a self-validating experience.

On the other hand, a naturalist believes either that no one has learned or that no one can learn the will of God. If, therefore, a proof for the existence of God is shown to be valid, this has no implications for the naturalist, for such a proof does not provide him with any information which he can utilize in his religious practice. If, on the contrary, a proof for the existence of God is shown to be invalid, this casts no doubt on the naturalist's religious views, since these views have been formulated independently of a belief in the existence of God.

Who, then, is concerned with philosophic proofs for the existence of God? First, there are those who believe that if such proofs are invalid, religion is thereby undermined. This is, as I have shown, a wholly erroneous view. Neither supernaturalist nor naturalist religion depends at all upon philosophic proofs for the existence of God. To attack religion on the grounds that it cannot provide a philosophic proof for the existence of God is an instance of *ignoratio elenchi.*

Secondly, there are those who believe that if the philosophic proofs for the existence of God are invalid, our moral commitments are necessarily undermined. This is also, as I have shown, a wholly erroneous view. It is, however, a common view, and one which underlies the so-called moral argument for the existence of God. According to this argument, it is only if one believes in the existence of God that one can reasonably commit oneself to respect the importance of moral values. This argument is invalid, however, for, as I have shown, belief in the existence of God is compatible with any and all positions on moral issues. It is only if one can learn the will of God that one can derive any moral implications from His existence.

Thirdly, there are philosophers who discuss proofs for the existence of God because of the important philosophical issues which are brought to light and clarified in such discussions. So long as philosophers are aware of the purpose which their discussions serve, all is well and good. It is when philosophers and others use discussions of this sort as arguments for and against religion that they overstep their bounds. Religion may be rationally attacked or defended, but to refute philosophic proofs for the existence of God is not to attack religion, and to support philosophic proofs for the existence of God is not to defend religion.

Chapter

FIFTEEN

FAITH AND REASON

THE ETHICS OF BELIEF
W. K. Clifford

From W. K. Clifford, *Lectures and Essays*, vol. II, *Essays and Reviews*, Macmillan, London and New York, 1879. Originally published in *Contemporary Review*, January 1877.

I. The Duty of Inquiry

A shipowner was about to send to sea an emigrant-ship. He knew that she was old, and not over-well built at the first; that she had seen many seas and climes, and often had needed repairs. Doubts had been suggested to him that possibly she was not seaworthy. These doubts preyed upon his mind, and made him unhappy; he thought that perhaps he ought to have her thoroughly overhauled and refitted, even though this should put him to great expense. Before the ship sailed, however, he succeeded in overcoming these melancholy reflections. He said to himself that she had gone safely through so many voyages and weathered so many storms that it was idle to suppose she would not come safely home from this trip also. He would put his trust in Providence, which could hardly fail to protect all these unhappy families that were leaving their fatherland to seek for better times elsewhere. He would dismiss from his mind all ungenerous suspicions about the honesty of builders and contractors. In such ways he acquired a sincere and comfortable conviction that his vessel was thoroughly safe and seaworthy; he watched her departure with a light heart, and benevolent wishes for the success of the exiles in their strange new home that was to be; and he got his insurance-money when she went down in mid-ocean and told no tales.

What shall we say of him? Surely this, that he was verily guilty of the death of those men. It is admitted that he did sincerely believe in the soundness of his ship; but the sincerity of his conviction can in no wise help him, because *he had no right to believe on such evidence as was before him*. He had acquired his belief not by honestly earning it in patient investigation, but by stifling his doubts. And although in the end he may have felt so sure about it that he could not think otherwise, yet inasmuch as he had knowingly and willingly worked himself into that frame of mind, he must be held responsible for it.

Let us alter the case a little, and suppose that the ship was not unsound after all; that she made her voyage safely, and many others after it. Will that diminish the guilt of her owner? Not one jot. When an action is once done, it is right or wrong for ever; no accidental failure of its good or evil fruits can possibly alter that. The man would not have been innocent, he would only have been not found out. The question of right or wrong has to do with the origin of his belief, not the matter of it; not what it was, but how he got it; not whether it turned out to be true or false, but whether he had a right to believe on such evidence as was before him.

There was once an island in which some of the inhabitants professed a religion teaching neither the doctrine of original sin nor that of eternal punishment. A suspicion got abroad that the professors of this religion had made use of unfair means to get their doctrines taught to children. They were accused of wresting the laws of their country in such a way as to remove children from the

505

care of their natural and legal guardians; and even of stealing them away and keeping them concealed from their friends and relations. A certain number of men formed themselves into a society for the purpose of agitating the public about this matter. They published grave accusations against individual citizens of the highest position and character, and did all in their power to injure these citizens in the exercise of their professions. So great was the noise they made, that a Commission was appointed to investigate the facts; but after the Commission had carefully inquired into all the evidence that could be got, it appeared that the accused were innocent. Not only had they been accused on insufficient evidence, but the evidence of their innocence was such as the agitators might easily have obtained, if they had attempted a fair inquiry. After these disclosures the inhabitants of that country looked upon the members of the agitating society, not only as persons whose judgment was to be distrusted, but also as no longer to be counted honourable men. For although they had sincerely and conscientiously believed in the charges they had made, yet *they had no right to believe on such evidence as was before them.* Their sincere convictions, instead of being honestly earned by patient inquiring, were stolen by listening to the voice of prejudice and passion.

Let us vary this case also, and suppose, other things remaining as before, that a still more accurate investigation proved the accused to have been really guilty. Would this make any difference in the guilt of the accusers? Clearly not; the question is not whether their belief was true or false, but whether they entertained it on wrong grounds. They would no doubt say, 'Now you see that we were right after all; next time perhaps you will believe us.' And they might be believed, but they would not thereby become honourable men. They would not be innocent, they would only be not found out. Every one of them, if he chose to examine himself *in foro conscientiae,* would know that he had acquired and nourished a belief, when he had no right to believe on such evidence as was before him; and therein he would know that he had done a wrong thing.

It may be said, however, that in both of these supposed cases it is not the belief which is judged to be wrong, but the action following upon it. The ship-owner might say, 'I am perfectly certain that my ship is sound, but still I feel it my duty to have her examined, before trusting the lives of so many people to her.' And it might be said to the agitator, 'However convinced you were of the justice of your cause and the truth of your convictions, you ought not to have made a public attack upon any man's character until you had examined the evidence on both sides with the utmost patience and care.'

In the first place, let us admit that, so far as it goes, this view of the case is right and necessary; right, because even when a man's belief is so fixed that he cannot think otherwise, he still has a choice in regard to the action suggested by it, and so cannot escape the duty of investigating on the ground of the strength of his convictions; and necessary, because those who are not yet capable of controlling their feelings and thoughts must have a plain rule dealing with overt acts.

But this being premised as necessary, it becomes clear that it is not sufficient, and that our previous judgment is required to supplement it. For it is not possible so to sever the belief from the action it suggests as to condemn the one without condemning the other. No man holding a strong belief on one side of a question, or even wishing to hold a belief on one side, can investigate it with such fairness and completeness as if he were really in doubt and unbiassed; so that the existence of a belief not founded on fair inquiry unfits a man for the performance of this necessary duty.

Nor is that truly a belief at all which has not some influence upon the actions of him who holds it. He who truly believes that which prompts him to an action has looked upon the action to lust after it, he has committed it already in his heart. If a belief is not realized immediately in open deeds, it is stored up for the guidance of the future. It goes to make a part of that aggregate of beliefs which is the link between sensation and action at every moment of all our lives, and which is so organized and compacted together that no part of it can be isolated from the rest, but every new addition modifies the structure of the whole. No real belief, however trifling and fragmentary it may seem, is ever truly insignificant; it prepares us to receive more of its like, confirms those which resembled it before, and weakens others; and so gradually it lays a stealthy train in our inmost thoughts, which may some day explode into overt action, and leave its stamp upon our character for ever.

And no one man's belief is in any case a private matter which concerns himself alone. Our lives are guided by that general conception of the course of things which has been created by society for social purposes. Our words, our phrases, our forms and processes and modes of thought, are common property, fashioned and perfected from age to age; an heirloom which every succeeding generation inherits as a precious deposit and a sacred trust to be handed on to the next one, not unchanged but enlarged and purified, with some clear marks of its proper handiwork. Into this, for good or ill, is woven every belief of every man who has speech of his fellows. An awful privilege, and an awful responsibility, that we should help to create the world in which posterity will live.

In the two supposed cases which have been considered, it has been judged wrong to believe on insufficient evidence, or to nourish belief by suppressing doubts and avoiding investigation. The reason of this judgment is not far to seek: it is that in both these cases the belief held by one man was of great importance to other men. But forasmuch as no belief held by one man, however seemingly trivial the belief, and however obscure the believer, is ever actually insignificant or without its effect on the fate of mankind, we have no choice but to extend our judgment to all cases of belief whatever. Belief, that sacred faculty which prompts the decisions of our will, and knits into harmonious working all the compacted energies of our being, is ours not for ourselves, but for humanity. It is rightly used on truths which have been established by long experience and waiting toil, and which have stood in the fierce light of free and fearless questioning. Then it helps to bind men together, and to strengthen and direct their common action. It is desecrated when given to unproved and unquestioned statements, for the solace and private pleasure of the believer; to add a tinsel splendour to the plain straight road of our life and display a bright mirage beyond it; or even to drown the common sorrows of our kind by a self-deception which allows them not only to cast down, but also to degrade us. Whoso would deserve well of his fellows in this matter will guard the purity of his belief with a very fanaticism of jealous care, lest at any time it should rest on an unworthy object, and catch a stain which can never be wiped away.

It is not only the leader of men, statesman, philosopher, or poet, that owes this bounden duty to mankind. Every rustic who delivers in the village alehouse his slow, infrequent sentences, may help to kill or keep alive the fatal superstitions which clog his race. Every hard-worked wife of an artisan may transmit to her children beliefs which shall knit society together, or rend it in pieces. No simplicity of mind, no obscurity of station, can escape the universal duty of questioning all that we believe.

It is true that this duty is a hard one, and the doubt which comes out of it is often a very bitter thing. It leaves us bare and powerless where we thought that we were safe and strong. To know all about anything is to know how to deal with it under all circumstances. We feel much happier and more secure when we think we know precisely what to do, no matter what happens, than when we have lost our way and do not know where to turn. And if we have supposed ourselves to know all about anything, and to be capable of doing what is fit in regard to it, we naturally do not like to find that we are really ignorant and powerless, that we have to begin again at the beginning, and try to learn what the thing is and how it is to be dealt with—if indeed anything can be learnt about it. It is the sense of power attached to a sense of knowledge that makes men desirous of believing, and afraid of doubting.

This sense of power is the highest and best of pleasures when the belief on which it is founded is a true belief, and has been fairly earned by investigation. For then we may justly feel that it is common property, and holds good for others as well as for ourselves. Then we may be glad, not that *I* have learned secrets by which I am safer and stronger, but that *we men* have got mastery over more of the world; and we shall be strong, not for ourselves, but in the name of Man and in his strength. But if the belief has been accepted on insufficient evidence, the pleasure is a stolen one. Not only does it deceive ourselves by giving us a sense of power which we do not really possess, but it is sinful, because it is stolen in defiance of our duty to mankind. That duty is to guard ourselves from such beliefs as from a pestilence, which may shortly master our own body and then spread to the rest of the town. What would be thought of one who, for the sake of a sweet fruit, should deliberately run the risk of bringing a plague upon his family and his neighbours?

And, as in other such cases, it is not the risk only which has to be considered; for a bad action is always bad at the time when it is done, no matter what happens afterwards. Every time we let ourselves believe for unworthy reasons, we weaken our powers of self-control, of doubting, of judicially and fairly weighing evidence. We all suffer severely enough from the maintenance and support of false beliefs and the fatally wrong actions which they lead to, and the evil born when one such belief is entertained is great and wide. But a greater and wider evil arises when the credulous character is maintained and supported, when a habit of believing for unworthy reasons is fostered and made permanent. If I steal money from any person, there may be no harm done by the mere transfer of possession; he may not feel the loss, or it may prevent him from using the money badly. But I cannot help doing this great wrong towards Man, that I make myself dishonest. What hurts society is not that it should lose its property, but that it should become a den of thieves; for then it must cease to be society. This is why we ought not to do evil that good may come; for at any rate this great evil has come, that we have done evil and are made wicked thereby. In like manner, if I let myself believe anything on insufficient evidence, there may be no great harm done by the mere belief; it may be true after all, or I may never have occasion to exhibit it in outward acts. But I cannot help doing this great wrong towards Man, that I make myself credulous. The danger to society is not merely that it should believe wrong things, though that is great enough; but that it should become credulous, and lose the habit of testing things and inquiring into them; for then it must sink back into savagery.

The harm which is done by credulity in a man is not confined to the fostering of a credulous character in others, and consequent support of false beliefs. Habitual want of care about what I believe leads to habitual want of care in others about the truth of what is told to me. Men speak the truth to one another when each reveres the truth in his own mind and in the other's mind; but how shall my friend revere the truth in my mind when I myself am careless about it, when I believe things because I want to believe them, and because they are comforting and pleasant? Will he not learn to cry, 'Peace,' to me, when there is no peace? By such a course I shall surround myself with a thick atmosphere of falsehood and fraud, and in that I must live. It may matter little to me, in my cloud-castle of sweet illusions and darling lies; but it matters much to Man that I have made my neighbours ready to deceive. The credulous man is father to the liar and the cheat; he lives in the bosom of this his family, and it is no marvel if he should become even as they are. So closely are our duties knit together, that whoso shall keep the whole law, and yet offend in one point, he is guilty of all.

To sum up: it is wrong always, everywhere, and for anyone, to believe anything upon insufficient evidence [. . .].

FAITH AND REASON AS GOVERNING SEPARATE REALMS

William James

From William James, *The Will to Believe* (originally published in 1893), Dover Publications, Inc., New York, 1956.

In the recently published Life by Leslie Stephen of his brother, Fitzjames, there is an account of a school to which the latter went when he was a boy. The teacher, a certain Mr. Guest, used to converse with his pupils in this wise: "Gurney, what is the difference between justification and sanctification?—Stephen, prove the omnipotence of God!" etc. In the midst of our Harvard freethinking and indifference we are prone to imagine that here at your good old orthodox College conversation continues to be somewhat upon this order; and to show you that we at Harvard have not lost all interest in these vital subjects, I have brought with me to-night something like a sermon on justification by faith to read to you,—I mean an essay in justification *of* faith, a defence of our right to adopt a believing atti-tude in religious matters, in spite of the fact that our merely logical intellect may not have been coerced. 'The Will to Believe,' accordingly, is the title of my paper.

I have long defended to my own students the lawfulness of voluntarily adopted faith; but as soon as they have got well imbued with the logical spirit, they have as a rule refused to admit my contention to be lawful philosophically, even though in point of fact they were personally all the time chock-full of some faith or other themselves. I am all the while, however, so profoundly convinced that my own position is correct, that your invitation has seemed to me a good occasion to make my statements more clear. Perhaps your minds will be more open than those with which I have hitherto had to deal. I will be as little technical as I can, though I must begin by setting up some technical distinctions that will help us in the end.

I

Let us give the name of *hypothesis* to anything that may be proposed to our belief; and just as the electricians speak of live and dead wires, let us speak of any hypothesis as either *live* or *dead*. A live hypothesis is one which appeals as a real possibility to him to whom it is proposed. If I ask you to believe in the Mahdi, the notion makes no electric connection with your nature,—it refuses to scintillate with any credibility at all. As an hypothesis it is completely dead. To an Arab, however (even if he be not one of the Mahdi's followers), the hypothesis is among the mind's possibilities: it is alive. This shows that deadness and liveness in an hypothesis are not intrinsic properties, but relations to the individual thinker. They are measured by his willingness to act. The maximum of liveness in an hypothesis means willingness to act irrevocably. Practically, that means belief; but there is some believing tendency wherever there is willingness to act at all.

Next, let us call the decision between two hypotheses an *option*. Options may be of several kinds. They may be—1, *living* or *dead*; 2, *forced* or *avoidable*; 3, *momentous* or *trivial*; and for our purposes we may call an option a *genuine* option when it is of the forced, living, and momentous kind.

1. A living option is one in which both hypotheses are live ones. If I say to you: "Be a theosophist or be a Mohammedan," it is probably a dead option, because for you neither hypothesis is likely to be alive. But if I say: "Be an agnostic or be a Christian," it is otherwise: trained as you are, each hypothesis makes some appeal, however small, to your belief.

2. Next, if I say to you: "Choose between going out with your umbrella or without it," I do not offer you a genuine option, for it is not forced. You can easily avoid it by not going out at all. Similarly, if I say, "Either love me or hate me," "Either call my theory true or call it false," your option is avoidable. You may remain indifferent to me, neither loving nor hating, and you may decline to offer any judgment as to my theory. But if I say, "Either accept this truth or go without it," I put on you a forced option, for there is no standing place outside of the alternative. Every dilemma based on a complete logical disjunction, with no possibility of not choosing, is an option of this forced kind.

3. Finally, if I were Dr. Nansen and proposed to you to join my North Pole expedition, your option would be momentous; for this would probably be your only similar opportunity, and your choice now would either exclude you from the North Pole sort of immortality altogether or put at least the chance of it into your hands. He who refuses to embrace a unique opportunity loses the prize as surely as if he tried and failed. *Per contra,* the option is trivial when the opportunity is not unique, when the stake is insignificant, or when the decision is reversible if it later prove unwise. Such trivial options abound in the scientific life. A chemist finds an hypothesis live enough to spend a year in its verification: he believes in it to that extent. But if his experiments prove inconclusive either way, he is quit for his loss of time, no vital harm being done.

It will facilitate our discussion if we keep all these distinctions well in mind.

II

The next matter to consider is the actual psychology of human opinion. When we look at certain facts, it seems as if our passional and volitional nature lay at the root of all our convictions. When we look at others, it seems as if they could do nothing when the intellect had once said its say. Let us take the latter facts up first.

Does it not seem preposterous on the very face of it to talk of our opinions being modifiable at will? Can our will either help or hinder our intellect in its perceptions of truth? Can we, by just willing it, believe that Abraham Lincoln's existence is a myth, and that the portraits of him in McClure's Magazine are all of some one else? Can we, by any effort of our will, or by any strength of wish that it were true, believe ourselves well and about when we are roaring with rheumatism in bed, or feel certain that the sum of the two one-dollar bills in our pocket must be a hundred dollars? We can *say* any of these things, but we are absolutely impotent to believe them; and of just such things is the whole fabric of the truths that we do believe in made up,—matters of fact, immediate or remote, as Hume said, and relations between ideas, which are either there or not there for us if we see them so, and which if not there cannot be put there by any action of our own.

In Pascal's Thoughts there is a celebrated passage known in literature as Pascal's wager. In it he tries to force us into Christianity by reasoning as if our concern with truth resembled our concern with the stakes in a game of chance. Translated freely his words are these: You must either believe or not believe that God is—which will you do? Your human reason cannot say. A game is going on between you and the nature of things which at the day of judgment will bring out either heads or tails. Weigh what your gains and your losses would be if you should stake all you have on heads, or God's existence: if you win in such case, you gain eternal beatitude; if you lose, you lose nothing at all. If there were an infinity of chances, and only one for God in this wager, still you ought to stake your all on God; for though you surely risk a finite loss by this procedure, any finite loss is reasonable, even a certain one is reasonable, if there is but the possibility of infinite gain. Go, then, and take holy water, and have masses said; belief will come and stupefy your scruples,—*Cela vous fera croire et vous abêtira.* Why should you not? At bottom, what have you to lose?

You probably feel that when religious faith expresses itself thus, in the language of the gaming-table, it is put to its last trumps. Surely Pascal's own personal belief in masses and holy water had far other springs; and this celebrated page of his is but an argument for others, a last desperate snatch at a weapon against the hardness of the unbelieving heart. We feel that a faith in masses and holy water adopted wilfully after such a mechanical calculation would lack the inner soul of faith's reality; and if we were ourselves in the place of the Deity, we should probably take particular pleasure in cutting off believers of this pattern from their infinite reward. It is evident that unless there be some pre-existing tendency to believe in masses and holy water, the option offered to the will by Pascal is not a living option. Certainly no Turk ever took to masses and holy water on its account; and even to us Protestants these means of salvation seem such foregone impossibilities that Pascal's logic, invoked for them specifically, leaves us unmoved. As well might the Mahdi write to us, saying, "I am the Expected One whom God has created in his effulgence. You shall be infinitely happy if you confess me; otherwise you shall be cut off from the light of the sun. Weigh, then, your infinite gain if I am genuine against your finite sacrifice if I am not!" His logic would be that of Pascal; but he would vainly use it on us, for the hypothesis he offers us is dead. No tendency to act on it exists in us to any degree.

The talk of believing by our volition seems, then, from one point of view, simply silly. From another point of view it is worse than silly, it is vile. When one turns to the magnificent edifice of the physical sciences, and sees how it was reared; what thousands of disinterested moral lives of men lie buried in its mere foundations; what patience and postponement, what choking down of preference, what submission to the icy laws of outer fact are wrought into its very stones and mortar; how absolutely impersonal it stands in its vast augustness,—then how besotted and contemptible seems every little sentimentalist who comes blowing his voluntary smoke-wreaths, and pretending to decide things from out of his private dream! Can we wonder if those bred in the rugged and manly school of science should feel like spewing such subjectivism out of their mouths? The whole system of loyalties which grow up in the schools of science go dead against its toleration; so that it is only natural that those who have caught the scientific fever should pass over to the opposite extreme, and write sometimes as if the incorruptibly truthful intellect ought positively to prefer bitterness and unacceptableness to the heart in its cup.

> It fortifies my soul to know
> That, though I perish, Truth is so—

sings Clough, while Huxley exclaims:

> My only consolation lies in the reflection that, however bad our posterity may become, so far as they hold by the plain rule of not pretending to believe what they have no reason to believe, because it may be to their advantage so to pretend [the word 'pretend' is surely here redundant], they will not have reached the lowest depth of immorality.

And that delicious *enfant terrible* Clifford writes:

Belief is desecrated when given to unproved and unquestioned statements for the solace and private pleasure of the believer. . . . Whoso would deserve well of his fellows in this matter will guard the purity of his belief with a very fanaticism of jealous care, lest at any time it should rest on an unworthy object, and catch a stain which can never be wiped away. . . . If [a] belief has been accepted on insufficient evidence [even though the belief be true, as Clifford on the same page explains] the pleasure is a stolen one. . . . It is sinful because it is stolen in defiance of our duty to mankind. That duty is to guard ourselves from such beliefs as from a pestilence which may shortly master our own body and then spread to the rest of the town. . . . It is wrong always, everywhere, and for every one, to believe anything upon insufficient evidence.

III

All this strikes one as healthy, even when expressed, as by Clifford, with somewhat too much of robustious pathos in the voice. Free-will and simple wishing do seem, in the matter of our credences, to be only fifth wheels to the coach. Yet if any one should thereupon assume that intellectual insight is what remains after wish and will and sentimental preference have taken wing, or that pure reason is what then settles our opinions, he would fly quite as directly in the teeth of the facts.

It is only our already dead hypotheses that our willing nature is unable to bring to life again. But what has made them dead for us is for the most part a previous action of our willing nature of an antagonistic kind. When I say 'willing nature,' I do not mean only such deliberate volitions as may have set up habits of belief that we cannot now escape from,—I mean all such factors of belief as fear and hope, prejudice and passion, imitation and partisanship, the circumpressure of our caste and set. As a matter of fact we find ourselves believing, we hardly know how or why. Mr. Balfour gives the name of 'authority' to all those influences, born of the intellectual climate, that make hypotheses possible or impossible for us, alive or dead. Here in this room, we all of us believe in molecules and the conservation of energy, in democracy and necessary progress, in Protestant Christianity and the duty of fighting for 'the doctrine of the immortal Monroe,' all for no reasons worthy of the name. We see into these matters with no more inner clearness, and probably with much less, than any disbeliever in them might possess. His unconventionality would probably have some grounds to show for its conclusions; but for us, not insight, but the *prestige* of the opinions, is what makes the spark shoot from them and light up our sleeping magazines of faith. Our reason is quite satisfied, in nine hundred and ninety-nine cases out of every thousand of us, if it can find a few arguments that will do to recite in case our credulity is criticised by some one else. Our faith is faith in some one else's faith, and in the greatest matters this is most the case. Our belief in truth itself, for instance, that there is a truth, and that our minds and it are made for each other,—what is it but a passionate affirmation of desire, in which our social system backs us up? We want to have a truth; we want to believe that our experiments and studies and discussions must put us in a continually better and better position towards it; and on this line we agree to fight out our thinking lives. But if a pyrrhonistic sceptic asks us *how we know* all this, can our logic find a reply? No! certainly it cannot. It is just one volition against another,—we willing to go in for life upon a trust or assumption which he, for his part, does not care to make.[1]

As a rule we disbelieve all facts and theories for which we have no use. Clifford's cosmic emotions find no use for Christian feelings. Huxley belabors the bishops because there is no use for sacerdotalism in his scheme of life. Newman, on the contrary, goes over to Romanism, and finds all sorts of reasons good for staying there, because a priestly system is for him an organic need and delight. Why do so few 'scientists' even look at the evidence for telepathy, so called? Because they think, as a leading biologist, now dead, once said to me, that even if such a thing were true, scientists ought to band together to keep it suppressed and concealed. It would undo the uniformity of Nature and all sorts of other things without which scientists cannot carry on their pursuits. But if this very man had been shown something which as a scientist he might *do* with telepathy, he might not only have examined the evidence, but even have found it good enough. This very law which the logicians would impose upon us—if I may give the name of logicians to those who would rule out our willing nature here—is based on nothing but their own natural wish to exclude all elements for which they, in their professional quality of logicians, can find no use.

Evidently, then, our non-intellectual nature does influence our convictions. There are passional tendencies and volitions which run before and others which come after belief, and it is only the latter that are too late for the fair; and they are not too late when the previous passional work has been already in their own direction. Pascal's argument, instead of being powerless, then seems a regular clincher, and is the last stroke needed to make our faith in masses and holy water complete. The state of things is evidently far from simple; and pure insight and logic, whatever they might do ideally, are not the only things that really do produce our creeds.

IV

Our next duty, having recognized this mixed-up state of affairs, is to ask whether it be simply reprehensible and pathological, or whether, on the contrary, we must treat it as a normal element in making up our minds. The thesis I defend is, briefly stated, this: *Our passional nature not only lawfully may, but must, decide an option between propositions, whenever it is a genuine option that cannot by its nature be decided on intellectual grounds; for to say, under such circumstances, "Do not decide, but leave the question open," is itself a passional decision,—just like deciding yes or no,—and is attended with the same risk of losing the truth.* The thesis thus abstractly expressed will, I trust, soon become quite clear. But I must first indulge in a bit more of preliminary work.

---

[1]Compare the admirable page 310 in S. H. Hodgson's "Time and Space," London, 1865.

It will be observed that for the purposes of this discussion we are on 'dogmatic' ground,—ground, I mean, which leaves systematic philosophical scepticism altogether out of account. The postulate that there is truth, and that it is the destiny of our minds to attain it, we are deliberately resolving to make, though the sceptic will not make it. We part company with him, therefore, absolutely, at this point. But the faith that truth exists, and that our minds can find it, may be held in two ways. We may talk of the *empiricist* way and of the *absolutist* way of believing in truth. The absolutists in this matter say that we not only can attain to knowing truth, but we can *know when* we have attained to knowing it; while the empiricists think that although we may attain it, we cannot infallibly know when. To *know* is one thing, and to know for certain *that* we know is another. One may hold to the first being possible without the second; hence the empiricists and the absolutists, although neither of them is a sceptic in the usual philosophic sense of the term, show very different degrees of dogmatism in their lives.

If we look at the history of opinions, we see that the empiricist tendency has largely prevailed in science, while in philosophy the absolutist tendency has had everything its own way. The characteristic sort of happiness, indeed, which philosophies yield has mainly consisted in the conviction felt by each successive school or system that by it bottom-certitude had been attained. "Other philosophies are collections of opinions, mostly false; *my* philosophy gives standing-ground forever,"—who does not recognize in this the key-note of every system worthy of the name? A system, to be a system at all, must come as a *closed* system, reversible in this or that detail, perchance, but in its essential features never!

Scholastic orthodoxy, to which one must always go when one wishes to find perfectly clear statement, has beautifully elaborated this absolutist conviction in a doctrine which it calls that of 'objective evidence.' If, for example, I am unable to doubt that I now exist before you, that two is less than three, or that if all men are mortal then I am mortal too, it is because these things illumine my intellect irresistibly. The final ground of this objective evidence possessed by certain propositions is the *adaequatio intellectûs nostri cum rê*. The certitude it brings involves an *aptitudinem ad extorquendum certum assensum* on the part of the truth envisaged, and on the side of the subject a *quietem in cognitione,* when once the object is mentally received, that leaves no possibility of doubt behind; and in the whole transaction nothing operates but the *entitas ipsa* of the object and the *entitas ipsa* of the mind. We slouchy modern thinkers dislike to talk in Latin,—indeed, we dislike to talk in set terms at all; but at bottom our own state of mind is very much like this whenever we uncritically abandon ourselves: You believe in objective evidence, and I do. Of some things we feel that we are certain: we know, and we know that we do know. There is something that gives a click inside of us, a bell that strikes twelve, when the hands of our mental clock have swept the dial and meet over the meridian hour. The greatest empiricists among us are only empiricists on reflection: when left to their instincts, they dogmatize like infallible popes. When the Cliffords tell us how sinful it is to be Christians on such 'insufficient evidence,' insufficiency is really the last thing they have in mind. For them the evidence is absolutely sufficient, only it makes the other way. They believe so completely in an anti-christian order of the universe that there is no living option: Christianity is a dead hypothesis from the start.

VI

But now, since we are all such absolutists by instinct, what in our quality of students of philosophy ought we to do about the fact? Shall we espouse and indorse it? Or shall we treat it as a weakness of our nature from which we must free ourselves, if we can?

I sincerely believe that the latter course is the only one we can follow as reflective men. Objective evidence and certitude are doubtless very fine ideals to play with, but where on this moonlit and dream-visited planet are they found? I am, therefore, myself a complete empiricist so far as my theory of human knowledge goes. I live, to be sure, by the practical faith that we must go on experiencing and thinking over our experience, for only thus can our opinions grow more true; but to hold any one of them—I absolutely do not care which—as if it never could be reinterpretable or corrigible, I believe to be a tremendously mistaken attitude, and I think that the whole history of philosophy will bear me out. There is but one indefectibly certain truth, and that is the truth that pyrrhonistic scepticism itself leaves standing,—the truth that the present phenomenon of consciousness exists. That, however, is the bare starting-point of knowledge, the mere admission of a stuff to be philosophized about. The various philosophies are but so many attempts at expressing what this stuff really is. And if we repair to our libraries what disagreement do we discover! Where is a certainly true answer found? Apart from abstract propositions of comparison (such as two and two are the same as four), propositions which tell us nothing by themselves about concrete reality, we find no proposition ever regarded by any one as evidently certain that has not either been called a falsehood, or at least had its truth sincerely questioned by some one else. The transcending of the axioms of geometry, not in play but in earnest, by certain of our contemporaries (as Zöllner and Charles H. Hinton), and the rejection of the whole Aristotelian logic by the Hegelians, are striking instances in point.

No concrete test of what is really true has ever been agreed upon. Some make the criterion external to the moment of perception, putting it either in revelation, the *consensus gentium,* the instincts of the heart, or the systematized experience of the race. Others make the perceptive moment its own test, —Descartes, for instance, with his clear and distinct ideas guaranteed by the veracity of God; Reid with his 'common-sense;' and Kant with his forms of synthetic judgment *a priori.* The inconceivability of the opposite; the capacity to be verified by sense; the possession of complete organic unity or self-relation, realized when a thing is its own other,—are standards which, in turn, have been used. The much lauded objective evidence is never triumphantly there; it is a mere aspiration or *Grenzbegriff,* marking the infinitely remote ideal of our thinking life. To claim that certain truths now possess it, is simply to say that when you think them true and they *are* true, then their evidence is objective, otherwise it is not. But practically one's conviction that the evidence one goes by is of the real objective brand, is only one more subjective opinion added to the lot. For what a contradictory array of opinions have objective evidence and absolute certitude been claimed! The world is rational through and through,—its existence is an ultimate brute fact; there is a personal God,—a personal God is inconceivable; there is an extra-mental physical world immediately known,—the mind can only know its own ideas; a moral imperative exists,—obligation is only the resultant of desires; a permanent spiritual principle is in every one,—there are only shifting states of mind; there is an endless chain of causes,—there is an absolute first cause; an eternal necessity,—a freedom; a purpose,—no purpose; a primal One,—a primal Many; a universal continuity,—an essential discontinuity in things; an infinity,—no infinity. There is this,—there is that; there is indeed nothing which some one has not thought absolutely true, while his neighbor deemed it absolutely false; and not an absolutist among them seems ever to have considered that the trouble may all the time be essential, and that the intellect, even with truth directly in its grasp, may have no infallible signal for knowing whether it be truth or no. When, indeed, one remembers that the most striking practical application to life of the doctrine of objective certitude has been the conscientious labors of the Holy Office of the Inquisition, one feels less tempted than ever to lend the doctrine a respectful ear.

But please observe, now, that when as empiricists we give up the doctrine of objective certitude, we do not thereby give up the quest or hope of truth itself. We still pin our faith on its existence, and still believe that we gain an ever better position towards it by systematically continuing to roll up experiences and think. Our great difference from the scholastic lies in the way we face. The strength of his system lies in the principles, the origin, the *terminus a quo* of his thought; for us the strength is in the outcome, the upshot, the *terminus ad quem*. Not where it comes from but what it leads to is to decide. It matters not to an empiricist from what quarter an hypothesis may come to him: he may have acquired it by fair means or by foul; passion may have whispered or accident suggested it; but if the total drift of thinking continues to confirm it, that is what he means by its being true.

VII

One more point, small but important, and our preliminaries are done. There are two ways of looking at our duty in the matter of opinion,—ways entirely different, and yet ways about whose difference the theory of knowledge seems hitherto to have shown very little concern. *We must know the truth;* and *we must avoid error,*—these are our first and great commandments as would-be knowers; but they are not two ways of stating an identical commandment, they are two separable laws. Although it may indeed happen that when we believe the truth *A*, we escape as an incidental consequence from believing the falsehood *B*, it hardly ever happens that by merely disbelieving *B* we necessarily believe *A*. We may in escaping *B* fall into believing other falsehoods, *C* or *D*, just as bad as *B*; or we may escape *B* by not believing anything at all, not even *A*.

Believe truth! Shun error!—these, we see, are two materially different laws; and by choosing between them we may end by coloring differently our whole intellectual life. We may regard the chase for truth as paramount, and the avoidance of error as secondary; or we may, on the other hand, treat the avoidance of error as more imperative, and let truth take its chance. Clifford, in the instructive passage which I have quoted, exhorts us to the latter course. Believe nothing, he tells us, keep your mind in suspense forever, rather than by closing it on insufficient evidence incur the awful risk of believing lies. You, on the other hand, may think that the risk of being in error is a very small matter when compared with the blessings of real knowledge, and be ready to be duped many times in your investigation rather than postpone indefinitely the chance of guessing true. I myself find it impossible to go with Clifford. We must remember that these feelings of our duty about either truth or error are in any case only expressions of our passional life. Biologically considered, our minds are as ready to grind out falsehood as veracity, and he who says, "Better go without belief forever than believe a lie!" merely shows his own preponderant private horror of becoming a dupe. He may be critical of many of his desires and fears, but this fear he slavishly obeys. He cannot imagine any one questioning its binding force. For my own part, I have also a horror of being duped; but I can believe that worse things than being duped may happen to a man in this world: so Clifford's exhortation has to my ears a thoroughly fantastic sound. It is like a general informing his soldiers that it is better to keep out of battle forever than to risk a single wound. Not so are victories either over enemies or over nature gained. Our errors are surely not such awfully solemn things. In a world where we are so certain to incur them in spite of all our caution, a certain lightness of heart seems healthier than this excessive nervousness on their behalf. At any rate, it seems the fittest thing for the empiricist philosopher.

VIII

And now, after all this introduction, let us go straight at our question. I have said, and now repeat it, that not only as a matter of fact do we find our passional nature influencing us in our opinions, but that there are some options between opinions in which this influence must be regarded both as an inevitable and as a lawful determinant of our choice.

I fear here that some of you my hearers will begin to scent danger, and lend an inhospitable ear. Two first steps of passion you have indeed had to admit as necessary,—we must think so as to avoid dupery, and we must think so as to gain truth; but the surest path to those ideal consummations, you will probably consider, is from now onwards to take no further passional step.

Well, of course, I agree as far as the facts will allow. Wherever the option between losing truth and gaining it is not momentous, we can throw the chance of *gaining truth* away, and at any rate save ourselves from any chance of *believing falsehood,* by not making up our minds at all till objective evidence has come. In scientific questions, this is almost always the case; and even in human affairs in general, the need of acting is seldom so urgent that a false belief to act on is better than no belief at all. Law courts, indeed, have to decide on the best evidence attainable for the moment, because a judge's duty is to make law as well as to ascertain it, and (as a learned judge once said to me) few cases are worth spending much time over: the great thing is to have them decided on *any* acceptable principle, and got out of the way. But in our dealings with objective nature we obviously are recorders, not makers, of the truth; and decisions for the mere sake of deciding promptly and getting on to the next business would be wholly out of place. Throughout the breadth of physical nature facts are what they are quite independently of us, and seldom is there any such hurry about them that the risks of being duped by believing a premature theory need be faced. The questions here are always trivial options, the hypotheses are hardly living (at any rate not living for us spectators), the choice between believing truth or falsehood is seldom forced. The attitude of sceptical balance is therefore the absolutely wise one if we would escape mistakes. What difference, indeed, does it make to most of us whether we have or have not a theory of the Röntgen rays, whether we believe or not in mind-stuff, or have a conviction about the causality of conscious states? It makes no difference. Such options are not forced on us. On every account it is better not to make them, but still keep weighing reasons *pro et contra* with an indifferent hand.

I speak, of course, here of the purely judging mind. For purposes of discovery such indifference is to be less highly recommended, and science would be far less advanced than she is if the passionate desires of individuals to get their own faiths confirmed had been kept out of the game. See for example the sagacity which Spencer and Weismann now display. On the other hand, if you want an absolute duffer in an investigation, you must, after all, take the man who has no interest whatever in its results: he is the warranted incapable, the positive fool. The most useful investigator, because the most sensitive observer, is always he whose eager interest in one side of the question is balanced by an equally keen nervousness lest he become deceived.[2] Science has organized this nervousness into a regular *technique,* her so-called method of verification; and she has fallen so deeply in love with the method that one may even say she has ceased to care for truth by itself at all. It is only truth as technically verified that interests her. The truth of truths might come in merely affirmative form, and she would decline to touch it. Such truth as that, she might repeat with Clifford, would be stolen in defiance of her duty to mankind. Human passions, however, are stronger than technical rules. "Le coeur a ses raisons," as Pascal says, "que la raison ne connaît pas;" and however indifferent to all but the bare rules of the game the umpire, the abstract intellect, may be, the concrete players who furnish him the materials to judge of are usually, each one of them, in love with some pet 'live hypothesis' of his own. Let us agree, however, that wherever there is no forced option, the dispassionately judicial intellect with no pet hypothesis, saving us, as it does, from dupery at any rate, ought to be our ideal.

The question next arises: Are there not somewhere forced options in our speculative questions, and can we (as men who may be interested at least as much in positively gaining truth as in merely escaping dupery) always wait with impunity till the coercive evidence shall have arrived? It seems *a priori* improbable that the truth should be so nicely adjusted to our needs and powers as that. In the great boarding-house of nature, the cakes and the butter and the syrup seldom come out so even and leave the plates so clean. Indeed, we should view them with scientific suspicion if they did.

---

[2] Compare Wilfrid Ward's Essay, "The Wish to Believe," in his *Witnesses to the Unseen,* Macmillan & Co., 1893.

Moral questions immediately present themselves as questions whose solution cannot wait for sensible proof. A moral question is a question not of what sensibly exists, but of what is good, or would be good if it did exist. Science can tell us what exists; but to compare the *worths,* both of what exists and of what does not exist, we must consult not science, but what Pascal calls our heart. Science herself consults her heart when she lays it down that the infinite ascertainment of fact and correction of false belief are the supreme goods for man. Challenge the statement, and science can only repeat it oracularly, or else prove it by showing that such ascertainment and correction bring man all sorts of other goods which man's heart in turn declares. The question of having moral beliefs at all or not having them is decided by our will. Are our moral preferences true or false, or are they only odd biological phenomena, making things good or bad for *us,* but in themselves indifferent? How can your pure intellect decide? If your heart does not *want* a world of moral reality, your head will assuredly never make you believe in one. Mephistophelian scepticism, indeed, will satisfy the head's play-instincts much better than any rigorous idealism can. Some men (even at the student age) are so naturally cool-hearted that the moralistic hypothesis never has for them any pungent life, and in their supercilious presence the hot young moralist always feels strangely ill at ease. The appearance of knowingness is on their side, of *naïveté* and gullibility on his. Yet, in the inarticulate heart of him, he clings to it that he is not a dupe, and that there is a realm in which (as Emerson says) all their wit and intellectual superiority is no better than the cunning of a fox. Moral scepticism can no more be refuted or proved by logic than intellectual scepticism can. When we stick to it that there *is* truth (be it of either kind), we do so with our whole nature, and resolve to stand or fall by the results. The sceptic with his whole nature adopts the doubting attitude; but which of us is the wiser, Omniscience only knows.

Turn now from these wide questions of good to a certain class of questions of fact, questions concerning personal relations, states of mind between one man and another. *Do you like me or not?*—for example. Whether you do or not depends, in countless instances, on whether I meet you half-way, am willing to assume that you must like me, and show you trust and expectation. The previous faith on my part in your liking's existence is in such cases what makes your liking come. But if I stand aloof, and refuse to budge an inch until I have objective evidence, until you shall have done something apt, as the absolutists say, *ad extorquendum assensum meum,* ten to one your liking never comes. How many women's hearts are vanquished by the mere sanguine insistence of some man that they *must* love him! he will not consent to the hypothesis that they cannot. The desire for a certain kind of truth here brings about that special truth's existence; and so it is in innumerable cases of other sorts. Who gains promotions, boons, appointments, but the man in whose life they are seen to play the part of live hypotheses, who discounts them, sacrifices other things for their sake before they have come, and takes risks for them in advance? His faith acts on the powers above him as a claim, and creates its own verification.

A social organism of any sort whatever, large or small, is what it is because each member proceeds to his own duty with a trust that the other members will simultaneously do theirs. Wherever a desired result is achieved by the co-operation of many independent persons, its existence as a fact is a pure consequence of the precursive faith in one another of those immediately concerned. A government, an army, a commercial system, a ship, a college, an athletic team, all exist on this condition, without which not only is nothing achieved, but nothing is even attempted. A whole train of passengers (individually brave enough) will be looted by a few highwaymen, simply because the latter can count on one another, while each passenger fears that if he makes a movement of resistance, he will be shot before any one else backs him up. If we believed that the whole car-full would rise at once with us, we should each severally rise, and train-robbing would never even be attempted. There are, then, cases where a fact cannot come at all unless a preliminary faith exists in its coming. *And where faith in a fact can help create the fact,* that would be an insane logic which should say that faith running ahead of scientific evidence is the 'lowest kind of immorality' into which a thinking being can fall. Yet such is the logic by which our scientific absolutists pretend to regulate our lives!

X

In truths dependent on our personal action, then, faith based on desire is certainly a lawful and possibly an indispensable thing.

But now, it will be said, these are all childish human cases, and have nothing to do with great cosmical matters, like the question of religious faith. Let us then pass on to that. Religions differ so much in their accidents that in discussing the religious question we must make it very generic and broad. What then do we now mean by the religious hypothesis? Science says things are; morality says some things are better than other things; and religion says essentially two things.

First, she says that the best things are the more eternal things, the overlapping things, the things in the universe that throw the last stone, so to speak, and say the final word. "Perfection is eternal,"—this phrase of Charles Secrétan seems a good way of putting this first affirmation of religion, an affirmation which obviously cannot yet be verified scientifically at all.

The second affirmation of religion is that we are better off even now if we believe her first affirmation to be true.

Now, let us consider what the logical elements of this situation are *in case the religious hypothesis in both its branches be really true.* (Of course, we must admit that possibility at the outset. If we are to discuss the question at all, it must involve a living option. If for any of you religion be a hypothesis that cannot, by any living possibility be true, then you need go no farther. I speak to the 'saving remnant' alone.) So proceeding, we see, first, that religion offers itself as a *momentous* option. We are supposed to gain, even now, by our belief, and to lose by our non-belief, a certain vital good. Secondly, religion is a *forced* option, so far as that good goes. We cannot escape the issue by remaining sceptical and waiting for more light, because, although we do avoid error in that way *if religion be untrue,* we lose the good, *if it be true,* just as certainly as if we positively chose to disbelieve. It is as if a man should hesitate indefinitely to ask a certain woman to marry him because he was not perfectly sure that she would prove an angel after he brought her home. Would he not cut himself off from that particular angel-possibility as decisively as if he went and married some one else? Scepticism, then, is not avoidance of option; it is option of a certain particular kind of risk. *Better risk loss of truth than chance of error,*—that is your faith-vetoer's exact position. He is actively playing his stake as much as the believer is; he is backing the field against the religious hypothesis, just as the believer is backing the religious hypothesis against the field. To preach scepticism to us as a duty until 'sufficient evidence' for religion be found, is tantamount therefore to telling us, when in presence of the religious hypothesis, that to yield to our fear of its being error is wiser and better than to yield to our hope that it may be true. It is not intellect against all passions, then; it is only intellect with one passion laying down its law. And by what, forsooth, is the supreme wisdom of this passion warranted? Dupery for dupery, what proof is there that dupery through hope is so much worse than dupery through fear? I, for one, can see no proof; and I simply refuse obedience to the scientist's command to imitate his kind of option, in a case where my own stake is important enough to give me the right to choose my own form of risk. If religion be true and the evidence for it be still insufficient, I do not wish, by putting your extinguisher upon my nature (which feels to me as if it had after all some business in this matter), to forfeit my sole chance in life of getting upon the winning side,—that chance depending, of course, on my willingness to run the risk of acting as if my passional need of taking the world religiously might be prophetic and right.

All this is on the supposition that it really may be prophetic and right, and that, even to us who are discussing the matter, religion is a live hypothesis which may be true. Now, to most of us religion comes in a still further way that makes a veto on our active faith even more illogical. The more perfect and more eternal aspect of the universe is represented in our religions as having personal form. The universe is no longer a mere *It* to us, but a *Thou,* if we are religious; and any relation that may be possible from person to person might be possible here. For instance, although in one sense we are passive portions of the universe, in another we show a curious autonomy, as if we were small active centres on our own account. We feel, too, as if the appeal of religion to us were made to our own active good-will, as if evidence might be forever withheld from us unless we met the hypothesis half-way. To take a trivial illustration: just as a man who in a company of gentlemen made no advances, asked a warrant for every concession, and believed no one's word without proof, would cut himself off by such churlishness from all the social rewards that a more trusting spirit would earn, —so here, one who should shut himself up in snarling logicality and try to make the gods extort his recognition willy-nilly, or not get it at all, might cut himself off forever from his only opportunity of making the gods' acquaintance. This feeling, forced on us we know not whence, that by obstinately believing that there are gods (although not to do so would be so easy both for our logic and our life) we are doing the universe the deepest service we can, seems part of the living essence of the religious hypothesis. If the hypothesis *were* true in all its parts, including this one, then pure intellectualism, with its veto on our making willing advances, would be an absurdity; and some participation of our sympathetic nature would be logically required. I, therefore, for one, cannot see my way to accepting the agnostic rules for truth-seeking, or wilfully agree to keep my willing nature out of the game. I cannot do so for this plain reason, that *a rule of thinking which would absolutely prevent me from acknowledging certain kinds of truth if those kinds of truth were really there, would be an irrational rule.* That for me is the long and short of the formal logic of the situation, no matter what the kinds of truth might materially be.

I confess I do not see how this logic can be escaped. But sad experience makes me fear that some of you may still shrink from radically saying with me, *in abstracto,* that we have the right to believe at our own risk any hypothesis that is live enough to tempt our will. I suspect, however, that if this is so, it is because you have got away from the abstract logical point of view altogether, and are thinking (perhaps without realizing it) of some particular religious hypothesis which for you is dead. The freedom to 'believe what we will' you apply to the case of some patent superstition; and the faith you think of is the faith defined by the schoolboy when he said, "Faith is when you believe something that you know ain't true." I can only repeat that this is misapprehension. *In concreto,* the freedom to believe can only cover living options which the intellect of the individual cannot by itself resolve; and living options never seem absurdities to him who has them to consider. When I look at the religious question as it really puts itself to concrete men, and when I think of all the possibilities which both practically and theoretically it involves, then this command that we shall put a stopper on our heart, instincts, and courage, and *wait*—acting of course meanwhile more or less as if religion were *not* true[3]—till doomsday, or till such time as our intellect and senses working together may have raked in evidence enough,—this command, I say, seems to me the queerest idol ever manufactured in the philosophic cave. Were we scholastic absolutists, there might be more excuse. If we had an infallible intellect with its objective certitudes, we might feel ourselves disloyal to such a perfect organ of knowledge in not trusting to it exclusively, in not waiting for its releasing word. But if we are empiricists, if we believe that no bell in us tolls to let us know for certain when truth is in our grasp, then it seems a piece of idle fantasticality to preach so solemnly our duty of waiting for the bell. Indeed we *may* wait if we will,—I hope you do not think that I am denying that,—but if we do so, we do so at our peril as much as if we believed. In either case we *act,* taking our life in our hands. No one of us ought to issue vetoes to the other, nor should we bandy words of abuse. We ought, on the contrary, delicately and profoundly to respect one another's mental freedom: then only shall we bring about the intellectual republic; then only shall we have that spirit of inner tolerance without which all our outer tolerance is soulless, and which is empiricism's glory; then only shall we live and let live, in speculative as well as in practical things.

---

[3]Since belief is measured by action, he who forbids us to believe religion to be true, necessarily also forbids us to act as we should if we did believe it to be true. The whole defence of religious faith hinges upon action. If the action required or inspired by the religious hypothesis is in no way different from that dictated by the naturalistic hypothesis, then religious faith is a pure superfluity, better pruned away, and controversy about its legitimacy is a piece of idle trifling, unworthy of serious minds. I myself believe, of course, that the religious hypothesis gives to the world an expression which specifically determines our reactions, and makes them in a large part unlike what they might be on a purely naturalistic scheme of belief.

I began by a reference to Fitzjames Stephen; let me end by a quotation from him.

> What do you think of yourself? What do you think of the world? . . . These are questions with which all must deal as it seems good to them. They are riddles of the Sphinx, and in some way or other we must deal with them. . . . In all important transactions of life we have to take a leap in the dark. . . . If we decide to leave the riddles unanswered, that is a choice; if we waver in our answer, that, too, is a choice: but whatever choice we make, we make it at our peril. If a man chooses to turn his back altogether on God and the future, no one can prevent him; no one can show beyond reasonable doubt that he is mistaken. If a man thinks otherwise and acts as he thinks, I do not see that any one can prove that *he* is mistaken. Each must act as he thinks best; and if he is wrong, so much the worse for him. We stand on a mountain pass in the midst of whirling snow and blinding mist, through which we get glimpses now and then of paths which may be deceptive. If we stand still we shall be frozen to death. If we take the wrong road we shall be dashed to pieces. We do not certainly know whether there is any right one. What must we do? 'Be strong and of a good courage.' Act for the best, hope for the best, and take what comes. . . . If death ends all, we cannot meet death better.[4]

---

[4]Liberty, Equality, Fraternity, p. 353, 2d edition. London, 1874.

JAMES AND CLIFFORD ON "THE WILL TO BELIEVE"[1]

George Mavrodes

George Mavrodes, "James and Clifford on 'The Will to Believe,'" *The Personalist,* vol. XLIV, no. 2 (Spring 1963). Used by permission of the author and editor, Professor John Hospers.

In this paper I intend to examine certain logical aspects of William James's argument in his essay, "The Will to Believe." However, I shall not concern myself with the question of whether this general sort of justification is either proper or useful for religious belief. Instead, I am interested primarily in James's controversy with W. K. Clifford, and in the logical relations of their apparently different doctrines about believing.

James devotes section VII of his essay to what he calls "a small but important point." He distinguishes here between two "commandments" which set forth our duty in the enterprise of thought. They are "We must know the truth," and "We

---

[1]This paper was presented to the Western Division of the American Philosophical Association, May, 1960

must avoid error." James points out that these two are not variant expressions of a single principle, but two separate principles.

We might illustrate James's distinction by imagining that a man going to the races is given two pieces of advice; "Win a lot of bets," and "Don't lose many bets." If he is especially impressed by the latter, he will bet only a few times, if at all, and only on what look like sure things. Hence, he can lose only a few times, if at all; thus obeying the second injunction. But this same caution will prevent any large number of winning bets, and thus he will fail to follow the first injunction. On the other hand, if he is more impressed by the first piece of advice, he may bet a larger number of times, thus having a chance of winning often, but also risking many losses. It is evident that the two pieces of advice are not identical, since following one of them does not necessarily imply following the other.

Now, believing a proposition is something like betting on its truth. We want to believe true propositions, and we want not to believe false ones. But, faced with some proposition for which the evidence is not conclusive, what shall we do? We may play it safe, making no commitment. Then, even if it turns out to be false, we shall not have been guilty of believing an error. But neither is there any chance of this course of action yielding us a true belief, since we refuse to commit ourselves in belief at all. On the other hand, we may take a chance, committing ourselves one way or the other. Thus we risk being wrong and gain the chance of being right. We might imagine two men going through life, the one extremely cautious and the other more venturesome in the matter of belief. The first makes few commitments and hence few errors, but he never advances beyond a rather small stock of true beliefs. The second makes more commitments and runs more risk of error, but he has the chance of building up a larger stock of true beliefs.

James quotes Clifford as saying, "It is wrong always, everywhere, and for everyone, to believe anything upon insufficient evidence."[2] He interprets Clifford as urging that "avoid error" is by far the more important of the two commandments. Believe only sure things, take no chance of making a mistake—this is Clifford's principle. As James later sums up the doctrine, "Better risk loss of truth than chance of error" (Sec. X).

James, however, tells us that he himself cannot accept this. He is more attracted by the prospect of true belief than he is repelled by the chance of error, and he is "ready to be duped many times . . . rather than postpone indefinitely the chance of guessing true" (Sec. VII).

The distinction which James makes is, I think, quite valid. On the other hand, I do not wish to say anything here as to whether James's or Clifford's choice between the alternatives is better or even more congenial to me. I do wish to maintain that (1) the distinction which James has drawn is irrelevant to the "will to believe" as James defines that doctrine, and (2) in the only cited examples where the distinction is relevant James adopts Clifford's viewpoint instead of the one he has himself championed.

It is important to remember that, according to James, the "will to believe" can be applied only to options which have, among their other characteristics, the quality of being forced (Sec. I, IV). Of course, not all options are forced. "Call my

[2]Quoted in William James, "The Will to Believe," Sec. II. The statement may be found in W. K. Clifford, *Lectures and Essays,* p. 186. Further references to James's essay will be made in the text.

theory true or call it false," is not forced, since you can refuse to judge my theory at all. You need not bet either way. But "Accept this truth or do without it," is forced. There is no third alternative, no possibility of neutrality. We are bound to take one or the other of the stated alternatives (Sec. I).

James, of course, wants to apply this doctrine to religious beliefs. But he can do so only if the options with regard to them are forced. So we must ask, are the options of religious belief forced, or are they more like the unforced "Call my theory true or call it false?" It is not possible that we may suspend judgment on every religious question, deciding neither one way nor the other?

James replies that these questions are indeed forced, but his explanation is not as full as we might desire. Yet, it is one of the most crucial steps in his argument. He tells us that they are forced because indecision loses the possible good of religion just as surely as does outright rejection (Sec. X). And he contrasts them with other belief options. "What difference, indeed," he asks, "does it make to most of us whether we have or have not a theory of Röntgen rays." (Sec. VIII). This is no forced option, for we need not decide at all about the Röntgen theory.

Behind this view of the forced character of religious options there lies, I think, a pragmatic theory of belief, perhaps that beliefs are different only if their practical consequences are different. The ordinary man can avoid taking a position on the Röntgen theory because he never has to act in a situation to which that theory would make a practical difference. But it is different in the case of religion. Religious beliefs color our approach to so many situations and actions that they cannot be avoided. And there is no third alternative in action. We must act either as though the religious hypotheses were true or as though they were false. There is no practical third way of acting as if we were uncommitted, though we may talk this way. Thus, the agnostic gets the same sort of consequences as the atheist. Unwilling to build his life on the hypothesis that there is a God he must build it without that hypothesis, and so must build the same sort of life as the atheist (Sec. IX and note 4). Practically speaking, their beliefs are the same, and so the agnostic's position is not a third alternative.

If this is true, if we can interpret beliefs in this way, then religious beliefs represent forced options. If it is not true, then they are not forced options, and the "will to believe" is not applicable to them.

But what happens when we apply James's distinction to these cases of forced options in belief, to the cases where we have to bet? Here we discover that the distinction has lost its point. For, in this special case, "Believe the truth" *is* equivalent to "Don't believe error." It was the usual possibility of non-commitment which gave the distinction its validity. In such cases one might hold back, giving up his chance for truth in order to be safe from error, while another plunges in, risking error for the possibility of truth. But where the possibility of remaining uncommitted disappears, as it must in the forced options, there the distinction vanishes too. If we must bet, then we will either win or lose, and not both. Not winning will imply losing, not losing will imply winning.

Here, then, there can be no question of this temperamental difference, some fearing the loss of truth, others fearing the chance of error. For here all risk error, and all have a chance for truth. They cannot avoid it; there is no middle ground between the loss and the gain. None is merely a spectator here, if James has correctly identified the options of religious belief as forced options. Pascal said,

"You must wager. It is not optional. You are embarked."[3] Those who agree, taking the options to be forced ones, will have no need of James's distinction in handling them. They know that they cannot stand aloof and wait; it is not a matter of making a commitment but, rather, of either affirming or changing the commitment which they already have. On the other hand, those who do not believe the option to be a forced one cannot apply to it the "will to believe." In neither case, then, is this distinction relevant to that doctrine.

The distinction is relevant, of course, to unforced options. Here it can come into play. We are presented with some proposition, some theory, which is not sure. Shall we bet or not? Is the chance for truth worth the risk of error? Curiously, though James urges the more venturesome spirit, a certain light-heartedness in thinking about errors (Sec. VII), he takes the opposite tack when it comes to his own examples. On scientific questions, in human affairs in general, it is better to wait for the evidence. "Such options," he says, "are not forced. On every account it is better not to make them, but still keep weighing reason *pro et contra* with an indifferent hand" (Sec. VIII). Here, on the only sort of questions on which he might reasonably differ, he lines up solidly with Clifford.

James certainly formulated the distinction with which we have been con-cerned with the intent of using it to support the "will to believe" doctrine. He wants to use it to counter the "faith-vetoer" (Sec. X). He supposes, apparently, that Clifford's position is logically opposed to his own in its approach to these religious questions. And so he tells us that Clifford is over-emphasizing one of the commandments of our mental life, but that there is another which we will do well not to neglect. We must not let ourselves be guided entirely by our fear of error.

However, if we have been right, we have seen that, when it comes to the particular questions in which James is primarily interested, the distinction between these two commandments disappears. It has become superfluous.

There is a curious corollary which follows on this conclusion. It is that Clifford and James are not logically opposed in their approach to these questions. In fact, Clifford's own doctrine that "it is wrong always, everywhere, and for everyone, to believe anything upon insufficient evidence," can be made to yield, in any particular case, the same answer that the "will to believe" will yield. In other words, it will yield whatever answer we want.

To see this, we must note one further limitation which James places on the "will to believe." It is to be applied only to questions which cannot be decided on "intellectual grounds" (Sec. IV). The evidence must be insufficient for deciding the question either way. Let us suppose for the moment that the question, "Is there a God?," is forced and is undecidable on evidential grounds.

Let us then ask Clifford, "Shall I believe that there is a God?" He will pre-sumably answer, in accordance with his principle, "No, you must not believe that there is a God, since the evidence is insufficient." James would like to justify the opposite answer, or at least to open the possibility of it to those who want it. So he introduces the "will to believe" along with a distinction which has turned out to be irrelevant.

I suggest, however, that James has too quickly assumed that Clifford's prin-

---

[3]Blaise Pascal, *Pensées*, 233.

ciple is the villain. It is not. If we are not satisfied with the answer which it provides, we simply need to ask a different question. Let us ask Clifford instead, "Shall I believe that there is no God?" Presumably he must answer, "No, you must not believe that there is no God, since the evidence for that is insufficient."[4]

Now, if the option is really forced, this reply is equivalent to, "Believe that there is a God!" for that is the other alternative. Thus, whichever reply we desire, we can get it by phrasing our question properly. Clifford's principle, just like James's distinction, makes a difference only in cases where the option is not forced. But in those cases where it is forced and where the evidence is inconclusive, Clifford can exclude neither answer.

I conclude, therefore, that James has mistaken the point where his dispute with Clifford lies. It is not at all in this matter of risking error for a chance of truth. The possibility of applying Clifford's principle significantly to questions of religious belief turns on the assumption that it is really possible to suspend belief on those questions. And then the only thing he can consistently urge, if the evidence is not conclusive, is that we not believe either way. But James's view of such options as forced, if I understand it correctly, implies that such a suspension of belief is not inadvisable but rather impossible. If this is granted, then James can eliminate Clifford and his followers from this field without any special "will to believe" doctrine. But if this is not granted, then James's whole argument collapses. The "will to believe" will not apply to religious questions.

Their real differences then, if they have any, will center around this question: "Are there forced options with regard to believing, and if so, what are they?" This is one of the over-riding and crucial questions in the argument, and one to which James should have devoted more attention. If he could have eliminated all doubt as to the character of religious options and as to the nature of belief, then the logical relations between his own and Clifford's principles would have become clear.

---

[4]*Ex hypothesi,* the evidence is insufficient on either side. Otherwise this question is not a candidate for the "will to believe" at all. James, of course, is right in pointing out that people who urge views like Clifford's are usually really assuming that the evidence is all against the religious hypothesis. But this means that urging on them a "will to believe" will be futile. See sec. V.

FAITH AS TOTAL INTERPRETATION

John Hick

Reprinted from John Hick, *Faith and Knowledge,* 1st ed., © 1957; 2d ed., © 1966 by Cornell University. Used by permission of Cornell University Press.

We come now to our main problem. What manner of cognition is the religious man's awareness of God, and how is it related to his other cognitions?

We become conscious of the existence of other objects in the universe, whether things or persons, either by experiencing them for ourselves or by inferring their existence from evidences within our experience. The awareness of God reported by the ordinary religious believer is of the former kind. He professes, not to have inferred that there is a God, but that God as a living being has entered into his own experience. He claims to enjoy something which he describes as an experience of God. The ordinary believer does not, however, report an awareness of God as existing in isolation from all other objects of experience. His consciousness of the divine does not involve a cessation of his consciousness of a material and social environment. It is not a vision of God in solitary glory, filling the believer's entire mind and blotting out his normal field of perception. Whether such phrases correctly describe the mystic's goal, the ultimate Beatific Vision which figures in Christian doctrine, is a question for a later chapter.[1] But at any rate the ordinary persons's religious awareness here on earth is not of that kind. He claims instead an apprehension of God meeting him in and through his material and social environments. He finds that in his dealings with the world of men and things he is somehow having to do with God, and God with him. The moments of ordinary life possess, or may possess, for him in varying degrees a religious significance. As has been well said, religious experience is "the whole experience of religious persons."[2] The believer meets God not only in moments of worship, but also when through the urgings of conscience he feels the pressure of the divine demand upon his life; when through the gracious actions of his friends he apprehends the divine grace; when through the marvels and beauties of nature he traces the hand of the Creator; and he has increasing knowledge of the divine purpose as he responds to its behests in his own life. In short, it is not apart from the course of mundane life, but in it and through it, that the ordinary religious believer claims to experience, however imperfectly and fragmentarily, the divine presence and activity.

This at any rate, among the variety of claims to religious awareness which have been and might be made, is the claim whose epistemological credentials we are to examine. Can God be known through his dealings with us in the world which he has made? The question concerns human experience, and the possibility of an awareness of the divine being mediated through awareness of the world, the supernatural through the natural.

In answer to this query I shall try to show, in various fields, that "mediated"

---

[1]See Chapter 8.

[2]William Temple, *Nature, Man and God* (London, 1934), p. 334.

knowledge, such as is postulated by this religious claim, is already a common and accepted feature of our cognitive experience. To this end we must study a basic characteristic of human experience, which I shall call "significance," together with the correlative mental activity by which it is apprehended, which I shall call "interpretation." We shall find that interpretation takes place in relation to each of the three main types of existence, or orders of significance, recognized by human thought—the natural, the human, and the divine; and that in order to relate ourselves appropriately to each, a primary and unevidenceable act of interpretation is required which, when directed toward God, has traditionally been termed "faith." Thus I shall try to show that while the object of religious knowledge is unique, its basic epistemological pattern is that of all our knowing.

This is not to say that the logic of theistic belief has no peculiarities. It does indeed display certain unique features; and these (I shall try to show) are such as follow from the unique nature of its object, and are precisely the peculiarities which we should expect if that object is real. In the present chapter, then, we shall take note of the common epistemological pattern in which religious knowledge partakes, and in the following chapter we shall examine some special peculiarities of religious knowing, and especially its noncompulsory character.

"Significance" seems to be the least misleading word available to name the fundamental characteristic of experience which I wish to discuss. Other possible terms are "form" and "meaning." But "form," as the word is used in the traditional matter-form distinction, would require careful editing and commentary to purge it of unwanted Aristotelian associations. "Meaning," on the other hand, has been so overworked and misused in the past, not only by plain men and poets, but also by theologians and philosophers,[3] as to be almost useless today, except in its restricted technical use as referring to the equivalence of symbols. We may perhaps hope that after a period of exile the wider concept of "meaning" will be readmitted into the philosophical comity of notions. Indeed Brand Blanshard has long braved the post-Ogden and Richards ban by his use of the phrase "perceptual meaning."[4] I propose here, however, to use the less prejuged term "significance."

By significance I mean that fundamental and all-pervasive characteristic of our conscious experience which *de facto* constitutes it for us the experience of a "world" and not of a mere empty void or churning chaos. We find ourselves in a relatively stable and ordered environment in which we have come to feel, so to say, "at home." The world has become intelligible to us, in the sense that it is a familiar place in which we have learned to act and react in appropriate ways. Our experience is not just an unpredictable kaleidoscope of which we are bewildered spectators, but reveals to us a familiar, settled cosmos in which we live and act, a world in which we can adopt purposes and adapt means to ends. It is in virtue of this homely, familiar, intelligible character of experience—its possession of significance—that we are able to inhabit and cope with our environment.

If this use of "significance" be allowed it will, I think, readily be granted that our consciousness is essentially consciousness of significance. Mind could neither emerge nor persist in an environment which was totally nonsignificant to it.

---

[3] Cf. Ogden and Richards, *The Meaning of Meaning* (7th ed.; London, 1945), ch. 8.
[4] *The Nature of Thought* (London, 1939), I, chs. 4–6.

For this reason it is not possible to define "significance" ostensively by pointing to contrasting examples of significant and nonsignificant experience. In its most general form at least, we must accept the Kantian thesis that we can be aware only of that which enters into a certain framework of basic relations which is correlated with the structure of our own consciousness. These basic relations represent the minimal conditions of significance for the human mind. The totally nonsignificant is thus debarred from entering into our experience. A completely undifferentiated field, or a sheer "buzzing, booming confusion," would be incapable of sustaining consciousness. For our consciousness is (to repeat) essentially consciousness of significance. Except perhaps in very early infancy or in states of radical breakdown, the human mind is always aware of its environment as having this quality of fundamental familiarity or intelligibility. Significance, then, is simply the most general characteristic of our experience.

Significance, so defined, has an essential reference to action. Consciousness of a particular kind of environmental significance involves a judgment, implicit or explicit, as to the appropriateness of a particular kind, or range of kinds, of action in relation to that environment. The distinction between types of significance is a distinction between the reactions, occurrent and dispositional, which they render appropriate. For the human psychophysical organism has evolved under the pressure of a continual struggle to survive, and our system of significance-attributions has as a result an essentially pragmatic orientation. Our outlook is instinctively empirical and practical. Physiologically we are so constituted as to be sensitive only to a minute selection of the vast quantity and complexity of the events taking place around us—that precise selection which is practically relevant to us. Our ears, for example, are attuned to a fragment only of the full range of sound waves, and our eyes to but a fraction of the multitudinous variations of light. Our sense organs automatically select from nature those aspects in relation to which we must act. We apprehend the world only at the macroscopic level at which we have practical dealings with it. As Norman Kemp Smith has said, "The function of sense-perception, as of instinct, is not knowledge but power, not insight but adaptation."[5] For an animal to apprehend more of its environment than is practically relevant to it would prove a fatal complication; it would be bemused and bewildered, and unable to react selectively to the stimuli indicating danger, food, and so on. And it is equally true at the human level that the significance of a given object or situation for a given individual consists in the practical *difference* which the existence of that object makes to that individual. It is indeed one of the marks of our status as dependent beings that we live by continual adaptation to our environment; and from this follows the essentially practical bearing of that which constitutes significance for us.

Although the locus of significance is primarily our environment as a whole, we can in thought divide this into smaller units of significance. We may accordingly draw a provisional distinction between two species of significance, object-significance and situational significance, and note the characteristics of significance first in terms of the former.

Every general name, such as "hat," "book," "fire," "house," names a type of object-significance. For these are isolable aspects of our experience which (in

---

[5] *Prolegomena to an Idealist Theory of Knowledge* (London, 1924), pp. 32–33.

suitable contexts) render appropriate distinctive patterns of behavior. The word "hat," for example, does not name a rigidly delimited class of objects but a particular use to which things can be put, namely, as a covering for the head. Objects are specially manufactured for this use; but if necessary many other items can be made to fulfill the function of a hat. This particular way of treating things, as headgear, is the behavioral correlate of the type of object-significance which we call "being a hat." Indeed the boundaries of each distinguishable class of objects are defined by the two *foci* of (1) physical structure and (2) function in relation to human interests. Our names are always in part names for functions or uses or kinds of significance as apprehended from the standpoint of the agent.

Significance, then, is a relational concept. A universe devoid of consciousness would be neither significant nor non-significant. An object or a sense-field is significant *for* or *to* a mind. We are only concerned here with significance for the human mind, but it is well to remember that the lower animals also are aware of their environment as being significant, this awareness being expressed not in words or concepts but in actions and readinesses for action.

There is, I hope, no suggestion of anything occult about this fundamental feature of our experience which I am calling "significance." The difficulty in discussing it is not novelty but, on the contrary, overfamiliarity. It is so completely obvious that we can easily overlook its importance, or even its existence. There is also the related difficulty that we do not apprehend significance as such, but only each distinguishable aspect of our experience as having its own particular type of significance. For significance is a genus which exists only in its species. Just as we perceive the various colors, but never color in general, so we perceive this and that kind of significance, but never significance *simpliciter.*

After this preliminary characterization of the nature of significance, we may take note of the mental activity of interpretation which is its subjective correlate. The word "interpretation" suggests the possibility of differing judgments; we tend to call a conclusion an interpretation when we recognize that there may be other and variant accounts of the same subject matter. It is precisely because of this suggestion of ambiguity in the given, and of alternative modes of construing data, that "interpretation" is a suitable correlate term for "significance."

Two uses of "interpretation" are to be distinguished. In one of its senses, an interpretation is a (true or false) *explanation,* answering the question, Why? We speak, for example, of a metaphysician's interpretation of the universe. In its other sense, an interpretation is a (correct or incorrect) *recognition,*[6] or attribution of significance, answering the question, What? ("What is that, a dog or a fox?") These two meanings are closely connected. For all explanation operates ultimately in terms of recognition. We explain a puzzling phenomenon by disclosing its context, revealing it as part of a wider whole which does not, for us, stand in need of explanation. We render the unfamiliar intellectually acceptable by relating it to the already recognizable, indicating a connection or continuity between the old and the new. But in the unique case of the universe as a whole the distinction between explanation and recognition fails to arise. For the uni-

---

[6] This is a slightly off-dictionary sense of "recognition," equating it, not with the identification of the appearances of an object at different times as appearances of the same object, but with the apprehension of what has been discussed above as the "significance" of objects.

verse has no wider context in terms of which it might be explained; an explanation of it can therefore only consist in a perception of its significance. In this case, therefore, interpretation is both recognition and explanation. Hence the theistic recognition, or significance-attribution, is also a metaphysical explanation or theory. However, although the explanatory and the recognition aspects of theistic faith are inseparable, they may usefully be distinguished for purposes of exposition. In the present chapter we shall be examining interpretation, including the religious interpretation, as a recognition, or perception of significance.

An act of recognition, or of significance-attribution, is a complex occurrence dealing with two different types of ambiguity in the given. There are, on the one hand, interpretations which are mutually exclusive (e.g., "That is a fox" and "That is a dog," referring to the same object), and on the other hand interpretations which are mutually compatible (e.g., "That is an animal" and "That is a dog"; or "He died by asphyxiation" and "He was murdered"). Of two logically alternative interpretations only one (at most) can be the correct interpretation. But two compatible interpretations may both be correct. We shall be concerned henceforth with this latter kind of difference, in which several levels or layers or orders of significance are found in the same field of data.

The following are some simple examples of different levels or orders of object-significance.

(a) I see a rectangular red object on the floor in the corner. So far I have interpreted it as a "thing" (or "substance"), as something occupying space and time. On looking more closely, however, I see that it is a red-covered book. I have now made a new interpretation which includes my previous one, but goes beyond it.

(b) There is a piece of paper covered with writing. An illiterate savage can perhaps interpret it as something made by man. A literate person, who does not know the particular language in which it is written, can interpret it as being a document. But someone who understands the language can find in it the expression of specific thoughts. Each is answering the question, "What is it?" correctly, but answering it at different levels. And each more adequate attribution of significance presupposes the less adequate ones.

This relationship between types of significance, one type being superimposed upon and interpenetrating another, is a pattern which we shall find again in larger and more important spheres.

We have already noted that significance is essentially related to action. The significance of an object to an individual consists in the practical difference which that object makes to him, the ways in which it affects either his immediate reactions or his more long-term plans and policies. There is also a reciprocal influence of action upon our interpretations. For it is only when we have begun to act upon our interpretations, and have thereby verified that our environment is capable of being successfully inhabited in terms of them, that they become fully "real" modes of experience. Interpretations which take the dispositional form of readinesses for action, instead of immediate overt activity, borrow this feeling of "reality" from cognate interpretations which are being or have already been confirmed in action. (For example, when I see an apple on the sideboard, but do not immediately eat it, I nevertheless perceive it as entirely "real" because I have in the past verified similar interpretations of similar apple-like appearances.) It is by acting upon our interpretations that we build up an apprehension of the world around us; and in this process interpretations, once confirmed, suggest and support further interpretations. The necessity of acting-in-terms-of to "clinch" or confirm an interpretation has its importance, as we shall note later, in relation to the specifically religious recognition which we call theistic faith.

We have been speaking so far only of object-significance. But, as already indicated, object-significance as contrasted with situational significance is an expository fiction. An object absolutely per se and devoid of context would have no significance for us. It can be intelligible only as part of our familiar world. What significance would remain, for example, to a book without the physical circumstance of sight, the conventions of language and writing, the acquired art of reading, and even the literature of which the book is a part and the civilization within which it occurs? An object owes its significance as much to its context as to itself; it is what it is largely because of its place in a wider scheme of things. We are indeed hardly ever conscious of anything in complete isolation. Our normal consciousness is of groups of objects standing in recognizable patterns of relations to one another. And it is the resulting situation taken as a whole that carries significance for us, rendering some ranges of action and reaction appropriate and others inappropriate. We live and plan and act all the time in terms of the situational significance of our environment; although of course our interest may focus at any given moment upon a particular component object within the current situation.

We do not, it is true, as plain men generally think of the familiar situations which constitute our experience from moment to moment as having "significance" and of our actions as being guided thereby. But in the fundamental sense in which we are using the term, our ordinary consciousness of the world is undoubtedly a continuous consciousness of significance. It is normally consciousness of a routine or humdrum significance which is so familiar that we take it entirely for granted. The significance for me, for example, of my situation at the present moment is such that I go on quietly working; this is the response rendered appropriate by my interpretation of my contemporary experience. No fresh response is required, for my routine reactions are already adjusted to the prevailing context of significance. But this significance is none the less real for being undramatic.

The component elements of situational significance are not only physical objects—tables, mountains, stars, houses, hats, and so on—but also such non-material entities as sounds and lights and odors and, no less important, such psychological events and circumstances as other peoples' thoughts, emotions, and attitudes. Thus the kinds of situational significance in terms of which we act and react are enormously complex. Indeed the philosopher who would trace the morphology of situational significance must be a dramatist and poet as well as analyst. Attempts at significance-mapping have been undertaken by some of the existentialist writers: what they refer to as the existential character of experience is the fact that we are ourselves by definition *within* any relational system which constitutes a situation for us. However, these writers have usually been concerned to bring out the more strained and hectic aspects of human experience, presenting it often as a vivid nightmare of metaphysical anxieties and perils. They are undoubtedly painting from real life, particularly in this anguished age, but I venture to think that they are depicting it in a partial and one-sided manner.

A "situation" may be defined, then, as a state of affairs which, when selected for attention by an act of interpretation, carries its own distinctive practical significance for us. We may be involved in many different situations at the same time and may move by swift or slow transitions of interpretation from one to another. There may thus occur an indefinitely complex interpenetration of situations. For example I am, let us say, sitting in a room playing a game of chess with a friend. The game, isolated by the brackets of imagination, is a situation in itself in which I have a part to play as one of the two competing intelligences presiding over the chess board. Here is an artificial situation with its conventional boundaries, structure, and rules of procedure. But from time to time my attention moves from the board to the friend with whom I am playing, and I exchange some conversation with him. Now I am living in another situation which contains the game of chess as a sub-situation. Then suddenly a fire breaks out in the building, and the attention of both of us shifts at once to our wider physical situation; and so on. There are the wider and wider spatial situations of the street, the city, the state, continent, globe, Milky Way, and finally, as the massive permanent background situation inclusive of all else, the physical universe. And there are also the widening circles of family, class, nation, civilization, and all the other groupings within the inclusive group of the human species as a whole. The complex web of interplays within and between these two expanding series gives rise to the infinite variety of situations of which our human life is composed.

Finally, enfolding and interpenetrating this interlocking mass of finite situations there is also, according to the insistent witness of theistic religion, the all-encompassing situation of being in the presence of God and within the sphere of an on-going divine purpose. Our main concern, after these prolonged but unavoidable preliminaries, is to be with this alleged ultimate and inclusive significance and its relation to the more limited and temporary significances through which it is mediated.

Our inventory, then, shows three main orders of situational significance, corresponding to the threefold division of the universe, long entertained by human thought, into nature, man, and God. The significance for us of the physical world, nature, is that of an objective environment whose character and "laws" we must learn, and toward which we have continually to relate ourselves aright if we are to survive. The significance for us of the human world, man, is that of a realm of relationships in which we are responsible agents, subject to moral obligation. This world of moral significance is, so to speak, superimposed upon the natural world, so that relating ourselves to the moral world is not distinct from the business of relating ourselves to the natural world but is rather a particular manner of so doing. And likewise the more ultimately fateful and momentous matter of relating ourselves to the divine, to God, is not distinct from the task of directing ourselves within the natural and ethical spheres; on the contrary, it entails (without being reducible to) a way of so directing ourselves.

In the case of each of these three realms, the natural, the human, and the divine, a basic act of interpretation is required which discloses to us the existence of the sphere in question, thus providing the ground for our multifarious detailed interpretations within that sphere.

Consider first the level of natural significance. This is the significance which our environment has for us as animal organisms seeking survival and pleasure and shunning pain and death. In building houses, cooking food, avoiding dangerous precipices, whirlpools, and volcanoes, and generally conducting ourselves prudently in relation to the material world, we are all the time taking account of what I am calling (for want of a better name) the *natural* significance of our environment.

We have already noted some instances of natural significance when discussing the recognition of objects and situations. It is a familiar philosophical tenet, and one which may perhaps today be taken as granted, that all conscious experience of the physical world contains an element of interpretation. There are combined in each moment of experience a presented field of data and an interpretative activity of the subject. The perceiving mind is thus always in some degree a selecting, relating and synthesizing agent, and experiencing our environment involves a continuous activity of interpretation. "Interpretation" here is of course an unconscious and habitual process, the process by which a sense-field is perceived, for example, as a three-dimensional room, or a particular configuration of colored patches within that field as a book lying upon a table. Interpretation in this sense is generally recognized as a factor in the genesis of sense perception. We have now to note, however, the further and more basic act of interpretation which reveals to us the very existence of a material world, a world which we explore and inhabit as our given environment. In attending to this primary interpretative act we are noting the judgment which carries us beyond the solipsist predicament into an objective world of enduring, causally interacting objects, which we share with other people. Given the initial rejection of solipsism (or rather given the interpretative bias of human nature, which has prevented all but the most enthusiastic of philosophers from falling into solipsism) we can, I think, find corroborations of an analogical kind to support our belief in the unobserved continuance of physical objects and the reality of other minds. But the all-important first step, or assumption, is unevidenced and unevidenceable—except for permissive evidence, in that one's phenomenal experience is "there" to be interpreted either solipsistically or otherwise. But there is no event within our phenomenal experience the occurrence or nonoccurrence of which is relevant to the truth or falsity of the solipsist hypothesis. That hypothesis represents one possible interpretation of our experience as a whole, and the contrary belief in a plurality of minds existing in a common world represents an alternative and rival interpretation.

It may perhaps be objected that it does not make any practical difference whether solipsism be true or not, and that these are not therefore two *different* interpretations of our experience. For if our experience, pheonomenally considered, would be identical on either hypothesis, then the alternative (it will be said) is a purely verbal one; the choice is merely a choice of synonyms. I do not think, however, that this is the case. Phenomenally, there is no difference between a dream in which we know that we are dreaming and one in which we do not. But, nevertheless, there is a total difference between the two experiences—total not in the sense that every, or indeed any, isolable aspects of them differ, but in the sense that the two experiences taken as wholes are of different kinds. We are aware of precisely the same course of events, but in the one case this occurs within mental brackets, labeled as a dream, while in the other case we are ourselves immersed within the events and live through them as participants. The phenomena are apprehended in the one case as dream constituents and in the other case as "real." And the difference caused by a genuine assent to solipsism would be akin to the sudden realization during an absorbing dream that it *is* only a dream. If the solipsist interpretation were to be seriously adopted and wholeheartedly believed, experience would take on an unreal character in contrast with one's former nonsolipsist mode of experience. Our personal relationships in particular, our loves and friendships, our hates and enmities, rivalries and co-operations, would have to be treated not as transsubjective meetings with other personalities, but as dialogues and dramas with oneself. There would be only one person in existence, and other "people," instead of being apprehended as independent centers of intelligence and purpose, would be but human-like appearances. They could not be the objects of affection or enmity, nor could their actions be subjected to moral judgment in our normal nonsolipsist sense. In short, although it must be very difficult, if not impossible, for the sanely functioning mind seriously to assent to solipsism and to apperceive in terms of it, yet this does represent at least a logically possible interpretation of experience, and constitutes a *different* interpretation from our ordinary belief in an independently existing world of things and persons. It follows that our normal mode of experience is itself properly described as an interpretation, an interpretation which we are unable to justify by argument but which we have nevertheless no inclination or reason to doubt. Indeed as Hume noted, nature has not left this to our choice, "and has doubtless esteem'd it an affair of too great importance to be trusted to our uncertain reasonings and speculations. We may well ask, What causes induce us to believe in the existence of body [i.e., matter]? but 'tis vain to ask. Whether there be body or not? That is a point, which we must take for granted in all our reasonings."[7]

But the ordering of our lives in relation to an objective material environment thus revealed to us by a basic act of interpretation is not the most distinctively human level of experience. It is characteristic of mankind to live not only in terms of the natural significance of his world but also in the dimension of personality and responsibility. And so we find that presupposing consciousness of the physical world, and supervening upon it, is the kind of situational significance which we call "being responsible" or "being under obligation." The sense of moral obligation, or of "oughtness," is the basic datum of ethics. It is manifested whenever someone, in circumstances requiring practical decision, feels "obligated" to act, or to refrain from acting, in some particular way. When this occurs, the natural significance of his environment is interpenetrated by another, ethical significance. A traveler on an unfrequented road, for example, comes upon a stranger who has met with an accident and who is lying injured and in need of help. At the level of natural significance this is just an empirical state of affairs, a particular configuration of stone and earth and flesh. But an act or reflex of interpretation at the moral level reveals to the traveler a situation in which he is under obligation to render aid. He feels a categorical imperative laid upon him, demanding that he help the injured man. The situation takes on for him a

---

[7] *Treatise,* bk. 1, pt. IV, sec. 2 (Selby-Bigge's ed., pp. 187–188).

peremptory ethical significance, and he finds himself in a situation of inescapable personal responsibility.

As has often been remarked, it is characteristic of situations exhibiting moral significance that they involve, directly or indirectly, more than one person. The other or others may stand either in an immediate personal relationship to the moral agent or, as in large-scale social issues, in a more remote causal relationship. (The sphere of politics has been defined as that of the *im*personal relationships between persons.) Ethical significance, as the distinctive significance of situations in which persons are components, includes both of these realms. To feel moral obligation is to perceive (or misperceive) the practical significance for oneself of a situation in which one stands in a responsible relationship to another person or to other people. That the perception of significance in personal situations sets up (in Kant's terms) a categorical imperative, while natural situations give rise only to hypothetical imperatives, conditional upon our own desires, is a defining characteristic of the personal world.

Clearly, moral significance presupposes natural significance. For in order that we may be conscious of moral obligations, and exercise moral intelligence, we must first be aware of a stable environment in which actions have foreseeable results, and in which we can learn the likely consequences of our deeds. It is thus a precondition of ethical situations that there should be a stable medium, the world, with its own causal laws, in which people meet and in terms of which they act. The two spheres of significance, the moral and the physical, interpenetrate in the sense that all occasions of obligation have reference, either immediately or ultimately, to overt action. Relating oneself to the ethical sphere is thus a particular manner of relating oneself to the natural sphere: ethical significance is mediated to us in and through the natural world.

As in the case of natural situational significance, we can enter the sphere of ethical significance only by our own act of interpretation. But at this level the interpretation is a more truly voluntary one. That is to say, it is not forced upon us from outside, but depends upon an inner capacity and tendency to interpret in this way, a tendency which we are free to oppose and even to overrule. If a man chooses to be a moral solipsist, or absolute egoist, recognizing no responsibility toward other people, no one can prove to him that he has any such responsibilities. The man who, when confronted with some standard situation having ethical significance, such as a bully wantonly injuring a child, fails to see it as morally significant, could only be classified as suffering from a defect of his nature analogous to physical blindness. He can of course be compelled by threats of punishment to conform to a stated code of behaviour; but he cannot be compelled to feel moral obligation. He must see and accept for himself his own situation as a responsible being and its corollary of ethical accountability.

Has this epistemological paradigm—of one order of significance superimposed upon and mediated through another—any further application? The contention of this chapter is that it has. As ethical significance interpenetrates natural significance, so religious significance interpenetrates both ethical and natural. The divine is the highest and ultimate order of significance, mediating neither of the others and yet being mediated through both of them.

But what do we mean by religious significance? What is it that, for the ethical monotheist, possesses this significance, and in what does the significance consist?

The primary locus of religious significance is the believer's experience as a whole. The basic act of interpretation which reveals to him the religious significance of life is a uniquely "total interpretation," whose logic will be studied in Part III. But we must at this point indicate what is intended by the phrase "total interpretation," and offer some preliminary characterization of its specifically theistic form.

Consider the following imagined situation. I enter a room in a strange building and find that a militant secret society appears to be meeting there. Most of the members are armed, and as they take me for a fellow member I judge it expedient to acquiesce in the role. Subtle and blood-thirsty plans are discussed for a violent overthrow of the constitution. The whole situation is alarming in the extreme. Then I suddenly notice behind me a gallery in which there are batteries of arc lights and silently whirring cameras, and I realize that I have walked by accident onto the set of a film. This realization consists in a change of interpretation of my immediate environment. Until now I had automatically interpreted it as being "real life," as a dangerous situation demanding considerable circumspection on my part. Now I interpret it as having practical significance of a quite different kind. But there is no corresponding change in the observable course of events. The meeting of the "secret society" proceeds as before, although now I believe the state of affairs to be quite other than I had previously supposed it to be. The same phenomena are interpreted as constituting an entirely different practical situation. And yet not quite the same phenomena, for I have noticed important new items, namely, the cameras and arc lights. But let us now in imagination expand the room into the world, and indeed expand it to include the entire physical universe. This is the strange room into which we walk at birth. There is no space left for a photographers' gallery, no direction in which we can turn in search of new clues which might reveal the significance of our situation. Our interpretation must be a *total* interpretation, in which we assert that the world as a whole (as experienced by ourselves) is of this or that kind, that is to say, affects our plans and our policies in such and such ways.

The monotheist's faith-apprehension of God as the unseen Person dealing with him in and through his experience of the world is from the point of view of epistemology an interpretation of this kind, an interpretation of the world as a whole as mediating a divine presence and purpose. He sees in his situation as a human being a significance to which the appropriate response is a religious trust and obedience. His interpretative leap carries him into a world which exists through the will of a holy, righteous, and loving Being who is the creator and sustainer of all that is. Behind the world—to use an almost inevitable spatial metaphor—there is apprehended to be an omnipotent, personal Will whose purpose toward mankind guarantees men's highest good and blessedness. The believer finds that he is at all times in the presence of this holy Will. Again and again he realizes, either at the time or in retrospect, that in his dealings with the circumstances of his own life he is also having to do with a transcendent Creator who is the determiner of his destiny and the source of all good.

Thus the primary religious perception, or basic act of religious interpretation, is not to be described as either a reasoned conclusion or an unreasoned hunch that there is a God. It is, putatively, an apprehension of the divine presence within the believer's human experience. It is not an inference to a general truth, but a "divine-human encounter," a mediated meeting with the living God.

As ethical significance presupposes natural, so religious significance presupposes both ethical and natural. Entering into conscious relation with God consists in large part in adopting a particular style and manner of acting towards our natural and social environments. For God summons men to serve him *in* the world, and in terms of the life of the world. Religion is not only a way of cognizing but also, and no less vitally, a way of living. To see the world as being ruled by a divine love which sets infinite value upon each individual and includes all men in its scope, and yet to live as though the world were a realm of chance in which each must fight for his own interests against the rest, argues a very dim and wavering vision of God's rule. So far as that vision is clear it issues naturally in a trust in the divine purpose and obedience to the divine will. We shall be able to say more about this practical and dispositional response, in which the apprehension of the religious significance of life so largely consists, when we come in Part IV to examine a particular form of theistic faith. At present we are concerned only with the general nature of the awareness of God.

Rudolf Otto has a somewhat obscure doctrine of the schematization of the Holy in terms of ethics.[8] Without being committed to Otto's use of the Kantian notion, or to his general philosophy of religion, we have been led to a parallel conception of the religious significance of life as schematized in, mediated through, or expressed in terms of, its natural and moral significance. As John Oman says of the Hebrew prophets,

> What determines their faith is not a theory of the Supernatural, but an attitude towards the Natural, as a sphere in which a victory of deeper meaning than the visible and of more abiding purpose than the fleeting can be won. . . . The revelation of the Supernatural was by reconciliation to the Natural: and this was made possible by realising in the Natural the meaning and purpose of the Supernatural.[9]

In one respect this theistic interpretation is more akin to the natural than to the ethical interpretation. For while only *some* situations have moral significance, *all* situations have for embodied beings a continuous natural significance. In like manner the sphere of the basic religious interpretation is not merely this or that isolable situation, but the uniquely total situation constituted by our experience as a whole and in all its aspects, up to the present moment.

But on the other hand the theistic interpretation is more akin to the ethical than to the natural significance-attribution in that it is clearly focused in some situations and imperceptible in others. Not all the moments of life mediate equally the presence of God to the ordinary believer. He is not continuously conscious of God's presence (although possibly the saint is), but conscious rather of the divine Will as a reality in the background of his life, a reality which may at any time emerge to confront him in absolute and inescapable demand. We have already observed how one situation may interpenetrate another, and how some sudden pressure or intrusion can cause a shift of interpretation and attention so that the mind moves from one interlocking context to another. Often a more

---

[8] *The Idea of the Holy,* trans. by J. W. Harvey (London, 1923), ch. 7.
[9] *The Natural and the Supernatural* (Cambridge, 1931), p. 448.

important kind of significance will summon us from a relatively trivial kind. A woman may be playing a game of cards when she hears her child crying in pain in another room; and at once her consciousness moves from the artificial world of the game to the real world in which she is the mother of the child. Or an officer in the army reserve may be living heedless of the international situation until sudden mobilization recalls him to his military responsibility. The interrupting call of duty may summon us from trivial or relatively unimportant occupations to take part in momentous events. Greater and more ultimate purposes may without warning supervene upon lesser ones and direct our lives into a new channel. But the final significance, which takes precedence over all others as supremely important and overriding, is (according to theism) that of our situation as being in the presence of God. At any time a man may be confronted by some momentous decision, some far-reaching moral choice either of means or of ends, in which his responsibility as a servant of God intrudes upon and conflicts with the requirements of his earthly "station and its duties," so that the latter pales into unimportance and he acts in relation to a more ultimate environment whose significance magisterially overrules his customary way of life. When the call of God is clearly heard other calls become inaudible, and the prophet or saint, martyr or missionary, the man of conscience or of illumined mind may ignore all considerations of worldly prudence in responding to a claim with which nothing else whatever may be put in the balance.

To recapitulate and conclude this stage of the discussion, the epistemological point which I have sought to make is this. There is in cognition of every kind an unresolved mystery. The knower-known relationship is in the last analysis *sui generis:* the mystery of cognition persists at the end of every inquiry—though its persistence does not prevent us from cognizing. We cannot explain, for example, how we are conscious of sensory phenomena as constituting an objective physical environment; we just find ourselves interpreting the data of our experience in this way. We are aware that we live in a real world, though we cannot prove by any logical formula that it *is* a real world. Likewise we cannot explain how we know ourselves to be responsible beings subject to moral obligations; we just find ourselves interpreting our social experience in this way. We find ourselves inhabiting an ethically significant universe, though we cannot prove that it *is* ethically significant by any process of logic. In each case we discover and live in terms of a particular aspect of our environment through an appropriate act of interpretation; and having come to live in terms of it we neither require nor can conceive any further validation of its reality. The same is true of the apprehension of God. The theistic believer cannot explain *how* he knows the divine presence to be mediated through his human experience. He just finds himself interpreting his experience in this way. He lives in the presence of God, though he is unable to prove by any dialectical process that God exists.

To say this is not of course to demonstrate that God *does* exist. The outcome of the discussion thus far is rather to bring out the similarity of epistemological structure and status between men's basic convictions in relation to the world, moral responsibility, and divine existence. The aim of the present chapter has thus been to show how, if there be a God, he is known to mankind, and how such knowledge is related to other kinds of human knowing. I hope that at least the outline of a possible answer to these questions has now been offered.